'Abdu'l-Bahá in Europe, 1912–1913

‘The Sun is only just beginning to rise in Europe; soon will the divine light grow more intense, and then will you all behold what has come to pass.’

Words of ‘Abdu’l-Bahá spoken in Paris, 15 March 1913

‘Abdu’l-Bahá in Europe, 1912–1913

The Talks and Travels of the Master as Recorded by Mírzá Maḥmúd Zarqání

translated by

Adib Masumian

with the assistance of

Farnaz Masumian

GR

George Ronald
Oxford

George Ronald, Publisher
Oxford
www.grbooks.com

A catalogue record for this book is available from the British Library

ISBN 978-0-85398-667-6

Cover photograph: Train waiting to leave London, 1913.
Photo by F.H. Stingemore,
used with permission of the Stephenson Rail Archive.

Cover design Steiner Graphics

MIX
Paper from responsible sources
FSC® C013056

Printed and bound in Great Britain by
TJ Books Limited, Padstow, Cornwall

Contents

Foreword by the Translator vii

A Brief Chronology of 'Abdu'l-Bahá's Travels Covered in this Volume ix

Preface by Mírzá Maḥmúd Zarqání 1

Voyage to England 9

England 25

Scotland 76

Return to England 92

France 122

Germany 269

Hungary 294

Austria 319

Return to Germany 336

Return to France 368

Voyage to Egypt 465

Egypt 473

The Holy Land 500

Appendix: Selected Biographical Notes 507

Bibliography 589

Notes and References 597

Index 757

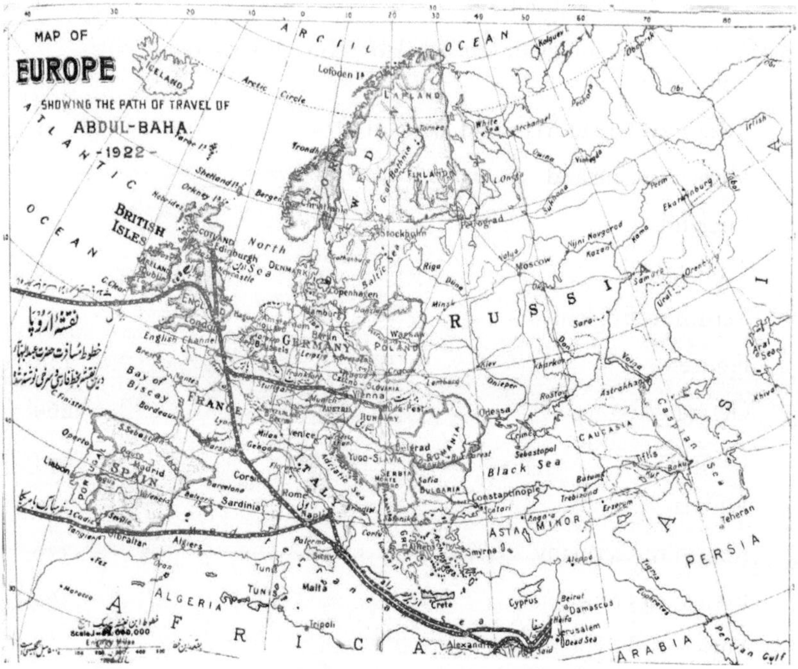

Map of 'Abdu'l-Bahá's European travels

Foreword by the Translator

This translation of the second volume of Mírzá Maḥmúd Zarqání's diary recounts 'Abdu'l-Bahá's voyage from America to Europe (December 1912); His travels to the United Kingdom, France, Germany, Hungary, and Austria (December 1912–June 1913); and, toward the end of the book, glimpses from His sojourn in Egypt (June 1913–December 1913) and return to the Holy Land (December 1913), where He remained for the rest of His life. This account does *not* cover 'Abdu'l-Bahá's first visits to France and England in 1911, since Zarqání did not accompany Him on those travels.

This book was originally published in Persian a little more than a hundred years ago as the second of two volumes of *Kitáb-i-Badáyi'u'l-Á<u>th</u>ár fí Asfár-i-Mawli'l-A<u>kh</u>yár ilá Mamáliki'l-<u>Gh</u>arb bi'l-'Izzati va'l-Iqtidár* (A Book of the Wondrous Traces of the Master's Glorious Travels to the West) – often shortened among Persian-speaking Bahá'ís to *Badáyi'u'l-Á<u>th</u>ár* or *Safar-Námih* ('travelogue'). The first volume was translated into English in 1998 and published by George Ronald under the title of *Maḥmúd's Diary*. Though the present volume had not been rendered fully and directly into English until now, a considerable amount of its contents had previously been summarized by H. M. Balyuzi in his exquisite biography of 'Abdu'l-Bahá,[1] several of the anecdotes He relates in it were adapted by Amir Badiei for inclusion in *Stories Told by 'Abdu'l-Bahá*,[2] and certain snippets of His other remarks recorded in it were translated by Marzieh Gail in 'A Sampler from Maḥmúd's Diary'.[3]

In a letter to the National Spiritual Assembly of the Bahá'ís of the United States dated 30 April 1984, the Universal House of Justice stated that it

> . . . attaches great importance to this work which . . . is regarded as a reliable account of 'Abdu'l-Bahá's travels in the West and an authentic record of His utterances, whether in the form of formal

> talks, table talks, or random oral statements. Mírzá Maḥmúd was a careful and faithful chronicler and engaged in assembling and publishing his work with the permission of the beloved Master, as he states in the Introduction. Indeed, Shoghi Effendi drew upon it for details about the Master's visit to the West in writing *God Passes By* . . .

It should, however, be noted that the words Zarqání has attributed to 'Abdu'l-Bahá in this chronicle do not have the status of Sacred Text, and the accounts included herein should be corroborated by His Writings where possible.

For those who wish to learn more about the people and events covered in this volume, I have prepared a freely accessible digital resource, *A Supplement to 'Abdu'l-Bahá in Europe, 1912–1913*,[4] which includes fuller English translations[5] of those talks by 'Abdu'l-Bahá that Zarqání has mentioned in passing or quoted partially; my renderings[6] of nearly thirty selections from the Writings of 'Abdu'l-Bahá in which He discusses His journey to the West, several of which He composed while still there; and my translation of a biography of Zarqání authored by 'Azízu'lláh Sulaymání.

Given Zarqání's relative unfamiliarity with the Gregorian calendar, it is understandable that he made the occasional mistake in dating his entries. In these instances, I have retained the erroneous dates in the body of the chronicle but mentioned the correct ones in accompanying endnotes with reference to other sources from that time. For the most part, I have restricted the multitude of reverent titles Zarqání used for 'Abdu'l-Bahá in the original account to 'the Master' and 'the Centre of the Covenant'. The translations used for the Biblical verses quoted in this chronicle are all taken from the King James Bible. For Quranic passages, I have used Shoghi Effendi's translations or renderings authorized by the Universal House of Justice where available; in every other case, I have relied on Rodwell's translation. All parenthetical text in the body of the account is Zarqání's, while all bracketed commentary is mine. All footnotes and endnotes are likewise my own. Zarqání withheld the names of certain Persian dignitaries who met with

'Abdu'l-Bahá, and this was done at His own instruction.[7] I have denoted these omissions with two em-dashes wrapped in brackets, thus: [——].

The original volume concludes with a sixteen-page collection of poetry by Zarqání in which he illustrates the coming of 'Abdu'l-Bahá from the East to the West after forty years of imprisonment, emphasizing the significance of that momentous journey; extols the greatness of 'Abdu'l-Bahá, lauding the talks He gave in the West and more generally the message of peace He delivered there; exhorts his fellow believers to follow 'Abdu'l-Bahá's example of serving and teaching the Cause with self-sacrifice; glorifies the return of 'Abdu'l-Bahá from the West to the East, and more specifically from Egypt to the Holy Land, highlighting the importance of this event; depicts the fulfilment of scriptural prophecies, including those pertaining to Mount Carmel, through the advent of the Bahá'í Faith and the construction of the Shrine of the Báb which is situated on that mountain; rebukes the Bábís who failed to recognize Bahá'u'lláh as the Promised One; and expresses his own love for Bahá'u'lláh, as well as his devoted servitude to Him. Those poems have not been included in this translation, and Zarqání's one reference to them in this book – found at the end of his entry for 21 June 1913 – has consequently been left out.

In rendering a translation of this size and substance, I benefited immensely from the assistance of various people. The lion's share of my gratitude goes to my mother, Farnaz Masumian, who sat with me and spent more hours than I can count checking every word of my translation against the original text as I produced it over a period of three years (July 2017–July 2020). I am also grateful to the Research Department of the Universal House of Justice, who reviewed all my provisional translations of 'Abdu'l-Bahá's words and approved them for publication in this book following the incorporation of some recommended revisions.[8] Additional thanks are due to the team at George Ronald, including May Hofman, who edited the manuscript with patience and meticulous precision; and Erica Leith, who typeset the book, added the images, and undertook other production work. My father,

Bijan Masumian, pored over the entire manuscript to identify names, places, and other suitable candidates for the aforementioned images that enrich this translation. With the help of my cherished and erudite mentor, Naeem Nabiliakbar, I gained insight into some of the older meanings of terms and phrases intended by 'Abdu'l-Bahá, Mírzá Maḥmúd Zarqání, and others featured in this account – and through his skillful and tireless tutelage over many years, he developed my command of Persian to a point that enabled me to take on this project in the first place. The 'brother I never had', Joshua D.T. Hall, offered several suggestions for improvement after reviewing an early draft of the full translation, and also provided, for my use in this work, his own superb renderings of certain lines of Persian poetry that have been quoted in this chronicle. Through the assistance of Edward Sevcik at the U.S. Bahá'í National Archives, I procured facsimiles of contemporaneous diary letters by Ahmad Sohrab which cover many of the same events recorded by Zarqání and thus served as a useful counterweight to his account. Jan Jasion and Amín Egea supplied me with a wealth of historical material relevant to the contents of this volume. Robert Stockman shed light on several allusions Zarqání made to the American Bahá'í community and to events that were concurrently unfolding in that country. Still more friends, diligent historians of the national Bahá'í communities to which they belong, reviewed chapters of the manuscript that aligned with their areas of expertise: David Merrick (United Kingdom), Ulrich Gollmer and Alexander Meinhard (Germany), Ágnes Ambró (Hungary), and David Menham (Austria). The recent release of *The Bahá'í Community of the British Isles, 1844–1963* – a new book printed by George Ronald and prepared by the late Adam Thorne, Moojan Momen, Janet Fleming Rose, and Earl Redman – proved serendipitous, in that George Ronald generously supplied me with a pre-publication copy just before they began editing this book. The fresh light shed by that definitive history of the Bahá'í Faith in Britain – especially in chapter 3, which covers 'Abdu'l-Bahá's time there – enabled me to make several corrections and clarifications to my notes to the corresponding period in this volume, and I cannot recommend it enough to any student of the Cause's development in that part of the world. Jan Jasion's impressively comprehensive *'Abdu'l-Bahá in France: 1911 & 1913* was of similarly great help as I worked through the portions of this account dealing with 'Abdu'l-Bahá's time in that country.

I have tried my best to produce an accurate and adequately researched translation that avoids wording anachronistic to Zarqání's time, reflects his elevated tone, and maintains fidelity to his attitude of respectful admiration. I can only hope that I have done right by him and by that Mystery of God Whose talks and travels he has so lovingly striven to immortalize.

Adib Masumian
November 2023

A Brief Chronology of 'Abdu'l-Bahá's Travels Covered in this Volume

1912	5 December	'Abdu'l-Bahá concludes His journey throughout America and sets sail for England
1912	13 December	Arrives in England
1913	6 January	Departs England for Scotland
1913	10 January	Returns from Scotland to England
1913	21 January	Departs England for France
1913	1 April	Departs France for Germany
1913	8 April	Departs Germany for Hungary
1913	18 April	Departs Hungary for Austria
1913	24 April	Returns from Austria to Germany
1913	1 May	Returns from Germany to France
1913	13 June	Sets sail from France to Egypt
1913	2 December	Sets sail from Egypt to the Holy Land
1913	5 December	Arrives in the Holy Land

Preface by Mírzá Maḥmúd Zarqání

In the Name of God, the Most Powerful

Praise be to the All-Bountiful Creator, Who has adorned the firmament of existence with the rays of the sun of benevolence, and illumined the dawn of creation with the stars of insight and understanding. He has taught the divine anthem to the pure souls; He has kindled the fearless hearts with the fire of the love of God. With His heavenly message, He has instilled a fresh spirit and breathed new life into the world. With His divine glory, He has endowed the human race with limitless endurance. He has summoned all His servants to the tabernacle of unity, and has made the exalted pavilion of peace the resting-place of the hearts and souls of humankind. He has illumined the West with the sun of the East. He has perfumed the nostrils of the truly liberated with the fragrance wafting from the firmament of the Covenant – a fragrance so enchanting that it stirs even the rose-gardens to jealousy. He has influenced the leaders of the West with His counsel, and has – through His aid and assistance – given the wise ones of the East a religion which has granted them salvation, that they may become the envy of the world and the cause of its perpetual prosperity, for this has always been, and will always be, the method of God.

The Sovereign of the Kingdom of glory has demonstrated His extraordinary power, and perfected His divine proof, by choosing the holy Manifestations from among the most backward of people. Through His spiritual power, He has enabled such people to surpass even the most glorious of nations. Unaided by earthly hosts, and void of acquired knowledge, they have conquered the religions and great nations of the world. He has made those Manifestations the greatest means of the unification of all peoples and races. With the advent of the prophet Abraham, for instance, God bestowed blessings and eternal glory upon his descendants. With the coming of Moses, He freed the Israelites from captivity, and made them even as the kings of the earth. With the breath of Jesus Christ, He unified the diverse nations of Assyria, Chaldea, Egypt, and Syria, and breathed eternal life into them. With the rising of the Muhammadan countenance, He made the peoples and pagan tribes of the Arabian desert the inheritors and caliphs of the earth. And now we arrive at this brilliant age and heavenly century, in which the Sun of Bounty [Bahá'u'lláh] shed its splendour from the horizon of Persia. With His advent, He made the East the dawning-place of God's ancient grace and glorious triumph. With the light of divine civilization, He has illumined scores of the people of advanced societies, and has made the renowned philosophers of the West to fall for the Beloved of the East. It behooves the learned ones of the East, then – especially those of Persian extraction – to lift up their voices to the highest heaven in gratitude of this honour and privilege, and cry out, 'Glad tidings! Glad tidings!' It befits them to sing the song that hails the loving Lord as they pluck the harp and strike the drum. They should so excel in this arena of grace that the signs of their supremacy will forever endure in both this world and the next, and so hoist the standard of felicity in this soul-stirring space that the banner of its glory shall wave throughout the ages and centuries to come. They must so move in the world of existence as to become the clear tokens of this most great dispensation and this supreme era. Even as a brilliant star must they rise over the horizon of these blessed words: 'Erelong will God bring forth treasures of the earth – men who shall aid Him with a power born of Him,'[9] and come to completely exemplify this irrevocable promise: 'There lay concealed within the Holy Veil, and prepared for the service of God, a company of His chosen ones who shall be manifested unto men, who shall aid His Cause, who shall be afraid of no one, though the entire human race rise up and war against them.'[10]

Were the peoples of the world to consider, with fairness and insight, the sacred teachings of this most great Cause, as well as the momentousness of this journey to the West – and also to ponder the grandeur, the glory, the majesty, and the transcendence that 'Abdu'l-Bahá (may the souls of all existence be a sacrifice for His bounty) evinced as He travelled throughout the cities of America and Europe – they would account all these as the most conclusive proof, the most perfect evidence attesting to the truth of the Revelation of the Blessed Beauty (magnified be His glory), and regard them as the supreme sign of the Sun of Truth shining resplendent from the Most Exalted Horizon and the Most Glorious Kingdom. Thereby would they be apprised of the secrets and truths of the divine religions, and moved to turn their faces from the darkness of prejudice and blind imitation to the luminous realm of oneness and unity. Indeed, every people would cleave tenaciously to this most great Cause as a source of life and a path to salvation, and all humanity would deem it their obligation to promote these blessed precepts. This applies in particular to the people of the East, whom the peerless Lord has once again deigned to honour with a crown so exquisite, a diadem so refulgent, that it shall arouse the envy of all humankind, and exalt that people to a most illustrious station in both this world and the world to come. I beseech God, blessed and glorified be He, to prepare them for this supreme bestowal and to make them grateful for this most magnificent gift. I pray, moreover, that He may aid them to preserve this imperishable glory and enable them to promulgate His sacred commandments, through which every weak one is strengthened, every lowly one is exalted, every poor one is enriched, every sick one is healed, and every soul is empowered to soar to the loftiest summits of redemption and reach the celestial heights of tranquillity. He, verily, is the Most Compassionate, the Lord of grace abounding.

Praised be God, Who out of His all-encompassing grace and all-pervading bounty has aided this poor servant to record the significant events of the Master's journey throughout the states of America, and helped him to complete and present the first volume of this chronicle.[11] Upon completing this introduction, I shall finish writing this vivid account of the Master's travels to the cities of Europe, and thus bring the second volume of this chronicle to completion. Having set my face towards the horizon of God's assistance and favour, I hopingly supplicate the paradise of His support and protection to make me vigilantly heedful of such things as beseem the majestic greatness of His Cause and the powerful might of His Covenant, and to protect me from errors and omissions. He is, in truth, the Protector, the Helper, the Giver of victory, and He is the Sustainer, the All-Knowing, the All-Wise.

The most important detail which the reader will glean from perusing these pages is surely the majesty and might which 'Abdu'l-Bahá (may my spirit be a sacrifice for the dust which the footsteps of His loved ones have trodden) demonstrated in the sundry churches and gatherings where He spoke; the transformation experienced by the celebrated philosophers who met Him, as well as the deference they showed Him; and the humble reverence extended to Him by religious leaders and the heads of various other groups, for in addition to captivating the hearts of the friends at Bahá'í gatherings, the profound impression which His blessed utterances made at other assemblies invariably revolutionized the hearts of eminent persons, and roused His distinguished listeners to genuine veneration and vigilant attention. Even our esteemed compatriots, who were residing in London and Paris when we journeyed to those cities, were, for the most part, witnesses to these things themselves, and have testified to the power and grandeur of the Master. Many were the matters of major importance that came to pass, the like of which I have previously discussed in my preface to the first volume of this chronicle, and countless the fruits of the power displayed, the resolve evinced, and the talks given by the Master in America and Europe.

What is surprising is that the most inveterate enemies of this Cause in Persia have not been able to deny this power and might. In Tehran, the Azalís – who today are meddling, both secretly and openly, in the political spheres of Persia with a view to disordering its affairs – have repeatedly said:

> 'Abbás Effendí has gifted precious objects and given large sums to the ministers of churches and the heads of societies. It is for this reason that the respected people of the West have, in their houses of worship and other gathering-places, lavished such lofty praise upon Him and held Him in such high esteem.

Here is an evidence of true power – that even the tongues of our Eastern enemies should bear ample testimony to the praise and respect which the Master received in the West, as well as the deference and reverence which the esteemed people of that land accorded Him at numerous gatherings. Ignorant as our opponents are of the pervasively prevailing might of the Word of God – which, though ever bereft of earthly means, has always reared humankind aright, and subdued its hearts and souls – they, in their idle fancy, have ultimately imagined the influence of the Cause of God and the power of 'Abdu'l-Bahá to have stemmed from material possessions. It is true that the Master's displays of generosity constituted just one of His distinctive behaviours that would invariably cause people to rejoice, but He gave this money to care for the weak and help the poor. It is also the case that, on certain occasions when He was the guest of a respected person – or when He Himself had a guest who was dear to Him (as it is the custom among the people of every nation to conclude their visits with friends for whom they feel respect by giving them a souvenir of some sort) – the Master would likewise extend His beneficence to people as He bade them farewell, but He Himself never accepted a single gift from anyone. To them that judge fairly, the Master's demonstrations of this munificence – as well as the self-sufficiency and independence He exhibited – all undoubtedly serve as testaments to the loftiness of His grandeur and the highness of His rank.

Such is the notion that these people, in accordance with their vain imaginings and selfish motives, have conceived – that with the ephemeral vanities of this world, one can transform the hearts of humanity and unite their inner realities beneath the shade of a single Word. Yet if that were truly possible, then it should be the Christian missionaries – with their wealth and capability, their schools and seminaries, their political power and influence – who achieve the outcome they so dearly cherish in summoning the peoples of the East to embrace their cause. Why should the Bahá'ís – the objects of hatred and wrath, the outcasts and prisoners of the nations – have received so much attention in the highly developed countries of the West and so completely captivated the hearts of their inhabitants?

During my sojourn in India, I met a great many people in the various provinces of that country (which is today one of the realms of the mighty British Empire) who had all been born into villages and farms in the utmost poverty and hardship, and taken by Christian missionaries to their schools on the condition that they convert to Christianity. The missionaries clothed them, fed them, and taught them, and every day they would read the sacred texts and learn religious subjects. In those schools and quarters, every one of the servants and other attendants had to first accept Christianity before they were employed there. They were expected to attend church regularly, at fixed times, where they would be taught spiritual topics. Yet despite all this, once they left the schools and quarters of the Christians after studying there for a few years, they, like their fellow Indians, returned to supporting their own people, reverted to the religion of their forefathers, and grew more entrenched in their prejudices of race and nationality, thus rendering all the efforts and outlays of the Christian missionaries and teachers entirely fruitless in the domain of religion; indeed, their endeavours had consequences in the political sphere that were the very opposite of what they had hoped to achieve.

Tremendously powerful confirmations, then, are needed to effectively spread divine guidance, not the expenditure of the transitory wealth of this world, for if the confirmations of God consisted in the riches of men, the Christians would have been able to protect the basis of divine religion from the pervasive onslaught of Western materialists, such that pure spirituality and divine civilization – the indispensable foundation of human welfare and prosperity – could have withstood the influence of material civilization. Not only this, but through divine confirmations, those spiritual forces could have even prevailed over the libertine civilization of the materialists, which can culminate only in sheer animality, and exalted the souls and inner realities of humankind to stations holy and eternal.

It is this aid and assistance from on high that has, in this day, sustained the Cause of the Blessed Beauty [Bahá'u'lláh] and supported the Centre of His Covenant ['Abdu'l-Bahá], Who in spite of His dire afflictions, the plundering of His possessions, His displacement in various climes and countries, and His incarceration in the Most Great Prison, has been able, in so short a span, to spread the Word of God in sundry regions of the world and penetrate the hearts of humanity with the teachings of Bahá'u'lláh. The ray of the Sun of Truth, beaming down from the horizon of the East, has been so cast upon the farthest corners of the West that, as soon as the Master had been freed from prison as a result of the Young Turk Revolution, special invitations were sent to Him not only from the Bahá'ís of America, but even from the leaders of churches and other significant assemblies in that land, imploring Him repeatedly to travel to their countries and speak to the new and wondrous teachings – all this notwithstanding that they had yet to meet Him in person, or receive any gifts or other transient treasures from Him. Had those who raised their cavils against the Master been aware of the invitations He had received before embarking on His journey, they would have attributed the praise and respect He was given only to the power of God, and were they to reflect, however briefly, on what could possibly be the source of such wealth as this – which has so remarkably noised abroad the Cause of God and glorified His Word in those prosperous lands – they would realize at once that this wealth has come from the treasuries of the Most Glorious Kingdom, and that this aid and assistance are rendered by hosts from the Concourse on High.

This glory, this wealth, this aid vouchsafed from the realm above are all the fruits of the calamities which the loved ones of Bahá'u'lláh have sustained in the path of God, and the results of their renouncing their lives, their riches, their prestige, and their repose, consenting instead to bear toil and trouble, abasement and vagrancy, as they follow in the footsteps of that One Beloved – ever afflicted, ever captive, ever faced with the threat of the blade.

Voyage to England

Thursday, 5 December 1912

[New York City → En route to Liverpool, on board the *Celtic*]

The Master's retinue set sail from America to England that day. After seeking confirmation and assistance from the Blessed Beauty, and invoking His Greatest Name, the Master spoke these blessed words:

> The significance of this journey will become known in the future. Up until the present time, such a thing has not happened before, and has never been witnessed in any age – that a person from the East should travel to the farthest cities of the West, teaching the Cause of God, promulgating its new precepts, and expounding upon questions of theology, in temples and in gatherings of various peoples – with such resolve and conviction that none is able to reject or object to them. On the contrary, all have been enamoured of and enraptured by these ideas, and express their deepest reverence for them.
>
> In His own land, Jesus Christ visited Jerusalem often, and entered the gatherings of the Israelites many times, offering admonitions and giving sermons. Consider how the Christian divines eventually came to ascribe such great importance to these acts. It is clear, then, what significance this journey – in which we have raised, in ringing tones, the call of Yá Bahá'u'l-Abhá in great churches and large gatherings – will acquire in the future, for we have, in most eloquent language and with most convincing proofs, hailed the glad-tidings of the Kingdom of God, and enunciated the teachings of the Blessed Beauty. In the synagogues of the Jews, we arose to vindicate the message of Christ and demonstrate the truth of Islam. In the churches of the Christians, we expatiated upon the greatness of Muhammad, the Apostle of God – may the blessings of God and His salutation be upon Him. In gatherings

of communists, we explained the laws that will conduce to the establishment of peace and order in the world. In materialist assemblies, we proved and established the extraordinary power of the supernatural. In congregations consecrated to the establishment of peace, and in the conferences of various peoples, we have raised the call of the Ancient Beauty, and have expounded upon that which leads to the advancement of universal peace, and promotes the unity of humankind, in such wise that in every gathering, heads were bowed in humility and tongues were unloosed in praise, hearts were enraptured by the sweet savours of God and souls were rejoiced at His glad-tidings. Behold, now, how great is this thing that has come to pass!

As a result of hearing these blessed words – and the anguish and bitter wailing raised by the devoted friends on the New York pier at the time of farewell, inasmuch as their separation from their Beloved was close at hand – the hearts of those in his retinue were deeply touched, and the minds of those who witnessed that power and grandeur were utterly astounded as they wondered to themselves, 'What a display of glory is this, and what peerless beauty He has!' His retinue on that voyage [from America to England] consisted of three people: Mirza Ahmad Sohrab, Áqá Siyyid Asadu'lláh [Qumí], and this lowly servant (Maḥmúd Zarqání).

The Master's room[12] was on the upper deck of the *Celtic* (from the White Star Line company), where passengers rode first class, while the members of His retinue sailed second class. Yet, at all other times apart from when the Master was eating or sleeping, we had the honour of being with Him in the first class.

Every morning and afternoon, tea would be brewed for the Master according to Persian custom. At times He would take His tea in His room, while at others He would have it outside. Most days, before having lunch and dinner, He would take walks in front of His room. That particular day, He had His lunch at the table. The weather was very pleasant, and the ocean was calm. The Master's face was brimming with the utmost joy.

That evening, a respected woman attained the presence of the

Master. This woman was sailing first class, and had been moved by the Master's talk – which He gave on the ship before it had set sail – and had sought permission through the Bahá'ís of New York to visit the Master. After receiving permission to make this visit, she sat down and asked Him, 'How are You faring with this voyage across the ocean?' The Master said in response:

> When God entrusts one to do something, He also gives one the capacity to endure it. We should not be constantly preoccupied with bodily comfort; rather, we should strive for lofty goals, even if those goals are incompatible with physical comfort.

The woman then remarked, 'I fear hardship and death', to which the Master responded:

> In that case, do something that will cause you never to die, but rather to become more alive with every passing day, and will confer eternal life upon you. According to the words of Christ, those who enter the Kingdom of God will never die. Enter, then, into the Kingdom of God, that you may have no fear of death. One should seek that life which has no end. This mortal life lasts for only a few days. This eating and sleeping will come to an end; it has no significance. What should be sought is that life which ends not in death, that day which is not succeeded by night, and that joy which is not followed by sorrow. Strive to the utmost; be not content with the ease and comfort of the flesh.

Afterwards, the subject of the stillness of the ocean and the gentle course of the ship was raised. The Master stated:

> One must embark upon the divine Ark, for this world is a turbulent ocean. All the people of the earth, more than two billion in number, shall all be drowned within the next hundred years, except for them that have boarded the divine Ark; they shall be saved. That Ark is the Ark of the Kingdom; it is a heavenly Ark. He that embarks thereon shall never drown. How many the kings

who came into the world! How many the men of stature who lived in it! And yet they all drowned, while the apostles of Christ were spared. My meaning is this, that those who are illumined with the light of God will shine from the horizon of everlasting glory. One must be wise; one should not be content with this earthly life, which will eventually come to an end. A wise person is one who seeks eternal life and perpetual glory.

The woman then asked, 'Will they that are not wise, then, be deprived of everlasting life?' The Master replied:

The permanence of those souls, when compared with that of the sanctified souls, is even as non-existence itself. It is similar to this wood, which does exist, but has no real life when compared with the world of humanity. Therefore, the existence and permanence of worldly souls, when compared with heavenly existence and permanence, cannot truly be called life. If this mortal life had any real significance, Jesus Christ would not have consented to be crucified. This ephemeral life is nothing but grief and sorrow. With every passing day, people grow anxious about their hopes and dreams, or mourn the loss of a loved one, or suffer an unforeseen calamity. What sort of life is this? The real life is the life which is everlasting. Let your thoughts be fixed upon that which is eternal, that you may have no fear of death, and ever regard yourself as one alive. Be courageous! A person's heart must overflow with life, his spirit must be filled with gladness, and his understanding must be vast and all-embracing; otherwise, he is like the animal – no, baser would he be! If merit lies in material existence, then the birds fare better than we. How hard must one work to live, and what hardships one must endure to survive! Yet, the birds of the mountains and prairies live effortlessly on the highest peaks and branches of trees. The fields and plains are their scenery, and the seeds and crops their wealth. No human knows such peace! If physical comfort were the only criterion, the lives of these birds would assuredly be superior to human life.

The Master continued to discuss subjects along these lines, until the music began to play, when singing and the sound of the piano could be heard. To entertain the passengers, an orchestra would play on a stage inside the ship several times after each meal over the course of the day. That night, the Master's food was brought to His room at 9 p.m.

Friday, 6 December 1912

[En route to Liverpool, on board the *Celtic*]

In the morning, 'Abdu'l-Bahá went to take a warm bath, which very much helped Him to relax. He then expressed how pleased He was with that bath.

At lunchtime, He joined the others at the table. After having His food, He said to the attendant:

> This chair and table of mine are by the door. It is cold here. You have other chairs and tables available; kindly put my chair somewhere else.

After resting for a short while, the Master took His tea in the saloon. He then went for a brief stroll, and after taking His seat again, He said the following:

> A seed has been planted in the states of America. Many people have become stirred and roused to excitement. The rest is now in God's hands. Praised be God, we have acted in accordance with the injunction of Jesus Christ – in every land and city through which we have passed, no dust has settled on our hem or on our shoes,* and we have spread the sweet savours of God and promulgated His Word with the utmost detachment.

* cf. Matt. 10:14: 'And whosoever shall not receive you, nor hear your words, when ye depart out of that house or city, shake off the dust of your feet.'

That night, the Master's food was brought to His room at 9 p.m. He retired shortly after having His dinner.

Saturday, 7 December 1912

[En route to Liverpool, on board the *Celtic*]

The Master was very happy that morning. He remarked, 'I was comfortable last night. Praised be God, the waters are calm and the ship is steady.' Afterwards, the letters which the American believers gave to the Master as He was preparing to depart were translated into Persian and read to Him. This continued until lunchtime, when He joined the others to have His meal. It was very cold outside, and since the Master could see from afar that His chair had once again been placed by the door, He returned to His room and did not come back outside. He said:

> Since the people of the East have not treated the attendants of this ship well, they now look upon those people with contempt. Inasmuch as it behooves one to respect the nobility of all humankind, I will assume an attitude of austerity and regard these people with indifference in order to educate them.

The Master was then asked to have a seat at the table, but He declined. He refused to eat their food, and did not disclose His reason for doing so. Eventually, the attendants of the ship themselves discovered the reason, and asked the Master for His forgiveness. With every passing day, He would show more generosity towards them. He would tip the attendants handsomely, and on a few occasions, He gave their supervisor some coins. At last, He said:

> I shall come to the table, but will first content myself with eating separately for a few more days, for the people of the East do not wish to behave imperiously. It is possible that the Europeans believe themselves to be superior to us, but we consider all people the servants of God and regard all humanity the same way.

From then on, whenever He spoke, He would do so with a smile. He would, moreover, relate anecdotes and offer His counsel. Those attendants so came to respect the Master that, from afar, they would humble themselves in deference even to the members of His retinue, and express their sincerest respect for them.

The Master spent most of that day writing responses to the letters of some of the believers. At His request, Áqá Siyyid Asadu'lláh prepared some rice and strained yogurt for His dinner.

Sunday, 8 December 1912

[En route to Liverpool, on board the *Celtic*]

From the morning till the afternoon, the Master was busily engaged in writing a number of lengthy Tablets on the subject of divine wisdom. For His meal that day, He contented Himself with some bread and cheese. The attendants' supervisor came several times to express his remorse, and to convey his deepest regret that the Master was not taking a seat at the table. He said to the Master, 'I fear that we might have offended You.' The Master offered him some comfort, and said, 'Rest assured that I am not at all upset.' He then proceeded to go for a stroll outside. Up until that day, the weather was very pleasant and the water was calm. At one point, He said, 'It would be good for the waters to become turbulent and tempestuous. I would not mind such a thing; it would be interesting to watch.' Early that night, the Master saw a shining star that had just appeared in the sky. He called out to His retinue and said, 'Come and see what a brilliant star this is! I cherish the hope that the loved ones of the Blessed Beauty may be like this shining star.'

After going for a lengthy stroll on the deck, the Master seated Himself and said:

> I have taken 4,600 steps. This is the distance between the city of 'Akká and the Shrine of Bahá'u'lláh. I wish to practise walking, that I may be able to travel to the Shrine of Bahá'u'lláh on foot. In the latter days of my time in the Holy Land, I had grown so weak as to be deprived of the bounty of making pilgrimage on foot.

Afterwards, He had occasion to speak at length about the condition and actions of the Covenant-breakers. He related humorous anecdotes about the Azalís and Mírzá Yaḥyá himself.[13] His meals that day and night consisted of bread and cheese.

Monday, 9 December 1912

[En route to Liverpool, on board the *Celtic*]

The waters were somewhat turbulent, and the turbulence grew stronger with every passing hour. The weather was rainy, and tempestuous gales were blowing. Yet, since the ship was large and sturdy, none of the passengers felt any turbulence; indeed, one could hardly tell that there was a storm going on. The Master went outside to watch, occasionally while walking, and sometimes while standing. He said humorously:

> A surging ocean is more enjoyable to watch. These mountain-like waves, with their rising and falling, are truly a sight to behold. If this ship were not large, all the passengers would have felt seasick by now.

His meals that day and night consisted of rice. The attendants and their supervisor approached the Master several times, asking Him if He would like them to bring some of the ship's food to His room, but He declined their offer.

That afternoon, the Master read some of the letters that had arrived from Shiraz and Qazvin. In spite of the stormy weather, He began to dictate responses without delay. Even the remembrance of the friends in Persia was enough to bring great joy to His heart; it would light up His face and wreathe it in smiles. He said, 'The handkerchiefs are filled with letters from Persia. All these other letters still remain, but until we reach the Shrine of Bahá'u'lláh, we will not be able to respond to them.'

He made repeated mention that day of Áqá Riḍá Shírází Muhájir[14] and his illustrious son;[15] after the ascension of his father's pure soul, the character of that youth was transformed. Likewise, in the evening, He made repeated mention of Mírzá Abu'l-Faḍl,[16] the late Mírzá Muḥammad Riḍá Yazdí,[17] and the days in which they were imprisoned in Tehran, relating stories of their integrity, firmness, and steadfastness. He continued this until eventually He had his dinner, and returned, with the utmost joy, to His room to rest.

Tuesday, 10 December 1912

[En route to Liverpool, on board the *Celtic*]

The ocean was more turbulent, and the storm had grown fiercer, but the Master's condition nonetheless improved with every passing day. He showed no signs of fatigue whatsoever – only prior to the storm, when, owing to weariness and an upset stomach, He would suffer from sleeplessness and a slight fever, yet even those symptoms subsided with the onset of the storm. Because it was raining and hailing, the Master would not go outside for walks as often. Before and after noon, He read the letters from the friends of Persia, and would issue Tablets in response. At the insistence of the steward, the Master's food was sent directly from the kitchen to His room. At night, He gave instructions on how to prepare chicken and rice for His dinner.

On that same day, the Master offered a fruit basket to one of the attendants.[18] As it happened, a small box that belonged to Him had fallen into that basket. After a few minutes, the attendant brought the box back to the Master. The Master rejoiced at the trustworthiness of this attendant, so much so that He gave the box back to him and tipped him a dollar. He said to the attendant, 'Your honesty and trustworthiness have pleased me greatly.' The Master then gave a lengthy exposition on the merits of trustworthiness; this talk was enlightening, and served to remind those present of the benefits of this virtue.[19]

The Master inquired as to the salary of the attendants and their supervisors. They replied, 'Our pay ranges from $15 to $20.' The Master then said:

> This is little compared to America. Though expenses are lower in England, still their workers' wages are too low. This is the reason they go on strike; the workers join forces with one another, and then refuse to work. The communists are given to starting revolutions. Proper rules and regulations must be established and enforced for the benefit of workers.

And on another occasion, He said, 'Were the companies to give a share of their profits to their workers, not only would they cease to strike, but it would also result in the advancement of the masses.'

That day and night, in spite of the storm outside, the Master was feeling very well, and He slept and ate better than He did on the previous days and nights.

Wednesday, 11 December 1912

[En route to Liverpool, on board the *Celtic*]

The storm was raging fiercely, and the ocean was rising and falling violently. The waves were like mountains, and we were battered on every side by the rain, the wind, and the hail. In spite of all this, however – because the ship was large, because it was carrying a heavy load, and because its Passenger was none other than the Mariner of the Ark of the Covenant – the ship rocked gently from side to side like a cradle, priding itself in the precious Burden it was carrying. Although it was difficult to walk on the ship with the storm raging outside, the Master would go there nonetheless and lean against a wall to see what was taking place. What a sight it was to see the Master smile and joke with the attendants! He demonstrated a calm, unruffled demeanour. Despite the great multitude of towering waves, truly a frightening sight for anyone to behold, yet the Master was happier that day than on any other. The dining tables were fastened to the floor to prevent the serving dishes from being overturned by the strong winds. The tranquil behaviour, the cheerful attitude which the Master maintained throughout that storm, were so readily apparent that everyone around Him felt gladdened and reassured.

In the evening, the intensity of the storm subsided a bit. While the orchestra was playing music on the deck,[20] the Master made some comments, among which were the following:

> There are strange relationships in the world of creation. Although melody and voice are ordinary phenomena – mere vibrations in the air, and properties of the material realm – yet when they reach the auditory nerve, it causes the spirit to rejoice.

At night, the storm intensified once again. The Master, however, stayed seated on the deck, and said these words:

> What would you say if I were to suddenly enter the Masjid S̲h̲áh[*] in Tehran, and say to the enemies of the Faith, 'You have sought after me, and here I am now'? The early days of Náṣiri'd-Dín S̲h̲áh's reign were a time for self-sacrifice. The very moment the believers would enter [the mosques], they would straightway be hanged or beheaded. Now, however, the times have changed. Siyyid 'Alí-Akbar Ás̲h̲tíyání once alleged that 'that person'[†] was amassing an army in the vicinity. When I heard this allegation, I wrote lengthy expositions in response. Among the things I said, I disavowed any intention of amassing an army to wage wars, and stated that I had, rather, prepared an arena where people may lay down their lives [for this Faith]. Furthermore, I said, 'You may choose to believe me or not, but I say to you that if the Persian government were to ask the Ottoman government [to allow me to go to Persia], and the Ottoman government were to consent to this arrangement, then I would hasten to Tehran. Prepare the means; if I come right away, you will see for yourself that I am a man of my word.'

In the midst of the intense storm, He talked and made more jokes than He would at other times. Among the things He said was the following:

---

[*] The S̲h̲áh Mosque.
[†] 'Abdu'l-Bahá.

> My mind was preoccupied last night with the materialist philosophers, and how oblivious they are. Although the new philosophers have conclusively denounced the mistakes of their ancient predecessors, yet they have made their own senses the standard by which they pass judgement. The philosophers of old believed in the four elements, and contended that the element of fire was above ether, but these materialist philosophers now maintain that all these elements are compounded rather than uncompounded, and that, while ether cannot be detected by the senses, it nonetheless encompasses all creation. Although these philosophers believe ether to be intangible, yet they deny the existence of other intangible forces – this notwithstanding that the inability to perceive something with the senses does not necessarily prove the non-existence of that thing . . .

The Master had a bit of rice for His food that day. With every passing day, an increasingly greater number of passengers and crewmen came to see Him. Even the officers would visit Him and inquire after Him with the utmost deference. One of the members of His retinue said, 'The people on this ship, whether high or low, show us great reverence.' In response, the Master said:

> Wherever you may be, the Blessed Beauty has exalted you there. Appreciate the value of this bounty and give thanks to God for it.

The storm grew fiercer after midnight that night.

Thursday, 12 December 1912
[En route to Liverpool, on board the *Celtic*]

The intensity of the storm had waned by the morning. Consequently, the doors of the ship's third floor, which had been closed up to that point, were opened. The ship continued to sail, and the storm ended altogether at nighttime. That night, the ship sailed past the pier of Queenstown. The Master said:

> We will arrive at the pier of Liverpool in England tomorrow, then. We have made commitments to speak at several places, and following the conversations at those meetings, it will take us four and a half hours to reach London by train.

Since the waters were calm that night, all the passengers of the ship attained the Master's presence in the main room of the first class. The women were seated and the men were standing. They were all completely captivated by the exchange of questions and answers that took place, and profoundly awed by His utterances.

The Master spoke of the unity of humankind and universal peace. In this talk, He likened this world to a garden, and compared the different peoples and races to variegated flowers. He stated that if all the flowers in a garden were to be of one kind, that garden would not appear very beautiful, but that if flowers of varying colour were arranged next to one another, this would embellish and add to the beauty of the garden. He continued in that vein, stating that if all the peoples of varying colour in the garden of the world of humanity – even as Eastern flowers, Western flowers, Italian flowers, American flowers, and French flowers – were to come together in groups and become united with one another, one could imagine the beauty and splendour that garden would acquire. These analogies so moved everyone present that they beamed with joy, like budding flowers themselves, and they expressed their gratitude to the Master.

When He spoke of the time He was in prison, He said, 'I entered prison a young man, and left it an old one.' Those who were present were greatly moved by this remark; indeed, even the interpreter (Mirza Ahmad Sohrab) fought back tears as he translated. After the meeting was concluded, each of the attendees came to shake hands with the Master. They humbled themselves in deference before Him, and were then dismissed. Some of them acquired the addresses of the Bahá'ís living in London, that they might have the honour of visiting the Master there. Many of them expressed the hope of attaining the presence of the Master tomorrow, which would be the last day of their voyage.

Praise be to God that, in the wilderness and on the sea, in the cities and villages, on the hills and mountains – in all these places, the power of the Covenant of God and the might of His Cause is evident. Every heart that came into the presence of the Master was enamoured of Him, and the confirmations of the Abhá Kingdom would descend upon them.

Friday, 13 December 1912

[En route to Liverpool, on board the *Celtic* → Liverpool]

This was to be the last day of our voyage; the skies were cloudy and the waters were calm. One by one, passengers and members of the crew attained the presence of the Master and expressed their gladness. Some of them invited the Master to their homes, which were in the vicinity of London, and the members of the crew sang His praises for the generosity He showed them; they were all like lowly servants.

The Master's talk that day concerned the education of the human race through the divine religions. According to Him, the purpose of religion is for the image of God to be reflected in the world of humanity; otherwise, if religion is the cause of discord and strife, it is better to dispense with it – and under such circumstances, ferocious beasts would be superior to humans. One of those present inquired about the possibility of a world war. In response, the Master said:

> In America, I stated that the Balkan War* was the beginning of the world war to which you refer.

At that moment I recalled that, when we were in America, Mirza Ahmad Sohrab told me that the Master had previously made this same remark when asked about the prospect of a world war.

The ship eventually reached the pier at Liverpool, and it was moored that afternoon. As they stood on the pier, the friends from London and Paris saw the Master, and they expressed their great

* The First Balkan War (8 October 1912–30 May 1913).

longing and adoration towards Him from a distance. The first to attain the presence of the Master was Mr [Hippolyte] Dreyfus.[21] Following that, a number of reporters – who were already aware of the Master's imminent arrival – entered His presence. They asked about His journey, and inquired about His purpose in undertaking it. He replied:

> I come from America, where I spent nine months as a traveller. I spoke at many churches and synagogues, and called on those present to embrace the unity of humanity. I summoned them, moreover, to universal peace – peace among nations, peace among religions, peace among the races, and peace among all lands. I discussed the benefits of peace, and explained the detriments of war and strife. I proclaimed that the foundation of all the divine religions is one, and that these dissensions have stemmed from blind imitation. Were the followers of religion to renounce this blind imitation, they would all become united. In brief, I summoned everyone to love and unity, and guided them to promote universal peace, that war and strife may cease to exist among humankind. All shall become as the members of one family, conducting themselves and associating with one another in a spirit of utmost love and fellowship. Thus will the East and the West embrace one another. These teachings had a profound effect on the hearts of those who heard them. At every gathering, a number of those present came to agree on the necessity of universal peace. In America, people are now greatly disposed to peace, and I cherish the hope that significant results will be gained therefrom. Indeed, this is the very purpose of my journey to London.

The Master was asked if He was the Messiah. He replied, 'I am a servant of God.'

Afterwards, Mr Dreyfus and I disembarked the ship at the Master's request, and accompanied Him to the hotel. Mirza Ahmad Sohrab and Áqá Siyyid Asadu'lláh passed the luggage through customs and came as well. When the Master came ashore, the friends from Liverpool, London, and Paris leapt with joy, and derived imperishable bounties from having the privilege of meeting Him and hearing Him speak.

The Master lodged at the Midland Adelphi hotel,[22] which was located in the best part of the city. After getting settled there, Mr Dreyfus informed the Master that Mr [Edward Granville] Browne[23] had expressed sentiments of regret and indicated that he had learned from his past mistakes; he mentioned how great an honour it would be to see the Master during His visit here, and accounted his failure to see Him during His previous travels as one of his losses in this life. Upon hearing this, the Master said:

> One should not place one's trust in such people. What he has said is of no importance to me whatsoever. During my sojourn in America, there were people who showed deference to me and fellowship with me, compared with whom people such as Browne are not worthy of mention. Even in New York, the renowned Carnegie* – the richest man in America – invited me to his home several times, and I declined. The consul general of Persia† made repeated entreaties on Carnegie's behalf, and I said, 'If he were poor, I would visit him at his home. Since, however, he is the richest person in America and enjoys great fame there, it would not be prudent [for me to visit him].' What I mean to say is that I pay no mind to people like Carnegie, though they show me the utmost deference. What, then, can be said of people like Browne, whose only aims are to advance their own interests and pursue their ulterior motives?

Sometime later, the Master happily ate His dinner and went to rest.

---

* Andrew Carnegie.

† H. H. Topakyan.

England

Saturday, 14 December 1912[24]

[Liverpool]

The leader of the Theosophists[25] attained the presence of the Master, and expressed the hope that He would speak at the Theosophical Society of Liverpool that night. After that, the minister of the Pembroke Chapel [Reverend Donald B. Fraser] also attained the presence of the Master, and invited Him to speak at his church the following night. The Master accepted both of these invitations. His utterances completely captivated and greatly elated those two individuals.

That day, one of the Bahá'ís of the East, Aḥmad Effendí Yazdí,[26] came from London to visit the Master, Who showed him great kindness. Telegrams were sent to gatherings of the East and West, announcing that the Master had arrived at the pier of England.[27] When He had finished sending some mail and telegrams of His own, the Master went outside for a stroll, after which He came back inside and had His lunch in the hotel. The Master relaxed for a bit, and some newspapers were then translated for Him. These newspapers reported that when the ministers of various countries had arrived to establish peace between the Balkan states and the Ottoman Empire, an Eastern prophet had also come from America at the same time. They accounted this a happy coincidence – one that would upraise the call of peace, and cause the signs of war and strife to dwindle away. Afterwards, the Master raised up His hands and said:

> The Blessed Beauty has showered His grace and bounty upon everyone. All are sheltered beneath the wing of His protection and assistance. The aid and confirmations of His Kingdom have cast their shadow upon all humankind. The effects and pervading influence of His teachings are evident in every clime and country.

And when Mr Dreyfus entered the room, the Master said:

> After this journey, the call of the unity of humanity and universal peace must be upraised in the Ottoman territories. Their turn shall come; perhaps an effort will be made to unite their various peoples. We are now in Britain and will depart for Haifa in a few months; let us see what the Will of God has in store.

Afterwards, the Master spoke of the Azalís. He gave detailed accounts of their chaotic state and the number of wives [Mírzá] Yaḥyá [Ṣubḥ-i-Azal] had taken to himself. Mr Dreyfus told the Master how Mírzá Yaḥyá Dawlatábádí[28] had disgraced himself:

> When it had become known that, in Lausanne [in Switzerland], Yaḥyá Dawlatábádí had had an affair with the wife of a certain man, in whose house he had taken up residence, that man threw [Mírzá Yaḥyá Dawlatábádí] out of his house. The news of this shameful act was spread far and wide, and when I myself asked him, 'People are saying this about you. Why did you do this?' He replied, 'This is natural instinct.'

The Master said:

> The foundation of these [Azalís] is chaos and confusion. From this act which their very leader committed, one can discern the conduct of the others in their ranks. These foolish people wish, in their depraved state, to oppose a Cause that has stirred both East and West and directed the attention of humanity to the kingdom of sanctity.

In this vein, the Master talked at length about the greatness of the Cause of God, as well as the captivating beauty and glorious power of Bahá'u'lláh, before Whose holy threshold every stranger and enemy would humble themselves upon attaining it. The Master said that even Browne himself was like a lowly servant in the presence of Bahá'u'lláh. He made these remarks with the utmost majesty and grandeur as He walked to and fro.

At eight o'clock, the leader of the Theosophists arrived with a special vehicle for the Master. When He entered the gathering of the Theosophists, He gave a lengthy talk, masterfully executed and highly effective, on the subject of the independent investigation of truth, the limitless sovereignty of God, the outpourings of God's grace, the appearance of Holy Manifestations in every dispensation, and the gathering together of diverse peoples under the shadow of the Bahá'í Cause.[29] At the end of that gathering, all who were present shook the Master's hand with the utmost humility, and expressed their joy and gratitude to Him. They remained by His side until the moment He embarked the vehicle.

For dinner that night, the Master had a traditional Persian meal consisting of rice and *khoresh*.[30] In the highest of spirits, He ate this meal in the room where the members of His retinue were staying. In addition to the Persian attendants, Mr Dreyfus also had the honour of dining in the presence of the Master.

Sunday, 15 December 1912
[Liverpool]

In the early morning, the Master called out to the members of His retinue and invited them to pray and have tea together.[31] Afterwards, the Master thanked the Blessed Beauty for His confirmations:

> From the day I left Haifa to the present time, the confirmations of the Kingdom have encompassed me more and more with every passing day. In Egypt, confirmations were vouchsafed to me; in Europe, powerful assistance was rendered me; and in America, more than anywhere else, the light of aid and protection from the unseen Kingdom dawned over me. All these are the confirmations of the Blessed Beauty; without them, we are but wretched servants, powerless and destitute in every respect. Day and night, all our thoughts should be fixed upon one thing only; we must devote our time to service. Europe is submerged in the ocean of materialism; its inhabitants are even as cows that have busied themselves with grazing in the pasture. They can see nothing at all, for their gaze is ever cast down. America, at least, fares better than they.

In the afternoon, a number of the friends from London and Liverpool; a Theosophist youth, who upon meeting the Master became a Bahá'í;[32] and one of the friends from Manchester [Sarah Ann Ridgway] all attained the presence of the Master. After giving a lengthy talk, and showering every one of those people with His loving-kindness, He went to the Pembroke Chapel at 6:30 p.m. He seated Himself in one of the rooms of the church, and the ministers gave Him a warm welcome. They told Him that this church was open to all, and that eminent people from every religion had spoken here. The Master said:

> It is good that this church is open to everyone, and is the cause of fellowship among every sect and creed, inasmuch as whatever is universal is of God, and that which is particular is of humanity. The Sun of bounty shines upon everyone, and the showers of mercy rain upon all, for they are divine bestowals.

The church began to teem with people, so much so that even the seats in the upper balcony were all taken.[33] The Master relocated to the lower level of a platform attached to the church altar. That platform had two levels; one of the ministers repeatedly implored the Master go to the upper level, but He refused. The minister eventually said, 'The whole audience will not be able to hear You if You stand on the lower level of the platform, and everyone here is yearning to see You and hear Your blessed voice.' The Master then consented to the minister's request, and went to the upper level of the platform.

To introduce the Master, the minister gave an account of His life from the time He entered the Most Great Prison until the journey He undertook to promote the Cause of God. He mentioned, moreover, the large number of adherents this Cause enjoyed in both the East and the West, as well as its sublime teachings and how they will conduce to peace on earth. This minister encouraged the audience to treat the Master with the utmost reverence, and to reflect carefully upon the teachings He presented. He remarked, furthermore, that he accounted the Master's visit to his church as a source of pride. At that point, the Master rose. Though this gathering was taking place in a church, all who were present applauded Him with sheer joy, and expressed their utmost delight and happiness. The Master's talk on that occasion dealt with the essential unity of all religions, the detriments of blind imitation, the spread of this new and wondrous Cause, and the greatness and veracity of Islam.[34] The audience listened with the utmost deference. When the Master concluded His talk, they applauded Him once again, and expressed even more eagerness and joy than before. Indeed, they made quite a commotion. As the minister drew the gathering to a close – heaping repeated praise upon the Master all the while – he asked the audience to rise, and requested the Master to recite a prayer. The Master rose and, lifting His arms up in supplication, began to recite a prayer. When He had concluded the prayer, He went to another room of the church,[35] and a number of the attendants expressed their desire to attain His presence. They demonstrated the utmost deference towards Him, and entreated that He pray for them to be confirmed.

In brief, in a city wherein the Cause of God had yet to be proclaimed, a number of people grew enamoured of the Master, and turned their faces towards the Most Glorious Horizon.

That night, the Master had dinner in the hotel. Weary and fatigued, He then went to His room to rest.

Monday, 16 December 1912
[Liverpool → London]

In the morning, the Master's car set out for London. After performing His obligatory prayer and reciting other prayers, He instructed His retinue to gather their things.

At nine o'clock, the Master went from the hotel to the train station [Lime Street Station]. The members of His retinue consisted of Áqá Aḥmad Yazdí, Mr Dreyfus, Mirza Ahmad Sohrab, Áqá Siyyid Asadu'lláh, Mrs [Isabel] Fraser, Miss [Elizabeth] Herrick, and this lowly servant.[36] The weather was temperate and very clear. The fields and meadows we saw on the way were lush and verdant, and the Master was in the highest of spirits.

When we arrived in London,[37] Lady Blomfield and her daughters [Mary and Rose], along with Mrs [Ethel] Rosenberg and a great number of other believers,[38] gathered around the Master. The cries of jubilation they raised were so loud as to draw the attention of those around them, and demonstrate to those onlookers the ardour of their devotion to the Master. Once the Master had inquired after each and every one of them, and showed them His characteristic kindness, He went to Lady Blomfield's home by way of a special vehicle. Despite the instruction the Master had given in America for a house to be secured in England where He would lodge, Lady Blomfield excitedly implored Him to bless her house with His presence. [To prepare that house for the arrival of the Master,] she had moved to another house a few days previously.[39] She insisted upon this offer, and begged the Master to accept it, so He eventually consented but said that He would pay for His own expenses. From the moment He entered that house, He would spend every waking moment in the company of friends and others alike. Likewise, a number of reporters also attained His presence and recorded His utterances in detail.

Tuesday, 17 December 1912
[London]

In the morning, a number of believers, some of whom lived in the area – as well as some seekers from London – all attained the presence of the Master. When His audience, which consisted of both believers and others, swelled to a great number, the Master spoke of more general subjects – the rejection of blind imitation, the barriers created by religious superstitions, the necessity of abandoning those imaginings and imitations which are contrary to science and reason, and the need to cast aside the hearsay of one's forefathers – to demonstrate to them that the essences of religious matters, which accord with science and reason, conduce to the intellectual growth and perpetual prosperity of peoples and nations. When He had concluded His talk, the majority of those present expressed their desire to have a private audience with the Master. One by one, they attained His presence. This continued until close to noon, when the Master received a telephone call through Lady Blomfield, the purpose of which was to make this request: 'Since the Master will be speaking at our gathering next week, with His permission, we would like to ask Mr Browne to preside over that gathering.' The Master replied, 'I will give my answer tomorrow.' Lady Blomfield and a number of the other believers remarked that Browne had changed, and mentioned that, if he were to preside over that gathering, he would introduce the Master with such reverent praise, and expatiate upon His qualities with such admiration, that it would disabuse people of the notion that he was opposed to the Cause. The Master, however, paid no mind at all to their remarks.

In the afternoon,[40] the Master went to a dignified gathering that was held in His honour [at Caxton Hall, Caxton Street, Westminster] by Mrs [Mary, or 'Minnie', Thornburgh-]Cropper, and was attended by a large number of friends and others. In a separate room, tables had been set with flowers, sweets, and *sharbats*.* It was a lively, glorious gathering. For His talk, the Master gave an account of His journey to America. He discussed the addresses He delivered in various gathering-places, churches, and synagogues, and underscored the profound effect and pervading influence of the teachings of Bahá'u'lláh. He concluded this address by describing how all things, including the religion of God, have been made new. The words of the Master generated a new level of excitement in the hearts of His listeners, and added to the ardour of their desire for Him. Once He had concluded His talk, a number of believers gave special speeches which expressed their joy at His arrival there, and praised and glorified the Cause of God. As a result, the Master rose again to show His kindness to those friends, and encourage them to serve at the divine threshold. As the gathering was drawing to a close, those present approached the Master, one by one, and shook His hand as they expressed their devotion and deference to Him. This continued until it was time to depart, at which point the Master remarked, 'I wish to go for a walk.' Consequently, a number of the respected friends – men and women, from both East and

* A sweet, refreshing fruit drink, usually served chilled in the summertime.

West – accompanied the Master until He reached His residence.

At night, a great number of people attained the presence of the Master, Who spoke at length on a variety of subjects.[41] Among His utterances was the following:

> Whenever a prophet would appear, people would say to them, 'We were enjoying ourselves in accordance with our own thoughts and desires. We would eat, sleep, sing, and dance. We had neither fear of God, nor hope of the Kingdom; we were content with what we had, and were occupied with our own whims. Despite all this, you came and deprived us of our pleasures and robbed us of our delights. At one time, you would frighten us with the wrath of God; at another, you would speak of the fear of punishment and the hope of reward in the hereafter. In short, you ruined all our joy.' The divine prophets, however, would reply, 'You had satisfied yourselves with the lives of animals; We desired only to elevate you to the rank of humans. You were enveloped in darkness; We wished for you to be luminous. You were as dead; We wanted you to be revived. You were terrestrial; We willed that you be celestial.'

After giving an extensive account of the [First] Balkan War, the Master said:

> In the world of humanity, love is a manifestation of the splendour of God. Without love, this world would be even as the animal kingdom. The distinction of the world of humanity is love. Until there is love among humankind, complete tranquillity and perfect prosperity will never be achieved. Consider how a person is filled with excitement and delight when he sits next to his friend, and how he is overcome with torment and dread alongside his enemy. Therefore, you must promulgate universal love and promote the brotherhood of all humanity. Now, we are from the East, and you are from the West, and we are gathered here in a spirit of utmost love and fellowship. Is this not better than if we were to be embroiled in conflict and contention? Is it not preferable to the

shedding of one another's blood, or the uprooting of each other's families? We must awaken the souls, that they may learn the secret of the world of existence, and recognize the gifts and bounties of God. Otherwise, people will continue to toil unnecessarily and be afflicted with calamity. They see that which is outwardly apparent, not what lies within. They see only lamps of varying form, not the reality of the light and the mystery of its manifestation.

Wednesday, 18 December 1912
[London]

In the morning, the daily gathering at the residence of the Master was convened. The number of those present, consisting of both believers and others, was so great that there were not enough chairs to seat everyone. As a result, most of the attendees stood. For His talk, the Master spoke of the contrast between the benightedness and ephemerality of material pursuits, and the radiance and permanence of spiritual endeavours. He explained, moreover, that the fruit of the world of existence is the acquisition of the perfections of God. Among those who were present that day, and attained the presence of the Master, was Mr Browne. When the gathering was concluded, a number of the attendees expressed their desire to have a private audience with the Master, even though they had already attained His presence earlier. This included the aforementioned [Browne], whose meeting with the Master proved lengthy.[42] I have recorded the words with which the Master addressed Browne exactly as they were spoken to him. The gist of what took place is as follows:

After showing deference to the Master, Browne immediately began to discuss matters of the past. He wished to explain himself, and sought the Master's forgiveness for what had taken place. The Master replied, 'We should discuss other matters – matters that will generate feelings of love.' Realizing that the Master had no interest in dwelling on the past, Browne changed the subject. He inquired about the current situation in Persia and the Ottoman Empire. The Master replied:

> I have previously written that, for as long as the government and the people are not mingled together like milk and honey, prosperity shall remain unattainable. Persia shall fall into ruin, and as a result, the governments of neighbouring countries will work to meddle in its affairs.

The Master elaborated further on the same subject, saying:

> You must strive to transform the characters of the people, such that they will become receptive to constitutionalism and other matters. Should this not occur, fresh problems will beset you with every passing day, and anguish and despair will increase. Consider how acquired knowledge, when not aligned with a refined character, becomes the cause of harm. Indeed, if the acquisition of knowledge is coupled with the best of characters, that knowledge will bring about marvellous results . . . Material progress and civilization alone will not suffice, and the acquisition of knowledge by itself will not result in complete prosperity.

Afterwards, the aforementioned [Browne] remarked that the people of Europe have categorically disregarded the promises of the prophets, and have rejected spirituality altogether. At that moment, the Master gave an extensive explanation of supernatural power, and adduced conclusive proofs in support thereof, in such a way that his interlocutor could do nothing but agree with Him and show greater and greater humility towards Him with every passing moment. Browne was eventually dismissed; he departed with the utmost deference and requested the Master's permission to have a second meeting with Him.

That afternoon, one of the teachers of Esperanto[43] – as well as a number of respected men and women who had recently arrived[44] – attained the presence of the Master, Who spoke extensively of divine subjects. Up until the very end of the day, people were constantly entering and leaving the Master's presence.

RMS Celtic

Midland Adelphi Hotel, Liverpool, where 'Abdu'l-Bahá stayed

Interior of the Pembroke Chapel, Liverpool, where 'Abdu'l-Bahá spoke on 15 December 1912

Maḥmúd Zarqání, chronicler of 'Abdu'l-Bahá's travels in the West

Ahmad Sohrab, a member of 'Abdu'l-Bahá's retinue during His travels in Europe and Egypt and whose diaries provide unique insights into His daily activities

Aḥmad Effendi Yazdí (Mírzá Aḥmad Yazdí), son-in-law of 'Abdu'l-Bahá, who met Him at the pier in Liverpool and became part of His retinue

Ethel Rosenberg

Sara, Lady Blomfield

Marion Jack, Canadian Bahá'í painter who arranged a meeting for 'Abdu'l-Bahá in London

Mary (Minnie) Thornburgh-Cropper

The Salvation Army Centre, Great Peter Street, London, visited by 'Abdu'l-Bahá on 25 December 1912

The Cedars Club, Battersea High Street, London, visited by 'Abdu'l-Bahá on 27 December 1912

Essex Hall where 'Abdu'l-Bahá spoke to the Women's Freedom League on 2 January 1913

Felix and Margaret Moscheles

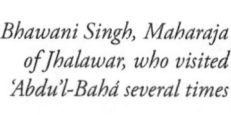

Bhawani Singh, Maharaja of Jhalawar, who visited 'Abdu'l-Bahá several times

Annie Gamble

Elizabeth Gibson Cheyne

Sir Richard Stapley

Alice Buckton

Lord Lamington

Jean Stannard

Yuhanna Dawud Archive, National Library of Israel

Yuhanna Dawud

Thomas Kelly Cheyne

Edward Granville Browne

Thursday, 19 December 1912
[London]

At a gathering that morning,[45] the Master gave a talk on the rights of women:

> Women must educate themselves and strive to acquire virtues. Moreover, they must win their rights through education, and not by force or obstruction, for it befits the wise to seek equality through prudent and educative means. Indeed, the wise seek to secure their rights through the acquisition of virtues, while the ignorant attempt to do this through compulsion. For instance, when a child reaches the age of adolescence, all testify to his growth and maturity.

To conclude His utterance, the Master expatiated upon the goodly character of the Bahá'í women of Persia, who demonstrate soundness of speech and rectitude of conduct in their dealings with others, rather than force and obstruction. When the Master finished His talk, a number of seekers expressed their desire to have an audience with Him, even though they had already attained His presence earlier. Each and every one of them was honoured and gladdened by the wondrous bounties the Master bestowed on them.

Mr Browne was also present in the gathering that day. After that gathering had concluded, he and his wife were summoned by the Master to His room. During their discussion,[46] Browne did not have a chance to mention matters of the past, inasmuch as the Master's aim was to bring about love and fellowship, and not to give Browne the opportunity to express his designs and views. Therefore, with exceeding kindness and a great willingness to overlook the past, the Master spoke of scientific subjects and conveyed anecdotes concerning the affairs of the East. With every passing minute, Browne grew more and more humble before the Master. This continued until the Master eventually dismissed Browne, at which point he kissed the Master's hand. With genuine deference, Browne took his leave.

Afterwards, a reporter entered the Master's presence. Listening attentively, this reporter recorded the words of the Master as He discussed economics from the perspective of the divine teachings. The reporter was eventually dismissed, and he departed with the utmost deference.

In brief, all throughout the day, there was a constant stream of people attaining the presence of the Master, in both public and private settings. Every neck was bowed in humility before the Centre of the Covenant. That day, Ḥájí Amín and his [three] dear travel companions – all of whom had come from Paris the night before[47] – attained the Master's presence.[48] The Master showered them with countless bounties, and their presence brought great joy and gladness to the friends. Amín was asked:

> In those days when you were in the prison of our enemies, and shared a cell with 'Alí-Akbar[49] – may my life be a sacrifice for his resting-place – did you ever imagine that a day would come when you would go to London and attain the presence of the Master, and behold at so festive an occasion this Friend who brings us such great joy?

Ḥájí Amín replied:

> No, I could never have imagined that such assistance, such confirmations would be vouchsafed so swiftly from the Kingdom of the Unseen; that the all-subduing power of the Cause of God would overtake both East and West in this way; and that those who are firm and steadfast in the Covenant would so clearly behold the truth of these words: 'Verily, We . . . shall aid whosoever will arise for the triumph of Our Cause with the hosts of the Concourse on high and a company of Our favoured angels.'[50]

In the afternoon, when the Master went for a stroll outside, He saw some things that could be used for cooking. He purchased these items, and took them back with Him to His residence. When He arrived, a number of those who were waiting for Him asked Him about several subjects, such as the progress of the construction of the Mas͟hriqu'l-Ad͟hkár [in Wilmette], the rights of women, and the like. Late into the night, the Master spoke on all these subjects. Afterwards, He sat at the table to have dinner. In addition to the respected English guests who were there, nine members of the Master's retinue – as well some other Persian friends – were honoured and nourished with His presence.

Friday, 20 December 1912
[London]

Before the Master commenced His address that morning to the public gathering, a number of women inquired about divorce. The Master gave an explication of verses from the Kitáb-i-Aqdas, and this gladdened those present greatly. He remarked that the absence of divorce in certain Christian countries has led to general corruption, noting that even if the husband becomes insane, or both parties grow to hate one another, the enforcement of divorce is virtually impossible. The Master then related anecdotes which illustrated how the inability to execute divorces has led to the shedding of blood, and has caused even the most esteemed individuals to fall into disrepute.[51] He continued, stating that divorce – if carried out in moderation, and done with legitimate reasons – must take place to the extent that it is needed. He noted, moreover, that there is a firm commandment and clear ordinance from Bahá'u'lláh to this effect.[52]

When the daily gathering was commenced, and the drawing room of the residence was teeming with people, the Master gave a profoundly impressive talk on the lack of happiness and tranquillity which characterizes this physical life, and the sadness and sorrow which afflict the people of this mortal world.[53] He observed:

> There is not one among us who is without hope or desire. The king and beggar alike are afflicted with some sorrow, and are both beset by some problem. In reality, there is no such thing as a heart that does not cherish some desire, nor does a desire exist that is not

> without some measure of suffering and anguish. Every hope, therefore, leads to some toil or trouble, and is the barrier to happiness and joy, except for the hopes of such people as have set their affections on the divine realm. Such people shall find spiritual happiness, and their hearts will rejoice. They remain joyous in the midst of calamity, and are free in the direst affliction.

At both the beginning and the end of that gathering, a respected woman who had lost a loved one attained the presence of the Master. With exceeding compassion and tender mercy, the Master consoled her, and after making some extensive remarks, He told her repeatedly:

> Do not cry or lament! Do not wail or let tears rain from your eyes! The happiness and sorrow of this world last only for a time, and its glory and abasement are both fleeting.

The effects produced by the Master's utterances were such as to deeply move every heart. His words liberated those present from every attachment to this world of dust, and drew their attention to the realm of purity.

On that day, too, a number of esteemed individuals attained the Master's presence, and received the outpourings of His imperishable grace.[54] One of the venerable people who had the honour of attaining the Master's presence that afternoon was the ambassador of Persia, and it gladdened him greatly to have had that privilege.[55] Among the remarks which the Master made to that ambassador were the following:

> Since we discerned no fruit from the counsel we gave our countrymen, nor could we find a hearing ear among them, we felt it necessary to turn our attention to the West. While our compatriots busied themselves with the destruction of their families, we were engaged in securing everlasting victories – victories which, in the future, will redound to the unfading glory of the people of the East, and crown Persia and its inhabitants with the diadem of honour . . .

In the evening, a great gathering was held in a spacious room at the Westminster [Palace] Hotel, where the Master was to give a talk.[56] The number of those present was so great that that room, with all its vast space, was unable to accommodate any more people, nor was there room for anyone to stand.[57] The man who presided over that gathering was Sir Thomas Barclay. That man – among the great ones of England, and a respected individual – commenced[58] and concluded that gathering by talking about the Master and showering Him with praise, even expressing how honoured and privileged he felt to be in so illustrious a presence as the Master's. Sir Thomas stated, moreover, that all humankind is in need of these teachings, which he characterized as the means through which the rehabilitation and progress of the peoples of the world can be achieved.[59] When the Master entered that great gathering, all who were present arose. After Sir Thomas had concluded his introductory remarks – while seated on a chair on an elevated platform reserved for oratory, located in the centre of the room – the Master took a seat next to him, and began to give a talk with the utmost glory and majesty.[60] In this talk, the Master observed that life consists of a composition of elements, and that death and extinction entail the decomposition and dispersion of those elements. With rational proofs and trenchant utterances, He summoned His audience to perfect unity and fellowship. The Master then proceeded to talk extensively about the advent of Bahá'u'lláh and enumerate His teachings, and this discussion captivated all those who were present. They all beamed with joy; their hearts were filled with ecstasy and excitement, and had become enamoured of the divine teachings, to such a degree that the entire audience readily expressed the depths of their delight. They applauded the Master numerous times and treated Him with exceeding reverence.

Once the Master had concluded His talk,[61] and after Sir Thomas had showered Him with acclaim and approbation, Miss [Alice] Buckton made some very fitting remarks in praise of the Centre of the Covenant and the teachings of the Blessed Beauty.[62] Afterwards, one of the women – a supporter of women's rights who had spoken at that gathering, named Mrs [Charlotte] Despard – stood up. She, too, spoke eloquently of the necessity and significance of the teachings of this most great Revelation – among which are the education of women and their equal status to men – and underscored the pervasive power of this irresistible Cause.[63] Although she was not a Baháʾí, this woman characterized the message of this Faith as the rehabilitator of the world's religions, and the answer to the needs of the present age. Following this, Mr Dreyfus rose, and began his remarks by expressing how grateful he was that the Cause of God had been introduced to the city of London in this way, and engaged the attention of its most respected inhabitants.[64] He then proceeded to list the distinctive attributes of the Master – the Centre of the Covenant – and also discuss spiritual subjects. When Mr Dreyfus concluded his remarks, Sir Thomas thanked and praised the speakers once again.

Afterwards, the Master rose and began to recite, with great feeling and emotion, a most eloquent prayer in Persian, which implored God to vouchsafe His confirmations and establish world peace.[65] With that, the gathering was concluded – and what a great gathering it was! Everyone was so very excited. Every neck was bowed in reverence; every heart was enraptured and profoundly gladdened. Most of those present expressed their desire to attain the Master's presence a second time, and some of them even requested a private audience with Him. Such a gathering would surely not have been held had it not been for the confirmations of the Abhá Beauty, Who would render fresh assistance to that peerless servant of His threshold [the Master] at every one of the impressive assemblages where He spoke.

That evening, when a number of people had gathered in the Master's presence at His residence, He spoke in particular of love and fellowship among the nations, and the oneness and brotherhood of the peoples of the world.

Saturday, 21 December 1912
[London]

After a great number of people had attained the presence of the Master, these were among the remarks He made:[66]

Last night, we discussed the subjects of love and brotherhood. Love is of several kinds. One of these is the love a person feels for his immediate family and other relatives. This love alone, however, is not sufficient. How often have the bitterest hatred and the most rancorous enmity developed among the members of a family! It is evident, then, that familial love by itself is not enough. The same likewise applies to the love a person feels for the members of his own race; this love, too, is inadequate. How many the times when animosity has sprung up between peoples and races, and grown so fierce that it has led each party to shed the other's blood and plunder his property! Another kind of love and brotherhood is one that is nationalistic in nature. How numerous the countrymen that have risen up against one another with enmity and hatred, and uprooted each other's families! It is clear, therefore, that nationalistic love and brotherhood are likewise insufficient. Still another kind involves love and brotherhood among one's own kind. How frequently have discord and strife ravaged entire clans and tribes! It is apparent, then, that love and brotherhood among one's own kind is not enough. Any fruits which these kinds of love may bear are all ultimately limited and temporary. They will not conduce to the edification of the soul, nor will they result in the gladness of the spirit. Thus, that divine love and spiritual brotherhood which is instilled through the breaths of the Holy Spirit must exist amidst humankind. The fruits of this love and brotherhood are infinite and eternal; they will never be subject to change or alteration. So long as this love and brotherhood exist among a people, their spiritual and physical progress alike shall be limitless. Animated by this love and brotherhood, such a people would readily yield up their lives for one another, inasmuch as this heavenly love and brotherhood go hand in hand with eternal life; the

> one is inextricably bound to the other. The world of humanity is illumined with these ideals. Its glory lies in this love, and its exaltedness depends on this brotherhood. I cherish the hope, therefore, that you will cling to this love. Indeed, I hope that you may cause the appearance of this love in the world, and also become the dawning-places of this brotherhood and the means through which these sweet savours are diffused, that the outpourings of Bahá'u'lláh's grace may be made manifest in the world of humanity, and the bounties of God encompass all humankind. I hope that you all shall be the recipients of such confirmations.

In addition to the various people who visited the Master's room and attained His presence up until the afternoon, a number of respected women's rights activists also requested an audience with the Master that evening. The Master admonished these women greatly; He exhorted them to moderation, a goodly character, and commendable deeds. In those days, the opposition these women showed to men in the government was so vehement that they had concocted a solution similar to nitric acid, and applied it to the mailboxes of every street. Their aim in doing this was to corrode the people's mail – thinking this would render the statesmen powerless – and thus force the government to grant women their rights and subsequently protect them. The Master, therefore, forbade these women repeatedly to commit acts of this nature, and then counselled them to spiritual edification – to demonstrate praiseworthy conduct, and show forth a goodly character – observing that women's progress and the preservation of their rights is conditioned and dependent solely upon moderation in their affairs, their acquisition of a good education, their obtainment of a godly demeanour, and their attainment of human perfections.

Sunday, 22 December 1912[67]
[London]

After a number of people had had private and public audiences with Him, and He had become unoccupied once again, the Master was invited to speak at an event [at Church House Westminster] that involved a theatrical performance about the birth of Jesus Christ, which portrayed the anticipation felt by those seekers at the time of His advent, peace be upon Him.[68] Once that gathering had concluded, the Master went to stand backstage of that hall. As all the backstage actors looked upon Him and listened intently to His words, the Master gave an extensive talk on the sense of anticipation felt by the peoples of the world before the day of Revelation, as well as their heedlessness and debarment following the appearance of Him Who was the Speaker on Sinai and the Dawning-place of light. The Master described all this with such vividness that those present were able to imagine it, and this moved them deeply. From there, the Master went to the Persian legation.[69]

When He returned to His residence afterwards, a number of the European and Persian attendants gathered around the dinner table and attained the Master's presence. After they had finished eating, the Master seated Himself in the drawing room, where He related an account of Mary Magdalene and the notable services she rendered:

> Following the martyrdom of Jesus Christ, among the services Mary Magdalene rendered was that, by some means or other, she secured a meeting with the emperor of Rome.* That meeting took place at a time when Pontius Pilate and Herod Antipas were both aware that the Jews had levelled unfounded allegations against Jesus Christ, and that He was in fact innocent of any crime. Pilate and Herod, therefore, began to persecute the Jews. When the emperor of Rome inquired about the reason for her visit, Mary Magdalene replied, 'I have come on behalf of the Christians; they have asked that the executioners of Jesus Christ be spared punishment, and the Jews be left undisturbed. Since Pilate and Herod persecuted the Jews, even though the Jews were responsible for killing Christ, He would not at all be pleased if anyone attempted to exact vengeance upon them.' These remarks from Mary Magdalene pleased the emperor greatly and made a profound

* Apparently a reference to Tiberius, the second Roman emperor.

impression on him. As a result, the emperor decreed that the Jews were to be left alone.

Monday, 23 December 1912[70]
[London]

The Master's talk to the gathering that morning dealt with the theatrical performance about the birth of Jesus Christ, as well as the unawareness and repudiation that the children of Israel exhibited toward the coming of Christ, despite their search for Him and their anticipation of His advent.[71]

When the Master had concluded His talk, He summoned a number of Persians to His room.[72] He spoke to them extensively of how the peoples of the world were shut out as by a veil, and discussed the signs of the Day of Revelation, observing that the Christians of this day are victims of the same vain imaginings and blind imitation that afflict the Jews, inasmuch as they continue to wait for the stars to fall from the heavens, oblivious of the fact that the size of a star is infinitely greater than that of our planet. Thus has it been revealed in the Qur'án: 'Thou* truly canst not guide whom thou desirest; but God guideth whom He will.'† Therefore, the confirmations of God and His guidance are necessary, and the ability to receive the outpourings of His mercy is essential. Otherwise, every person is immersed in the oceans of idle fancy and vain imaginings, to such a degree that even if you were to rend one of his veils asunder, he would be hindered by yet another veil that would take its place.

In the afternoon, the Master spoke of the obstructive veils and the blind imitations of certain religionists, as well as the benighted thoughts of some of the materialists. He described how these two attitudes have enveloped the world of humanity in darkness, and thoroughly rendered its inhabitants the victims of selfish motives and harmful views.

---

* Muhammad.

† Qur'án 28:56.

Tuesday, 24 December 1912[73]
[London]

The rooms of the Master's residence were teeming with people; every heart was filled with a remarkable sort of joy and ecstasy from the love He showed. The talk the Master gave that day dealt with the improvement of the character of all humankind, as well as their edification, emphasizing in particular that one must first educate oneself before devoting one's attention to the education of others.[74] When the gathering was concluded, a number of seekers attained the presence of the Master, to whom He said:[75]

> God made manifest the True Shepherd to gather together all His flocks, and that kind Shepherd was Bahá'u'lláh. He brought together the scattered flocks, and fostered fellowship among various peoples. Wishing to protect and support the peoples of the world, He made Himself even as a shield – and in so doing became the target of the darts of calamity, and prey to the onslaught of ravenous wolves – so that the sheep of God may be kept safe from the cruelty of ferocious and relentless beasts, and sheltered from the oppression of the wolves of self and desire, with the aim that these sheep may enjoy protection and eternal life. My hope is that we, too, may succeed in gathering together the scattered flocks beneath the shade of the True Shepherd, guiding them to the pasture of divine bounty and protecting them from the wolves. Thus shall these scattered flocks come together and live out their days in the utmost happiness.

After dismissing those seekers, a number of reporters entered the Master's presence.[76] In response to their questions about where He came from, and what the purpose of His journey was, the Master said the following:

> I have come from America. For nine months, I visited the various places of America. I went to every city. I spoke at the churches, synagogues, and gatherings of every town. I attended numerous

conferences – such as the conference at Lake Mohonk,[77] to which I was invited – and was present at many colleges. Wherever I was invited to speak, there I went, and the basis of all my talks was the teachings of Bahá'u'lláh. With these teachings, I summoned everyone to universal peace among the religions, universal peace among the races, and universal peace among the nations, and adduced proofs which attested to the need to establish peace. Through these intellectual proofs, I demonstrated that the most vital and pressing issue of this day is that of establishing universal peace, which will bring tranquillity to the world of humanity and serve as the most effective means of solving the problems which beset us, inasmuch as this is the century of light. It is the century of the progress of minds and thoughts, and the century of the education of souls. It is the century of the revelation of the mysteries of creation, and the era of the dawn of the Sun of Truth. It is the era of peace and tranquillity, and the era of love and fellowship. In such an era, it befits all the nations to become harmonized, and all the religions to become united. The countries of the world must become even as one country, for the world of humanity is even as a single tree, and the religions and nations are like its branches and offshoots. Humankind, therefore, must exist in a state of perfect fellowship; it must be nurtured with the warmth of the Sun of Truth, and grow and develop with the showers of divine bestowals. Thereby shall the world of humanity become illumined and heavenly. Thus will perfect unity exist amidst the people, and concord among the nations be realized. In truth, numerous gatherings devoted to the subject of peace have been held. The people have eagerly sought such gatherings, and they have accepted our summons with the utmost receptivity.

Now, I have come to Europe. Praised be God that a peace conference has been convened in this city![78] This truly is a cause of happiness – that in this important centre of society, and before the representatives of the nations, a conference such as this has been held. It is my hope, therefore, that the lights of universal peace will shine forth. I hope, moreover, that this noble nation and this just government will establish in this place what shall lay the firm

> foundation of universal peace, which is the basis for the appearance of tranquillity in the world of humanity. I hope that the Balkan War shall come to an end, and that the rights of both belligerents* be protected and preserved. Otherwise, the flame of this war shall devour the earth – in particular Europe, which is even as an arsenal filled with explosives, and needs only a single spark to utterly obliterate the entire continent. Thus, there is no recourse but to embrace universal peace. This, indeed, is the most pressing issue of the day; I pray God that this peace will be realized. America and Europe have advanced to the utmost in terms of material civilization; day by day, they continue to make material progress. My hope, however, is that divine civilization shall likewise be established in these countries – a civilization whose foundation was laid by the prophets of God, whose success depends on the realm of saintly character and spiritual education, and whose existence shall be the cause of spiritual advancements in the world of humanity.

Afterwards, the Master related an anecdote about Stanford University (in California) and spoke highly of its president.

In the evening, a group of people were eating dinner at the table in the presence of the Master when He told this joke:

> Though I am not hungry, I sit here at the dinner table only for the sake of Lady Blomfield. She insists and she compels! Two despotic kings in the East were powerless to dictate over me or subdue me. The women of America and Europe, however, rule over me because they are free!

Following this, He addressed these words to one of those present:[79]

> The property of heat exists in all things, but a power is needed for that heat to be made manifest. In the realm of religion, it is the power of Bahá'u'lláh that causes the heat of the love of God – that power which lies dormant and hidden within every heart – to

* The Ottoman Empire and the Balkan League.

appear, and widens the ken of the human mind. This heat confers gladness and imparts guidance. You, too, must now manifest this heat. With this power, you must pave the way to the Kingdom and deliver humankind to the abode of salvation. Such a path is even better than the tracks of railroads! Lift up your voice, then, to the Kingdom of God. Yea, lift it up even as John the Baptist lifted up his voice, that you may pave the way, for the Kingdom of God is at hand. Such a way must be paved, and to such a path must humanity be guided.

Wednesday, 25 December 1912[80]
[London]

It was Christmas Day. Even though everyone was busy celebrating the holiday, a greater number of people than ever before had gathered at the Master's residence. A woman, who was one of the Master's neighbours, attended His presence early in the morning, and said: 'I have come here to celebrate my holiday in Your blessed presence, and also in the presence of the Bahá'ís of the East and West.' Among the remarks which the Master made in response to this woman were these:

> The Bahá'í Cause consists of the same principles inherent in all the divine religions. 'Now that one hundred hath come, ninety is with us also.'*

After explaining some of the Bahá'í teachings, the Master said:

> Yesterday, the editor-in-chief of *The Christian Commonwealth* requested that I write something for publication in his newspaper. I wrote a piece for him describing how, because of his quarrel with Satan, Adam was banished from Paradise, and explaining how, for

* A hemistich from the *Mathnaví* of Rúmí. The first hemistich of this couplet reads: 'The name of Ahmad [Muhammad] is the name of all the Prophets.' 'Abdu'l-Bahá, then, is citing the second hemistich here to reinforce the oneness of the Manifestations of God and the unity of the divine religions.

> this reason, it is not permissible to quarrel even with the devil.* It is likewise forbidden to engage in conflict and contention with one's enemies, inasmuch as this would render one deprived of the grace of the loving Lord. One must leave one's opposers to themselves.

At this point, one of the attendees inquired: 'How, then, are we to defend ourselves?' To this, the Master replied:

> This is a different matter altogether. Indeed, reward and punishment constitute the basis of order in this world. For instance, were a person to come here and attempt to strike you – or even murder you – it would be unseemly for me to sit and remain silent. In such a situation, I must certainly rise up to defend you.

It was then asked: 'What is Satan?' The Master responded:[81]

> One's insistent self. Were you to leave a child to persist in his natural state, he would develop a character that is reprehensible and fiendish – even as the inhabitants of Central Africa, who are the embodiments of every base attribute.† For instance, they shed one another's blood; this is a prompting of one's nature. These corrupt inclinations all stem from human nature, and the force which compels him to indulge those inclinations is the struggle for survival. The divine Manifestations have come to save humankind from the darkness of their natural state, for humanity shall not acquire knowledge without the presence of a teacher. By what means have people come to know that honesty is good? Through education and training, of course; otherwise, a person's natural

---

* See *Selections from the Writings of 'Abdu'l-Bahá*, no. 220.

† 'Abdu'l-Bahá is using the contemporarily popular example of 'uncivilized' peoples in Central Africa to highlight the importance of education and refute the then-prevailing theory that a person's race determined their intellect. In a Tablet on this subject, He states, 'What difference is there between the blacks of Africa and the blacks of America? . . . It is certain that education has led to the glory of the latter, while the lack thereof has resulted in the abasement of the former' (*Khiṭábát-i-Ḥaḍrat-i-'Abdu'l-Bahá*, vol. 3, p. 48; provisional rendering by the present translator).

> inclination is to lie. The difference which now exists between you and the inhabitants of Central Africa is education. Indeed, there is a restraining force – that is, an internal inhibitor – latent within people, but this force can only begin to exert its influence through the acquisition of education and the cultivation of godliness.

When the Master went to the gathering that had assembled outside,[82] He gave a talk on the birth of Jesus Christ, and the days that witness the inauguration of the dispensations of the divine Manifestations, through which the thoughts of people are renewed, the behaviour and general states of the nations and peoples are restored, and the minds and souls of humanity are advanced.[83] The Master observed that, in the days that witnessed the dawning of the Christian Sun, a great many superstitions prevailed even in the philosophy of the Greeks, and that the advent of Jesus Christ led to a transformation in their way of thinking.

That afternoon,[84] the Master went to the residence of Lord Lamington [Charles Wallace Alexander Napier Cochrane-Baillie].[85]

Afterwards, as the evening was beginning to set in, He gave a talk to a gathering of the poor who had convened at the Salvation Army [Centre on Great Peter Street] – a gathering of some 500 souls in all.[86] In this talk, the Master explained, at length, that poverty and indigence are beloved by God.[87] Those in the audience were so moved by these words, stirred to their very cores, that they repeatedly applauded the Master and raised uproars of jubilation. When the Master had concluded His talk, since it was Christmas Day, He distributed a sum of twenty pounds[88] to treat everyone to dinner for a night.[89] So great was the clamour raised by those present, and so vigorous the praises and benedictions they heaped upon the Master, that the walls of that space seemed to shake.

Afterwards, the Master went to the upper floor of that building to go for a stroll. While there, He observed the beds and other places to sleep that had been laid out for the poor. For every day and night that a homeless person wished to lodge in this building – and avail themselves of the food, bathrooms, and other basic home amenities that were offered there – they needed only to pay three pence, which amounts to fifteen shāhís.[90] The Master considered this arrangement highly commendable, inasmuch as it was a kind service that provided support to the poor.

From there, the Master went to visit the children of the poor.[91] When He eventually returned to His residence, He expressed how profoundly it had affected Him to see just how destitute and distressed those poor souls truly were.

Thursday, 26 December 1912
[London]

The Master gave a talk to the gathering which had convened that morning[92] on the birth of Jesus Christ and the true meaning of baptism.[93] From the moment that talk had concluded until the afternoon, a number of illustrious souls and highly respected individuals attained His presence. The Master discussed numerous subjects with these people.[94] At one time, He spoke of the unity of the world of humanity; at another time, He talked about unity and universal peace; at yet another time, He discussed the elimination of religious, racial, national, and political prejudice; and at still another time, He expatiated upon the pre-existence of the Essence of God, the Ancient of Days, as well as the constant and perpetual nature of the grace of the Greatest Name. The Master spoke without ceasing, and the hearts of his listeners were enraptured by His utterance.

A question was then posed concerning the reincarnation and ascension of souls.[95] The Master stated:

> Existence itself consists of perpetual permanence. Show me something that does not exist perpetually! Ultimately, all things come to occupy different degrees of existence and undergo a transformation in their forms. Consider even this flower; it shall never be totally effaced from the earth. In the end, its present form shall be altered; it will not simply fade into nothingness. Neither does existence end in obliteration, nor can complete nonexistence ever come into existence in this world. Nonexistence is darkness, while

> existence is light. When light comes, darkness is driven out. It is not the case that darkness shall ever become light.

The Master then gave an explication on the subject of reincarnation:

> This reincarnation in which people have traditionally believed is contrary to what has been revealed in the Books of God. What is truly meant by 'return' is the reappearance of past attributes in future creatures, and the similarity of the perfections possessed by successive generations to the characters and qualities of their precursors. It is like when we say that this flower is the same flower of last year; the meaning is that the same colour and fragrance of the previous flower are now manifest in this one.

Afterwards, the Master spoke at length on material and spiritual civilization, as well the effects of one's thoughts and occupations, observing that some of these lead to joy while others lead to sorrow. He also gave an extensive talk on the meaning of the Word of God, education, and the equality of men and women. At that juncture, a question was posed concerning the realm of divine transcendence. The Master addressed this question in a way that discredited the vain imaginings of the Sufis, and expounded upon both the meaning of the exclusive individuality of the soul and also the purity of the heart. So extensive were His explanations that, if they were to be written down, it would require entire books to be written – one for every day of the year!

That evening,[96] a gathering of Bahá'ís convened at the home of that handmaid of God,[97] Miss [Marion Elizabeth] Jack. There, too, the Master spoke at length on the importance of encouraging one's fellow Bahá'ís, and the distinctions of the world of humanity. After having some tea and sweets, He departed for the night.

Friday, 27 December 1912
[London]

Before attending the public gathering, the Master's utterances to a number of respected souls who had just attained His presence that day fell from His tongue like a copious rain. When those present asked Him about His journey,[98] the Master responded in this way with the utmost majesty and power:

> I have come to promote divine civilization. This is a civilization that Bahá'u'lláh established in the East. It is a civilization that tends to the domain of character; it is a civilization that conduces to universal peace; it is a civilization that promotes the unity of the world of humanity.

When another group of people attained His presence,[99] the Master spoke of the education of their children:[100]

> Children must first be trained in divine virtues and encouraged to improve their characters. When this has taken place, every effort must be made to teach them sciences, crafts, and other excellences – for if godly training and a goodly character are absent, the acquisition of sciences and crafts alone are inadequate. In such a state, there would be nothing to safeguard the child's character against corruption, or to protect him from the harmful influence of self and desire. On the contrary, such a void would generate idle thoughts, and strengthen the compelling power of personal interests. Such an outcome can be avoided only when this secular education is imparted in conjunction with the conferment of godly training and the cultivation of a goodly character.

After expounding, to another group of people, the wholly sanctified nature of the Essence of God, and expatiating upon the divine teachings and similar subjects, the Master delivered an extensive talk at the aforementioned public gathering, in which He gave a commentary on the first verse of the New Testament, and offered an interpretation of the meaning of 'the Word'.[101] The audience gave the Master a round of applause and, seized with complete rapture, they humbled themselves in deference to Him, and expressed their sincerest respect for Him.

Afterwards, Mrs [Thornburgh-]Cropper readied her car, and told the Master that she wished to take Him on an excursion. The Master consented and entered her car, and they set out for a large park in that city [Battersea Park]. They stopped and exited the car when they had reached the middle of the park, situated on the banks of a lake. For nearly one hour, the Master went for a stroll in that park. He was generous and benevolent to all the children He encountered along the way, giving them money[102] and caressing them tenderly. At this juncture, the Master began to speak of the consequences that the Persians will face for their deeds – such as the loss of their majesty and independence, brought about by their own hand:

> Though admonitions were given to both sides,* though the right path was shown to them, and though they were warned about meddling from their neighbours, all these counsels were given in vain. The believers, therefore, have been categorically forbidden to participate in these affairs, and have distanced themselves from corruption. Undoubtedly, those who pursue selfish interests and oppress the loved ones of God will never achieve success; indeed, their efforts shall avail them nothing but manifest loss. Know, of a certainty, that whatever occurs will conduce to the exaltation of the Cause of God, the promotion of His Word, and the protection of His loved ones, and that divine wisdoms are hidden therein.

Following this, the Master commented on the spaciousness and pleasantness of the park:

> It is indeed uncrowded and peaceful here. The weather is lovely, and the grass is verdant and beautiful. To walk in such places causes one to feel more spiritual, and grants tranquillity to one's

* The constitutionalists and monarchists of Qájár Persia.

> heart. This is especially the case when one is alone, and may enter into a state of reflection and transcendence.

Shortly after nightfall, the Master went to a gathering of poor women and children. He began with an address to His audience,[103] in which He consoled them and spoke of the education of children.[104] So openly did those present rejoice at the Master's address that they practically leapt with joy. Afterwards, the women and children stood up from their seats, so as to form two separate lines by their respective tables. The Master then circled each table, and – with His characteristic heavenly conduct and divine bounty – He kissed the children, caressed them tenderly, and gave each one of them a present. When the audience witnessed the kindness and generosity the Master had shown to these children, they became so overjoyed that they all began to sing, in unison, a poem about the coming of Khiḍr[105] and the guidance he imparts. Some among them cried out in jubilation, and heaped benedictions and praise upon the Master. Whenever the children would attain His presence, cherishing the hope of His grace, they would invariably declare, 'This is the divine Khiḍr! These are heavenly showers of grace!' This is because the children of America and Europe believe that Khiḍr appears to children at Christmastime and gives them presents.

Upon returning from that place, the Master saw a number of other poor people, to whom He showed great kindness and good cheer. He then related an anecdote from the days when He lived in 'Akká:

> A number of souls, destitute and famished, approached me and begged me to give them something to sustain them. I directed their attention to a grocer's stall, on which every kind of food imaginable had been laid out, and said to them, 'Throw yourselves upon this stall. Whatever is there, seize it, eat it, and take it with you. The responsibility for your actions will rest with me.' Upon hearing these words, these impoverished, desperately hungry souls immediately ransacked the stall and began to plunder its wares.

> However much the shopkeeper loudly objected, 'You are stealing my goods!', these impoverished people paid him no heed whatsoever. They even ate dry, uncooked rice, and took all sorts of merchandise with them.[106]

In the evening, a banquet was held at the home of Lady Blomfield,[107] who had invited a number of dignitaries to attend. Each and every one of those dignitaries attained the presence of the Master,[108] and this they did with the utmost courtesy and deference. Shortly thereafter, the Master gave a most eloquent talk on the all-encompassing nature of the outpourings of God's grace, as well as the unending conferment of divine bestowals and perfections in the world of existence.[109] He noted, in particular, that the ability to witness these liberal effusions of God's grace is dependent on the spiritual insight and conscientious perceptiveness of the beholder.

After dinner, the Master asked that someone chant a prayer. An Arabic prayer was recited, and this prompted the Master to say:

> Praised be God, for groups from both the East and the West have come together in this gathering. All here are like a single kind; no difference is there in their thinking. Their hearts are linked one to another, and their spirits rejoice with gladness. I hope that, day by day, these ties will grow stronger, and this love and fellowship increase, that this gathering may become the means through which the hearts of humankind grow closer together, and all peoples begin to show love to one another. Thereby will the world of humanity be illumined, and the darkness of prejudice and ignorance be driven out entirely.

There was truly a remarkable spirituality about that gathering, and those present exhibited a peculiar kind of rapture and love. This was especially the case as the Master was dismissing His audience, when, one by one, they thanked Him with the utmost reverence and expressed their sincerest respect for Him.

Saturday, 28 December 1912
[London]

At the gathering that morning, the Master gave a talk on the unity of the Essence of God, that Necessary Being, and the limitlessness of the outpourings of divine grace. The hearts of those present were totally captivated, and they expressed tremendous joy and enthusiasm. The number of people who thronged to attain the Master's presence once that gathering had concluded was greater than that of any other day. So it was, too, in the afternoon. Up until the time had come to retire for the evening, a constant stream of respected people attained the presence of the Master, one after the other, and they would depart with the utmost devotion and rapture. The Master spoke of the degrees of divine unity, as well as the appearance of the Manifestations of singleness. He noted that, in every age in which they lived, the Cause of God at first mattered little to the people of that day, but observed that – with the passage of time – the Word of God eventually pervaded the realities of all things, and its penetrating power was ultimately manifested amidst the greatest of peoples.

Late into the evening, the Master gave an extensive talk on people's temperaments and capacities, as well as the need to train and educate the world of humanity.

Greatly fatigued, the Master then had a little dinner and retired for the evening.

Sunday, 29 December 1912
[London]

Before the public gathering had convened, a number of reporters[110] – as well as a respected Rajah from India[111] – attained the presence of the Master. Among the subjects He discussed with them were the history and teachings of the Faith. Afterwards, the Master expounded upon the diversity of views that exists among people, stating:

> This diversity is of two kinds. The first kind of diversity involves innate and temperamental differences, which do not preclude the establishment of universal concord and fellowship; on the contrary, such diversity aids its appearance. It is like the various colours and kinds of flowers in a garden; this diversity adds to their beauty and adornment. Similarly, it is even as the different limbs of the human body, each one of which assists the other and causes its perfections to become apparent. Since all the limbs operate under the influence of a single spiritual power, the differences inherent in each of them do not prevail; rather, they work in concert with one another, and become a thing worthy of veneration. The second kind of diversity involves acquired or otherwise imposed differences. This diversity leads to a lack of proper education; it lays the foundation for ignorance and disloyalty, and results in oppression, hatred, and hostility. Such diversity shall, in the end, cause the peoples of the world to enter into war and strife with one another. Diversity of this kind must be eliminated, so that the various peoples of the world may draw on spiritual power and repose together beneath the shade of a single Word . . .

When the reporters had finished recording the words of the Master, they were dismissed from His presence. Shortly thereafter, the Master went to the drawing room to meet with the public gathering. He remarked on the sun and the temperate weather of that day, observing that such conditions were rather rare for the winter in London. In this connection, the Master gave a talk in which He likened the dissipation of the clouds to the dispersion of the smoke of vain imaginings, and the brilliance that radiates from the purity of people's hearts to the effulgences that emanate from the Sun of Truth.

The gathering for that afternoon[112] was convened at the home of that handmaid of God, Miss [Annie Eliza] Gamble,[113] and yet another gathering was held later that evening at the King's Weigh House Church.[114] The hearts of those present at the latter gathering were filled to the brim with ecstasy and rapture, and the number of attendees exceeded that of any other gathering theretofore convened. The opening remarks of the priest [Rev. Edward William Lewis], in which he introduced the Master, only added to the excitement of the crowd. When the priest had finished making his remarks – and had completed his effusive praise of the Master[115] for the talk He had just given on the degrees of love and unity, as well as His explication of spiritual subjects and His explanation of the divine teachings[116] – the hearts of those present had become so spiritually enraptured that, when the gathering was concluded, they all hovered around Him like moths, beseeching His confirmations and spiritual blessings.

Monday, 30 December 1912
[London]

At the gathering which was convened that morning, the Master gave a talk whose thrust was that every cause has a focal point. He remarked that the focal point of universal fellowship, the education of humanity, and the instilment of a godly character were the holy Manifestations of God, Who, bereft of earthly influence and outward power though They were, nonetheless promulgated teachings that pervaded the hearts of humankind.

When the Master had finished expounding upon various subjects, the majority of those present expressed their desire to have a private audience with Him. In addition to that group of attendees, a constant stream of other respected people attained and departed the Master's presence up until the evening.[117] The only times when such visits were not taking place were before lunchtime, when the Master had gone for a stroll in a park [Battersea Park] to dispel His fatigue,[118] and after lunchtime, when He decided to rest for a few minutes and relax His nerves. Apart from those times, He spoke constantly, expatiating on divine subjects, and tenderly encouraging His audience to acquire human perfections and occupy themselves with diffusing the fragrances of God.

That evening,[119] a Nineteen-Day Feast was held at the home of that handmaid of God, Mrs [Mary Letitia] Robinson,[120] at which the Master gave a talk on such subjects as love, the bonds between hearts that had been forged through the advent of the Manifestations of God, and the divine teachings.[121] These words roused all those present to great excitement and jubilation. Indeed, they received these glad-tidings with great warmth, and aligned themselves with this message enthusiastically. So great were they in number that most of them had to stand by the door.

Tuesday, 31 December 1912
[London → Oxford → London]

After prayers and meditations, and once a number of dear and virtuous souls had had the honour of attaining the presence of the Master, He set out for the University of Oxford – a renowned and prestigious institution of higher education. The train departed from London, and after two hours they reached the city of Oxford. From the train station, the Master went straight to the residence of Professor [Thomas Kelly] Cheyne, one of the well-known philosophers and authors of England. While the Professor was ill and afflicted with paralysis,[122] he had read a number of letters and newspapers that discussed the Master's travels in the West, and had become apprised of the divine teachings. As a result, he embraced the Faith and sent a letter to the Master while He was in America, in which he explained his situation and asked the Master to promise to meet with him someday, as he very much wished to attain His presence. It was for this reason that, when the Master arrived in London, Professor Cheyne arranged for a special gathering to be held at the University of Oxford,[123] and invited the Master to speak there.

Upon reaching the city of Oxford, the Master immediately went to visit Professor Cheyne at his home,[124] and then engaged the Professor in conversation with the utmost solicitude. Professor Cheyne, for his part, showed the Master the things he was presently writing about the Faith in spite of his poor health, and expressed to Him the intensity of his devotion and allegiance to the religion. So commendable did the Master find these sentiments – and so profoundly moved was He by them – that He repeatedly kissed the Professor's forehead and cheeks, and tenderly stroked his face and hair with His blessed hand.

The Master had lunch at the residence of Professor Cheyne. At the table were seated the professor, his wife [Elizabeth Gibson Cheyne], a number of friends from London and Oxford, the Master's attending servants, and the Master Himself.

In the afternoon, after the Master had had some tea, two special cars were prepared. Accompanied by a number of friends, as well as the members of His retinue, the Master set out for the University of Oxford.[125] When He reached His destination and alighted from the car, a number of the high-ranking officials of the university – who had been waiting for the Master to arrive – welcomed Him with the utmost reverence. The Principal of the college [Joseph Estlin Carpenter] gently took the Master by the arm, and led Him to one of the halls of the university. Notwithstanding that it was winter and the university was on break, that room still teemed with people – and despite the fact that the majority of those present consisted of professors who taught at that university, the priests of the city of Oxford, and a number of other respected English individuals, all of whom were later introduced to the Master, they all arose when He entered the room. The Master then motioned to the audience to be seated. The Principal of the college stood up, and gave – with the utmost compassion and precision – an account of the history of the Faith; its teachings; the calamities the Master had endured in 'Akká during His forty years of imprisonment there; the prophecies of Isaiah concerning this most great and most exalted age, such as the exaltation of the children of Israel to glory; and the arrival of the Centre of the Covenant in Egypt. The Principal expressed, on behalf of all those present, his exceeding gratitude to Professor Cheyne, since he was the reason such a splendid gathering had been convened in the first place. He spoke highly, moreover, of Professor Cheyne's august rank. The Principal then introduced the Master with the utmost respect. When the Master arose with His beautiful stature, all those present at once leapt into applause, and began to make a jubilant commotion.

The Master then launched into an extensive talk on the significant value of knowledge, the virtues that characterize this long-awaited era, the teachings of this most great Dispensation, and the power of the supernatural to subdue the laws and forces of nature.[126] Even as a copious rain, pouring down from the heaven of bounty, the Master expounded on a myriad heavenly meanings and mysteries. This roused the audience to fervent excitement. Indeed, they listened attentively and wholeheartedly to the words of the Master; they relished the subtle wisdom of His remarks, and took great delight in hearing Him convey the truths of various subjects.

When He had concluded His talk, and the jubilant uproar raised by the audience had subsided, the Principal arose once again to give an account – one which proved to be more informative and influential than the first – of the Master's imprisonment, and also to emphasize the importance of the new and wondrous teachings. Additionally, the Principal prayed for the Master; he implored God to keep the Master healthy and happy, and entreated Him to vouchsafe His confirmations to the people of Bahá. The Principal then turned to the audience and said, 'Whoever here has a question, whatever it may be, let him feel free to ask 'Abdu'l-Bahá, that he may hear the answer to his query.' All those present expressed abundant gladness, gratitude, and praise; hearing the Master's talk made them thankful and content.[127] Shortly thereafter, the Principal requested that the Master conclude the gathering with a prayer. The Master consented to this request, and His chanting evoked great tenderness and humility in the hearts of His audience.

Afterwards, the Master returned to the home of Professor Cheyne, where a number of the professors and other university officials attained His presence, repeatedly humbled themselves in deference before Him, and expressed the importance they ascribed to the blessed Cause and the divine teachings. This continued until the crowd had assumed great proportions, at which point that illustrious gathering was commenced. The Master spoke of the underlying unity that exists between the teachings of all the divine religions, which are primary and spiritual in nature, and the change which the laws of the religions, which are secondary and social in nature, undergo according to the exigencies of the time. He spoke, moreover, of economics and similar subjects. So moved were all those respected people by His words that they implored His confirmations in the dissemination of these blessed teachings, and expressed their sincere desire to render service to this most great Cause – and this despite the fact that, until that very moment, they were not as apprised of the nature of this blessed Cause as they should have been.

In brief, the Master then departed Oxford to return to London.[128] He spent the night in deep gratitude to the Abhá Beauty for the aid and assistance He had rendered, saying:

> Praised be God for the help that has come from the Abhá Kingdom – for in such a country as this, the sweet savours of holiness are diffused, and the Word of God quickens the hearts and souls.

Since the Master has made repeated mention of Professor Cheyne, both orally and in writing – and because he is one of the most illustrious and renowned people of England – the text of an extensive article that he has written concerning this most great Cause has been provided below, that it may demonstrate the glory of the Cause of God and the power of the Covenant of the Abhá Beauty:[129]

THE UNION OF RELIGIONS

29 January 1913

Published in *The Christian Commonwealth* (London), pp. 324–325

> Is it possible that there should be a union of religions? An increasing number of persons would answer in the affirmative, because ideally the union of religions exists already. Religion is not of earthly, but of heavenly origin; it is not a branch of magic, not a department of State policy, but a revelation. Now revelation is worldwide; there is probably no people in which the light of sympathetic study does not disclose signs of contact between the

human and the divine. More especially is revelation a characteristic of the great religions – those which have had the advantage of a rich and varied development. Jews would have no right to place their prophetic revealer (MOSES, or those unknown personages for whom MOSES may stand) above the prophetic revealer or revealers of the Zoroastrians nor are Mohammedans justified in promoting their prophet MOHAMMED to a place above JESUS, the revealer worshipped by the Christians.

This appears a favourable time for asking English Christians to reconsider their attitude towards Eastern religions, because of the visit of the leader of the Bahai movement, ABDUL BABA [sic] ('Servant of the All-Glorious'), who is conspicuous for his avoidance of the errors into which so many leaders have fallen. Of greater or lesser rank he says nothing; each prophet must be studied with reference to his period and surroundings. That his own father stands for him in the foreground becomes natural and right as soon as we recognise that BAHA'O'LLAH has a special mission to this age, and acknowledge the transcendent beauty and grandeur of his character. There have been many who have set a noble moral example, but there are elements in BAHA'O'LLAH's inner life and consciousness for which the biographer would find it difficult to produce a parallel.

Space forbids us to dilate upon the singular phenomena of the lives of this father and this son. It is only necessary to add that writers in the newspapers have done what in them lay to make known ABDUL BAHA's deep love for all his fellow-men. His love of GOD is a secret between him and EL-ABHA ('the Most Glorious One'). Nor must we enter into details respecting ABDUL BAHA's teaching. He is doubtless not original; he claims only to be an interpreter of his father's written revelations. These are in a high degree adapted to the wants of the present age. But the central truths are those of Judaism and Christianity – the love of GOD and the love of man.

ABDUL BABA [sic] is not a Mohammedan, and it is a mistake to describe Bahaism as a Mohammedan sect. But there is no reason why a really broad-minded Mohammedan should not be a Bahai, or, for that matter, why a broad-minded Christian or Jew or Zoroastrian should not enter the community. Just as the moulders of the doctrine gather pearls of truth in all seas, so neophytes of the community may adhere with affection to the church, synagogue, or sect to which they owe their spiritual birth. The Bahai community is really not so much a church as a fighting religious order, whose members are, to adopt the beautiful phrase of HEINRICH HEINE, *Ritter des Theologengeist.*[130]

Bahais are not subject to the decrees of any Council or Pope; both BAHA'O'LLAH and ABDUL BAHA have had to make pronouncements on difficult points which involve disputable matters of historical criticism and Biblical exegesis. Those of us who have spent life and energy in the battle for freedom of inquiry are not likely to change even for the sake of a new spiritual power. There is no ground for supposing that in this new Catholic Church any real difficulty from the presence of free inquirers will arise. There will, however, always be differences between North and South, East and West.

T. K. CHEYNE

Wednesday, 1 January 1913
[London]

At the gathering that morning, the Master began His talk with these words:[131]

> I have now travelled for two years in America and Europe. My purpose in so doing has been to announce the unity of the world of humanity and herald the glad-tidings of universal peace, ideals which Bahá'u'lláh has established . . .

After that gathering had been concluded, the Master went to the home of that handmaid of God, Mrs [Thornburgh-]Cropper, where a highly elaborate gathering was being held.[132] That which would lead to the happiness and spiritual upliftment of those present had, in every respect, been prepared there. A number of the

Bahá'ís, hailing from the East and the West alike, were completely captivated with hearing the Master's most sweet voice in that gathering, wherein they had the privilege of being with Him and meeting Him. This was especially true of the attending servants and the members of His retinue, who felt thoroughly gratified to witness the beauty and majesty of the Master, and to be present at that gathering in such a state of gladness and jubilation. Indeed, they rendered thanks for the aid and confirmations that had come from the unseen Abhá Kingdom.

In the early hours of the evening, a well-ordered gathering of clerics was convened [by the Cosmos Club] expressly to have the Master give a talk to them.[133] As the Master entered the room, all those present at the gathering arose in unison. With the utmost respect, they asked Lady Blomfield to offer some introductory remarks concerning the Master. It is perhaps obvious how effusively that faithful handmaid of God went on to praise the Master and illustrate the greatness of the Cause of God, and this was enough to render all those present totally enamoured of the person of the Master. They were all ready to hear Him speak, so the Master arose and delivered an extensive explication, replete with all manner of proof, on the subjects of unwavering constancy; progress; and the exaltedness of the spirit, that second reality of humankind.[134] So enraptured were the attendees with these divine breaths on that blessed night that it defies description. As the gathering was drawing to a close, one of those present requested that the Master recite a prayer. With His hands upraised, the Master began to chant – and with every sentence He intoned, a translation was given.

When the gathering was concluded, and the Master had finished His talk and His recitation of the aforementioned prayer, He went to another room. At this time, the leaders of that gathering requested that one of the Persian attendants recite a prayer in Arabic for those present. Consenting to this request, Mírzá Muḥammad Khán Qazvíní took the seat of honour and began to chant, in a state of wholehearted rapture, a prayer revealed by Bahá'u'lláh. From that point forward, a request would be made at most gatherings for someone to chant a prayer, and those present would invariably take great pleasure in hearing these recitations. It is truly remarkable that – notwithstanding that those in the audience could not understand Arabic – they were nevertheless stirred to their cores and thrust into a deeply spiritual state as they listened to those sweet and wondrous words.

Mr [J.W.] Sidley had invited a number of the friends,[135] both Easterners and Westerners, to have dinner that evening [at Eustace Miles Restaurant][136] in the presence of the Master. When the gathering was concluded, He went to a hall that had been decorated for the guests and in which a variety of food had been laid out. All this delectable food, in fact, had been prepared in a way that accommodated a vegetarian diet, inasmuch as the majority of those who were to attend this banquet – in particular, the respected host himself – abstained from eating meat.

When all those present had finished eating dinner, Mr Sidley, who was quite fond of the Master, rose first. With the utmost gratitude, he stated what an honour it was to have the Master in attendance, wished Him a happy New Year, and lauded Him as 'the Leader of the East' and 'the Prophet of Peace'. After him rose Sir Richard Stapley, one of the political leaders of England, who, with complete humility and reverence, rendered praise and thanksgiving for the blessed bounties of the Master; he acclaimed the divine teachings, and magnified the heavenly power that animates this Cause. He spoke also of the penetrative influence which the Master's utterances have exercised in a myriad grand gatherings. At that juncture, the Master arose and expressed His joy at having heard the remarks of these respected persons. He then extended His New Year's greetings to all those present, spoke of religious subjects, and then took His seat.

After Him rose Mr Felix Moscheles,[137] who was one of the leaders of various gatherings and societies dedicated to the establishment of peace and unity – a man who eventually became enraptured by the Word of God and set His face towards the heavenly Kingdom. So effusive was the acclaim he lavished upon the Cause of God, and in such glowing terms did he characterize the

Centre of His Covenant, that he seemed to have flung open the door to manifold mysteries. At times, owing to the delight he felt at having embraced the Word of God, Mr Moscheles would dance with ecstasy. At others, he rendered thanks and praise for his unwavering confidence in the truth of this new and wondrous Cause, as well as his recognition thereof; he openly prided himself in having the honour of standing in the presence of the Master, and magnified the confirmations of God for having aided him to attain so glorious a bounty.

In response to this touching display of gratitude, the Master once again gave a brief but informative talk on the importance of rendering thanks for the confirmations vouchsafed from the Abhá Kingdom. He, moreover, enunciated those teachings of the Blessed Beauty whose application will conduce to the establishment of fellowship and unity among the people of the world. With His utterance, the Master unsealed the choice wine of true understanding, and those present listened with wholehearted attentiveness. Every face was beaming with irrepressible excitement, and every heart was immersed in oceans of gladness. Truly, that gathering was a particularly significant one, and that day and night were among the most blessed of all days and nights.

Thursday, 2 January 1913
[London]

After a number of people were honoured with hearing the tender counsels and exhortations of the Master,[138] He went to the drawing room and addressed the gathering that had assembled there with a talk on the degrees of love, knowledge, and detachment,[139] and those present seemed to have felt awakened and freshly vigilant upon hearing these words. After that gathering had been concluded, a number of the respected people of London attained His presence.[140] They were eventually dismissed, and expressed the utmost gratitude as they departed. They rendered thanks for the bounty of having met Him, and attested that in having the inestimable privilege of standing before Him they had achieved their highest aspiration, experienced the greatest possible joy, and attained to the very fruit of their existence.

In the evening,[141] a truly glorious gathering was assembled [at Essex Hall] expressly to have the Master give a talk to a group of respected women [the Women's Freedom League] who actively championed the cause of women's rights. When the Master entered that gathering, all those present arose immediately, and raised a remarkable sort of clamour.[142] However, before the Master commenced His talk, Mrs Despard – a highly respected speaker among the women of England – first gave a very moving speech that included the following remarks:[143]

> We have with us, today, an Eastern prophet who has travelled a great distance to come here, who has brought us the message of peace, who will speak to this gathering presently, and among whose teachings is the equality of the rights of men and women. Among the first leaders of this religion to appear in Persia was the Báb, Who was martyred, and many of Whose followers were likewise killed. This continued until the advent of Bahá'u'lláh, Who laid the foundation for peace and equality. Among those individuals in Persia who offered up their lives for this Cause with the utmost bravery was a woman by the name of Ṭáhirih, who was even as a flame of fire, heralding unremittingly the tidings of this Cause. And 'Abdu'l-Bahá, this prophet of the East Who has brought us the message of peace, is the son and successor of Bahá'u'lláh. You should not expect him to discuss political subjects, inasmuch as his teachings are confined to spiritual matters. It is a great joy and honour for us to have him present at this gathering.

At that point, the Master rose, and the crowd raised a great uproar once again. The talk He gave, in which He enunciated the new and wondrous teachings and discussed the equality of the rights of men and women, generated great excitement among all those present.[144] When the Master had concluded His talk, Lady Blomfield gave a moving speech concerning the far-reaching influence of the divine

Message, which had pervaded the various regions of the world, as well as the harm and imprisonment which the Blessed Beauty sustained during His lifetime. Following this, Mr Sidley rose, stood before the Master, and gave a most sweet and enchanting talk concerning the wisdom, the illustriousness, the power, and the perfection of the Master and the teachings of Bahá'u'lláh. He spoke, moreover, of the unity and oneness that must be established among the various peoples and religions beneath the shade of the Word of God. To conclude the gathering, Mr Sidley requested the Master to recite a prayer.

The devotion with which those present at that gathering thronged the Master, as well as the degree of reverence they showed Him, are truly beyond description.

Friday, 3 January 1913
[London]

In addition to other remarks that the Master addressed at a certain public gathering to various people, believers and others alike, He also gave two most eloquent talks on spiritual power and supernatural perfections. The first of these was delivered in the morning at His residence to a certain group of people, and the second – which was an especially detailed and extensive talk – was given in the evening to the Theosophical Society.[145] The latter talk had such an extraordinarily revolutionizing and captivating effect on those present that every heart was bubbling over with irrepressible zeal and ardour; indeed, every face seemed to burst with frenzied jubilation as it beheld the beauty and perfection of the Master. His remarks that evening made an unforgettable impression on the hearts of His audience; every tongue rendered Him thanks and sang His fervent praise. So intense was the devotion they felt that, once that gathering had concluded, each and every one of them approached Him, expressed their sincerest love and respect for Him, and conveyed their heartfelt excitement at having had the privilege of hearing Him speak and standing in His presence.

As to the address which the president [Daniel Dunlop][146] of that gathering gave, in which he introduced the Master to the audience – this was an extensive address, but I did not record the remarks that were made.

Eventually, the Master departed and returned to His residence. He was very fatigued – so much so that He did not eat dinner, and instead retired to His room to rest.

Saturday, 4 January 1913
[London]

When the members of the Master's retinue attained His presence, He said to them, 'I did not sleep at all last night; I was very tired.' Consequently, the Master did not go out that day, and no one attained His presence – except for a certain few who truly needed to see Him, whom He received in His room.[147] To these individuals, the Master repeatedly gave exhortations to achieve unity with all the peoples of the world, as well as encouraging admonitions to disseminate the Writings of this most great Revelation.

For lunch and dinner, the Master ate only a bit of *áb-gúsht*[148] without bread.

Sunday, 5 January 1913
[London]

After prayers and meditations, and once some of the friends had had the honour of attaining the presence of the Master, He went to meet the large crowd that had gathered in the drawing room, and said:

> I was not feeling well; I have come outside purely for your sake. And yet, tomorrow I must go to Edinburgh (Scotland); I have promised to be there, so there I shall go. I have spoken at many gatherings in London. My hope is that my words shall be like pure seeds cultivated in rich soil. Christ has said that the blessed Word is even as a pure seed,* but at times some of these seeds fall by the

* These remarks may come from the Biblical parable of the farmer scattering seeds; see Matt. 13:3–8.

wayside, are trampled underfoot, and are destroyed. Although the seed is pure, since the ground in which it has been planted is not fertile, it will ultimately rot. Other such seeds are scattered upon rocks; although these germinate for a short while, they shall eventually wither and fail to ever give fruit, inasmuch as they could never take root. And yet, other seeds of this kind that have been planted in pure earth and nourished with water will yield an ample harvest.

I am hopeful, then, that London may prove to be rich soil – in other words, that the hearts of its people shall be pure and detached, in order that praiseworthy results may appear therefrom. These results are the love and knowledge of God, the advancement of conclusive proofs and arguments, the promulgation of universal peace and the oneness of the world of humanity, the close union of the hearts that must be forged with the power of the spirit, and the divine philosophy. These are some of the results; it is my hope that they shall be gained in London.

I have placed my trust in God and put my reliance on His endless confirmations. I believe that this pure seed shall flourish, for I see that it has been planted in the rich soil of the human heart. The Cloud of divine mercy rains upon it, and the warmth of the Sun of Reality shines upon it. It is certain, then, that this seed will thrive. I foresee harvests that will ultimately be yielded by these pure seeds – that is, the divine teachings.

I am hopeful that London shall become the centre of peace, that the banner of the oneness of humanity shall be hoisted therein, and that this city shall become the cause of fellowship among all people. I hope, moreover, that ignorant prejudices shall vanish altogether – prejudices that have disrupted the order of the world, such as religious prejudice, racial prejudice, and national prejudice. May these prejudices, these outworn imitations, dwindle away into nothingness, for such imitations and vain imaginings conduce ultimately to conflict and contention, and have no relationship whatsoever to the religion of God. These are among the things which people have instituted, and not what the Manifestations of God have established. The foundation of the divine religions is exalted and sanctified from such vain imaginings – and this is especially true of this luminous age, in which most have come to realize that these vain imaginings are fruitless and detrimental to the well-being and tranquillity of the world of humanity. This is an age in which the light of love must shine brilliantly; the hearts of humankind mirror forth the attributes of the All-Merciful, conferring their bestowals upon one another; and the celestial effulgences encompass all things, for the effulgences of God vouchsafe undying spirituality and perpetual happiness to the world of humanity. The love of God caused humanity to come into existence; His mercy led to the creation of every person on this earth. Praised be God that this age is a luminous age, and this century a divine century. I entreat God to grant such aid as beseems this era.

The Master was in better health that day. He ate His dinner with zest, and then retired to rest.

Monday, 6 January 1913
[London → Edinburgh]

That morning,[149] the Master's retinue departed from London and set off for Scotland. A number of Bahá'ís, hailing from the East and West alike, rode with the Master to the train station [Euston Station] in a state of consummate rapture. Among the Persian members of His retinue who accompanied Him on the journey to Scotland were Mirza Ahmad Sohrab, Áqá Siyyid Asadu'lláh, Mírzá Luṭfu'lláh [Ḥakím], and this lowly servant. As the train began to depart from London, lush and verdant meadows came into view, which caught the Master's eye. Although it was wintertime, the sky was clear and the sun was shining brightly. Indeed, it seemed that such things as would cause every heart to rejoice and every soul to exult had been prepared in every respect.

The Master had His lunch in the dining car[150] and asked the members of His retinue to come join Him. After lunch, He rested for a short while.

As the afternoon was approaching, and the train was nearing Edinburgh, the Master summoned His attendants and began to counsel them, saying:

> We are now going to Edinburgh, where the divine fragrances have only just begun to be spread. You must associate with its denizens with such rapture, such ardour, and such spirituality that they will all testify that you are heavenly; that you are servants whose gaze is ever fixed upon the Abhá Kingdom; that your hearts are brimming with light; and that your souls, filled as they are with celestial secrets, are the envy of every rose-garden.

Following this, the Master told a story about Núr-'Alí Sháh:[151]

> This man had been banished by his government and rejected by his people, and was left to wander in exile. He repaired to the *'atabát*,[152] and there too he languished under the oppression of the divines, until he perished at last in Baghdad. A number of his servants, who were then afflicted with the utmost poverty, were deeply affected by the harm he sustained and the vagrancy he endured. As a result, with complete sincerity, they began to mention his name and sing his praises far and wide. So profoundly had they been moved, and with such rapturous devotion did they arise, that each and every one of them gained immense renown and was elevated to conspicuous glory amid their fellow men. Their fame was such as to render everyone astonished. Even the majority of the ministers of the court and the divines of Islam became their close friends and admirers – and all this notwithstanding that the cause for which these people had arisen was of no importance! Imagine, then, what we who are servants at the divine threshold and guardians of the Kingdom of eternity will accomplish if we arise to serve the Almighty with perfect tenderness, heartfelt devotion, and conscientious attraction!

The train reached Edinburgh at five o'clock in the afternoon.[153] That handmaid of God, Mrs [Jane Elizabeth] Whyte, along with a number of other distinguished notables, had gathered at the train station [Princes Street Station] to receive the Master. It was an honour and source of perpetual happiness for them to attain His presence; they showed Him great reverence, and expressed their delight at His arrival. Mrs Whyte was one of the highly respected women of that city. Her husband [Dr Alexander Whyte], moreover, served as one of its chief divines,[154] and her son [Sir Frederick Whyte] was a Member of Parliament. When Mrs Whyte had previously attained the Master's presence in London, she had become totally enamoured of Him and subsequently embraced the Cause. With great insistence, she implored the Master to promise [to stay at her home during His visit to Edinburgh]. It is for this reason that, upon the Master's arrival, she entreated Him to bless her home with His presence. Since she importuned a great deal, the Master consented to her request, and went to her home accompanied by an interpreter. As for the other members of His retinue, the Master sent them to a hotel close to Mrs Whyte's home,[155] but they stayed there only to eat and sleep; at all other times, they remained in the Master's presence.

On the first night in Edinburgh, a number of august individuals attained the Master's presence in the drawing room.[156] Once the Master had been properly introduced, and those present made their displays of courtesy and deference to Him, He gave an extensive talk on the new and wondrous teachings, the nature of the advent of the divine Manifestations, and the benightedness demonstrated by the people when the Sun of Truth had risen. So profoundly did these explications affect His esteemed audience that they were all stirred to their very cores, and gave vent to abundant joy and fervour. As they were being dismissed from His presence, they all thanked the Master profusely for His enlightening remarks and expressed great delight.

The Master kept all His attendants with Him for dinner. Mrs Whyte; her husband, the good doctor himself; and their entire family were all present at the table, and they repeatedly expressed their joy and gratitude to the Master for gracing their home with His presence, and for giving them the privilege of hearing His enunciations of the divine teachings.[157]

Scotland

Monday, 6 January 1913 [sic][158]
[Edinburgh]

Following the recitation of humble and heartfelt prayers,[159] and when a number of seekers had attained the Master's presence,[160] two cars were prepared[161] for Him and a group of friends and attendants, and they all went to visit a school that specialized in geography.[162] When the Master entered the school, the director [Patrick Geddes] gently took Him by the arm, and showed Him to every one of the building's rooms. As the Master was being conducted, the director presented various objects and maps to Him. They proceeded in this way until they reached the top floor of the building. When they subsequently entered the Outlook Tower that had been erected on the building's roof, elevated very high up in the air, they arrived at a room in whose centre was suspended a large, round surface resembling a flat table, over which was draped a white cloth. This surface was placed opposite a small window in the middle of the tower's dome. In that window, a special camera[163] had been installed, which could capture aerial scenes from the centre of the city as it rotated, and project those scenes, as they were happening, onto the aforementioned surface.[164] All the buildings and streets, the carriages and trains, the coming and going of various people, even the smoke billowing from the factories – all these took on the form of motion pictures, and this was met with ample praise from the Master.[165] The director remarked, 'Three hundred years have passed since this apparatus was invented, but it had not been used until this very moment.'

Following the tour of the remaining rooms of the school, the Master took His leave. At the request of the friends, He went by car to see the citadel [Holyrood Palace] and other ancient edifices that once composed the king's estate. He proceeded until He left the city and reached high ground, to which kings would retire for recreation (King's Drive).[166] It was a pleasant and beautiful place, from which one had a view of the entire city below them. The Master then returned to Mrs Whyte's residence.

After He had some lunch and rested for a short while, seekers began to come and attain His presence in groups; they asked Him various questions about the Cause of God, and this continued until the evening had just begun to set in. So immensely gladdened were these people at the privilege of hearing His most sweet voice, and listening to Him articulate the teachings of the Cause, that they hailed the laws and ordinances revealed by Bahá'u'lláh as the remedy for the incurable ills which afflict this age.[167]

That day,[168] the members of the Esperanto Society convened a special gathering, presided over by the most august ministers of the city, in Freemason's Hall,[169] which had a very large main room. Because the gatherings in Edinburgh where the Master was scheduled to speak had been announced in the newspapers a few days beforehand, the number of attendees at this one was so great that some three hundred people were forced to remain outside the building, as there was no room inside even to stand.[170] First, the Reverend [John] Kelman made some remarks about the blessed Cause, among which was the following:

> This Cause is not opposed to the foundation which Jesus Christ has laid; on the contrary, it is born of the Spirit of God, which is at work exerting its influence over the hearts beyond the churches and Christendom in general. Though the advent of Christ will not be followed by another, the door of God's grace is not closed. This is because the teachings of Christ must be renewed and expounded upon. We in the West have laid the foundation for a great civilization, but it is now bound for instability and disorder. It is incumbent upon us, therefore, to welcome and worship the light of peace and rehabilitation wherever we behold it, regardless of the land from which it hails or the tongue it speaks.

Notwithstanding that this gentleman was among the great leaders of the Christian faith, observe how he was nonetheless so profoundly affected by the majesty of the Cause of God and the power of His Covenant as to attest that this religion is born of the Spirit of God – whose active influence extends beyond the ken of Christendom – and to affirm, moreover, that it is itself the door of God's grace; the means through which the foundation laid by Christ will be renewed, and peace and rehabilitation spread; and a Cause worthy of acceptance and worship.

When the Master arose from His seat on the podium to give His address, the audience greeted Him by arising, in turn, from their seats in unison. The Master's talk concerned the subject of a universal language, which is one of the teachings of this manifest Cause and the proofs of the greatness of this momentous century.[171] His address evoked great astonishment from His audience and profoundly affected the hearts of His listeners.

At the end of the gathering, Professor Geddes rose and extended His gratitude to the Master on behalf of all those present.

Tuesday, 7 January 1913[172]
[Edinburgh]

A number of articles concerning the Master's coming to Edinburgh, as well as the new and wondrous teachings of this Cause, had been printed in the newspapers,[173] and this led to a great increase in the number of seekers who met with Him. A group of these seekers attained His presence before noon;[174] they heard from Him the tidings of the Revelation of Bahá'u'lláh, and expressed humility and deference before Him.

Afterwards,[175] at the request of Mrs Whyte, the Master went to visit a vocational college[176] and a school for poor children.[177] He went into every one of the rooms of the college, and offered words of praise and encouragement to those students who were studying sculpting,[178] carpentry, painting, and other crafts. He also rendered aid and assistance to the children at the orphanage.[179] Following these visits, the Master went again on a swift excursion to the verdant hills and mountains that lay just outside the city.

When the Master returned to Mrs Whyte's residence, a constant stream of people began to attain His presence. When they were apprised of the teachings and Writings of this most great Revelation, it plunged them into a veritable sea of joy and happiness.

That evening, an impressive gathering was convened at Rainy Hall (a divinity school),[180] through the arrangement of the Outlook Tower Society, expressly to have the Master give a talk there. The entire audience consisted of the priests, clergymen, grandees, and other notables of Scotland. Patrick Geddes presided over that gathering, and among the remarks he made to introduce the Master were these:

> Last night, 'Abdu'l-Bahá spoke of the benefits of a universal language, insofar as its implementation would engender fellowship amidst humankind, bring about ease during one's travels and journeys, conduce to the progress of industry, and dispel misunderstandings among the various religions. Tonight, however, the Master will give a talk which concerns the teachings of Bahá'u'lláh. The Bahá'í Faith was founded more than fifty years ago; it has ever been subjected to torture and beset with affliction. Such a history brings to one's mind those martyrs of the early days of Christianity. This religion had its beginnings in Persia, but it later spread to other Islamic countries, and was promulgated among Jews and Christians. Though this spiritual Cause emerged in prison, every one of its teachings accords nonetheless with this century of civilization.

The talk that the Master then gave[181] – in which He enunciated the teachings of Bahá'u'lláh; depicted the calamities which befell the Cause of God; and described how, despite the enemies that had besieged it on every side, His Word was exalted nonetheless – so profoundly moved the hearts of His audience, and stirred them to such great vigilance, that Professor Geddes [sic] [182] rose from his seat once again to thank Him on behalf of all those present. He remarked that everyone felt wholehearted gratitude to the Master for having delivered, with consummate eloquence, an account of those teachings which are indicative of the spirit of progress for this century. The professor observed, moreover, that:

> This is a Cause which spread with the utmost speed throughout the East, like the affairs which are now transpiring and effervescing in the West. That which most captivated us, however, was that 'Abdu'l-Bahá seemed to be voicing the hopes of our hearts as He spoke. We embrace, with the utmost delight, the teachings of this Cause – in particular those which concern the spreading of knowledge, emphasize the incumbency upon everyone to engage in some profession, liken the world of humanity to a bird with two wings, and state that material civilization and spiritual civilization must be intertwined. In conveying these ideals, 'Abdu'l-Bahá has truly described the hopes of our hearts. That which is the cause of still greater astonishment, however, is the fact that – in spite of the persecution, the threat of murder, and the imprisonment He faced – 'Abdu'l-Bahá was able to spread these teachings nonetheless.

Afterwards, the Reverend [Alexander B.] Robb rose and said:

> We in the West have always sent our missionaries to the East. Today, however, we see that a teacher from the East has come to the West to promulgate the precepts of the Holy Books of old, as well as the new and wondrous teachings. But in spite of this, the life of 'Abdu'l-Bahá produces a greater effect than words. His is the right to speak, for He has spent forty years of His life in prison, and God has unveiled to Him many mysteries. Last night, the Reverend Kelman stated that 'Abdu'l-Bahá has not come here to invite people to His religion. I, however, believe that this is actually the case, for I know that we ministers are engaged in spreading these same glad-tidings. Not only this, but it is, in fact, our desire to disseminate such teachings. It is our hope, therefore, that this talk of 'Abdu'l-Bahá shall protect us, encourage us, and confirm us.

Following this, the Reverend [Robert B.] Drummond offered kind remarks of praise and thankfulness. The chairman of that gathering [Patrick Geddes] likewise extended his gratitude. The meeting was brought to a close with the utmost enthusiasm and zeal. That gath-

Jane Elizabeth Whyte with her husband Rev. Alexander Whyte and two of their children in about 1894. Mrs Whyte invited 'Abdu'l-Bahá to Scotland

Dr Alexander Whyte

Sir Patrick Geddes

The Outlook Tower, Edinburgh

St Giles Cathedral, Edinburgh, where 'Abdu'l-Bahá heard a performance of Handel's Messiah

Reverend John Kelman, who introduced 'Abdu'l-Bahá at Freemason's Hall, Edinburgh

Lutfu'lláh Ḥakím, who accompanied 'Abdu'l-Bahá to Scotland

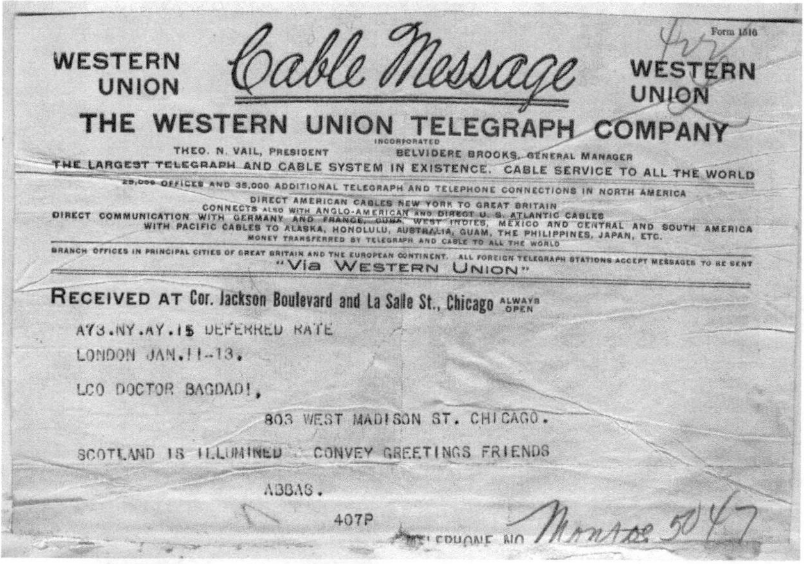
Form 1516

WESTERN UNION

Cable Message

WESTERN UNION

THE WESTERN UNION TELEGRAPH COMPANY

INCORPORATED

THEO. N. VAIL, PRESIDENT BELVIDERE BROOKS, GENERAL MANAGER

THE LARGEST TELEGRAPH AND CABLE SYSTEM IN EXISTENCE. CABLE SERVICE TO ALL THE WORLD

25,000 OFFICES AND 35,000 ADDITIONAL TELEGRAPH AND TELEPHONE CONNECTIONS IN NORTH AMERICA

DIRECT AMERICAN CABLES NEW YORK TO GREAT BRITAIN

CONNECTS ALSO WITH ANGLO-AMERICAN AND DIRECT U. S. ATLANTIC CABLES

DIRECT COMMUNICATION WITH GERMANY AND FRANCE, CUBA, WEST INDIES, MEXICO AND CENTRAL AND SOUTH AMERICA

WITH PACIFIC CABLES TO ALASKA, HONOLULU, AUSTRALIA, GUAM, THE PHILIPPINES, JAPAN, ETC.

MONEY TRANSFERRED BY TELEGRAPH AND CABLE TO ALL THE WORLD

BRANCH OFFICES IN PRINCIPAL CITIES OF GREAT BRITAIN AND THE EUROPEAN CONTINENT. ALL FOREIGN TELEGRAPH STATIONS ACCEPT MESSAGES TO BE SENT "Via WESTERN UNION"

RECEIVED AT Cor. Jackson Boulevard and La Salle St., Chicago ALWAYS OPEN

A73.NY.AY.15 DEFERRED RATE

LONDON JAN.11-13.

LCO DOCTOR BAGDADI,

803 WEST MADISON ST. CHICAGO.

SCOTLAND IS ILLUMINED CONVEY GREETINGS FRIENDS

ABBAS.

407P

TELEPHONE NO Monroe 5047

Cable from 'Abdu'l-Bahá to Dr Zia Bagdadi on leaving Scotland

ering was the strongest proof and the greatest evidence demonstrating the truth of this mighty Cause, as well as the power and influence of the irrefutable Covenant and Testament, that in a city such as this within the realms of Britain – a city holy to the Christians and home to their leaders – the choicest of people, and the most august of divines and sages, should so unequivocally attest to the power, the might, the influence, and the significance of the blessed teachings, and become so enamoured of the utterances and conduct of the Master, that all the articles published in the newspapers, in addition to featuring ample praise of the Master, also included the praise extended by the leaders of various groups. Thereby have the fame of the greatness of the Cause of God, as well as the majesty of His Covenant, made the pillars of the world of existence to tremble.

Wednesday, 8 January 1913
[Edinburgh]

A new development, involving some very interesting remarks, recently occurred. The owner of the *Edinburgh Evening Dispatch* wrote the following: 'If our ministers have so quickly lauded the glory and perfection of an Easterner, what will become of the rest of us?' Truly, they have every right to feel as they do, for they have witnessed how, just three days after the arrival of an Eastern personage in Edinburgh, He has made such a profound impression on the hearts of distinguished individuals. When He enters any gathering, all those present rise at once to show Him their respect, and many honourable souls pay Him great tribute. Most people treat Him with such deference that, at the end of every gathering, they shake His hand and express their wish to see Him again. Every day, the newspapers describe the greatness of His glory and the transcendence of His perfection – though, to be sure, some of them speak jealously of Him and succumb to fear. They warn their readers to be wary of embracing this Cause, lest it shake the pillars of their so-called independence and deal a blow to the foundation of their blind imitation.

That day, a constant stream of people from all walks of life attained the presence of the Master; they benefited from the celestial outpourings of His grace, and received His imperishable favours. This continued until the evening, when a pleasant gathering was held in the large drawing room of Mr Whyte's residence for a number of students who had come from India, Egypt, and Japan.[183] They all attained the presence of the Master and had the privilege of hearing His words. When they were apprised of the Master's arrival in Edinburgh and informed of His talks, and had learned of the influence which the holy teachings had exerted at a myriad illustrious gatherings, these students prided themselves in the fact that such a majestic Sun as this had dawned once again over the horizon of the East, granted sight to the peoples of the West, and illumined the pure hearts of them that reside there. It is for this reason that all these students had asked Dr Whyte to convene such a gathering. Among the remarks with which Dr Whyte commenced that meeting and addressed to the Master were these:

> Dear Sir! I have convened many a gathering here in my life, but never before have I seen one such as this. In witnessing these gatherings of fellowship, I am reminded of these words from Peter [sic], [184] 'God hath created all of one blood,' as well as this utterance of Jesus Christ, 'On that day, the East, the West, the South, and the North shall all enter the Kingdom of God.'[185]

When Dr Whyte had concluded his remarks, one of the Indian students rose and addressed these words to the Master on behalf of his compatriots:

> All my countrymen who are present salute and welcome the arrival of 'Abdu'l-Bahá to this part of the world. There is no need for me to offer any words in praise of these holy teachings, since all are aware that they are conducive to the progress of the world of humanity. They realize that, to this day, whatever advancements have been made in Persia – and the degree to which its inhabitants have been saved from the vain imaginings and blind imitations that have

> heretofore hindered the establishment of unity – must be attributed to this Cause. These developments, moreover, are not confined only to Persia; rather, they have spread to other regions of the earth. This progress has continued until the present day, in which 'Abdu'l-Bahá has now come here to remind us of what we had forgotten – namely, that we are all of a single kind, that we are all brothers, and that we are all the servants of one God. There is no doubt that, through the pervading influence of this great teacher, the condition of the world shall be rehabilitated, and these teachings will bring about the tranquillity of all humanity. It is for this reason that we, one and all, extend our greetings to 'Abdu'l-Bahá.

Following this, one of the Egyptian students rose and said:

> This gathering is a source of pride, for we place our sincere and heartfelt conviction in the illustrious Person of 'Abdu'l-Bahá, Who is the greatest teacher of the East. Among the teachings He promulgates are the elimination of religious, national, political, and racial prejudice, inasmuch as these prejudices are the cause of dissension, dissipation, and ruin. For this reason, God has always chosen a Messenger from every people to train humankind in the ways of unity and promote brotherhood among them, and, in this way, bring together the various religions, even as this Cause is doing. As far as we all are concerned, this is the right thing to do, and we eagerly await the day when the peoples of the world shall be united. We are, therefore, indebted to this blessed Personage for His bountiful favour, inasmuch as He has guided us in this way, and has summoned us to universal peace. I will not go on any longer, lest I become a hindrance to your hearing the address of 'Abdu'l-Bahá. On behalf of all my compatriots, as well as the other students present, I extend my greetings to Him.

By that point, the remarks made by these souls had caused every heart in attendance to brim with longing and receptivity to hearing the utterances of the Centre of the Covenant. Shortly thereafter, the Master rose and delivered a most excellent talk on the oneness of the principles of the divine religions, the need to eliminate blind imitation, the truth of Islam, the modification of secondary religious laws[186] according to the exigencies of the age, and extraordinary spiritual power. So potent was His talk that all those present voiced their effusive praise and gratitude to Him – among them Dr Whyte, who, at the conclusion of the gathering, once again expressed his joy and thankfulness to Mrs Whyte for her prodigious efforts, insofar as she had arranged for the Master to come to Edinburgh, and was ultimately responsible for all this bounty and happiness to which we had attained.

When the gathering was concluded, many people of all kinds came once again to attain the presence of the Master. Upon hearing His utterances, including His enunciations of the blessed teachings, they all expressed rapturous zeal.

A number of people that day were taking up a collection to donate to the poor. Those who wanted to donate would exit the main room and give however much they wished. The Master, too, donated a few pounds, and this act greatly moved those who were attentive to this charitable effort – in particular the members of the Whyte household, as they had not expected a display of such generosity.

That night, Mrs Whyte and her family insistently expressed to the Master their wish for Him to attend a choral performance [of Handel's *Messiah*] that was going to be held in one of the ancient churches [St Giles' Cathedral].[187] She noted that this was an annual event that was held to uplift the poor and provide them with some recreation. Continuing her description, Mrs Whyte said that several groups of people, arranged in a special order, stand in the centre of the main hall of that house of worship, singing various hymns to musical accompaniment, and observed that thousands of people – people of every stripe, poor and rich alike – attend this event to hear these melodies. Since Mrs Whyte insisted, and because it was obvious that she herself very much wanted to go, the Master consented and accompanied her there. The Master found the performance highly commendable; when they had all returned to Mrs Whyte's residence, He said:

It was a good gathering. I saw that the poor were very glad. Truly, the hearts of the poor are very tender; they are easily affected. When we were living in Baghdad, and a poor soul came to our home, he noticed a small rug laid out on the ground. He brushed it with his hand and said, 'This is very soft. Were a person to repose on it, he would be thrust into deep sleep and rest with great comfort.' I replied to him, 'Take it; this carpet is yours.' I saw him again some time later, and he said to me, 'I had imagined that reposing on that rug would enhance my sleep, but eventually I realized that it made no difference whether I slept on that rug or on a mat of straw. Having reached this conclusion, I sold the rug.' The hearts of the poor are easily broken. Thus, whenever a person can bring gladness to them, it is the right thing to do. When I was in 'Akká, I constantly extended invitations to the poor. You are, however, unaware of the dire straits in which the poor ones of the East live. What can those poor souls do?

Thursday, 9 January 1913
[Edinburgh]

From that morning until noon, so steady was the stream of reporters and other respected people that attained the Master's presence that He did not stop speaking for so much as a single minute. He was engaged constantly in answering questions, rending veils, and expounding perspicuous verses. Various people asked questions about every conceivable subject, and upon hearing the answers given by the Master, their faces would beam so widely that they seemed almost to blossom like roses. They inquired about the differences between the Bahá'í Faith and Christianity. In response, the Master discussed the oneness of the fundamental tenets of the divine religions, as well as the need for their secondary principles to change according to the exigencies of every age. They inquired also about the difficulty of fostering unity and fellowship among the various peoples, as well as reconciling their opposing views and temperaments. The Master answered this question with a tangible proof; He observed that all creation is composed of diverse elements that have been unified by a spiritual power, and that, through this composition, the perfections and attributes of God have been made manifest in the contingent world. He stated, moreover, that our innate differences cause the world of humanity to resemble a garden, and rejected the notion that such differences hinder the appearance of unity and fellowship among the various peoples and religions. He noted also that those differences which are born of aggression, prejudice, and ignorance can be eliminated through a proper education and the observance of prudence. The Master would speak of such subjects repeatedly and extensively. Every heart in attendance was filled with joy, and every neck was bowed in reverence. All those present expressed their gratitude to the Master and sang His praises.

In the afternoon,[188] an impressive gathering attended by two groups was held at Dr Whyte's residence. One of these groups consisted of respected and illustrious women from the city who were all supporters of women's rights and advocates for their freedom; the other consisted of distinguished men who were opposed to the views of the first group. Despite their differences, both sides showered the Master with vigorous praises and benedictions, inasmuch as His talk dealt with the subjects of the well-being, peace, happiness, and unity of the world of humanity. In that talk, moreover, the Master enunciated the divine teachings, and discussed the need to so educate and inculcate a rectitude of conduct in women that they shall be ready and worthy to possess rights equal to those of men. All those present were satisfied with these utterances and expressed their gratitude to the Master. Both sides were profoundly affected and enraptured by Him to such a degree that the explanations He gave on every subject were the very fulfilment of their greatest desires, and they came to regard the teachings of Bahá'u'lláh as the cure for every ailment and the balm for every wound. Most of those present considered this kind of discourse, as well as the effect and influence of the Master's blessed words, to be extraordinary, inasmuch as it was able – in the span of a single gathering – to satisfy the opposing groups, and to be regarded by them, in spite of their differing tastes and tendencies, as the object of their ultimate desire. The Master elucidated the truth and articulated it clearly. It is for this reason that every neck was bowed in reverence and every heart was revolutionized. Indeed, every discerning clergyman was deeply moved in the course of such a significant gathering, and came to realize that their well-being could be secured, in every respect, through obedience and deference to the teachings propounded by the Master. Without willing it, moreover, every fair-minded soul in attendance found itself attesting to His grandeur and glory. Everyone present, regardless of the station or rank they occupied, had no recourse but to humble themselves before the Centre of the Covenant of God. How can the heedless ones of Europe and America be compared with the humility and reverence exhibited here before this Eastern Master, or them that boast of Western civilization with them that express submission to this Eastern religion? Consider how immeasurable is the difference between these two ends of the spectrum!

The more impressive gathering of that evening was held in the main hall of the Theosophical Society of Edinburgh.[189] It was a lively gathering; the audience raised a great commotion after hearing the Master's talk. Beyond the inhabitants of the city, a number of Theosophists from the surrounding areas were also present that night – since they had seen the gathering advertised in the newspapers and other written media – and so great was the number of attendees that the main hall, immensely spacious though it was, could not accommodate them all,[190] such that the majority had to form rows and stand outside the hall. Before and after the Master's talk, the president of that gathering [Major David Graham Pole] remarked on His characteristics in a way that astonished every mind in attendance.[191] The exact words of those remarks have since been published in the Theosophical Society newsletter, whose contributors asserted that perfect unity exists between the Bahá'ís and themselves. Among those who shared such opinions was Mr Graham Pole, the editor of the Edinburgh Theosophical Society newsletter, who wrote:

> The spiritual power of 'Abdu'l-Bahá is intense. He seems to me to be the focal point of spiritual, intellectual, and divine power in

> this century and in the next. When one learns of the source from which He derives His power, he will come to have no doubt that this Cause will effect immense transformations in the spheres of religion and economics.

Given the degree to which even the leaders of that society had been enraptured by the lucid utterances and trenchant remarks of the Master, one can imagine the state of the others who were present.

When the Master rose in the midst of that most excellent gathering with that ravishing stature of His, He gave a talk in which He expressed His gladness that the members of this society had discerned the truth and were free of any partiality. He discussed, moreover, the harmful consequences of the blind imitation exhibited by the members of certain religions; the nature of the extraordinary power possessed by humanity, which is their second reality; and the rising of the Sun of Truth over various horizons in every age.[192] So vigorous was the clamour raised by those present that the walls of that space seemed to shake. Eventually, when it was time to depart, each of the attendees, one by one, demonstrated their utmost reverence for the Master as they passed Him by. They voiced their desire to have the opportunity to express their servitude to Him, as well as their fervent hope that He would bless and confirm them – but it was not possible for every one of those present to attain this goal. It was evident that all the attendees were in a state of rapture and yearning, and that they had no desire whatsoever to leave the Master's side and be separated from Him.

Following that gathering, the leaders of that society prepared dinner in the same building. All the members of the society dined in the Master's presence in a state of indescribable zeal and fascination.[193] They all truly expressed their sincerest love and reverence for Him.

After dinner, two youth who intended to marry knelt before the Master's chair; took hold of the hem of His garment; and implored Him, with the utmost tenderness and love, to confer His blessings and aid upon them. They expressed, moreover, their hope to the Master that they would be confirmed and successful, that they would be the recipients of His favour, and that they would be remembered in His prayers.

Following this, a number of people who had portraits of the Master approached Him and requested that He sign them. The leader of the Theosophists then presented the Master with a special notebook belonging to their society, and asked Him to inscribe a prayer in it. The Master consented and wrote this brief supplication:[194]

He is God!

O Divine providence, shed a ray from the Sun of Truth upon this gathering that it may become illumined.

—'Abdu'l-Bahá 'Abbás

That same leader then presented the Master with one of his personal notebooks, and requested that He inscribe a prayer in it in his honour. Accordingly, the Master wrote:

He is God

O God! Graciously assist the bearer of this book.

—'Abdu'l-Bahá 'Abbás

In brief, that gathering was the last which the Master attended in Edinburgh, and that night was the last He spent there. The transformation of the hearts in that city is surely the greatest sign of His majesty and power.

Friday, 10 January 1913
[Edinburgh → London]

The Master was departing Edinburgh and setting off for London. He instructed His attendants who were staying in the hotel to gather their belongings and pay for the cost of lodging. When Mrs Whyte learned of this, she became upset and insisted on covering this expense, but the Master would not accept her offer. He had, moreover, donated ten pounds to aid the sick.[195] Afterwards, He went downstairs, summoned all the servants and attendants of the house, and began offering them counsels on dutiful service, right conduct, trustworthiness, honesty, and servitude to God. He expressed His great satisfaction with the services they had rendered, and tipped each of them one pound.[196] The way the Master spoke with the servants of that home and conducted Himself with them was such as to fill their hearts with tenderness and sorrow. Even Dr Whyte, that illustrious gentleman, was like a lowly servant before the Master, exhibiting the utmost courtesy and expressing the shame he felt in falling short of his own service to Him. Dr Whyte then presented the Master with a book, and requested that He inscribe a prayer in it. The Master consented to this request, and Dr Whyte was blessed with words from His most pure pen.

A number of people accompanied the Master to the train station.[197] When the time had come for the train to depart,[198] all those present were overcome with intense grief, and they implored His blessings and confirmations – in particular Mrs Whyte, the leader of the Esperanto Society, and the members of the Theosophical Society. Two hours into the train ride, the Master said the following in one of the railway carriages:

> The transformations of souls like the ones we have witnessed are possible only through the power and confirmations of the Abhá Kingdom, through which we, some Persian individuals, were enabled to spread the holy verses with such power and might before the gatherings of this city, and even in the home of the archbishop, and there to vindicate the truth of Islam and demonstrate the glory and grandeur of Muḥammad, the Apostle of God – that all were humbled thereby, and moved to show great reverence. Never before has the eye of creation beheld such confirmations; we must appreciate their value and be grateful for them.

That day in the train, the Master was deeply gladdened, and He rendered constant thanks for the confirmations from the Abhá Kingdom.[199]

The train reached London at five o'clock in the afternoon.[200] A number of the friends who were awaiting His arrival at the train station began to hover around Him like moths.[201] The Master's intention that day was to take up lodging in one of the hotels of London, but when Lady Blomfield and her family learned of this, they became distraught and threw themselves at the Master's feet.[202] As a result, He agreed to stay at her residence once again.

A number of the friends, hailing from both the West and the East, attained the Master's presence. When they beheld His conspicuous joy, it roused them to great zeal and ecstasy. Owing to the Master's fatigue, some of the guests were dismissed earlier, but a number of Persian travellers remained in His presence until after dinner. His utterances and His most sweet voice totally enamoured and intoxicated these guests with the wine of favour and bounty.

Return to England

Saturday, 11 January 1913

[London]

Believers and others from the East and West alike came in groups to attain the Master's presence and receive the outpourings of His abiding grace. Each of them benefited, in proportion to their respective capacities, from the Master's discussions of the truths and inner meanings of spiritual subjects. Among them were a group of respected Persians,[203] who felt abundant joy and gladness at having had the privilege of meeting the Master. One of these individuals was a particularly distinguished Persian, who without any introduction entered the main hall of the building. When the members of the Master's retinue asked him for his name, he replied, 'Simply mention my name to 'Abdu'l-Bahá. I have come here strictly to see Him, and for no other purpose than this.' Immediately thereafter, this gentleman was summoned to the Master's room, where he was showered with abundant kindness. From that point onward, this gentleman would be by the Master's side most of the time. With every passing day, he learned something new about the Cause of God; he began to exhibit an attitude of sincere devotion and demonstrate immeasurable rapture.

In the afternoon,[204] an important gathering was convened in Caxton Hall expressly to have the Master give a talk there.[205] Both prior to the Master's talk and following it, a number of the Bahá'ís of London gave impressive addresses of their own before that great assemblage on the history and teachings of the Cause of God. For His part, the Master's talk explored the prophecies of Isaiah, discussed this most great and most glorious Revelation, and explained the teachings of Bahá'u'lláh.[206] It was a talk that enamoured all those present of the Master, and enraptured them with the Word of God.

Afterwards, those who had attended the aforementioned gathering went to another room of that majestic building, where high tea had been prepared for them. While there, they went – one by one and two by two – to attain the Master's presence and shake His hand. They expressed their thanks and praise to Him upon hearing His enunciation of the blessed teachings. They humbled themselves in obedience to Him, and swelled with pride at having had the bounty of attaining His presence. So charged was the room with spiritual potency that the two distinguished persons of the East who were seated to the Master's left and right were profoundly affected by the sight of the impressive influence of the Cause of God, as well as the rapture and utter humility demonstrated by the illustrious men and women who were present. Several times they expressed their gratitude that the people of the East had now become so dear and precious to the West, owing to the influence exerted by the blessed Cause in those countries, and had become the object of the devoted reverence of the civilized peoples of the Occident.[207] The Master showed tenderness and loving-kindness to each and every one of those souls.

After having some *sharbat*, sweets, tea, and ice cream, the Master departed that place. He entered the car of that handmaid of God, Mrs [Thornburgh-]Cropper, and they returned to His residence. He showed great loving-kindness to Mrs [Thornburgh-]Cropper, for she truly strives to the utmost to spread the verses of God, and is always ready to serve His Cause.

Sunday, 12 January 1913
[London]

As there were a great number of people present at His residence, and it was not possible for each and every one of them to attain His presence, the Master stated that He would meet with everyone in the drawing room all at once. He then went to meet them there, and gave a brief talk on spiritual and material civilizations. He noted that, at one time, the East was the more materially advanced civilization, and the West was deprived of this progress. He offered counsel, moreover, that the East must avail themselves of the material civilization of the West, and the West benefit from the spiritual civilization of the East.

Following that gathering, a number of seekers, as well as others who truly needed to see the Master, attained His presence. In hearing His utterances, they partook of spiritual delights, and received the outpourings of eternal grace – and this continued until the afternoon.[208]

In the evening, a kingly banquet to receive the Master – charged with abounding love and spiritual sentiments – was held in the home of Sir Richard Stapley,[209] one of the political leaders of the English people. Truly, that gentleman and his honourable wife [Annie (Elizabeth) Jenner, Lady Stapley] showed the utmost servitude and respect. Additionally, a number of dignitaries and seekers – most of whom were engaged in political pursuits – had also been invited solely so that they might attain the Master's presence. To give a detailed account of that gathering, as well as the etiquette and decorum which characterized it, would prove overly lengthy. What is more necessary to mention – a thing that will bring abundant joy to the friends of God, and which demonstrates the power and might of the Covenant of Bahá'u'lláh – is that, once everyone had had their dinner and coffee,[210] all the guests went to a special room[211] where the Master was seated, and attained His presence there.

First, the esteemed host arose and said:

> I wish to express my deepest gratitude on behalf of all those present, for 'Abdu'l-Bahá is with us at this gathering. Most of us have some degree of familiarity with the history of this Cause, and we feel the sincerest respect and deepest humility towards it. Those present are aware that a spiritual power has been manifested from this Bahá'í Cause – a power which is the cause of edification and salvation, and is stronger than all the powers of war and strife – for despite the fact that 'Abdu'l-Bahá endured prison for forty years, and that the Bahá'ís of the East have always contended with affliction and torment, this flame was ultimately never extinguished; on the contrary, it burned even more brightly. Most of those present have been to 'Akká and witnessed firsthand the kindness and solicitude 'Abdu'l-Bahá would show to all kinds of people, in particular the poor. And now, having gained His freedom, He

> journeys to every corner of the world, striving to the utmost to spread the cause of peace and unity. We hope that He may, with abounding gladness, accomplish this lofty goal and attain to His heart's desire.

That esteemed host then concluded his remarks, and all those present expressed great joy and humility. Shortly thereafter, the Master began to speak while seated. He first remarked upon the goodly comportment and conscientious sentiments of the attendees, observing that for them to show such respect to a stranger from the East was a sign of their consummate love. He then gave an extensive talk on the unity and fellowship that must be fostered between the peoples of the East and West through divine power, and the establishment of a spiritual civilization, noting that all other powers are ultimately impotent and limited – and all beings subject to the laws of nature – except divine power and spiritual civilization, which exert extraordinary influence upon the realities of humanity.

Afterwards, Sir Richard Stapley rose once again and expressed his thanks to the Master for giving His talk. He then asked the Master if He would entertain questions from those in the audience who wished to ask Him something, that they might be honoured with hearing His reply. When the Master consented to this request, one of those present first asked Him, 'To what extent have sentiments of peace gained currency in the East?' The Master replied:

> To the extent that all the Bahá'ís of the East are ready to give up their lives in their efforts to promote peace. Twenty thousand souls have sacrificed themselves in the cause of peace, inasmuch as the foremost teaching and injunction enjoined by Bahá'u'lláh is that of universal peace. Thus, the Bahá'ís consider the promotion of this peace to be a religious obligation.

Another attendee then inquired, 'If a person should transgress their limits and encroach on the possessions of others, what must be done?' The Master replied:

> In brief, to protect the rights of humans and to repel wickedness is a matter separate from conflict and contention. Of course, this does not give a person the right to take revenge; it is, rather, the duty of society to protect and defend him. For example, should a person murder your child, you cannot kill the child of that person. Should a person blind the eye of another, the victim has no right to blind the eye of his attacker solely for revenge. Should a person steal your possessions, it is not for you to steal his in return. Rather, society must take steps to defend the victims, and protect the lives and substance of their kind. Cruelty and oppression must be prevented through good governance; otherwise, chaos and confusion will ensue . . .

A question was then asked about striking children who have a propensity to misbehave. The Master responded:

> It is not permissible even to strike an animal. When an animal is trained properly, it becomes domesticated. Thereby is the crooked branch made straight, and the thorny thicket transformed into a rose-garden. The Arabs do not strike their horses as they train them, for they say that striking the horse will make it ill-tempered and unruly.

The following question was then asked: 'How can the power of love be manifested in a nation that attacks another nation solely out of cruelty?' The Master responded:

> This subject has been discussed among people for some time. As was mentioned previously, no one has the right to take revenge. If, however, a nation acts oppressively, and arises with murderous and plunderous intent, it is the bounden duty of society to defend the target of such an onslaught, inasmuch as this oppression has ramifications for the general population. If a person acts unjustly towards you alone, you must forgive him – but if that person acts unjustly towards the general population, you have no right to forgive the perpetrator on their behalf. Society, therefore,

must arise to defend and protect the victims of such an act.

This question was then posed: 'If a country should be in the midst of great turmoil, and if the denizens of that country should begin to act unjustly towards one another, may the denizens of another country intervene to defend and protect the victims of these wrongful deeds?' The Master replied:

> In this Cause, all humanity is regarded as a single family, and the whole earth accounted as one country. People must cooperate with one another, and this cooperation is a prerequisite of their protection. Their efforts, however, to counsel and improve the human condition must be unsullied by selfish motives . . .

In brief, the answers given by the Master induced a remarkable and conspicuous kind of astonishment and transformation in His audience. All those present expressed their thanks and gratitude – in particular the president of that assembly consecrated to peace, Mr Moscheles, and the esteemed host, Sir Richard Stapley, who expressed his praise and gratitude on behalf of all those present in these vivid terms:

> Though it is necessary to consider certain material subjects, yet we had grown completely forgetful of spiritual power. But praised be God, for through His utterances, 'Abdu'l-Bahá has tonight made us aware of that spiritual power which is born of God.

In consequence of these remarks, the ocean of beneficence surged once again, and the Master offered these words of vigilance and encouragement to His audience:

> It is so; spiritual power is necessary. The Cause of Jesus Christ, Muhammad, Zoroaster, and the other Prophets of God was promoted through spiritual power. As you are the pillars of peace, it is my hope that you shall be aided by this spiritual power. Furthermore, since you have noble aspirations – and because you desire

peace with all your heart – I firstly express my thanks that you cherish these high-minded ideals, and I secondly beseech God to add to your confirmations.

Following this, all those present repeatedly praised the Master with the utmost reverence. They also thanked Sir Richard Stapley for having convened such a memorable gathering, and for having served as the means through which they were able to have the tremendous honour and bounty of attaining the Master's presence.

Monday, 13 January 1913
[London]

The weather in London was smoggy and rainy. It had become so dark that the cars were forbidden from driving on the roads for fear that they would collide.[212] This day stood in stark contrast to every other one during the Master's time there, when conditions were clear and the sun shone brightly – so much so that the people of the city expressed their amazement, observing that the weather in London during the wintertime had never been so clear.

Occasioned by the dark conditions that day, the Master gave a talk before a certain gathering that dealt with the darkness of the vain imaginings and blind imitation that exist among people and act as barriers preventing them from beholding the light of divine guidance and the Sun of Truth.

In the afternoon, while before a great gathering [at Caxton Hall] devoted to the establishment of peace,[213] the Master gave an extensive talk on the foundations of peace and well-being, which have always been the primary aims of the Prophets and the Manifestations of God. The Master concluded this talk by expounding the teachings of this most great and most glorious Revelation.

Shortly thereafter, the president of that gathering of peace, Mr Moscheles, rose and said:

On behalf of all those present, I would like to express my praise of 'Abdu'l-Bahá as well as my gratitude to Him. The attendees made

> a special request of me to openly laud and appreciate these teachings and utterances, for we are all aware of the trials and tribulations this Cause has suffered in the East. Not only have its adherents raised the call of peace, but thousands of them have even given their lives for it, and sustained all manner of affliction and calamity in its path. And now, we who had forgotten the essential principles promoted by Christ are being guided aright, and summoned to build a spiritual civilization. Surely, there is no matter more vital or pressing than this. Furthermore, this is a Cause which forbids conflict and contention, and promotes the ideals of peace and the oneness of humanity – ideals whose fulfilment will realize the ultimate prosperity and demonstrate the greatest glory of humankind. We, therefore, are exceedingly grateful that the land of Christ has once again given such magnificent teachings to the West.

When the president of that gathering had expressed his remarks with perfect courtesy and reverence – and the audience had been roused to great clamour and excitement, several times breaking out into applause – the Master rose once again and spoke these lofty words:

> I am most grateful to you all for your sentiments, inasmuch as universal feelings are divine, whereas particular matters are born of humankind. Indeed, the regions of the West are in need of divine civilization. There material civilization has made great strides and continues to advance with every passing day, yet divine civilization has been discarded. This material civilization is like a clear glass, but divine civilization is even as a shining lamp. When that glass is illumined with this lamp, then will divine perfection be made manifest. Material civilization, therefore, is like an exquisite form that, regardless of its beauty, is still in need of a spirit. Material civilization was established by philosophers, whereas divine civilization was established by the Manifestations of God. Jesus Christ established a civilization that cast a ray upon the realm of morality, and thus became the means through which fellowship was fostered

among the people. This is a feat which material civilization alone is powerless to accomplish. Rather, material civilization produces the Krupp gun, firearms, dynamite, and other such things, whereas spiritual civilization conduces to the development of a goodly character, the promotion of human welfare and tranquillity, the illumination of the world of humanity, and the realization of perpetual prosperity. It is my hope that humankind may succeed in both respects, inasmuch as material civilization contributes to the realm of physicality, and divine civilization to the realm of morality. I rejoice with exceeding gladness at all of you and at this gathering.

As the Master departed that meeting, He said, 'I wish to go for a walk.' Consequently, the Master went for a stroll, accompanied by a few of the friends and His attendants, until they eventually reached a rug-seller's shop. After taking His seat, conversing a while with some of the Ottomans who were there[214] and relating accounts concerning the Cause of God, the Master and His companions entered two cars[215] and set out for the Persian legation, where He had made a commitment to speak that evening.

The nobility, intelligence, and fair-mindedness of the ambassador and his dear compatriots[216] brought great joy to the hearts of the members of the Master's retinue. The ambassador commenced the gathering by expressing his gratitude for the Master's arrival at this place, voicing his abundant joy that He had travelled to Scotland, and recounting the humble deference and reverence shown to Him by the esteemed people of Edinburgh. To that end, a number of the newspapers of Edinburgh had been prepared which discussed the talks that the Master had given there. The secretary of the legation read most of these articles aloud, and also offered translations of them into Persian. The fact that the people of the East had now reached such high ranks in the countries of the West, and were exerting such notable influence there, brought great happiness to the Master. It was indeed a blessed night, and a perfect and most illustrious banquet. The Master had a wonderful time. Eventually, that gathering drew to a close with a spirit of joy and love.

'Abdu'l-Bahá with His attendants in Bristol

'Abdu'l-Bahá at the Shah Jahan Mosque, Woking

The Shah Jahan Mosque, a modern photograph

Sir Syed Ameer Ali (Amír 'Alí)

Tuesday, 14 January 1913
[London]

After reciting prayers and meditations, voicing supplications to God, and expressing gratitude for the aid and assistance vouchsafed from the Abhá Kingdom, a number of the believers requested permission to attain the Master's presence, and they subsequently received His tender mercies.[217] Among these friends was that handmaid of God, Mrs Rosenberg, whose services and character were most pleasing to the Master.

When the number of people who were gathering, believers and others alike, had swelled to large proportions, the Master went to the drawing room to see them. He then gave a talk in which He expressed His happiness at the fruits of this journey, and also at the steadfastness and spirituality exhibited by the believers of London. Furthermore, He encouraged His audience to spread the sweet savours of God, and exhorted them to acquire imperishable perfections.

Likewise, a great number of people attained the Master's presence in the afternoon,[218] and benefited immensely from His abiding favours and loving-kindness.[219]

In the evening, a spirited gathering was held at the New Congregational Church.[220] The priests of that church expressed their heartfelt praise for the Master. When the Master had entered the room where He was to speak, but had not yet appeared before the audience, one of the priests [the Reverend John James Pool] commenced the gathering by giving an account of the history of the Cause, which included a discussion of the Dispensations of the Báb and Bahá'u'lláh. He then said:[221]

> 'Abdu'l-Bahá, who is with us tonight, is the third teacher of this most great Cause. He spent forty years of His life securing the good-pleasure of God while incarcerated in the prison-city of 'Akká, and has summoned and guided the people to the ways of brotherhood, love, universal peace, and the oneness of humanity. It is our inestimable privilege to have so esteemed an individual

> with us tonight – a man eminently forbearing, illustrious, kind, generous, eloquent, and wise. He is truly the king of all humankind, and it is our great honour to benefit – in a spirit of the utmost joy – from the bounty of His presence. I have no doubt that you all will show the utmost reverence to such a luminous personage, and that you will arise to receive Him when he appears before you. It behooves us to be exceedingly grateful and to feel immensely privileged, that in spite of His fatigue – and in the absence of a more favourable opportunity – 'Abdu'l-Bahá has nonetheless chosen to honour us tonight. Though He is regarded by all as their lord and their master, He considers Himself a mere servant of God – and it is through this servitude that He possesses a heavenly sovereignty.

Following the address of that high-minded priest, the Master went up to the platform of the sanctuary. All those present rose, and showed Him complete humility and respect. The Master then began to give His talk, in which He discussed the need to educate people with the divine teachings, as well as the subject of spiritual power. His talk captured the undivided attention of His audience, and conferred upon them a state of perfect spirituality. When the Master concluded His talk, each and every person in the audience attained His presence. They shook His hand, showered Him with praise, and implored His confirmations and blessings.

Wednesday, 15 January 1913
[London → Clifton, Bristol]

In the morning, the Master set off for Bristol and Clifton. After having some tea, and when a number of believers and friends had attained His presence, the Master departed London [via Paddington Station] at ten o'clock.[222] At one o'clock in the afternoon, He arrived at Clifton, where He was to stay at the hotel of Mr [Wellesley] Tudor Pole.[223] After having some lunch, the Master rested for a short while.

A number of believers and seekers had the honour of attaining the Master's presence. From Him they heard discussions of various spiritual subjects, explanations of the purposes for which the Manifestations of God appear from time to time, exhortations to dispel the vain imaginings and blind imitations which stem from religious fanaticism, and admonitions to eliminate all manner of harmful prejudice.

After His audience had been dismissed, expressing their humility and sincere devotion to Him as they departed, the Master and Mr Tudor Pole – at the request of the latter – went on an excursion by car and then returned to the hotel.[224]

In the evening,[225] an impressive gathering was held in the main hall of that hotel. Since the Master's arrival had been announced in the newspapers a few days in advance, the number of attendees was so great that most of them had to stand outside.[226] With perfect praise and total humility, Mr Tudor Pole commenced the gathering by discussing the history and teachings of this new and wondrous Revelation, and giving an account of the Master's travels. Following this, the Master entered the hall,[227] and all those present rose at once. The Master bade everyone be seated, and then gave an extensive talk on the Lesser Peace, which He described as one of the exigencies of this age. As part of this talk, the Master stated that the nations and religions of the world are in need of universal peace and the oneness of humanity.[228] These explanations of the blessed teachings and other spiritual subjects roused the audience to immeasurable joy and gladness. So brightly were their eyes and hearts illumined thereby, and so humbled were their necks in reverence, that as they were being dismissed, each and every one of those respected men and women knelt before the Master's chair, clung to the hem of His robe, and implored His grace and blessings.

As this scene was taking place, my eyes fell upon the Mu'ayyiru'l-Mamálik,[229] who had accompanied the Master on this trip [to Clifton, Bristol]. I noticed that he was looking, with complete astonishment, upon the reverence and humility that the most distinguished people of England were showing before the power of this Cause and the might of the Master, and I saw that he was crying profusely – so much so that it aroused great tenderness within me. Indeed, to see this gentleman so profoundly affected by this scene moved me, in turn, to shed tears of ecstasy. I rejoiced in my heart of hearts, and gave thanks for those promised confirmations that had been vouchsafed from the Abhá Kingdom.

At the most impressive of gatherings convened throughout the realms of Britain, we have on numerous occasions seen people such as this gentleman, who in the presence of the Master are moved to lament the ignorance and wretchedness of their countrymen, and say to themselves:

> What conspicuous glory has God deigned to bestow upon us Persians! How great is this prosperity, which is even as a mighty sun that has risen over the world's horizon and shines with dazzling resplendence! But alas, we have failed to recognize its value. As a result, we find ourselves now burdened with weariness and facing the consequences of our actions.

That gentleman had truly been stirred to a remarkable degree of vigilance, and the Master was most pleased with his sincere devotion, his undivided attention, and his prayerful supplication.

At the end of that gathering, a number of Egyptian students,[230] as well as some journalists, attained the Master's presence. They all felt immense honour and delight at having had the privilege of hearing His utterances.

The Master's heart brimmed over with joy that night. With perfect felicity, He sat at the table, had His dinner,[231] and spoke happily and lovingly of the services of Mr Tudor Pole.

Thursday, 16 January 1913
[Clifton, Bristol → London]

In the morning, as they lay in the comfort of their beds, the Master's attendants woke to the sweet sound of His voice as He walked outside, giving thanks for the aid and assistance from the Abhá Kingdom. His heart was rejoicing with exceeding gladness, for in the span of just one night, a single talk of His had sufficed to bring awareness to a great multitude and captivate scores of pure hearts.

Afterwards, when the Master expressed His intent to set off for London, Mr Tudor Pole and his wife remarked to Him that a car had been prepared to take Him for a stroll. At first, the Master excused Himself, stating, 'We have already resolved to depart soon, and are not in the mood for excursions and other recreation.' Notwithstanding, Mr Tudor Pole and his wife importuned, and the Master eventually acceded to their request. This excursion by car lasted for more than an hour,[232] during which time the Master saw the exquisite scenery of Clifton and Bristol.

Upon their return, a special photographer was waiting for them, by prior arrangement that had been made with him. He took two photographs of the Master: in the first one, He was in the company of His Persian servants; in the second, He was with a number of friends and members of His retinue.[233]

Following this, the Master departed quickly. Some of the Bahá'ís accompanied Him only to the railway station, while others followed Him all the way to London.

When the Master alighted the train, a number of the friends of London had already formed a line to receive Him at the station. Even as moths they hovered around Him, thrust into a rapturous frenzy by the intensity of their zeal and fervour.

That night, Lady Blomfield presented the Master with a piece of paper that featured a number of the teachings of the Cause, as well as discussions of other significant subjects. This paper also included an invitation to the King of Britain [George V] to meet with the Master. Lady Blomfield sought the Master's permission to submit this paper to the King's court, so that he might have the bounty and privilege of standing in the Master's presence. The Master praised the contents of that paper, but said:

> Such a meeting would prove effective and useful. However, we have come to meet with the poor, not to consort with kings and rulers. We will, with heartfelt love, receive everyone who seeks us, but have no desire or inclination to meet with heads of state. In addition to this, our association with those who boast such ranks

may alarm the people, arouse their suspicion, and create misunderstandings among them. Do not send this paper, then, as there is absolutely no need to do it.

Friday, 17 January 1913
[London → Woking → London]

The Master was scheduled to speak at two grand gatherings of Muslims.[234] Each of these served as proofs of His remarkable power, and spoke to the pervading influence of this Cause. Both gatherings were held at a mosque outside of London in Woking.[235] That morning, Sir Richard Stapley and his wife prepared a car for the trip to Woking, and the two of them accompanied the Master and His retinue to that city.[236] The Muʻayyiru'l-Mamálik also travelled with the Master's retinue that day.

At the first gathering [at the *Asiatic Quarterly Review* building], which was of a private nature, a number of Muslims from the East – as well as the dignitaries and Christians of London – attained the Master's presence. The attendees of this gathering were seated at the table, where they ate their lunch and had the honour of listening to the Master as He spoke of the unity and fellowship that must be established among the various peoples of the world.

From there, the Master went to the second gathering, which was open to the public and had been convened at the [Shah Jahan] mosque. As that gathering had been announced in the newspapers beforehand, a great number of people – believers and others, Christian and Muslim – were present at the mosque. When the Master entered the mosque, he found that it had no room to accommodate Him. For this reason, He stood outside on top of the staircase of the mosque. The attendees – who consisted of the wealthiest people of England, a number of respected Egyptians and Indians, and grandees of Constantinople – formed lines on both sides from end to end to stand in His presence. Before He began to speak, a special photographer set up his equipment and took two photographs of the gathering.[237]

Following this, the Master gave a most excellent talk in which

He discussed the foundation and the truth of the divine religions, and expounded upon the teachings of universal peace and the oneness of humanity.[238] Despite the light rain that had begun to fall, every one of the illustrious attendees remained standing and listened intently with the utmost deference.[239] They received the divine teachings as if they were being delivered by an angel from above.

When the Master concluded His extensive talk, a certain august person [Dr John Pollen] expressed – on behalf of Lord Lamington [sic],[240] and in a most clear voice – his thanks to the Master for delivering His address and articulating the divine teachings. Following that, Judge Amír-'Alí Ṣáḥib[241] – one of the eminent Muslims of India – stood before the Master, extended to Him his abundant gratitude, and lauded the Bahá'í teachings and other spiritual subjects that had just been discussed. He then urged everyone to appreciate the value of this privilege and to show reverence to the Master. After the effusive praise lavished by such distinguished individuals, one can imagine the humility and deference that was demonstrated by the others in the audience. All those present were as lowly servants before the Master. They supplicated His aid and assistance, and sought His grace and blessings. They shook His hand, and clung to the hem of His bounty. They expressed their sincere devotion to Him, and showered Him with their heartfelt love.

Saturday, 18 January 1913
[London]

After a great number of people, believers and others alike, attained His presence at public and private gatherings,[242] the Master went to the home of [the Reverend Reginald John] Campbell, where He had a lunch appointment that day. Upon entering that residence, He addressed a number of young ministers who were waiting in that room to attain His presence.[243] He said:

> My hope is that you purify your hearts until they resemble this mirror, that they may reflect the light of the perfections and grace

> of the Sun of Truth. May you unloose your tongues in praise of the Lord of the Kingdom, that like this piano, your melodies may bring happiness to people and confer heavenly life upon them. May the breezes wafting from the garden of loving-kindness bestow such freshness upon you that, even as these flowers, you may grow verdant and flourish, that every heart may rejoice with ecstasy. May you be graciously aided to spread the divine fragrances perpetually.

The young ministers were humbled and gladdened by the Master's utterances and comparisons; indeed, His manner of speaking made a profound impression on them.

Following this, the Master gave an extensive talk [to the same group of young ministers] on the meaning of the first verse of John in the New Testament,[244] in which He interpreted the term 'the Word of God'. Through this talk the Master unravelled a myriad mysteries. In unsealing this choice wine, and disclosing the secrets enshrined in these words, all those present had become inebriated with spiritual ecstasy.

In the afternoon, a large number of people, hailing from both the East and the West, visited the Master's residence and attained His presence. They all had the honour of listening to His encouraging counsels and exhortations.

One of the people who that night had the honour of attaining the Master's presence in that gathering replete with grace and bounty was a woman [Gabrielle Enthoven] who happened to live in the neighbourhood.[245] As this woman was a celebrated playwright, the Master spoke to her of the spiritual drama, discussing at length the circumstances attending the advents of the Manifestations of God:[246]

> Whenever the promised Manifestations had yet to appear, the masses sought after them desperately and eagerly awaited their appearance. They offered their fervent prayers and humble supplications at the threshold of God, cherishing the hope that they might sacrifice themselves on the day of the advent. It was chiefly

the clergy – as well as others who led the people in some capacity – who claimed to be able to recognize the promised Manifestations, and interpreted the signs mentioned in the Holy Books according to their own imaginings. And yet, whenever the day of the advent arrived, the deficient understanding of those same leaders caused them first to reject the Promised One, and then provoke the people to oppose Him. To seize the belongings and spill the blood of the Promised One were deemed as lawful acts by these leaders, who moreover issued edicts for their death, plundered their possessions, condemned their companions before the rulers of the realm as stirrers of sedition, arose to slander and persecute them, sentenced them to imprisonment, and put them to death. In spite of all this, the people grew more earnest in their quest with every passing day. They ultimately came to be numbered with the faithful, and strove to oppose the endeavours of the deniers. These believers resolved those spiritual questions which up to that time had perplexed those in their midst, and made apparent the meanings of a myriad secrets and signs. They destroyed the foundation of vain imaginings and blind imitations, and apprised others of the essential basis of the divine religions.

In the early days of every Dispensation, these souls were but base wanderers, bereft of all earthly means and power. The ascendant influence of their adversaries relegated them to the remotest wildernesses, where they spent their days lost and confused, and the unyielding cruelty demonstrated by the exponents of enmity drove them to vagrancy. In stark contrast to these hapless souls stood the deniers, all well-equipped and invested with consummate power, who before their congregations denied that the Promised One had appeared, and arose proudly to reject Him with the utmost endeavour. In the end, however, the fame of the Cause of God spread all over the world, and belief in the advent of His Promised Manifestation became a source of pride for all humanity, whether high or low, in such wise that kings prostrated themselves before them, and bowed their heads before even a mere servant of theirs.

Such were the explanations and accounts the Master gave to illustrate the circumstances attending the advents of the Manifestations, by way of describing the views, the words, the deeds, and the behaviour of both the faithful and the deniers. It then so happened that the aforementioned playwright went to record a word-for-word translation of all the Master's utterances on this subject.

Sunday, 19 January 1913
[London]

Since the Master was preparing for His imminent journey to Paris, He gave the following address that morning to a gathering of the friends:[247]

> I will be here for two more days, after which I shall depart for Paris. I must go to the East soon. It has been two years since I left the Holy Land. I have travelled throughout most of the states of America. In all the cities I visited, I have raised the call of the Abhá Kingdom, and summoned all people to the love and knowledge of God. It is necessary first to possess the knowledge of God, inasmuch as this knowledge is the fruit of human existence. Should the effulgences of the knowledge of God cast their rays in the world of humanity, every good would be obtained and the light of love would shine resplendent. In every heart would the candle of the knowledge of God be lit; in every aspect of existence would people progress, and their breasts be suffused with light.
>
> The world of nature is darkness upon darkness. Its illumination is contingent upon the knowledge of God, and the glory of the world of humanity is born of the love of God. The goal of one's earthly life should be to gain admittance into the Kingdom of God, and the fruit of one's existence must be to adorn oneself with heavenly virtues. Should a person remain deprived of these divine splendours, his state would be lower than that of the animals. If, however, his face should be illumined with the light of the love of God – and his heart adorned with the ornament of the knowledge of God – he would soar above this contingent realm,

and become attuned to innumerable realms of existence. He would be privy to supernatural power, gaining deliverance from the world of extinction, and discovering celestial life and heavenly splendour. He would disclose the realities of things, and unravel the secrets contained in the Holy Books. In all things would he discern a sign of wisdom, and from every direction would he hear glad-tidings. In the direst of calamities would he remain joyous, and in every hardship would he perceive a token of mercy. He would be potent to do all this, for his heart would be well-assured, his soul would rejoice with delight, his eyes would be illumined by beholding the most resplendent signs, and his nostrils would be perfumed with the sweet savours that waft from the Abhá Paradise. As a result, he would ascend day by day towards the pinnacle of glory, in such wise that he would behold all created things reposing beneath the shade of his existence.

I hope that this journey I have undertaken will bring about such results. May people learn of the knowledge of God and be apprised of the celestial realm. May they so soar in these supernal heights that they shall transcend the world of nature. May they draw on spiritual power to govern nature, and not allow themselves to be subjected to it. May they make nature their captive, and not suffer themselves to become its prisoner. These are the outpourings of grace and the heavenly perfections I desire for you – that you may be illumined with the light of the Kingdom of God, and secure your portion of supernatural power, inasmuch as the world of nature is the realm of corruption. It is the world of imperfection and the dominion of darkness. The Kingdom of God, however, is the world of perfection. It is the realm of manifold excellences, and the focal point of heavenly virtues. It is the world from which the liberal effusions of God's grace are vouchsafed, and every one of His signs and splendours are sent down.

Among the remarks the Master made that afternoon to a number of believers and seekers who had attained His presence were these:[248]

In the future, people will inevitably arise to oppose the Cause and write treatises against it. But what fruit will these efforts bear, except to make the people more aware and better informed of the Cause? In Persia, the divines and other leaders have written many books in repudiation of this Cause, with the aim of uprooting it and completely obliterating the foundation on which it rests. Among these people was Ḥájí Muḥammad Karím Khán, who wrote several books to that end – but they have all been totally forgotten, while the Cause of God has gained renown in both the East and the West, and been promulgated amidst the peoples and kindreds of the earth. Consider how the Jewish leaders arose to oppose Christ at the time of His advent, and even denounced Him as the Devil himself. Our ears, therefore, are well acquainted with such idle murmuring.

The Bahá’ís of Persia would travel to every city and hamlet expressly to teach the Faith. They would persist in their efforts until all the people there had been informed of the Faith – and, as a result, these people would at times be roused to agitated excitement, engaging in assaults, issuing words of slander, and raising great clamours. When the Bahá’ís were certain that all the people in that area had been apprised of the Faith, and had been stirred to their cores after learning of it, they would depart from that place and travel to another where they would continue to teach the Faith.

How pleased will I be when we are reviled in the streets, and made the objects of reproach and persecution! This would be a cause for celebration; it is nothing short of our greatest wish and ultimate aspiration. What could be better than this, that one should become a wanderer abased in the path of God? From this abasement, he will discover such delight as can never be described. When we first arrived in ‘Akká, we were in the direst of straits, all stricken with some toil or calamity – and yet, so great was our joy and delight that it cannot be put into words. At one point, seventy of our companions were imprisoned in the fortress, and they had all fallen sick with a fever so debilitating that it robbed them even of the ability to move. This illness had afflicted everyone but me

> and Áqá Riḍá; consequently, we tended to the believers, preparing medicine and soup for them. It so happened that I had been made to dwell in a room of that fortress whose floor had been paved with stones. It was an exceedingly humid room – one that had originally been built as a place where the dead were to be washed. And yet, despite all these tribulations, so joyous were we beneath the sheltering shade of Bahá'u'lláh that we accounted every toil and trouble as comfort and ease.

As the Master had spent the past few days in London, a constant stream of people attained His presence from the morning up until the afternoon.[249] The soul-stirring ardour felt by the people in these gatherings is a thing which eludes all description.

That night,[250] the Master – as well as a number of His servants and some of the friends – had been invited to the home of the Maharaja of Rajputana [sic],[251] one of the princes of India. A number of other illustrious souls from both the East and the West were also seated at the dinner table at that exquisite gathering,[252] where they had the honour of attaining the Master's presence and benefiting from His most tender grace. While in His presence, they had the privilege of dining on an array of colourful foods and a variety of Eastern dishes. And yet, the spiritual counterparts to these delectable delights – which moved all those present to express their profound gratitude and extend their effusive praise for this abundantly beneficial gathering that had been convened – were the Master's sweet and ravishing utterances. He first spoke of the detriments of prejudice:

> It is prejudice that has uprooted families. It is prejudice that has led people to shed each other's blood. It is prejudice that has prompted them to hate one another. If this prejudice were to be eliminated entirely, this lowly earth would become the most exalted Paradise. Every soul would be like a celestial rose-garden, and every heart the mirror of the highest heaven.

The subject of abstinence from eating meat was then raised, to which the Master replied:

> If one can content oneself with vegetables for one's sustenance, this would be preferable, for the food of humanity consists in vegetables. However, given the great extent to which people have become accustomed to their ways of life, it is not possible for them to abstain from eating animals.
>
> When I was living in Baghdad, I saw an Indian who insisted on abstaining from eating meat. I asked him, 'Do you yourself eat a great number of animals?'
>
> 'No,' he replied.
>
> Following this, I asked him, 'Do you drink water?'
>
> 'Yes,' he replied.
>
> I then asked him, 'Do you eat cheese?'
>
> 'Yes,' he replied again.
>
> I responded, 'Observe with a microscope, and behold how many animals you will find in all these things you admit to consuming! When you boil water, see how many microbes you kill in the process!'
>
> To this he replied, 'But such animals are tiny!'
>
> I responded, 'They all feel pain nonetheless. When the microbes in the water are boiled, and the sheep and the cow raise their cries of anguish, both sets of organisms feel the agony of torment and murder.'
>
> In former times, it was difficult for people to conceive of such matters, but it is easy to do this now that we have entered the century of progress and education. In ages past, every people had their own vain imaginings, but now they have become educated through proper instruction, and the veils which once hindered them have been rent asunder. This is true even of the Muslims, who formerly believed that the angel Gabriel literally possessed wings, but now understand that this symbol represents the holy power of revelation and descent. They have come to realize that its true meaning is exemplified in the verses, 'the Faithful Spirit* hath

* A reference to the angel Gabriel.

> come down with it[*] upon Thy[†] heart,'[‡] and that all other interpretations are but idle fancies.
>
> Praised be God that the century of vain imaginings has passed! Consider this: if those prejudices and vain imaginings still existed in our midst, would it have been possible for such intimate fellowship to have been fostered among the various peoples gathered here – who belong to foreign religions and hail from distant lands – and for us to have shown such love and kindness to one another?

Following this, the subject of the travels of the believers was raised – in particular, the matter of the illness which Mr [Sidney] Sprague contracted while in the Indian state of Punjab. The Master stated:

> When the Pársí believers of Bombay learned of Mr Sprague's illness, one of them – a man named Kay-Khusraw[§] – arose with the utmost alacrity, and rushed to Punjab to serve him. This he did in spite of the intensity of the heat in that place, or the various plagues and diseases that were rampant there. So devotedly did he tend to Mr Sprague – forgoing sleep and sustenance, and ever remaining by his side – that Mr Sprague's illness infected Kay-Khusraw. Mr Sprague recovered, while Kay-Khusraw fell sick and eventually succumbed to his disease. Behold what a power this is – a power that compels people to sacrifice themselves for each other, and brings them to a station where they demonstrate such love! . . .

Every heart in the audience was profoundly moved by the Master's utterances and anecdotes. They all expressed their gratitude – in particular the Maharaja, who, as he was preparing to depart, expressed his sincerest respect for the Master, and asked Him to promise that He would travel to India someday, as this was a prospect the prince very much cherished.

---

* The Qur'án.
† Muhammad's.
‡ Qur'án 26:193–94.
§ Kay-Khusraw Isfandíyár.

Monday, 20 January 1913
[London]

The Master once again gave a farewell address to the believers and friends,[253] in which He spoke of the seeds that had been planted in London, remarked on the fertility of the soil of its denizens' hearts, commented on the fresh and flourishing flowers that had bloomed in the divine rose-garden, and described the luxuriance and verdure of the trees that had grown in the garden of humanity.

Following this, two of the believers who had come from the island of Honolulu attained the Master's presence.[254] They implored Him to pray for the people of that land and convey a message in their honour. The Master consented, and spoke these exalted words:

He is God

> Convey my greetings and kindest sentiments to the Bahá'ís of Honolulu, and inform them that they are ever in my thoughts; that I supplicate Almighty God, tearfully and fervently, on their behalf; that I beseech Him to grant His pardon and confer His bounties upon them; that I cherish heavenly confirmations for them; that I pray for the breathings of the Holy Spirit to vivify them; and that I wish for a ray of the Sun of Truth to be cast upon them, that thereby those friends may become fruitful trees. Await the appearance of this divine gift. Soon will the lights of the Abhá Kingdom illumine the hearts, and the outpourings of the Sun of Truth encompass the earth. Then will the glory of the believers be made known and manifest. Therefore, strive day and night to become even as the dwellers of paradise, and develop such firmness in the divine Covenant that even if all the peoples of the world were to unite against you, they would fail to make you falter in your faith – for firmness in the Covenant of God will bring about every one of His bestowals, and steadfastness in His Cause is the means through which every token of His grace and bounty is made manifest.

In the afternoon,[255] a significant gathering was convened in the home of the president of the Peace Society, Mr Moscheles, who was sincerely devoted to the Master.[256] A great many of the grandees and nobles who had theretofore not had the honour of attaining the Master's presence were now in attendance expressly to hear His address, and they became totally captivated as they listened to His discussions of spiritual subjects. That handmaid of God, Lady Blomfield, commenced the gathering with a most sweet address in which she gave the glad-tidings of the advent of Bahá'u'lláh, and she concluded this address by recounting the attributes of the Centre of the Covenant. Afterwards, the president of the society rose and said:

> We all extend our greetings to this most holy personage, who has traversed wildernesses, crossed seas, and endured great toil and trouble, all so that the message of peace and the oneness of humanity may gain renown among the peoples of the West. Although each and every one of us here has striven to further the causes of peace and unity, yet we have not travelled great distances, or suffered imprisonment, or sustained trials and tribulations in the fulfilment of these noble goals. We, therefore, feel the utmost pride and joy that this blessed being, who has consented to bear such great afflictions in His life, is with us today. It is our great pleasure and ardent desire to hear those blessed teachings which He has come to propound – teachings that will unite humankind, liberate it, and grant it salvation. I offer my most fervent gratitude that this blessed soul has attended our gathering.

Following these remarks, the Master gave an immensely powerful talk on the teachings of this Most Great Dispensation, as well as the oneness of the divine religions and the unity that must be established among the peoples of the world.[257] The Master's talk evoked such ecstasy and delight in His audience – and roused them to such irrepressible excitement – that they all unloosed their tongues to lavish their praise and gratitude on Him, and were enamoured of His most impressive demeanour.

The Master then went to another room reserved for an afternoon meal, where tea, sweets, and *sharbat* had been prepared. All who were present there expressed their sincerest respect for Him, and bowed their necks in humble reverence before Him. They attested to the glory of the Cause of God, and affirmed the vital importance of the teachings of this Most Great and Most Glorious Dispensation.

Shortly after nightfall,[258] the Master went to the Higher Thought Society at the Doré Gallery,[259] where an impressive gathering had been arranged expressly to have Him give a talk there. Despite the Master's fatigue after having met with scores of people and engaging in so many conversations with them, He nonetheless gave a talk on the essential basis of the divine religions, humanity's indispensable need for the new and wondrous teachings, and the unveiling of divine realities – a talk which brought about a prodigious transformation in His listeners, and had a profound effect on their hearts.[260] This applied even to a number of the Persians there that night, who were not Bahá'ís and listened only from the periphery, but bore witness nevertheless to the pervading influence of the Cause of God and the consummate power of His Word.

That gathering was the last at which the Master spoke in London – a gathering that clearly demonstrated His power and might.

Tuesday, 21 January 1913

[London → Paris]

The Master was preparing to set off for Paris. A great number of people, consisting of both friends and others, had gathered at the Master's residence, and they were all deeply saddened by the news of His imminent departure. During the last few days of His sojourn in London, the believers would express such sentiments as these to the Master:

> The people of London have only just now become aware of Your stay here, and immeasurable ecstasy and rapture have taken root

> in their hearts. It would be a shame to distance them from the grace of Your presence so soon.

However much they insisted and implored, and expressed their wish for Him to stay a while longer, the Master replied:

> It is imperative that I go. This sojourn has taken a great deal of time. The Bahá'ís in other countries are expecting me; we must depart.

It can truly be said that, with every passing day, a new group of people attained the Master's presence. Among these people were the owners of various newspapers, the majority of whom would – in addition to recording the words of the Master, and printing descriptions and characterizations of Him – implore Him to make some special statements for their readership. The Master made numerous remarks and revealed many Tablets to this end. One of these Tablets, revealed during Christmastime at the request of the editor-in-chief of *The Christian Commonwealth* for the readers of that publication, is as follows:[261]

He is God

> The Lord of all humankind hath fashioned this human realm to be a Garden of Eden, an earthly paradise. If, as it must, it findeth the way to harmony and peace, to love and faithfulness, it will become a true abode of bliss, a place of manifold blessings and unending delights. Therein shall be revealed the excellence of humankind, therein shall the rays of the Sun of Truth shine forth on every hand.
>
> Remember how Adam and the others once dwelt together in Eden. No sooner, however, did a quarrel break out between Adam and Satan than they were, one and all, banished from the Garden, and this was meant as a warning to the human race, a means of telling humankind that dissension – even with the Devil – is the way to bitter loss. This is why, in our illumined age, God teacheth

> that conflicts and disputes are not allowable, not even with Satan himself – yet now, on the contrary, the world of humanity is filled with war and strife. There is war among the religions; war among the nations; war among the peoples; war among the rulers. What a welcome change would it be, if only these black clouds would lift from off the skies of the world, so that the light of reality could be shed abroad! If only the darksome dust of this continual fighting and killing could settle forever, and the sweet winds of God's loving-kindness could blow from out the wellspring of peace. Then would this world become another world, and the earth would shine with the light of her Lord.
>
> If there is any hope, it is solely in the bounties of God: that His strengthening grace will come, and the struggling and contending will cease, and the acid bite of blood-dripping steel will be turned into the honey-dew of friendship and probity and trust. How sweet would that day be in the mouth, how fragrant as musk the scent thereof.
>
> God grant that the new year will bring a promise of the new peace. May He enable this distinguished assemblage to conclude a fair treaty and establish a just covenant, that you may be blessed forever, across the unborn reaches of time.[262]

When the Master had first arrived in London, a number of representatives for peace had also come to that city on behalf of the Ottoman government and the various Balkan regimes, and planned to hold a meeting there.[263] Thus, in His remarks, the Master alluded to the success of their efforts to achieve peace between the two parties. Likewise, He made this remark several times:

> When they have concluded their war with the Ottomans, the Balkan regimes will fall into conflict with one another.

Eventually, it did indeed come to pass that the Balkan nations waged war against themselves.[264]

The Master left His residence for the railway station, and a number of people came to see Him off.[265] They implored Him constantly for His grace and bounty, and entreated Him to bless and confirm them in the path of service. When the train began to depart, they all grew distraught and began to moan and wail with such bitterness as to cause astonishment. To think that the Cause of God should have exerted such pervading influence throughout a country like this one, and the power of the Covenant of the Abhá Beauty so revolutionized and enraptured the hearts of its inhabitants! Though the winters of London are typically cloudy and foggy, its denizens were in disbelief as they had the good fortune of basking in the brightness of the sun and enjoying the temperate climate during the Master's sojourn there. Indeed, most of the days of that sojourn were marked by clear skies and moderate weather – especially on this particular day, whose mild temperature and verdant views were wonderfully pleasant to experience. The Master's heart rejoiced with gladness, and He rendered thanks for the confirmations vouchsafed by the Abhá Kingdom.

The train eventually reached the shore at a juncture when the waters were calm.[266] All those present remarked that it was impossible for the waters to be so peaceful at this time of year, and that, over the course of this one-hour voyage, ships would cross in the face of violent turbulence. On that day, however, the waters were perfectly still, and our ferry arrived at the French shore in complete tranquillity. When the Master passed through customs, He embarked a train once again. Shortly after nightfall, He arrived in Paris, and went to a special apartment on Rue Saint-Didier which Mr Dreyfus had secured for Him.[267]

By the time the train had reached the station, a number of the Bahá'ís of Paris – as well as some Persian dignitaries – had gathered at the railway station to receive the Master. Upon attaining His presence, these friends expressed the utmost joy and ecstasy. With perfect reverence, they saluted Him on His arrival, and showered Him with fervent praise.

For dinner, Mr and Mrs Dreyfus-Barney prepared a Persian dish consisting of rice and *khoresh*. The Master partook of this meal at the dinner table with great delight, and then went to rest.

France

Wednesday, 22 January 1913
[Paris]

Among the Persian travellers who had come from Persia to London and Paris that morning purely to attain the Master's presence – and thereby be present day and night at the table of His grace, and thoroughly sustained with His imperishable favours – were as follows:

- Ḥájí Amín
- The sons of that soul martyred in the path of God [Mírzá 'Alí-Muḥammad Varqá],[268] Mírzá 'Azízu'lláh Khán [Varqá] and Mírzá Valíyu'lláh Khán [Varqá]
- Mírzá 'Alí-Akbar Rafsanjání
- Áqá Mírzá Áqá Khán Qá'im-Maqámí
- Mírzá 'Abdu'lláh, the illustrious son of Áqá Siyyid Naṣru'lláh Báqiroff
- Áqá Siyyid Aḥmad Báqiroff
- Mírzá Muḥammad Khán Qazvíní
- Mírzá 'Alí ibn Adíb
- Mírzá Faraju'lláh Khabbáz Káshání
- Mírzá 'Alí-Akbar Nakhjavání

Two of these lofty souls, Mírzá Valíyu'lláh Khán and Mírzá 'Alí-Akbar Nakhjavání, had first travelled from Persia to America expressly to attain the Master's presence. While in that prosperous country, they took great delight and received perpetual benefits as they beheld in a number of impressive gatherings the pervading influence of the Cause of God – as well as the power and might of His Covenant – and from there they attained His presence yet again in London and Paris.

Although Mr and Mrs Dreyfus-Barney had not informed anyone of the Master's impending arrival in Paris – so that He would have time to rest and relieve Himself of the fatigues of His journey, undisturbed by troubles of any kind – yet a number of believers and those who were well disposed to the Faith had hastened with abounding ecstasy and delight to meet Him nonetheless. Likewise, a number of Persians – including the Intiẓámu's-Salṭanih; Jináb-i-Qá'im-Maqámí; and the Mu'ayyiru'l-Mamálik, who had accompanied the Master's retinue from London – also attained His presence. The Master related for His audience anecdotes from the impressive gatherings and religious assemblies at which He had spoken in America, and described the exaltation of the Cause of God in that country. As He was discussing this subject, the Master stated:

> While the Persians were occupied with themselves, neglecting their country in the process, we journeyed to the vast expanses of America, where we were engaged in securing spiritual victories and promoting unfading glory.

That night, the Master expounded upon those verses from Bahá'u'lláh's Tablets to the kings and rulers of the earth which specifically concerned the prophecies and other matters pertaining to the Ottoman territories, and recited verses from the Lawḥ-i-Ra'ís. He then said:

> Instruct the friends to read and disseminate these Tablets. How impressive are the commentaries which the Muslims of former times wrote concerning these verses: 'The Romans have been defeated . . . but after their defeat, they shall defeat their foes.'* And yet, they wilfully disregard this knowledge and power that have now been manifested from the Blessed Beauty in this Most Great Dispensation.

On numerous occasions over the course of this journey, the grandsons of Náṣiri'd-Dín Sháh would express their humble supplications to the Master in their letters to Him. He would then recount the transgressions committed by their forefather and say:

* Qur'án 30:2–3.

> Would that he could now lift up his head from out of his grave and behold what has come to pass!

Thursday, 23 January 1913
[Paris]

Since people of every stripe were meeting with the Master – to the extent that a number of them would always be seated, waiting to attain His presence – He designated the hours between nine o'clock and twelve o'clock every morning[269] as a time when seekers and people of importance who had not previously met with Him were permitted to attain His presence. This they did, one by one and two by two, sometimes before a gathering had commenced and sometimes after it had ended. Others would attain the Master's presence in the setting of a public gathering, where they would feel a fresh joy and rapture from hearing His blessed utterances.

At the public gathering that morning, the Master gave a talk in which He stated that one must be receptive if one is to acquire the divine bounties and perfections.

To dispel His fatigue and maintain His good health, it was the Master's daily custom to go on an excursion – whether on foot or by car – before having lunch and dinner.

That afternoon, when the Master had dismissed a number of respected Persians from His presence – including the secretary of the Persian legation[270] – He walked along some of the streets, and remarked:[271]

> All the inhabitants of this city are immersed in this world, and its buildings resemble the hives of bees. Its people are engaged constantly in building, constructing, and preparing for themselves the means of their physical comfort. They are exactly like honeybees!

That night, the Master described the capability and insight of the Qá'im-Maqám,[272] recounted the grave mistake made by Muḥammad Sháh in ordering his execution, and spoke extensively about the history of Persia. Among the words He spoke were these:

> Had they not killed the Qá'im-Maqám, Persia would never have fallen into ruin, and had they heeded the divine counsels, its ancient glory would not have been cast to the wind.

He then stated:[273]

> We, of course, do not at all involve ourselves in the political affairs of Persia. Had this Cause, however, appeared in the midst of any one of the peoples of the West, that people would vaunt this bounty over all the world.

Friday, 24 January 1913
[Paris]

At the public gathering that morning, the Master gave a talk which dealt with the second reality of humankind.[274] He observed that every being possesses one reality, with the exception of humans, who have both a natural reality and a spiritual one. His audience was completely captivated by the explanations He gave on this subject, as well as His unveiling the secrets which had theretofore been stored within that spiritual reality, His exhortation to inculcate goodly character, and His summons to promote the oneness of humanity and universal brotherhood.

Among the people who were perpetually blessed and immensely delighted to attain the Master's presence that afternoon were two respected Persian gentlemen who had not met with Him before. The Master spoke extensively on several subjects; the following are some of the statements He made: [275]

> The assault of one people against another, and the aggression which a person exhibits toward another, are demonstrations of natural behaviour. They stem from the dictates of nature, which actuate in every person the desire to preserve himself and harm all others.
>
> Consider the ravening wolf, which if given the chance would tear every sheep in the world to pieces, or how every animal wishes

to have all the grass of the field for itself. The nursing babe suckles his mother's breast – but if another babe should also begin to suckle milk from that breast, the first babe will strike him. This he does according to the dictates of nature.

There is no barrier, then, which prevents people from engaging in reprehensible behaviour, except for education – and education is of two kinds. The first is material education, which deters people from committing overt crimes. The second is divine education, which deters people from committing crimes and exhibiting aggression that is both overt and covert. Without this second kind of education, it would be utterly impossible for one to be protected. Such are the evidences of the dictates of nature, which is none other than the self that is susceptible to evil. The same holds true of the ferocious lion and the ravening wolf. Can it be asked of either of them why they tear sheep to pieces? No, for they are compelled by the dictates of nature. 'The right to rule rests with him who conquers.'*

All this is part of the struggle for survival, in which every living thing seeks to preserve its own life and harm or kill other creatures . . .

The Master continued His talk at great length, and it instilled awareness and vigilance in the hearts of His compatriots – so much so that afterwards they expressed their sincere devotion and gratitude to Him, and departed His presence most appreciatively. From that point forward, these Persians would, on most days, attain His presence in a spirit of devotion, receptivity, humility, and deference.

That night, a majestic gathering was held at the home of Mr and Mrs Dreyfus-Barney. In the talk which the Master gave there,[276] He offered words of encouragement to the believers, described how the sun of divine guidance had risen to dispel the darkness of ignorance and oppression, enumerated the teachings of this Most Great and Most Exalted Cause, and illustrated the pervading influence which the Word of God had exerted in the remotest regions of the world. All those present listened to these

* An Arabic saying attributed to Abú Ḥamíd al-Ghazálí.

blessed counsels and utterances with an accepting ear, and in hearing them the eyes of their understanding were opened wide. Furthermore, as the Persian believers and attendants beheld the potency of the Covenant of God and the supremacy of His Cause, they unloosed their tongues in thanksgiving for the confirmations that had so clearly been vouchsafed by the Abhá Kingdom – that souls in a city such as this had been enraptured by the Word of God, notwithstanding that previously they had grown weary even of the word 'religion', and cherished no aim but to soar in the world of nature.

Saturday, 25 January 1913
[Paris]

When the Master had finished rendering praise and thanksgiving to the Abhá Beauty – and after some of the believers had attained His presence – He gave a talk in which He discussed the rising of the Sun of Truth and the Focal Point of humanity's prosperity, and observed that, by turning towards this Sun, earthly souls would become heavenly, the vices of the nether world would be changed into the virtues of the celestial Kingdom, the dissension among peoples would be transformed into fellowship, and the darkness of blind imitations and vain imaginings would be totally dispelled by the brilliant splendours of knowledge and understanding.[277]

In the afternoon, a number of respected Persians had the inestimable bounty and privilege of attaining the Master's presence, and He spoke to them of Persia and the Persian people:

> The wise one does not counter the corrupt with a more corrupt person. In their desire to counter foreign encroachment upon their independence, the Persians ultimately became the cause of such interference themselves, and gave a pretext for meddling in their nation's affairs to them that had been seeking it. At the very least, these constitutionalists should have perused the histories of the various nations and civilizations of the world – such as those of France, a country that first formed a government rooted in law

and order – so that, under the influence of this law, its people would become prepared for progress. Then, with the passage of time, attention can be directed to other affairs.

As regards the nation of Persia, which was for years in ruin – a nation whose denizens are completely ignorant of law and are entirely without experience in such matters – how can it possibly adopt, preserve, and promote a constitutional government all of a sudden? How can a person who advocates for independence in his own household, but is himself a hindrance to the attainment of freedom, exhort others to embrace constitutionalism and freedom? The constitutionalists failed to realize that, although constitutionalism itself is good, its promoters seek to advance their personal interests in promulgating their message.

The Master then related an anecdote concerning the Armenians residing in Turkey:

A certain government provoked them, but as their situation grew dire, and because they were murdered and tortured, it did not support them at all. Not only this, but they said, 'You did not act in the way that behooved and befitted you.'[278]

After some additional detailed discussion, the Master concluded His talk with these remarks:

There is, in this day, no hope left but in unseen aid and divine power. There is an account in the Qur'án which describes a decomposed corpse, whose pieces had been scattered and whose bones had been disconnected from one another.* It was asked, 'How can this decomposed corpse now be revived?' The inquirer watched as the bones were suddenly joined together, enveloped with flesh and skin, and endowed with vigorous life and potent ability. At that moment, the inquirer recognized the power of God, for he had witnessed and come to know how life shall be given to bones, mouldering though they be.

* Qur'án 36:78.

> My meaning is that Persia can be likened to a decomposed corpse. Should unseen aid and divine power be vouchsafed to it – and heavenly assistance and confirmations conferred on it – the various peoples and contending kindreds of that nation would be gathered together through spiritual power, and become united in that which will secure everlasting life and glory. Now, we must strive to advance the progress of Persia's agriculture, its industry, and its commercial enterprises. Even if it should lose its independence, Persia will not cease to exist. When we turn our attention to improving the character of our compatriots, this act will conduce to every conceivable form of progress. If the Bahá'ís arise to carry out what they have been bidden, their highest aspirations will be realized in no time at all, and Persia shall become the envy of every Paradise.

The Master's heart was heavy that night; He was visibly despondent and upset.

Sunday, 26 January 1913
[Paris]

As the attendants and other members of His retinue were gathered in His presence, the Master asked this lowly servant to chant a prayer, and I did as I was instructed. Some of the Bahá'ís who had come from America and Europe had heard that prayers would be chanted every morning in the Master's presence, and they requested permission to be present on these occasions. When they heard a few lengthy prayers intoned, their eyes were illumined with the light of the Perspicuous Beauty. Although these friends from the West did not understand Arabic, they began nonetheless to feel such great tenderness for the Bahá'ís of both the East and the West that they were moved to tears, and their hearts were set ablaze with the fire of love.

The public gathering was then convened, where the Master gave an extensive talk on the sanctified reality and special station of the Prophets of God in response to a question that had been raised.

He stated:

> The progress of any thing occurs within its own station. When one considers the mineral, vegetable, animal, and human stations, one will see that each of these progresses within its own station. However much the vegetables advance – however exquisite the elegance, freshness, colour, flavour, and distinction they may come to acquire – they will remain vegetables nevertheless. They shall never become animals, neither will they ever develop the five senses. The same principle applies to the other aforementioned stations. Thus, the progress and elevation of every person occurs within his own station; in other words, he is confined to the world of humanity. As to that brilliant Reality which encompasses the world of being, however, this station is unique to the Manifestations of God . . .

On that day, too, a great number of people gradually attained the Master's presence. Every one of them expressed to Him their wishes, their hopes, and their supplications, and humbly implored His grace and bounty. This continued until nightfall – a juncture when, as most of these people were still present before the Master, He expounded upon those Writings of Bahá'u'lláh that were addressed to the Ottoman government. Among the remarks He made were these:

> Now, despite the fact that the Ottomans were victorious in their war with Crete,* other governments seized Crete from them nevertheless and gave it to Greece. How, then, can their protection now be imagined? Fifty years ago, at a time when such plans were not at all being designed or carried out, the Blessed Beauty proclaimed that they must leave Europe. This will inevitably come to pass. But praised be God, for we engage in war and strife with no one, and are weary of contention in all its forms. We are forbidden to interfere in such affairs, and are charged with establishing peace and tranquillity. We are to give up our own lives, not take the lives of others.

* A reference to the Greco-Turkish War of 1897.

Well into that night, the Master spoke of the friends of the East and sent this telegram to Muḥammad-Taqí Iṣfahání:[279] 'Prepare the means of comfort for Mírzá Abu'l-Faḍl; he is even as my own self.' The Master also revealed a Tablet for Mírzá Abu'l-Faḍl which discussed the treatment of his ailments and the prospect of regaining his good health – may my life be a sacrifice for his resting-place. Likewise, the Master spoke of Ḥájí Mírzá Ḥaydar-'Alí,[280] and said repeatedly: 'The value of these two blessed souls is not yet known.'[281]

Over the course of that day and night, the Master would make humorous remarks to Ḥájí Amín, observing that he had brought seven hundred pounds to present to Him,[282] notwithstanding that he had already obtained more than a thousand pounds from Him for this and that. One truly marvelled at the way the Master administered His finances – how He would spend them to care for the poor, support the weak, and nurse the sick, in addition to still other expenses made to promote the Cause of God and carry out His laws, while He Himself did not even have a winter coat. Indeed, He had no regard for His own necessities; His attendants had to beg Him for permission to have a new coat made for Him, as His present one was tattered and worn out.

Monday, 27 January 1913
[Paris]

In the morning, after some prayers were chanted, and a number of Bahá'ís had attained the Master's presence, He went to the drawing room to meet with the public gathering. He gave to them a talk on the stars and the heavens, in which He discussed celestial bodies and similar subjects. When that gathering was concluded, the seekers in attendance expressed their wish to meet with the Master. One by one and two by two, they attained His presence and were filled with a fresh longing and rapture upon hearing His discussions of spiritual subjects.

That afternoon, the Envoy Extraordinary and Minister Plenipotentiary of Persia [in Paris], 'Abdu'ṣ-Ṣamad Khán, as well as a number of respected persons from both the East and the West, attained the Master's presence. To them He spoke at length of chronicles from the days of Islam, and this included an episode involving the tyrant Ḥajjáj,[283] who issued a command for the tent of his minister to be burned to the ground to preserve order in his camp:

> When Ḥajjáj was named chief of the camp, following a period of disorder, he first issued an edict ordering that all its tents be pitched at once, and then brought down immediately thereafter. As the tents were being lowered, Ḥajjáj noticed that his minister's tent was still standing, and he ordered at once that it be burned to the ground. This matter served to alert those in the camp and establish order therein. Had it been permissible to make exceptions, and had the law accorded such distinction to the elite as to set them apart from the indigent, the affairs of the camp would have been thrown into disarray, completely obstructing the path to order.

The Master then related accounts involving the former ministers of Persia and other countries. Among these was a story featuring the nocturnal meetings of the ministers of Fatḥ-'Alí Sháh:

> Nighttime afforded these ministers peace of mind, as they would be undisturbed by the chattering and clamouring of the people, along with other such noise. As a result, they would come together at a certain place every night and hold gatherings characterized by intimate fellowship. The space at these gatherings would belong to the ministers alone; even their attendants were not permitted to be present. Bringing to bear the full measure of their concentration, and animated by a spirit of abundant joy and perfect concord, these ministers would consult on matters of great importance. They would dedicate an entire night or more to the discussion of each matter. When they would conclude their deliberations, such that they all regarded the subsequent course of action as having been decisively established, they would put their decision in writing. From that point onward, they would not give the matter

> a second thought, and nothing would hinder them from executing their decision. They dispensed with intermediaries, and refused to accept any vetoes. On every one of these occasions, the ministers were engaged in consultations and discussions from dusk till dawn. They would disperse at the approach of morning, having only just eaten their dinner, and on the following day they would carry out what they had put into writing. What exhilarating gatherings these must have been, and how fruitful they were – not at all like those gatherings which begin and end with mere words and trivial preoccupations . . .

The Master spoke extensively of such subjects; His audience was made alert and vigilant through His words, and they expressed their gratitude to Him. So enraptured were these souls in the presence of the Master that even to see the trappings of that gathering – the Eastern attire and etiquette, the samovar, the tea set, and other Persian furnishings – was enough to thoroughly gladden them and fill their hearts with consummate joy. These friends would remark:

> At this gathering, convened in Your blessed home, one receives the impression that he is in Your native Persia – not at a gathering in Paris held in a European residence. This gathering has a special sort of spirituality about it, and it grants a unique kind of delight.

In brief, illustrious souls always expressed their appreciation and gratitude to the Master at these gatherings replete with grace and bounty, and were totally enamoured of Him under all conditions.

Shortly after nightfall, a pleasant gathering was held in the home of Mr [Frank Edwin] and Mrs [Josephine Sanford] Scott.[284] As the Master related anecdotes from His travels in America, with specific regard to the four criteria of comprehension[285] and the holy power of the Manifestations of God, the hearts of His listeners burned even as temples of fire consecrated to the love of God.[286] They were filled with frenzied ecstasy as they beheld the beauty and perfection of their Beloved, the Epitome of grace and bounty. How astonishing, how bewildering it is that such gatherings as that one were convened in a city like Paris – gatherings that demonstrated the extraordinary power of the Cause of God.

In the evening, after that gathering was concluded, the Master repaid a visit to the aforementioned envoy of Persia.[287] When He returned to His residence, He said:

> Consider the places where God has taken us – how He has made us wanderers upon the plains and across the seas. Truly, this passage from Ḥáfiẓ is relevant to our situation:
>
> That fair gazelle go gently chide,
> O westward blowing wind that brings
> Whate'er a hopeful lover sings.*
> And the question kindly press:
> 'Why cast our heart to wilderness?'†

Tuesday, 28 January 1913
[Paris]

That morning, the Master said:[288]

> The people of this country are far removed from spirituality. They cling firmly to material things and have become immersed in this world.

He then went to the drawing room, where He took a seat and asked for some tea. When the samovar and tea were brought before Him, He remarked, 'There is no tea so delightful as the kind prepared with a samovar.' Before the Master had His tea, some travellers and other friends, all of Persian extraction, attained His presence. He then asked for a prayer to be chanted, and this caused the hearts of all those present to become wholly engrossed in the remembrance of God.

* Which is to say that the message of the lover is carried on the breeze.
† Translation by Joshua D.T. Hall.

Following this, the Master went outside to go for a stroll. When He returned, He began to speak at length of the vocations and avocations of the people of Paris, which were rooted in worldly affairs:[289]

> They are like the pitiable worms that dwell in the depths of the earth, unaware of the supernal realm.

The Master then exhorted His audience to turn to the Abhá Kingdom, that imperishable dominion where eternal life and perpetual prosperity can be found, observing that:

> This is the very purpose of creation. Otherwise, what fruit would this fleeting existence bear? Of what avail would this creation be, and what meaningful mark would it make?

After concluding His talk and extending His loving-kindness to those present, the Master and some of the Bahá'ís[290] went outside to go for a stroll once again. He said, 'I cannot sleep at night, and at times I develop a slight fever.' From the moment we departed London up until that day, the Master had been in excellent health. He said:

> As we travel from one city to another, owing to the change in climate and conditions, my health improves. When, however, we remain in a certain place for an extended period, I become ill once again and contract a fever.

That evening, a number of Ottoman Páshás and their respected wives listened to the Master's counsels. So profuse was their gratitude to Him, and so profound their delight, that on most of the following days they continued to attain His presence. Of these individuals, Aḥmad Páshá and [Ṣáliḥ] Munír Páshá, as well as their relatives, evinced the greatest degree of fascination with the Word of God and enchantment with the Master.

After dismissing the Ottomans from His presence, the Master directed His attention to a number of esteemed Persians and stated:

> Though the independence of Persia has been cast to the wind, yet does it continue to progress with every passing day. You must not despair, for each person has his turn for only a short while. Nothing remains the same forever. Come what may, the future of Persia will be exceedingly great.

Before retiring that evening, the Master took a warm bath in His residence.

Wednesday, 29 January 1913
[Paris]

That morning, the Master said:

> Because I took a bath last night, I was able to fall asleep with relative ease.

He then expressed His delight at how the gatherings convened in London had turned out, and rejoiced at the confirmations vouchsafed by the Abhá Kingdom and the fragrances of God that had been diffused in the realms of Britain, stating that:

> Although my health has been better these past few days in Paris than it was during my final days in London, I was happier there nonetheless.

Following this, Mírzá ʻAzízu'lláh Khán Varqá translated and conveyed to the Master the contents of a newspaper that concerned the Ottoman Empire and had been relayed to him by telegraph. The Master then stated:

> The doors are closed on every side, and the way to salvation is barred, unless one is aided with spiritual power and hidden confirmations. Were they aware of this, they would turn towards the horizon of the Cause. We do not say that they must necessarily become believers; indeed, were they to regard this Cause with even

> the slightest favour, this would suffice for hidden confirmations and divine assistance to be granted them . . .

When the crowd had assembled, and the daily gathering was convened, the Master gave a talk in which He discussed the preoccupations of the people of Paris with material matters, and encouraged the Bahá'ís to diffuse the fragrances of God.[291]

When all those present had attained the Master's presence and shaken His hand, one by one, and He had subsequently dismissed them, He went for a stroll. Afterwards, He remarked, 'The Persian travellers must be here every day for lunch and dinner.'

That afternoon, when the Master had taken a seat in the drawing room and asked for tea, Ras͟híd Pás͟há – who in the days of the Young Turk Revolution, and during the hardships brought on by the inspectors in 'Akká, had been the governor of Beirut and an inveterate opponent of the Cause – suddenly entered the premises and requested permission to attain His presence. Consequently, the Master summoned Ras͟híd Pás͟há to His room and showered him with loving-kindness. Up until he was dismissed, every moment that Ras͟híd Pás͟há spent in the Master's presence only added to the humility and reverence he showed Him, eventually going so far as to bow himself before Him. In His conversations with him, the Master related to Ras͟híd Pás͟há anecdotes from His travels in America, and spoke also of other subjects. As they watched this scene unfold, the Persian Bahá'ís in the vicinity celebrated the appearance of these heavenly confirmations, rejoiced at the subduing power of the Cause of God, and lauded the aid and assistance that had been bestowed by the Blessed Beauty, declaring:

> Praised be God that we were alive to witness such people as this humble and prostrate themselves in the presence of the Master, and behold how the Cause of God has prevailed over all things while the hopes of every other host have been frustrated!

That night, when the Master had returned to His residence after repaying a visit to Ras͟híd Pás͟há, He told a story illustrating the nefarious activities of the Covenant-breakers in the days of Ras͟hı́d Pás͟há's rule. He explained how these stirrers of sedition had worked to provoke an outcry from the former president of the American University of Beirut, to the point where he said:

> We have come to the East to educate the Muslims, but we see 'Abbás Effendí proselytizing to the people of our country (Americans), and attempting to demonstrate the truth of Islam.

As fate would have it, the Muslims objected when they eventually heard these remarks, stating that the president of the university had insulted Muslims. Consequently, to placate the Muslim community and set their minds at ease, Ras͟hı́d Pás͟há said to the president, 'You have come here to teach at a school, not to protest against others or make statements that will excite and agitate people.' After that remark, the president remained absolutely silent.

The Master then gave an account of the events involved in a conflict that had broken out between the Muslims and Christians, and described the capability and insight of Ras͟hı́d Pás͟há. He recounted, moreover, an episode from the past in which Ras͟hı́d Pás͟há had striven rapaciously to obtain money from the Master:[292]

> Ras͟hı́d Pás͟há came to Haifa, but I paid no attention to him. He even sent his son to 'Akká. He executed one strategy after another, but it availed him nothing. Eventually, when he came to Haifa, he made an arrangement with the *mutaṣarrif* of 'Akká for me to meet with him there, despite the fact that I had been confined by official decree to the limits of 'Akká's city walls. Ras͟hı́d Pás͟há made hints and allusions, but he saw that these were entirely disregarded, and realized that he would not achieve his end through bribes and gifts.
>
> It so happened that, on the day we went to Haifa, the *mutaṣarrif* lost a valuable ring on the way. He informed me of this as we were returning to 'Akká, and I said to him, 'Do not worry at all; it will be found.' When we entered 'Akká, I alighted by a goldsmith's shop. I told him that a ring would be brought to him, and that he should bring it to me. I then re-entered the carriage and went home

with the *mutaṣarrif*. On the following morning, the goldsmith brought the very ring. I took it and handed it over to the *mutaṣarrif*, who was astonished. He went to Ras͟híd Pás͟há and said:

> 'Abbás Effendí is versed in the Imám 'Alí's art of divination! My ring had been lost, and He found it so easily. You, therefore, should let Him alone altogether, for He is aware – and has even stated as much – that if all the hosts of the world were to unite and attempt to free Him from His imprisonment before the appointed time, it would be impossible for them to do so, and that if the rulers of the earth should join forces and work to prevent His liberation when the moment arrives, they would be powerless to accomplish their goal.

Inasmuch as Ras͟híd Pás͟há placed his confidence in this *mutaṣarrif*, he relented for a time in his hostility and restrained his greed. And now, this man – mighty and manly as he is – visits us with such remarkable deference.

Thursday, 30 January 1913
[Paris]

At that morning's gathering,[293] the Master gave a talk on the ways in which the soul, spirit, and mind all differ from one another in response to a question posed by one of the members of His audience.[294] His words filled the hearts of His listeners with exceeding gladness, and stirred their very souls with abundant joy.

In the afternoon, as the Master was writing Tablets while seated in the drawing room with the tea set laid out before Him, a number of people – friends and others alike – attained His presence. One of these individuals was the Indian professor 'Ináyatu'lláh K͟hán, who styled himself an instructor of music. Accordingly, the Master's remarks to him dealt with music, and eventually concluded with a discussion of the divine melody, the call of the Kingdom of God, and the pervading influence of the teachings of Bahá'u'lláh.

When the Master had dismissed those people from His presence, Mírzá Mihdí Khán[295] – an associate of Ḥájí Amín's who had come from Persia to see the Master, and had just arrived that very day – attained His presence. The Master inquired after the Bahá'ís of the Holy Land, as well as those residing in Egypt, the Caucasus, Rasht, and Qazvin. Mírzá Mihdí Khán delivered to the Master numerous letters addressed to Him from the Bahá'ís of the East, which He perused. Among these was a letter from Mírzá Músá Khán [Ḥakím-Báshí, known as] Ḥakím-i-Iláhí; as the Master read it, He expressed sentiments replete with the utmost loving-kindness, and His face was wreathed in conspicuous joy. Several times, each with consummate tenderness and delight, He asked after Mírzá Abu'l-Faḍl and Ḥájí Mírzá Ḥaydar-'Alí.[296]

Following this, a number of Easterners, as well as some individuals in the employ of the Persian legation,[297] attained the Master's presence. Among the remarks which He addressed to them were these:

> At a time when the Europeans did not yet enjoy this ascendancy and influence, I had written to 'Abdu'l-Ḥamíd,* indicating to him what would come to pass. He, for his part, expressed his gratitude, but then forgot my admonitions. At the outset of that revolution in Persia known as the Constitutional Revolution, I wrote again and again that until such time as that government and its people become commingled, even as milk and honey, their success and prosperity will remain entirely unattainable. Persia shall fall into ruin, and the governments of its neighbouring realms will ultimately meddle in its affairs . . .

Friday, 31 January 1913
[Paris]

That morning, Mírzá 'Azízu'lláh Khán Varqá, who had telegraphically been apprised of current events that had been reported in the newspapers, presented the Master with a translation

---

* Sulṭán 'Abdu'l-Ḥamíd II.

of this news into Persian. Shortly thereafter, the Master stated:

> When the Prime Minister of Persia went to Qum, and thence conducted certain divines to Tehran while lavishing them with reverence, Mullá 'Alí-Akbar wrote the following upon their arrival at that city:
>
>> Even when the government had not yet aligned themselves with the divines, they perpetrated dire calamities. What will they do now that they treat the divines with such honour and respect?
>
> In response to him, I wrote:
>
>> Concern not yourself with the glory and majesty which those divines now enjoy; this glory will soon be turned into the most abject abasement. 'Vileness and poverty were stamped upon them, and they returned with wrath from God.'* These divines will uproot their foundations by their own hand, even as it has been said: 'They demolish their homes with their own hands.'† These divines have seen the stable, but not the end which awaits them.‡

On numerous occasions in those days, the Master would make the following remarks about the Easterners:

> How impressive the dominions that have passed through their hands! How conspicuous the glory they once could boast, and how wretched the abasement which now defines them! How precious the bounty, how priceless the gift from which they have withheld their gaze, and how miserable the misfortunes which

* Qur'án 2:61.

† Qur'án 59:2.

‡ An original aphorism by 'Abdu'l-Bahá that involves a play on words, *á<u>kh</u>ur* being the original for 'the stable' and *á<u>kh</u>ir* for 'the end which awaits them'. This same letter by 'Abdu'l-Bahá to Mullá 'Alí-Akbar is also mentioned in Thompson, *The Diary of Juliet Thompson*, pp. 102–03.

> now bedevil them by reason of what their hands have wrought on the Day of Recompense!

After reciting some prayers, the Master went for a brief stroll outside. Áqá Mírzá 'Alí-Akbar Rafsanjání and Áqá Mírzá Faraju'lláh Ká<u>sh</u>ání had come from Persia expressly to attain the Master's presence, and had arrived that very day. When the Master returned to His residence, He found the two of them there, and they promptly threw themselves at His feet. They cried tears of ecstasy and bellowed from the depths of their hearts, and the Master showered them with His grace and bounty.

The talk which the Master later gave at the public gathering, in response to a question posed to Him by a member of His audience, dealt with the immateriality and immortality of the soul.[298] He spoke, moreover, of the duty incumbent upon every Bahá'í to love and consort with the followers of all religions, and to be the well-wishers of all humanity – including one's enemies.[299]

In the afternoon, a number of Russian women attained the Master's presence,[300] and were overjoyed as they listened to Him discuss matters pertaining to the Cause. Some students then met with the Master, and to them He spoke extensively of agriculture, industry, and commerce, observing that Persia was in need of iron-smelting plants, since agriculture and industry alike depend on foundries. At that juncture, the Master was shown a newspaper from the Egyptian press, in which the transcript of a talk He had given at a synagogue had been printed. Upon seeing this, the Master said:

> Take note of how, in the churches and synagogues, we have established the truth of Islam, and consider the calumnies which, in spite of this, the Muslims have hurled at us, and the things they have said about us – how the Bahá'ís are the enemies of the people and of the state, and sundry other condemnations of this sort. Yet, if we were truly a party to such corruption, then what better pretext, what more propitious opportunity would we have had to advance it than when giving those talks? Despite our endeavours

> to vindicate their faith, these Muslims remain heedless; they are content to pursue their selfish interests, and are immersed in the depths of their pride.

After two Persian men had spent more than an hour in the Master's presence, and had expressed their effusive praise and gratitude for having heard His blessed utterances and tender counsels, He went to the drawing room, where before a large crowd He hailed the glad-tidings of God's imperishable grace and everlasting bounties. The talk the Master gave at that gathering that afternoon concerned the prophecies mentioned in the divine Scriptures, as well as the advent of this Most Great and Most Glorious Dispensation, and He specially noted that the Sun of Truth has always risen above the horizon of the East. Though here they attained the Master's presence in a public setting, most of those present expressed their wish to have a private audience with Him. With the aid of an interpreter, numerous questions were submitted to the Master, and those inquiring souls had the bounty and privilege of hearing His answers to them.

That evening, another gathering was convened at the home of Mr and Mrs Dreyfus-Barney.[301] This was a weekly gathering, in which believers and seekers alike would come together on a certain evening,[302] and the crowd would eventually swell to a great size. At that particular gathering, marked by the bliss of reunion with their Master, every heart was thoroughly illumined with the lights of His grace and bounty. At the outset of the gathering, the Master went to another room to rest for a while. In the meantime, Mr Dreyfus spoke of various subjects pertaining to the Cause, and also recited a number of Tablets that had been translated into French. Following this, with the Master's permission, Áqá Mírzá 'Alí-Akbar Rafsanjání delivered a message that was laden with sentiments of longing and ecstasy felt by the Bahá'ís of the East for their fellow Bahá'ís in the West. He spoke, moreover, of the spiritual ties, the celestial love, and the heartfelt yearnings which bind the friends to one another.

Shortly thereafter, the Master joined this assemblage of souls who had so eagerly been awaiting Him, and delivered to them an impressive address in which He exhorted them to eliminate all forms of prejudice and dispel the darkness of estrangement, depicted the brilliance of the light of love and unity, described the goodwill which the Bahá'ís must show all peoples and creeds, articulated the divine teachings, and offered heavenly counsels. So aglow with the fire of the love of God had this crowd of seekers and lovers been set as a result of this talk, and so captivated had they become by His sublime fragrances, that they raised a commotion greater than any other that had theretofore been made. Indeed, they were most reluctant to depart from this gathering. The Master asked for a prayer to be chanted, and Mírzá 'Alí-Akbar intoned some verses of the Blessed Beauty accordingly. That blessed gathering, by now suffused with an air of utmost rapture and ecstasy, was then brought to a close.

Saturday, 1 February 1913
[Paris]

That morning, some Eastern Bahá'ís attained the Master's presence. The sweetness of the prayers that were chanted moved them to cry tears of ecstasy, and they unloosed their tongues in fervent praise as they witnessed the Master's loving-kindness. Up until the time when that day's gathering was scheduled to commence, a number of Western Bahá'ís and seekers received their share of the Master's generous grace.

When the Master arrived at the gathering, He gave an extensive talk in which He discussed the veils that have always hindered humanity at the advent of every Manifestation, and also explained the meanings of various divine verses, thereby unravelling the mysteries enshrined in their words. It was a talk that rent asunder the barriers of vain imaginings and blind imitations, and removed from the beauty of Truth the veil that had once concealed it.

At noon, the Master went to the home of Mr and Mrs Dreyfus-Barney for lunch.[303] Among those invited to this event were Ḥájí Amín; Áqá Mírzá 'Alí-Akbar Rafsanjání; Mirza Ahmad Sohrab; Áqá Mírzá Mihdí, Ḥájí Amín's associate;[304] and this lowly servant. The esteemed guests, moreover – all of whom were filled with joy at that gathering, so profoundly marked by the Master's benevolence – included the envoy of Persia, the [first] secretary of the Persian legation, and the Intiẓámu's-Salṭanih. When the Master had entered the room, and after He had related some anecdotes and extended His tender kindness to each and every one of those present, He took a seat at the table. He then began to give an account of the Niẓámu'd-Dawlih, illustrating the pervasive authority he enjoyed up until the events which occurred on the day of his death, when in the end he cried out, 'My riches avail me nothing, and my sovereignty hath perished!'[305]

After lunch, the Master sat awhile in the drawing room, where He counselled His listeners to be alert and heedful.

In the afternoon, once some prayers and Tablets had been recited, a group of respected Persians – along with a number of Parisians, including one of their religious leaders[306] – attained the Master's presence. He spoke at length to disabuse this clergyman of his vain imaginings, and grew very weary as a result. Consequently, when that gathering had ended, the Master departed and walked outside for an hour. As He was returning to His residence, He asked Mírzá 'Alí-Akbar how the Bahá'ís of Persia were faring. In response, he conveyed to the Master the rapturous cries and prayerful humility of those lovers from the East, among which were supplications from the poet Na'ím Sidihí[307] and Dr Yúnis Khán Afrúkhtih.[308] To these the Master responded with the utmost tenderness and kindness:

> Though I have been in the West throughout this span of time, yet my face has ever been turned towards the Bahá'ís of the East, and I have entreated the Abhá Kingdom unceasingly to confirm them. However, the myriad thoughts which assail me constantly, and the numerous preoccupations which demand my attention, have left me with no opportunity to write to them. My hopes for the Bahá'ís of the East have always been high, for they constitute the very essence of this Faith, and it is through them that the Cause of God has taken firm root in Persia. How, then, could I possibly forget them for so much as a single moment?

The Master then made repeated mention of Áqá Riḍá Muhájir Shírází and his family, stating, 'I wish to go and make pilgrimage to him myself, and pray before that pure tomb of his.'

On that day, the Master sent Mirza Ahmad Sohrab to Nice to meet with a number of respected Eastern gentlemen.[309] As these illustrious men had witnessed the evidences of the pervading influence which the Cause of God had exerted in the West – and taken note of how widely renowned the perfection, the glory, and the beauty of the Master had become – they would readily express their humility and deference to the Cause, whether in the presence of the Master Himself or that of one of His deputies, and derive abundant pride and joy therefrom.

Sunday, 2 February 1913
[Paris]

More believers and seekers had gathered that morning than on any other. The talk the Master gave them dealt with the subject of existence and preexistence, and the effect it had on the hearts of his listeners once He had concluded was so profound that they – at first wishing to have a private audience with Him, where they might pose their questions to Him – now remarked, 'This blessed talk was the answer to all our questions.' In a spirit of perfect joy, they expressed sentiments of servitude and humility in His presence.

In the afternoon, the Master travelled by car to the outskirts of Paris to tend to some poor children.[310] After walking among these children, extending His loving-kindness to them, and giving each of them a sum of money, He prepared to depart, at which point these children – as well as all the other people who were present – expressed their fervent gratitude and praise to Him with the utmost love and rapture. Whether young or old, they all showed Him reverence and extolled His luminous being.

From there, the Master went to the home of that handmaid of God, Miss [Edith] Sanderson, that night.[311] The evening began with a gathering of people at her table – a gathering charged with frenzied ecstasy. As the Master entered, one of those present asked Him, 'Were you happier in America, or are you happier here?' The Master replied:

> I am happy wherever I go; this happiness is never separated from me. What brings me happiness, moreover, is the exaltation of the Word of God. Wherever people are more engaged in diffusing the fragrances of God, I will certainly be more gladdened thereby – and the degree of engagement in this pursuit was greater in America.

Mr [Alfred] Bernard and his wife [Claire Bernard] then expressed to the Master their regrets that they were possessed of little capacity. In response, the Master said:

> If the love of Bahá'u'lláh is present in a heart, it will be endowed with capacity. Divine love is like a spirit; when a spirit is present in a body, that body is endowed with the capacity to do anything. We were passing by a church today that was built according to the principles of Greek architecture when my companions observed that this church was dedicated to Mary Magdalene. When one considers her outwardly, what capacity did Mary Magdalene have? She was a woman who hailed from a village. There have been many women greater than she was – women descended from the kings of the earth, or numbered with the most renowned of its denizens. Yet, since the love of Christ was present in Mary Magdalene's heart, that love endowed her with such capacity that a church in France such as this one was built in her name. Thus, anyone who discovers their relationship with God will be endowed with every conceivable capacity. Then do not say 'we are bereft of capacity'; when the love of Bahá'u'lláh is present in your hearts, you will possess every conceivable capacity and every measure of worthiness.

The Master then remarked on the vocations and other restrictive preoccupations of the Parisians:

There is a poem in Persian which states:

'Tis truly for the sake of living
And praising God that one should eat.
'Tis thy belief life *is* for eating,
As if such made thy life complete.*

The denizens of Paris, as well as the majority of Europeans, believe that people have been created to work, not that work has been created for people.

Such were the remarks which the Master made at the dinner table, and those Bahá'ís from Paris and Persia who were present derived the utmost ecstasy and delight from being in His presence.

Sometime thereafter, the Master left the table to join the public gathering that had already assembled in a large drawing room of the residence, and gave a talk that began in this way:

He is God

In one of His prayers, the Blessed Beauty states: 'O God! Every eye is asleep, and all are reposing on the bed of ease – but I sleep upon the dust, and await Thy limitless favours.' Now, too, the nights of the Carnival are upon us;[312] all are busy walking about and spectating in the theatres, and are occupied in some way. One is a singer, another a dancer; one has busied himself with drinking alcohol, while another boasts the fame of his name and the highness of his rank. They all have tainted themselves with these pursuits; immersed are they in the world of nature, and oblivious of God and the realms above. That place which is itself the remembrance of God – the place where every eye is awake and every heart enraptured by the divine breezes – is right here. All gatherings are earthly, but, God be praised, this is a heavenly assemblage. All are confined to the world of nature, but, thank God, you have set your faces towards the Abhá Kingdom . . .

* From the *Gulistán* of Sa'dí; translation by Joshua D.T. Hall.

Hippolyte Dreyfus-Barney

Laura Dreyfus-Barney

Apartment at 30 rue Saint-Didier, Paris

Paris, the Bois de Boulogne, where 'Abdu'l-Bahá would take the air

'Abdu'l-Bahá at the Eiffel Tower, 8 February 1913, accompanied by believers and friends. Members of his retinue include Valíyu'lláh Khán Varqá (far left), Siyyid Asadu'lláh Qumí (second from left), Maḥmúd Zarqání (sixth from right), Ahmad Sohrab (third from right) and Hájí Abu'l-Ḥasan Ardakání (Ḥájí Amín) (second from right)

'Alí-Akbar Rafsanjání

'Alí-Akbar Na<u>kh</u>javání

Credit: Creative Commons/Momtaz

'Abdu'ṣ-Ṣamad <u>Kh</u>án Mumtáz (the Mumtázu's-Salṭanih), who visited 'Abdu'l-Bahá several times in Paris

Áqa Mírzá Jálal, Hippolyte Dreyfus-Barney, and Rúḥá <u>Kh</u>ánum in Paris

© USBNA

Inayat Khan, Indian Sufi leader and musician who visited 'Abdu'l-Bahá in Paris and sang for him

Courtesy Necati Alkan

Ra<u>sh</u>íd Pá<u>sh</u>á, former Governor of Beirut during the Young Turk Revolution. He and 'Abdu'l-Bahá visited each other many times in Paris

Ṣáliḥ Munír Pá<u>sh</u>á, Ottoman dignitary. He and 'Abdu'l-Bahá visited each other many times in Paris

Ḥájí Mírzá Ḥaydar-'Alí and Mírzá Abu'l-Faḍl. 'Abdu'l-Bahá spoke often of them, and said: 'The value of these two blessed souls is not yet known'

Áqá Aḥmad Siyyid Báqiroff, who travelled from Persia to be with 'Abdu'l-Bahá in Paris

Mírzá Músá Khán Ḥakím-Báshí

Áqá Khusraw, 'Abdu'l-Bahá's Burmese servant who accompanied Him on His journeys to the West and was with Him in Paris, spending 'most of his time in the kitchen'

Siyyid Naṣru'lláh Báqiroff

Mírzá Áqa Khán, Qá'im-Maqámí

Mírzá Valíyu'lláh Khán Varqá (left) and Mírzá 'Azízu'lláh Khán Varqá, who travelled from Persia to be with 'Abdu'l-Bahá in Paris

Charles Blech,
of the Paris Theosophical Society

Carlo Bourlet,
French Esperantist and mathematician

Edwin Scott,
American Bahá'í painter in Paris

Mirra Alfassa Richard, French Hindu leader, with her husband Paul Richard, so active in the Paris Bahá'í community that many believed her to be a Bahá'í

Edith Sanderson

Stanwood Cobb,
American Bahá'í who visited
'Abdu'l-Bahá in Paris

Henri Moser

Photograph taken of 'Abdu'l-Bahá with his entourage by Elize Cabot on 15 August 1912 on the lawn of the Partons' home. Mírzá 'Alí-Akbar Na<u>kh</u>javání (third from left) and Siyyid Asadu'lláh Qumí (far right)

Monday, 3 February 1913
[Paris]

In the morning, once a number of Persian believers and attendants had visited the Master – and after some prayers had been chanted – a French youth, firm in his religious beliefs, attained the Master's presence. The Master spoke to him of the veils which hindered the Jews during the days of Christ, and He described their failure to apprehend the true meaning of the signs mentioned in the Torah. He concluded that this day is no different, observing that if we should fail to understand correctly the meaning of the words of the Gospel, we would remain veiled like the Jews on the day of the promised advent. As this was an intelligent youth, the Master's words made him alert and heedful. From that point forward, he would be present at most of those gatherings of blissful reunion, and rendered totally captivated by the Master's utterances.

At that day's public gathering, before the Master Himself had arrived and spoken to the audience, Mrs Richard[313] gave a talk at His request on subjects pertaining to the Cause of God. It was a most effective address that roused her listeners to great vigilance. Consequently, the Master saw fit to repeatedly encourage this woman, along with a number of Bahá'ís who were competent to speak at public gatherings, to arise and give talks at such events and thereby spread the fragrances of God. When He arrived at that gathering, the Master gave a talk on the mental faculty and rational faculty of humankind, in which He averred that these were the two greatest gifts from God. He stated, moreover, that if a person opens his mouth to speak when his thoughts and aims are aligned with the divine teachings, and his face is turned towards Bahá'u'lláh, spiritual intimations and heavenly inspirations will encompass him.

In the afternoon, the Master told a story about the poor of Paris to a group of people. He said:

> We went to visit the children of some poor souls yesterday and saw their pitiful living conditions. As we were returning, I noticed that people were coming out of certain buildings in groups. I asked my

companions, 'Where had these people gone?' They replied, 'To the theatre.' These people have elaborate buildings on every street corner where they can enjoy themselves and spectate for their amusement, yet they have left the poor in their midst to languish in hardship and distress.

That night, the Master went to the public gathering held at the home of Mr and Mrs Scott. It was similar to the one convened at the residence of Mr and Mrs Dreyfus-Barney, in that it was a weekly gathering[314] attended by the friends. Mr and Mrs Scott were devoted believers, and the Master regularly showed them His loving-kindness. A large crowd – one that consisted of many seekers – had gathered on that occasion, and to them the Master delivered an extensive address on the history and teachings of this new and wondrous Dispensation. To conclude the gathering, Mírzá 'Alí-Akbar Rafsanjání chanted a prayer at the Master's request, and this moved everyone in attendance to fervent joy and ecstasy.

It was the Master's custom on most days to pay visits to various dignitaries and princes, whether they were sick in the hospitals or staying at their own residences. On that day, however, He did not have the opportunity to do this, so He sent some of His attendants to go in His stead and inquire after these individuals, among whom were certain grandees and princes who were especially dear to the Master.[315]

Afterwards, a number of people from Rasht and Tabriz,[316] along with some other illustrious souls, attained the Master's presence. I will provide a more detailed account of this episode in the future.[317]

Tuesday, 4 February 1913
[Paris]

The public gathering that morning was held with consummate grandeur in the Master's residence. Carried away by transports of spiritual ecstasy, His audience cried out in jubilation, and thoroughly afire with the love of God, they bubbled over with frenzied clamour. For such gatherings of remembrance and sanctification as that one to have been convened in Paris is surely the greatest testimony to the pervading influence of the Word of God.

The talk the Master gave that day dealt with universal peace, the oneness of humanity, the promotion of harmony and fellowship, and the uprooting of prejudice and tyranny. He articulated, moreover, the teachings of the Ancient Beauty, and discussed the establishment of unity among the peoples of the world.

When that gathering was concluded, the Master asked a number of Easterners to stay for lunch. At the table, He showed them all such loving-kindness, and spoke to them with such good cheer and humour, that 'each and every one of those servants well-nigh regarded Him their Lord'.[318]

Among the friends who were in His presence day and night were Ríyáḍ Salím Effendí and Dr [Muḥammad] Ṣáliḥ Effendí.

In the afternoon, after a number of other people had attained His presence, the Master went outside to go for a stroll. From there, He went to the home of Miss Sanderson, to whom He gave this instruction:

> Praise and encourage, on my behalf, some of those seekers who can speak and communicate well. Say to them, 'Turn towards the Abhá Kingdom, and diffuse the fragrances of God at various gatherings.'

Eventually, the Master departed Miss Sanderson's residence and walked to the Bois de Boulogne. Among the remarks which He made along the way were these:

> Every power and ability that is utilized for the Cause of God shall produce perpetually enduring effects and yield eternally abiding results; otherwise, it is a thing unworthy of mention.

He also stated:

> As to those souls endowed with the power of oratory – should this power of theirs be coupled with a spirit of sanctification and rapture, tremendous influence will be manifested from them, and they shall succeed in rendering distinguished services at the threshold of God.

Wednesday, 5 February 1913
[Paris]

The talk the Master gave at the public gathering that morning dealt with the degree to which the spirit of every living thing flows through it in accordance with its potential. The crowd at that gathering consisted of all kinds of people – English and French, American and Persian. They were all captivated by the Master's utterances, and astounded at the penetrating influence of the Covenant of God – namely, how it has made various peoples and contending groups to gather together, with the utmost ecstasy and delight, beneath the shade of a single Word.

In the afternoon, Dr Muḥammad Khán accompanied the Master as He went to repay a visit to certain distinguished Easterners and inquire after their health. As they were returning from that visit, notwithstanding the Master's great fatigue, He nonetheless conversed with a crowd of respected individuals who had attained His presence, telling stories, giving historical accounts, and making humorous remarks. To speak with the Master in this way filled these people with delight, and plunged their hearts into oceans of joy and ecstasy. Words can hardly illustrate the nature of that occasion, and should I attempt to recount it to one who did not witness for themselves the remarkable quality which attended it, they would scarcely comprehend it – for that most sweet voice of His which adorned every utterance He imparted on so many subjects, the brightness of His beautiful eyes as they scanned His audience, the graceful gestures of His hands, the soul-stirring wonder of His smile, the due consideration He gave to the exigencies of the time and place in which He was speaking, the keen attention He paid to the temperament and understanding of His listeners, the solutions He presented to resolve the problems that have plagued nations and religions, the captivating effect which His words had on the hearts of His hearers, and the reverence and deference shown to Him at that juncture were such as to defy all description or comparison.

Thursday, 6 February 1913
[Paris]

The Persian friends and attendants had the bounty and privilege of listening to chanted prayers and being in the Master's presence at a certain gathering that morning. Afterwards, the attendees of this gathering had some tea, and the Master showed special loving-kindness to each and every one of them. With every passing day, these tender kindnesses from the Master infused these souls with new life, and filled them with immeasurable gladness.

Shortly thereafter, several believers and seekers began to attain and depart the Master's presence. They came and went, one by one and two by two, and expressed their desire to have a private audience with Him. Accordingly, the Master would summon these people to His room, where an interpreter was also present. As they listened to the Master's replies to the numerous questions they posed to Him, they were filled with spiritual joy and heartfelt delight.

Eventually, the Master went to speak to the public gathering,[319] to which He delivered an address that dealt with the renewal of all created things, the progress of various sciences and industries, and the gradual changing of humanity's views. He remarked that this is a new era with unprecedented exigencies, observing that the laws of a former age will not suffice this momentous century, and concluded that the spiritual laws – which is to say secondary religious laws – must be renewed, and divine truths revitalized.

When the Master finished His talk, He went to His room, and a number of seekers expressed their ardent wish to once again have a private audience with Him. He received each and every one of these souls, and showed them His loving-kindness. They, in turn, expressed to Him their heartfelt gratitude and delight at having been blessed with such favour. It took some time for the Master to dismiss them all from His presence.

Following this, the Master summoned Mr Dreyfus, who then took the Master by car to see the Palace of Versailles. There they remained until shortly after nightfall, at which time they returned to Paris, where an Indian professor named 'Ináyatu'lláh Khán attained the Master's presence. 'Ináyatu'lláh Khán had previously had this honour on several occasions, and expressed his desire to spend an evening in the Master's presence to share some information about music with Him.[320] For one hour, 'Ináyatu'lláh Khán sang and played instruments,[321] and the Master then began to give biographical accounts of various celebrities and masters of music.[322] Additionally, He told stories about Fárábí and recited some of the poetry of Rúdakí. Such was the way in which this meeting proceeded, ultimately culminating in that celestially melodious voice of the Master which unfailingly granted abundant gladness and abiding bliss.

Friday, 7 February 1913
[Paris]

The Master's talk that morning[323] made reference to professor 'Ináyatu'lláh Khán, and dealt with such subjects as the melody of the Concourse on High, hearkening to the call of God, and the outpourings of grace from the Sun of Eternity.[324] These, He concluded, are the means to divine happiness and the true goals of human life.

That afternoon, a number of Persian grandees and dignitaries attained the Master's presence. After one of them, Áqá Mírzá Ḥusayn 'Árif, entered the room and expressed his reverence for the Master, he arose and began to recite, with the utmost courtesy and deference, a number of poems he had composed in His praise.[325] These compositions, however, were not met with the Master's approval. He stated:

> My one aim is to serve at the divine threshold – and that alone. Despite this, some have gathered poems such as these from the friends and even sent them to the editor of the *Star of the West* in Chicago with a view to having them printed in that publication.

Once Áqá Mírzá Ḥusayn 'Árif had repeatedly recited some verses from his poetry, expressing his personal beliefs in so doing, the Master said: 'You must rhyme your verses with the attributive article, not the indefinite.' Those verses which this gentleman recited in spite of the Master's objections were these:

> Benighted do we languish in the darkness
> And there's no light more glorious than Thee
> In truth I swear upon Bahá Himself
> That no better Bahá'í is there than Thee
>
> Though all see themselves as slaves to the Lord
> This slave is sure no God can surpass Thee
> Could Moses see Thy Face upon the Mount
> 'All hail this best encounter!' would say He
>
> If Asia should be sick and sore afflicted
> And Europe its fatal calamity
> There's no physician better for this illness
> Indeed no better remedy than Thee

A great many individuals, not affiliated with the Faith and belonging to every land imaginable, composed such poems of praise and adoration, and presented them before the Master. The majority of these He refused to accept, and He forbade them from being disseminated and published. For instance, when one of the eloquent orators of Egypt attained the Master's presence in Alexandria, he recited an ode that he had composed in His honour, and this roused the believers in attendance to great ecstasy. When, however, this gentleman requested the Master's permission to have this ode published, the Master refused to grant it, stating, 'This person has not composed these poems with purity of motive.' Indeed, even the sincere praises that believers and others alike would express were, for the most part, not compatible with the Master's temperament and contrary to His complete and total servitude at the divine Threshold, and He would reject them accordingly.

In brief, that gathering clearly demonstrated the majesty of the Master. All those in attendance, irrespective of their class or rank, expressed their gratitude to Him and sang His praises.

Among the remarks which the Master made about Persia were these:

> A person of action and an active force are needed, and in this day the confirmations and assistance of God are likewise essential. Otherwise, talk is plentiful, and it is easy to make commotions and create disturbances.

In the afternoon, someone[326] broached the subject of law. The Master stated:[327]

> The concept of law is ancient. Just as God and His creation have always co-existed, so too have humankind and law. At most, the establishment and execution of laws have ever been confined to the limitations of a given era. Even industries are ancient. Ancient traces of the city of Nineveh, whose existence the historians of Europe once denied, were eventually discovered in the environs of Mosul – and these vestiges attested to the industries that had been developed and the advancements made in that age.

The Master concluded His remarks by discussing some caveats of law, observing that:

> Although people have no right to exact vengeance, reward and punishment must be carried out, for these are the two pillars upon which the canopy of world order rests.

At that juncture, a car which Mr Dreyfus had sent to the Master to use for excursions arrived.[328] When His attendants informed Him of this, the Master said, 'It is your turn to go on an excursion today; I have no time for that now.' The attendants complied, and their outing proved so grand as to be almost kingly. After beholding and passing by some exquisite scenery, they returned to the Master and expressed their exceeding reverence for Him.

That night, the Master gave a talk at Mr Dreyfus's home that dealt with spiritual life; the advent of Bahá'u'lláh, as well as the incalculable calamities He endured; and the pervading influence of the Cause of God, observing that even its enemies have borne witness to its greatness in this supremely glorious Dispensation.

Saturday, 8 February 1913
[Paris]

At the gathering that morning, the Master gave a talk on the Intermediary between the Creator and His creation – the Dawning-place of the Cause of God in every age – and how one can come to recognize Him.

When that gathering was concluded, the Master spent some time writing Tablets in response to important letters that believers had sent Him. As He was doing this, a great many people attained His presence once again. The Master showered them with the outpourings of His imperishable grace, and this filled them with fresh joy and bliss. He would say repeatedly:

> The letters from the believers of the East have all gone unanswered; I have had no opportunity whatsoever to respond to them. In the past, I would sometimes awaken at night to write something, but now I cannot even do that.

Among the people who attained the Master's presence with the utmost rapture and irrepressible ecstasy, and gazed spellbound on His radiant face, were a number of believers from Germany. These friends had brought with them some letters from the Bahá'ís of

Stuttgart, in which they invited the Master to visit that area, and described how eagerly they anticipated such a prospect. The Master commended those denizens of Stuttgart and expressed His loving-kindness for them – in particular Mr [Wilhelm] Herrigel, one of the eloquent Bahá'ís of Germany, and Miss [Alma] Knobloch, the first American teacher of the Faith who along with Dr [Edwin] Fisher went, at the Master's instruction, to Stuttgart to spread the divine fragrances.

The Persian believers wished to take a photograph with the Master that day, and it was taken as He was standing underneath the Eiffel Tower alongside a number of believers and servants of the sacred threshold.[329] Both before the picture was taken and afterwards, those devoted souls brimmed with delight as they relished the elegant majesty and graceful grandeur of the Master's gait.

Sunday, 9 February 1913
[Paris]

As the Master was drinking His tea and observing the scenery before Him that morning, He said:[330]

> Just as the birds and other beasts think, from the break of day, only of seeds and prey, so too is it with these people, who think constantly of the means by which to secure their livelihood. How preoccupied they are! What hopes they cherish, and what felicities they enjoy – especially in these countries, which are very much developed. It is truly like a beehive. All are immersed in material matters. Indeed, the only difference between these people and the inhabitants of Central Africa is that the former are city animals, while the latter are wild animals. They are all bereft of the breathings of the Holy Spirit – all deprived and oblivious of eternal life.

When the daily gathering was convened, the Master gave a talk in which He established proofs for the existence of God, that Necessary Being, and discussed accidental composition, necessary composition, and purposeful composition.[331] As they listened to the Master's talk, many of the attendees evinced signs of satisfaction and reassurance. They were roused to great ecstasy and delight, and expressed their gratitude for the tender kindnesses which the Master had shown them.

That day, some Persians who were awaiting the Master's beneficent aid were summoned to His room, and He gave each of them a sum of money.

Among the people of Europe who had the honour of attaining the Master's presence that afternoon were the wife [Madeleine Sacy] and [four] daughters [Mercedes, Giselle, Edmée, and Gabrielle] of the late Gabriel Sacy.[332] The Master began His remarks to them by describing how the body of Gabriel Sacy was moved, and relating an anecdote concerning the repair of his grave in the days when the Master was living in Egypt. He then expressed His loving-kindness, stating:

> The late Gabriel was a pure believer in the Cause of God, and he composed a treatise to logically prove its truth.* I hope that you all will become the luxuriant branches and verdant leaves of that goodly tree, and come to bear the choicest of fruits.
>
> A public banquet was held one night in 'Akká, where many believers from every land imaginable were in attendance and an extensive spread had been prepared. A great many of the friends, consisting of various kinds of people – hailing from Isfahan, Shiraz, Tabriz, Paris, London, America, Egypt, Syria, and India – were all gathered at the table in a spirit of the utmost joy, radiance, and oneness. In truth, the light of love shone brilliantly from their faces. A number of the believers had leapt into service on that occasion – among them the late Gabriel Sacy, who tended to the friends with complete devotion, sincerity, and purity. I will never forget that spirit of service and humility. It is, then, a matter of God's inscrutable wisdom that Gabriel has left us while Khayru'lláh† (his brother) has remained.

* Likely a reference to *Du Règne de Dieu et de l'Agneau, connu sous le nom de Babysme* (1902), a short pamphlet arguing that the Bahá'í Faith has fulfilled various Biblical prophecies.

† Ibrahim George Kheiralla.

At that juncture, the envoy of Persia entered; he was subsequently summoned to the Master's room, and the two of them were engaged in conversation for some time. When the wife and children of the late Gabriel Sacy requested permission to be dismissed, the Master bestowed them with a considerable sum of money, and offered them words of great comfort and consolation.[333]

Shortly after nightfall, the Master went outside to go for a walk.[334] When He returned, He said:

> Tonight, we went outside to go for a stroll, and it so happened that we saw some of the illuminated streets and bylanes of Paris that we had not seen before. We then went on an excursion by car and made our way back.[335] The cab fare is far less expensive here than it is in America.

Monday, 10 February 1913
[Paris]

In the morning, following prayers and meditations, and after having some tea, the Master summoned Áqá Faraju'lláh Ká<u>sh</u>ání to meet with Him outside, where He showed great loving-kindness to that servant of His.[336] When the Master had returned from that visit, He complained of His inability to sleep at night and His overall fatigue. And yet, despite His tired state, He appeared before a crowd and gave an extensive talk on the differences and commonalities between humans and animals, calling attention to the necessity of the holy power of God, divine relationships, and spiritual attractions. All those present were roused to alertness and vigilance through mystic power, pure spirituality, and imperishable perfections.

After lunch and a bit of rest, a reporter[337] – along with a number of respected individuals – attained the Master's presence. Among the remarks which the Master made to them were these:

> [Napoleon] Bonaparte was a powerful person in this earthly dominion. His conquests, however, were limited. They eventually

came to an end, and all his gains were lost. But as for them that summon people to the Kingdom of God, they shall receive everlasting grace and enjoy imperishable sovereignty. Consider how the sovereignty of the kings of the earth is finite, whereas the sovereignty of the Apostles of Christ is eternal and without limit. Whatever pertains to the Cause of God, whatever service is rendered to the divine threshold, is unconstrained by limitations. It befits the wise, then, to summon people to the Kingdom of God, and thereby be granted eternal life. This is that imperishable sovereignty, that manifest power, with which the love of God is obtained. It is our hope that this meeting and discussion may yield good results – like the encounter between the pure soil and the vernal shower, and even as the morning breeze that stirs the blossoms and spreads their fragrance.

A gathering was held at the home of Mr and Mrs Dreyfus-Barney that evening.[338] Some prayers were recited, and both Mr Dreyfus-Barney and Mrs Richard spoke of subjects pertaining to the Cause. Shortly thereafter, the Master joined that gathering of ardent lovers, and gave an extensive talk about how the peoples of the earth have always anticipated and sought out the Manifestations of God prior to their advent. The Master observed how, despite their expectant state, some of those who had been exhorted to this anticipation in their scriptures nonetheless rejected and waxed proud before the Manifestation when He did appear, whereas others accepted Him and were numbered with the unconstrained, for they were not hindered by a single veil. 'Praised be God, then,' were the Master's words of approval to that gathering, 'that you all were not only exhorted to such anticipation, but have also recognized and embraced the object of your expectation.'

When that talk was concluded, all those in attendance approached the Master with heartfelt humility and overwhelming love as their faces beamed with joy. They shook His hand, expressed their gratitude to Him, and rendered Him praise.

Tuesday, 11 February 1913
[Paris]

Before the public gathering was convened, a number of people had the honour of attaining the Master's presence and the privilege of conversing with Him. Among the remarks He made to those people were these:

> One must look at things with a view to learning from them. Should he fail to open the eye of receptivity to such lessons, of what avail will this life be to him? Myriads of people are born into the world and leave it every day, yet we must consider what their end shall be, and look to the fruits of their lives. What harvests from the farm of this life will they take with them, and what services to the realm of real significance have they rendered?
>
> A person's duty consists in service to the world of humanity and thraldom to the divine threshold – to pray ardently, remain vigilant, and maintain an attitude of detachment. Should we succeed in cultivating these virtues, it would be most excellent; otherwise, we will have naught to our names but empty hands. The Blessed Beauty has established for us so wondrous a foundation that all the implements and instruments of the world seem like the playthings of children in its light, for what He has given us is no less than the very spirit of this world, while every one of its other matters and affairs can be likened only to a lifeless corpse. It is, of course, the spirit which vivifies the body.

When that day's gathering had convened, the Master gave a talk in which He explained that human perfection lies in the love and knowledge of God.[339] With this talk, the Master set the hearts of his audience towards the Abhá Kingdom, and turned their faces towards the Most Exalted Horizon. Their hearts and souls thoroughly captivated, each and every one of them expressed their deference and assurance before the Master.

In the afternoon, a number of Persians attained the Master's presence, and felt abundant delight as they listened to His kind counsels and tender admonitions. Shortly thereafter,[340] Mr Dreyfus arrived with the car, and he took the Master to the home of a respected woman,[341] where a number of the city dignitaries had gathered to attain His presence. While there, the Master instilled in those captives of this nether world an awareness of the peace and tranquillity of the heavenly Kingdom.

When the Master returned to His residence shortly after nightfall,[342] He first gave an account from His days in Mazandaran to a group of Persians whom He had instructed to remain at His home to have dinner. He spoke of the bravery and valour of Riḍá Khán,[343] and described his trek from Qazvin to Mazandaran – a journey that ended with his martyrdom in the divine path, which caused him to attain to God's supreme bounty and greatest favour. When the Master then seated Himself at the dinner table, He told stories and recounted episodes from the histories of early Islam at length, eventually concluding His remarks with this account:[344]

> Notwithstanding that the Jews had made a pact with the Prophet Muhammad, a pact which guaranteed the protection of the Jews so long as they remained faithful to it, they formed an alliance nonetheless with the tribes of Quraysh and arrayed themselves against Islam. This development forced the Prophet Muhammad and His companions to dig a trench, where they remained confined for some time. It so happens that one of the Jews themselves was responsible for sowing the seeds of dissension between the tribes of Quraysh and the Israelites, which compelled the former to flee, and presented an opportunity for Islam to be safeguarded from the deceit and wickedness of the tribes of Quraysh. Seven hundred of those covenant-breaking enemies were massacred in the span of a single day. If this massacre had not taken place, the Jews would have made pacts with like-minded tribes once again – bending every effort to lay axe to the root of Islam, and rendering its firm and secure establishment a most difficult prospect. And yet, those who know nothing of divine wisdom, and are uninformed of historical events as they actually occurred, let loose their tongues in ample protest, and object to the incident due

strictly to their ulterior motives or out of their ignorance of the facts.

Wednesday, 12 February 1913
[Paris]

As the Master was having tea that morning, He said:[345]

> Our enemies have beset us on all sides. Do you not see what the Azalís are doing? They have not given us so much as a moment's peace. The Muslims assail us from one direction, and the Covenant-breakers from another. The prejudiced priests burn with the fire of jealousy and rancour more fiercely than ever before, and yet the debility that now plagues me is still more dire than all this. The blows have rained down from every side, but since we endure these calamities in the path of God, we bear them with the utmost joy.

The Master then asked for a prayer to be chanted. Mírzá 'Alí-Akbar Rafsanjání acceded to this request, and when he had finished chanting a few prayers in a spirit of ardent supplication, the Master remarked:

> How strange it is that such prayers as these should be intoned in the city of Paris! It is as if its inhabitants are enveloped in three darknesses,* one after the other. Were one to light a lamp, they would behold how the darkness of materialism and preoccupation with worldly affairs has encompassed them from one direction, the darkness of immorality and unseemly behaviour from another, and the darkness of pride and prejudice from yet another.

The talk which the Master then gave to the gathering dealt with the essential unity of the divine religions, as well as the renewal of their secondary teachings, which must be changed with every new dispensation in accordance with the exigencies and requirements of the time.

---

* Possibly an allusion to Qur'án 39:6.

In the afternoon, a number of the German friends attained the Master's presence.[346] This brought immense happiness to His heart, and even as a blooming flower, His face beamed with joy. He said:[347]

> The Cause of God will make such great progress in Germany as to excel every other place. Although London and its environs surpass Paris in this respect, yet will Germany achieve a measure of advancement greater than that of any other place.

Then, owing to the stifling weather, the Master related this anecdote:

> When, as a child, I would hear descriptions of Ptolemy's model of the universe, which consists of seven spheres that resemble seven concentric circles, it would bring much grief to my heart. Even from childhood, I have disliked spaces that are small and closed. Yet one day, in a prayer revealed by the Blessed Beauty, I heard mention of 'a limitless space' and, immediately, I felt a joy that I could not possibly describe.

That day, the Master received an invitation in the form of a letter that had come from Budapest.[348] The authors of this letter were Mr [Lipót, or Leopold] and Mrs [Karolina] Stark, who had heard about the Cause of God and had become acquainted with some of its teachings through what they had read in American and European newspapers and magazines that discussed the Master's talks and described His travels. So enraptured had they become with what they had read about the Cause that they repeatedly sent such letters as this one to the Master, in which they invited Him to come to Budapest.

In the evening, a special banquet was held in the Master's honour by the Paris Esperanto Group, and in spite of His great fatigue and weakness, the Master departed His residence to attend it.[349] The banquet had been prepared in one of the halls at the Hôtel Moderne,[350] and when the Master arrived at the hotel, He first went to one of the other rooms to rest for a few minutes.[351] While there, some of the members of the Esperanto group approached the Master to introduce their friends to Him. The Master showed them all His characteristic loving-kindness, and they expressed to Him how joyful and honoured this made them feel.

Eventually, the Master went to the room where the banquet had been prepared, whereupon all those present rose.[352] The president of the Esperanto group, Carlo Bourlet, also rose to express his gratitude to the Master for having attended the banquet. He enumerated, moreover, some of the subjects that the Master had discussed at the gatherings held by the Esperanto Society of Edinburgh. The transcripts of these talks had been published and translated into Esperanto; Bourlet read some passages from these transcripts, and then said:

> It is a great joy and honour for us to have 'Abdu'l-Bahá, the leader of the Bahá'í Cause, in our midst, for He shares the views of our group on the question of a universal language. It became clear to me, as I was reciting the text of 'Abdu'l-Bahá's past talks, that you all are brimming with delight, and that you understood His words well. 'Abdu'l-Bahá will exhort His friends to learn the language of Esperanto, and there is no doubt that, through His pervasive influence, this language will gain currency in the East, inasmuch as millions of people today identify themselves as the devotedly obedient adherents of the Cause He propounds. In Edinburgh, 'Abdu'l-Bahá stated well that a universal language would dispel misunderstandings, promote the growth of a universal religion, and establish ties between the hearts of all humankind. We are all different peoples – we believe in different religions and hold different views – yet it is our hope that a universal language will conduce to universal concord, even as the universal Bahá'í religion has united people in the domain of morality. For this do we all pray, and indeed cherish as our highest aspiration – that with every passing day, this religion continue to be noised farther and farther abroad, and these lofty ideals spread to the greatest possible extent.

> On behalf of all the Esperantists, I extend the profoundest gratitude to 'Abdu'l-Bahá, for in spite of His fatigue, He has nonetheless graced this gathering with His presence.

The Master then rose from His seat, at which time all those present broke into vigorous applause and expressed their unbridled joy. The Master began His address to the members of this group with these words:

> Every matter in this world belongs to one of two categories – it is either universal or particular. Every particular matter is of humankind, and its benefits are limited, whereas every universal matter is of God, and its benefits know no limits . . .

The Master's talk roused His audience to such irrepressible excitement that they punctuated His delivery with rapturous laughter, praise, and applause.[353] Such was their state even as they had dinner afterwards, and as the banquet drew to a close, each and every one of them approached the Master and expressed their sincere devotion and deference to Him. Those who had not previously had a chance to attain the Master's presence requested permission to do so, and when it was granted them, they asked Him for the address of the residence where He was staying.

Thursday, 13 February 1913
[Paris]

The talk which the Master gave at the gathering that morning dealt with the two kinds of influence which the human soul exerts in the world of existence: the first, through the body; the second, without any intermediary at all.

When the gathering was concluded, a number of Persians attained the Master's presence. The Master spoke to them,[354] and concluded His remarks by recounting the unseemly behaviour of Mírzá Yaḥyá and discussing the power and might of the Cause of the Abhá Beauty. He gave, moreover, an extensive account of the calumnies and lies of the Azalís; enumerated the names of thirteen women who were all the wives of Mírzá Yaḥyá; and spoke at length of the fear, the weakness, and the misdeeds of that doomed soul. He then said:

> When the Blessed Beauty returned from Sulaymáníyyih to Baghdad, He permitted the general population to attain His presence. Among the first to do so were one or two Persians, who were hostile to the Cause and had come to oppose Him, as well as a number of others who said, 'The Bábís are showing their faces again!' The Blessed Beauty silenced them in such a way that they realized they could not make such remarks.[355]
>
> Gradually, He assumed leadership of the community and raised the Cause of God to new heights. He rent the veils asunder, and exhorted the people to sanctity and detachment. At that time, Mírzá Yaḥyá, actuated by his cowardice, had begun to disguise himself as a peddler, for he would always run away in times of distress. Ultimately, when he noticed in Constantinople how, in spite of the imprisonment and calamities Bahá'u'lláh was then facing, the Cause of God had gained such renown that even the Ottoman grandees and pás͟hás would go to see Him and show Him the utmost courtesy and deference, he concluded that he no longer had any reason to fear, as no harm could possibly come to him under such favourable circumstances. Consequently, he rushed out onto the scene – and yet, what could he accomplish? As he lived out his days in Cyprus, enjoying as he did the freedom afforded him by the English government, did he guide even a single soul aright? And this despite the fact that he was neither a prisoner, nor the object of the cavils raised by the peoples of the world. I swear by God, besides Whom there is none other God, that whenever I am reminded of the weighty chains around the Blessed Beauty's neck, it causes every limb of my body to tremble. How severe the blows that were dealt Him – how dire the calamities that so copiously rained down on Him! Yet in the end, these trials and tribulations notwithstanding, He propelled the Cause to triumph, and made the Voice of God to be heard throughout the world.

In those days, Mírzá 'Alí-Akbar Rafsanjání and some of the other friends had gone to the public libraries of Paris and London, where they had found some of the compositions of that grievously misguided Mírzá Yaḥyá written in the hand of his son, Riḍván-'Alí. The believers were delighted to know that these worthless works would remain stored in those libraries, and forever bear sufficient testimony to the feeble-mindedness, the ignorance, and the stupidity of Mírzá Yaḥyá. Had the works given to those libraries not been transcribed by his own son, no one generations from now would believe that his father was the source of these unseemly words and unsightly phrases – and had his words been recorded some other way, and anyone then rejected the notion that he was their author, it would be difficult to prove that this is actually the case. Yet, things being as they are, anyone can easily visit the British Museum (the London Library) [sic][356] and the Paris Library for themselves to become informed and well-assured of the truth of the matter.

On this particular day, some of those compositions which were especially ridiculous were read aloud, and this moved everyone to laughter. Among the passages recited were these:[357]

> The hunters set their traps, and the wicked seek to accomplish their purpose. I am bound in their fetters, and I boil in their snares. My existence is extinguished, and my non-existence toil and trouble. I come from the right to the left, and I hasten from the left to the right . . .

> Praised be God, He Who loves whatever He wills unto whatever He wills from whatever He wills however He wills! Lo, He captivates whomever He wills however He wills unto whomever He wills by whatever He wills in whatever He wills from whatever He wills of whatever He wills through whomever He wills from whomever He wills in whatever way He wills . . .

> In recognizing the name of God, 'The Hidden' – in the Name of God, the Most Existent, the Most Existent! God, no God is there

> but Him, the Most Existent, the Most Existent. Say: God is the Most Existent above all other existers . . .

As these are apparently the choicest of Mírzá Yaḥyá's words, one can only imagine how his other compositions must read! As we recited these passages, the Master would make the following remarks again and again:

> With this fatuous tactic of theirs, these ignorant fools have sought to call attention to themselves by pitting these ridiculously meaningless words against the shrill voice of the Supreme Pen. Vain indeed is that which they have imagined! The people, uninformed as they are, have mistakenly ascribed a Heavenly Source to such words as the ones we have just read.

A gathering charged with ecstasy was convened that night[358] at the Paris Theosophical Society.[359] As with other gatherings of this sort, all those in attendance rose as soon as the Master entered. Before He spoke, the president of the gathering, Charles Blech, rose and introduced the Master with the following remarks:

> We regard 'Abdu'l-Bahá as the very embodiment of spiritual love, and a prophet who promotes in this age the brotherhood of all humanity. His life-giving utterances set an example for us all to follow. Seventy years have passed since this new Cause was established. First, the Báb appeared in the midst of the Muslims to improve the condition of the world; then, Bahá'u'lláh, the greatest of God's Manifestations, laid the foundation for the establishment of universal peace and concord among the peoples of all nations; and now, 'Abdu'l-Bahá works to promote these ideals. He has spoken at Theosophical societies on many occasions, and in every country He has visited, our fellow Theosophists in those lands have sought out His utterances and been captivated by His writings. It is a great honour, then, for us to have the chance to lend our ears to His lofty words. Let us set aside our own thoughts and convictions for the moment, and reflect deeply on His utterances,

> which are even as a wellspring of wisdom and knowledge. 'Abdu'l-Bahá will conclude His talk by chanting a prayer in Persian; no translation of this prayer will be provided, but there can be no doubt that simply hearing the words He intones will cause our souls to ascend to the most sublime of stations. And now, it is my great joy to present 'Abdu'l-Bahá to you all.

The Master then rose with that beautiful stature of His, and began to pace the podium with majestic elegance. The Master started to speak – and whenever He finished a sentence, Mr Dreyfus would interpret it for the audience. In His talk, the Master stated that the life of every living thing comes from the divine grace and power with which God has imbued it, as well as a mighty force, unlimited in its potency, that pervades the material world. Observing that the physical realm has attained to so glorious a rank as to benefit from a limitless share of God's grace, the Master then asked how the outpourings of that grace, and likewise God's heavenly perfections, could ever possibly be limited in the spiritual realms.

The Master's talk,[360] as well as the eloquent prayer He chanted in a most melodious voice,[361] filled all those present with godly gladness, and moved them to turn their faces towards the Horizon of Truth.

Friday, 14 February 1913
[Paris]

As the Master was having His tea that morning, He said:

> The president of last night's gathering stated that Bahá'u'lláh was the greatest of God's Manifestations, and spoke of the greatness of the Cause of God. Yet, the inhabitants of Paris do not share the spirituality and zeal of the Americans, who are truly something else.

A number of Easterners then attained the presence of the Master, Who spoke to them of the heedlessness and cavilling of the people at the outset of every divine Revelation:

> How utterly heedless are the people! In the time of the Prophet Muhammad, those who rejected Him would scorn Him with extreme derision, going so far as to write poetry in which they would ask how long He would 'trot', even as a camel, around the Kaaba. In the end, however, the Word of God so triumphed over its opponents as to leave no trace of them whatsoever.

The Master gave the following talk to the gathering that morning:[362]

> People are the possessors of two kinds of abilities: the first, inborn; the second, acquired. In this respect, they are like other beings, which have natural abilities and traits, as well as virtues that are cultivated under the influence of an educator. Though the natural traits inherent in all things are praiseworthy in their own right, yet when such a trait is brought under the influence of an educator, it will develop into a different kind of virtue altogether. Thus, while natural traits are themselves worthy of praise – inasmuch as these traits will still exert their own measure of influence – yet their perfection depends on the education, the ability, and the personality of their possessor. But alas, people squander their inborn abilities. Rather than use a poison to create its antidote, they make it the cause of death and destruction . . .

Following that gathering, some people made reference, while in the Master's presence, to certain articles that had been published in the newspapers of the day. This prompted the Master to say:

> Though these newspapers will, if written impartially, inform the people, yet we have written articles in the newspapers of the Kingdom. These are articles of perpetual influence, and they will never be forgotten. You all must work to write spiritual articles in these sorts of newspapers, and make a significant mark thereby.

Afterwards, letters from the Bahá'ís of Washington were read aloud and translated into Persian in the Master's presence. He spoke at length of the Bahá'ís of America, and in that connection, He sent the following telegram:[363]

He is God

To Mr Remey* and Mrs Parsons†

I am 'Abdu'l-Bahá. Bahá'u'lláh is without likeness or peer; all must turn towards Bahá'u'lláh in their prayers. This is the way of 'Abdu'l-Bahá. Announce that to be firm in the Covenant is to be lovingly devoted and obedient to the instructions of 'Abdu'l-Bahá.

—'Abdu'l-Bahá 'Abbás

In the afternoon, some letters from the Bahá'ís of the East were presented to the Master. One of these letters was from Mírzá 'Alí-Akbar, the Muḥibbu's-Sulṭán,[364] and when the Master read it, He began to recount the services rendered by that friend:

Praised be God, for that soul has always been ready and willing to serve. I beseech the bounty of the Blessed Beauty that, with every passing day, he may be granted ample confirmations and given an ever-increasing measure of success.

The Master then related an account from the days when Bahá'u'lláh was living in Mazandaran:[365]

On a certain day, when He was in the prime of His youth, the Blessed Beauty entered the residence of Mírzá Muḥammad-Taqí, the well-known *mujtahid*, in the village of Yálrúd. Present there were four of the *mujtahid*'s trusted seminarians, as well as a number of other students. To the four seminarians, all of whom were close to attaining the rank of *mujtahid* themselves, Mírzá Muḥammad-Taqí posed the following Islamic tradition: 'Fáṭimih is the best of all the world's women, except for the one born to

* Charles Mason Remey.
† Agnes Parsons.

Mary.' Since Mary did not give birth to a daughter, as the word 'except' suggests, the *mujtahid* asked the seminarians to make sense of the tradition. Each offered his own commentary and justification, but Mírzá Muḥammad-Taqí rejected all their responses. At that moment, the Blessed Beauty remarked:

> This statement – that, with the exception of the one born to Mary, Fáṭimih is the best of all the world's women – is predicated upon an impossibility. Since Mary never gave birth to a daughter, the stated exception referreth to an impossibility. The purpose of this purported exception is to emphatically affirm the initial statement in the tradition – that Fáṭimih is indeed the best of all the world's women. It would be as if we were to say that a certain king was the best of all the earth's kings, except for the one who cometh from heaven. As kings cannot actually descend from heaven, the statement serveth to emphasize the peerlessness of the king initially mentioned. The descent of a king from heaven, just as the birth of a daughter to Mary, is predicated upon an impossibility.

Mírzá Muḥammad-Taqí fell silent. When the Blessed Beauty left the room, the *mujtahid* said to his seminarians, 'I did not at all expect that a Youth, sporting the hat of a layman, would be able to so expound a tradition as to render you all – approaching the rank of *mujtahid*, and clothed in the garb of learned divines – unable to apprehend His commentary.'

That night,[366] the weekly gathering was held at the home of Mr and Mrs Dreyfus in a spirit of the utmost love and fellowship. First, Mr Dreyfus read, for the audience, some historical accounts of the Faith, as well as French translations of Bahá'u'lláh's Tablets to the kings and rulers of the earth.[367] Afterwards, Mrs Richard gave a talk on subjects pertaining to the Cause, and then Mírzá 'Alí-Akbar Rafsanjání chanted a prayer.[368] Following this, the Master entered the room, and all those present rose at once. After the Master bade everyone be seated, He delivered a sweetly eloquent talk on those verses of Bahá'u'lláh pertaining to His prophecies regarding future events, as well as His references to the fulfilment of God's promises. He expounded, moreover, certain passages from the aforementioned Tablets to the kings and rulers of the earth, and described the power and might which those sovereigns enjoyed.[369]

To conclude His talk, the Master chanted a plaintive prayer that moved everyone profoundly; it was a prayer that stirred His audience to vigilance, and roused within them the most intense of emotions.[370]

Saturday, 15 February 1913
[Paris]

The Master's address to the gathering that morning[371] dealt with Bahá'u'lláh's prohibition of asceticism, which deprives its practitioners of the bounties of God. He spoke, moreover, of moderation in one's affairs, the meaning of detachment, and charity to the poor.[372]

When the gathering was concluded, the Master addressed these words to Mírzá 'Alí-Akbar Rafsanjání, whom He had instructed to travel to Switzerland:[373]

> The most important thing in this day is to teach the Cause of God; this will bring salvation and grant eternal life. The good-pleasure of the Blessed Beauty consists in this, and also in self-effacement – in other words, that one regard oneself as utter nothingness. I am sending you to teach; God willing, you will succeed in this endeavour. Go with the utmost courage and valour. Pay no mind to the pride and protests of the people. Nothing whatever will be of any avail unless it promotes the Cause of God. It is for this reason that I have set aside all my other affairs and engaged myself in teaching the Cause.
>
> When Jamál Burújirdí[374] came to 'Akká, I noticed he was bereft of mental focus. I asked him, 'As you were en route to here from Tehran, did you teach the Cause to anyone?' He replied that he had not, remarking that the opportunity to do so had not

> presented itself. I then counselled him, 'To teach the Cause of God in this day is most necessary for you; it will benefit you.' How low, in truth, will one be brought by unseemly ambition! Contrary to an attitude of complete self-effacement, he wished for everything and gained nothing. In stark contrast to him, we have Ḥájí Mírzá Ḥaydar-'Alí, who wished for nothing and gained everything. As the days went on, the extent to which Jamál Burújirdí's ever-increasing desire remained unfulfilled was precisely the measure of fulfilment granted to the already-contented Ḥájí Mírzá Ḥaydar-'Alí. The one began high and was brought to naught, the other began as nothing and was raised to the heights of enlightenment.

Among those who had the great joy of attaining the Master's presence that afternoon[375] were a group of Persian youth who had come to Paris to pursue a higher education.[376] The Master's responses to their questions – which concerned the impermissibility of individuals to exact vengeance upon one another, as well as the duty of society to protect the rights of all people – filled these students, as well as their esteemed instructor [Théophile Cart], with such profound ecstasy; moved them to express such profuse gratitude; and instilled in them such humble devotion to the Master, which they evinced as they departed that gathering, as to defy all description.[377]

Shortly after nightfall,[378] once the Master had returned from a visit He had made to the residence of Rashíd Páshá, He set out for a gathering of Parisian ministers. This grand gathering was held at the home of the minister [Henri] Monnier,[379] who had personally extended an invitation to the Master to attend. What a gathering it was – one that, in every respect, served as supreme proof vindicating the Cause! Up to that time, it had never come to pass that such an exalted personage as the Master should enter a gathering of religious leaders, and so eloquently discuss matters of religion, so remarkably unravel the mysteries enshrined in the verses of scripture, and so convincingly answer the questions raised by His audience as to move them, one and all, to attest to the force of His utterances, the power of His proofs, the greatness of His knowledge, the loftiness of His wisdom, and the captivating charm of His person. No minister could be seen who did not express his humble gratitude to the Master, and not one of them made so much as a single remark in protest to His words. Much to the contrary, up until the moment He departed the gathering, each and every one of the attendees showered Him with benedictions and sang His praises, and glowingly extolled the teachings He had come to propound. A record of that gathering, which has been published elsewhere,[380] itself bears witness to the greatness of the Cause of God, testifies to the power of the Covenant, and constitutes the means by which every fair-minded seeker of truth will take vigilant heed.

Sunday, 16 February 1913
[Paris]

In the very early hours of the morning, the Master summoned His attendants to the main room.[381] Once some prayers and other verses had been chanted, the Master asked for some tea – and as He drank it, He related this account from His days in the Holy Land:

> A Christian archbishop[382] came to see me and said:
>
>> Mírzá Muḥammad-ʻAlí[383] met with me, and I noticed that he was very quiet and deep in thought.
>>
>> I asked him, 'Why are you so pensive?'
>>
>> He replied, 'What can I say? My Brother seized all my possessions, and this I accepted without objection. He then called on me to be His obedient servant; this, too, did I tolerate and take in stride. Yet now He demands that I give Him a document bearing my testimony that He is Christ Himself! Of course, my oral testimony to that effect will not satisfy Him – He demands a written document wherein I refer to Him explicitly as Christ.'
>>
>> Mírzá Muḥammad-ʻAlí then sheepishly tilted his head from side to side, and asked me, 'Does this seem right to you – that I should regard Him as Christ?'

> Mírzá Muḥammad-‘Alí astonished me with this deceitful behaviour, by which he hoped to instil in me feelings of hatred and animosity towards You. Having discerned his intent, I paid no mind to his words.

> Mírzá Muḥammad-‘Alí would spend his every waking moment attempting to incite this sort of sedition. For instance, he would send to the authorities in Constantinople ostensible letters of advice intended to misrepresent us. As another example, he would say to Muslims, ‘Bahá’u’lláh has not brought any new teachings; He was simply inclined to Sufism and other forms of mysticism. That Brother of mine, however, has established a new religious law which He now actively promotes; He holds gatherings and summons the people to accept Him.’ Indeed, he wrote many things of this sort to excite the people and foment sedition. Eventually, the Commission of Inquiry aligned themselves with the makers of mischief, who cherished the hope of inciting a grievous sedition – but in the end, God thwarted all their plans at once. All those seditious souls were dispersed; some of them were killed while others fled.

The talk which the Master gave to the gathering that morning dealt with the blind imitations and vain imaginings that have always been endorsed by the leaders of religion, who – wishing to propagate these idle notions and superstitious practices, while at the same time recognizing their incompatibility with the standards of science and reason – have denounced those standards as inapplicable, and portrayed adherence to the beliefs they enjoin as a sign of religious devotion. By contrast, the Master observed that, in this perspicuous age, Bahá’u’lláh has brought teachings that dispel these vain imaginings and promote the essential truths of the divine religions – among these teachings the compatibility that must exist between matters of religion and proofs that are scientific and rational in nature.

Brimming with unbridled ecstasy, all those present approached the Master, one by one, to express their sincerest sentiments of servitude to Him, whereafter they were each dismissed. Acceding to a request which some of these people had made, the Master went to the home of a certain photographer who was to take a colour photograph of Him.[384] Two photographs, in fact, were taken on that occasion: one colour, the other a profile.

While seated in the main room that afternoon, the Master spoke of some friends from the East – in particular Jináb-i-Samandar and his family, of whom He made many a loving and tender remark. He described how that family had suffered numerous calamities and yet maintained an unwavering steadfastness in the Cause, having sacrificed everything in the path of God.

When another group of people attained the Master's presence, He spoke to them at length on the divine teachings, and also related anecdotes from His travels to America, such as the talks He had given at various synagogues and churches.

Shortly thereafter, a respected Persian entered the premises and requested a private audience with the Master. Accordingly, the Master summoned this gentleman to His room. This man had come to convey the humbly devoted sentiments of [——],[385] who was seeking the Master's permission to attain His presence, and had requested that the Master determine a time at which he would come to see Him. In response, the Master stated repeatedly, 'I will go to him for this meeting,' which prompted His interlocutor to say, 'This individual has specifically requested that they first come to meet with You, and have the privilege of receiving You only after this first meeting has taken place.' The Master then granted permission to that effect, and promised to have the requested meeting the following morning.

Monday, 17 February 1913
[Paris]

In the early morning, the aforementioned individual attained the Master's presence in His room. To him the Master addressed such words as these:

In truth, there is not a single person in Persia today who is adept and knowledgeable, nor can any individual keenly aware be found. Now they hope that some of the Easterners who have been educated in Europe will go to Persia and help it prosper. Let us suppose that such people have received a proper education and will apply that knowledge correctly. Even under such circumstances as those, it would take a thousand years for Persia to truly flourish, or for Tehran to become like Paris – and even then, Persia would still be unable to withstand the power of Europe.

Though Mírzá Taqí Khán,* the former prime minister of Persia, meted out to the Cause an unprecedented measure of injustice, yet in spite of this fact, he laid what can truly be called the firmest of foundations in matters of politics and governance – and this he accomplished without having ever entered the schools of Europe. A proper education will benefit one who is knowledgeable, cognizant, and confirmed. Should, however, a person not possess innate knowledge or lack divine confirmations, then of what avail to him would such an education be? . . .

A considerable amount of time passed before the aforementioned individual was dismissed, evincing the utmost humility and devotedness as he departed.

Afterwards, a public gathering was held in the main room of the apartment where the Master was residing. Occasioned by the clear weather that Paris was enjoying that day, the Master gave a talk to this gathering on the lights of divine bounties and the rising of the Sun of Truth, observing that this Sun has shone over the horizon of oneness in every age to dispel the humidity of ignorance and obliterate the darkness of heedlessness, thereby allowing the warmth of unity and oneness It imparts to rouse the people to fresh excitement and movement, and kindle within their hearts the fire of the love of God.

In the afternoon,[386] a gathering charged with a spirit of friendliness and fellowship was held at the home of that American handmaid of God, Mrs [Lilian Haydon] Hieston,[387] and the

---

* Amír Kabír.

majority of those in attendance were Americans. It is for this reason that the Master began His address to that gathering by remarking on the receptivity of the Americans to the Cause, noting that their receptivity stood out as superior even in Paris. Additionally, He implored God to bestow confirmations on the people of Paris, and expressed His hope for the development of their spiritual receptivity. He encouraged the believers, moreover, to derive their share of eternal life and of God's everlasting bounties – and so impressive were these exhortations that, to a degree theretofore unseen, all those present became enraptured with the Abhá Kingdom and were moved to set their faces towards the Most Glorious Horizon.

After having some tea, *sharbat*, and sweets, the Master departed that gathering for His third meeting of the day, which was held at the home of Mr and Mrs Scott. The Master's talk that night dealt with the new laws and teachings of this Most Great Dispensation, and also the equality of the rights of men and women. In that vein, He made reference to a number of renowned Eastern women, and told stories about Ṭáhirih, the mother-in-law of the King of Martyrs,[388] and the like.[389]

Tuesday, 18 February 1913
[Paris]

A number of seekers attained the Master's presence that morning. As they entered His room, one by one and two by two, they felt greatly privileged as they posed their questions to Him and listened to His responses, and this moved them to ecstasy and delight.

The Master then gave a talk to the public gathering that dealt with the need for spiritual education and divine civilization, making such observations as these:[390]

> Material education and civilization will not improve the character of humanity. Unlike the teachings of the prophets and the divine civilization they have come to establish, these material measures will not conduce to the edification of humankind. They could

> never have exalted a people as base as the Israelites to the lofty heights they ultimately attained, nor formed a community as illustrious as that of the Christians. Furthermore, they could never have civilized the desert-dwelling wild ones of Arabia so thoroughly as to empower them to conquer great cities and transform the hearts of differing peoples, to the extent that that once brutal people had become enabled to so quickly establish the schools of Andalusia – schools which the denizens of Europe attended to learn the hallmarks of civilization, and returned to the West to promote the arts and sciences they had studied. Had it not been for the foundation laid by the prophets of God, Europe would never have attained to the degree of material civilization which it now boasts, and but for the planting of that seed, this blessed harvest would never have been yielded – for if it were possible for such progress to be made unaided by spiritual power and divine civilization, the renowned philosophers of old should have been able to educate the masses, elevate the lowly kindreds of the earth to the pinnacle of glory, and unite the hearts of varying peoples.

Following that gathering, the Master went outside to go on a lengthy excursion – first on foot, and then by car. When He returned, a number of Persians – believers and others – attained His presence and were seated at the table for lunch. The Master enjoyed His meal in a way that gladdened those around Him, and He regaled them with humorous anecdotes. He then went to His room to rest for a bit.

Most of those who attained the Master's presence as the afternoon approached were Persian. Accordingly, the Master addressed to them the following words:

> We have spoken and written about such things as will conduce to the good and betterment of Persia and its people, yet our counsels have gone unheeded. Even at the outset of the Constitutional Revolution, we explicitly wrote: 'Until such time as that government and its people become commingled, even as milk and honey, their success and prosperity will remain entirely unattainable.

> Persia shall fall into ruin, and the governments of its neighbouring realms will ultimately meddle in its affairs . . .' In His *Tablet of the World*, the Blessed Beauty has stated, 'Certain laws and principles are necessary and indispensable for Persia.'*

A number of Persian students then attained the Master's presence, and to them He said:[391]

> Those who attend the schools of Europe will find, upon their return to Persia, that the means by which they might practise the disciplines they have studied do not exist, leaving their efforts in vain.

Wednesday, 19 February 1913
[Paris]

After chanting the divine verses that morning, and also rendering praise and thanksgiving to the Abhá Beauty, the Master began to speak of the greatness of this momentous century and perspicuous dispensation, as well as the manifold wonders of this unprecedented time. In the course of this discussion, He remarked, 'It would now be fitting to prepare the means of travel to other planets!'

A strange incident took place that morning. Two Persians, who were not Bahá'ís, had come to the Master's residence to attain His presence, and it so happened that these two people were on very bad terms. They entered the Master's residence, and when they saw and recognized each other, they both realized that it was too late to turn back now. They quickly went inside, one after the other, and seated themselves in the main room as each of them glowered with resentment for the other. The Master's attendants beheld these two people in their rancorous state and began to engage each of them in separate conversation. Eventually, each of the two guests was summoned, individually, to the Master's room. He offered them both many counsels and spoke to them at great length. Eventually,

* Bahá'u'lláh, *Tablets of Bahá'u'lláh Revealed after the Kitáb-i-Aqdas*, p. 92.

these two guests came away from their respective meetings with a kind of gladness and assurance that I cannot possibly describe.

Afterwards, a number of students, some of whom were young believers, attained the Master’s presence. They had all been given scholarships by the Persian government to study in Paris. As school was not in session that day, the Master insisted that they stay at His residence for the day. They felt greatly privileged and deeply gladdened by the tender kindnesses which the Master extended to them, and His extensive utterances and compassionate counsels roused them to exceeding joy and vigilance. Among the remarks He addressed to those students were these:

> The well-known Persian students of the past were unable to bring about any advancements in their native land, but God grant that you all, on the other hand, will be able to render some service to Persia – that you will study such disciplines as will redound to the rehabilitation of that country, such that you will, upon your return there, become the very means of its revival, and the instrument through which the Cause of God is spread; that you will resolve to rectify the character of all humankind, and promote holiness and sanctity; that your efforts to make progress and bring prosperity will be granted divine confirmations and crowned with heavenly success; and that you will achieve outstanding proficiency in agriculture, industry, and commerce. Indeed, may you be given such divine confirmations as will compensate for the failure of your precursors and resplendently manifest the ancient glory of Persia.

As part of His talk that day, the Master discussed the need for all humanity to be educated, observing that the prophets of God, as well as the world’s sages and philosophers, have always ascribed paramount importance to the matter of education. He remarked, moreover, that education will transform a jungle into a garden, and turn thickets of thorns into beds of roses. Education, He said, will cause hidden gems to emerge into visibility, and adorn the world of existence with the flowers of inner realities.

In the afternoon, a number of Persians came to the Master’s

residence at a time when He had gone out to repay a visit to certain respected individuals. In His absence, these Persians began to converse with the Master's attendants and extol His virtues. Among these visitors was a man who, although he was not a Bahá'í, recounted this anecdote:

> Yesterday, an exceedingly prejudiced Persian sent me a letter laden with censure and rebuke, in which He asked why I had begun to visit the Master and had grown enamoured of Him. I addressed these reproofs with an extensive response, which included the following points:[392]
>
> > Third: In the face of kindness, love, and tenderness, even a wild animal will be tamed and captivated by these displays of affection. Woe to that one who in reacting otherwise would be lower than an animal!
> >
> > Fourth: Thousands of people better than I have rendered praise to 'Abdu'l-Bahá. How, then, can I refrain from doing the same?
> >
> > Fifth: If this noble personage were indeed bereft of a special rank and majesty, then by what power could He have so enraptured all these souls as to render them stunned and spellbound, or transformed so many of the masses into obedient servants?
> >
> > Sixth: Of the fifteen million Persians who exist today, has any one of them left their homeland devoted to so prodigious an endeavour, such that whatever city or clime where He has set foot has attained the highest degree of dignity, and the denizens of every country He has reached have gone to kiss His hand in fulfilment of their highest aspiration?
> >
> > Let us now suppose that, as you say, 'Abdu'l-Bahá does not enjoy such a position as the one I have attributed to Him. What objections would you raise to His other distinctions,

> which are themselves the pride of Persia and the glory of the East? . . .

Thursday, 20 February 1913
[Paris]

The Master was very tired as He drank His tea that morning. He said:

> I did not have any dinner whatsoever last night, nor did I sleep at all. I was engaged in writing until morning approached, and I did fall asleep for a brief period before the break of day. It was simply delightful to have fallen asleep in the early hours of the morning while overcome with fatigue; this granted me a bit of rest. Sleep truly brings great tranquillity to the body and relieves one altogether. A sleep so deep that it can be likened to death itself, a sleep which renders one utterly oblivious of the world, grants rest to the body and preserves one's physical health. Reflect: of what significance is the sort of life spent in pursuit of such blissful oblivion as only sleep can confer? And yet, to sleep is still better than to eat. Sleeping grants the greater measure of relief, for eating makes one heavy and listless. Were one to spend his life solely eating and sleeping, then all his days on this earth will, in truth, have yielded no fruit.

The Master then made this remark about Paris:

> As to this city, which the people so thoroughly enjoy, I behold it even as a carcass infested with a great many maggots, endlessly creeping up and down their carrion with much excitement.

Once the public gathering had been convened, and the members of the audience had arrived, the Master gave a talk on the purpose of human existence, in which He stated that people are the very spirit of this contingent world, and noted that their purpose consists in the knowledge of God, the building of divine civilization, the acquisition of spiritual perfections, and the obtainment of heavenly outpourings. Were this not the goal, He said, then despite all the material progress that may be made in this world, it would nonetheless resemble a beautiful statue or a lifeless form.[393]

Once the gathering was concluded – and everyone in attendance had gone, one by one, to shake the Master's hand and demonstrate their sincere devotion to Him, whereupon they were each dismissed – the daughter of Horace Holley [Hertha Holley] went running towards the Master, Who immediately took her into His arms with a tenderness that brought abundant joy to all those present. It was always a happy occasion when children attained the Master's presence, and He would show them such tender kindness, such genuine love, and such heartfelt fondness as no father would ever accord his own child. He then said:

> Children are a great source of gladness and solace. I myself had a child (Ḥusayn Effendí); when he was three or four years of age, he would crawl quietly into my bed as I lay asleep, and there was a sweetness to this that I cannot possibly describe.

The Master then discussed the rearing of children:[394]

> In the time of Lycurgus, parents would raise their children with a set of rules and a particular structure in place. When the time came for these children to marry, their parents would permit them to wed only those who were in good health. From the moment they conceived their children, the women engaged in arduous work, so that even in the womb the child would be reared with hardship. Once the children were born, they would be washed thoroughly with cold water. In the event that the mother fell sick, her child was nourished with the milk of another woman. These children were not shielded from the cold. Beginning at the age of three, they were accustomed to a great deal of walking. From the age of eight onwards, the children would spend one half of their day in educational pursuits, and the other engaged in recreational activities intended to strengthen their bodies. The children,

moreover, were given such food as would fortify them. The result of all these measures was that these children came to possess a robust constitution and enjoy proficiency in various arts and sciences by the time they had reached the age of twenty.

Though it was only the children of the noble and lofty that were raised along these particular lines, yet whatever the extent to which any child is reared, from the beginning of his life, in a way that accustoms him to toil and trouble – for instance, the less he is shielded from the cold and the heat – the better it will be for him.

On a certain day when I was residing in 'Akká, an administrative officer, a judge, and the commander-in-chief of the army and I had left one of the gardens and were returning to the city when we saw that a camel had fallen in a ditch. The animal was on the verge of death; its driver was sobbing, unable to do anything for his steed. I assembled a large group, nearly a hundred persons in all, but try as they might, they could not bring the camel from out the ditch. Yet then I called out to a few Bedouins, who happened to be passing by, to ask for their assistance. Despite the fewness of their number, these Bedouins handily rescued the camel from the ditch, and this is because those men were accustomed to arduous exertion.

On that day, the Master went to repay visits to certain respected persons, and He sent some of His attendants to meet with a number of esteemed Persians. The Master had composed tender letters for each of these gentlemen, and these He entrusted to His servants to deliver to their respective recipients.

When the Master returned, He was holding a letter from Áqá Siyyid Naṣru'lláh Báqiroff of Tehran. He perused some of the matters mentioned in that letter, including reports that sentiments of unity and enrapturement were present among the loved ones of God, and that the signs of the greatness of the Cause of God were being spread. That the believers of Tehran had so readily arisen to serve and aid the Cause moved the Master to express His exceeding joy, and also extend great praise to Áqá Siyyid Naṣru'lláh for the things he had written and the services he had rendered.

The Master was busily engaged that afternoon in composing Tablets in response to the letters of various Bahá'ís, and also to the owners of English newspapers. Having been fatigued by all this writing, the Master then went outside to go for a stroll.

Friday, 21 February 1913
[Paris]

The Master began His address to the gathering that morning with these words:[395]

> Some are of the opinion that, by practising asceticism and withdrawing from society, one can rectify one's character and draw closer to God. Yet all the Prophets of God have enjoined a way of life, and have articulated a set of teachings, that call on people to maintain good health and be engaged in some kind of work, that thereby they may render service to all humanity. Were a certain person, physically weak and disengaged from work, never to wrong anyone, this would hardly be a demonstration of virtue on his part. On the contrary, real virtue would consist in his refraining from such oppression while he is able-bodied and engaged in some work. For example, if we consider a person who does not have even a cent to his name, we cannot determine from his indigence alone whether he is generous or miserly. A person who enjoys great wealth, however, is in a position where his generosity or miserliness can be clearly demonstrated . . .

Following that gathering, the Master spoke to a number of Persians about the Cause of God, remarking that it has so penetrated and moved the hearts of humanity that even its opposers and deniers attest to the momentous significance of its teachings.

In the afternoon, a certain Ottoman consul general, as well as a group of respected Egyptians, attained the Master's presence. The Master spoke to these people primarily in Turkish and Arabic as He discussed the detrimental consequences of prejudice, observing how it had ruined the East and prompted various groups and tribes to rise up in opposition to one another. The Master remarked, moreover, that in whatever country and among whatever people such prejudices have been found, abasement and turmoil have always appeared in their midst. He then related extensive accounts of prejudice against the Jews, as well as other peoples, admonishing His audience against such matters as would result in discord and degradation, and exhorting them instead to embrace the basis of unity and oneness.

The Master then departed His residence to attend a gathering of Spiritualists at 14 Rue de Trévise,[396] which had been convened expressly to have the Master give a talk to them, and had been advertised a week in advance. In that spacious room, and before an impressively large audience, the Master gave a comprehensive talk that dealt with various spiritual subjects, including the teachings, the supremacy of divine power over material forces, and the advancement and edification of all humankind.[397] This talk roused everyone to such great excitement – and so illumined the minds of His audience – that both before and after He had delivered it, the president of that gathering [Mrs Jeanne Beauchamp] and its other members[398] rose to render repeated praise to the Master, laud the divine teachings, and emphasize the need for a spiritual force, openly priding themselves all the while in having the privilege of so effusively hailing the Master in such a setting as that one.

What follows are some of the remarks of Mrs Jeanne Beauchamp, which she made at the beginning of that gathering as she stood before the Master, and were later published in some newspapers:[399]

> The Alliance Spiritualiste is happy to receive again Abdoul Baha [sic] the leader of the Behai [sic] movement who, a year ago for the first time spoke to its members & friends. We are happy to listen to him again with a religious spirit.
>
> You noble & generous hearts, who are willing to work for the happiness of human kind [sic], instruct harmony, to think, to reason; see what she [sic][400] needs . . .
>
> It is an ideal who[401] will carry her[402] above this physical plane. Humanity must raise its high destiny! To the great thinkers of our

> time, I ask them if they don't believe that our Century hasn't more intelligence than heart, and I beg of them to find the reason.
>
> For myself I believe the reason is the lack of ideal. The simple faith of our fathers not being sufficient for us now, the heart not being able to find in it, the necessary food, has become atrophied.
>
> Intelligence on the contrary, owing to the marvellous discovery of science, has found everywhere a great variety of food and in abundance, and has thus been able to develop itself, at the expense of the heart, who cannot then perceive the secrets of its destiny.
>
> O century! if you wish to accomplish your task, you must see that the heart vibrates with the intelligence. For this you must work incessantly to give the world a scientific faith.
>
> At all times, thinkers have had for mission to enlighten the nations and to bring them to the greatest conceptions of the human mind. At our time, and in men's desire of reasoning all the transcendental laws of nature have united the modern thinkers in a world fraternity . . .
>
> At this meeting Abdoul Baha [sic] represents the spiritual force of the Orient. All the spiritualists of the Occident are hoping that the universal Spiritual mind may bring about this law of love, who alone can unite the Orient and the Occident.

At both the beginning of that gathering and at its end, all those present evinced their abundant delight, broke out into jubilant applause, and expressed their overwhelming gratitude to the Master for the teachings and other matters He had come to propound. They each had the opportunity to shake His hand, and this they did with the utmost devotion and rapture.

The Master then departed that event for a gathering of believers held at the home of Mr and Mrs Scott.[403] At the outset of that gathering, a number of the friends, among whom were both men and women, conversed with one another and recited some French translations of certain Tablets. Sometime thereafter, the Master, Who had been in another room up to that point, joined the gathering of friends. Owing to His great fatigue, the Master excused

Himself from giving one of His customarily extensive talks, and asked that some prayers be chanted instead.[404] Following this, each of the believers and seekers in attendance approached the Master to shake His hand; express to Him their sentiments of devotion, rapture, and servitude; and implore Him to confirm them in their efforts to serve.

Saturday, 22 February 1913
[Paris]

The Master's talk that morning dealt with prophecies of the past concerning the promised advent, as well as the lack of understanding on the part of the clergy and other leaders of former peoples who, having failed to comprehend the meanings and secrets enshrined in the scriptural verses of God, remained deprived of the breathings of the Holy Spirit.

That day, the subject of the Zoroastrians was mentioned before the Master. He stated:

> From the moment the Supreme Pen first wrote of the Persians, glorifying them and showing His respect for them, that people grew increasingly exalted and began to make ever greater strides. Some of them, however, remained oblivious of Bahá'u'lláh; they did not know the reason for this glorification. They were swayed, rather, by pride and heedlessness, and failed to appreciate the bounties that had been given them. As a result, they fell into tests and difficulties.

A Bahá'í by the name of Mihtar Khusraw Bimán had repeatedly sent letters to the Master, from his residence in the Indian city of Pune, entreating Him to arrange for some recordings of His voice to be produced.[405] Because these numerous letters had reached the Master, He consented to Khusraw Bimán's request on that day. The Master went to a special facility,[406] where two recordings of His most sweet utterances in Persian and Turkish were produced. They were excellent recordings; the quality of the Master's voice was very clear. He promised to return to the facility another day to have two more recordings produced. These were truly gifts that the Master bequeathed to future generations – and likewise the photographs of Him that had been taken at various occasions, among them a colour photograph and the other a profile portrait, at the request of some of the friends.

At His residence that afternoon,[407] the Master spoke to a number of believers and others about His time in Baghdad, as well as the period of the Blessed Beauty's absence from that city when He had withdrawn to Sulaymáníyyih. Afterwards,[408] the Master's neighbours, who lived one floor below Him, invited Him to their home, and He accepted their invitation. The Master then gave an account of the history of the Faith and the teachings of Bahá'u'lláh, and recounted some of the calamities and afflictions He had been made to suffer. The Master departed sometime thereafter, His respected audience having become totally enamoured of His remarkable temperament.[409]

Sunday, 23 February 1913
[Paris]

Before prayers were chanted that morning, the Master said:

> I am most unhappy in Paris. As much as I was happy in America and London, here I am just as sad. However much I wish to set myself to work, I find that it is no use.

Once prayers had been chanted and tea had been served, the Master went to the home of Mr Dreyfus;[410] he and his wife had only recently awakened.[411] They made mention of a high-ranking Persian who had been deeply gladdened by a visit he had had with the Master.[412] This gentleman had sung the Master's praises, and expressed great joy upon learning of His travels to America and Europe.

The Master then returned to His residence, where the daily gathering was convened. He gave a talk on the differences between divine philosophy and natural philosophy, the adherents of which regard their powers of perception as the only means by which things can be known. The Master observed that, in contrast to this belief, the prophets of God have ever stated that one's inability to perceive a given thing in this nether world does not necessarily indicate the nonexistence of that thing in the realm above. The warmth of the Master's lofty words roused every despondent heart in attendance to fervent excitement.[413]

When that gathering was concluded, the Master went to His room to issue Tablets in response to some important letters He had received from the Bahá'ís of America and Europe.

After lunch and a bit of rest, a number of Parisians attained the Master's presence, among them the wife and daughters of the late Gabriel Sacy.[414] Over the course of the Master's discussions, one of the daughters[415] heard Him state that the Christian priests do not understand the true meaning of the Gospel, and this remark offended her deeply.[416] In response, she said, 'That is entirely untrue. The words of the priests are the same as the words of Christ; there is no difference between them.'[417]

At that juncture, two Ottoman páshás[418] attained the presence of the Master, Who spoke to them at length[419] on His travels, as well as matters pertaining to the Cause.

When they had been dismissed, two Persian men[420] attained the Master's presence. Among the remarks which He made to these gentlemen were these:[421]

> Forty years we were held captive in the prison of 'Akká. How great the efforts we would have seen in other nations had we been free, and how significant the results thereof that would have redounded to the glory of the East!

He then stated:

> Among the things I did in recent times, in spite of the great severities which confronted me, was to forward two hundred and fifty letters I had received from the Bahá'ís of America to Sulṭán 'Abdu'l-Ḥamíd, that thereby he might see that the Bahá'ís make no

mention of politics whatsoever. All this correspondence was translated and read for the Sulṭán by his amanuensis, who added, 'This group does not at all interfere in political affairs.' The Sulṭán then thought to himself and stated, 'Let us suppose that we were to eradicate all the Bahá'ís living in Persian and Ottoman lands. What can we possibly do about the Americans? It would behoove us, then, to leave them be.' The amanuensis then remarked to the Sulṭán, 'Should any harm come to 'Abdu'l-Bahá, the Americans will grow exceedingly indignant with you.'

Ras̲h̲íd Pás̲h̲á, who was here with us only a short while ago, was once the governor of Beirut. All the inhabitants of Syria trembled with fear towards this man, who was one of Sulṭán 'Abdu'l-Ḥamíd's most trusted men. For years we were held captive by such people, until strictly through [divine] power, the Word of God was raised up, and every neck was bowed in reverence.

The gentlemen then remarked that, despite His imprisonment and confinement, the Master had made efforts that yielded such monumental results as to surely redound to the glory and prosperity of every Easterner. To this the Master said:

Even with the presence of freedom and the means of accomplishment, no effort will advance without divine confirmations. With divine confirmations, goals will be achieved even without the means of accomplishment. Through these confirmations, foes are turned into friends, and the proud and haughty are made to prostrate themselves, bowing their necks in humility.

The Master then told a story from the early days of Islam – one that illustrated the abasement and calamities which the Prophet Muhammad endured at that time:

As the Prophet Muhammad and His companions were digging a hole to defend themselves during the Battle of the Trench, the Prophet made a promise to those alongside Him that Islam would prevail over the Persians and the Romans. This prompted some of the *munáfiqín** in His company to say to one another, 'Muhammad has promised us that we will be nourished by the treasuries of Khusraw and Caesar, even as our fear prevents us from leaving this trench!' In short, they would scorn the promise of the Prophet. Yet because the religion of Islam was aided with divine confirmations, those same *munáfiqín* ultimately cried out these words at the moments of Islam's victories: 'This is what God and His Prophet had promised us!'

Monday, 24 February 1913
[Paris]

Before that day's gathering was convened, the Master spoke of the worthlessness and ephemerality of worldly affairs, which He contrasted with the grandeur of the eternal dominion and the sovereign majesty of God. A large crowd had already gathered, and some of those present expressed their desire to have a private audience with the Master. These individuals had the privilege of visiting the Master in His room, where they were honoured with hearing more of His soul-stirring utterances.

As part of the talk He gave to the public gathering that day, the Master observed that the measure of a person's belief has historically been reflected in the declaration of their faith, but stated that, in this most mighty Cause, a person's faith must be demonstrated through goodly deeds and a seemly character.[422]

When that gathering was concluded, yet another group of people requested to have a private audience with the Master in His room. These individuals listened to His blessed utterances and responses to their questions, which captivated their attention and filled them with gratitude.

That afternoon, some respected persons of Persian and Ottoman extraction, who were not Bahá'ís, attained the Master's

* A historical group, often referred to as 'the hypocrites' – outwardly Muslim but inwardly opposed to the religion – who were condemned repeatedly in the Qur'án for their duplicity.

presence.[423] They extended their utmost courtesy and reverence to Him, and were addressed with His gracious and bountiful words. With these individuals the Master discussed the blessed teachings, and to them He imparted His tender counsels. With perfect humility, they heaped their benedictions upon the Master and sang His praises. It was a remarkably delightful thing to witness the meeting which the Master had with those esteemed persons – to see their necks bowed in humility before Him, and their hearts captivated by His presence – for most of them belonged to that class of people who, with exceeding pomp and vanity, had once persecuted the Bahá'ís in their realms and took pride in this oppression. It was this show of reverence that prompted the Master to say repeatedly:

> The wisdom of my sojourn here in Paris, as well as the results it will yield, consist in the admonitions I have imparted to the people of the East, and the awareness I have instilled in the Persians – and this to a degree greater than has been achieved with the inhabitants of Paris themselves!

That evening,[424] a grand gathering was held at the home of Mr and Mrs Scott. As a large number of seekers were in attendance, the talk the Master gave on that occasion dealt with the steadfastness of the believers, in particular that of the martyrs of the Cause.[425] He discussed the sacrifices they had arisen to make, and told extensive stories about the martyrdom of Sulaymán Khán. To conclude His talk, the Master described the plight of Jesus Christ, as well as the perplexity and flight of His apostles. In this vein, the Master made special mention of Peter, who was the most steadfast of all the apostles, and yet still denied Christ three times and spoke ill of Him. So impressive was the Master's talk that His audience was rendered speechless, and they demonstrated their fervent admiration for Him once He had finished speaking.

The Master then returned to His residence, where He made these remarks:

> The people are oblivious indeed. One must take great pains to help them appreciate the degree of agitation that had seized the apostles of Christ – even Peter, who thrice disavowed Him – whereas, in this Most Great Cause, the companions and loved ones of Bahá'u'lláh remained so steadfast that they rushed forth into the arena of sacrifice with alacrity and joy. Truly, the extent of their perseverance and zeal was such as to astound the minds of humankind.

The Master then said:

> In every land and city of the West we have raised the divine call with all our might, and to vindicate the truth of the Manifestations of God we have adduced the most conclusive of proofs for the disbelievers. We have heralded the glad-tidings of the promised advent, announcing the dawning of the Sun of Truth over the horizon of the East, and promoting the unfading glory that has been vouchsafed to that land – but the Persians themselves are unaware of this supreme bestowal, and know nothing of this most great bounty.

Such were the remarks that the Master would make time and again with the utmost power and force.

Tuesday, 25 February 1913
[Paris]

As mention of Manúchihr Khán,[426] the Mu'tamidu'd-Dawlih, had been made, the Master began to relate accounts of the sense of justice, the capability, and the pure intentions he demonstrated during his tenure as governor of Isfahan:[427]

> I am filled with happiness at the thought and mention of such blessed souls as him. Whenever I hear a reference to him – or to Mírzá Abu'l-Qásim, the Qá'im-Maqám – it stirs me to my very core.
>
> At a meeting with Manúchihr Khán, this question was posed

to the Báb: 'Was the Qur'án intended only for those who were present at the time of its revelation, or was it addressed also to those who were absent?' The Báb responded, 'There is no distinction between present and absent in the estimation of God.' At that moment, the son of Ḥájí Muḥammad-Ibráhím Kalbásí* declared, 'My late father has not said any such thing in his treatise!' After considering this man's remark, along with the unfairness of the other mullás more generally, and comparing it with the decisive answer the Báb had given, Manú<u>ch</u>ihr <u>Kh</u>án underwent a transformation and pledged his allegiance to the Báb at once. Consider how fortunate was the life he lived as a result of his justice and fairness, and how doomed were the fates of those who practised tyranny and oppression. How high was his rank, and how low the estates of Mírzá Áqá <u>Kh</u>án and Mírzá Taqí <u>Kh</u>án!†

The Master then said:

I strove to the utmost so that Mírzá 'Alí-Aṣ<u>gh</u>ar <u>Kh</u>án, the Amínu's-Sulṭán,‡ might be aided, but he paid no heed. In the days when Mullá 'Alí-Akbar§ and Ḥájí Amín were imprisoned, the Amínu's-Sulṭán spoke of them favourably; as a result, the Blessed Beauty said [to me]: 'Send a letter to him.' Accordingly, I wrote the Amínu's-Sulṭán to the following effect: 'Every edifice shall ultimately fall into ruin, except for service to the threshold of God. Render service, then, to the court of God, that you may find the path to His threshold.'

As Náṣiri'd-Dín <u>Sh</u>áh had removed the Amínu's-Sulṭán from office by that point, I dispatched Jamál Effendí¶ to travel from

---

* The chief of the 'ulamás of Isfahan. It is mentioned in Sohrab's diary, but not Zarqání's account, that he was the one who had asked the question about the intended audience of the Qur'án.

† Mírzá Áqá <u>Kh</u>án Núrí and Mírzá Taqí <u>Kh</u>án, the latter more commonly known by his title of Amír Kabír, were both prime ministers of Persia.

‡ The prime minister of Persia at the time of this anecdote. For more on this episode, see Taherzadeh, *Revelation*, vol. 4, pp. 185–8.

§ Ḥájí Á<u>kh</u>und.

¶ This is a reference to Jamál Burújirdí (discussed in endnote 374), not Sulaymán <u>Kh</u>án Tunukábuní, who also happened to have been known as

> 'Akká to Qum to give him this letter, in which I assured him that he would be aided and confirmed. The Amínu's-Sulṭán received this letter with the utmost respect and even kissed it. Yet when he returned to Tehran and regained the premiership, on the one hand his affinity for the Bahá'ís was chilled by that old hyena,* and on the other he himself waxed proud and heedless with the passage of time. As a result, divine confirmations were withheld from him and grievous dangers befell him.

Among the remarks the Master made in the talk He gave to the public gathering that morning[428] were these:

> Nothing but the Cause of God is worthy of your attachment. All affairs but those which pertain to God are fleeting and undeserving of mention.

That day, the Master repeatedly encouraged the Bahá'ís, in particular Miss Sanderson, to teach the Cause, exhorting them with these words:

> Speak at the gatherings! Be as a flame of fire and a brilliant star; thereby you shall illumine this city. I work day and night to help you spread your wings, that you might help others to progress, and guide them to promulgate the Cause in turn. Otherwise, should a person not be aided and confirmed in the Cause of God, he will bear no fruit, and his life shall have failed to make its mark. Every lamp will ultimately be extinguished, and every melody is destined to be forgotten.

That afternoon, the Master visited the residences of some dignitaries from the East, to whom He related extensive accounts of the supreme confirmations vouchsafed to the Cause of God, as well as examples of humanity's haughtiness and heedlessness.

Jamál Effendí and whom Bahá'u'lláh sent to teach the Faith in India (see Balyuzi, *Eminent Bahá'ís*, pp. 116–128).

* Again, Jamál Burújirdí.

Wednesday, 26 February 1913
[Paris]

The Master caught such a severe cold that He did not come out of His room that day. As a result, His would-be visitors were deprived of the bounty of His presence, and this saddened them very much. No one attained His presence except for a few particularly important individuals, among them a certain leader of the clergy.[429] This gentleman entered the Master's room, and despite His illness, the Master spoke at length to this clergyman about kindness towards all men, universal peace, and the unity of all humanity:[430]

> The Will of God is that these ideals should be promoted. It is certain that anyone who arises to promote them shall be aided, but a spiritual power is needed to succeed in this task. Without the aid of such a subduing power, these ideals can never be promoted as they must. Indeed, there are many who think along such lines, and are yet powerless to act upon their goals. Let us suppose there are some who can distinguish between those deeds which are good and those which are bad. This knowledge notwithstanding, when the time comes to act, they are dominated by self and passion.
>
> At a time when a certain convention had been held at The Hague, and a great number of individuals had assembled to represent various governments and peoples and deliver addresses on universal peace, I wrote a letter to the Bahá'ís of Persia to tell them that the actions of these statesmen resembled those of wine-sellers who hold a gathering devoted to the prohibition of wine, wherein they engage in extensive discussion on the harmful effects of that substance, only to continue selling it, just as they had before, once they depart the gathering.

In response, the aforementioned clergyman remarked, 'The matter is as You say. Here, too, there are a great many people who are inclined to peace and unity, but few are willing to act or have the power to work towards such ideals.'

That day marked the beginning of the Master's illness. His

cold, along with a fever and a cough He had developed, grew worse over the succeeding days.

Thursday, 27 February 1913
[Paris]

The Master's cold had grown more severe, and His fever and cough had worsened. By that point, His voice was so hoarse that He really could not speak. He remained in His bed, and a number of respected people from Europe, America, and Asia who had come to visit Him entered His room and attained His presence, where they remained for a few minutes and received the outpourings of His grace.[431]

Despite His own poor health, the Master turned His attention to the care and treatment of His daughter, Rúḥá Khánum.[432] In response to some letters she had sent, the Master sent a telegram to His son-in-law, Áqá Mírzá Jalál, with the following message:[433]

> Bring Rúḥá and Sikkínih Sulṭán[434] along with you at once.

However much the Master's servants and friends implored Him for permission to summon a physician to treat Him, He refused despite the severity of His weakness and illness. He took only a bit of castor oil and said:

> A cold must be left to run its course; hasty attempts to treat it will just make it worse.

He had only a little *áb-gúsht* for dinner that night.

Friday, 28 February 1913
[Paris]

The Master's condition was essentially the same as before, and His throat was also very sore.[435] Yet in spite of His state, He spent most of the day speaking with and giving counsels to the believers and servants from His bed.[436] Among the remarks He made were these:

> We are in Paris at present, engaged in the remembrance of God. At a time when all are preoccupied with material affairs and in pursuit of political motives, we repose beneath the sheltering shade of the Blessed Beauty.

He likewise said:

> When the Apostles of Christ embraced His Cause, this was not seen as a significant development at the time. The people would scorn them, wondering aloud what station or worth a mere fisherman could possibly possess. In sum, they were the objects of ridicule and derisive laughter. Yet, with time, those same people came to recognize just how important the Apostles were. In our case, too, the significance will eventually become known, and people will long for every moment of these days.
>
> To outward seeming, Abú Dhar Ghaffárí was but a humble shepherd, and Abú Ayyúb Anṣárí likewise a man of low rank. Yet because they were among the companions of the Prophet Muhammad, their descendants take great pride in their lineage to this day. The Aws and the Khaḍraj were two tribes from among the Prophet's companions; the one accompanied Him on His emigration from Mecca to Medina, while the other were themselves the inhabitants of Medina. At that time, the station and worth of these two tribes were entirely unknown; indeed, they were the objects of ridicule, and if anyone had told them that after a thousand years their descendants would revere them, they would have refused to believe it – yet this is precisely what happened.
>
> You must, therefore, be vigilant. You must be alert. You must busy yourselves with mention of the Blessed Beauty, and be glad that you dwell beneath His shade. You must claim your portion from the kingdom of His grace. Every eye is blind, and every ear is deaf – but praised be God, for you have embraced His Cause and are firm in His Covenant. You must show abundant gratitude at every minute for this bounty – that such inestimable favours have been vouchsafed to you, every one of which deserves a thousand thanks on your part.

For His food that day, the Master had only a bit of soup, and He slept very little at night over the course of His illness.

Saturday, 1 March 1913
[Paris]

The Master was feeling better. He had regained some of His strength; He coughed less frequently, and was not as fatigued as He had been before. The hearts of His visitors were cheered by this improvement in His health, and their eyes illumined with the light of His presence. One by one and two by two, people entered His room and attained His presence – and this continued until the afternoon, when the Master went to the drawing room to sit for a while.[437]

As part of the Master's remarks that day, He discussed the reconciliation of spiritual matters with scientific and rational principles, stating that the duty of religious leaders is to promote matters of spirituality, not interfere in political affairs:

> When we consider the history of the people and government of France, it becomes clear that the reason for their irreligion, as well as their reluctance towards matters of spirituality, stems from the blind imitation of those religious leaders of the past who promoted, in the name of religion, all sorts of vain imaginings that were contrary to science and reason. As a result of their actions, the people developed an aversion to religion. Similarly, their meddling in political affairs resulted in their own abasement and degradation, for the more the priests opposed and interfered in matters of state, the more resentful the government and masses alike became of religion altogether – and this resentment eventually grew so profound that all those priests were cast out from the seat of government in such a manner as to utterly humiliate and bewilder them. Thereafter, religion itself was pronounced as contrary to the consolidation of government and state, and at odds with science and reason. Even now, these sentiments of opposition have continued to increase with every passing day, such that the very mention of God in political gatherings is enough to elicit ridicule and scorn. The reason for this

attitude must be traced only to the vain imaginings propagated by the leaders of religion, as well as their interference in political affairs. Their vain imaginings, their ulterior motives, led the people to remain unaware of the truth of divine religion, and ultimately drove them away from it. These people have failed to realize that divine religion is totally opposed to such vain imaginings and blind imitation, and that, in every age, God's religion has been founded upon the advancement of nations and the progress of peoples. Even those secondary teachings which in this day and age seem inappropriate to us were perfectly suited to their own time. It is the changing of these secondary teachings, with the passage of time and in accordance with the circumstances of each era, that conduces to the security and prosperity of all humankind.

Sunday, 2 March 1913
[Paris]

As a large crowd had gathered at the Master's residence that morning, and they had all expressed their intense desire to see Him, He came out of His room and gave a talk on the baseness and heedlessness of the animal world, the worthlessness of the physical body, and the extraordinary power of humanity.[438] The sweetness of the Master's words, as well as the joyfulness of His most pure heart, roused all those in attendance to fervent excitement.

That day, a number of the German Bahá'ís – Mr [Wilhelm] Herrigel and his wife [Marie Herrigel], Mrs [Annemarie] Schweizer, and Miss Anna Köstlin – had come from Stuttgart to see the Master, to Whom they conveyed, ardently and repeatedly, the wish of the German Bahá'ís that He might visit the cities of Germany. The Master showed the utmost tenderness and generosity to these German visitors.[439]

In those days, the Master's illness prevented him from attending outside gatherings for a number of weeks – even the weekly gatherings that were held at the residence of Mr and Mrs Dreyfus-Barney, and also at the home of Mr and Mrs Scott. Yet in spite of His condition, the Master continued to create souls anew, praising the friends for having accompanied Mr and Mrs Dreyfus-Barney to speak on religious subjects at various gatherings.

The Master's health improved that day, but His cold had not yet run its full course. He still had a fever and was unable to sleep at night, making Him very weak and tired as a result.

Monday, 3 March 1913
[Paris]

That morning, once He had had some tea after prayers were chanted, the Master remarked on the calamities perpetrated by the Azalís, and gave the account of a Persian philosopher who, while in Baghdad, renounced the Cause of God entirely as a result of certain things that Mírzá Yaḥyá had said and done. The Master remarked also on calamities that had resulted from the conduct of the Covenant-breakers:

> They have melted my bones. I treated them with exceeding kindness and forbearance; even when they took two coffers containing the writings of Bahá'u'lláh which had been entrusted to me, I still did not wish to embarrass them by mentioning the matter, hoping that they would come to their senses and return what they had taken. In spite of these trials and tribulations, I arose alone and unaided; I hoisted the banner of the Cause, and promulgated the Word of God to the East and the West. This I have done to the present day, in which every neck is bowed in reverence. Even the people of prominence all throughout the world, though they are not Bahá'ís themselves, nonetheless show humility before the Faith. Indeed, should the renown of this Cause spread just a bit more, it will suffice. But God forbid that problems should arise! God forbid that a blow should be dealt! God forbid, God forbid, God forbid!

The Master then said:

> A respected person[440] once wrote me the following:

> Although I am a Muslim, I love to be of service to the Bahá'ís. It is not fear which motivates me to say that I am not a Bahá'í, for in this day the Bahá'ís have nothing to fear. On the contrary, the Bahá'ís are beloved everywhere – this in stark contrast to the Muslims, who are largely regarded with contempt and condescension. The intent of my words, then, is to make it clear that my service to this Cause is rendered sincerely and from the bottom of my heart.

The Master then made mention of respected persons who had attained His presence in Paris and London:

> In no other age has the Cause of God manifested such greatness at its outset as it has in this one. Much to the contrary, it was reviled, and rather than humble themselves before it, such eminent souls as those would wax proud in its presence, and condemn as ignoble the companions of the Manifestation in every age. How abundant, then, must be the thanks we render the Blessed Beauty for His bounties, without which we would be absolutely nothing.

A number of Easterners had attained the Master's presence that afternoon. As mention had been made of certain upheavals in the Ottoman territories, the Master said:

> I had brought these very matters to the attention of Sulṭán 'Abdu'l-Ḥamíd forty years ago, but alas for him, he failed to heed my words. He occupied himself with his own pursuits, and this has resulted in the state of affairs you see today.

The Master was very sick and weak that day – and to compound His illness, His heart had been made heavy by the lack of spirituality He had theretofore seen from the people of Paris.

Tuesday, 4 March 1913
[Paris]

That morning, the Master spoke of the Conference of Badasht, as well as the grievous tests which attended that gathering, from which 'all but a few of the early believers fled'.[441]

A crowd of people had gathered that day to attain the Master's presence; their hearts were filled with ecstasy as they each made their request to see Him, and He eventually joined the gathering.[442] He gave to this audience a brief talk on the first and second trumpet blasts mentioned in the Qur'án,[443] and also the subject of spiritual life.[444] He then rose and, as on other days when that gathering was concluded, people of every stripe went to His room to attain His presence. Among the Master's visitors on that occasion were a number of illustrious Easterners, who bowed their necks in reverence before Him, and departed His presence with enraptured hearts when they had been dismissed.

As the afternoon approached, the Master began to write a number of Tablets, one of them in response to an article written by Professor Cheyne. As the Master was composing this particular Tablet, He made repeated mention of the Professor's writings in contrast to those of his historical counterparts:

> In previous dispensations, such people felt that they had no need for spiritual teachings, and they would condemn the companions of their respective Manifestations with the most scathing of words. Some would say, 'We see in Thee[*] but a man like ourselves; and we see not any who have followed Thee except our meanest ones of hasty judgment';[†] others would say, 'He is certainly a lunatic';[‡] and likewise it is said, 'When they see Thee, they do but take Thee in mockery.'[§] Yet now such people openly praise the Manifestation of their day. This matter will acquire great importance in the future. For instance, the writings of Professor Cheyne will be

* Muhammad.
† Qur'án 11:27.
‡ Qur'án 68:51.
§ Qur'án 25:41.

weighed against the writings of his peers from former times, and the greatness of this Cause will then become known.

What follows is the text of Professor Cheyne's article as it was published in *The Christian Commonwealth* (London) on 29 January 1913,[445] as well as a Tablet of the Master to Professor Cheyne in response to the publication of his article, with the hope that these will add to the insight and vigilance of the readers.

THE UNION OF RELIGIONS

29 January 1913
Published in *The Christian Commonwealth* (London), pp. 324–325

Is it possible that there should be a union of religions? An increasing number of persons would answer in the affirmative, because ideally the union of religions exists already. Religion is not of earthly, but of heavenly origin; it is not a branch of magic, not a department of State policy, but a revelation. Now revelation is worldwide; there is probably no people in which the light of sympathetic study does not disclose signs of contact between the human and the divine. More especially is revelation a characteristic of the great religions – those which have had the advantage of a rich and varied development. Jews would have no right to place their prophetic revealer (MOSES, or those unknown personages for whom MOSES may stand) above the prophetic revealer or revealers of the Zoroastrians nor are Mohammedans justified in promoting their prophet MOHAMMED to a place above JESUS, the revealer worshipped by the Christians.

This appears a favourable time for asking English Christians to reconsider their attitude towards Eastern religions, because of the visit of the leader of the Bahai movement, ABDUL BABA [sic] ('Servant of the All-Glorious'), who is conspicuous for his avoidance of the errors into which so many leaders have fallen. Of greater or lesser rank he says nothing; each prophet must be studied with reference to his period and surroundings. That his own father stands for him in the foreground becomes natural and right as soon as we recognise that BAHA'O'LLAH has a special mission to this age, and acknowledge the transcendent beauty and grandeur of his character. There have been many who have set a noble moral example, but there are elements in BAHA'O'LLAH's inner life and consciousness for which the biographer would find it difficult to produce a parallel.

Space forbids us to dilate upon the singular phenomena of the lives of this father and this son. It is only necessary to add that writers in the newspapers have done what in them lay to make known ABDUL BAHA's deep love for all his fellow-men. His love of GOD is a secret between him and EL-ABHA ('the Most Glorious One'). Nor must we enter into details respecting ABDUL BAHA's teaching. He is doubtless not original; he claims only to be an interpreter of his father's written revelations. These are in a high degree adapted to the wants of the present age. But the central truths are those of Judaism and Christianity – the love of GOD and the love of man.

ABDUL BABA [sic] is not a Mohammedan, and it is a mistake to describe Bahaism as a Mohammedan sect. But there is no reason why a really broad-minded Mohammedan should not be a Bahai, or, for that matter, why a broad-minded Christian or Jew or Zoroastrian should not enter the community. Just as the moulders of the doctrine gather pearls of truth in all seas, so neophytes of the community may adhere with affection to the church, synagogue, or sect to which they owe their spiritual birth. The Bahai community is really not so much a church as a fighting religious order, whose members are, to adopt the beautiful phrase of HEINRICH HEINE, *Ritter des Theologengeist.*[446]

Bahais are not subject to the decrees of any Council or Pope; both BAHA'O'LLAH and ABDUL BAHA have had to make pronouncements on difficult points which involve disputable matters of historical criticism and Biblical exegesis. Those of us who have spent life and energy in the battle for freedom of inquiry are not likely to change even for the sake of a new spiritual power. There is no ground for supposing that in this new Catholic Church any real difficulty from the presence of free inquirers will arise. There will, however, always be differences between North and South, East and West.

T. K. CHEYNE

And here is the Tablet which the Master wrote in honour of Professor Cheyne:

He is God

O renowned and respected personage! Though to outward seeming it appears we are far removed from one another, in reality we are always together, ever present as each other's companions in both heart and soul. I shall never forget the kindness and gracious hospitality you showed me on that blessed day. I am grateful to you indeed, and most satisfied with your efforts – in particular with that fair and truth-propounding article of yours, published in *The Christian Commonwealth*. It can honestly be said that, to this day, no one has written an article like it, free as it is from the taints that typically defile the writings of other European authors. Never before has a writing such as this appeared in the dispensation of Bahá'u'lláh. This article will be regarded with profound significance in the centuries to come. It will be included in every text, be it a historical chronicle, or a work of literature, or a treatise on religion. It is certain, moreover, that every scholar will have a copy of this article in their home, and that your favourable mention, being the knowledgeable philosopher you are, will grace the pages of countless books and adorn the lips of a myriad people. The fame of your perfections shall spread throughout East and West generations hence, and reach the ears of both young and old alike.

I give my regards to your esteemed wife, who is the embodiment of a wholly virtuous character, and stands out as truly distinguished from her peers.

Upon you be the glory of God, the All-Glorious.

That day, a number of orientalists who had not previously met with the Master attained His presence. Though they were not

Bahá'ís, these gentlemen nonetheless showed the utmost reverence and humility before the Master, and revelled in having the privilege of visiting Him and hearing Him articulate the tenets of the Faith. They showed great gladness and mirth, particularly as they listened to the Master discuss how certain eminent philosophers regarded the lack of spiritual perception as a source of pride, notwithstanding that the absence of this perception befits the station of the animal. He observed that anything which occupies a lower rank of existence can never perceive the existence of anything higher than it, adding that this inability to perceive the existence of such things as the divine realms and spiritual degrees, far from serving as proof of their non-existence, is in fact is a deficiency and a sign of powerlessness.

Once He had departed the meeting that afternoon, the Master went on a brief excursion around the city by car and then returned to His residence.[447]

Shortly after nightfall, a gathering of Bahá'ís convened at the home of Mr and Mrs Scott. The Master instructed all His attendants to go to the gathering, stating that, 'I myself cannot attend on account of my illness and weakness.'

Wednesday, 5 March 1913
[Paris]

A number of Bahá'ís from Germany – including Miss [Alma] Knobloch, who had taught the Faith to these Germans and had, at the Master's instruction, departed America for Stuttgart with Dr Fisher to teach the Cause there – recently attained the Master's presence.[448] To these visitors He extended His loving-kindness and commendation. Moreover, He joked with Miss Knobloch repeatedly. Here is one of the remarks which the Master made to her:

> How is it that a young lady such as yourself, with your small size, could have possibly given birth to all your tall boys and girls, with their elegant physiques and graceful statures?[449]

In response, Miss Knobloch said:

> It was possible through divine confirmations and bounties, and also the extraordinary power of the Abhá Kingdom. I take pride in my spiritual children, who confer upon me such honour as will persist throughout all the worlds of God.

Among the remarks which the Master made to the German Bahá'ís were these:[450]

> So great is my love for the Bahá'ís of Germany that if even a single flame of the fire of this love were to reach them, it would suffice to wholly consume them.

He continued:

> Now is the time to build, and in this foundation we are building, every stone shall be put to some use. You friends in Germany must serve as the cornerstone, and announce to others the glad-tidings of the foundation on which God's Cause is based.

The Master gave a very brief talk to the public gathering that morning; He stated:[451]

> Though I cannot speak with you all for very long, yet do my heart and soul converse with you, unravelling mysteries without any need for a physical tongue.

Time and again that day, the Master extended His loving-kindness to Áqá Siyyid Aḥmad Báqiroff, who had come from Persia to Paris the previous day expressly to see the Master, and He also made inquiries to Báqiroff as to how the Ibtiháju'l-Mulk[452] and the other Bahá'ís of Rasht were faring.

That evening,[453] when a number of people who had attained His presence had been dismissed, the Master went, in spite of His infirmity, to pay a visit to the envoy of Persia. Sometime after His arrival, the Master and the envoy were joined by one of the grandees of Persia,[454] and the three of them discussed several subjects at length.

After the Master had returned to His residence, He perused a letter from that handmaid of God, Mrs Whyte, to whom He wrote the following Tablet in response:

He is God

O my respected daughter! Your letter has arrived; its contents were infused with radiant joy and laden with pleasant themes.

You had written about relations between France and Scotland. The divine power of Bahá'u'lláh shall bind together the East and the West, the North and the South, and hoist the waving banner of the unity of humanity in the midmost heart of the world.

As regards the consumption of alcohol, this has been forbidden in the Tablets of Bahá'u'lláh. It is certain that, in all the worlds, this grievous menace shall, with the aid and assistance of Bahá'u'lláh, be removed in the end.

Concerning those women who champion their rights – this, too, pertains to the teachings of Bahá'u'lláh. But rather than taking inappropriate measures, such women must secure their rights by acquiring virtues, developing their minds and souls, and seeking that power which is spiritual and divine in nature.

As for those Eastern students pursuing their education in Scotland, aid must certainly be rendered them, and the means of their comfort prepared for them; this to ease their financial burden, for the people of the East have little money.

With regard to that occasion when I entered your home and received your love and kindness, know that the account thereof shall forever adorn the pages of history and never be forgotten. Though such hospitality holds little significance for humankind at present, in the future it shall be the melody that reverberates throughout the ages and centuries to come.

Convey my Abhá greetings to your esteemed husband, Mr Whyte, and also to your respected sons and daughters. The glory of God, the All-Glorious, rest upon you.

—'Abdu'l-Bahá 'Abbás

Thursday, 6 March 1913
[Paris]

The Master's weakness and fatigue that morning stemmed chiefly from His lack of sleep. In light of His condition, He did not leave His room that day, and it was not possible for every one of His visitors to attain His presence. Exceptions were made only for those with important letters or other matters to present, and also for seekers. These individuals visited the Master in His room, and expressed their abundant gratitude as they listened to Him discuss spiritual subjects and impart heavenly counsels.

In the evening, a number of Persian and Ottoman grandees attained the Master's presence, and they each heard His concise and valuable utterances on the basis for establishing the felicity of humanity.[455] They were dismissed from His presence in turn, each expressing the utmost purity of heart and sincerity of intentions as they left.

Among the things which gladdened the Master in those days as He contended with His infirmity were the visits by Áqá Faraju'lláh Khabbáz Káshání. The remarks and poems of that sincere believer would bring a smile to the Master's face, and in His weak and weary state – suffering from a lack of sleep and assailed by countless thoughts – even a few minutes of joy and happiness did wonders for Him.[456]

Mr and Mrs Dreyfus-Barney sought the Master's permission to have a physician come and examine Him, but He refused to grant their request. Eventually, however, the Master grew so fatigued as a result of His sleeplessness that a physician did come that afternoon to see Him. To remedy His lack of sleep, the physician prescribed a sort of carrot juice, which He drank that night and then rested for a bit.

Friday, 7 March 1913
[Paris]

All were immensely delighted that morning to see that the Master's health had improved. He attended that day's gathering and gave a brief talk on divine favours, invisible realms, the lofty stations of those who have embraced the Cause, and holy realities.[457] When the gathering was concluded, a great number of people expressed their desire to have a private audience with the Master. In groups they poured into His room, where they were privileged to receive His abundant grace. Among the Master's visitors were a few Indians and one American,[458] who had recently arrived for the purpose of attaining His presence. What follows are some of the remarks which the Master made to His audience:

> Our hope is that the East and the West shall embrace one another, and that the various peoples and nations of the world shall become even as one nation and a single family. May the differences and vain imaginings that exist among us today be dispelled, and the prejudices of religion, nation, politics, and sex be entirely removed, such that all may gather beneath the shade of a single pavilion. How great is this bestowal – how supreme this bounty! I cherish the hope that, through the endeavours of sanctified souls, these divine bestowals will be obtained. You all, for your part, must make an effort, and do your utmost to attain this station. Many are the favours of God, and infinite the effusions of His grace. The acquisition of that grace, however, is conditioned on the unity of humankind. When that ideal is realized, the confirmations of God will encircle the world on all sides. Then shall the gates of paradise be flung open, and the hosts of triumph come rushing forth – every hope shall be fulfilled, and all will be surrounded by light – for this era is a new era, and this century a wondrous century.
>
> I love you all dearly. You are all even as my own children; this is the reason I wish, from the bottom of my heart, that you all may be well and happy, and it is why I hope that you all may succeed in promoting the oneness of humanity. For fifty years, Bahá'u'lláh

endured every conceivable affliction. At one time He was in prison, at another He was beneath the sword, and at yet another He was in chains and fetters. Not a day did He spend in peace, nor a night did He pass in tranquillity, all so that humankind may come together beneath the tabernacle of unity, gather at God's bounteous banquet replete with heavenly bestowals, drink from one wellspring, and repose in the shade of a single tree. This is the supreme bounty; this is the greatest glory. By this means shall humanity receive the grace of God and enter His kingdom. My hope is that you all will be graciously aided to achieve this goal.

In the afternoon, the Master repaid visits to certain dignitaries[459] – and at every moment, He had some occasion to speak extensively of the necessity of spiritual power, divine confirmations, and a heavenly character.[460] Subsequently, upon returning to His residence, the Master was overcome with profound weakness and fatigue.

He did not go that evening to the home of Mr and Mrs Dreyfus-Barney, where a gathering of believers had been convened, but He did instruct all His servants to attend, stating that, 'You must go, and there make mention of the Blessed Beauty with the utmost joy and radiance.'

Saturday, 8 March 1913
[Paris]

As the weather that morning was clear, still, and mild,[461] the Master went out for a stroll after some prayers and other verses had been chanted, and a number of believers and travellers from Persia had attained His presence. When He returned from His excursion, the Master gave the following talk to the public gathering:[462]

He is God

I wish very much to speak with you all, but I am not feeling well. Pray for my full recovery, that I may be able to converse with you at length. My powers have been exhausted in Paris, but I have persevered in spite of my infirmity, and not left the city.

I am exceedingly fond of you all. I hope that my condition improves before too long so I can speak with you extensively. Of course, there is a wisdom in this illness of mine; it is not without reason, and the wisdom thereof will become clear in the future. Otherwise, I would not have developed an illness in Paris for no reason. I have been travelling now for two and a half years, and nowhere did I fall sick but here, where I have had to extend my stay on account of my illness. Had I not fallen sick, I would not have remained in Paris for more than a month. Thus, there is a wisdom in this. I am subject to the Will of God, not the laws of nature – that nature should overpower me and reduce me to illness! No, rather it is the wisdom and Will of God that bring about whatever they ordain. This has been the case from the beginning of my life; the wisdom of whatever has happened to me has become clear with time.

When I was a child of seven in Tehran, I contracted tuberculosis and there was no hope of my recovery, but the wisdom in this eventually became clear. Had I not fallen sick, I would have been sent away to Mazandaran, yet owing to my illness, I remained in Tehran and was there while the Blessed Beauty was imprisoned; hence, I accompanied Him and His retinue to Iraq. When the time came to embark on that journey, I suddenly regained my health – this despite the fact that all the doctors had given up hope that I would recover, and everyone had said it would be impossible to cure my affliction. My meaning is that a consummate wisdom underlies everything that takes place. In this present illness of mine, too, there is a wisdom that will manifest itself, for I have ever been subjected to the Will of God, and whatever has happened has conformed to the dictates of divine wisdom. So too with this illness, one wisdom of which is that it has allowed me to meet you all. My hope is that is that this meeting may bear great fruit, and that that fruit may be made manifest.

In the afternoon, the Master read Persian translations of letters that had been sent to Him by the Bahá'ís of America and wrote responses to some of them. He spoke very fondly of Mrs [Helen] Goodall and Mrs [Ella] Cooper, and expressed His praise for the Bahá'ís of California.[463]

As a great number of people would attain His presence in those days, the Master gave talks that were appropriate to each of His audiences. At times, He discussed the prophecies concerning this momentous day and the fulfilment of the divine promises mentioned in religious scriptures; at others, occasioned by questions from His audience, He spoke of the differences between the utterances of the prophets and the sayings of the mystics. Some of the Master's remarks on the latter subject were as follows:[464]

> The Sufis believe only in God and in creation, rejecting that any third party exists between them or apart from them. They regard God even as a sea and creation as the waves of that sea. The divine Manifestations, however, speak of a third party, which consists of the Will of God and the intercession of His invisible and unfathomably sublime bounties in the world of creation.

After dismissing His audience, the Master had a brief opportunity to go on an excursion; He walked to the Eiffel Tower and went for another stroll upon reaching it.[465]

From there, the Master went to the home of Munír Pá<u>sh</u>á,[466] where He spoke so impressively on a variety of subjects that the esteemed men and women in His audience became engrossed in listening to His blessed utterances and enchanted with the divine teachings He was propounding. On numerous occasions, they expressed such sentiments as these:

> Oh, would that our compatriots had the ability to attain this exalted Presence and hear His most sweet statements! Thereby would everlasting glory and salvation be theirs.

This effusive praise came especially from the respected Munír Pá<u>sh</u>á, who implored the Master for special confirmations to be vouchsafed to him.[467]

Sunday, 9 March 1913
[Paris]

The Master devoted most of His addresses to the public gathering that morning to prayers for the people of Paris and the nation of France, expressing His hope that, through the grace of the divine spirit, that 'delicate body' might gain eternal life, and that that 'clear lamp' might shine the light of divine guidance and attain to everlasting joy.[468] These sentiments from the Master were prompted by the profound despondency He felt at the sight of the preoccupations and defilements of the people of Paris; time and again He would make these remarks:

> The results from our sojourn here will stem from our meeting and guiding those esteemed denizens of this city who hail from other countries and belong to other ethnicities.

In brief, after that gathering, the Master summoned a group of believers to His room and addressed them with these blessed words:

> He is God
>
> I wish to leave Paris and leave you as my memento in this city. Strive day and night to illumine this city and make its people heavenly, and know that, if you arise as you should, confirmations will reach you even as the waves of the sea.
>
> I wish, moreover, that there may be abundant love among you all. May you become intimate companions with one another, and gather together at your homes and also the home of this daughter of mine (Miss Sanderson). May you all hold pleasant conversations with each other, guide the people, and serve as the means through which the hearts are strengthened. Therein lies imperishable glory; therein lie eternal life and everlasting happiness.

Afterwards, two Persians who had recently arrived requested to have a private audience with the Master.[469] At the beginning of their visit, the Master addressed them with these words:

> The people of Paris are oblivious indeed; a grievous danger and dire affliction await them as a result.

Following this, some Jewish students of Persian extraction attained the presence of the Master, Who greatly encouraged them to both study academic disciplines and cultivate heavenly characters.

Then, immediately after lunch, a number of respected Persians, along with Ḥájí Khalílu'lláh Khán Rashtí, all attained the Master's presence. On account of this meeting, the Master did not rest that day. As He was engaged in conversation with this audience, Mr Browne (from Cambridge) and his wife entered the room. After requesting permission, they seated themselves and were treated most kindly by the Master. Mr Browne remarked, 'I am deeply grateful to you for sending me that blessed Book.' The Master replied:

> I wanted you to become acquainted with Bahá'u'lláh's latter Tablets and epistles. Know that, in the scriptures of every dispensation – even in the Bayán – reference is made to two trees: the tree of affirmation, which is good, and the tree of negation, which is evil. Yet Bahá'u'lláh has done away with these things. He has proclaimed:
>
>> O peoples of the world! Ye are the fruits of one tree, and the leaves of one branch.*
>>
>> Take pride not in love for yourselves but in love for your fellow-creatures.†
>>
>> It is not his to boast who loveth his country, but it is his who loveth the world.‡

* Bahá'u'lláh, *Gleanings from the Writings of Bahá'u'lláh*, CXXXII.
† idem. *Tablets of Bahá'u'lláh*, p. 138.
‡ idem. *Gleanings*, XLIII.

> O people of Bahá! Ye are the dawning-places of the love of God and the daysprings of His loving-kindness. Defile not your tongues with the cursing and reviling of any soul, and guard your eyes against that which is not seemly. Set forth that which ye possess. If it be favourably received, your end is attained; if not, to protest is vain. Leave that soul to himself and turn unto the Lord, the Protector, the Self-Subsisting. Be not the cause of grief, much less of discord and strife.*

> The fundamental purpose animating the Faith of God and His Religion is to safeguard the interests and promote the unity of the human race, and to foster the spirit of love and fellowship amongst men. Suffer it not to become a source of dissension and discord . . .†

> If religion be the cause of disunity, then irreligion is surely to be preferred, for the potential to stir up dissension and strife exists in all our natures, and we have no need of yet another vehicle for their expression.‡

In brief, the Master spoke to these divine verses and teachings with such majesty and power as to transform His audience, so profoundly impressing some of those in attendance that they had practically become intoxicated by His utterance.

As Mrs Browne had a prior engagement, she left with Mrs Dreyfus-Barney. Mr Browne, however – along with Mr Dreyfus – met with the Master for more than an hour,[470] and they both showed great delight as they listened to Him discuss the effects and fruits of the advent of the Manifestations of God and their

---

* idem. *Tablets of Bahá'u'lláh*, p. 27.

† idem. *Gleanings*, CX.

‡ The wording of this passage from 'Abdu'l-Bahá up to 'is surely to be preferred' comes from *Bahíyyih Khánum, the Greatest Holy Leaf: A Compilation from Bahá'í Sacred Texts and Writings of the Guardian of the Faith and Bahíyyih Khánum's Own Letters*, p. 203. The remainder is a provisional rendering by the present translator approved at the Bahá'í World Centre for publication in this volume.

prodigious aims. Over the course of this conversation, the Master had occasion to speak briefly on the Universal House of Justice and the Lesser Peace. With regard to the latter, He remarked that it would certainly come to pass, and that it will be close at hand when the peoples of the world have been provoked to cry out, unable to suffer the prohibitive cost of war any longer. It is then, the Master observed, that the rulers of the earth will summon the people to peace, noting that anything which reaches a degree of extremity must ultimately return to a lower state. He then spoke extensively of the French and German military forces, showing such forbearing kindness to Mr Browne that, as he departed the Master's presence, he expressed the utmost contrition and gratitude for the favour He had shown him. Mr Browne's displays of deference extended even to the Master's attendants. They, however, were aware that people like Mr Browne have no interest at all in matters of religion – and this was a point they had discussed among themselves – since, during his second visit with the Master in London, Mr Browne had repeatedly remarked that the people of this age, particularly in that corner of the world, were entirely uninterested in religion. These attendants maintained that Mr Browne's own attitude towards religion could be inferred from his remark – namely, that he professed no belief in any creed whatsoever, unless to do so would be politically expedient for him and afford him the chance to promote, whether in speech or in writing, his own racialist and nationalistic ideas. The attendants were of the opinion that, in making their remarks and producing their publications, Mr Browne and his peers were in fact furthering their own agenda while claiming complete objectivity.

So profoundly affected were some of those present at the beginning of the Master's conversation with Mr Browne that most of them let out cries of astonishment, saying:

> No fair-minded soul can deny these divine teachings or this blessed Personage. In every country they will be accepted and captivate the hearts of humanity.

What can I possibly say that might illustrate how the power and influence of God's Covenant pulsated like throbbing arteries in their bodies and souls, or the way in which their hearts were revolutionized and their minds bewildered?

As Mr Browne was being dismissed, the Master instructed that a pamphlet consisting of His talks, which included remarks on the immortality of the human soul, be given to him.[471] When he had left, others likewise entered the Master's room and attained His presence in a state of enthralled devotion. There they listened to Him speak at length on such matters as the divine teachings, and expressed their heartfelt praise and gratitude.

The Master was very tired that night; He said:

> We have now been travelling for two and a half years. That is enough! Let us go and retire to some corner in Haifa or ʻAkká!

Monday, 10 March 1913
[Paris]

The Master gave this most impressive talk to the public gathering that morning:[472]

He is God

> I am feeling a bit better today. For the past few days, I have had to keep my discussions with you all very brief, as it was difficult for me to converse. Today, however, my health has improved, and I have come to speak with you, awaken you, and announce to you the glad tidings, that you may appreciate the significance of the day in which you are living. You, of course, have read in the holy scriptures that a day will come that shall be known as the King of Days – a day when the Lord of Hosts will descend from the heavens; a day when all the world will gather together beneath the shade of the divine Word; a day when God will reign as the true Lord of the world; a day when the East and the West will be united; a day when every trace of war and strife will have

> vanished, and all the peoples will have established peace among themselves. This is none other than that blessed day, and this age the very same as that momentous age. It is the beginning of the appearance of light, even as the light that shines from the dawning sun . . .

The Master's talk roused the already-excited crowd to even greater enthusiasm, and stirred them to a remarkable degree of awareness and vigilance.

At that time, the Master had intended to return to the East, but the entreaties of the German Bahá'ís for Him to visit Stuttgart, along with other factors, resulted in the postponement of these plans. Consequently, that afternoon, the Master instructed that the following message be written to Ḥájí Mírzá Ḥaydar-'Alí, who was then in the Holy Land:

> We were about to depart for the Holy Land, but have had to delay that journey as a result of these obstacles. God willing, after a brief sojourn in Germany, we will quickly set off for Port Said and then the Holy Land.

On that day, those two honourable souls, Áqá Mírzá Áqá Khán Qá'im-Maqámí and Áqá Mírzá Faraju'lláh Khabbáz, departed France for Persia. When they had left, the Master made repeated mention of their services and steadfastness. The Master would indeed become conspicuously happy whenever He mentioned the staunchly devoted Bahá'ís of Persia.

Tuesday, 11 March 1913
[Paris]

Among the letters from the Bahá'ís of Persia which the Master perused that day was one from Mírzá 'Alí-Akbar Khán, the Muḥibbu's-Sulṭán, with regard to whom the Master repeatedly remarked:

> He has succeeded and is aided in serving the Cause of God and diffusing the divine fragrances. I beseech the favours of the Blessed Beauty to assist and protect him.

The Master's talk to the gathering that day[473] dealt with the differences between material education and spiritual education, as well as the need for a mystic protector to be present and true bonds to be established among the hearts of all humanity.

Both before the gathering and afterwards, a great many people expressed their wish to have an audience with the Master. One by one and two by two, accompanied by an interpreter, they entered the Master's room, where each and every one of them listened to Him speak about spiritual subjects, the divine teachings, and the factors that have so conduced to the ignorance and deprivation of former generations as to have resulted in their abasement and agitation. As each member of the Master's audience was dismissed, they departed His room in a state of complete ecstasy and rapture.

In the afternoon, the Master sent a telegram to various corners of the East and the West alike to inform the friends that He was in high spirits and good health.[474]

After some other people had attained His presence, the Master asked for a car to take Him to the residences of a number of illustrious individuals.[475] Dr Muḥammad Khán was the only one of the Master's attendants who accompanied Him in His retinue on that occasion.

Shortly after nightfall,[476] the Master returned weak and weary to His residence.

Wednesday, 12 March 1913
[Paris]

While having tea after some prayers had been chanted, the Master discussed the irreligion of the people of Paris:[477]

> Their contempt for religion and spirituality stems from the meddling of the Catholic clergy in political affairs. On the one hand,

> the clergy were opposed to constitutionalism and republicanism, and on the other, they promoted blindly imitative customs and beliefs that were contrary to science and reason. Consequently, the government arose in vehement opposition to them, and declared their hatred for and weariness of religion altogether, deigning to make mention of the subject only to scorn and ridicule it. This state of affairs can be attributed only to the mistakes made by the leaders of religion, who rather than serve as channels to promote the tenets of the religion of God, instead became the cause of hatred and ruin. As a result, the people of this country have strayed entirely from the path of moderation, or fallen victim to the blind imitations and vain imaginings propounded by religious leaders, or clung to the motives of the materialists and arisen in hostility against the people of religion.

This irreligious state of the Parisians had deeply saddened the Master. Furthermore, He contended with great weakness and hardship during those few weeks due to His intense fever and cold. But the Master was in very good health that day, and since it was nearly time for Him and His retinue to depart Paris, His talk to the gathering that day was focused on encouraging the believers to exalt the Word of God and promote His Cause, that in striving to diffuse the fragrances of God, they may become the clear signs of His Covenant.

In the afternoon, the Master instructed, at the request of some of the friends, that treatises on the Faith be translated into French, published, and disseminated.

Afterwards, Mr Dreyfus brought a well-known physician to examine and treat the Master.[478] Among the remarks that the Master made to this physician were the following:

> I have no illness whatsoever. It is simply that the severe hardships I endured in prison have harmed my nerves, which have become exceedingly weak. Owing to the many preoccupations that have demanded my attention over the course of this journey, my body has grown very frail.[479]

In brief, after examining the Master, the physician wrote a prescription for some medicine, which Mr Dreyfus and Dr Muḥammad Khán fetched and offered to Him, but the Master refused to take any medicine. Time and again, He would mention simple remedies and foods, recounting this anecdote from the life of the Blessed Beauty:

> During Bahá'u'lláh's seclusion in Sulaymáníyyih, He mostly drank milk and ate bread with rice pudding; this is truly excellent sustenance.

An elaborate banquet was held by Mr and Mrs Dreyfus-Barney at a local hotel that night;[480] they had invited the Master, all His servants, and other Persian friends to attend. It was a wonderful time, and as with all the other services rendered by that couple, this banquet was most pleasing to the Master, Who was wreathed in smiles from start to finish.

Thursday, 13 March 1913
[Paris]

After tea and prayers that morning, the Master went outside, both before and after the gathering, for a stroll in the sun to the Eiffel Tower, occasionally seating Himself by parks along the way. During these excursions, the Master spoke of the many materialistic preoccupations that had captured people's attention, as well as their devotion to hedonistic pursuits.

The Master's talk to the public gathering that day dealt with the differences among the various religions and the need for the independent investigation of truth, stating that, if the peoples of the world were to abandon their blind imitations and investigate the truth for themselves, they would all become united, for blind imitations are many, but the truth – the foundation underlying all the divine religions – is one. The Master concluded that these differences, therefore, stem from blind imitation, and not from the tenets of divine religion.

In the afternoon, a number of the Eastern friends attained the presence of the Master, Who offered them such kind and tender counsels as to thoroughly gladden them.

Shortly thereafter, the Master went to the [Persian] legation,[481] and thence to the home of a distinguished Persian gentleman. Among other topics, the Master discussed the Eastern youth living in these Western countries, observing that their morals had, for the most part, been corrupted, and that this corruption had so impaired their health and retarded their condition as to prevent them from living a useful life. The Master went on to say that such people are entirely oblivious of spiritual character, which protects them, inhibits them, and keeps them vigilant, comparing them to beasts that have no one to look after them.

The Master then commented on the homes of the East. In addition to His remarks on how neatly their furnishings were arranged – as well as their spaciousness, cleanliness, and the overall pleasantness of their interiors – He also recounted the hospitable demeanour of the Easterners.

After departing that place,[482] the Master went on an excursion through some of the illuminated streets of the Bois de Boulogne,[483] and then returned to His residence.

In those days, the Master and His retinue were about to set off for Germany when the news arrived that His daughter, Rúḥá Kh́ánum, was coming from Port Said to treat her illness. As a result of this development, the Master's plans to travel to Germany were postponed.[484] Furthermore, He decided that a change of lodging was in order, as the rental period for His current residence was about to expire.

Friday, 14 March 1913
[Paris]

The Master was seated in the drawing room that morning and asked that prayers from Bahá'u'lláh be chanted. As the attendants and other friends listened to those divine verses, their hearts swelled with tender affection and their spirits brimmed with sweet ecstasy.

Afterwards, the Master stated the following in response to a question raised by one of those in attendance:[485]

> It has indeed been revealed in the wondrous verses that to engage in some occupation is equivalent to worship, but this does not mean that one should dispense with such remembrances and acts of worship as have been expressly recorded in the Holy Writ, inasmuch as acts of worship have been enjoined in the Book of God. Such acts make the hearts vigilant and the characters of humanity spiritual; they stir people's souls, dilate their breasts, manifest divine love within them, and rouse them to wholehearted reliance [upon God] and complete detachment at the heavenly threshold. Apart from this, all other thoughts shall disturb the minds and chill the hearts of humankind. This sort of talk has always existed amongst people; in every age, these exchanges have perplexed humanity and led to their disunity. The believers must always act in accordance with what has been explicitly revealed in the Holy Writ and remain united; otherwise, they could each interpret the verses to accord with their own desires, and this would conduce to discord . . .

When the crowd had assembled for the daily gathering, the Master gave a brief talk on the steadfastness of the Bahá'ís in the Cause, as well as their readiness to spread the divine fragrances.[486] As the members of the audience approached the Master with devoted humility to shake His hand, they were each dismissed in turn, and He then went to the home of Mr Dreyfus. From there, partly by car and partly on foot, He returned to His residence.

Until nightfall, despite the coming and going of those wishing to attain His presence, the Master was busily engaged in preparing mail and composing Tablets in response to the important letters of some believers.

A gathering of friends was held that night at the home of Mr and Mrs Dreyfus-Barney, but the Master did not attend.[487] He said to His attendants:

I feel very weak and fatigued, and cannot speak at the gathering. You all, however, should go there and make mention of God.

Saturday, 15 March 1913
[Paris]

Before the public gathering was held that day, a group of the friends attained the Master's presence in His room, where they listened as He addressed them with such remarks as these:[488]

True significance lies in states of spirituality. Should you all be captivated by the sweet savours of spirituality, then I shall always be with you. This is a splendid companionship – a companionship that knows no separation. You must ever strive to spread the divine fragrances; I will be with you always. The Sun is only just beginning to rise in Europe; soon will the divine light grow more intense, and then will you all behold what has come to pass.

The Master then went to the public gathering, where He gave a talk on the subject of distinction, in which He discussed the qualities that have ever distinguished the loved ones of God from their peers in the days of every divine Manifestation.

A number of letters arrived that day for the Master from Mrs [May] Maxwell and some of the American friends, who were requesting that He allow the believers to write a refutation of the futile attacks of that benighted Shu‘á‘[489] against the first volume of this chronicle, which documents the Master's sojourn in Los Angeles. In response, the Master stated:

This matter is of no importance and is unworthy of a response. It is a matter that rests on a foundation weaker than a spider's web. Of what significance is it? Attention must be devoted to spreading the divine fragrances. I have laboured for years in hopes that these people might not leave the Cause, but the more I have striven, the more brazen they have grown.

The Master then spoke at length about the extraordinary kindnesses he had shown Mírzá Badí'u'lláh:[490]

> In spite of all the love and support I gave him, Mírzá Badí'u'lláh caused a fresh adversity with every passing day. How utterly regrettable! And to make matters worse, he wrote to those outside the Cause entreating them to find some sort of occupation for him, hoping that he might be able to pursue this livelihood with the help of people like Browne.

In the afternoon, after composing some wondrous Tablets addressed to the Bahá'ís of the West, the Master went to the home of one of the grandees of the East,[491] where He related extensive historical episodes and told other stories that were laden with enlightening lessons.

As He was returning to His residence, the Master said:

> I regard the people of Paris even as bees or ants, coming and going in clusters, surging to and fro like a wave, preoccupied to the utmost. And yet, should you ask them what they are doing or why they are moving as they do, you would find that they are entirely oblivious of where they have come from and where they are destined to return, and that they cherish no desire but to eat, sleep, and indulge in the most hedonistic of pursuits.

Such were the remarks of the Master on that occasion. His words made a profound impression on those who were privileged to be in His presence, and roused them to great vigilance.

Sunday, 16 March 1913
[Paris]

That morning, Mirza Ahmad Sohrab translated and conveyed to the Master the contents of some newspapers that had been relayed to him by telegraph. The Master then said:

> The Ottomans still do not know what must be done, despite their full knowledge that their present position affords them the opportunity to embroil their opponents in conflict with one another, and prepare the means for their own security in so doing. They are like the Persians, whose affairs stand in such dire disarray that their women have desperately placed their hopes in a certain German woman, whose support they have sought even as they shut their eyes to and remain ignorant of such a Cause as this, around which the kingdoms of might and power revolve. Their situation can be attributed only to their wretchedness, as well as the fact that heavenly confirmations and success have not been granted them.

Before that day's gathering was held, the Master went outside for a stroll. When He returned, He addressed the gathering with a talk on the necessity of motion in the world of creation.[492]

In both the afternoon and the evening that day, a number of Persian grandees, including the envoy of Persia, humbly attained the Master's presence one by one.[493] They each posed their questions, and the Master would give an answer. Among the esteemed individuals who with every passing day derived ever greater benefit from the outpourings of the Master's grace, and grew increasingly vigilant with every gathering he attended, was [——].[494] As the Master was relating anecdotes from the talks He gave at various gatherings in America, as well as the lectures He delivered at the great churches and synagogues of that country, He was asked about the receptivity of the Americans to the Cause, to which He replied:

> The Americans are a satiated people who hunger – this in contrast to the Persians, who in their state of hunger and privation believe themselves to be satiated and without need.

Along those lines, the Master then gave the following explanation:

> The East has always been able, through the aid of a spiritual power, to withstand the West and ultimately prevail over them. When the companions of Christ were subjected to the torture of

the Romans, they saw themselves as powerful and victorious over the world. At that time, they suffered blows and endured adversities, yet now the leaders of Christendom have made their present glory and tranquillity the means by which to selfishly advance their own interests.

The Master then told this story:[495]

In one of the cities between Canada and California, a certain cardinal – one of the most eminent leaders of Christendom – denounced us as the enemies of Christ, and forbade the people from meeting with us.* A church had just been built in those days, and the cardinal had gone to open it with excessive pomp and pageantry. At that time, some said that the cardinal had participated in a ceremony to officially open that church. I responded in the affirmative, confirming that the public display of that cardinal was the very same as that of Christ, but I then noted some 'minor' differences between the two. Christ flung open the gates of heaven, whereas this cardinal has opened the door of an earthly church. Christ was surrounded by a large group that scorned and condemned Him as an enemy of the prophets, whereas this cardinal has gathered a great crowd of people who all revere him. Christ wore a crown, albeit one of thorns; this cardinal also wears a crown, but his is studded with gleaming gems. Christ wore clothing, though it was badly tattered; this cardinal, too, wears clothes, but his are made of silk and gold. One had a cross for His kingly seat, while the other has a golden altar and throne. One gave His life to edify humankind, while the other uses the means and lives of people to secure his own glory and comfort. Such is the difference between the display of Christ and the display of this cardinal. How minor is the difference – how minor indeed!

Then, occasioned by the mention of Ka'bu'l-Aḥbár and the blindly imitative practices of the Muslims, the Master said:

* This was probably John Murphy Farley (1842–1918).

Ka'bu'l-Aḥbár was an Israelite who lived in the time of Mu'ávíyyih and feigned belief in Islam. Whenever anything concerning historical chronicles or religious traditions and commentaries was asked of him, he would immediately fabricate some lie in response. When he was asked what the term 'Iram of the Pillars' mentioned in the Qur'án referred to,* he replied:

> This was a garden situated opposite the garden of Paradise itself and created by Shaddád.† It was a garden whose leaves, flowers, and trees were all made of emerald; whose blossoms were made of gems; whose pebbles were made of pearls; whose walls were made of gold and silver; and whose servants were this and that. When Shaddád had finished creating his garden, he decided to go there and enter it. As he was alighting from his steed by the entrance of the garden, he had not yet taken both his feet from out his stirrups when the angel of death came all of a sudden and claimed his life.

As soon as the Muslims heard this story, they documented it and deemed it a credible commentary.

Monday, 17 March 1913
[Paris]

The Master was slightly ill. He did not sleep the night before, and thus did not leave His room that day; He remained in bed and had some soup. Those who came to visit the Master and truly needed to see Him were called into His room for a few minutes at a time.[496] Among these visitors were a group of Jewish youth and also a number of Bahá'ís from Honolulu, who asked the Master to compose a Tablet for the friends in that city. The Master consented to this request; the text of the Tablet He wrote is as follows:

---

* Qur'án 89:6–14.

† Shaddád bin 'Ád.

He is God

> Humbly and ardently, I supplicate constantly the Abhá Kingdom on their behalf, praying that they may be confirmed and successful, and also steadfast in His Cause and firm in His Covenant. Should one stealthily come to your vicinity and attempt to weaken your faith in the Covenant, do not hesitate in the least. Know that such a one is a wicked soul, an exponent of Satan whose company you must certainly avoid. Whoever summons you to embrace the divine Covenant is to be reckoned with God's chosen ones, whereas he who vacillates is an enemy of the Blessed Beauty. The aim of these people is to incite dissension in the Cause of God and destroy the unity of the Bahá'í Faith as they work to further their own interests all the while.

Although the Master was not in good health that day, He felt much better in the evening once He had had some soup, after which He decided to rest.

On that day, the Master sent Mírzá 'Alí ibn Adíb to Marseilles to receive Rúḥá Khánum, who had come from the Holy Land to Paris to treat her illness.[497]

As the rental period for the Master's residence had now expired, He said, 'Gather our belongings; tomorrow, we will take them from here to the hotel.'

Tuesday, 18 March 1913

[Paris]

The Master was in very good health that day. That morning,[498] as He was having tea while seated in the main room, He spoke of the Parisians:[499]

> They are all immersed in hedonistic pursuits, and are entirely bereft of tranquillity. Some of their monks are better, at least, but this does not apply to the ones who seclude themselves in monasteries – which they enter while they are alive and leave only after

they have died, having lived undeveloped and altogether fruitless lives – but rather to the ones who serve in hospitals with all their heart and soul. I once saw one of these monks when I was walking along the slope of Mount Carmel; he was murmuring in a spirit of humble supplication as he ascended the mountain, and this made a profound impression on me. I took great pleasure as I stood in place and listened to him. The effect that purity has on us is truly remarkable.

The Master then discussed the sincerity and humility of Mírzá Abu'l-Faḍl:

> I am delighted to hear that Mírzá Abu'l-Faḍl is in good health. I would, in truth, be content to fall sick so that blessed souls like him might be protected from illness. How great was my joy when he visited me in the Holy Land! Though time and again Siyyid Mihdí Dihají[500] would mention some service he had ostensibly rendered with regard to the imprisonment of Mírzá Abu'l-Faḍl in Tehran, when this subject was raised on a certain occasion, Mírzá Abu'l-Faḍl immediately said the following with the utmost candour:
>
>> The truth is that none of us did anything worthy of mention. The real effort was made by Mullá Riḍá Yazdí, who became well-known for his consummate courage, perseverance, and sincerity, and openly discussed matters of religion with the princes of Persia. As he had gained a reputation for his honesty and truthfulness, when he stated that the Bahá'ís do not involve themselves in political affairs, his words were accepted by his audience. My companions and I, however, preferred to speak more cautiously, and saw fit to give the vicegerent the impression that Mullá Riḍá Yazdí was a Sufi or Gh́álí.* Mullá Riḍá Yazdí, for his part, would candidly say to the vicegerent, 'That which I have said is the very truth. When Mírzá

* A Ghálí (literally, 'exaggerator') is one who belongs to a Muslim sect that ascribes divine qualities to the Imáms.

> Abu'l-Faḍl and his companions gather at each other's homes, they say precisely the things I am saying.'

So great was the gladness of the Master as He spoke of the sincerity of Mírzá Abu'l-Faḍl and the steadfastness of Mullá Riḍá Yazdí that I cannot possibly describe it.[501]

In the afternoon, a number of Parisian and American Bahá'ís attained the presence of the Master, Who addressed them with these words:[502]

> Though Paris is today sunk in apathy, its soul will soon be stirred, for I have spent many a night here praying that heavenly confirmations may be granted it. I have neither slept nor enjoyed a moment's ease – all peace and tranquillity have escaped me. I have prayed constantly and fervently, and I hope, therefore, that you all will arise to exalt the Word of God, inasmuch as the hosts of divine aid and success are rushing forth and awaiting devoted reinforcements to assist them. The one who arises shall be aided to victory; the one who is detached shall be assisted.

A question was then raised as to whether one will necessarily become more spiritual if one comes to possess fewer things. The Master replied:[503]

> Detachment is not to be found in the absence of material possessions, but rather in the freedom of one's heart from attachments. While living in Tehran, one night we possessed everything imaginable, and the following morning it had all been plundered. Things came to such a pass that we lacked the most basic provisions to sustain us. I went hungry; as we did not even have bread, my mother would pour some flour into the palm of my hand, and I would eat that instead. Yet we remained happy in spite of our plight.

The Master then told this story:

There were once two friends: a wealthy detached man and a poor worldly man. At the request of the poor man, the two of them suddenly went to embark on a journey, leaving all their attachments and belongings behind. The poor man, noticing that his wealthy friend had actually abandoned all his possessions and forsaken all the trappings of his good fortune with no intention of returning, said to his friend, 'Now that we are resolved to go, wait here until I return; I have a donkey that I wish to bring along.' His wealthy friend replied, 'You are not a travelling man. You could not forgo just one donkey, yet I have renounced all my wealth and power. I have come here at your prompting with no thought of returning, despite the fact that I had everything in my possession, but you are already anxious to return, notwithstanding that you have only a mere donkey to your name.' Detachment, then, consists in the freedom of the heart from attachments, and not in the lack of possessions. When the heart is freed from attachments and kindled with the fire of the love of God, the things of this world will become the means of promoting one's spiritual perfections; otherwise, one's heart would be immersed in oceans of defilement, completely penniless though one be.

The talk the Master gave to the public gathering that day dealt with 'the lesser world' and 'the greater world'.[504]

That evening, Rúḥá Khánum and her husband, Áqá Mírzá Jalál – along with Munírih Khánum's niece, the wife of Áqá Mírzá Ḥusayn Ḥájí – arrived safely and lodged at the home of Miss Sanderson. The Master and His attendants moved their belongings to the Pension hotel on Lauriston street.[505]

Wednesday, 19 March 1913
[Paris]

The Master's talk to the public gathering that morning concerned the fact that the divine teachings have been revealed in every age through the Will of God in accordance with the exigencies of that age. He concluded His talk with a discussion of the new and wondrous teachings of this most glorious dispensation, stating that, in this day, these blessed teachings are the most potent antidote for the ills afflicting the peoples and kindreds of the earth.

Following that gathering, and up until noontime, a constant stream of people attained and departed the Master's presence in the main room of the hotel.

Towards the afternoon, a number of students studying at (a Persian) school attained the Master's presence. Here are some of the statements He made to those students:

> In every affair one undertakes, one must arise to pursue it with great effort, acting in a way commensurate to the requirements which that task demands of that person, that thereby one may reach the milestone of perfection. If one is studying a certain discipline, one should have no other desire than to study. If one is engaged in commerce, one must meet the demands of that occupation. If one is in government, it behooves one to arise to discharge one's essential duties with the utmost justice and trustworthiness. One must carry out every affair with consummate purity, sincerity, honesty, and fairness, which all conduce to the attainment of perfection and the attraction of progress and confirmations. Had the people of Persia acted in this way, they would not have been afflicted with distress. Rather than serve as the protectors and trusted ones of the Qá'im, they became His traitors. For instance, if the members of every administrative department in Persia were all Bahá'ís, extraordinary progress would be quickly achieved – even where entire governments are concerned – for the Bahá'ís keep their distance from those who are tainted and impure, and involve the trustworthy and compassionate in their affairs. Thus would emerge once again the ancient glory of Persia, and the light of justice and fairness dispel the smoke of tyranny and oppression.

The Master then addressed these remarks to a few of the others among those respected Persians:

How many are the impossible imaginings which occupy the minds of certain people, who, by emulating the Europeans, wish to achieve such great progress in material pursuits, and so develop the countries of the East, as to protect themselves from the encroaching hand of the West! What they fail to realize is that even if they remain undisturbed by their prodigious problems, such as the opposition and strife that characterize the internal affairs of their countries – and that if the people of the East were to spend a whole century studying the arts and sciences which currently prevail in the West, and come to achieve the level of progress enjoyed there today – the Europeans will have advanced by another ten degrees in that time. If the Easterners take one step, the Europeans will cross entire valleys, for they are far swifter in the strides they make.

Thus, every thought that may occur to a person will remain unattainable, and every object of one's tenacious attachment nothing but an idle fancy, unless it is aided by the power of God and His invisible confirmations. Indeed, to study the various disciplines and receive an education are of the utmost importance, but without the power of these heavenly confirmations, they will not result in prosperity. It is this penetrating power, this subduing force, that has enabled the lowliest of people to conquer the mightiest of men, and made the most advanced societies to suffer defeat at the hands of the most primitive tribes. In the time of each and every one of the Manifestations of God, this extraordinary power has appeared resplendently as the sun shining with its noontide splendour – but alas, the people of the East are oblivious to what will restore their former glory. They are unaware that every power has always revolved around the power of God, and that all goodness and virtue have ever consisted in obedience to the divine teachings. Until spiritual perfections become apparent through adherence to those teachings, universal peace and tranquillity will never be secured, nor will complete comfort and happiness ever be attained.

Thursday, 20 March 1913
[Paris]

In the [Martha-Pension] 'Family Hotel'[506] that morning, the Master read letters from the Bahá'ís of the East and wrote Tablets in response to some of them.

On that day, the Master spoke of His illness; He remarked that people must be cautious, observing that they have often consulted incompetent physicians, and that this yields adverse results.

The Master then turned to the subject of teaching the Cause of God in America:

> Should any detached souls be found, they could render great services in America. Indeed, were even a few eloquent and severed souls to be found, this would suffice to achieve spectacular success in America. The Cause of God will be exalted in this day through sanctification and detachment. And yet, behold how, when one is granted wings, one transgresses the bounds of moderation at once, and becomes preoccupied with oneself. For instance, had Ibráhím Khayru'lláh been safeguarded from self and passion, he would have shone over the horizon of that land* even as a brilliant sun.

In brief, once a great number of people had attained His presence, and after He had made many remarks, the Master departed the hotel for the home of Miss Sanderson – to whom He had given the title 'Rúḥíyyih Khánum' – to see His daughter.[507] The majority of the Bahá'í women would visit the Master at Miss Sanderson's residence, and on most days from that one onward, the gatherings of Bahá'í women were held at her home. The Master's other visitors would attain His presence at the hotel where He was staying, and at still other times they would come to see Him at the homes of various illustrious persons. It was not possible to be present and record the Master's remarks at every place or gathering where He spoke – only at the public gatherings convened at His residence

* America.

(and just some of His statements even then), and also at the hotel to which He had recently relocated.

As Áqá Siyyid Aḥmad Báqiroff was already lodging at that same hotel, he repeatedly begged the Master day and night to allow him to defray His expenses for the duration of His stay there. The Master consented to this request and would often make this comment [to Báqiroff]: 'The five *siyyids* have consistently served the Cause of God.'[508] This was the first act of service [of that sort] in this period of the Master's journey that He accepted; it had been rendered by an old Persian friend, no less, and the Master was his guest for those few days.

As is mentioned in the first volume of this chronicle, the Master refused to accept a single thing from among the gifts and sums that were offered to Him – by believers and others alike – at the large conferences He attended in the various cities of America. If it so happened that He stayed at someone's home for a few days as their guest, He would, as He was leaving that place on His last day there, give the attendants of that household a tip greater than what it would have cost Him to stay at a hotel for those few days. He would make donations to every church, and show special generosity to the poor ones of each city. Wherever He went, the Master would exhibit such remarkable self-sufficiency and independence as to astound the minds and captivate the hearts of the people of that place. Even in certain cities, such as New York, the Bahá'ís so strongly wished to emulate the Master's demeanour and disposition that they all made an arrangement among themselves to the effect that, whenever He visited a group of impoverished souls on a certain day and gave them some money, they, too, would visit that same group each year on that very day, and give those souls a sum equal to the one He had previously given them, as if to commemorate the presence of 'Abdu'l-Bahá in that city and reenact the generosity He showed to the poor ones who lived there.

It was in this way that people of great importance were always fascinated by the Master's utterances; they were enamoured of Him in every respect, and their gaze was fixed constantly on Him.

Friday, 21 March 1913
[Paris]

That day was the festival of Naw-Rúz – and a most auspicious day it was. Those from among the Master's attendants and devoted servants who had the bounty of being with Him that morning were Siyyid Aḥmad Báqiroff, Mirza Ahmad Sohrab, Siyyid Asadu'lláh, and this lowly servant; we were all summoned to His presence, and He showered us with tender kindnesses too many to count.

After the recitation of prayers and meditations, the chanting of divine verses and supplications, and the preparing of certain letters for mailing,[509] the Master departed the hotel for the home of Miss Sanderson to see His daughter. He said:[510]

> Decorate the main room with bouquets of flowers, and also prepare some tea and sweets. I will return soon.

When He came back, a large crowd of people from Persia, America, England, and France approached the Master holding bouquets of flowers.[511] They extended their New Year greetings to Him, and were visibly honoured to have had the privilege of showing Him their utmost reverence. Among those in that crowd was the poet Mírzá Ḥusayn ['Árif], who implored the Master's permission to recite an ode he had composed in His praise, and also in commemoration of a prosperous New Year. But no matter how much this poet begged, the Master did not grant him the permission he sought, and instead bade him be seated.

The Master then proceeded to make the following poignant remarks on Naw-Rúz:

> In former times, the Persians held grand celebrations on such a day as this, but in these days they are afflicted with distress. Truly, the Persian kings of old would treat their subjects even as a father would his own child; they were compassionate indeed. Although they ruled independently, the majority of them exercised that rule only after consulting their ministers. How splendid were the harmony

> and fellowship that resulted from the celebrations of Naw-Rúz in those days! Every gathering that was held during this festival would lead to acts of charity and conduce to considerable reforms.

The Master then discussed this Most Great Cause and the teachings of the Ancient Beauty:

> Most of the people are unaware of this Cause. Were they to become properly apprised of it, every person would attain to their desire through it. In truth, every sick one would find the cure for his illness through this Most Great Cause. It is for this reason that, in whatever place we have explained these blessed teachings, every soul has humbled himself in lowliness upon hearing them. My hope is that Paris may be similarly illumined. There is a time for everything . . .

When the lunch bell was rung, the Master called a number of people to join Him at the lunch table. So remarkable was the sight of the people in His presence, hailing from both East and West and dressed in their diverse clothing – and so astonishing the humility and reverence they showed Him – that all those present turned to look at that gladsome scene, and were utterly enamoured of the Master's glory and beauty.

In the afternoon, another group of Persian grandees came to see the Master. Some of those Eastern dignitaries who stood in His presence had not previously met one another; each had not imagined or expected the other to be as he was in reality. They all listened, with blissful joy, to the utterances of that Epitome of gladness. Among other things, the Master's remarks to them concerned the hope that follows despair, and also how pure intentions, thoughtful reflection, and goodly deeds all attract the confirmations of God. When the Master discussed these and similar subjects at length, some of those in attendance posed their questions to Him and brimmed with ecstasy as they listened to His extensive replies, among them the following explanation of the wisdom behind the permissibility of polygamy in Islam:

> Prior to the Revelation of the Prophet Muhammad, the Apostle of God (may the blessings of God rest upon Him), the practice of polygamy was so prevalent among the Arabs that it would not have been possible to enjoin monogamy on them all of a sudden. This notwithstanding, the Prophet Muhammad declared that if a man was incapable of treating all four of his wives equally, he would need to choose just one of them to be his wife.* It is clear from this verse that, in reality, it is the practice of monogamy which is allowable and acceptable in the sight of God, since it is impossible to treat multiple wives equally.

In brief, the gathering that afternoon was a most glorious and impressive occasion.

Following that gathering, a group of people from the Master's retinue requested to be dismissed, and asked for His permission to visit the Persian legation[512] and convey their New Year greetings there. To these attendants, the Master said, 'You may go.'

An elaborate meeting had been convened at the legation, and all those present were Persian.[513] Mírzá Ḥusayn ['Árif], the poet, arose and recited some of his compositions, written in both verse and prose, in which he hailed the advent of the New Year, prayed for the government and people of Persia, and praised the Persian ambassador. Afterwards, all those in attendance went to sit at the table and have some tea and sweets. The members of the Master's retinue made the acquaintance of their fellow Persians and engaged them in brief conversation. They left that gathering early, and upon returning whence they had come, the attendants learned that the Master and Mr Dreyfus-Barney had also departed for the Persian legation sometime after they themselves had already left that place. There were still a number of people present at the legation when the Master delivered a most impressive and stirring talk on the New Year, and His audience was immensely grateful to have heard it – but since no one from the Master's retinue was in attendance, the content of His talk was not recorded anywhere.[514]

The weekly gathering of friends was held at the home of Mr

---

* Qur'án 4:3.

and Mrs Dreyfus-Barney that evening, and the believers and seekers who had come were filled with excitement. The Master's address to them once again concerned the festival of Naw-Rúz and the results that proceed from gatherings of heavenly love and fellowship. Additionally, He encouraged His audience to be as one and help bring about the unification of humanity.[515]

Both that day and night were truly auspicious. Every soul had been roused to excitement by the fire of love for the Master that had been kindled within them, and every heart was thoroughly cheered by witnessing His bounty and beneficence. To see the Master in such good health and high spirits moved all those friends to abundant joy. The best gift those ardent lovers could have received to celebrate the arrival of that new year and the advent of that prosperous springtime was the descent of these divine confirmations. Dazzling indeed was the Master's splendour on that occasion – a splendour that seemed to shine throughout the world.

Among the wondrous Tablets the Master composed Himself that morning was the following, written in honour of the Báqiroff family:

He is God

> O family sacrificing yourselves in the path of God! It is the auspicious morning of the new year, and the splendours of the Sun of Truth can be readily discerned. In a spirit of consummate rapture, 'Abdu'l-Bahá has now taken up the pen to extend His wishes for a prosperous new year to that renowned and blessed family. May each and every one of its members thank the All-Glorious Lord, inasmuch as they all repose beneath the shade of His bounty; are encompassed by His limitless glory; and have, in this Revelation of Him Who shone forth on Mount Sinai, become enamoured of the Ever-Forgiving. Assist them, O my God, with Your most vehement might.
>
> —'Abdu'l-Bahá 'Abbás

Saturday, 22 March 1913
[Paris]

The Master composed a wondrous Tablet in honour of the son of the late Muḥammad Muṣṭafá Ba<u>gh</u>dádí [Dr Zia Bagdadi], which He concluded with these words:[516]

> I beseech God to make blessed this joyous new year for all His loved ones, and to assist them with fresh confirmations. Verily, my Lord is powerful over all things.
>
> —'Abdu'l-Bahá 'Abbás

Among the people who had the honour of attaining the Master's presence that morning was one of the teachers of the 'travelling school',[517] Mr [Stanwood] Cobb, a sincerely devoted American Bahá'í who, along with a few other teachers and students from that school, was travelling and teaching throughout the various countries of Europe.[518] Wherever they went, they acquired the necessary information for education. Once he had met the Master and received the outpourings of His grace, Mr. Cobb said:

> I have discussed the Cause with the other teachers and students; they eagerly request Your permission to have the privilege of meeting You at an appointed time.

The Master agreed to this request.

As the afternoon approached, the Master visited Aḥmad Pá<u>sh</u>á and Ra<u>sh</u>íd Pá<u>sh</u>á, with whom He spoke extensively of many matters pertaining to the Cause, history, and other subjects.[519]

That evening, a number of important persons attained the presence of the Master,[520] Who related the following account:

> When the Blessed Beauty was sent to Baghdad and 'Akká, the people responsible were certain that the Cause would be wiped out altogether and that no trace of it would remain. How dire the calamities that befell Him – how deplorable the schemes they

> conceived to uproot the tree of the Cause of God! But they were totally oblivious of the prevailing power of this Cause, and entirely unaware of the confirmations vouchsafed from the Abhá Kingdom, which are capable of changing afflictions into bounties and turning toil [into ease]. Were a person to reflect on this very matter – that is, the exile of the Blessed Beauty – it would become apparent to him that His banishment to the Holy Land, which His enemies deemed the most effective means of abasing and annihilating this Cause, in fact served as the most conclusive proof of its validity, and the vehicle through which the prophecies and promises mentioned in the Scriptures of old were at last fulfilled. The result of this exile was that various peoples turned their attention to this Cause and embraced it, and that fellowship and unity were fostered among differing groups, inasmuch as they were all expecting the Promised One to appear from that hallowed land, and were awaiting the brilliance of His splendour to shine from the horizon of that clime upon the farthest reaches of the earth.
>
> Consider how sustaining is the Word of God, and how victorious His Cause, that whatever friend and foe alike have done – be it their acceptance of this Cause or their rejection thereof, their praise for this Faith or their condemnation of it – all this has redounded to its glory and exaltation, so much so that this Cause has become a source of pride for those Easterners, in particular the Persians, residing in the well-developed lands of Europe and America.

The remarks of this nature which the Master made on that occasion so revolutionized the hearts of His distinguished listeners that they unloosed their tongues in praise and gratitude, openly testifying to the power and greatness of this Cause. They uttered 'what the blamers aforetime exclaimed, that there shall be made manifest in the end that which appeared in the beginning'.[521]

Sunday, 23 March 1913
[Paris]

After prayers and meditations that morning, the Master summoned His attendants and asked them to chant some supplications and other divine verses. These intonations of the words of God cleansed away the rust from their hearts, and then warmed those hearts with the imperishable outpourings of eternal life.

The Master then went to the main hall and gave a talk on Bahá'u'lláh's addresses [to the kings and rulers of the world] regarding future events. Among the Master's remarks were these:

> When Jesus Christ entered Jerusalem, He proclaimed: 'Verily I say unto you, there shall not be left here one stone upon another that shall not be thrown down.'* When Titus conquered Jerusalem forty years later, the Christians wrote explanations and commentaries in which they accounted the aforementioned prophecy as an example of the omniscience and supernatural ability of Christ.
>
> Similarly, when the Persians conquered Rome in the beginning of the Islamic dispensation, those who disbelieved in Islam let loose their ridicule and scorn, as the Muslims did not consider the Persians to be 'people of the Book', whereas they believed the Romans to belong to that group. Consequently, those disbelievers would say: 'If the people of the Book are superior to other peoples, then how could the Romans have suffered defeat at the hands of such a people as the Persians?' It was this very matter that occasioned the revelation of this blessed verse: 'The Romans have been defeated . . . but after their defeat, they shall defeat their foes.'† Afterwards, when Rome was indeed victorious, the divines of Islam likewise accounted, in their own commentaries, this victory as a most conclusive proof and miraculous development.
>
> As to this Revelation, however, they reject its verses and utterances, and utterly fail to take heed. What grave injustice this is! How plainly it was predicted in the verses of Bahá'u'lláh that the

* Matt. 24:2.

† Qur'án 30:2–3.

> Land of Mystery (Adrianople) would pass out from the hands of the Ottoman Sultan; so too with His addresses to the other sovereigns of the earth, and also His allusions to the upheavals in Tehran. But heedless as they were, no fruit could be discerned from them – and during my sojourn in America, I advised my listeners not to await any good news from that part of the world.

In the afternoon, the Master paid a visit to His daughter, and from there went to meet with a number of Easterners. Following this, the Master went on an excursion by car up to the Bois de Boulogne, and was then taken back to His residence.[522]

Monday, 24 March 1913
[Paris]

That morning, the Master sent Siyyid Aḥmad [Báqiroff] and this lowly servant, with copies of the Kitáb-i-Mubín[523] and the Kitáb-i-Aqdas in hand, to visit one of the Persian dignitaries, with whom we had been instructed to share specific passages from those books that pertain to Tehran and other places. To that end, the Master had said:

> Read for him these passages exactly as they were revealed; then say to him that Bahá'u'lláh had predicted these upheavals with the utmost clarity forty years prior to their occurrence, and that these blessed Writings were published in Bombay twenty-three years ago and have since been disseminated in every country. Bahá'u'lláh's addresses to the Ottomans are replete with wrath and despair, while His utterances concerning Tehran mention the tranquillity and security that will follow intense upheaval. There can be no doubt that whatever has taken place until now has happened in accordance with what Bahá'u'lláh revealed, so much so that some of the mischievous enemies of this Cause in Tehran and Shiraz, wishing to advance their own interests and subject the Bahá'ís to further aggression, have recited passages from the Kitáb-i-Aqdas from atop their pulpits, declaring, 'These are the upheavals which

> have been predicted in this book, and the Bahá'ís have incited tumult and stirred up sedition to fulfil these prophecies!'

From the outset of the [Constitutional] revolution, the statements which the Master has made emphatically and repeatedly to the people of Bahá have been as follows:

> Until the government [of Persia] and its people become commingled, even as milk and honey, their success and prosperity will remain entirely unattainable. Persia shall fall into ruin, and the governments of its neighbouring realms will ultimately meddle in its affairs. Then strive, O loved ones of God, to foster perfect harmony between the government and the people, and should you find yourselves unable to achieve this, then withdraw from the matter entirely. Beware, beware, lest you involve yourselves in shedding the blood of a single Persian . . .

As we shared the relevant passages with the esteemed gentleman mentioned above – and because we conveyed to him, on the Master's behalf, that heavenly confirmations would descend upon him in the event that he arose to promulgate the Cause of God and promote His Word – he listened with complete deference, and extended his heartfelt praise and gratitude for these divine bounties and blessed favours.

At a gathering of believers that day, the Master read from some of the compositions of [Mírzá] Yaḥyá.[524] Originally recorded in a book held at the British Museum and written in the hand of Yaḥyá's son, Riḍván-'Alí, one of the Bahá'ís of Khorasan had transcribed these phrases and other constructions from Yaḥyá's books and sent them to the Master, Who would smile as He read them and say:

> These pitiful people wish to contend with the power and might of the Supreme Pen through the use of these meaningless phrases and ridiculous constructions. Alas for them!

Tuesday, 25 March 1913
[Paris]

The Master's talk that day dealt with the following theme:

> The grandeur of this Cause is such that even its disbelievers have testified to its power and greatness. Not one of the dispensations inaugurated by any of the previous Manifestations of God enjoyed such grandeur as this one; on the contrary, all the deniers of those past revelations would ridicule them and say, 'We see no excellence in you above ourselves.'* But how many are the learned ones in this most great dispensation who, though not affiliated with this Cause, have rendered it countless praises nonetheless!
>
> In 'Akká, the first to throw himself at the feet of Bahá'u'lláh and kiss the hem of His robe was none other than the *muftí* of that city himself. We had made every effort to persuade the Blessed Beauty to relocate to the garden [of Mazra'ih], but He refused every time, and would say, 'We are prisoners, and prisoners must be confined.' Eventually, as the *muftí* of 'Akká was a highly respected and insistent individual, I said to him, 'Could you do something that will convince the Blessed Beauty to leave His confinement?' Animated by his intense devotion, the *muftí* arose at once and went to see Bahá'u'lláh. After obtaining His permission to attain His presence, the *muftí* threw himself at the feet of Bahá'u'lláh and said, 'I have a request to make of You, and I will not rise up from this spot until You agree to do it.' The *muftí* insisted and implored repeatedly, until at last the Blessed Beauty consented to his request. He left the fortress to which He had been confined and went to the Mansion of Mazra'ih, which had been prepared to receive Him. So great was the grandeur of this Cause even then that, despite the fact that Bahá'u'lláh was a prisoner, not one person was able to attain His presence without first obtaining His permission to do so. This applied even to the *mutaṣarrif* of 'Akká, who for several years had besought the Blessed Beauty's permission to see Him, but was paid no mind.

* Qur'án 11:27.

> In His state of imprisonment, Bahá'u'lláh pitched His tabernacle on the summit of Mount Carmel with the utmost ascendancy. Such a triumph has never before been witnessed in any of the dispensations of the Manifestations of the past.

In those days, the Master was resolved to go to Germany – owing to the promise He had made to the German Bahá'ís, in acceptance of their earnest request, that He would travel to their country – and He and His retinue had planned to leave Paris imminently. However, as Mírzá Yuḥanná Dávúd, a Persian Bahá'í of Jewish extraction, was coming from London to see the Master[525] – and because Dávúd had mentioned how Mr [Henri] and Mrs [Sophie] Moser, English [sic][526] dignitaries who would also be travelling to Paris in the next few days, were expecting to visit the Master, and had also described how ardently they wished to have the honour of attaining His presence – the Master acceded to this request, and once again postponed His plans to travel by another day or two.

Wednesday, 26 March 1913
[Paris]

That morning,[527] Mr. Cobb, along with the other teachers and students from the (American) travelling school – previously mentioned on 22 March – attained the Master's presence, and were roused to fervent excitement by His talk on the history and teachings of this Most Great Revelation, as well as the Writings of the Blessed Beauty.[528] Up until the moment they were dismissed, each and every one of those present voiced their praise and gratitude, their hearts completely captivated by the Master's utterance.

In the afternoon, a number of Persian dignitaries attained the Master's presence. Among the remarks He addressed to them were as follows:

> It is my hope that Persia, too, may attain order and stability, achieve renown, and be granted mighty confirmations. Nothing is improbable for the power of God to accomplish. Through His

confirmations, thickets of thorns become beds of roses, the lowly ant becomes a glorious Solomon, the atom becomes a world-illumining sun, the drop becomes an ocean, the abased become glorious, the poor become rich, and the despairing become hopeful. Indeed, none of this would be hard for God. Before the advent of Islam, the Arabs of Mecca and Medina ate lizards. It was the power of God and His confirmations that enabled them to prevail over the treasuries of Khusraw and Caesar.

The situation of Persia is now beyond saving, unless it be through divine confirmations and spiritual power. The government of Persia has not been powerful as of late, and yet behold how humiliating was the defeat which the army of the Ottomans – with all their power, their might, and their preparation – suffered at its hands!* Why were the Ottomans deprived of divine confirmations? Why did they occupy themselves with their selfish imaginings and pursue their personal interests?

Despite all this, none of it will stay the same; the abasement of Persia will not last, nor will the glory of Paris persist. There shall come a time when this city will fall into ruin, and become the inheritor of every pain and sadness. There is no doubt that things will not remain as they are now. Everything is subject to change, and is in a constant cycle of ascent and descent. It is like the human body, which from the age of childhood is in a state of progress and maturation, but then, having reached the peak of its development, begins to droop ever closer toward the ground. One's duty, however, is to strive, endeavour, and remain hopeful of God's confirmations; one must not be heedless, or wax proud, or sink into apathy. As people cannot know the end of any affair before it unfolds, they must always take the path of vigilance and righteousness, and learn from their past in a way that will benefit their future.

It is said in the Qur'án: 'Behold, then, the end of the wrongful doers!'† Look at this field and its hills. Here there are armies defeated, regiments scattered, which have all become one with the

* Likely a reference to the Ottoman–Persian War of 1821–23, in which the Persians handily defeated the Ottomans despite their being heavily outnumbered and having to contend with an epidemic of cholera.

† Qur'án 28:40.

dust. Where there was once a grand pavilion now stand dilapidated ruins, and the palaces of the past are today the nests of the menacing raven and the rapacious owl. Every gain shall in the end be lost, save one's longing to be a thrall of God, one's servitude at His celestial court, and one's achievement of heavenly success. Pray, then, that God may grant His confirmations and cast the glance of His favour – that same God Who can turn barren soil into a verdant refuge for the heart and soul; Who can make the environs of ruins into flourishing rose-gardens; and Who, with but a single look, can transform the whole of Persia, restoring serenity to its troubled peoples, changing the signs of its decay into the hallmarks of prosperity, and moving the saddened hearts of its people to rejoice with exceeding gladness.

Thursday, 27 March 1913
[Paris]

In both the morning and the afternoon that day, a great number of illustrious individuals from the East and the West alike attained the Master's presence; they received the outpourings of His imperishable grace, and were immeasurably gladdened by His tender kindnesses. Among the Master's visitors were Mr and Mrs Moser, English [sic] dignitaries who had come to meet with Him through the assistance of Mírzá Yuḥanná Dávúd, and on whom the Master bestowed His ample bounties.[529] After observing the proper etiquette and demonstrating their complete deference to the Master, Mr and Mrs Moser expressed their gratitude for having the privilege of attaining His presence. The Master then addressed them with these words:

He is God

You are aware of the situation in the East; you know how grievously its horizon was enveloped with the darkness of ignorance and prejudice. The religions of the East opposed each other with the utmost hatred and strife, so much so that the Jews could not leave their homes when it was raining outside, as the followers of other religions would not touch them when they were damp, regarding them as impure. The peoples of the East once deemed it lawful to shed one another's blood.

It was at such a time as this that Bahá'u'lláh rose over the horizon of the East even as a sun. He first proclaimed the oneness of humanity, stating that all were the sheep of the flock of God, the True Shepherd, Who sustained them and nurtured them with the utmost kindness – for if He were not kind and did not love them, He would neither have created them nor given them their daily sustenance.

The second teaching of Bahá'u'lláh concerns the independent investigation of truth, the intent being that when the people of religion investigate the truth independently, they will all become united, for the truth is one. The truth is incompatible with plurality; on the contrary, it is blind imitation which exists in various forms. So long as humanity persists in such imitation, they will remain in conflict and contention.

Third, religion must be the cause of love and fellowship among humankind. Should it become the cause of dissension and strife, irreligion would be preferable, for religion is like a remedy: If a remedy becomes the cause of illness, it would be better to dispose of that remedy. God has sent down religion to unite the hearts and foster love and fellowship among them, not to create strife and animosity.

Fourth, religion must accord with science and reason. Should a matter of religion not be compatible with science and reason, it would be nothing more than superstition.

Many were the teachings of this sort which Bahá'u'lláh proclaimed, but the people of Persia condemned Him as an infidel, plundered His possessions, cast Him into prison, and subjected Him to persecution. Eventually, He was exiled to Baghdad, and thence to Constantinople and Rumelia. But despite their efforts, they saw this Lamp shine only more brightly, and watched the power of this Cause grow only stronger. In the end, they sent Bahá'u'lláh to the prison of 'Akká, but He raised up the Cause of God while bound with chains and fetters, and His teachings were spread to every land. He promoted the principles of peace in spite of His imprisonment.

Fifty years ago, Bahá'u'lláh announced that the time to establish universal peace had come. He wrote to the Ottoman Sultan and the Shah of Persia, saying: 'A Prisoner though I be, afflicted with oppression and assailed by sedition, yet this glory and sovereignty you now enjoy shall not last; they will ultimately be changed into toil and abasement.'* Those Tablets were published in India and are today readily available.

In brief, through the pervasive spread of these teachings in the East, various peoples have become united, and a great many souls – Jews and Zoroastrians, Muslims and Christians – now enjoy such intimate fellowship, and gather together in a spirit of such perfect oneness and brotherhood, that were a person to enter their gathering, he would not know which was the Jew and which the Zoroastrian, and find himself unable to distinguish the Christian from the Muslim. To him it would seem that they were all brothers and sisters – all the members of a single family.

Mr and Mrs Moser then stated, 'We are well-informed of this Cause. It is truly a light from the East, and it will surely become the means through which peace is established.' The Master replied:

Indeed, God willing this world may find peace. How numerous are the calamities that have afflicted humanity! How many the mothers who have lost their sons, and the sons who have lost their fathers! Every war and conflict have stemmed from prejudice. A friend of mine here mentioned that there were six villages in the East that once enjoyed abundant prosperity, but the news was eventually received that they had all been totally razed to the ground, such that no sign of its flourishing remained.

---

* A paraphrase of this passage from Bahá'u'lláh's Súriy-i-Ra'ís: 'Have ye fondly imagined your glory to be imperishable and your dominion to be everlasting? Nay, by Him Who is the All-Merciful! Neither will your glory last, nor will Mine abasement endure. Such abasement, in the estimation of a true man, is the pride of every glory' (*Summons of the Lord of Hosts*, p. 165).

The Mosers then said, 'The thing about this Cause which truly demands careful attention is that spiritual power that will conduce to peace and unity. Were it not for this, we, too, have held many gatherings that were all devoted to peace, yet every one of them has proven futile and yielded no fruit.' The Master replied:

> Yes, this is so. In the world of humanity, peace and unity have ever been brought about only through patriotic bonds, formed through the shared nationality of a given group; or through racial bonds; or through political bonds – yet none of these will prove sufficient. How often have people from the same country fallen into conflict and strife with one another! Furthermore, as a person will feel love only for their own country, that love will itself become the cause of animosity towards others. So too with racial and political bonds, which create dissension among peoples and, owing to their differing political interests, set them at odds with one another. These bonds cannot bring about universal peace. What, then, is left to us? It is the power of God. Such a spiritual power as this is needed to establish universal peace and oneness.

The Mosers then asked how one should treat people who are immoral. The Master replied:

> The power of God is capable of moderating a person's morals. There was once a highwayman from the Caucasus who had killed a great many people. Upon becoming a Bahá'í, he assumed so gentle a demeanour that, when he was thrown a handgun, he refused to take it. A man as ferocious as this became so gentle a servant. The morals of the people, therefore, must be so moderated as to make them heedful, and this is possible only through the power of God.

The Mosers then inquired as to which country boasts the largest number of Bahá'ís. The Master replied:

> The majority of Bahá'ís reside in Persia, where this Cause has been firmly established. In America, too, there are Bahá'ís of every stripe.

The Mosers then said, 'Praised be God that, in this age, the people of every nation have acquired such great capacity that they yearn for universal peace. They do not say, "We are Jews," "We are Christians," or "We are Muslims." Rather, they are seekers of fellowship, though they have distanced themselves from matters of religion.' The Master replied:

> This century is the century of truth. The signs of extraordinary progress in this world are clear and evident from every direction. As to the distance which people now seek from the divine religions, this is because those religions of the past no longer enjoy the level of influence they once did, and the exigencies of the time have completely changed. Thus, religion can be likened to a tree with no fruit, or a shell without its pearl. Moreover, Jesus Christ said that if any one should treat you with cruelty or aggression, you must show them goodness in return: 'Whosoever shall smite thee on thy right cheek, turn to him the other also.'* Yet in this day, the people of Christ have busied themselves with war, and gone so far as to deem this war 'holy'. What relevance does this have to the divine teachings, considering that Christ consented to be crucified and interceded on the behalf of murderers? . . .

The Master's utterances of this sort evoked such sincere devotion and fascination in the hearts of the Mosers that they insisted He come to their summer residence, where they would arise with all their heart and soul to serve Him and spread the wondrous teachings. The Master replied:

> This journey of mine has become protracted, and we cannot possibly delay our plans any more than we already have. I must return to the East sooner rather than later.

The Master concluded His talk with a discussion of Islam:

> For thirteen years, the Apostle of God (may the blessings of God

* Matt. 5:39.

rest upon Him) was in Mecca, where He was subjected constantly to persecution from His enemies. They would harass Him, murder His companions, and plunder their possessions. Some of those companions fled, while others were taken as captives. They were intent on slaying the Prophet Muhammad Himself; hence, His eventual migration. Yet even there they pursued Him and came upon Him, intending to kill every man and capture every woman. It is for this reason that He commanded those in His company to defend themselves. This laid the foundation for war in Islam, and although these wars were defensive in nature, the Prophet Muhammad and His companions would nonetheless put their enemies to rout. But as His enemies thirsted for blood, they continued to wage war against Him. Without end they mounted attack after attack, taking pride in their killing and robbing of men, and also in their capturing women and children . . .

Friday, 28 March 1913
[Paris]

The Master counselled the believers that morning to embrace the single foundation underlying all the divine religions, and warned them against differences and prejudices:

> The people of every religion, nation, and race – all the peoples of the world – must so abandon their idle prejudices, and so forsake the illusory distinctions they have made among themselves, that they will visit the places of worship of every community and creed, inasmuch as the mention of God is made in every church and mosque. They have all been built to praise God, and also to edify humanity and foster fellowship in its midst. All the peoples of the world worship one God; none are the worshippers of Satan. Should the eye of truth be focused on this, what difference would one find among these places of worship? The fundamental purpose of all these buildings is to facilitate the remembrance of God and the vigilance of humankind, not to promote illusory imitations and fanciful customs. How wonderful will it be when the

> Muslims enter the synagogues of the Jews and the churches of the Christians – and, likewise, when the Jews and the Christians enter the mosques of the Muslims – and then all worship the same single God, renounce those empty traditions and prejudices that are incompatible with this foundation, and remove every trace of antipathy and aversion from their midst.
>
> Whether in the churches of the Christians, or the synagogues of the Jews, or the mosques of the Muslims – in all these places, I have seen them worship only one God. Each of them regards their respective prophets as the intermediaries of divine grace, and considers the religion of God to be the cause of progress, prosperity, and love in the world of humanity. This being the case, they are all united in the fundamental principles. What harm would there be if they were to come together on this foundation, which will conduce to the oneness of humankind, and dispense with the differences among them, which can lead only to estrangement and contention? In so doing, they would come to truly understand the primary goal of the divine Manifestations, and their hearts and souls would arouse the envy of the garden of Paradise itself. It is for this reason that Moses called on the Israelites to worship the perpetual God of Abraham; it is why Jesus Christ proclaimed: 'I am not come to destroy, but to fulfil,'* and why in the Qur'án the following has been revealed with perfect clarity: 'Verily, they who believe,† and they who follow the Jewish religion, and the Christians, and the Sabeans – whoever of these believeth in God and the last day, and doeth that which is right, shall have their reward with their Lord: fear shall not come upon them, neither shall they be grieved.'‡

As the Master would soon be travelling to Stuttgart, He spent most of His time during those [last] few days [in Paris] repaying visits and bidding farewell to various people. On that particular day, His car was travelling constantly from the afternoon up until night-

* Matt. 5:17.
† Muslims.
‡ Qur'án 2:62.

time, and for the most part, no one but Mr Dreyfus accompanied Him on these visits.

According to the Master's own instructions, in most cases I did not write down the names of the Persian dignitaries He visited, nor did I go into any detail about their meetings. At times, I described what took place as briefly as possible, while at others I recounted these meetings without mentioning the names of the Master's visitors, recording only the remarks which He addressed to them. However, since Mirza Ahmad Sohrab was writing letters to Americans at the time, he would recount such details more explicitly by including the names and positions of those dignitaries in his correspondence.[530]

Saturday, 29 March 1913
[Paris]

The Master spoke to the believers that morning, recounting the early days of the Cause and the calamities which occurred in Tehran. His remarks to that effect included the following anecdote:

> When I was a boy, just nine years of age, I was in the crucible of calamity, assailed and beset by our enemies, who had pelted us with so many stones that our house had become filled with them. We had no one but our mother, my sister,* and Áqá Mírzá Muḥammad-Qulí.† To protect us, my mother took us through the gate of Shimírán to the district of Sangilaj. While there, my mother found a residence along one of the bylanes. She kept us safe in that place, and forbade us to go outside.
>
> Ultimately, the matter of our subsistence came to such a dire pass that my mother said to me: 'Could You go to the home of Your aunt and tell her to somehow find a few coins for us?' My aunt resided in the *tikíyih*‡ of Ḥájí Rajab-'Alí, near the home of

* Bahíyyih Khánum, known to Bahá'ís as the Greatest Holy Leaf.

† The faithful half-brother of Bahá'u'lláh.

‡ Also known as a *khánqáh*, 'A place of religious retreat, a sanctuary, a meeting place of dervishes, or a pilgrim inn' (Glassé, *The Concise Encyclopedia of Islam*, p. 394). A *tikyih* can alternatively refer to a place where

Mírzá Ḥasan Kaj-Damágh. I went as instructed. After searching very hard, my aunt finally found a coin worth five *qiráns*;* she wrapped this in a handkerchief, which she then gave to me. As I was returning, the son of Mírzá Ḥasan Kaj-Damágh recognized me in the *tikíyih* and immediately said, 'This is a Bábí!', which prompted the other children to chase me. The home of Ḥájí Mullá Ja'far Astarábádí was close by; upon reaching it, I crossed the threshold and entered the residence. The son of Ḥájí Mullá Ja'far saw me, but he neither prevented me from coming inside nor made any effort to disperse the children. I remained there until nightfall, and when I went outside, the children pursued me once again, raising a clamour and hurling stones. This continued until I had nearly reached the shop of Áqá Muḥammad Ṣandúq-Dár, at which point the children stopped chasing me and came no closer.

When I arrived home shortly thereafter, I collapsed from fear and exhaustion. 'What is the matter with You?' my mother asked me, but I was unable to respond and promptly fell to the ground. After taking the handkerchief with the money, she took me to bed and I fell asleep.

The Master also made these remarks that day:

At one time, when we lived in Tehran, we possessed all the trappings of a comfortable life, but they were all taken from us in the span of a single day. So extreme was our hardship that, one day, rather than give me bread, my mother poured some flour into the palm of my hand, and I ate it raw.

On another day, this time during the incarceration of the Blessed Beauty,† I requested insistently to attain His presence. Eventually, I was sent to the prison accompanied by a servant. Upon reaching the prison, and once the attendants had indicated

passion plays representing the martyrdom of the Imám Ḥusayn and others slain at Karbala are performed.

* The monetary unit of Persia during the Qájár era, superseded by the *rial* in 1932.

† In the Síyáh-Chál.

> to us where Bahá'u'lláh was being held, the servant put me on his shoulders and headed for that spot. I beheld before me an exceedingly dark place with a downward slope; we entered through a small, narrow door and began to descend two flights of stairs, though we could not see anything. All of a sudden, as we were descending the stairs, we heard the voice of Bahá'u'lláh ring out: 'Do not bring Him',* and He then bade us return. We sat outside, awaiting the time when the prisoners would be taken outdoors. Suddenly, the Blessed Beauty was brought outside, chained to a series of other prisoners. What weighty manacles they had cast about Him, so heavy as to hinder His movements! It saddened me profoundly to witness Him in that state. The calamities He sustained defy all description, and the tongue is powerless to recount them.

As that was the last day of His sojourn [in Paris],[531] the Master spent the morning visiting the residences of some páshás to bid them farewell.

The Master visited the hospital that afternoon to see His daughter, Rúḥá Khánum.

In the evening, the Master said [to the members of His retinue], 'Gather our belongings and be prepared for our departure.'

Sunday, 30 March 1913[532]
[Paris → Stuttgart]

The Master telephoned that morning to inquire after the health of His daughter. The friends were immensely delighted to learn that her condition had improved, and that she had high hopes of a speedy recovery. After having surgery on her throat and being admitted to the hospital, Rúḥá Khánum's health improved with every passing day. No sooner had she arrived at Paris than, at the instruction of the Master, Mírzá Jalál took up lodging at the Master's residence at the Pension hotel on Lauriston street.

---

* 'Abdu'l-Bahá.

The Master departed the hotel at nine o'clock that morning.[533] A few of the believers had readied their cars to accompany the Master and His retinue to the train station,[534] where a number of other friends were already waiting to see Him off. Their hearts filled with rapture, and their eyes fixed squarely upon Him, they all fervently implored the Master's bounty and assistance. Accompanying Him on that journey were Siyyid Aḥmad Báqiroff, Mirza Ahmad Sohrab, Áqá Siyyid Asadu'lláh, and this lowly servant. As the train was beginning to depart, the Master addressed these words to the Bahá'ís of Paris:

> We are now going to Stuttgart to raise a cry that shall reach the Most Glorious Kingdom. You all must arise with the utmost ecstasy and concord to serve the Cause of God and spread His fragrances, resting neither day nor night. I will not forget you; you are always in my thoughts, and I will see you again.

Once the train had set off, the Master said the following [to those with Him] in the railroad car:

> Morgan* was one of the wealthiest people of America, and now he has died. Every trace of his existence will vanish, but had he rendered even the smallest service to the Cause of God, the effects of that service would have endured forever, and he would have attained to eternal life.

The Master then stated:

> In view of a certain wisdom, we did not allow anyone to send a telegram to Stuttgart to convey the news of our departure from Paris. Hence, the believers of that city will be astonished; when all of a sudden they hear that we have arrived, this news will take them by surprise.

Before leaving Paris, the Master told the members of His retinue to set aside their Persian hats and other clothing and change into

* John Pierpont Morgan.

European dress, and also instructed the believers of Germany not to publish anything in the newspapers concerning His coming to their country.

The Master was in high spirits and excellent health throughout the train ride.[535] He said:

> With every passing minute, my health is improving, and my physical strength and spiritual sentiments are likewise increasing.

The Master had a wonderful time on the train, especially because it was the springtime and He could see plains, fields, and hills stretched out before Him – all lush and verdant – as well as picturesque cities and scenic rivers. All the grasslands on both sides of the tracks were studded with flowers.

At eight o'clock in the evening, the train arrived at the station in Stuttgart 'at a time when its people were unaware.'[536] The Master was to lodge at a hotel [the Hotel Marquardt] which was adjacent to the train station, and whose address He had obtained while still in Paris.[537] That hotel, a majestic building, was one of the best and largest hotels in all of Stuttgart. As the crown prince of Great Britain [Edward VIII] was also visiting Stuttgart in those days, a number of his attendants who had accompanied him from England happened to be lodging at that same hotel.

When the Master first arrived at Stuttgart,[538] the signs of His power and glory – His elegant gait and dignified bearing – all served to create so imposing a presence in the eyes of His onlookers that, at the train station, a person who spoke English asked me, 'What country are you from?' I told him we were from Persia. He then inquired, 'Is this resplendently magnificent personage a dignitary of your country, or perhaps one of its princes?' I replied, 'He is a spiritual teacher, a promoter of universal peace, and an advocate of the brotherhood and prosperity of all humankind.'

When the Master had finished settling in, He allowed us to telephone Mr Herrigel and Miss [Alma] Knobloch to give them the glad-tidings that He had come to Stuttgart.[539] The instant they heard this news, those yearning souls, along with some other friends – all filled with ecstasy and wonder – rushed to attain the Master's presence.[540] They rendered abundant thanks and expressed their great surprise that the Master had come without informing them of His plans in advance. In response, the Master addressed them with these words:

> I wished to come without apprising anyone. I love the Bahá'ís of Stuttgart very much. Wherever I have gone on this journey, I have said that the Bahá'ís of Germany are deeply sincere, enamoured, and steadfast. It is for this reason that the Cause will acquire great power in this place. I detected a pleasant fragrance the moment I entered Stuttgart.

As the Master was tired, He dismissed the believers early. He had dinner in His room, where the hotel's attendants had brought it at His request, and He instructed the members of His retinue to have their dinner in the hotel dining hall.[541]

Germany

Tuesday, 1 April 1913[542]
[Stuttgart]

The believers came in groups, filled with rapture and ecstasy, to attain the Master's presence. Some of them, out of the intensity of their longing to see Him, had been moved to tears, while others beamed with consummate joy. To each and every one of them the Master extended a special share of His tender kindnesses. Among the remarks He made to them were these:

> Behold what the grace and bounty of Bahá'u'lláh have done! Observe where we are and where you are. See how this grace and bounty have gathered us together in one place – how they have bound the hearts to one another, and delighted the souls with the glad-tidings of God. What bonds are these, what love is this, that derive their power from no earthly source? How many are the people who come from a single family or belong to one race, but oppose one another with the utmost antipathy and hostility! Compare them to us – we who were very far from each other, and were strangers to one another in every respect, but have each now come to feel such heartfelt love, fellowship, and oneness towards the other.
>
> To outward seeming, neither had we heard the name of Stuttgart, nor had you all heard the name of Núr. The power of the Word of God has rent the veils asunder. How wonderfully has this power united us! How completely has it bound the hearts together! How remarkably has it made the East and the West as one – how it has brought the far removed so close together, and turned strangers into friends! On the other hand, it has also separated brother from brother, and fathers from their sons.
>
> The extent to which the power of Bahá'u'lláh has revolutionized the hearts and enraptured the souls has yet to be fully realized; only later will it become known. People are still in need of moral

> and spiritual edification. When this has been achieved to the most conspicuous possible degree, such that it resembles a tree bearing the fruits of a goodly character, then will the extent of that power become evident. Until spiritual sentiments attain their highest consummation, and until the lights of sanctification shed their splendour, the perfection of humankind will never be made manifest. When these requirements have been completely satisfied, then will people have attained to the rank of true Bahá'ís. Only then will it become readily apparent what a brilliant light Bahá'u'lláh has shone forth, and what a resplendent ray He has cast down. Only then will remarkable displays of purity be witnessed from the world of humanity.

The Master then addressed these words to another group of people:

> Your receptivity is the reason God has sent me to Stuttgart, that here I might cry out: 'How blessed is this day!'
>
> What a cause of joy it is for me to meet with you all. We have come here at a good time; it is the beginning of the spring, and the gardens and fields are flush with verdure. The moment I entered Stuttgart, I felt a happiness suggesting that this city will become illumined.

Things were carrying on in this way – one after the other, the Master's visitors were continuously attaining His presence, and He was constantly engaged in speaking to them – when we suddenly heard the crying of a woman. Upon entering the Master's room, this woman threw herself at His feet and began to wail bitterly.[543] After showering her with loving-kindness and consoling her tenderly, the Master said:

> We arrived last night unbeknownst to anyone. Praised be God that we have met with the friends – and what wonderful friends are these! They are immeasurably firm and steadfast in the Cause of God; exceedingly luminous and enraptured are they.

Such were the events of that morning up until noon.[544] The Master had arranged His schedule to where the believers, and also some seekers, would attain His presence every morning, while at other times of the day He would attend other gatherings.[545] Accordingly, He dismissed the believers at noon that day, had His lunch, and then rested for a while.

Mr Herrigel came with his car sometime thereafter,[546] wishing to take the Master for an outing before going to a gathering of believers later in the day. Consequently, the Master and Mr Herrigel went on a very quick excursion around Stuttgart. On this outing, the Master saw many of the buildings, gardens, hills, and mountains of the city. They were remarkably pleasant sights, and this was especially true of one part of the city in particular – an elevated place where the car stopped for a few minutes, giving the Master a chance to look out over the entire city, with all its buildings and other places, and behold a breathtaking view. As we were returning, we passed by most of the magnificent edifices of the area, as well as several factories. The car eventually reached a public garden [Oberer Schlossgarten], which was so wonderfully luxuriant that the Master exited the car and walked the entire length of the adjoining street.

After re-entering the car through the other door, we resumed our course and arrived at the gathering of believers held at the home of Mr Herrigel,[547] where the sound of 'Alláh-u-Abhá' could be clearly heard from every direction. Notwithstanding His own vehement objections to such demonstrations of reverence, all those present threw themselves at the Master's feet; kissed the hem of His robe; and, when the time came to shake His hand, each and every one of them, young and old alike, would first kiss it and then rest their brow upon it.

To witness that moving scene evoked an unusual kind of tenderness; it was truly an astonishing sight to behold. All the believers of Germany evinced a level of attraction, deference, and courtesy that far exceeded the genuinely humble displays of the American friends. It can be said that, if the Cause of God were to be taught in the cities of Germany the same way it has heretofore been spread in America, the measure of progress which the Cause of God would make in Germany – and the extent to which His Word would be exalted – would considerably surpass the degree to which these have been achieved in America. Not one child from among the Bahá'ís of Germany attained the presence of the Master who did not kiss His hand and say 'Alláh-u-Abhá'. In seeing the children behave in this way, and witnessing the profundity of their fondness [for the Master], one could clearly discern the complete attraction, the fixed attention, the consummate love, and the utmost devotion which characterized the Bahá'í men and women of that place.

It is for this reason that the Master's address to that gathering of friends included His praise and gratitude for having seen them so rapturously embrace the Cause. He expounded, moreover, on the counsels of the Abhá Beauty, Whose commandments He exhorted His listeners to obey; urged them to arise and guide others; spoke of the end of ignorance and blindness; and discussed the revival of the peoples of the world through the fragrances and effects of the Greatest Name.

Once the Master had concluded His talk, those loved ones of God came before His chair once again; they each shook His hand and implored His confirmations.

The Master then went to another room, and as no one else was there apart from His attendants, He gave repeated thanks and praise to the Blessed Beauty.

Following this, a new group of people that included some seekers – among them a number of professors and dignitaries of the city – entered Mr Herrigel's residence.[548] The Master summoned them all to that same room where He and His attendants were. In response to the questions they asked Him, He began to expound on spiritual subjects – and as His audience listened to these explanations, they all expressed their sincere and humble devotion, and voiced their praise and gratitude. The Master's heart swelled with even more joy than before as a result of that visit from those souls.

The Master returned to the hotel. On the way there, He rendered constant thanks for the confirmations vouchsafed from the Most Glorious Kingdom, and made repeated mention of the capacity and staunchness of the Germans.[549]

A public gathering was held that evening at the home of Mr Herrigel once again. When the Master's car reached the residence shortly after nightfall, He found that the friends had formed a line outside and were waiting for Him to arrive.[550] With heartfelt devotion, they all raised the cry of 'Alláh-u-Abhá'. So great was the number of believers and seekers in attendance that both the drawing room and the dining area were completely filled with people.[551] Some of those present had to stand outside the rooms, where they listened to the Master's utterances and hearkened to His most sweet voice. The talk He gave to them concerned the debarment of the peoples of the world in the time of every Manifestation of God, the meanings of the prophecies and terms mentioned in the various holy texts, and the second coming of Christ from heaven.[552] From the clamorous ecstasy of those in attendance, as well as their devoted attention to the Master's words, it was evident indeed that the confirmations promised to us had descended there from the Most Great Paradise.

Following the conclusion of that public gathering, a number of the attendees who were seated in the Master's presence at the dinner table were brimming with such overwhelming excitement that I cannot possibly describe it. How effusive were the thanks they gave for having had the bounty of meeting 'Him round Whom all names revolve'![553] This was especially the case with the respected hosts of that occasion, Mr and Mrs Herrigel.

Wednesday, 2 April 1913[554]
[Stuttgart]

From morning till noon, a steady stream of Bahá'ís and their friends attained the Master's presence.[555] As they received His tender kindnesses and listened to His blessed words,[556] they were stirred to their very cores and roused to fervent excitement. They expressed their abundant gratitude, moreover, as He answered their questions on spiritual subjects and discussed the new and wondrous teachings. So enamoured of the beauty and the glory of the Centre of the Covenant had they become that, when they had been dismissed from His presence, they gathered once again at the Master's hotel, where they related for one another instances of His kindnesses and quotations from His utterances. They did not wish to leave the hotel, much to the astonishment of its employees, who would ask:

> What is all this commotion for a person from the East? Why all this coming and going of so many people, and what is the reason for the reverence they show Him and the clamour they raise?

It is for this reason that the Master exclaimed:

> The proprietor of this hotel would do well to leave this place and run away!

Among the remarks which the Master made to the Bahá'ís were these:

> I was very happy last night because I saw that your hearts are ablaze with the fire of the love of God, that the breathings of the Holy Spirit are readily apparent, and that the confirmations vouchsafed from the Most Glorious Paradise are clearly manifest. It was a good gathering; the effects thereof shall spread to every corner of the world, inasmuch as the ray of the Sun of Truth was shining upon it. That gathering was luminous indeed; every heart was turned towards the Abhá Kingdom, every eye was fixed on the Most Exalted Horizon, and every soul was rejoicing as it heard the glad-tidings of God. Those in attendance were baptized with the divine spirit and the fire of the love of God. I hope, therefore, that it will yield magnificent results, and that its splendour will shine throughout the world.

As groups of people continued to attain the Master's presence, He would expound on some subject or other for them. One of the believers[557] said to Him, 'People ask us, "Who is this blessed Personage?"' The Master replied:

> Say to them: 'He is a summoner to the Kingdom of God, a promoter of the religion of Bahá'u'lláh, a herald of peace and welfare, and one who calls on humanity to embrace their oneness.' Respond in this way, and then discuss the Cause of Bahá'u'lláh with them.

In the afternoon,[558] Consul [Albert] Schwarz and his wife [Alice Schwarz] brought their car and expressed the hope that they might take the Master on an excursion. The Master consented to the request of the consul and his wife, and they took Him to the grounds of the royal palace [Schloss Solitude] for their outing that day.[559] While there, the Master spoke of the ephemerality of this world and the immortality of the life to come.

Following this excursion, the Master went to the home of Consul Schwarz,[560] where a number of the consul's friends attained the Master's presence and learned about the teachings of this most great dispensation.[561]

The weekly gathering of Bahá'ís was convened at a certain hall [the Bürgermuseum] that evening.[562] In addition to the Bahá'ís, a great many seekers were also present at that gathering.[563] The Master's address to them all dealt with the impermissibility of blind imitation, the promotion of the single foundation underlying all the divine religions, the renewal of religious laws, and the establishment of a heavenly civilization.[564] To conclude His talk, the Master chanted a prayer supplicating success and confirmations for that gathering – a chant that only added to the rapture of those in attendance, and strengthened the firmness of their gaze on the Most Glorious Kingdom.[565]

At each of these gatherings, the Master's words would be translated twice: first from Persian into English by Mirza Ahmad Sohrab, and then a second time from English into German by Mr [Adolf] Eckstein (or Mr Herrigel).[566] Every single sentence was conveyed by the translators – and this double translation notwithstanding, the blessed utterances of the Master burned brightly nonetheless, even as a raging fire, within the hearts of His audience, and kindled the flame of love and ecstasy within their souls.

All those present on that occasion, friends and others, were totally captivated by the speech and conduct of the Master.

Thursday, 3 April 1913[567]
[Stuttgart → Esslingen → Stuttgart]

From the early hours of the morning until noon, the jubilant commotion of those who loved the Master and longed to be in His presence could be heard from His residence at the hotel where He was staying.[568] When Miss [Alma] Knobloch, a blessed and faithful handmaid of God – one of the first people, along with Dr Fisher, to travel from America to Germany to teach the Cause of God, which has caused the divine fragrances to be diffused in that land – attained the Master's presence, He said to her:[569]

> You are truly a summoner to the Kingdom of God. Your heart is pure, and you intend only to serve for the sake of God. It is for this reason that you have succeeded in spreading the divine fragrances; otherwise, how else could you have possibly risen to the occasion? It is your purity that has made you successful. When I was in America, I remembered you constantly; I never forgot you. I feel the utmost fondness for those who are sincerely devoted to the Cause of God.

A large crowd of believers – men, women, and sweet children, all ablaze to the utmost with the fire of the love of God – then attained the presence of the Master, Who began His talk to them with these words:[570]

> The bounty which has been given to Stuttgart is not yet known; only later will it become clear. When the clouds rain and the sun shines, the bounty they are giving is not known at first – only later, once the plants have sprung up, does it become clear . . .

In addition to the Bahá'ís in attendance, a number of Theosophists and members of the Esperanto Society were also present, and they evinced the utmost devotion and deference as they listened to the Master's lofty words. This was especially the case with one of the Theosophists in particular, who expressed his great joy at having had the privilege of attaining the Master's presence. To him, the Master said:

> I hope that our happiness may last forever – that we may be together throughout all the realms of God, and take refuge in the shade of the bounty of Bahá'u'lláh. Therein lies a union that knows no separation; it is a day not followed by night, a joy entirely free from sorrow, and a life that shall never end in death. My hope is that we may be together in the shade of such a bounty as this.

In the afternoon, a most majestic gathering was held in honour of the Bahá'í children at the children's school (in Esslingen).[571] The convener of that gathering was that handmaid of God, Miss Anna Köstlin – a sincerely devoted believer and one of the teachers of those children, to most of whom she herself had taught the Faith. But before that gathering was held, the Master, His attendants, and some other friends set out, in two cars, from Stuttgart to Esslingen.[572] For more than an hour, the Master's car passed by verdant hills, gardens, and forests.

When the Master arrived at the aforementioned school, He found that all the children, dressed in their school uniforms, had formed a neatly-ordered line extending from the entrance of the building all the way to its main room.[573] They all expressed their reverence for the Master and exclaimed 'Alláh-u-Abhá!'[574] The Master walked gracefully among those children, handing sweets to each and every one of them and caressing them tenderly.[575] He said:

> What precious children these are! I beseech God to send down from the heavens a blessing on these children, that even as the flowers of the most glorious garden, they may flourish with verdure. May the light of the love of God make each of them as brilliant lamps, and may they derive their portion of splendour shining from the Daystar of the Most Glorious Paradise.

> These children are the fruits of the tree of the love of God; they are the saplings of the Abhá Kingdom. Their hearts are pure to the utmost, and their souls are as undefiled and delicate as can be. I hope, therefore, that even as pearls, they may be nurtured in the shell of the love of God.

The Master then went to a large hall where high tea had been prepared, all sorts of sweets and flowers had been laid out on the tables, and other such arrangements for receiving Him had been made. All the believers had formed lines in that room and were waiting for the Master to enter – and as soon as He did, they began to sing songs in His praise. Most of them presented the Master with bouquets of flowers, and they kissed His hand and the hem of His robe.

Afterwards, the Master went to the platform, sat in the chair that had been specially reserved for Him, and bade everyone be seated. The absence of all those friends who could not attend that gathering, with all its ascendant majesty, was palpable indeed. As the believers were seated before the Master at their tables, on which were arranged all kinds of sweets and flowers – every inch of that space having been decorated, and *sharbat,* confections, and fruits of various colours all having been laid out – every one of their hearts was keenly attuned to the beautifully tender demeanour of the Master, and their eyes were fixed firmly on the light that seemed to radiate from His face. All this made for a scene so spectacular that it would surely have aroused the envy of kings – a scene that clearly demonstrated the sovereignty of Him Who is the King of glory and power.

At the beginning of that grand gathering, Mr Herrigel rose and gave an extensive address, in which He hailed the arrival of the Master and sang His effusive praises. Following this, the Master rose with that elegant stature of His and gave a talk on the promotion of universal peace, the oneness of humanity, and the love of God.[576]

Once those in attendance had had some tea, fruits, and sweets, a request was made for the Master to have His photograph taken with the children and other believers. The Master consented to this request and went outside the school. A photograph was taken as all the children and some of the friends were holding bouquets of flowers, evincing their blissful ecstasy as they basked in the Master's presence.[577]

The Master then entered the car, and as He did this, the believers raised such a clamour and showed Him such profound reverence that some others nearby gathered to watch this spectacle with astonishment.[578] Some of them approached the believers and asked:

> What is the meaning of this? How is it that an illustrious Persian, clad as He is in the garb of the East, has so conspicuously become the beloved master of a people as respected as the Germans?

The friends, for their part, seized this opportunity to discuss the Cause of God with them, and even bring some of them into the presence of the Master, whereupon they all shook His hand, expressed their joy, and showed Him deference.

Friday, 4 April 1913[579]
[Stuttgart]

The Master gave thanks that morning for the confirmations and support of Bahá'u'lláh, and His heart was immensely cheered by the fact that the sweet savours of God and the influence of His Word had spread in Germany.

After having tea,[580] the believers came in groups. With absolute servitude and perfect love, their faces radiant and joyous, they all had the honour of attaining the Master's presence, listening to His utterances, and receiving His tender kindnesses.

To the first group that met with Him, the Master interpreted the meaning of the dreams which some of those Bahá'ís had had. One of them had dreamed that he was dead; another had dreamed that he was holding a staff; and yet another, who was sick, had dreamed that he was fleeing in terror from Satan. To each of them, the Master said in turn:

> You will soon make a full recovery; be assured of the grace of God. That Satan is none other than the human self. Each person has a Satan, which is his own self, and it strives every hour – no, every minute! – to prevail over him. The staff is the staff of a shepherd; it symbolizes the acts of tending to God's flock and guiding His servants aright. The death represents the longevity of your life, and constitutes a sign of your salvation.

The Master then turned to a seeker[581] and said:

> I wish for you to be illumined with the light of God, that you may discover the secrets of truth – that you may acquire seeing eyes with which to see the Most Glorious Kingdom, hearing ears wherewith to hear the celestial voice, and that you may be baptized with the Holy Spirit, the fire of the love of God, and the Water of Life. This is the station I desire for you.

A certain woman then requested the Master to give her an Eastern name, and on her He conferred the title *qamar*.[582]

Another woman spoke to the Master about her husband's harmful habits, and expressed the hope that he might be rightly guided and find spiritual happiness. To her, the Master said:

> I pray God that both he and your son may become spiritual, and that divine munificence and generosity may be shown them.

The Master answered each question that was posed to Him, one after the other, and then discussed the subjects of spiritual happiness, divine love, the degrees of faith and understanding, the excellences of humankind, and eternal life. In so doing, it seemed He had flung open the gates of Paradise before the faces of all those present.

Afterwards, a number of Bahá'ís from Esslingen attained the Master's presence and spoke to Him of the effects of the gathering held there the day before. The Master said:

> I had a wonderful time yesterday. It was a spiritual gathering, well-attended and exceedingly luminous . . .

A highly intelligent child, who felt particularly close with the Master whenever he stood in His presence, approached Him accompanied by his mother and father, who said to the Master, 'This child mentions the Faith to everyone he meets; he has become a teacher of the Cause!'[583] The Master stated:[584]

> It is good to teach the Cause when one is young; I myself did it when I was this age. One of the believers had a brother who did not believe in the Faith; whatever efforts they would make, this man would not accept the Cause. They then brought him to me, and he said, 'The others have spoken to me at length regarding this Cause, but I have yet to be satisfied with their explanations.' I replied to him, 'You have not had the requisite readiness. It is the thirsty who enjoy water and are contented with it, the seeing who are satisfied with the light of the sun and the moon, and the hearing who take pleasure in soul-stirring melodies – not the deaf, the blind, and others of that sort.' My extensive conversation with him ultimately transformed him into a believer in the Cause.

It took some time for all the friends from Stuttgart and Esslingen, as well as their acquaintances and some seekers who had come with them, to attain the Master's presence.[585] They were all visibly enraptured, intoxicated with the wine of the Master's bounty.

In the afternoon, Consul Schwarz came with his wife and children in tow. He had brought two cars with him, and expressed his desire to take the Master and His attendants on an excursion.[586] With great swiftness, the cars travelled for an hour before eventually reaching a palace [Wilhelma] that had been modelled after the Alhambra, built by Andalusian Arabs. The Master walked throughout the buildings and rooms of the palace, examining many of its furnishings and precious antiques.[587]

Shortly after nightfall, once He had finished His stroll and tipped the caretakers of the palace, the Master returned to the city and headed straight for a gathering held by the Esperanto Society.[588] The talk He gave there, which concerned the oneness of humanity and the fellowship of all people – ideals that can be achieved through the implementation of a universal language, which is itself one of the laws enjoined by Bahá'u'lláh – roused all those present, friends and others, to abundant ecstasy. The very prospect of promoting the means for establishing unity was enough for them to bubble over with enthusiasm. Notwithstanding the brevity of that particular talk, the members of the society expressed their blissful joy and grateful praise nonetheless as that gathering was brought to a close.

From there, the Master went to the residence of Mr Eckstein, where a number of the friends had been invited for dinner.[589] As they were seated in the Master's presence, each and every one of those in attendance had their meal with the utmost delight, and voiced their thanks for having had the bounty of meeting Him.

Once everyone had had their dinner,[590] some of those present sang a song, put to accompaniment on the piano, in praise of the Master – a song that surely cleansed away the rust of sorrow from the mirrors of every heart.

Saturday, 5 April 1913[591]
[Stuttgart]

To the first group of people who attained His presence that morning,[592] the Master described the attraction which the Esperantists had shown the previous night. He then gave a talk that included these remarks:

> At the beginning of every religious dispensation, the Manifestations of God have always spoken in a way that is suited to the level of intelligence and knowledge of their audience, and phrased their utterance in the terminology of the people to whom they appear. Since, however, the terms belonging to the earlier eras of each dispensation would be discarded in its latter days with the changing of circumstances, the people would fail to grasp the

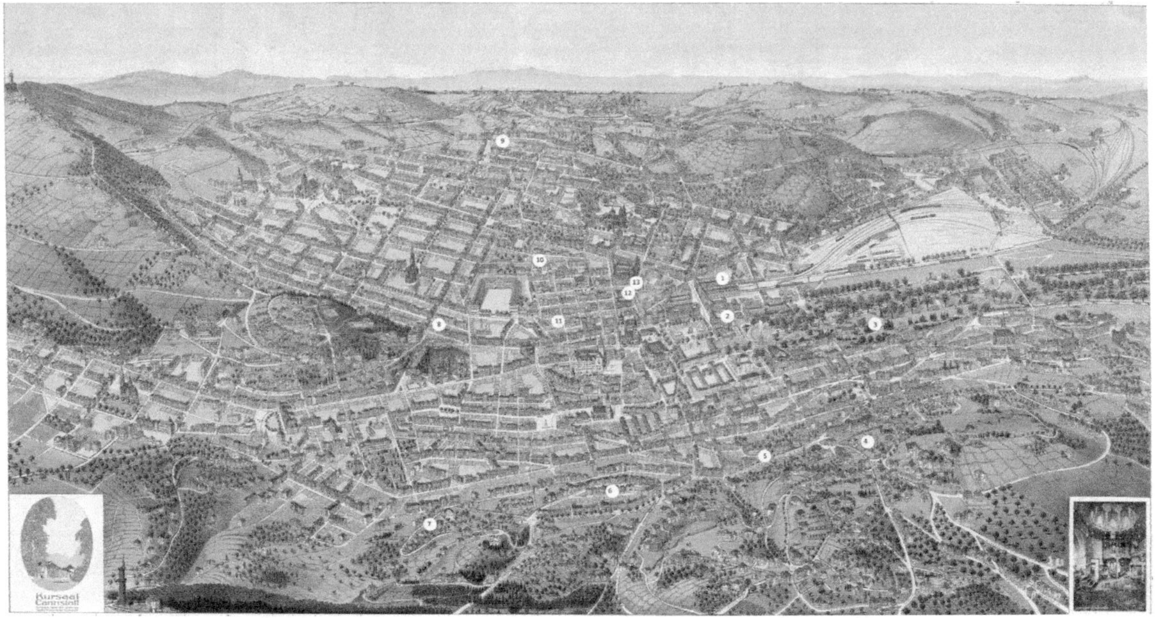

'Stuttgart from a Bird's Eye View'; Rudolf Hagmann, circa 1912. Places that 'Abdu'l-Bahá visited in 1913 have been numbered by Alexander Meinhard as follows: (1) Stuttgart Central Station; (2) Hotel Marquardt; (3) Oberer Schlossgarten (Upper Castle Garden); (4) Villa Wagenburg (at that time), Wagenburgstrasse 5; (5) home of Consul Albert Schwarz and Alice Schwarz, Alexanderstrasse 3; (6) home of Edwin Fisher, Stitzenburgstrasse 12; (7) home of Margarethe Döring and Alma Knobloch, Neue Weinsteige 23; (8) home of Adolf and Agathe Eckstein, Silberburgstrasse 175; (9) home of Wilhelm and Marie Herrigel, Hölderlinstrasse 35; (10) Bollwerk (Bastion); (11) Bürgermuseum (Citizens' Museum); (12) Obere (Upper) Museum, Kanzleistrasse; (13) Frauenklub (Women's Club), Kanzleistrasse 24

The old train station in Stuttgart where 'Abdu'l-Bahá arrived and departed

Hotel Marquardt

'Abdu'l-Bahá in Stuttgart, 6 April 1913: (1) Lydia Bauer, (2) Rosa Schwarz, (3) Helene Eger, (4) Hede Jäger, (5) Alma Knobloch, behind her left to right: Julia Stäbler, Elise Stäbler, then Wilhelm Herrigel, unidentified, Siyyid Asadu'lláh, Siyyid Aḥmad-i-Báqiroff, 'Abdu'l-Bahá, Alice Schwarz. Back row: (6) Katharine Eger, Margarethe Döring in white hat, Heinrich Schwab holding the Greatest Name, Adolf Eckstein (holding the darker version of the Greatest Name), Ahmad Sohrab, (8) Maḥmúd-i-Zarqání, (9) Christian Haug, (10) Mrs Jäger

'Abdu'l-Bahá in Stuttgart, 6 April 1913: (1) Julius Grünzweig, (2) Dr Edwin Fisher, (3) Max Bender,(4) Karl Goll, Mr Häfner,(5) Heinrich Schwab, then following, left to right: Siyyid Asadu'lláh, Maḥmúd-i-Zarqání, Christian Haug senior, Siyyid Aḥmad-i-Báqiroff, Hugo Bender, (6) Adolf Eckstein,(7) Richard Kohler, (8) Mr Schneebeli, (9) Wilhelm Herrigel, then following left to right: Axel Schwarz, Consul Schwarz, 'Abdu'l-Bahá, (10) Gustav Eger, (11) Emil Ruoff, (12) Friedrich Schweizer holding the Greatest Name, (13) Ahmad Sohrab, (14) Wolfgang Schwarz, (15) Otto Häfner

'Abdu'l-Bahá at the Esslingen Kinderfest, April 1913

Consul Albert Schwarz

Alice Schwarz-Solivo in later years

The Schwarz residence in Stuttgart

'Abdu'l-Bahá walking in the Schwarzes' garden in Stuttgart

Friedrich Schweizer

The Schweizer house, visited by 'Abdu'l-Bahá and today the seat of the Spiritual Assembly of the Bahá'ís of Stuttgart. 'Abdu'l-Bahá is reported to have said: 'In this house the call "Yá Bahá'u'l'Abhá" will always be heard and the teachings Bahá'u'lláh will be spread from this house . . .'

Wilhelm Herrigel

Alma and Fanny Knobloch in Stuttgart Stadtgarten, Spring 1913

Anna Köstlin

Adolf Eckstein

Olga (Ollie) Schwarz
at Bad Mergentheim

Edwin Fisher

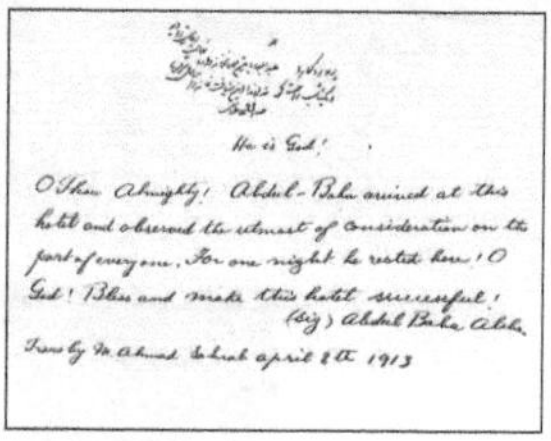

He is God!

O Thou Almighty! Abdul-Baha arrived at this hotel and observed the utmost of consideration on the part of everyone. For one night he rested here! O God! Bless and make this hotel successful!

(Sig) Abdul Baha Abbas

Trans by M. Ahmad Sohrab april 8th 1913

'Abdu'l-Bahá's entry in the Bad Mergentheim guestbook

Marker of 'Abdu'l-Bahá's visit to Bad Mergentheim

> meaning of the words of the prophets. Although Jesus Christ states explicitly in the Gospel, 'I have come down from heaven,'* He was born to Mary in corporeal form – and this notwithstanding, the Christians still expect Him to physically descend from heaven in His second coming!

To another group of people,[593] the Master gave a talk on divine confirmations and heavenly blessings, which He concluded with these words (addressed to one of the friends who was a leading figure in a certain monastic order):[594]

> There is no monasticism in this Cause, but a person who wishes to devote his time exclusively to teaching the Cause of God and serving the human race can still distance himself from the things of this world. It would certainly be preferable for him to spend his time in service to the Kingdom of God, but not to practise monasticism. The intention should be to consecrate one's life to serving the Cause of God, but if he should ever wish to marry, he is free to do so. My sister (the Greatest Holy Leaf) has consecrated her life to the Cause of God, but not with the goal of asceticism or seclusion; rather, she has dedicated herself solely to serving at the threshold of the Abhá Beauty.
>
> My meaning is that the choice is one's own to make: one can consecrate one's life to the Kingdom of God if one so wishes, or serve His Cause while also engaged in other pursuits. Therefore, I hope that you will occupy yourself with teaching the Cause of God. One can promote the Word of God in a variety of ways.

As the Master was giving this talk, His eyes fell upon Mr [Gottlieb] Pfund, a very devoted and courageous Bahá'í, whereupon He said:

> This man is like a lion – no, he is even better! – for the lion only has physical power, whereas this man has both physical and spiritual power.[595]

---

* Possibly a reference to John 6:38: 'For I came down from heaven, not to do mine own will, but the will of him that sent me.'

Owing to the magnificent humour of that remark, the crowd of believers in attendance began to laugh boisterously, and all those gathered raised an unusual uproar.

Another group of believers from Esslingen, as well as some friends from Stuttgart, then attained the Master's presence. Among those visitors was a weeping woman who fell at the Master's feet, and to this woman He said:

> It is evident from your face how pure your heart is; indeed, how sincere and enraptured it is!

After consoling and extending His tender kindnesses to her, the Master further said to this woman:

> The people of Stuttgart and Esslingen are very warm; they are genuinely attracted and excel other Europeans. They will raise a clamour in Europe and throw the continent into disarray. What times these are, and what glory this is!

After pausing briefly, the Master then said:[596]

> You must all be thankful that God has provided the means for us to meet, for this meeting cannot be compared to any other. This meeting is a meeting of radiant hearts. This meeting has been occasioned only by the power and glad-tidings of God. This is a meeting of the inmates of Paradise. This meeting is even as the meeting of the magnet with metal, or the vernal shower with rich soil, or the mirror with light, or the breeze with trees. Thus, it will yield prodigious results . . .

It was at the approach of afternoon when the Bahá'ís, both inside and outside the Master's room at the hotel, made a great commotion. Although the Master had dismissed them from His presence, they did not wish to leave. It is for this reason that the Master said to those friends, repeatedly and humorously:

> You all are going to do something that will cause the proprietor of this hotel to flee at the very sight of you!

With the Master's permission, the Bahá'ís gathered at the garden of Consul Schwarz that day to have a group photograph taken – but before that gathering took place, the consul, his wife, and his children came to the Master with two cars, and took Him and His attendants on an excursion that lasted for more than an hour.[597] With the utmost swiftness, the Master's car passed by all the villages, gardens, fields, hills, and plains on the outskirts of the city, and He beheld some truly breathtaking scenery. All the land had been cultivated; there was not one piece of it that had not been farmed.

Following that excursion, the Master went to the garden of Consul Schwarz.[598] How palpable was the absence of all the believers of the world, especially the Persian friends, from that rose-garden! If only they could have seen the fascinated ecstasy of those servants to the divine threshold, and witnessed the staunchness of those stalwarts of the Covenant in the land of Germany – for in beholding such a scene, they would surely have attained to their heart's desire.

As it was not possible to fit all the believers in the frame of a single photograph, they divided themselves into seven groups.[599] A number of excellent photographs were taken of the Master with others by His side. Some small photographs were also taken of the Master and the members of His retinue.[600] Afterwards, in the buildings where tea and sweets had been laid out for the afternoon meal, all those in attendance expressed their praise and gratitude for the Master's bounties.

Following this, Mrs Schweizer – a sincerely devoted believer, a real flame of the fire of the love of God – and a number of other friends implored the Master to honour her home with His presence. Consequently, a gathering was held at her residence[601] for fifteen minutes, and the friends in that vicinity seemed to be soaring in the heavens out of the intensity of their joy. As the Master began to render praise and thanks to the Abhá Kingdom, He said:

Praised be God! Through the grace and bounty of Bahá'u'lláh, we have come to your home, too. Every house in which the mention of Bahá'u'lláh is made shall be blessed; divine favours will descend upon it, the light of God will shine over it, and the breathings of the Holy Spirit will be breathed into it. My hope, then, is that your home may become blessed and heavenly, that in this home the mention of Bahá'u'lláh may always be lifted up, and that from this home the teachings of Bahá'u'lláh may spread to other homes. This is my hope.

Sunday, 6 April 1913
[Stuttgart]

Among the people whom the Master addressed in the gathering of Bahá'ís that morning was one of the ministers of Stuttgart.[602] This gentleman had become very intrigued after reading *Some Answered Questions*, and the Master gave him permission to translate that work from English into German. The Master's remarks to him were as follows:

The clouds of blind imitation have obscured the Sun of Truth, and the lights of the divine teachings have been prevented from shining forth. Praised be God that there is only one set of spiritual principles underlying the single foundation of the divine religions.

We are all united in thought. We must lend each other a hand by working to remove this blind imitation from our midst and promote the unity of religions, for the foundation of the divine religions is one. Blind imitation has provided the means for discord and strife among humanity. I hope you will succeed in awakening them that are fast asleep, and becoming the cause of Germany's illumination.

The Master's talk caused the darkness of nature to be dissipated and the mysteries of truth to be unravelled. So delightfully fascinated was the aforementioned minister by the Master's utterances that he said, 'With Your permission, I can convey these wondrous teachings to the Emperor of Germany [Wilhelm II] before anyone else.' The Master replied:

> Do not write to the emperor; he is proud and preoccupied, and will not take heed at present.

He then said:

> We will be leaving for Budapest soon. After a few days, we will return and meet with you again. Be very happy; speak with others moderately, not harshly, and do not at all interfere in political affairs.

When another group of people attained the Master's presence, He spoke to them of the divine seasons, the spiritual springtime, and the blossoming of the trees of the gardens of humanity.

A gathering was held that evening in a large hall of the Obere Museum to celebrate the Covenant. In addition to the Bahá'ís who were present, close to a thousand other people were also in attendance.[603]

At the front of that large, well-decorated room, there was a majestic arched veranda that had been adorned with verdant foliage. At the centre of this veranda was a platform, on which a rug made of velvet and silk had been spread out and variegated flowers had been arranged, and on that platform stood a golden chair where the Master was to sit. From the ceiling of the veranda hung the emblem of the Greatest Name, and on both sides were placed two velvet couches.

When the Master entered that room, all those present gave Him a standing ovation and expressed their reverence for Him. Two of the esteemed friends each took the Master by His arms and conducted Him to the veranda of that room, where they asked Him to have a seat. Those two friends then led four of the Master's Persian attendants to that same spot, and instructed them to sit on the velvet couches placed on either side of the Master. All the attendees sat spellbound before the Master and gazed on His luminous face with evident wonderment.

At that juncture, Consul Schwarz rose and began to recite, with the utmost humility and deference, a letter of salutation to the Master on behalf of all the believers. Following this, the consul made some remarks in praise of the blessed teachings and brought His address to a close.

The Master then rose and gave, with consummate power, a captivatingly eloquent talk on the peerlessness of the people of Bahá, the calamities which the Manifestations of God sustained to foster love and oneness among humanity, and the teachings of Bahá'u'lláh.[604] The transformation and fascination evinced by those in attendance can neither be depicted by the pen nor conveyed by the tongue. It would be impossible to befittingly describe how enamoured they were of the Master's incomparable beauty and glory, how entranced they were by His explanation of the blessed teachings, and how enraptured they were by the evidences of His conspicuous glory.[605]

Monday, 7 April 1913

[Stuttgart → Bad Mergentheim]

The Master was preparing to depart that day for Budapest, where Mr Stark had repeatedly implored Him to visit. Although this gentleman was not a Bahá'í,[606] he had arranged for a group of receptive souls to meet with the Master and organized gatherings where He was to speak – but His plans to travel that day were delayed. Consul Schwarz and his wife had insisted on taking the Master to Bad Mergentheim, one of the splendid towns in the German countryside where the consul himself owned a hotel and a mineral hot spring.[607] Consequently, at ten o'clock in the morning,[608] the consul came with his wife, children, and two cars,[609] and set out for Bad Mergentheim with the Master and His attendants.[610] The cars travelled for four hours, during which time the Master saw flourishing villages, pleasant rivers and valleys, verdant mountains and plains, wildflowers, gardens, and cultivated forests.

At noon,[611] the cars stopped at [a] hotel [in] Swabia,[612] which was on the way. After having lunch and resting for a bit,[613] we continued on to Bad Mergentheim, where the Master arrived at two o'clock in the afternoon.[614] The Master was so delighted by the beauty of its fields and the songs of its nightingales that He remarked:

> From the moment I left Persia until now, I had not heard such pleasant melodies from nightingales, or beheld such beautiful fields and gardens in such great abundance.

To relieve Him of the fatigues of His journey, Mr and Mrs Schwarz suggested to the Master that He stay in that city for at least a few days in private quarters, undisturbed by the coming and going of visitors wishing to attain His presence. 'Our intention and hope in bringing You here', they said to Him, 'was to bless this place and also afford You a few days of rest.' The Master replied:

> Our purpose is not to seek repose or go on leisurely excursions; rather, it is to serve at the threshold of God and spread His fragrances. Our comfort and happiness consist in service at the threshold of Bahá'u'lláh. This applies especially to the promise we have made to visit Budapest, where gatherings with us have already been scheduled and a great number of people are eagerly waiting to meet with us. It is, therefore, imperative that we leave soon.

It is for this reason that the Master did not sojourn at Bad Mergentheim for more than one night, and it is also why He was engaged constantly – even as He walked throughout the gardens and plains of that area – in conversations about the Cause of God. He would occasionally speak of the best interests [of the Cause] in that city and give instructions on how to achieve them. The Master's thoughts were so focused on His journey that He did not even go to the mineral hot spring. However much they pleaded with Him, the Master contented Himself with a stroll along the hot spring, taking note of the various baths with private chambers. He said:

> I am not in the mood for bathing, nor do I have the peace of mind needed for it; my thoughts are preoccupied with work.

Later on in the journey, when the Master was travelling from Stuttgart to Paris and His train passed by Baden-Baden, the members of His retinue remarked to Him:

> The water, the climate, and the mineral hot springs of Baden-Baden are world-renowned. It would be good for You to stay there, even for just one day.

The Master replied:

> I am not interested in recreation; I am interested in work and service.

Tuesday, 8 April 1913

[Bad Mergentheim → Stuttgart → En route to Budapest]

The Master departed Bad Mergentheim and returned straight to Stuttgart that morning.[615] He had lunch at the home of Consul Schwarz [in Stuttgart],[616] and a constant stream of believers attained His presence. When they realized that the Master's train would soon be departing [for Budapest], they did not forfeit this chance to visit Him. Up until the afternoon, that gladsome house was positively brimming with ecstasy and delight, and the Master's promise that He would return to Stuttgart filled the friends with blissful joy.[617]

When the Master arrived at the railway station,[618] a number of believers – adults and children, men and women – were there, too.[619] They were visibly despondent, yearning so intensely for the Master's presence that they lamented His imminent departure with heart-rending sighs of regret. All the friends in that spacious railway station had gathered around the Master's radiant face, circling the Centre of the Covenant in the atmosphere of their love for Him even as moths fluttering about a brightly burning candle – and this created so remarkable a spectacle that it drew the surprise of onlookers near and far, who brought their hands to their mouths in astonishment as they witnessed the ecstatic commotion the Bahá'ís were making.[620] This was especially the case when the Master approached the railroad tracks, at which point the believers formed a line in front of the train; tears streamed down their faces, and they lifted up cries of anguish. As the train began to depart,[621] they all waved their hats and handkerchiefs out of reverence to Him. To the extent that they were able, they kept their gaze fixed squarely on the train from a distance, and some of them[622] even accompanied the Master for a few stations to see Him off.

The friends in Esslingen had been informed through a telegram that the Master would be passing through their city quickly in a mail train but would not be stopping there. Consequently, all the friends in Esslingen stood near the railroad tracks, and as the train came into view, they began to raise a great clamour and cry out, 'Alláh-u-Abhá!' Though their 'visit' had lasted for only a brief moment, it had sufficed nonetheless to bring them great joy.[623]

The Master slept in the train that night. Among the Bahá'ís of Germany who accompanied Him on that train ride was Mr Herrigel.[624]

Wednesday, 9 April 1913

[En route to Budapest → Vienna → Budapest]

The outskirts of Vienna came into view at eight o'clock that morning. When the train arrived at the station,[625] a few of the Persian friends[626] were waiting to receive the Master. It took fifteen minutes to go from that place to another railway station that serviced Hungary.[627] From there, they set off for Budapest,[628] and that city was eternally blessed and honoured with the Master's footsteps.

Notwithstanding the fact that none of them was a Bahá'í at that time, Mr Stark, his wife, and the heads of various societies had unwittingly gone to a different railway station to receive the Master.[629] Since, however, they were aware that He would be lodging at the Ritz[630] – the most distinguished hotel in Budapest – they hastened there at once.

When the Master arrived [at the hotel],[631] all His visitors rose before Him.[632] One of them[633] welcomed and praised Him on behalf of all those present with the following remarks:

> On behalf of everyone here, I wish to salute You on Your arrival, extend to You my praise, and express to You my gratitude, for in spite of Your advanced age (69 years old), You have shouldered labours and faced difficulties during Your journey to secure the tranquillity of humanity. This toil and sacrifice serve as the greatest example for us to know how best to live our lives and serve humankind . . .

When that gentleman had concluded his remarks, the Master spoke these blessed words:[634]

He is God

> My hope is that we may all succeed in rendering service to humanity, for in this day there is no greater service than to promote the oneness of humankind and universal peace, that thereby people may be saved from age-old bigotries and harmful imitations, and sanctified from prejudices of religion, nationality, race, and politics. So long as these prejudices persist, the world will not know complete tranquillity and prosperity.
>
> At a time when the East was engulfed in such intense darkness, and beset on every side by the gloom of prejudice, Bahá'u'lláh rose even as a sun over its horizon; He proclaimed the oneness of humanity and declared that all people were of one kind, servants of one God, descendants of one source, and the sheep of one divine flock, observing that God, the true Shepherd, loves His flock dearly, and that all are precious to Him. Considering that God has always been kind to everyone, and that all are beloved by Him – sustaining and protecting them as He does – why, then, should we be unkind to one another, or quarrel and contend with each other? The divine Sun shines upon everyone; the showers of His mercy rain on everyone. Behold how kind is God towards all

humanity, that He has created them and bestowed on them all an equal measure of His bounties!

The human race is the handiwork of God. Is it fair of us to destroy that handiwork and then take pride in this destruction – to boast of our bravery as we killed countless people in the span of a single day, or laid an entire nation to waste in just one hour? It can be likened to the wolf priding itself on how ferociously it tore a flock of sheep to pieces. What foolishness is this? What ingratitude is this towards the blessings we have been granted? God has invested us with these powers and capabilities so that we might serve humanity with them, not bring about its destruction and distress.

Praised be God! This age is a luminous age. It is the age of arts and sciences – the age in which the realities of things will be discovered. It is the age of justice and fairness – the age of the progress of minds and souls. We must arise to do things that befit the magnitude of this momentous age.

A number of reporters were present, and they asked the Master about the basis of the blessed Cause. In response, the Master gave an explanation of the divine teachings, which the reporters wrote down immediately.

From that very night, several newspapers printed articles in German and Hungarian that discussed the Master's arrival and the wondrous teachings with the utmost praise. In such a city as this, where no more than just two or three people were apprised of this sublime Cause,[635] the fame of the Word of God and the power of His Covenant had, on our first day there, been spread to everyone and roused numerous souls to fervent excitement.

Hungary

Thursday, 10 April 1913
[Budapest]

Early that morning, the Master prepared the tea Himself and graciously served it to His attendants. He remarked favourably on how the skies were clear and the weather not overly warm, and commented also on the invigoratingly splendid view from His room. The Master's elevated vantage point, afforded Him by the third floor of that hotel overlooking the magnificent Danube River, enabled Him to see the large bridges of that river and the ships crossing its surface; the royal citadel [Buda Castle], along with certain ruins of that site from the days when the Muslims [Ottomans] had occupied it; and other buildings, trees, and gardens situated on the side of the river visible from His room. Although it was spring, the weather would at times become intensely cold, with snow even falling on some occasions.

Up until noon, a great many professors and heads of various societies – men of Ottoman, Arab, and European extraction – attained the Master's presence, and were roused to such fascinated excitement by His talk on the divine teachings that they openly testified to the greatness and significance of the blessed Cause. Among those present were Dr Ignác Kúnos, a university president; Dr Alexander [or Sándor] Giesswein, a member of parliament; Professor [Gyula, or Julius] Germanus; Mr [Nándor] Eigel, first secretary to a certain legation;[636] and Sarkar 'Azíz Aḥmad.[637]

Sometime thereafter, at the request of some of the owners of certain newspapers, a number of photographs of the Master were taken outside the hotel; in some of those pictures, the Master was by Himself, while in others He was with a crowd of people.[638] He then said, 'Let us walk for a bit.'[639]

While on this stroll, someone who had learned of the Master's arrival through a newspaper ran right up to Him, upon realizing He was the very Person he had read about, and requested that He autograph the margin of that same newspaper with his pen and honour him with an eternal memento in so doing.

After crossing the river, Sardar Umrao Singh [Sher-Gil] – an old friend [of mine] from the Indian state of Punjab – attained the presence of the Master, Who spoke to him and showed him loving-kindness. The remarks which the Master addressed to him concerned the Theosophists:

> In spite of all their awareness, and notwithstanding their quest for peace – knowing as they do that a Perfect Man is needed in this perspicuous age – most of them are ignorant of this Cause and the momentousness of the advent of Bahá'u'lláh, which is more manifest than the sun itself. Rather, they expect that a young Indian,* who at present is being groomed in Europe, will be the source of such a prodigious cause. They do not realize that to deem him who will be the World Teacher to be in need of education by others is like trying to create a resplendent Sun by using the oil and wick of a candle. But the light of this Perfect Man must be heavenly, not earthly; His perfections must be innate, not acquired; and His writings must be unbounded bestowals, not the products of the finite disciplines of this limited and contingent world.

The Master then looked at some of the ruins from the days of the Ottoman conquests, and this prompted Him to say:

> Had the Persians and the Ottomans not opposed one other, all these nations would now be under their control. Yet they fell into such grievous heedlessness that whenever the Ottomans were preoccupied with their conquests in Europe, the Persians would take note of this preoccupation and mount attacks against them. Likewise, whenever the Persians were similarly preoccupied, the Ottomans would assail them. Each refused to leave the other alone. Every day they held revels, pursued their selfish interests, and indulged their deep-seated rancour, until at last each cast the

* Jiddu Krishnamurti.

> glory of his foe to the wind and laid waste to a prosperous civilization. When Sultan Selim* conquered certain European lands, he was suddenly informed that Shah Tahmasp† had attacked some of his own territories. As a result, the sultan was forced to return whence he had come. Had they not opposed each other at that time with such vehement hostility, neither nation would have descended into its present abasement.

A youth[640] who happened to be passing by at that moment became so fascinated by the Master's utterances that, without even willing it, he joined the crowd of people who were already walking with Him. Every day thereafter, this youth was present at every occasion when the Master spoke, and grew increasingly enamoured of Him as he listened to His most sweet voice.

As they were walking that day, Sardar Umrao Singh mentioned the name of Professor [Ármin, or Arminius] Vámbéry to the Master. Vámbéry was a famous philosopher who had expressed an interest in learning more about this most great Cause, as well as his ardent desire to attain the Master's presence.[641] 'But alas!' said Singh, 'he is sick, and it would be difficult for him to leave his residence during Your brief time here.' The Master replied, 'We will pay him a visit.'

The Master was scheduled to speak that night at the Theosophical Society.[642] It was an auspicious night; the members of that society, similar to those of the Edinburgh Theosophical Society, leapt into service with the utmost zeal and devotion.

The first to speak was the president of the society [Róbert Nádler], who introduced the Master with these remarks:

> I welcome 'Abdu'l-Bahá 'Abbás on behalf of all the brothers and sisters of this society. Our hearts are immeasurably cheered by the presence of this blessed Personage in our midst. All the members of this society appreciate the value of this bounty, for some of the principles of this Cause are known well to them. Likewise, they

* Sultan Selim II.

† Shah Tahmasp I.

> have come to profess a belief not shared by the peoples of the West – that the East has always been home to immense treasures, and that those treasures have historically been, and are today still being, brought to the West. Thus, the members of this society hope that the inhabitants of the West – who are engrossed in the natural sciences, devote their energies exclusively to physical matters, and are entirely deprived of spiritual delights – may obtain nonetheless this supreme bestowal. This society is thrilled and thankful to the utmost that the greatest spiritual Teacher of the East is with them tonight, and that He will grant them all a share of God's bounties and blessings.

The Master then rose and gave an extensive talk in which He stated that both material and divine civilization have always appeared in the East, and that every advancement achieved in the West has stemmed from ancient Eastern civilization. He observed that this was especially true of spiritual civilization and celestial splendours, which have invariably shone from the East upon the West. The hearts of those present were so profoundly moved by this talk, which had stirred them all to great excitement, that the president of that society arose once again with conspicuous ecstasy, turned towards the Master, and said:

> Dear Sir! On account of Your eloquent remarks and beautiful utterances, the joy in our souls and the gladness in our breasts have swelled to such great proportions that the tongue is powerless to describe it, for when the heart has reached the pinnacle of happiness, the tongue cannot possibly depict that state. Hence, it is with the utmost gratitude and delight that we hereby conclude this gathering.[643]

It was indeed a gathering charged with fervour, and every heart in attendance had been plunged into oceans of blissful joy.

Friday, 11 April 1913
[Budapest]

The first people to have the honour of attaining the Master's presence that morning were a group of Theosophists,[644] who effusively expressed their genuine affection. To them the Master said:

> Praised be God that the means for us to meet were prepared. The meeting last night was very good; feelings of spirituality pervaded the hearts of those present. I hope that these feelings and bonds may grow stronger every day, such that Budapest may become the focal point from which the oneness of humankind may appear, and that these splendours may shine from this city in every other direction.

Following this, the Master discussed the perspicuous perfections of the Promised One, along with the signs of the power and grandeur of His advent.[645]

At that juncture, the Hungarian youth who had crossed paths with the Master the previous day attained His presence once again,[646] this time accompanied by one of his friends.[647] To that youth the Master said:[648]

> It is good that we met you in the street without some sort of intermediary; it is good to make one's acquaintance this way. Praised be God that sentiments of spirituality exist in Budapest. The people here investigate the truth; they wish to know more of the divine realm, and seek greater awareness of the Kingdom of God.
>
> I love Budapest and Stuttgart very much; there are good people in these two cities. Just as there are now earthly alliances between Germany and Austria, I hope that one day they may also form spiritual alliances. The true root of such alliances is spiritual, for political alliances can dissolve in the span of a single day, whereas heavenly alliances – along with spiritual love and fellowship – are perpetual.

A group of Ottoman youth[649] then requested [to attain the Master's presence].[650] They stood before the Master, Who was seated in His chair, and expressed to Him their utmost courtesy and reverence. One of them was holding a letter of salutation, which welcomed the Master's arrival [in Budapest] and which that youth recited – with an air of consummate dignity – on behalf of the Ottoman Society. He followed this with ample praise for the Master, 'Him round Whom all names revolve,' Who then bade those youth be seated and spoke these blessed words:

He is God

> My greatest hope is that the East and West may be united, for this is the greatest service that can be rendered to the world of humanity. In reality, there is no such thing as East or West; they are all just parts of the earth that should be considered one and the same. Any given place will be west of another place, and it will also be east of yet another place. Thus, they are all relative to one another. They are all the parts of a single planet and a single country, and all humanity are the members of one race and one family. It is for this reason that I am most delighted to behold this society, which has caused the advancement of the Eastern peoples and fostered their fellowship with peoples of the West. I desire success for you – that with every passing day, you may be aided with fresh confirmations and assistance.

Up until noon, people from various societies humbly attained the Master's presence in groups;[651] they benefited from His blessed words and unfading perfections, and thanked Him for His time.[652]

Furthermore, reporters were in the Master's presence on most occasions, and had the honour of listening to His most sweet utterances. On that particular day, prior to actually meeting with the Master, the owner of a certain newspaper had published an article in Hungarian that included the following remarks:

> 'Abdu'l-Bahá has arrived with consummate majesty and grandeur, and gives talks on the unity of religions, but He is a millionaire.[653]

Everyone viewed the Master’s power and glory through a certain lens; they attributed the effect and influence of His blessed utterances to various motives, and spoke of His greatness according to their own limited understanding. Upon seeing the aforementioned article, I was reminded of certain calumnies that had been levelled by those seeking an excuse to defame the Master. One such person had written that the Master had accepted gifts from Westerners, notwithstanding that, in every city and country, friends and others alike have attested to His financial independence, and always demonstrated their astonishment at the sums He bestowed on the poor at various gatherings while rejecting any gifts for Himself from the believers. So known was the Master for this behaviour that Dr [Howard Colby] Ives, the respected minister of the [Brotherhood] church in New Jersey, stated repeatedly and emphatically, in the remarks He made to introduce ‘Abdu’l-Bahá to the members of his congregation [on 19 May 1912], that:

> . . . this great teacher and proclaimer of the Cause of God, since His arrival in America, had stayed at the Hotel Ansonia and had not accepted any assistance from anyone, bearing all His expenses personally. Indeed, He had even liberally contributed to institutions and churches serving the poor.[654]

A truly majestic gathering was held that night[655] at a hall in the city’s old parliament building expressly to have the Master give a talk there, which had been announced some time in advance.[656] That stately room was filled to the brim with the dignitaries, leaders, and professors of that city.[657] The topics of the Master’s talk consisted of the oneness of humanity, universal peace, education, the rights of women, a universal language, the union of the East and the West through spiritual power, and the divine teachings[658] – all this at the request of the president of that gathering [Sándor Giesswein], who arose to commence the occasion by making these remarks to introduce the Master:

> O dear Master! You have travelled a great distance to promote the teachings of peace and the brotherhood of humanity. Such is the fellowship You have brought about among diverse peoples that, even in this very gathering, You have caused the people of the East and the West to come together. This is because these teachings, which Your blessed Self is engaged in spreading, are high-minded and will yield immense benefits for the world of humanity. This is why we are most grateful, and eagerly await Your discussions of brotherhood, peace, unity between the East and the West, and so on. We are all disposed and committed to achieving the progress of humankind . . .

When the Master then rose, the audience made a jubilant commotion, and they punctuated His delivery with ample applause.[659] When He had concluded His talk,[660] the aforementioned president of that gathering arose once again to praise and thank Him on behalf of everyone. The Master had repaid visits that afternoon to Professor [Ignác] Goldziher and a number of other respected individuals, and He had spoken so extensively at every one of those visits that, by the time He arrived at the old parliament building, he was intensely tired and did not at all have the strength for conversing. Yet in spite of His fatigue, the Master's talk stirred those present to such great excitement that, once the gathering had been concluded, they poured into a separate room to attain His presence and express their devoted servitude to Him.[661]

Such occasions as that one prompted the Master, time and again, to make these remarks:

> The confirmations vouchsafed by the Most Glorious Kingdom, as well as the effect of one's speech, are truly something else. These are not just idle words! All these confirmations are born of the bountiful aid of the Blessed Beauty, and stem from the support and assistance of the divine threshold.

Saturday, 12 April 1913
[Budapest]

That morning,[662] the Master spoke of the injurious effects of the deeds committed by malicious people, and discussed the pride and heedlessness shown by small bands of clamour-raising mischief-makers. He stated that, if such people belonged to the Cause of God, they would become the cause of grievous harm and their conduct would spread to others.

The [executive vice-]president of the Turanian Society [Alajos Paikert] came, accompanied by a group of others, to attain the Master's presence.[663] Once they had showered Him with praise, He said to them:[664]

> I hope you may acquire a power that will enable you to effectively unite and harmonize the various peoples, and also promote peace and brotherhood among all humanity. To fulfil these important ideals, a mighty and transcendent force is needed – an all-unifying agency of an entirely different sort – for today there exist many unifying agencies, but none of them resemble the power of the Word of God and His Cause.
>
> One example of a unifying agency is ethnicity. Consider the Hungarian people, or the French, or the Germans, or the English. Such ethnicity is an agency that unites many peoples, just as your Turanian Society fosters fellowship – but this agency will not conduce to the unity of all the peoples of the world. On the contrary, it will only impede the realization of universal peace and oneness. So long as Hungary is Hungary, Germany is Germany, and England is England – and so long as each of these nations pursues only its own interests – this very agency of ethnicity, as well as the ethnic prejudice which attends it, will hinder the achievement of fellowship among all the world's diverse peoples.
>
> Another unifying agency is nationality. This, too, is a barrier to the unity and concord of the various kindreds of the earth, inasmuch as the people of every country believe their own nation to be the greatest. The French say, 'All other countries should be

> under the control of our nation!' Similarly, when we consider the love of one's country, we see that each people ascribes certain distinctions to their respective nations, and wishes for all other countries to be subjugated by their own.
>
> Yet another unifying agency is the power of politics, which is also inadequate, for political interests are diverse and prevent unity.
>
> Therefore, we are in need of a unifying agency that embraces and encompasses all, such that it will leave no room for any other agency or force to exert its influence; rather, it will unite everyone. There is no doubt that this must be a spiritual power, and that no other power but a spiritual one can prevail over the material forces of today . . .

The Master's visitors then asked Him which place would become the centre of peace. He replied:

> Whichever place is the first to hoist the banner of peace will become that centre. Should England be the first to hoist that banner in this day, it will become the centre of peace. Likewise, if Germany or France wishes to have this distinction, whichever one of them takes the lead will become that centre.

Some of the city's officials and their wives attained the Master's presence. They expressed their great interest in the divine teachings, and the Master spoke to them of the history of the Cause and the advent of Bahá'u'lláh, which further captivated their attention. When they were dismissed, they departed the Master's presence with the utmost devotion and genuine love.

In the afternoon,[665] the Master paid a visit to the renowned philosopher, Professor Vámbéry, who was sick at the time. This professor had a strong command of Persian, Arabic, and Turkish. He was of Jewish heritage, but up until that time had not professed belief in any religion. Rather, he supported the Europeans and opposed the people of the East, especially the Muslims. He told stories from his travels throughout Eastern countries and the gatherings with Muslim leaders and divines he attended while dressed in their garb.[666] Yet in spite of the Professor's views, the Master related His own anecdotes from His travels, speaking at length about the talks He gave at various churches and synagogues, His efforts to convey the wondrous teachings of this Cause, His explanations of religious laws, and the single foundation underlying all the divine faiths. The Professor listened to the Master's words and was profoundly affected by what he heard. He considered the Master's powerful endeavours – His explanation and promotion of these teachings in those places of worship – to be truly extraordinary. On several occasions from that point forward, he lauded the principles and ordinances of this Revelation as the most potent cure for the inveterate diseases afflicting the peoples of the earth, and he arose to promote the principles of this Most Great Cause with the utmost devotion and conviction.

A most lively gathering was held that night by the Theosophical Society once again.[667] When the attendees had turned their attention to the Master, He gave an extensive talk on the life of the Blessed Beauty with such impressive delivery that it evoked the utmost tenderness in the hearts of all those present.[668] The members of that society were moved to unparalleled ecstasy and delight, to the point where, every so often, most of them would hasten to the Master's presence to express their acceptance of the Faith and implore Him to confirm them in their services to the Cause of God.[669]

Sunday, 13 April 1913
[Budapest]

A group of Theosophists attained the Master's presence early that morning.[670] Each of them had brought a photograph of the Master; these they asked Him to autograph, so that they would be kept in their families as a token of His memory and a source of everlasting honour. The Master then said:[671]

> Last night, I spoke to you of the life of Bahá'u'lláh; remember it

> well. This Cause is just beginning to dawn in Europe; eventually it will shed splendours of great intensity. The people did not accept the Cause of Jesus Christ at first, but with time, it cast a dazzling ray upon the realms of their hearts, and only then did they realize what had come to pass. It took three hundred years before His Cause was spread in Europe, but in the span of just sixty years, the Cause of Bahá'u'lláh has been promulgated in both the East and the West. Wherever we have gone during this journey, we have found a group of Bahá'ís. The fame of the Cause of God has even reached the island of Honolulu and enraptured its inhabitants. And now, having reached this place, we have kindled a flame here, and it is certain that a day shall come when the brilliance of that flame will grow to dazzling proportions. A tree is only a seed at first, but once it has grown and developed, it yields exquisite fruit.

At that juncture, a great number of people entered [and attained the Master's presence] one after the other; each derived his share of heavenly grace and was enamoured of the Master's conspicuous glory and power as He unraveled a myriad mysteries for them. The gathering crowd – consisting of the heads of the Esperanto, Theosophical, and Turanian Societies, as well as people from England, America, India, Germany, and Hungary – eventually grew so large that the Master's residence had no room left to seat them, and the majority of those present had to stand.[672] Until close to noon, they listened to the Master's utterances and hearkened to the sweetness of His voice with captivated attention.

Afterwards,[673] the Master went to the home of professor [Róbert] Nádler at his earnest request, so that he, being a skilled artist, could paint the Master's portrait.[674] While He was away, Professor Vámbéry came to the Master's residence to pay Him a visit. Among the remarks he made to me again and again that day were as follows:

> I have spent my life travelling throughout various countries, and until now I had not seen so noble a Personage – a Well-wisher of

> all humanity Who embodies every one of its virtues. Truthfully speaking, the perfections of this blessed Personage, as well as the teachings of this Most Great Cause, will benefit the present condition of all humankind. This applies in particular to the peoples of the East, and still more especially to the Muslims, whose entire civilization is headed for annihilation, and whose future generations are bound for inheriting every conceivable anguish and affliction. If there is to be any hope for their security, they must turn their attention to this Cause and cleave to it with all their might . . .

These remarks of his were deeply moving; it was evident that attaining the Master's presence and hearing Him speak of the divine teachings had immeasurably transformed him. The Professor profusely expressed his submissive devotion to the Master, and voiced the hope that he might spread the Cause of God in the most exalted and conclusive of ways. Professor Vámbéry waited a considerable length [for the Master to return from His visit with Róbert Nádler], but owing to his weakness and illness, he repeatedly expressed his humbly devoted sentiments and then rose [to excuse himself].

As it was snowing that afternoon, the Master went to the home of Sardar Umrao Singh.[675] After having tea and sweets, the Master spoke of His journeys from Tehran to the Most Great Prison, and then departed the residence.[676] Sardar Singh and his wife [Antónia Gottesmann] were most hospitable that day; they repeatedly expressed their humble devotion to the Master, and were among the people who – along with others like Mr and Mrs Stark – truly appreciated the bounty of being in His presence on most occasions, and always stood ready to serve Him.

Although it was springtime, a blizzard was raging that day – but even in spite of such inclement weather, a crowd of people gathered at the Master's residence and remained there until well into the night.[677] As they listened to the Master's talk on humanity's faulty powers of perception, which cause them to mistake a spinning brand of fire for a circle and a mirage for an oasis – and also to His

Leopold Stark, Hungarian Theosophist. He and his wife had invited 'Abdu'l-Bahá to visit Budapest

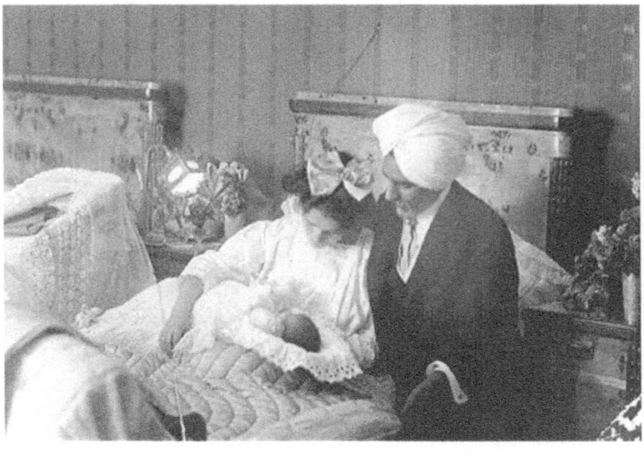

Sardar Umrao Singh with his wife and child. 'Abdu'l-Bahá visited their home in Budapest

Alajos Paikert,
executive vice-president of
the Turanian Society

Róbert Nádler,
who painted a portrait of
'Abdu'l-Bahá

Gyula (Julius) Germanus,
Hungarian Orientalist and
Islamist, who met 'Abdu'l-Bahá
in Budapest

Dr Alexander Giesswein, member of the Hungarian Parliament who met 'Abdu'l-Bahá in Budapest

Ignác Goldziher, who met 'Abdu'l-Bahá in Budapest. Considered by many to be founder of European Islamic studies

Ignác Kúnos, Hungarian scholar of Turkish folk literature who met 'Abdu'l-Bahá in Budapest

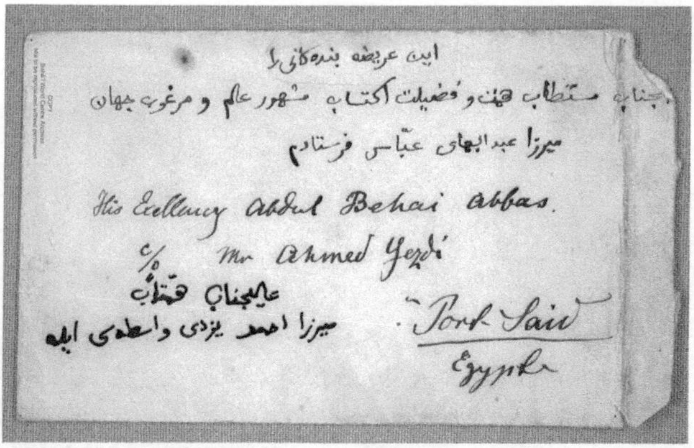

این عریضه بنده‌گانی را
بجناب مستطاب هنر و فضیلت اکتساب مشهور عالم و مرغوب جهان
میرزا عبدالبهای عباس فرستادم

His Excellency Abdul Behai Abbas.
c/o Mr Ahmed Yezdi

عالیجناب قمتاب
میرزا احمد یزدی واسطه‌ی ایله

Port Said
Egypt

Letter from Ármin Vámbéry to ʻAbdu'l-Bahá.
Copyright held by the Bahá'í World Centre and reproduced here by permission.

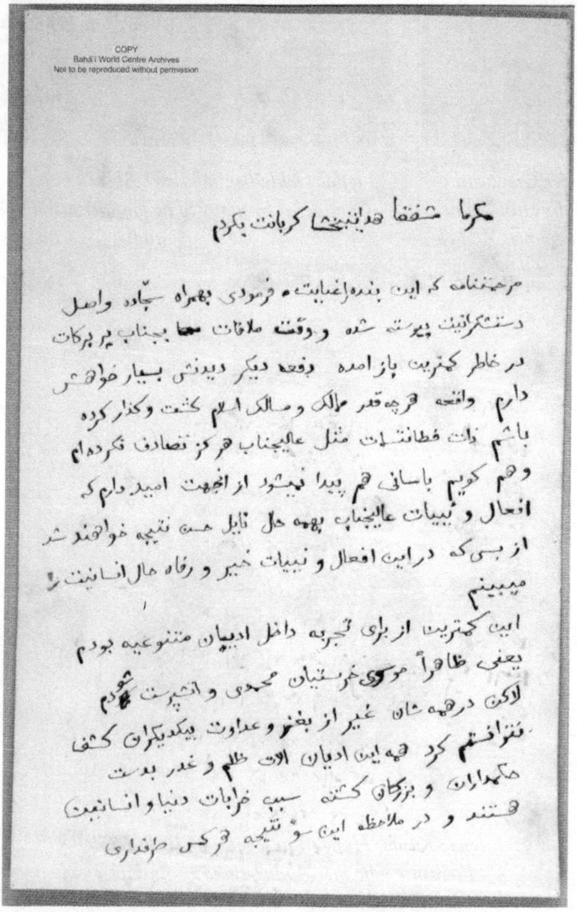

مکرما شفقا هداینبخشا کربانت بکردم

مرحمتنامه که این بنده را عنایت فرمودی بهمراه سجاده واصل
دستشکرانیت پیوسته شده و وقت ملاقات معا بجناب پر برکات
در خاطر کمترین باز آمده دفعه دیگر دیدنش بسیار خواهش
دارم واقعه هرچه قدر ممالک و ممالک اسلام گشت و گذار کرده
باشم ذات فطانتسمات مثل عالیجناب هرگز تصادف نکرده‌ام
و هم گویم باسانی هم پیدا نمیشود از انجهت امید دارم که
افعال و نیات عالیجناب بهمه حال نایل حسن نتیجه خواهند شد
از بس که در این افعال و نیات خیر و رفاه حال انسانیت را
میبینم
این کمترین از برای تجربه داخل ادیان متنوعه بودم
یعنی ظاهراً موسوی خرستیان محمدی و اتشپرست شودم
لاکن در همه شان غیر از بغض و عداوت بیکدیگران کشف
نتوانستم کرد همه این ادیان آلات ظلم و غدر بدست
حکمداران و بزرگان گشته سبب خرابات دنیا و انسانیت
هستند و در ملاحظه این سو نتیجه هرکس طرفداری

Armin Vámbéry, dressed in dervish robes, c. 1860 . . . *and in later years*

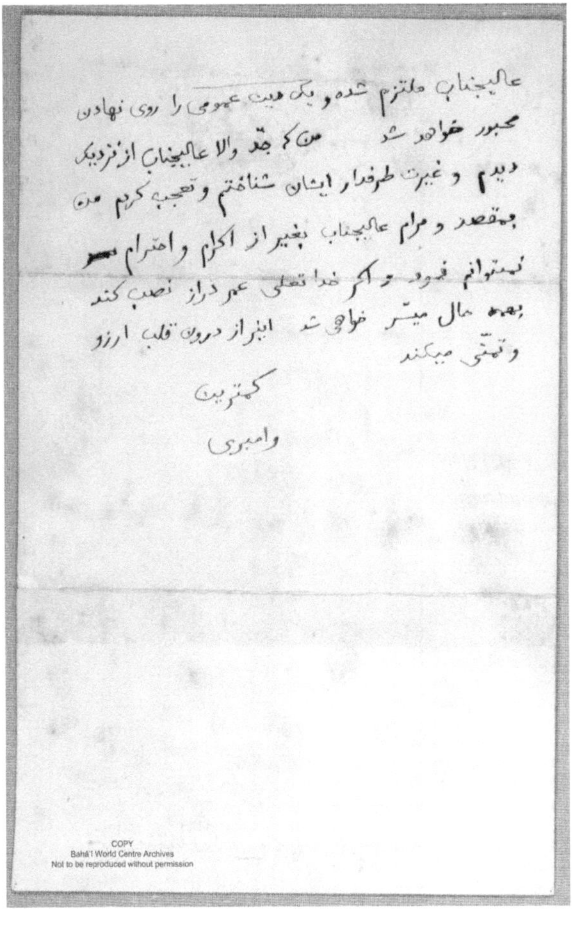

عالیجناب ملتزم شده و یک دین عمومی را روی نهادن
مجبور خواهد شد من که جدّ والا عالیجناب از نزدیک
دیدم و غیرت طرفدار ایشان شناختم و تعجب کردم من
بمقصد و مرام عالیجناب بغیر از اکرام و احترام
نمیتوانم نمود و اگر خدا تعالی عمر دراز نصب کند
بهمه حال میسّر خواهی شد ابراز درون قلب ارزو
و تمنّی میکند

کمترین

وامبری

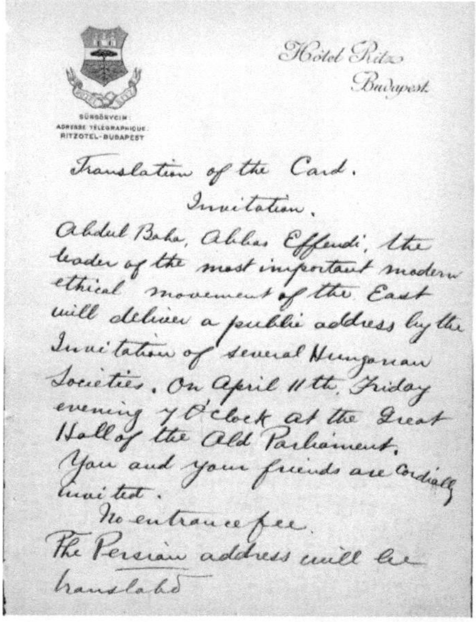

Hôtel Ritz
Budapest

SÜRGÖNYCIM:
ADRESSE TÉLÉGRAPHIQUE:
RITZOTEL-BUDAPEST

Translation of the Card.
Invitation.
Abdul Baha, Abbas Effendi, the leader of the most important modern ethical movement of the East will deliver a public address by the Invitation of several Hungarian Societies. On April 11th, Friday evening 7 O'clock at the Great Hall of the Old Parliament.
You and your friends are cordially invited.
No entrance fee.
The Persian address will be translated

Translation of the original Hungarian invitation to the talk given by 'Abdu'l-Bahá at the Old Parliament, Budapest

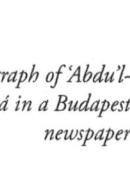

Photograph of 'Abdu'l-Bahá in a Budapest newspaper

discussions of the extraordinary qualities inherent in supernatural power – all those present were roused to exceeding delight, especially by one of His explanations that can be summarized as follows:

> If the inability of a thing which occupies a lower rank of existence to perceive that which occupies a higher rank was itself indicative of the [non-]existence of that higher rank, then in the estimation of an animal, all the degrees of a person's intellect and perfections would be inscrutable and imperceptible. Is the animal's inability to perceive the existence of human intellect or perfections sufficient grounds on which to reject them as falsehoods? How, then, can one claim that one's powers of perception encompass the divine realms, or rely on that deficient perception as the standard by which to prove [the existence of such realms]?

The Master concluded His talk with a discussion of the teachings of this most great Revelation, as well as the gathering of the various peoples and kindreds of the earth beneath the shade of a single, all-inclusive Word. This discussion motivated His audience to listen even more attentively, and only added to the humility they showed as they listened.

Monday, 14 April 1913
[Budapest]

At the Master's instruction, the members of His retinue finished their writing, gathered their belongings, and were nearly ready to depart when the [executive vice-]president of the Turanian Society [Alajos Paikert] attained the Master's presence.[678] This gentleman asked the Master to stay a while longer, as the Turanian Society had arranged a second public gathering to be held in His honour, and this gathering had already been announced in the newspapers. In light of this wish, expressed by both this gentleman and also a group of new friends who had accompanied him on this visit, the Master cancelled His plans to leave [Budapest] that day.

After dismissing His visitors, the Master repaid a visit to the home of the Ottoman consul,[679] where He spoke at length in this vein:[680]

> The East today cannot compete with the West in any way. Indeed, not only is the East incapable of rivalling the West, but the former cannot even protect itself from the latter. This it can only do by the power of God, which has always united the various peoples and kindreds of the earth. Beyond this cure, this feeble body will not be healed, and apart from this remedy, this affliction will have no end.

From there, the Master went to the residence of Professor Vámbéry.[681] On that day, that high-minded philosopher showed more humility in the Master's presence, and spoke more glowingly of the significance of the teachings of this most great Revelation, than ever before.[682] So commendable did the Master find the Professor's sincere devotion that, as soon as He returned to the East, He began to praise him both in His speech and in His writing. The Master also wrote him a sublime Tablet[683] and gave him a wondrous gift [a rug], bestowing eternal honour on him in so doing. Upon receiving those gifts, the Professor sent a letter of his own [written in Persian] to the Master, in which he indicated his sincerity and devotion, and expressed his desire to be of assistance and service.[684] In the days when the Master was in Ramleh (Alexandria), the newspapers of that area published translations of the Professor's letter to the Master in both Arabic and English,[685] which are now available in most countries. Among the places where the letter was featured is the first issue of the third year of the *al-Bayán* magazine (printed and distributed in March 1914), which published numerous articles from celebrities who extolled the virtues of the Master. The translation of the Professor's letter to the Master is as follows:[686]

> I forward this humble petition to the sanctified and holy presence of 'Abdu'l-Bahá 'Abbás, who is the centre of knowledge, famous throughout the world, and loved by all humankind. O thou noble

friend who art conferring guidance upon humanity – May my life be a ransom to thee!

The loving epistle which you have condescended to write to this servant, and the rug which you have forwarded, came safely to hand. The time of the meeting with your Excellency, and the memory of the benediction of your presence, recurred to the memory of this servant, and I am longing for the time when I shall meet you again. Although I have travelled through many countries and cities of Islam, yet have I never met so lofty a character and so exalted a personage as your Excellency, and I can bear witness that it is not possible to find such another. On this account, I am hoping that the ideals and accomplishments of your Excellency may be crowned with success and yield results under all conditions; because behind these ideals and deeds I easily discern the eternal welfare and prosperity of the world of humanity.

This servant, in order to gain first-hand information and experience, entered into the ranks of various religions, that is, outwardly, I became a Jew, Christian, Muḥammadan and Zoroastrian. I discovered that the devotees of these various religions do nothing else but hate and anathematize each other, that all these religions have become the instruments of tyranny and oppression in the hands of rulers and governors, and that they are the causes of the destruction of the world of humanity.

Considering those evil results, every person is forced by necessity to enlist himself on the side of your Excellency, and accept with joy the prospect of a fundamental basis for a universal religion of God, being laid through your efforts.

I have seen the father of your Excellency from afar.[687] I have realized the self-sacrifice and noble courage of his son, and I am lost in admiration.

For the principles and aims of your Excellency, I express the utmost respect and devotion, and if God, the Most High, confers long life, I will be able to serve you under all condition [sic]. I pray and supplicate this from the depths of my heart.

Your servant,
(Mamhenyn.)
VAMBÉRY.

The transformation which these important individuals experienced as a result of hearing the utterances of 'Abdu'l-Bahá is one of the signs of the power and greatness of Bahá'u'lláh's Covenant, as the articles and other writings of those illustrious persons – some of which have been quoted verbatim in the first volume of this chronicle – will amply attest. The praises and tributes offered by these luminaries in America and Europe were regarded by the peoples of those continents with such significance as to arouse the jealousy of the envious, so much so that some of these antagonists strove, through subtle deception, to snuff out the burning attraction of those enlightened souls to the Cause and dissuade them from pursuing it any further – but God has manifested whatsoever He has willed through His supreme power over all that are in heaven and on earth.

A majestic gathering was held by the Turanian Society that night at the grand hall of the National Museum expressly to have the Master give a talk there.[688] The imposing power He projected at that gathering captivated the attention and enraptured the hearts of those present more than on any other such occasion.[689] Indeed, their ecstasy and delight could be likened to the commotion of the gathering crowd on the Day of Resurrection. Following some remarks on the history of the Turanians as part of His discussion of this Most Glorious Revelation and the teachings of Bahá'u'lláh, the Master brought His talk to a close.[690] Those in attendance were visibly excited and profoundly affected. Up until the Master's departure from that gathering, they approached Him to express their devoted servitude; they shook His hand, and implored His confirmations to make them successful in their efforts to serve humanity and promote the divine teachings.

From there, He went to the home of 'Alí 'Abbás Áqá,[691] a rug merchant from Tabriz who had grown deeply enamoured of the Master's disposition. This gentleman had also invited a number of others who were in attendance, a diverse group consisting of Bahá'ís and seekers hailing from both the East and the West.[692] Among these guests was the Ottoman consul, who was privileged to have his dinner in the Master's presence. He was thoroughly delighted by the Master's stories and other utterances, and expressed his effusive gratitude to Him.

Tuesday, 15 April 1913
[Budapest]

Due to His fatigue and the cold weather the previous day, the Master fell sick with a cold. Consequently, He did not leave the hotel that day, and His plans to depart [Budapest] and proceed with His journey were once again delayed by a few days.

Early that morning,[693] Mr and Mrs Stark attained the presence of the Master, who showered them with His tender kindnesses. He said to them:

> You are the reason I have travelled to this city; it is from your earnest efforts that my own opportunity to serve here has presented itself.

Mr and Mrs Stark then asked the Master to confirm them in their endeavours to spread the sweet savours of God.[694] The Master replied:

> Rest assured; it is certain that you will be assisted. Such people will be raised up in this place as will be the cause of your eternal happiness. The Cause will make strides here, and you will see how remarkably you shall be aided to victory. Should you rise as you must, the hosts of the Concourse on High will assist you.

Among those who attained the Master's presence and were captivated by His loving demeanour were a few other individuals, to whom He explained how best to hold gatherings for teaching the Cause in this city.[695] Up until noon, the Master continued, in spite of His fatigue and His cold, to encourage such enamoured souls as these to spread the Cause of God and exalt His Word.

A group of Theosophists and Ottomans,[696] as well as a number of professors,[697] attained the Master's presence that afternoon.[698]

They were all profoundly impressed, to the point of fascination, by the Master's address to them on the subjects of philosophy, reincarnation, and the like. When they were then dismissed, they departed the Master's presence with the utmost humility and devotion.

Afterwards, a reporter[699] attained the presence of the Master,[700] Who spoke to him of economics. The reporter wrote down all the Master's words, along with a detailed portrayal of the Bahá'í teachings.[701] Then, with consummate deference to Him – prompted by the loving-kindness He had shown him – that reporter extended his thanks to the Master and sang His praises.

Sardar Umrao Singh stayed with the Master late into the night.[702] He was stirred to spiritual delight by the Master's remarks to him, which among other subjects included proofs of the existence of God as the Necessary Being. Sardar Singh then expressed his acceptance in a spirit of perfect humility.[703]

Wednesday, 16 April 1913
[Budapest]

The weather that morning was milder and the sky clearer than the previous day. The Master's cold was not as severe as before; His overall health had improved. While He drank His tea, and as He gazed out the window upon the Danube, stretched out before the hotel and shimmering in the sunlight even as a sparkling mirror, He said:

> All the floods of the world can be dammed up, except for the flood unleashed by the Cause of God. The power of the Cause of God is supreme over all the powers of this world.

Sometime thereafter, a group of Indians, Americans, and Hungarians attained the presence of the Master,[704] Who said to them:

> This is a luminous age, and these countries are in need of spirituality and divine civilization. Therewith may the foundation for the

prosperity of humanity be firmly established, and the virtues of all humankind be perfected . . .

After dismissing those visitors, the Master went to the residence of the [Ottoman] consul, then to see a few professors,[705] and finally to the home of Mr and Mrs Stark.[706, 707] There the Master remained until two o'clock in the afternoon, at which time He returned to the hotel with Mr Stark. The two of them had lunch together; the Master spoke to Mr Stark extensively of matters pertaining to the Cause, taking no time for Himself to rest.

Eagerly seeking souls came in groups that afternoon to attain the Master's presence. Their yearning hearts were roused to ecstasy as they listened to His utterances, hearkened to His sweet voice, and beheld His resplendent beauty. He began by speaking of reincarnation and subjects related to Sufism, in response to questions along those lines raised by His audience, and then concluded with the following remarks on the Theosophists:

Some of their principles are similar to the teachings of this Cause. The Cause of God, however, is the embodiment of every divine principle, and the possessor of that which is needed by the various peoples of the earth. These divine teachings, moreover, are supported by an invisible power and assisted by indisputable confirmations. This power, these confirmations, are unique to the religion of God and His Word. They transform the hearts and improve the characters of all people; they unite the kindreds of every clime and country, so unifying these various groups that they readily offer up their lives for one another, thus changing their abasement into imperishable glory, and causing their signs to persist perpetually throughout all the realms of God – even on this earthly plane. The following verse has been revealed in the Qur'án: 'Pilgrimage to the House* is a service due to God.'† Observe how, in obedience to these words, millions of people – travelling from distant lands and belonging to different groups – come together to

* Mecca.

† Qur'án 3:97.

> make the Islamic pilgrimage. Here is an example of how, on this earthly plane, the power of the Word of God can exert its influence in the realms of people's minds and souls, purifying their hearts and sanctifying their breasts. This is a power without peer in any of the world's societies or groups; other causes can never yield the fruits and effects that this Cause can produce.

A number of other people then attained the Master's presence, and to them He spoke extensively of how the leaders of religion have falsely interpreted the meanings of the divine verses and perverted the text of the Books of God.

Thursday, 17 April 1913
[Budapest]

That morning, the Master read translations of some letters from the friends in America. Among these was a letter from a woman in Washington [D.C.], on whom the Master had conferred the name Ásíyih.[708] In this letter, Ásíyih recalled how she had visited the Holy Land and the Shrine of Bahá'u'lláh, and how during her time there, she had expressed her ardent desire to have children. She mentioned that, as soon as she returned from that Most Exalted Spot, her prayer was answered, in that she now has two sweet and precious children, whom she has named Rawshan and Gulshan according to the Master's wish. Enclosed with her letter were strands from the hair of those dear children of hers, by which she hoped to remind the Master of her. This prompted the Master to say:

> What a devoted and blessed woman! She is always engaged in serving and teaching the Cause. Although her husband* is not a Bahá'í, he loves her and supports her in the services she renders to the Cause of God. I say this notwithstanding the fact that he took a second wife – an act that drew the objections of other believers, who insisted that I cease all contact with them, remarking to me

* Harrison Gray Dyar.

that paying them any mind would endanger the glory of the Cause. It is not forbidden for a man to have two wives, but since it is difficult to treat them both equally, a fair and pious person will not choose to have two wives.

My meaning is that the servants of the Cause cannot be cast out for such matters as these. Ásíyih now holds gatherings dedicated to teaching the Cause, and has sent strands from the hair of her children as a token of remembrance from her days in the Holy Land.

A great many people were intoxicated with the wine of the Master's utterance in both the morning and the afternoon that day. Among His remarks were the following, which He made in response to a question from one of those present regarding freedom:

He is God

Freedom is of three kinds. The first is divine freedom, which is confined to the Essence of God, inasmuch as He is the Embodiment of absolute freedom. Under no circumstance or condition can anyone compel Him to do anything. Through His irresistible bidding, the laws of God are renewed in every age, and His secondary ordinances are changed according to the exigencies of the times. We see this through the appearance of Him Who is the Dayspring of God's command and the Manifestation of His knowledge and will in this contingent world, even as the Blessed Beauty – magnified be His Most Glorious Name – has said: 'Were He to pronounce water to be wine, unto no one is given the right to say why or wherefore.'*

Another is the political freedom enjoyed by the Europeans, whereby a person is at liberty to do whatever he wishes so long as he does not harm anyone in the process. This is the freedom of the

* An abridgement of the following passage from Bahá'u'lláh: 'Were He to pronounce water to be wine or heaven to be earth or light to be fire, He speaketh the truth and no doubt would there be about it; and unto no one is given the right to question His authority or to say why or wherefore' (*Tablets of Bahá'u'lláh*, p. 108).

world of nature; its highest expression can be seen in the animal kingdom, and is thus a freedom befitting the animal. Consider these birds, and observe how freely they live. Whatever a person may do, he will never be as free as the animal, for order is an obstacle to complete and total freedom.

The third kind consists in the laws and precepts of God. This is the freedom of the human kingdom. When a person is reared beneath the shade of the Word of God, he will sever the attachments of his heart to every material thing, and be free of anguish and sorrow. Neither will earthly riches or temporal power deter him from moderation and justice, nor will poverty and indigence deprive him of happiness and serenity. The more one's conscience develops, the freer will be one's heart and the more joyous one's soul. In the religion of God, there is freedom of thought, for no one but God has power over the conscience of another, but this freedom exists only within the bounds of propriety. As to unrestrained freedom of action, this does not exist in the religion of God. A person cannot violate divine law, even if he inflicts no harm on another, inasmuch as the purpose of divine law is for one to edify both oneself and others. In the estimation of God, to harm oneself and to harm another are one and the same; both are equally reprehensible. The fear of God must be a present force in the human heart. One must not commit that which is condemnable in the sight of God; therefore, the sort of freedom enshrined in the laws of Europe does not exist in the religion of God. The freedom of one's thoughts must not transgress the bounds of propriety, and one's deeds must be conjoined with the fear of God and His good-pleasure.

I hope that you all will become the means by which these countries will be illumined, and the channels through which the characters of humankind will be refined.

Friday, 18 April 1913
[Budapest → Vienna]

The Master's retinue was preparing to depart that morning.[709] At His instruction, His attendants gathered their belongings and paid the expenses for their stay at the hotel.

Up until it was time to leave, a great many people[710] came to bid the Master farewell.[711] Having all been enraptured by the sweet savours of God and set ablaze with the fire of His love, they were now deeply sad to see Him go – but He extended the utmost love and compassion to each and every one of them, and counselled them all to spread the divine fragrances, promote the oneness of humanity, and promulgate universal peace and unity.

Similarly, when the Master reached the train station at two o'clock in the afternoon, He found that a number of friends from India, America, Hungary, and Turkey had come to see Him off.[712] They each voiced their effusive requests for His aid and assistance, and implored Him to confirm them in their services to the sacred threshold. Although there was not a single Bahá'í in Budapest prior to the Master's visit there, some thirty people had expressed their acceptance [of the Faith] by the time of His departure.[713] Of course, with regard to sentiments of love and friendship, the attendees of every gathering where He had spoken were humble and submissive before Him.

When the train began to depart, the Master offered His loving utterances; He exhorted them all to rise up and exalt the Word of God, and promised them that they would be confirmed in their efforts. As He did this, all the necks of those who had come to see Him were humbled in reverence; their eyes were fixed squarely on Him, and their arms were stretched out towards the car that carried Him.

The Master arrived in Vienna shortly after nightfall.[714] At first, He went to a rather small hotel,[715] whose address had been given to us by some of the believers[716] – but as this place proved unsuitable,[717] He left it and went to the Grand Hotel,[718] the finest of all the distinguished hotels of that city. Owing to the frigid weather in

Budapest, the strain of His sojourn in that city, and the aftereffects of the cold He caught there, the Master was so intensely tired that He did not sleep at all that night.

Austria

Saturday, 19 April 1913
[Vienna]

Despite His sleeplessness and fatigue, the Master was in high spirits that morning. He said:

> The Ottoman ambassador who is stationed here told the [Ottoman] consul in Budapest that he wishes to meet with us, and asked the consul to apprise him once we had left that city. Make inquiries today, then; when it has been determined that the ambassador is home, we will pay him a visit.

At twelve o'clock, we were informed by telephone that the ambassador had returned to his residence, so we set out to see him. Siyyid Aḥmad Báqiroff was also in the Master's presence on that occasion. Although the ambassador was set in his Islamic beliefs to the point of great prejudice, he was deeply moved nonetheless as he listened to the Master discuss His journey to America and recount the hardships He sustained during the days of His still-recent confinement in 'Akká. Once he had expressed his gratitude, the ambassador persuaded the Master, after much insistence, to stay for lunch. One of the remarks that the Master made regarding the ambassador once He had returned to the hotel was the following:

> The people had hoped that such individuals as these would revive the Ottoman government and population, but behold how the tables have turned!

Among the people who attained the Master's presence at the hotel that day were Mr [Johann] Kreuz[719] and Mrs [Marie] Thaler.[720] These were two Theosophists who had gone to the railway station the night before to receive the Master after learning of His arrival, and this illumined their hearts with the light of His grace and bounty. They remarked:

> Even in Your absence, we became enamoured of Your blessed utterances and wondrous writings – but praised be God, for now that we have attained Your presence, our rapture has only grown more fervent. Of course, our devotion and humility before You are evident; there is no need to convey it in words.

The Master replied:

> Your love is the reason I have come here. I have come to see you, not to go on leisurely excursions, for we are in search of people, and wherever we find them, it brings us matchless joy. We hope that this meeting with us will yield results that shall illumine the hearts and irradiate the souls with the light of supreme guidance. Thereby may every eye be brightened and every heart attain everlasting joy and bliss; thereby may all come together, with tranquil souls and well-assured hearts, beneath the shade of the pavilion of the oneness of humanity; and thereby may eternal peace, harmony, welfare, and prosperity be realized on earth, for we are all the members of humankind – all the servants of one loving God.

The Master then discussed the origin of the European languages, and also how the ancestors of the Europeans migrated from the East to the West:[721]

> From the banks of the Ganges River in India, they migrated to Persia. Then, as their population grew and became more diverse, some of them migrated to Caucasia, and from there they spread to Europe. Gradually, their languages became diverse, and their various groups began to multiply. Due to the varying climates of each region, the colours of these peoples also became diverse. Just as they were one family in the beginning, our hope is that they may be united in fellowship once again. If at first they were united physically, let them now be united spiritually.

Mr Kreuz and Mrs Thaler then spoke at length about the Theosophical Society of Vienna:

> Some of our members are aware of Your travels, and when we conveyed the glad tidings of Your arrival here last night, they expressed their eagerness to meet with You. They are now waiting to hear Your talks and discussions of the spiritual teachings.

Once Mr Kreuz and Mrs Thaler had been dismissed, the Master went outside the hotel to go for a stroll. It so happened that a festival was being held that day.[722] Every year, most of the respectable women and girls of the city would dress in their finest clothing, gracefully walk every street and bylane with smiles on their faces and bunches of flowers under their arms, give a flower to everyone who crossed their path, and hold out a container to collect money.[723] These donations were being collected for the poor, and everyone was free to donate whatever amount they liked. The Master encountered these people at every turn that day; they offered Him flowers, and He gave them each a donation.

The Master reached a park [the Stadtpark] in the centre of the city.[724] A group of children were playing there; He took them in His loving embrace, and gave them each a sum of money. Similarly, on the way back to the hotel, the Master gave away whatever money remained in His pockets and His attendants still had with them. He remarked, 'The people have made us penniless today!'

At seven o'clock that night, the Master went to the Theosophical Society.[725] There He gave a talk on the realities of animals and humans, as well as the progress of souls towards eternal stations, and His words filled the hearts of His audience with enamoured ecstasy.[726] When He had concluded His talk, all those in attendance fluttered about Him like moths, expressing their gratitude for having had the bounty of attaining His presence.[727] One could never have expected that, in the city of Vienna, a society such as that one would have held a gathering expressly for the Master to speak there, or that the people would have so completely surrendered their hearts to Him.

Although the Master was very tired as a result of the cold He had caught in Budapest, He walked up one hundred and twenty steps of that building nevertheless to get to the main hall of the Theosophical Society – this because the building was still new, and an elevator had not yet been installed to transport people.[728] When He reached the fourth floor, He did not enter the main hall at first owing to His great fatigue; instead, He initially went to a different room and conversed with certain individuals. One can well imagine the great strain that must have been placed on the Master's body when He then went to the public gathering!

Sunday, 20 April 1913
[Vienna]

A group of Theosophists attained the Master's presence that morning; they expressed their praise and gratitude for the gathering held the night before, and He said to them:

> I am most delighted to have been present at your society. This is a society whose members believe in spiritual values and are in search of a world that transcends material things. My hope, then, is that you will successfully overcome the world of nature and its leaders, who style themselves philosophers. In this day, nature has dominated godliness, inasmuch as the followers of religion are immersed in blind imitation, and the materialists are engrossed in the world of nature. It is certain that nature will prevail over blind imitation, but those who are spiritual, and are submerged in the outpourings of heavenly grace, will overcome all things. Thus, I hope that the splendours of spirituality may shine over this city and dispel the darkness of nature. You all, of course, must exert yourselves, and know of a certainty that a time shall come when Europe will be illumined with these splendours. At present, however, the gloom of prejudice, imitation, and materialism has encompassed it. Indeed, as the powers of humanity are incapable of subduing these forces, the power of the Holy Spirit is required to discover the truth, burn the veils of prejudice and imitation, and dispel the

darkness of nature, for the truth is one; it has no multiplicity or variation.

A question was then raised regarding the meanings of the terms 'teacher' and 'Heavenly Father'. The Master replied:

By 'teacher' is meant the True Educator, Who is the Manifestation of divine attributes, one of which is the attribute of a nurturer. Among the attributes of God, glorified and exalted be He, is the attribute of fatherhood, inasmuch as He is the Source of all existence, and the Dawning-place of the divine names and attributes. He is a Mirror that reflects the Sun of Truth.

In the parlance of the philosophers, the term 'teacher' refers to a person who is without peer. Until now, two such teachers have appeared in the midst of the philosophers. The first is Aristotle, who excelled at all the disciplines of his day, and the second is Fárábí, who once spoke these words: 'I am the second teacher.' The king of Fárábí's time convened a gathering to which he summoned the masters of every discipline; Fárábí competed with each and every one of them, even the foremost instructor of music, and defeated them all. Then was the title of 'second teacher' accorded him.

A third person who should be mentioned is Avicenna, in whose day a similar gathering was convened. He defeated all his competitors except for the instructor of music, who proved to be his equal in that field. For this reason, the title of 'teacher' was not given to him, though he was referred to as a 'leader', since he had a peer in the field of music.

This is the usage of these terms among the philosophers. According to our terminology, however, Jesus Christ was a Teacher, which is to say that He was a Focal Point of divine splendours, even as a perfectly stainless mirror that reflects the light of the sun. Our usage of the term 'teacher' refers to the Centre of all perfections in the world of humanity, and the supreme Intermediary between God and His creation.

Such were the Master's extensive comments on numerous subjects.

Afterwards, a Persian dignitary,[729] who in those days was about to depart for Persia, entered the room, at which time all the other visitors were dismissed from the Master's presence.

In the afternoon, the Master made the following remarks to Mr Herrigel, one of the German friends who had accompanied Him on that [stage of His] journey:[730]

> You all must leave Stuttgart and come here, where you should spread the divine fragrances and disseminate treatises on the Cause among Theosophists and other seeking souls, for this place is a significant centre. A great number of receptive souls will be found here.

When the Master went outside, He saw a very large church nearby known as the [St] Charles Church [or Karlskirche].[731] As there were not very many people inside, the Master entered the church. He looked around and said:

> How majestic and embellished it appears to be on the outside, yet how bereft of spirituality and truth it is on the inside!

The Master then went to the Persian embassy, and in the evening to the Ottoman embassy,[732] where He spoke extensively on numerous subjects that roused the hearts of His listeners to great vigilance.

Monday, 21 April 1913
[Vienna]

Among the subjects the Master discussed with the Persian ambassador that morning were philosophy and the four criteria of comprehension.

Afterwards, the Master repaid a visit to [——].[733] As He was returning, a certain person, who in the past had repeatedly implored the Master's permission to sculpt a bust of His likeness

– a request He had refused to grant – set himself to sculpting this bust for fifteen minutes nonetheless, albeit from a distance.[734]

Sometime thereafter, some of the friends came with a car[735] and expressed their desire to take the Master on an excursion. He consented to their request, and they went to a royal garden and palace [Schönbrunn Palace] that was situated on the edge of the city of Vienna. The Master walked a great deal there,[736] and spoke very highly of the state of that garden. The grounds [specifically, the Schönbrunn Zoo] had many animals, both terrestrial and marine, and their pathways were symmetrically lined with trees on either side, resembling walls built with the meticulous precision of an engineer or an architect.[737] The branches and leaves of these trees had been trimmed to appear in perfect harmony, ordered neatly as the greenery that adorns the street in front of the Eiffel Tower. The grounds also had elevated buildings and other places that allowed one to look at the grass, flowers, and a variety of birds and other animals from above. When the Master saw these animals, He remarked:

> Behold how these frightening and ferocious animals have become the captives of humanity! It is in this very way that all the forces of the world of nature have been subdued and encompassed by human power.

The Master had walked a great deal and grown tired as a result. He asked for the car and was taken back to the hotel to have lunch.[738]

A number of Persians and some Eastern Bahá'ís attained the Master's presence that afternoon.[739] As they listened to His tender counsels and historical anecdotes, they were roused to great vigilance and profoundly moved to poignant emotion by the power and glory of the Master.

In the evening, the Theosophical Society once again held a splendidly joyous gathering expressly to have the Master speak there.[740] The longing hearts of those in attendance were enamoured of the utterance and demeanour of that matchless Beloved.[741] The Master's talk dealt with how the spirit of every [living] thing flows through it, described the appearance of the perfections of the spirit in accordance with the capacity of its mortal frame, explained the complete bonds that exist between all beings, and discussed the perspicuous verses.[742] Both before and after that gathering, a great many people attained the Master's presence in a separate room, where they had the honour of expressing their devoted servitude to Him.[743] Each and every one of them was like a Bahá'í, captivated by His radiant face and submissive before His luminous person.[744] It is for this reason that, when the Master returned to His residence, He rendered thanks for the aid and assistance that had been vouchsafed by the Most Glorious Kingdom and said:

> One could never have hoped that such a gathering would be convened in this city – that so brilliantly spiritual an assemblage would come together, or that their faces would be so brightly illumined with the light of the love of God.

Tuesday, 22 April 1913
[Vienna]

After reciting prayers and other remembrances of God that morning, the Master composed Tablets in response to some letters from the American friends.

Sometime thereafter, a group of people from the Theosophical Society, as well as a number of Ottomans, attained the Master's presence. A most courteous and dignified editor [of a newspaper] likewise entered;[745] he raised several questions concerning the history and teachings of this wondrous Cause, and also the dissemination of the blessed Writings in various regions of the world. The Master gave extensive answers to these questions; this visitor listened to them all and recorded them for publication in his newspaper.[746] When he was dismissed, the Master addressed the others in His presence with these words:

> The distinction of humanity lies in spirituality and divine civilization, as well as their eternal peace and happiness – a state they

> will attain when they enter the Kingdom of God, and also when they act in accordance with the heavenly teachings. The virtues they will develop as a result can be likened to brilliant lights shining from the horizon of their spirit, and it is through the manifestation of these virtues that this happiness and spirituality are achieved. Every instance of happiness and perfection, of prosperity and glory, is to be found in the manifestation of these virtues.

He then said:[747, 748]

> I regard this city even as a colony of ants that have spread their wings and wish to fly. I hope that you may be among those people who will soar from the limits of materialism to a boundless space, and that you may set your faces towards the world of the Kingdom.

Once His visitors had been dismissed, expressing the utmost devotion and ecstasy as they departed, the Master said, 'Today is a good day; let us walk for a bit in the garden.'[749]

The Master went outside with His attendants, who were wearing their Persian hats and other attire. This drew the attention of onlookers from every direction, which prompted the Master to remark, 'This clothing of ours is itself an announcer of the Cause!'

When the Master reached the park in the centre of the city, He found a large number of people there. They all turned to look at Him, and most of them approached Him from the various corners of the park with curiosity. Mr Herrigel and some other friends discussed the Cause of God with them, and provided them with the addresses of both the Master's hotel and also the residences of certain believers.

While at the park that day,[750] a Bahá'í youth from Tabriz by the name of Áqá 'Alí-Akbar Áqá, the son of a certain Ḥájí Ismá'íl, noticed us, his fellow Easterners, from a distance. He quickly ran towards us, and was infused with new life when he realized that the Master Himself was in our company.[751]

The Master spent the entire afternoon repaying visits to certain respected individuals. Sometime later that night, He returned to the hotel and took a hot bath.

Wednesday, 23 April 1913
[Vienna]

Early that morning, two Theosophists attained the Master's presence with the utmost humility and implored Him to help them progress.[752] To them the Master said:

> Two kinds of progress exist for humanity: physical progress and spiritual progress. Physical progress is temporary and ultimately fleeting. Whatever the extent to which a person may progress in this respect, it will never grant him total peace or happiness, and the indications thereof will at last be effaced and forgotten. Spiritual progress, on the other hand, will lead to everlasting joy; it will serve to rear and support the world of humanity and bring it eternal prosperity.
>
> As to lending aid and protection to the human race – this, too, is necessary in both the physical and the spiritual domains, but relative to spiritual assistance, physical assistance is inevitably limited, for the effects of guiding people aright and lending them spiritual assistance are without limit. Yet should both kinds of assistance be present, it would be light upon light. It is certain that perfection lies in a combination of spiritual virtues and physical capabilities. When the brilliance of the lamp is coupled with the stainlessness of the glass, it will yield results that defy all comparison. If at first a person is incapable of imparting divine guidance or lending spiritual assistance to others, this should not sadden him, for he would be excused on account of his initial inability. Such a one must exert himself, that thereby he may be granted the grace of God and enabled to guide others. Similarly, should he have little substance to speak of, he must not despair. Many indeed are the people who have donated enormous sums to assist others, but as the aid they rendered was of a physical nature, its effects were ultimately limited. Yet consider a person who strives

to spread the signs of God's guidance and exalt His Word, such as the Apostles of Christ; observe how limitless are the marks they have made, and behold how everlasting is the life they have attained!

Bend every effort, then, to attain this divine grace and engage yourself in lending this sort of assistance to others.

The Master's visitors then asked Him, 'How might we acquire this power?' He replied:

Enter into the Kingdom of Bahá'u'lláh, that you may be aided in every respect. In Persia, there are women who are entirely bereft of wealth, yet they devote the utmost effort to imparting spiritual guidance and assistance. I hope that you, too, will strive in this way, that you may train and guide both others and your own selves.

The happiness of humanity consists in the severance of their minds and hearts from all attachments and affections. Viewed in this light, should a person lack so much as a single cent to his name, he would be glad regardless, and without this detachment, all the world's riches and sovereignty would never bring him happiness. Now imagine that you had been born a hundred years ago![753] Do not become attached to this world; such attachments befit a child. One must only set one's affections on the outpourings of divine grace, that one may come to personify all perfections, outward and inward alike. Every other affair is limited and fleeting.

Furthermore, the Cause of Bahá'u'lláh cannot be compared with any other, for within this Cause are all others included. The followers of every religion, the members of every assemblage, will find the basis of their own cause in this one. It is in this Cause, moreover, that people are reborn and created anew. Through this Cause, falsehood is changed into truth, and ignorance is turned into knowledge; the defiled are purified, and the fearful and agitated become courageous and confident; the dumb are empowered to speak, and the deaf are enabled to hear. Yet these results cannot be brought about by a shift in a person’s thought alone. Rather, one’s soul must advance day by day; one must promote the oneness of humanity, and enkindle the hearts of humankind with the fire of the love of God.

The Master then said the following to another group of people:

I wish for you all to become balls of fire, freed from every chain and fetter. This Bahá’í Cause is a fountain of healing that purges people of every defilement and wholly purifies them from every attachment. I hope that you will be immersed in this fountain, and obtain a power that shall enable you to guide others aright and instill awareness in them. This is the station I desire for you, that you may enter the Kingdom of God and know eternal peace and happiness. Otherwise, should you become the possessors of all the world’s treasures, you would remain afflicted with toil and adversity in the end.

It was then asked, ‘How can we enter the Kingdom?’ The Master replied:

Enter into the Cause of Bahá’u’lláh and act in accordance with His counsels. When you have attained to the pinnacle of your development in the Cause of Bahá’u’lláh, you will see how confirmations are granted you.

Afterwards, a number of Persians attained the presence of the Master, Who addressed them with these words:

We came to Europe and found that some Persians – individuals of no significance who are entirely unconcerned with religion or the maintenance of order in this world – stood in opposition to us, and that they even spoke ill of us to the Christians. Even if we failed to become the cause of Persia’s glory and prosperity, we have not caused its destruction, nor have we contributed at all to these tumults that have beset it. Still more strange is that those people

Grand Hotel, Vienna

The Palace of Schönbrunn, Vienna,
where 'Abdu'l-Bahá walked in the gardens and visited the zoo

The Stadtpark, Vienna, modern views

Baroness Bertha von Suttner, Austrian pacifist and novelist, who visited 'Abdu'l-Bahá in Vienna. She was the first woman to be awarded the Nobel Peace Prize (1905)

Statuette of 'Abdu'l-Bahá by Alexander Engelhardt

residing outside of Persia who at first behaved towards us in this way are themselves on bad terms with one another! Indeed, they are all opposed to each other, notwithstanding that what is needed now is for them all to come together, be united in thought, and ponder the question of their own exaltation and salvation. Though their leaders may hold varying opinions, the concourse of Persians must pursue an all-inclusive and spiritual power that will unite them.

Persia stands in need of this power at present. Observe how the wisest and most knowledgeable of people attest to the importance and greatness of this Cause! For instance, consider Mr Bryan,* the American Secretary of State, who has travelled to the East on several occasions and is widely known for his wisdom. He has explicitly written that the remedy of the Easterners, and in particular the prosperity of the Muslims, consists in their cleaving tenaciously to the Bahá'í teachings.† Such is the testimony to the greatness of this Cause given by those who are not even Persian, while the Persians themselves have remained heedless thereof. God has made such a glorious Sun as this to shine from the horizon of the East, and yet the Persians are still fast asleep. How often has perpetual fortune knocked at a person's door, only for him to reject it with all his might!

The Master then gave an account from the early days of Islam:

The children of those very people who at the inception of Islam made the Prophet Muhammad the object of their reproach and persecution became, in no time at all, the caliphs of that same religion. Examples include the descendants of Abú Sufyán and 'Abbás, who, upon aligning themselves with Muhammad and

* William Jennings Bryan.

† As part of his brief discussion of 'Abdu'l-Bahá in his *Old World and Its Ways*, published in 1907, Bryan wrote: 'How much ['Abdu'l-Bahá] may be able to do in the way of eliminating the objectionable features of Mohammedanism no one can say but it is a hopeful sign that there is . . . an organized effort to raise the plane of discussion from brute force to an appeal to intelligence' (p. 382).

> identifying themselves with Islam, attained to a cherished station and began to openly pride themselves on their affiliation with this Cause. So too with the present day, in which the value of this generous bounty that God has given the Persians has yet to become known. Soon will those people vaunt the blessed name of Bahá'u'lláh in the East and West alike, and swell with pride at the mention of Persia and its people.

That afternoon,[754] a number of respected persons had the honour of attaining the Master's presence both at His residence and at the [Persian] embassy.[755]

At a gathering of Theosophists (held at the home of Mrs Lukaneder),[756] the Master gave a talk that evening that concerned the teachings of Bahá'u'lláh, as well as the pervasive and all-encompassing signs of this Most Great Revelation. The Master's words only added to the gladsome delight that that eager crowd had already evinced, and so many of them were in attendance that they had filled every room of that residence to the brim. Their faces were afire with fervour, and their bodies resembled the wings of moths, singed by the scorching touch of the Master's love. When they all learned of His impending departure from Vienna, they became deeply upset. It is for this reason that the Master began His aforementioned address to them with these words:

> How ardently had I longed to meet you all, that I have crossed great distances to see you! In visiting you all, my soul is thoroughly cheered. I very much wish to remain with you all a while longer, but I must return to the East. Thus, tonight I will speak to you of the divine teachings and also bid you farewell . . .

Once the Master had concluded that gathering with a prayer,[757] the members of His audience approached Him, in a spirit of the utmost ecstasy, to shake His hand. They clung to the hem of His bounty and implored Him to bless them with success. Mrs Lukaneder and her son [Paul Lukaneder] were themselves the most profoundly affected of all those in attendance that night, so much so that, after the Master went to another room to relieve His fatigue and seated Himself on a couch, they and a few others fell at His feet and expressed their thanks for having had the bounty of meeting 'Him round Whom all names revolve'.

Thursday, 24 April 1913
[Vienna → Esslingen → Stuttgart]

That morning, Mrs Thaler, the first woman from Austria to declare her devoted allegiance to the Cause of God, made the following remarks to the Master:

> Matters have come to such a pass that my husband, notwithstanding his disinterest in religion, has begun to show prejudice and now forbids me from attending [Bahá'í] gatherings and listening to Your talks – but wherever I go, I mention that I am a Bahá'í.

The Master replied:

> You must treat your husband with the utmost kindness; show love to him and be considerate of his feelings. Do not grow resentful of him. Perhaps he will change with time and draw closer to God.

Afterwards, Mrs Lukaneder and her son attained the Master's presence with consummate deference and reverence. So deeply captivated and profoundly affected by Him were they that they hovered around Him constantly up until the moment of His departure. The intensity of their attraction to the Master moved them to show great submissiveness before Him as He addressed them with these words:

> Always hold gatherings at your home, and call to mind the things I have said. I, for my part, will pray that you be confirmed.
>
> Behold what spiritual sentiments can do! We are from Persia and you are from Vienna, yet how remarkable and unforgettable

are the affections that have developed between our hearts in just a few short days. My heart is ever with you. This earthly body is of no significance; what truly matters is the human heart, which must have spiritual connections.

Among the other important individuals who were thoroughly cheered and illumined by having had the bounty of being in the Master's presence was Baroness [Bertha] von Suttner.[758] This woman was an earnest promoter of peace; she was deeply respected and widely renowned, and the Master showed her great loving-kindness. He spoke to her of universal peace and the Bahá'í Faith, and this served to gladden her heart, broaden her mind, and brighten her soul. She was then dismissed, and she displayed the utmost devotion as she departed the Master's presence.

On the Master's last day [in Vienna], Mrs Stark also attained His presence.[759] She had come from Budapest with glad-tidings of having promoted the Word of God there, and to the Master she recounted the effects of His sojourn in that city and mentioned that a Bahá'í society had been formed there. Despite the fact that there were no Bahá'ís in Budapest or Vienna [before the Master visited those cities], the transformation experienced by the illustrious people of Hungary and Austria truly speaks to the presence of an extraordinary power – that in so brief a span, their nostrils were perfumed with the fragrances of God, and their hearts illumined with the light of the Most Glorious Kingdom. The Master's visits to those two cities were occasioned by just two people, Mr Stark in Budapest and Mr Kreuz in Vienna. Both these gentlemen were members of the Theosophical Society who had heard something of the Master's travels and talks, but were not Bahá'ís themselves. It is for that reason that the Master would say again and again:

One could never have imagined that such gatherings as these would be held in these two cities, or that these people would grow so attracted [to the Cause].

Additionally, He instructed the Bahá'ís of Germany time after time to travel to those cities to spread the divine fragrances, and not allow the fire that had been kindled in the hearts of the seekers there to go out.

The Master's train departed Vienna at nine o'clock that morning.[760] Shortly after nightfall, and prior to reaching Stuttgart, the Master – intensely tired, and still suffering from the fever, cold, sleeplessness, and weakness brought on by the frigid weather in Budapest – had only a little food and a bit of rest in the railway carriage.

At one o'clock the next morning, the Master's train arrived at Esslingen – and as soon as it pulled into the station, Miss Köstlin, Mr [Friedrich] and Mrs Schweizer, and some other friends entered our carriage.[761] Each and every one of them was like a blooming flower and a flame of fire.

When the Master's train pulled into the Stuttgart station at two o'clock in the morning,[762] Consul Schwarz and a group of other Bahá'ís who had been waiting there to receive Him began to make a jubilant commotion once they saw Him.[763] Tears fell from their eyes and sprinkled the hem of the Master's robe; they saluted Him on His arrival and rendered thanks for having the bounty of seeing Him once again.

Since the Master's cold and weakness had worsened, and owing to the lateness of the hour, He returned to the same hotel where He had lodged before (the Marquardt) and the believers were dismissed from His presence.[764]

Return to Germany

Friday, 25 April 1913
[Stuttgart]

The believers were enraptured in the Master's presence that morning, each one of them like a ball of fire as they beheld His peerless beauty.[765] They gave Him bouquets of flowers and kissed the hem of His robe, and until permission was given them to do so, not one of them took their seat.[766] Respected persons would often stand before the Master completely oblivious of themselves, filled with enamoured wonderment at His heavenly temperament, and when His gaze fell upon them, He would bid them with the utmost tenderness to be seated and ask them how they were faring. This sort of devotion, courtesy, submissiveness, and reverence was constant and common to all the Bahá'ís of Germany – even their children. Indeed, they were pure spirit personified in human flesh. The Master would shower them with His loving-kindness and say:

> We have come to Stuttgart once again. It is clear that this place is both receptive and worthy. God willing, the Cause of God will make great strides here and be spread far and wide.

It was asked, 'How can we become the means by which the Cause of God is spread?' The Master replied:

> Act in accordance with the teachings of Bahá'u'lláh. Many are the people who peruse the divine teachings, but promptly forget what they have read when the time comes to act. A true Bahá'í is one who acts in accordance with the blessed teachings.

A copy of the *[Stuttgarter] Neues Tagblatt* dated 24 April 1913 was presented to the Master. This particular issue of that newspaper conveyed the news of His arrival, along with an explanation of the history and teachings of the blessed Cause. As word of both the

Master's return [to Stuttgart] and the public gathering at which He was to speak that same night had been spread a week in advance, that grand occasion was also advertised in this newspaper. Here is a translation of the news that was printed:

> The leader and head of a great ethical movement in the Orient, the Bahá'í Movement – which has already found its way into the whole world from there, and has thousands of followers among Christians, Jews, and Muḥammadans – will give a talk on Friday, 25th at eight o'clock in the evening in the Great Hall of the Bürgermuseum. 'Abdu'l-Bahá from Persia, a descendant of an ancient line of princes, dedicates himself completely to the Bahá'í Movement. This is not a new religion. Love for humanity, as well as unity among the religious denominations and peoples, are to be realized by the Bahá'ís. The movement does not originate from 'Abdu'l-Bahá himself. His immediate predecessor was his father Bahá'u'lláh, who took over the mission from a person known as the 'Báb', who was the leader of the Bábís and who proclaimed his mission to the Persian people in May 1844. Inevitably there followed the martyrdom of thousands of Bábís and then the renewed growth of the movement, which under the leadership of Bahá'u'lláh also spread to the Ottoman Empire. Once again the consequence was persecution and imprisonment, first in Adrianople and later in 'Akká. In 1892, Bahá'u'lláh died and handed over the leadership to his son, who did not obtain freedom for the movement and the teachings until 'Abdu'l-Ḥamíd was overthrown. This marks the beginning of the spread of the Bahá'í Movement to the West. Towards the end of a long journey lasting almost one year, this tireless seventy-year-old man has come to Stuttgart for the second time at the request of his local friends and followers after staying here for a few days at the beginning of April.[767]

Once a translation of this article was read for the Master, some of the friends asked for permission to hold an afternoon gathering exclusively for the believers [and requested Him to speak there]. The Master replied:

> The cold I contracted from the frigid weather of Budapest has worsened. I still have a bad cough and feel intensely weak. Content yourselves, then, with the gathering that will take place in the evening.

However, the Master's respiratory illness grew more severe that afternoon, so much so that multiple doctors forbade Him from speaking, writing, or going outside when the weather was anything but sunny. When the Bahá'ís learned of this development, they grew deeply sad and voiced their laments – not only on account of His sickness itself, but also because of that night's important gathering, which had been announced a week ahead of time in the newspapers, and which a great number of people would be attending from near and far in their eager anticipation to attain His presence and listen to His talks.

Shortly after nightfall, the Master summoned all His attendants and some of the German Bahá'ís to His presence, and said to them:

> I am forbidden to attend the gathering tonight; therefore, you all must go there and speak in my stead. Recite prayers and share the perspicuous verses; the confirmations of the Most Glorious Kingdom will encompass you.

He then said to Mr Herrigel:

> Rest assured! When you place your trust in the Most Glorious Kingdom and set your face towards it, you will certainly be aided when the time comes to speak.
>
> I have not entered any school, but in spite of that fact, I spoke at a gathering in Baghdad when I was young,* and I tailored my speech to suit the capacity of my audience. Suddenly, I noticed that the governor entered, and I immediately realized that the remarks I had made up to that point would not be suitable for him. Hence, without any introduction, I recited the following

* Fifteen years of age, according to Sohrab.

verse: 'Moses said: "Show Thyself to me, O my Lord, that I may look upon Thee!"'* Moses would not have made an impossible request of God if it were indeed not possible to have an encounter with Him in this world. Thus, it is evident from this verse that divine encounters in this world are possible. Then, taking the capacity of the other members of my audience into account, I said: 'When Moses, peace be upon Him, quaffed the wine of the love of God, hearkened to the voice of God, and became enraptured by the sweet savours of God, He forgot all that was in this world and saw His own self in "the Garden of Repose"† – in other words, the station of beholding and meeting. It is for this reason that Moses, peace be upon Him, said: "Show Thyself to me, O my Lord, that I may look upon Thee!"'

The governor remained standing and listened attentively, and when I had concluded my speech, he invited us to his home. As some of those present claimed to be quite knowledgeable, this invitation evoked their resentment, and roused them to such rancour and jealousy that I cannot possibly describe it.

When a person is granted confirmations, and when he attains a state of reliance and trust, he will be able to put the hosts of idle fancy to rout, and rend every prohibitive veil asunder. I had never spoken at a gathering before that one. When I first wished to speak, sweat would fall from my brow! But the confirmations of the Blessed Beauty so surrounded me that at every gathering I was empowered to summon the people to the Most Glorious Kingdom. Attend that gathering, then, and be assured of the confirmations of the Blessed Beauty. I will stay here by myself.

After being dismissed, everyone attended the gathering in obedience to the Master's instruction.[768] When they arrived at the main hall (of the Bürgermuseum), they beheld a truly majestic gathering, and saw that the entire space, including the balcony and all the rooms, was teeming with people[769] – some standing, others sitting, and all waiting to see when the renowned 'Abdu'l-Bahá would

* Qur'án 7:143.
† Qur'án 53:15.

make His appearance and grace them with His soul-stirring utterance and most sweet voice. The Master's attendants[770] observed this state of affairs and came to regret His absence from this event. They began to vacillate: at times, they refused to regard the gathering so highly as to be worth risking the Master's health for it, and prepared themselves to speak and spread the divine fragrances on their own; but at others, as they stood and looked at the glorious state of that gathering, they cherished the hope that the Master might deign to attend it, if only for a single minute. After some discussion among themselves, they eventually decided to take a car back to see the Master and implore Him to come – strictly so that the attendees would have the honour of attaining His presence, and without any expectation that He would give a talk – inasmuch as those eager souls were sure to be filled with rapture at the very sight of Him. When they entered His presence and inquired after His health, the Master rose at once and said:

> It is the doctors who have required me not to go; otherwise, I wish for good health only so that I might expend it in service to the Cause of God and the loved ones of the Abhá Beauty.

As Mr Herrigel was speaking on the Cause of God from the podium,[771] and as the audience was growing despondent over the Master's absence from that gathering, He suddenly made His appearance, immediately stirring all those in attendance to such intense delight that they raised cries of ecstatic jubilation and voiced their grateful praise. In an even stranger turn of events, despite the Master's infirmity and illness – and notwithstanding that there was neither hope nor expectation that He would be able to speak – He gave a most effective and extensive talk nevertheless on universal peace:[772]

> This sort of peace is one of the exigencies of this age. Though all the Prophets of God have summoned humankind to peace and unity, they had always lacked the requisite capacity to achieve it until now. It is for this reason that, in all the divine religions, the

> Prophets have said with respect to 'the Latter Days' that the religion of God would encompass the whole world, and be the refuge and saviour of all who dwell therein. It is true that there are now many societies devoted to peace, which itself attests to the throbbing pulse of this age and the fresh requirements it demands, but the only Cause that can become the focal point of the world's Great Peace is one that can penetrate the hearts of humanity and embrace every other divine principle, which is to say that it meets the needs of all humankind – a Cause that can be a remedy for every ill and a balm for every wound.

Once the Master had concluded His elaborate talk on universal peace and the divine teachings, and rejoiced at the fairness and nobility of the government and people of Germany, a wave of such irrepressible excitement came over the members of His audience that each and every one of them felt impelled to betake himself to His presence. On account of His poor health, however, the Master quickly left the hall – but no sooner had He done this than the sound of crying could be heard. The Master stood up and said, 'Go see who that is.' Following some investigation, it was discovered that the crying was coming from a woman who had wanted to approach the Master but, despite her best efforts, was unable to make her way through the crowd and reach Him, and that the anguish she felt in her heart as a result had moved her to moaning and wailing. When this woman did attain the Master's presence at last, she clung to the hem of His bounty while He consoled her with words that brought her heavenly joy. One can well imagine the remarkable spectacle which took place that night, as well as the profound degree to which those people evinced the transformation they had experienced up until His car departed that place.[773]

Saturday, 26 April 1913
[Stuttgart]

The symptoms of the Master's illness and weakness were the cause of sadness that morning, but He Himself was feeling a bit better than the day before, and His heart was immensely cheered. He said:

> Though leaving the hotel last night posed harm to my chest, we went to the gathering and spoke nonetheless. In the end, God granted His assistance and protection, and the gathering went very well.

Afterwards, when a translation of a newspaper article concerning the Balkan War was read for the Master, He remarked:[774]

> Speak of our own war, wherein the hosts of aid and confirmation fight against the legions of the darkness of the world of nature, and in which we, armed with knowledge and wisdom, handily defeat the forces of ignorance and illusion. The former war is the cause of life, while the latter leads only to death. The one is entirely without danger and always ends in victory, while the other results in perdition, toil, and harm. Reflect on this: that to give one's life for this war is to attain true existence. Jesus Christ waged this war while on the cross, and at the moment He yielded up His life, He reigned supreme over every king and vassal of this earth.

Believers and seekers alike then came in groups to attain the Master's presence. They all spoke highly of the previous night's gathering, and this prompted the Master to say again and again:

> Although last night I lacked the strength to take even a single step, I attended the gathering nevertheless. I said to myself, 'I will go there even if it is dangerous to do so, and will sacrifice myself to the Cause of God and the friends of the Abhá Beauty. What could be better than this?' But praised be God, we had a wonderful time.
>
> Now that my poor health has forced us to remain in Stuttgart for a protracted period, we must stay here for yet another few days. On our previous sojourn [in Stuttgart], too, we had come intending to stay only for a few days, but in the end it lasted for a week.[775]

The Master then said the following to another group of people who had just attained His presence:[776]

> You are among the people whom God has chosen to receive His love. It behooves you to be abundantly joyous that He has guided you aright, and crowned your heads with the diadem of imperishable glory. You must be exceedingly grateful to God. The value of this bounty is not yet known; it will become clear in the future. The matter can be likened to the time of Christ, when the value of those who accepted Him was unknown, and the people scorned and ridiculed them.

To yet another group who was visibly thrilled to have the bounty of being in His presence, the Master said:[777]

> I, too, am most delighted to be meeting with you all. When I see each and every one of you, it is as if I am beholding one who is near and dear to my heart.

They then inquired after the Master's health, and He replied:

> The gathering last night proved to be potent medicine; my condition has improved. There must be a wisdom to these days of illness and my stay here. It is a testament to the devotion of the Bahá'ís of this city that the circumstances for my lengthier stay here have now been arranged. This will certainly yield prodigious results; only later will it become known. One of these results is the establishment of absolute love among the Bahá'ís, the second consists in the vigilance and progress of God's chosen ones, and the third is the pervading influence of the Word of God.

A person from Switzerland then attained the Master's presence,[778] and to him He said:[779]

> The Swiss are a receptive people. Should this Cause be spread in that land, blessed souls would be raised up as a result. I spent a few

days at a hotel in Geneva,[780] but I saw very little of the people of that place.

I hope that all of you may progress in the love of God and become the means through which people are guided aright. I pray for all of you and beseech God to confirm you, that you may become so spiritual as to attract the people in your midst. My hope is that these tokens of your love may grow more numerous with every passing day, and that your hearts may be increasingly ablaze with the fire of the love of God, that thereby the splendours of the Most Glorious Kingdom may illumine these regions.

I love you all very much and am well-pleased with you. Truly, the people here are receptive; the faces of those who attended last night's gathering were radiant indeed.

The believers presented the Master with a newspaper that afternoon. Once a translation of its contents was read for Him, it was conveyed to Him that the owner of a certain newspaper had listened to Him speak at the previous night's gathering, and that this person had written a completely honest account of that occasion. Upon hearing this news, the Master said:

Although he is not a Bahá'í, behold how he has testified to the greatness of the Cause of God and the greatness of the blessed teachings!

The name of that newspaper is the *[Stuttgarter] Neues Tagblatt*, and the article in question, published on 26 April [1913],[781] begins thus:

An illustrious, dignified, and elderly man with a flowing white beard, wide brow, and luminous face attended the gathering last night. The appearance of that grand personage was reminiscent of Abraham Himself . . .[782]

And concludes with these words:

The Stuttgart Obere Museum, where 'Abdu'l-Bahá spoke. Many Bahá'í talks were held here; it was destroyed in the Second World War

View of Bebenhausen

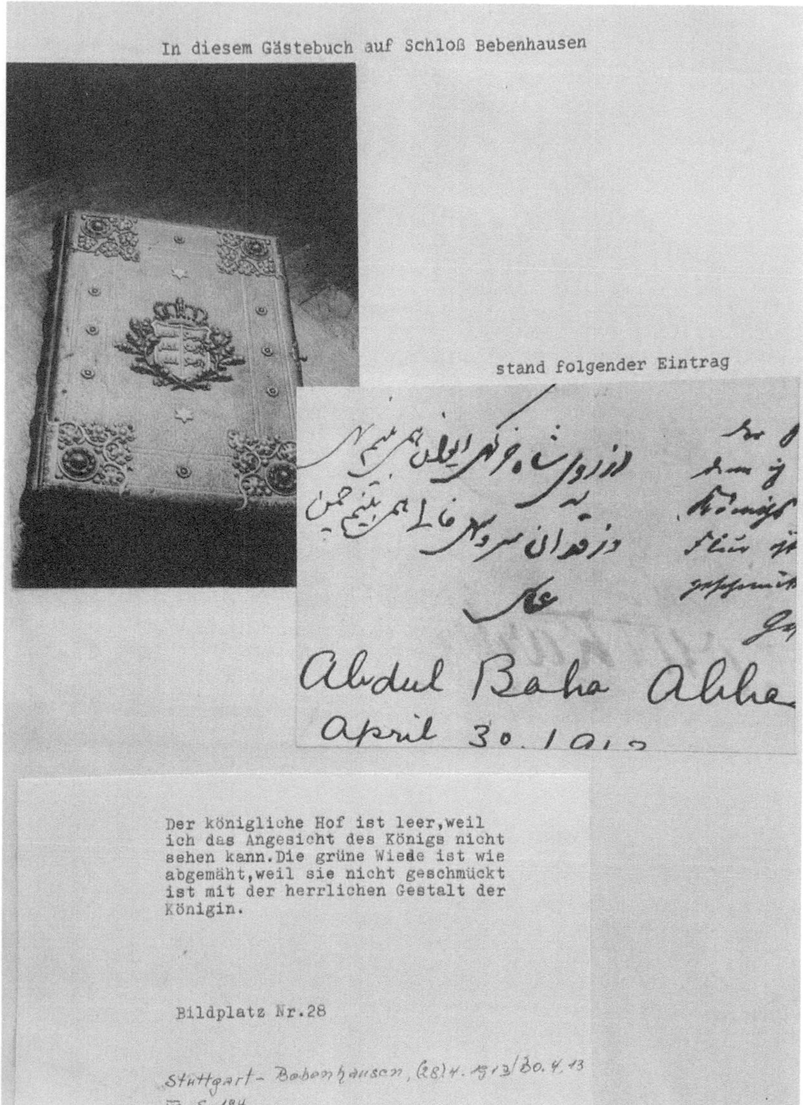
In diesem Gästebuch auf Schloß Bebenhausen

stand folgender Eintrag

Abdul Baha Abbas
April 30. 1913

Der königliche Hof ist leer, weil ich das Angesicht des Königs nicht sehen kann. Die grüne Wiede ist wie abgemäht, weil sie nicht geschmückt ist mit der herrlichen Gestalt der Königin.

Bildplatz Nr. 28

Stuttgart- Bebenhausen, (28) 4. 1913/30. 4. 13
IV, S. 194

30 April 1913, the guest book in the Palace of Bebenhausen where the King of Württemberg did not come to meet 'Abdu'l-Bahá, so 'Abdu'l-Bahá wrote in the guest book: "The Imperial court is empty because I cannot see the face of the king. The green pasture is as if mown down, because it is not adorned with the glorious figure of the Queen" After the First World War the King was forced to abdicate the throne and he fled to the palace of Bebenhausen where he passed away

> Even on behalf of those who belong to no religion and profess no such belief, we welcome the arrival of 'Abdu'l-Bahá.[783]

At the end of that day's gathering, the Bahá'ís implored the Master's permission to look for another physician to treat Him.[784] He replied:

> I am in better health today and the weather is mild. There is no need for this at the moment; let us see what happens. God will cure me; He is my Physician.

Since the Master was feeling better that day, the believers asked if He might attend a gathering of Bahá'ís the following day, and He consented to their request.

Sunday, 27 April 1913
[Stuttgart]

Early that morning, a group of the friends came with their children to see the Master. When they attained His presence, some of those children immediately ran up to Him and began touching His robe. Their parents remarked, 'The children were crying in the wee hours of the morning, saying, "We want to go see 'Abdu'l-Bahá!"' The Master took them in His embrace and said:

> Observe how pure is the love of children, and how stainless are their hearts! The purity of their love can be seen in their faces. This is how the love in one's heart must be, and this applies especially to the hearts of the loved ones of God. When the love of God is manifest in the human heart, it will have attained to the utmost purity. It will be even as the heart of a child, which is entirely free of guile and deceit, and is controlled more by his emotions than his volition. If a child is fond of someone, his affinity for that person will be evident, and when he dislikes someone, he will straightway keep his distance from them; he does not behave deceptively in the least.

> Children must be raised well, for they are even as fresh and tender saplings; however you train them, that way will they accept. The love of God must be instilled in their hearts when they are young. Then will they be raised well – then will they be radiant and demonstrate a goodly disposition.

The friends expressed their gratitude for the Master's stay [in Stuttgart]. He replied:

> The believers here are worthy. I am now sick with a cold and a fever, and you all have benefited from this turn of events!

(This remark moved them to boisterous laughter.)

> Though I will leave this place, I will ever be waiting to hear good news from you all – that with every passing day, you are increasingly ablaze with the fire of the love of God, and are constantly progressing from one spiritual station to the next. It is certain that when the heat of the sun emanates forth, and the vernal shower rains down, the trees will grow and develop. My hope, then, is that you may always be advancing and ascending.

Yet another group of people arrived, with their very precious children in tow and colourful flowers in hand, to attain the Master's presence. With the utmost tenderness, the Master took these children in His embrace and said:

> I love children very much, for they are close to the Kingdom of God. I hope that a day may come when these fresh saplings will bear abundant fruit. Because they are Bahá'ís, they will receive a spiritual education beneath the shade of Bahá'u'lláh.
>
> At every hour, you must render a thousand thanks to God that He has guided you, edified you, and singled you out amidst all creation. The Voice of the Kingdom has reached your ears. All humanity is asleep, but you are awake; all are blind, but you are seeing. You are beneath the shadow of divine grace, and have taken

refuge in heavenly aid and protection.

The value of this bounty is not known at present; in time its lustrous gems will gleam forth, shining throughout the ages and centuries to come. Consider the advent of Jesus Christ; how remarkable was the crown He placed on the heads of His loved ones, but the value thereof was not known at the time. Rather, the people subjected them to scorn and reproach. Whenever a Christian passed them by, they would mock him, saying: 'Here now is one of the followers of Christ. He must be mad to follow a youth from Nazareth!' Eventually, however, the glorious crown He had placed on their heads became apparent, to the extent that its jewels still shine to this day. Appreciate, then, the value of this bounty and arise with gratitude, that these divine splendours may shine brilliantly throughout every region of the earth.

I pray for you all and have high hopes for the Bahá'ís here, inasmuch as their faces are radiant and their hearts are attracted to the Kingdom of God. Thus, I promise you all that you are close to God, that you are commendable in His sight, and that the gates of Paradise are opened to your faces. Soon will you witness the evidences of these things for yourselves.

Still another group of people then came, but as there was no room for them to sit, everyone arose and formed lines in which to stand. The Master then spoke these exalted words as He walked to and fro:

I wish for you all to be granted divine confirmations and imperishable glory – that you may be so aided as to free you from the circumstances of the world of nature, that thereby every defilement may be changed into peace.

I shall never forget this city, for I inhale from it the sweet savours of God. Unlike certain other cities, the people of this place are not engrossed in materialism; they are staunch and spiritual. Other cities, however, are so steeped in the world of nature that no trace of spirituality whatsoever can be found there. All the people of such cities are concerned only with eating and sleeping, or

> dancing and making merry; they are entirely oblivious of the divine realm. Stuttgart, on the other hand, is not this way. It is for this reason that I hope Stuttgart will become luminous.

At that juncture, the Master's gaze fell upon Mr Gottlieb Pfund, who boasted a robust physique and wore a substantial mustache, and whom the Master had previously likened to a lion. To him He said once again:

> This man is a lion, which is to say the lion of the forest of God's love. There is a difference between the lion of the reed-beds and the lion of God; both are courageous, but the former is ferocious while the latter gives life. You are indeed a lion of God! A person's courage consists in the stoutness of his heart, through which he will fear nothing whatever, and achieve outstanding success in the arena of sacrifice as he treads the path of God.

Mr Pfund remarked, 'Thanks to the blessed teachings, I have now become a different person.' The Master replied:

> This is as it should be; otherwise, one does not become a Bahá'í by simply adopting the name. In Persia, there were people who lived in a state of the utmost defilement and ferocity, yet when they became Bahá'ís, they assumed so gentle and holy a demeanour as to result in their harassment and murder, and not once did they retaliate because of this treatment.

As the believers were being dismissed, the Master took the children in His embrace and remarked:

> Oh, what precious children they are! My God, who are these children, and who could have imagined that I might meet with them here someday?

The Master was invited to have lunch at the home of Consul Schwarz that day. The consul and his wife brought two cars to take the Master and the members of His retinue, who all went in the same car, and then set off. The Master was first taken on a lengthy excursion outside the city, where He passed by wonderfully scenic hills, rivers, villages, gardens, and forests. At certain elevated spots,[785] from which one could look out over the outskirts and other environs of the city, the Master's car would stop for a few minutes. A considerable amount of time passed before He arrived at the consul's residence and had lunch.[786]

After a bit of rest, a number of the city's dignitaries and other grandees came,[787] as they had previously been invited, to attain the Master's presence. He gave an extensive talk that dealt with the nobility and spirituality of the Germans, the need for the promulgation of universal peace, the oneness of humanity, and the single foundation underlying all the divine religions. So moved were the hearts of these respected persons by the Master's words that they openly declared the promotion of the blessed teachings to be their highest aspiration, and were conspicuously delighted and honoured to have the bounty of being in His presence.

On that day, the daughter of Consul Schwarz [Olly Schwarz] presented the Master with all her jewelry and said, 'I wanted to give you my most precious possessions so that they will remind You of me.'[788] The Master replied:

> We do not need such things as these to remember you by. Know of a certainty that I will never forget you.

Despite all her pleading, He refused to accept her gift.

From there,[789] the Master went to a gathering of Bahá'ís,[790] where He gave a sweet talk on the fervour of the friends and rendered thanks for the confirmations vouchsafed by the Most Glorious Kingdom.[791] He then bade the friends be seated and invited them to have some tea and sweets, as an afternoon meal had been prepared and a variety of delectable food laid out on all the tables. Every heart demonstrated the utmost tenderness and purity on that occasion, and every eye was fixed squarely on the Master – the Embodiment of grace and bounty.

Because the Master had spoken a great deal that day, His respiratory illness worsened once again; He coughed violently and developed a slight fever.

Monday, 28 April 1913
[Stuttgart]

A steady stream of believers came in groups that morning to attain the Master's presence with the utmost delight. In spite of His illness, He spoke at length to each group of visitors – among them Miss Helen Wieland and Mr Eugene Diebold,[792] who stated that they intended to marry. To them He said:

> Marriage is necessary according to the Law of God, so your plans are most auspicious. The fruits and blessings of marriage are not apparent when one is young, but with time, one will see how delightful and beneficial it is to start a family. Marriage, moreover, is a fortress for humanity that protects it from self and passion and conduces to its purity and chastity. In the sight of God, there is no matter more important than that of purity and chastity; they are the highest stations to which humankind can attain, and are among the traits of this divine creation. To be without them is to resemble an animal. In the estimation of God, then, marriage is a most auspicious and highly commendable affair, and your union will be blessed as a result. God grant that it may likewise yield a blessed family.

A respected minister whom the Master had met during His previous journey then attained His presence. To him He said:[793]

> I have met with you previously. There are many ministers in the world, but few of them are confirmed. There were many leaders of religion at the time of Christ, but among them only a single Paul was confirmed. All were deprived, but he so benefited as to become the king of the divines. Thus, I hope that you, too, may be confirmed and surpass all others in your distinction – that even

as Paul, you may be granted an ample portion of the liberal effusions of heavenly grace, and obtain eternal life from the breathings of the Holy Spirit. This is my hope.

Focus not on your own self; rather, set your face towards the Kingdom of God. When a person is freed from the fetters of this world and vivified by the breaths of the Holy Spirit, he will be so aided with divine confirmations as to leave him utterly astounded. Turn towards God, then; focus on His favours, not on your own ability. Though the soil may be barren, yet through the bounty of the rain and the heat of the sun, in time it will yield plants and flowers and come to bear wholesome fruit.

When another group of people then attained the Master's presence, He said to them:

Though I completely lacked the strength for it, I attended the gathering yesterday strictly for your sake because a gathering of Bahá'ís is an assemblage of spiritual ones. The spirit of God descends upon such gatherings; hence, they are the cause of great joy.

Towards the end of His life, Jesus Christ came together as one with His companions; they sat around a single banquet-table and proclaimed this 'the Lord's Supper', inasmuch as heavenly conversations were had at that gathering. It is evident, then, that any gathering which produces discussions pertaining to the Kingdom of God is a heavenly gathering. You must strive that your gatherings may always be heavenly – that they may be radiant and cause the souls to rejoice at the glad-tidings of God. Then will you know of a certainty that that gathering is a heavenly one – that it is the means by which the world of humanity will be illumined and the source of everlasting life. I hope that you may hold many gatherings of this sort.

Consider the gatherings which today are convened and devoted to the various sciences – to industry, agriculture, commerce, and politics – and observe how none of the effects they produce endure like those of a divine gathering. This is a gathering

> that yields eternal effects and perpetual results. Strive, then, that your gatherings may be divine and heavenly. In other words, when the time comes to gather, may your hearts be pure and entirely purged of all natural emotion; may you conduct yourselves with the utmost sanctification; may you make mention of God in a spirit of perfect love and fellowship; may you recite the celestial words; and may you bear in mind the counsels of Bahá'u'lláh. Thereby you will be purified of all that is not of God, your souls will wing their flight, your minds will be broadened, and your spiritual sentiments will prevail. Through such gatherings, you will be liberated from earthly circumstances and moved to commune with the breathings of the Holy Spirit. Such is the station I desire for you, and it is my hope that you shall be aided to attain it.

A seeker asked,[794] 'As to the saying that Jesus Christ illumined the eyes of the blind and enabled them to see, is this also possible in the present age?' The Master replied:

> Anything is possible, but Jesus Christ, quoting the words of Isaiah, has said, 'They have eyes, but do not see; they have ears, but do not hear; they have hearts, but do not understand – yet I will grant them healing.'[*]

The Master then spoke of the intense racial prejudice that exists between the white and black people of America:

> That prejudice notwithstanding, at Bahá'í gatherings the blacks and the whites were like brothers and sisters. Even marriage between the black and the white has taken place in the Bahá'í Cause – namely, the union of Miss Mathew,[†] a white girl, and Mr Gregory,[‡] a black youth – and this was regarded as an extraordinary occurrence. It was made possible only by the power of the Word of God; otherwise, in America the people do not admit a

* A paraphrase of Matt. 13:13–15, originally from Isa. 6:9–10.
† Louise Mathew.
‡ Louis Gregory.

> single black person into their homes or gatherings, let alone establish fellowship with them.

Once the believers had been dismissed, His weakness and cough grew more severe and the condition of His chest became much worse. As a result, that morning a Bahá'í physician – and later that afternoon, a second physician – attained His presence to treat Him.

Tuesday, 29 April 1913
[Stuttgart]

A physician came once again that morning. After examining the Master's chest several times, he forbade Him, emphatically and categorically, from speaking, writing, or attending any gatherings. The physician told Him that, if He refrained from giving talks for two or three days and took the medicine prescribed for Him, His illness would so subside as to allow Him to continue travelling; otherwise, it would not be possible for Him to do this.

The physician's medicine and treatment proved most effective and were met with the Master's praise. While He did take His medicine, some of the believers attained His presence nonetheless, and to them He extended His loving-kindness and spoke of necessary matters, though He did this only briefly.[795]

Among His visitors that day[796] was Mr Schweizer, who was preparing to travel to discharge certain duties and had requested the Master's permission to attain His presence.[797] He implored the Master to confirm him and grant him success in his efforts to teach the Cause of God, both in word and in deed, and to him the Master said:

> In you I see such ability that if you should arise to teach the Cause, you would be so confirmed in your efforts as to leave you utterly astounded. I promise you that you will be successfully aided to action. Indeed, if one takes no action, one's speech will have no effect whatsoever. The matter can be likened to a person who summons the people to peace, but himself engages in the killing of

others. The Revelation of Bahá'u'lláh is for action; peruse *The Hidden Words* and see what He has said therein.

Mr Schweizer then mentioned the translation of certain books written for the Cause of God, and spoke highly of *The Brilliant Proof* of Mírzá Abu'l-Faḍl in particular.[798] The Master said:

I love him very much. In order to leave himself free to serve the Cause of God, he has not married. He is always occupied with promoting the Word of God. He has not rested for a single moment of the days of his life; he has either engaged himself in teaching the Cause, or set himself to composing treatises, or devoted himself to travelling, or spent his days in prison. He is an exceedingly blessed individual, and it is for this reason that I love him dearly.

A number of the friends who had brought their children in hopes that the Master would bless them then requested to attain His presence.[799] After extending His tender kindnesses, He said to them:[800]

Blessed souls will be raised up from among these children. Saplings that are tended by the Perfect Gardener will assuredly grow and develop to unparalleled proportions. Children must be raised with a spiritual education. They must be given such means as will add to their intellect with every passing day and conduce to the broadening of their mind. Children should be educated from their earliest years, even before they are enrolled in school; indeed, knowledge should be imparted to them through the use of toys and other objects, that they may learn the various subjects with joy and eagerness. By this means, when the time comes to play, they will engage one another in conversation and ask each other questions; each will benefit from the other and give his answer according to some law or principle. When a question concerning any given subject is asked them, whichever child offers the best answer should receive a prize so as to embolden them to speak on future occasions, and spiritual subjects should be taught them in the same way.

The Master then said:

> It would be very good if the friends of Germany and America began to correspond with one another; this would increase their fellowship and strengthen the bonds between their hearts. It is a cause of great joy that the power of the Cause of Bahá'u'lláh has gathered us together – that despite the distance between us, this Cause has brought us so close to each other. Though the sun appears to be far from the earth, yet do its rays reach our soil. Jesus Christ has said: 'The children of the Kingdom shall be cast out, but the people will come from far-off corners and distant paths and enter the Kingdom of God.'*
>
> Notwithstanding that the Persians hail from the native land of the Blessed Beauty, the majority of them have failed to take heed, but you all, who are far from Persia, have derived abundant bounty and benefit from the Kingdom of Bahá'u'lláh. You have heard His Voice from thousands of leagues away, but most of those who were near it have failed to hear it. This is due strictly to divine favour; render thanks that you have attained it.
>
> My hope is that you may draw nearer to the Kingdom of Bahá'u'lláh with every passing day – that you may be increasingly ablaze with the fire of the love of God, and be granted an ever-greater share from the breathings of the Holy Spirit. I pray that hidden confirmations may be vouchsafed to you all.

When the physician attained His presence that afternoon,[801] the Master said:

> It would be good if there were some way we could leave sooner rather than later.

* Perhaps a paraphrase of Matt. 8:11–12: 'And I say unto you, that many shall come from the east and west, and shall sit down with Abraham, and Isaac, and Jacob, in the kingdom of heaven. But the children of the kingdom shall be cast out into outer darkness: there shall be weeping and gnashing of teeth.' See also Luke 13:29: 'And they shall come from the east, and from the west, and from the north, and from the south, and shall sit down in the kingdom of God.'

The physician replied:

> Your health has improved, but stay here for two more days. Do not go out, and be very brief in your conversations with others. God willing, it will be possible for You to travel the day after tomorrow.

Thus, a telegram was sent to Paris stating that the Master's retinue would be departing for that city at nine o'clock the morning after next.

Wednesday, 30 April 1913
[Stuttgart]

When the believers heard the good news that the Master was feeling better, they made arrangements that morning to visit Him.[802] With overwhelming excitement, they attained His presence and gazed spellbound on His face. Among the remarks He made were as follows: [803]

> We will leave Stuttgart tomorrow. Praised be God that we came here and met with you all, and that sentiments of the utmost spiritual affection have developed between us. We will strive that perfect bonds may be established between the East and the West, and my coming here marks the beginning of that process. The sun has only just begun to dawn. I hope that the splendours of the daystar of oneness may shine upon all regions of the earth.
>
> The peoples of the world are like drops; when they come together, a mighty ocean is formed. My hope is that all may be united, so that the sea of the oneness of humanity may surge – that this scattered flock may gather beneath the nurturing shade of the Divine Shepherd, where they may find the most peaceful repose in the meadow of prosperity and beneficence, and drink their fill from the wellspring of eternal life. This is our purpose, inasmuch as the children of humanity can be likened to scattered sheep, wandering the plains, hills, and mountains in bewilderment and

distress. How excellent would it be if they should all come together to live in the divine pasture with the utmost fellowship and tranquillity under the protection of the True Shepherd! These people are even as children, and God is the True Father. How beautiful would it be if these children should come together around the banquet-table of divine favour beneath the shade of the Heavenly Father and be reared with the training of that Loving Provider!

Dr Faber[804] then said:

In the course of a discussion I was having with a respected individual, I shared the blessed teachings with them. They remarked, 'There can be no doubt that these principles have the potential to bring about the welfare of all humanity and manifest the virtues of humankind, but to put them into practice would be impossible.' I responded, 'Before the telegraph, the telephone, and the lightbulb, no one ever imagined that such things could be invented.'

The Master replied:

Indeed, the hallmarks of this age were all deemed impossible by the wise ones of former times. Could anyone have previously imagined a time when women would not only seek to have rights equal to those of men, but actually attain to that desire? At present, women have earned the right to vote in nine states of America. You answered well – that before the appearance of these inventions which exist today, no sage considered such developments to be possible. What wise one ever said that a time may come when the vehicles of humankind would be able to fly – that, by means of an aeroplane, one could travel through the air from city to city? What sage ever declared that a day may come when – without the use of an apparatus, and strictly through waves in the air – people would be able to convey news to one another?

Furthermore, some say that war and strife are natural – that the differences between the various natures of people are innate, and that reconciliation and unity are thus impossible. We maintain firstly that ferocity and corruption are characteristics of the world of nature, whereas peace and welfare are characteristics of the world of humanity. If the characteristics of nature were sufficient for humankind, they would have no need for education; the jungles and forests would be even as paradise for them, and thickets of thorns would never have been turned into beds of flowers. Secondly, the differences between the various natures do not indicate the impossibility of achieving unity between them. Rather, they suggest the possibility of this prospect, inasmuch as every being in the world of creation is composed of conflicting elements that have come into existence through the agency of a dominating power. Through composition and unification, then, the differences between these constituent elements have given rise to the power and perfections of sanctified realities and pure souls. If the inherent differences between these elements rendered unity and concord impossible, then no being would exist in this contingent world. Those who contend such a position should consider the world of existence, whose foundation rests on the combination of various members, and in which the differing natures of people only add to the glory and beauty they manifest. Perfect examples include the human body, which demonstrates the supremacy of the human spirit through one's various limbs and members; the country, which prospers through the various classes of people; the sovereignty of a monarch, which orders affairs through various noblemen, officials, and servants; and the mass of a nation, which is formed through people possessed of various views and differing intellects. Hence, according both to the laws of nature and the dictates of reason, the establishment of universal peace and oneness in the world of humanity is not impossible; in fact, it is necessary, and its fulfilment will constitute the fruit and perfection of humankind.

Such people likewise contend that war and strife conduce to the appearance of honour and valour, as well as the superiority and advancement of certain nations over others. We maintain that, if by ‘honour’ and ‘valour’ are meant physical pride and courage, and thus the appearance of animalistic instincts – and if it is the case that, the more ferocious one is, the happier one will be – then why limit this war and strife to the level of nations? It would be better for such conflict to take place between individuals! What need would there be for safety or order? Tumult and confusion would surely be preferable. If, however, by 'honour' and 'valour' are intended the preservation of the foundation of glory and prosperity, as well as the protection of human rights, in this case war and strife would destroy that foundation and trample underfoot the rights of the world's inhabitants. How could the honour of a man of moderation, or the valour of a person of wisdom, ever be content to see thousands of their brethren welter in pools of their own blood, all to conquer a piece of land or gain some fame? How could such a one bear to hear the heart-rending cries of the wives and children of those slain in battle, or find a once flourishing city now in ruins? All the wealth and substance which the labour, the agriculture, the commerce, and the industry of the people of a given nation have produced over many years are summarily expended, in the span of a single day, to kill others and violate their women. In this day, the honour and valour of humankind must eliminate these dire calamities and weighty burdens, not add to them.

Moreover, war and strife are not needed to demonstrate the superiority and advancement of certain nations over others. There exist today a myriad laudable means and countless commendable channels to this end, and not one of them depends on the shedding of blood, or the meting out of destruction, or the infliction of harm. Examples include the repairing of one's country; the dissemination of knowledge; the promotion of the arts and sciences; the expansion of the spheres of commerce and agriculture; and the realization of perfect security, justice, tranquillity, comfort, and the like. All these are vehicles for superiority and advancement. Were the exorbitant sums that today are spent on warfare and bloodshed to be devoted to these important ideals, every country would become a token of the Most Exalted Paradise. If these ideals, which are all conducive to the joy and prosperity of the peoples of the world, do not result in the superiority and advancement of a given people over others in this day, then how can war and strife, which bring ruin and destruction, ever possibly be the means for effecting that superiority and advancement? Perhaps in some of the past ages, in which fewer sorts of these means for the progression of people's minds existed, one could cite these kinds of national and political prejudices as pretexts for going to war, arguing that warfare will edify the proud and primitive people of a given nation, and establish order in their underdeveloped country. In an age as glorious as this one, however, the hideousness of conditioning the advancement of peoples on war and bloodshed between civilized nations and governments is clear and apparent to every person of wisdom.

What is strange indeed in this connection is that, in such a day and age as this one, these nations and governments of Europe regard racial and political prejudices, along with warfare and bloodshed, as vehicles for superiority and advancement – yet when the subject of past religions is mentioned, their first objection is to religious prejudice. The greatest proof they adduce in favour of dispensing with religious belief, and among its detriments which they cite, is the war promoted by leaders of religion in former times. How well and true is the saying of Jesus Christ: '. . . why beholdest thou the mote that is in thy brother's eye, but considerest not the beam that is in thine own eye?'*

Afterwards, a young soldier and teacher of music requested the Master to speak about his profession. He replied:

Music is one of the signs of God. Even as your kind of music stirs the bodies to motion and rouses them to excitement, divine music and the Heavenly Voice animate the hearts and souls. It is this spiritual music which is taught by the Prophets of God. I hope, therefore, that you will hearken to this celestial melody – that just as you spur the army and the nation to movement with earthly music, you will likewise use this heavenly music to confer abiding joy and ecstasy on the minds and spirits.

---

* Matt. 7:3.

The weather that afternoon was sunny and mild. Thus, at the request of the believers, and because the Master wished to get some fresh air, He went on an excursion by car, and the physician saw fit to let Him do this. He beheld wonderfully scenic gardens, meadows, valleys, hills, and forests, and eventually arrived at an ancient royal palace known as 'Palace Bebenhausen'.[805] The Master saw the rooms on every floor of the palace, which were filled with antique and valuable furnishings – as well as its corridors, whose walls were bedecked from the lower levels to the upper floors with various weapons and other instruments of war, including armor, helmets, and other military attire – and this prompted Him to speak extensively on the transience of material things and the significance of spiritual life.[806]

When the Master went to a village [Steinenbronn] that was on the way, and also when His car departed the palace [sic],[807] the children and other residents of the village thanked and praised the Master effusively for the generosity and beneficence He had shown them.[808]

Thursday, 1 May 1913

[Stuttgart → Paris]

The Master's retinue was preparing to depart and the friends made a jubilant commotion as they met with Him. The Master was feeling much better; the physician permitted Him to continue travelling, but told Him that too much writing or speaking, and also going outside when the weather was anything but sunny, would be very harmful to His health. Yet as today was the day of His farewell, the believers came in groups from the early morning and hovered around that beautiful face of the Master, Who spoke to them constantly up until it was time to leave. He addressed His first group of visitors with these words:[809]

> What a love this is that has been established in our midst through the power of Bahá'u'lláh! The Shah of Persia made two visits to Stuttgart, and even though he was a king, the state merely welcomed him with a formal ceremony and hosted him as their

official guest; he did not have two true friends there, nor was there anyone who genuinely loved him. We, on the other hand, who were once prisoners and exiles, came here and found all these sincere friends, and such ties of love formed between our hearts as are beyond compare, for this sort of love and fellowship are born of an extraordinary power that can be seen only from the Word of God. Were it not for this power, how else could all these hearts be so profoundly affected, or the people be this attracted to us? It is clear from this that the holy Manifestations, from Whom a power as subduing as this one proceeds, are the very Essences of existence and are greater than all the kings of the world. Behold what splendours are shining from the Most Glorious Kingdom, and observe how they have illumined the corners of people's hearts! The gracious outpourings of that Kingdom have bound the souls one to another, and its teachings have made the denizens of the East and the West even as a single person. Soon will you see for yourselves how it has encompassed the East and the West alike.

When another group of people attained the Master's presence, He said:

Today I will bid you farewell, but farewells are of two kinds. One is a farewell in which people say their goodbyes and then forget one another with the passage of time. This is a farewell that suits the inhabitants of this nether world. But a farewell that carries no forgetfulness is the one that befits the denizens of the Kingdom and the loved ones of Bahá'u'lláh – a farewell in which people only draw closer to one's heart as they go farther away from one's sight, and in which a bond so strong exists between them that it shall never be severed. There are Bahá'ís whom I have not seen for many years, yet I am with them day and night. Although they are in Persia and I am in Europe, we are companions who are together at present. Even this child I will not forget.[810]

His visitors then said:

Yesterday we heard this child say a strange thing. When we told him, 'Say "Alláh-u-Abhá" ninety-five times every morning and we will count your repetitions, in hopes that the Master will get well sooner,' he replied, 'Very well, but when the Master has recovered, He will leave us sooner.'

This story moved those present to smile with great astonishment. The Master said:

My hope is that you may be increasingly aided with every passing day and that you may illumine the souls, for all the peoples of the West are enveloped in the darkness of nature, and the splendours of God are nowhere to be seen. Though in the physical realm they have attained to the highest degree of civilization, yet they have remained entirely deprived of spiritual benefits. Indeed, God willing you will be the means through which the brilliance of divine civilization will be made manifest.

Place your hope in the confirmations of the Most Glorious Kingdom. When divine confirmations are obtained, every difficulty becomes easy. The horizon of Persia was much darker than it is now, but it was illumined with the rising of the Sun of Truth. It is His confirmations that change a drop into an ocean, a dried-up plant into a blessed tree, and a gnat into an eagle. Indeed, they grant power to the powerless, make known the nameless throughout earth and heaven, and endow the lowly ant with the majesty of Solomon.

With that, I bid you all farewell. I commend you to the refuge of God, and will ever be waiting to hear good news from you.

The Master then said the following to another group:

I want to say goodbye to you, but at the same time my heart wishes to stay with you. Meeting is just as sweet as parting is bitter, but neither our farewells nor the distance between us will prevent our nearness to one another, inasmuch as the love of Bahá'u'lláh has bound us with ties that can never be broken. Should the distance between the farthest ends of the earth be between us, it would never preclude the closeness of our hearts and souls, for spiritual sentiments are beyond any doubt. When people meet one another, it is their spirits that take pleasure in this meeting, not their bodies, and their souls that experience degrees of spiritual feeling, not their flesh. Thus, it is this spiritual feeling which is continually present. I commit you all to the sheltering shade of the protection and aid of Bahá’u’lláh.

The Master then addressed these words to yet another crowd:

This is the last day of our stay in Stuttgart and the first day of your entrance into the Most Glorious Kingdom because, in your absence, I shall supplicate the divine threshold with the utmost ardour, praying that you all may be firm and resolute, for it is easy to enter the Kingdom but difficult to remain staunch and steadfast. I hope that you may be exceedingly firm in the Cause of God, and that the favours of Bahá’u’lláh may encompass you from every side. Divine tests are grievous indeed, and perseverance is needed to endure them. How often does a thing go contrary to the way one believes it should, and how frequently do these experiences shake one’s faith! Yet when one perseveres, every problem will fade into nothingness.

Furthermore, you all must show consummate love and fellowship towards one another. You must never grow distant or resentful of each other, for trivial occurrences are fleeting and will eventually pass. Should a person fall short in some way, others must forgive him and not hang it over his head; then will God overlook their failures, too.

One must be firm – not like a stalk of straw that the wind may carry every which way, but rather like a mountain, fixed and immovable.

I commend you all to the care of God, that you may abide in His refuge and remain safe and secure – that with every passing day, your characters may improve increasingly and your detachment may wax ever greater. Thereby may you become birds of the

Kingdom, winging your flight to the summit of happiness in heights divinely protected.

To still another group of visitors the Master said:

I wish to speak with you, but my chest is in poor condition. To put it briefly, I shall leave imminently, but will ever be waiting to hear glad-tidings from you. I await the news that you are showing the utmost unity and love to one another – that with every passing day your firmness and steadfastness in the Kingdom of Bahá'u'lláh are increasing constantly, and that your perfections are steadily growing in number. I have sown a pure seed in this place; my hope is that you all may water these seeds and tend to them, that they may sprout forth and form ample harvests. This is what I am waiting to see. I shall never forget you; you are always in my thoughts.

And to a further crowd He said:

Welcome! I love you all from the bottom of my heart, and this is all that is needed. This is an eternal love. The distances of time and place between you and me will never serve as barriers. Even if I should be in the East, my heart and soul will still be with you. I sense your inner feelings. Whenever news from you reaches me, it gladdens me immensely. Know of a certainty that I will not forget you. We are all beneath the sheltering shade of Bahá'u'lláh, and repose in the shadow of the pavilion of His Covenant. Thus, separation is of no importance. What truly matters is heartfelt love, which is perpetual and always with us. We will all gather in the Kingdom of Bahá'u'lláh, which is to say the divine realm; that will be an everlasting meeting. Rest assured that I am not far from you and that I am always with you.

And to the final group He said:[811]

We are all the drops of a single ocean; the drops are not separate from the ocean. We are the trees of one orchard, and the flowers of a single bed. Hence, there is no separation between us. We all dwell beneath the bountiful shade of Bahá'u'lláh; the lights of His grace shine upon us all, and we all derive benefit from that Sun of Truth. Our nostrils are all perfumed by the breeze of a single garden, and we all drink our fill from a single spring. Therefore, we are always together; we are not separated from one another.

Although the days of my sojourn in Stuttgart were limited, I hope nevertheless that the results thereof will prove limitless – that each of you may become a lamp of the love of God, and the means through which these regions are illumined.

When the Master had gone from the hotel to the railway station,[812] He found that all the believers had formed a line there and were waiting for Him to arrive. The Master walked in their midst with His graceful gait, and His visitors gazed on His glorious beauty. The friends approached Him on both sides to show their reverence, and He unloosed His tongue to beseech their confirmation and success.[813] Even the children, whose lips were occupied with the mention of 'Alláh-u-Abhá', presented the Master with bouquets of variegated flowers that were fragrant and exquisite. All those present were deeply saddened by His impending distance from them, and they wiped away the tears that streamed down their faces. The Master offered words of tender consolation, and counselled them to set their minds at ease. He told them He was well-pleased with the services they had rendered, and exhorted them to spread the divine fragrances. As others in the vicinity watched the remarkable scene that was unfolding before them, they grew so astonished that they stayed right where they were, and fixed their undivided and undeviating attention on what was taking place.

The Master's train departed at nine o'clock that morning.[814] All those who had come to see Him off stood alongside the train, wailing and sighing as they looked squarely upon His beautiful face.[815]

While en route, an American passenger[816] and a few Pársís[817] sought to attain the Master's presence. These visitors were thoroughly delighted as they listened to His most sweet utterances, His counsels, and His enunciations of the teachings of Bahá'u'lláh.

At nine o'clock that evening,[818] the Master's train arrived in Paris [at the Gare de l'Est]. Áqá Mírzá Jalál and a number of other eager souls were filled with fresh joy and immeasurable gladness when they saw Him at the railway station.[819]

As the Master was very fatigued from both the train ride itself and the cold weather that attended it, He had a bit of bread and milk and then retired to rest.

Return to France

Friday, 2 May 1913
[Paris]

That morning, a number of the Bahá'ís of Paris attained the presence of the Master,[820] Who was rejoicing at the journey He had made to Germany, Austria, and Hungary.[821] He recounted the fervour of the Bahá'ís of Stuttgart, and described the seeds that had been planted in Budapest and Vienna. He then said:[822]

> In truth, material civilization has pitched its tent in all the nations of Europe. Every one of those countries is flourishing with the utmost prosperity; they are only in need of divine civilization.

Parcels that had been sent from both the East and the West were presented to the Master. He was greatly delighted to hear of the attraction of the Bahá'ís of Tehran; He made mention of certain respected persons, and also related an anecdote concerning Tehran and Geneva. Following this, the contents of a copy of a programme which had been prepared for a gathering [the National Bahá'í Convention] held at the House of Worship in America, and had been sent to the Master from New York, were translated for Him. The substance of the programme indicated that the heads of other societies acted as helpers to the people of Bahá at that gathering, and that they were rendering service with all their heart and soul. The Master said:

> At every gathering, we have stated things in the best of terms – terms that accord with the truth and agree with a diversity of temperaments. For instance, we have said that our purpose is that the various sects and peoples should gather beneath the shade of a single Word and be friends with one another . . .

The fame of the grandeur of the Master's journey had reached such great proportions that a French newspaper featuring an extensive article which discussed His travels and mentioned the spread of the teachings of peace and unity was shown at that gathering. Included in the article was a full-page colour illustration of the Master, in which He was standing before a large crowd of Muslims at a mosque in Constantinople.[823] He had been depicted while speaking, suggesting that He was imparting counsels; His hands were raised up, and all those present were listening with the utmost humility. The caption accompanying the image stated that a new prophet of Islam was summoning the followers of the various religions to oneness and unity.[824] Seeing this image brought an ample smile to the Master's face.

Among the remarks which the Master made to the Bahá'ís of Paris at His residence that afternoon were the following:[825]

> The abilities of anyone who enters beneath the shade of Bahá'u'lláh will increase with every passing day, even as a tree that is tended by the hand of the Perfect Gardener. It is certain that such a tree will grow and develop, and be nurtured in the most perfect way. Consider what blessed people were raised up beneath the shade of Jesus Christ, and what lofty stations were attained by the poor fishermen among them. When the bounties of God are made manifest, and the breathings of the Holy Spirit lend their assistance, the matter of one's own ability becomes irrelevant.

Some of those present implored the Master to confirm them in their efforts to teach the Cause. He replied:

> The Cause of God is taught in two ways: in word and in deed. My hope is that you will succeed in both.

A public gathering of the friends was held that night at the home of Mr and Mrs Dreyfus-Barney. The Master remarked:

> My health does not permit me to attend; you all go in my stead.

Accordingly, all the members of the Master's retinue – as well as the other believers and friends in attendance at that gathering – occupied themselves with the mention and remembrance of the Master, and discussed the Revelation of Bahá'u'lláh with the utmost zeal and ecstasy.[826] To conclude the gathering, a prayer was chanted by Riḍváníyyih Khánum.[827]

Saturday, 3 May 1913
[Paris]

The Master was feeling much better and His infirmity had completely disappeared. As He walked to and fro in the reception room of the hotel – a most majestic room that was adorned with variegated flowers – He looked out at Avenue Kléber, along which His hotel (Hotel California) [sic][828] was situated.

At that juncture, a number of respected Persians attained the Master's presence. After extending His tender kindnesses to these visitors, He said to them:

> In the East, the mention of one's own native land has never conduced to the excitement or unification of the Easterners, nor has it ever produced any great results. Rather, what have invariably united the people of the East – and have resulted in their dominance and might – are spiritual power and godliness. Their distinction has always consisted in this power; so too will this be for the present . . .

According to a previous arrangement, two Bahá'í women from America[829] had their lunch in the Master's presence that day. While seated at the table in a special hall of the hotel, the Master spoke of the spiritual life of Jesus Christ. His guests apprised Him of certain descriptions that had been written about Him, among them an account from an American magazine which had written something to this effect:

> 'Abdu'l-Bahá is the first illustrious Person Who did not accept so

much as a penny from a single soul as He gave important talks at various churches and grand gatherings during His journey to America; rather, He Himself gave money to a great number of people.

The Master said:

> We have acted in accordance with the commandment of Jesus Christ, and the dust of any given city has not settled on our hem or on our shoes.*

His guests then mentioned the transformation experienced by one of the members of their family, who had been profoundly affected by hearing the Master speak at a certain church. The Master said:

> Things were said at those churches that no person could deny or raise the slightest objection against.

His guests then remarked:

> The greatest objection that was raised in Your absence by some of those who are prejudiced against this Cause was this: 'Contrary to former times, most of the people who become Bahá'ís here [in America] are wealthy or leaders of some sort.'

The Master said:

> If this is indeed the case, then it is an evidence of supreme power, as it is more difficult for the wealthy and noble to profess religious belief than it is for the poor to do this. To accomplish a difficult task is surely a glorious thing. At any rate, he who cavils is merely seeking an excuse to do so; he himself is giving testimony to the greatness of the Cause without even realizing it.

* cf. Matt. 10:14: 'And whosoever shall not receive you, nor hear your words, when ye depart out of that house or city, shake off the dust of your feet.'

He then rose from His seat at the table and said:

> Weariness is overtaking me; I feel fatigued. I will go rest for a bit. You two stay seated and have your meal; do not get up.

Miss Sanderson and Mrs Moreau,[830] as well as a number of other friends, attained the Master's presence that afternoon.[831] The Master's talk on that occasion dealt with two subjects. The essence of the first was as follows:[832]

> Every great undertaking has a focal point which possesses a penetrating power and subduing might. In relation to the mighty centre of that circle, all other things can be likened to its circumference; the latter is dependent on the former, without which their powers would be limited and lacking.

And this was the substance of the second:[833]

> If outward perfections and physical well-being are the fruits of the world of humanity, then any flock of birds or hive of bees already possesses these perfections. A person must study geometry and architecture for years, and yet the bee possesses such excellence without having acquired an education. A person must toil his entire life to procure wealth and buildings, but the birds of the gardens and meadows dwell on the tallest of branches and in the most splendid of heights without having expended any effort. The seeds, the vegetation, the refreshing waters – all these have already been prepared for the birds, and they have felt no weariness in the process.
>
> Civilization is a very good thing, and perfection in any matter is worthy of praise. Yet material civilization must not hinder divine civilization or spiritual training; rather, the former must aid and assist the latter.

Afterwards, Mr Dreyfus attained the Master's presence. Since the weather was pleasant and the Master's health had improved, He and Mr Dreyfus went on an excursion by car at the latter's request.

Aḥmad 'Izzát Páshá, a former Ottoman government official. 'Abdu'l-Bahá visited his home in Paris in June 1913

The Holley family in 1916 or 1917. Horace is holding Marcia and Hertha is seated on Bertha's lap

Muḥammad-'Alí Bey, Prince of Egypt, who visited 'Abdu'l-Bahá

Beatrice Irwin, British-American Bahá'í who was 'almost constantly' in the presence of 'Abdu'l-Bahá when He was in Paris

Sunday, 4 May 1913
[Paris]

At His residence that morning, the Master related anecdotes from His travels to Germany, Austria, and Hungary with the utmost delight:[834]

We have returned to Paris to see what the believers have done and observe how they have become channels for spreading the divine fragrances here. We went to the nations of Germany, Austria, and Hungary; we saw that everyone was immersed in the world of nature, and that they were all oblivious of the divine realm. We spoke at some gatherings; a number of people were awakened, and they set their faces towards the Most Glorious Kingdom. Although our time in those countries was short, yet extraordinary advancements were made with every passing day. We have sown a seed and returned. Can you all now go and water it? When a farmer cultivates a crop, his heart is set on that cultivation. If he sees that the crop is growing and is likely to yield an ample harvest, he will rejoice with exceeding gladness – but if he sees that the crop is withering, he will be deeply saddened.

I wish for you to become spiritual farmers, that you may nourish the farms of people's hearts with the water of true understanding. Every person is a farmer of some sort, but the manner of cultivation practised varies from person to person, consisting in commerce, or industry, or politics. All these grow verdantly, but they do not yield any lasting abundance or eternal benefit, except for spiritual cultivation and heavenly guidance. Consider how the seed which Christ planted still bears fruit to this day. It is for this reason that He said: 'My Words are like unto seeds that are sown by the hand of the farmer. Seeds which are scattered along the path, or in the midst of grass, or upon the rocks will bear no fruit, yet that which is strewn over soil that is fertile will grow and bear such abundant fruit as to become a source of blessings.'* We, too,

* A reference to the Parable of the Sower; see Matt. 13:1–30, specifically verses 1–9.

have now planted such a seed in fertile soil. Since the seed is pure, it is sure to grow; it will certainly bear ample fruit and yield prodigious results.

After making these remarks, the Master rejoiced at the services rendered by Mr [Horace] Holley:[835]

I am well-pleased with you, for you are attracted to the Kingdom and are promulgating the Word of God. You are an active army and are victorious on the battlefield. The attention of a king is always focused on his active army, which is occupied with securing victories at the frontiers and borders. Know of a certainty, then, that the Sovereign of the Kingdom is your Sustainer and that the power of His confirmations is with you.

Some of those present then asked about healing through prayer.[836] The Master said:

Healing is of two kinds: physical and spiritual. God has not created remedies without reason; He has made the various things to have certain effects. Thus, medicine is needed to treat physical illnesses, while prayer is required for the treatment of spiritual diseases or wayward characters.

The Master then discussed the contraction of diseases:

When an excess or deficit occurs in some component substance of the body, such as the sugar or starch component, illness develops as a result. In such cases, treatment must be provided through medicines that will restore balance among those components; otherwise, whatever the invocations one may recite or the thoughts one may produce, one's thirst will remain unquenched. There can be no doubt that the gladness of a person's heart will at times help with his healing and alleviate his pain, but this is not true in every case. At present we are discussing divine healing and spiritual medicine, in relation to which physical treatments are of no importance.

> My hope is such that you will acquire healing and good health both by setting your faces towards the Kingdom of God and by spreading the knowledge of Him. How many are the people whose bodies are weak, yet their spirits boast the utmost power and might! And conversely, there are some whose bodies are in perfect health, yet their spirits suffer from the utmost weakness and despondency.

The Master then spoke of divine happiness and spiritual attractions,[837] and this prompted one of the women in attendance to say: 'My husband is not a Bahá'í, but he says that I should raise [our] children with the Bahá'í teachings.' The Master replied:

> The greatness of the Cause and the significance of the teachings of Bahá'u'lláh are indisputable to every person of wisdom. The bestowals of the Most Glorious Kingdom in this day are even as an endless sea; all that is required is for one to turn towards them, and in sum one must be receptive and ready to arise.

As it was the Master's custom to take a stroll or go on an excursion every morning and afternoon, usually on foot and occasionally by car, He went outside after the believers were dismissed to walk down some of the streets and then returned.

Most of the time, the Master's lunch and dinner were brought to His room, but on that day He came to one of the tables at the dining hall to have those meals.[838]

Monday, 5 May 1913
[Paris]

A number of Persians were in the presence of the Master, Who addressed them with various counsels:[839]

> A person's life is a profoundly precious thing, and one must devote this precious life to a great cause. It is good and necessary to occupy oneself with industry, commerce, and the like, but one

must not content oneself with only these pursuits. One must spend one's time on such undertakings as will yield abiding results and conduce to the spreading of humanity's virtues and perfections, rather than limit it to physical pursuits and transient affairs.

Be not silent! Be not dismayed! Hold not your tongues, and be not disheartened! You must be souls personified; you must be enkindled with the spirit. Not many in this world can live as comfortably as Morgan,* one of the millionaires of America, yet what was his fate in the end? Therefore, you must be occupied with teaching the Cause. Indeed, people must be engaged in some trade or profession – this so they will not be burdens to others, and be equipped to meet their basic needs.

A person's primary goal must be to progress in the development of human perfections, such that each of his days will be better than the day that came before; otherwise, he would be doomed to loss and disappointment. Each day he must reflect on what he has said and done that day, and ponder the fruits his existence has yielded. If these fruits are confined to eating and sleeping, he should know that this would be sheer loss. How base must one be to content oneself with these things! People must be servants to the world of humanity and thralls at the threshold of God. One must plant a tree and lay a foundation that will bear abiding fruits and produce enduring effects. Think not that one can find real happiness or assurance, or acquire essential joy or peace, in anything other than the Cause of God. The human heart is perpetually vexed, and the people are always agitated. The greatest existence under such conditions would be one whereby a person drinks alcohol at one time, dances at another, and laughs at still another – but at another moment, he will fall into profound sadness, and be afflicted with various pains and sorrows.

After dismissing the Bahá'ís, the Master composed a number of wondrous Tablets in response to letters from some of the American and German friends. He was deeply saddened to hear news of the

* John Pierpont Morgan.

upheaval in Hamadan and the cruelty of the enemies of the Faith towards the Bahá'ís there.

Tuesday, 6 May 1913
[Paris]

As the Master was seated in the reception room of the hotel and drinking His tea, He told extensive stories to the members of His retinue about the days of exile in Adrianople, as well as the severe hardship and distress that came from various directions.[840] He spoke of the cruelty and fear which Sultan 'Abdu'l-Ḥamíd showed towards Bahá'u'lláh, and began to give thanks for the confirmations of the Abhá Beauty:

> Through the confirmations and bounties of the Blessed Beauty, the banner of the Cause of God is now hoisted above the highest of flags, and the hosts of aid and assistance are rushing forth from every side.

The Master then discussed those who had broken the Covenant of God:

> Those people, filled as they are with pride and ignorance, deemed themselves to be worthy or deserving, oblivious of the fact that their glory stemmed from their relationship to the Cause of God. It is through the aid and protection of Bahá'u'lláh that the eyes of people are opened and their ears become hearing. Who are we otherwise, and what is so special about us? Were it not for the ray of His grace, who would pay any mind to people like us? I swear by God, besides Whom there is none other God, that if it had not been for His confirmations, no one in the West would have paid any attention even to me.

A large crowd of visitors, made up of people from every walk of life, then attained the Master's presence. One of them [Ethel Patterson Fraser], a Bahá'í from South Africa and a friend of Mrs

Goodall's, inquired after the Master's health. He replied:

> I attach no importance to physical health. So long as one is not bedridden, one must be satisfied with this amount of health. What is of real significance is spiritual health, which is enduring. A person's soul must be strong and healthy; this is what is important. Otherwise, whatever you may do, this body will decompose in the end. Whatever precautions you may take, this edifice will be destroyed. Mr Morgan possessed a fortune amounting to millions of dollars; how great were the lengths he went to in order to preserve himself, yet where at last did he go, and what happened to him in the end?
>
> The human soul, which is a manifestation of divinity, is an eternal bounty. That is where true significance lies. That is where our thoughts should be centred – that it is a splendour of God. Of what significance is this glass which surrounds it? The radiant lamp is the soul, which illumines the world of existence and delivers it from the darkness of nature. The human eye can see as far as a mile away at most, but the brilliance of the soul can behold an infinite number of realms. It encompasses both East and West, and unravels matters which are hidden. It unveils heavenly things underground; it becomes apprised of the mysteries of created beings, and plumbs the depths of the earth. These are the powers of the soul in this world of dust; imagine now what pervading influence it has when it comes to spiritual discoveries, invisible faculties, and divine mysteries! Among these invisible faculties are intellect and knowledge, which are endless. True significance consists in these faculties, which change darkness into light. Through them, one will remain dry even in a sea of tribulations, and live with the utmost firmness and composure in the fiery crucible of calamity and affliction.

Some of those present remarked, 'We have many things to say to You, but whenever we attain Your presence, we forget all about them.' The Master replied:

> Remember well whatever is good and of great importance, and devote no attention to anything that is trivial.

Following that gathering, accounts from some newspapers that concerned the East were read for the Master,[841] and this prompted Him to say:

> Behold how they have cast their ancient glory to the wind with their ignorance and thoughtlessness! And yet they continue to suffer from vainglory, and are far removed from heedfulness and vigilance.

In the afternoon,[842] the Master summoned Áqá Mírzá Jalál, the son of the King of Martyrs – may my life be a sacrifice for the tomb that holds him – and decided to pay a visit to his daughter, Rúḥá Khánum. When He returned from the hospital, He said the following as He walked down Avenue Kléber with that elegant gait of His:[843]

> My heart is very heavy here in Paris, and my patience easily wears thin.

He raised a great deal of criticism as He watched the people indulge in hedonistic pursuits and beheld their immodest movements.

A gathering of believers was held at the home of Mr Scott that evening. The Master said:

> I am not feeling well, but you all must attend.

Wednesday, 7 May 1913
[Paris]

That morning, Mirza Ahmad Sohrab said to the Master that, if it pleased Him, it would be a good idea for Him to go on an excursion to the Palace of Fontainebleau near Paris to get some fresh air.[844] To this the Master replied:

The people who are attached to this earth are bound by palaces, but the friends of God have their thoughts fixed on the grave. God has built for you all an eternal palace that shall never be destroyed. That palace is our place of recreation – a perpetual palace which is none other than the promotion of the Cause of God and the dissemination of the divine signs. The rooms of this palace are the verses of the King of Light; its young servants and fair maidens are the virtues and secrets of the Day of Resurrection. Its foundation is the Word of God, and its veranda is the knowledge of God. Its flag is universal peace among the peoples and nations of the earth, and its banner is the Most Great and Most Glorious Name. Its gardens are adorned with the flowers of inner meanings and realities, and its trees are laden with the fruits of secrets and subtleties. Its battlements reach the Most Exalted Throne, and its soul-stirring space encompasses both earth and heaven. Its attendants are the denizens of the Most Glorious Kingdom, and its gatekeeper is 'Abdu'l-Bahá. Such is the palace on which our thoughts are fixed. Praised be God, moreover, that we have neither palace nor abode, nor do we desire any sort of dwelling. We have shelter wherever we go. 'Wherever a dervish may be when night falls, there is his home.'*

The Master spoke these words with such remarkably majestic power that the feeling one felt in witnessing that scene defies all comparison.

When a crowd of believers gathered and attained the Master's presence in the reception room of the hotel, He gave a talk that began as follows:[845]

Some people are like lamps that must be lit, while others are lamps that are already lit but do not light other lamps. The blessed people, however, are those who are themselves lit and also light others. They both edify themselves and counsel others to the path of divine guidance. Whoever gathers with them will acquire seeing eyes and hearing ears. They are the blessed people.

* From a *ghazal* by Sa'dí.

After that gathering, the Master went outside for a stroll. As He was returning, He made the following remarks to some of the friends:[846]

> I happened to see today that the king of Spain* was arriving in Paris. What a clamour the people raised for a single person purely for their own amusement! How superficial they are, and how distant from truth and inner realities!

He then summoned Áqá Siyyid Asadu'lláh and said:

> For the love of God, bring me a cup of coffee! I feel very weak; the food here does not agree with me, and to order a meal is even worse. Yet in spite of all this, it would still be best to go and sit at the dining table.

When Mr and Mrs Scott came with a crowd of believers to visit the Master, He said to them:[847]

> I very much wished to attend the gathering last night,[848] but alas, I was unable to do this. Praised be God that you are the flowers of Paris and sanctified Bahá'ís. All the people of this city think only of commerce, industry, and revelry – except for you few, whose thoughts and remembrances are also focused on God. In this jungle that is Paris, it is only you, a few fruitful trees, who have understood the purpose of life. Hence, you are most conspicuous and exceedingly great. In the days when we were leaving Persia for Baghdad, we did not encounter a single believer on the way, until at last we reached that Abode of Peace. There we found two or three believers, and when we met them, it made a very strong impression on us. But now that the loved ones of God can be found in every city and village, the impression they make is not as strong. It is for this reason that, you, too, now make a strong impression here in Paris and are conspicuous indeed.

* Alfonso XIII.

The size of the crowd began to grow, and the Master gave an extensive talk in which He rendered thanks for the confirmations vouchsafed by the Most Glorious Kingdom, spoke of the ties between pure hearts, and discussed the unification of diverse peoples beneath the shade of the blessed Word. He concluded that gathering with a discussion of the advancement of women in the East.

In the afternoon, the Master went to the residence of Aḥmad Pá<u>sh</u>á, and from there went to the home of Miss Sanderson. As He was returning, He said:[849]

> I saw the Blessed Beauty in a dream last night. He was speaking in a tongue different from the languages that exist today, and everyone was able to understand it. I said to myself, 'How strange! Is this that universal language, and have the blessed Tablets been translated into this tongue?' At that moment, I heard the sound of someone's voice. Bahá'u'lláh said, 'Go see who it is.' I went outside and saw that it was a tall Man with white hair, dressed in a beautiful cloak, and that He was saying: 'I have come from Jábulṣá and Jábulqá . . .'* He then remarked that these two cities were in the heavens, whereupon I said, 'Then You are heavenly,' and took Him to the presence of the Blessed Beauty. I then awoke from the intensity of my joy.

Thursday, 8 May 1913
[Paris]

Áqá Mírzá Jalál and Riḍváníyyih <u>Kh</u>ánum were preparing to depart for the Holy Land.[850] Rúḥá <u>Kh</u>ánum was still at the Maison de Santé,[851] and through the grace and bounty of God, her health was improving with every passing day.

The Master spoke to Miss Sanderson of the love of God, which is an eternal foundation, and He likewise imparted His tender

* 'According to <u>Sh</u>í'ih traditions, the twin cities of Jábulqá and Jábulṣá are the dwelling place of the Hidden Imám (the Promised One), whence He will appear on the Day of Resurrection' (Bahá'u'lláh, *Gems of Divine Mysteries*, p. 82, n. 35).

kindnesses and counsels to Áqá Mírzá Jalál and Riḍvániyyih Khánum.

At the public gathering,[852] the Master related anecdotes from His sojourn in California and His encounters with Japanese Bahá'ís, remarking in particular how profoundly attracted a certain Japanese poet [Takeshi Kanno] became to the divine fragrances. After eventually concluding this talk by discussing episodes from the history of the Cause, mentioning the martyrdom which certain Bahá'ís had suffered,[853] and recounting their steadfastness, He went outside.

A travelling reporter from America attained the Master's presence that afternoon.[854] He gave a comprehensive summary of the teachings of this Most Glorious Revelation to that reporter, who wrote as the Master spoke.

Among the remarks which He made in His address to the Bahá'ís at that afternoon's gathering were these:

> God has given you abilities so that you might use them to serve His Kingdom. When you employ your abilities in any undertaking, the fruits of your efforts are limited – but this does not apply when those abilities are used in the Cause of God to promote the oneness of humanity or spread the spiritual perfections, for the fruits of these endeavours are limitless.
>
> Anyone who sacrifices in the path of God shines even as a candle in the assemblage of humankind. Consider the Apostles of Christ; [uneducated] commoners though they were, because they consecrated their abilities to the path of God, observe how they continue to shine from the horizon of eternal glory! To this day, their signs foster love and fellowship among the hearts, and they still cast their splendours with the utmost brilliance. The mention of their greatness is renewed in every dispensation, and leads in every world to the happiness of them that believe in God's unity. Mary Magdalene, in whose name such an important church has been built in Paris, was a woman from a village – but because she used her capacities for the Cause of Christ, behold what signs have appeared from her! Strive, then, to expend your own abilities in service to the Cause of God, and to gather together beneath the

> shade of His Word. The gathering of people in the Cause of God attracts the confirmations of the Most Glorious Kingdom, and the rapture and unification of hearts and souls in the shadow of the Word of God conduces to salvation and deliverance. They that are well-assured are the variegated flowers of the garden of the knowledge of God; the differences in their colours only add to their beauty, and the meeting of minds leads to the clash of opinions. When one mind reinforces another, observe how effectively that mind is strengthened! It is in this way that when one seeks or receives the help or bounty of another, this causes the gracious bestowals of Him Who is the All-Glorious, the Most Great, to be made manifest. The hosts of confirmation rush forth, and the gates of triumph and victory are flung open – and this is due to the gathering and unification of devoted souls. Thus, the believers must help each other and make sacrifices for them. Consider what peace and tranquillity the sheep enjoy when they are gathered beneath the shadow of the kind shepherd, and how protected they are from the threat of wolves!

The Master concluded His address with these words:[855]

> The Blessed Beauty trained and taught me to lift the burdens of others, not to place my own burdens on their shoulders.

As the Master was walking down the Champs-Élysées after that gathering had been concluded, He saw an aeroplane flying overhead and remarked:[856]

> Now this is a sight to behold! With but one bomb, this aeroplane can kill all these people and destroy all these cities.

When the Master returned, He met with a respected American Bahá'í woman and teacher of music, with whom He discussed the etymology and derivation of the word 'music', the melody of the bird known as *músíqár*,[857] and anecdotes concerning Rúdakí and Fárábí.[858]

Following this, Aḥmad Pás͟há attained the Master's presence.

The pá<u>sh</u>á was stirred to abundant ecstasy as he listened to the Master speak about the history of the Cause of God and His own journey to America.[859]

At the approach of sunset, the Master went to the homes of Miss Sanderson and Mr and Mrs Dreyfus-Barney to see how they were doing.[860]

Friday, 9 May 1913
[Paris]

As the Master was serving tea to His attendants that morning, and also drinking that tea Himself, He mentioned the bounties of the Blessed Beauty and gave thanks for the confirmations of the Most Glorious Kingdom.

Some friends from America attained the Master's presence,[861] and they implored Him to confirm their efforts to teach the Cause of God. To them He said:

> When you converse with those who are not religious, alert them to the detriments and corruptive influences of the world of nature, and mention to them that these are attributes befitting the station of the animal. Humans, on the other hand, are distinguished from other creatures through their rational faculties and sentiments of the heart, which enable them to deepen themselves in spiritual matters, unveil the realities of things, become attracted to the Most Exalted Kingdom, work for the common welfare of all humanity, and promote the means for justice and fairness. Conclude your remarks to them with these words: 'You have explored the world of nature and its appurtenances; come now for a while to the world of the spirit and the realm of light. Should you encounter any harm, return whence you came.' Speak with them along such lines as these.
>
> As to those who are religious, summon them with the glad-tidings of God in this way: 'How long will you remain heedless like the peoples of the past? Are you asleep, or perhaps blind? The Sun of Truth is shining, and the gates of the Kingdom are opened.

> The divine bestowals have been made manifest, and the liberal effusions of heavenly grace have pervaded all things. How long will you remain unaware?' They are like the Jews, who are still oblivious to the advent of Christ, and exhibit the utmost prejudice and hatred toward His name and Revelation.

The Master's address to the public gathering dealt with the melodies of heavenly birds and the knowledge of the loved ones of God, in which He remarked:[862]

> It is through these songs that I am stirred to joy; otherwise, of what significance are the other melodies in this physical world?

At the end of that gathering, the Master responded to the questions of the friends in attendance, and their hearts were immeasurably enraptured by the effect of His holy utterances.

After going for a stroll,[863] having His lunch, and resting for a bit, the Master went with Mr Dreyfus to visit Rúḥá Khánum. Upon His return, He spoke to a group of the friends[864] about the requisites for teaching the Cause of God, among them the following:

> One must first teach the Cause to one's own self. A person must become attracted and detached himself so that his words might have an effect upon others. Furthermore, he must speak to each person according to the search, capacity, and thirst of that person. Whenever he finds a thirsting soul, let him proffer the living waters of guidance to that person. We have bought these precious gems at a high price; we will not sell them cheaply. The loved ones of God have accepted this mighty Cause through sacrifice, and they have been subjected to great torment. Therefore, one must give the thirsty to drink from the living waters of guidance, for if a soul is not athirst, he will never relish the taste of water, no matter how refreshing it may be.

The weekly gathering of Bahá'ís was held at the home of Mr and Mrs Dreyfus-Barney.[865] The Master said:

> You all attend; I am very tired, and do not have the strength to go there and speak.

Saturday, 10 May 1913
[Paris]

Letters from the believers of California[866] were presented to the Master that morning. They all contained the good news of the promulgation of the Word of God and the advancement of His Cause, as well as abundant praise of the Master. He said:

> Behold what abounding ecstasy the Covenant of the Abhá Beauty has kindled within the people, and how it has caused the believers to gather together and promote the Word of God! The Blessed Beauty formed this Covenant to preserve the power of the Cause of God and to spread His Word in the East and the West. Were it not for this Covenant, you would see how scattered the community of believers would become – how the fire of the love of God would die out, and the memory of His Cause slip away from people's minds. Some have imagined that the Blessed Beauty merely took the sort of measure that a father might take with his own child. They do not realize that He has invested the Covenant with power for the dissemination of the Cause of God and the triumph of His Word.

Time and again, the Master made remarks like these with the utmost majesty and power. He also spoke fondly of Mrs Goodall and Mrs Cooper.

At the gathering that day, the Master gave an extensive talk on the beliefs of the Sufis, who liken God to an ocean and living beings to the waves of that ocean – little more than mere phantoms. He observed, however, that the divine Prophets consider God to be sanctified from incarnation and other limitations, and concluded His talk with an explanation of the meanings of the terms '*símurgh*'[867] and 'Mount Qáf',[868] as well as the phraseology of the Sufis.[869]

The Master then composed Tablets in response to letters from the Bahá'ís of America. Among them was a Tablet to the friends in Denver, [Colorado,] which contained these holy words:[870]

He is God

> You had asked about making contributions to the Tarbíyat schools. Assistance and cooperation constitute the foundation of the religion of God. The East must aid the West, and the West must do the same for the East.

In another Tablet addressed to [the Bahá'ís of] Fruitport, [Michigan,] the Master wrote:[871]

> You had written that you wish to render some service to the Orient–Occident Unity. The East and West must certainly assist one another, in particular where the Tarbíyat schools are concerned. The Bahá'ís of the East contributed to the development of the House of Worship in America, notwithstanding their abject poverty and in spite of their internal upheaval. If the Bahá'ís of the West can lend assistance to the Tarbíyat schools, this would assuredly be the cause of joy.

That same day, Mrs [Maud] Lillienthal [von Behr] offered a sum of five hundred francs to the Master, but He refused to accept it. After insisting and pleading with Him a great deal, the Master said that the money should be sent to Tehran through Dr [Susan] Moody for the Tarbíyat school.

In the afternoon, the Master paid visits to Ras͟híd Pás͟há and the mother of Mr Dreyfus.[872] Upon His return, He commented on the divine confirmations He had received during His sojourn in California.[873] Then, while mentioning the names of certain European professors and teachers,[874] He remarked:

> Most people are celebrated only because they speak several languages, and they are thus numbered with people of knowledge and learning. Some are truly learned, while others are merely famous.

Sunday, 11 May 1913
[Paris]

The Master was seated in the reception room of the hotel that morning, and through the door of the building He looked out at Avenue Kléber. He spoke of the high-mindedness of the Americans when it came to the matters of peace and welfare.[875]

Letters from the Bahá'ís of Persia were then presented to Him, and He said:

> I will peruse the letters from Persia, but I do not have time to respond to them. From the outset of my journey, I have asked the Bahá'ís of Persia to excuse me from writing them during these days of travel. Everyone is under the impression that I am corresponding only with them. If I wanted to write responses to all their letters, it would be impossible. The Bahá'ís need to realize that I must exchange letters with people from all over the world.

A group of Bahá'ís and seekers then attained the presence of the Master, Who addressed them with a talk in which He discussed the mirror of nature and the mirror of humanity:[876]

> The lights of the virtues and perfections of the world of humanity are reflected in the second of these mirrors. Just as there is the struggle for survival in the world of nature, and this is the means through which the things of that world grow and progress, in the world of the spirit there is the acquisition of human perfections, and this law conduces to the advancement of souls and the obtainment of spiritual bestowals. In relation to this, the world of nature is a prison, as well as an obstacle to peace of mind and freedom of conscience.
>
> In the world of nature, humans are captives to eating and sleeping. They are subject to the corruptive influences of nature; imprisoned are they by greed and covetousness, and afflicted with folly and deceit. It is possible for them to be liberated from these harmful conditions and attributes – such as wrath and pride, or

cruelty and treachery – inasmuch as these are among the imperfections of the world of humanity. It is necessary, however, for one to eat, sleep, and the like, for these are essential to one's life. To observe moderation in them, moreover, will help one to acquire spiritual perfections and attain to eternal stations. Captivity in darkness is tantamount to ignorance, oppression, heedlessness, and blindness, all of which abase one's station. With the power of the spirit, a person is able to free himself from this captivity, and through the laws of God, he can rescue himself from these perilous vices. In this way can the benighted one become radiant. Such a one is dead, but can be brought back to life; blind, but granted the power to see; limited, but enabled to transcend all limitation.

Yet since the efforts of people are diverse, one will consequently arrive at this station through great toil, another will reach it with the passage of much time, but still another will be immediately transformed through the power of faith. It is for this reason that Bahá'u'lláh has said: ‘Take thou one pace and with the next advance into the immortal realm . . .’* In a similar vein, He has stated that time and space do not exist in the spiritual realm and the divine kingdom, for time and other such limitations are relative constructs, along with east and west, north and south, the day and the night, and the month and the year. All these exist in relation to the earth, not the sun in the sky. So too with the divine realm, the heavenly Kingdom, and everlasting life, which all transcend time and space, and lie beyond the confining properties of this world. This is why Jesus Christ declared: ‘I am now in the heavens.’ Thus, although sanctified realities do exist in the world of limitations, they are free of all fetters. With regard to the body, they are compelled to eat and sleep, but with respect to the spirit, they are sanctified from and independent of this world of dust, for in relation to the eternal stations just mentioned, the transitory trappings of this world resemble the playthings of children. It is because the gaze of blessed souls was fixed on those stations that, when the time came for them to sacrifice themselves, they attached no importance to their physical bodies.

---

* Bahá'u'lláh, *Hidden Words*; from the Persian, no. 7.

In the afternoon, the Master spoke to a group of European and Persian friends. To them He told stories about the hardship and severity of the days of His still-recent confinement in 'Akká, and spoke of the measures He took to fend off the calumnies of the seditious and the perdition of the enemies, highlighting the abasement to which they had all been reduced in so short a span.[877]

When that gathering was concluded, the Master went on an excursion by car through some of the streets of Paris and the Bois de Boulogne.[878] He made extensive remarks on His journey to the West, among which were the following:

> I wished to succeed in travelling to various regions of the earth and sounding the call to the Most Glorious Kingdom. Yet even if this should not come to pass, souls will assuredly rise up after me to render this service, and they will be sustained through confirmations from the unseen world.

Monday, 12 May 1913
[Paris]

As the Master was having His tea that morning, He mentioned how fatigued He was by the multitude of cares and concerns that assailed Him, remarking, 'I have a thousand thoughts at every moment.'

After He had revised some of His letters and prepared them to be sent by mail, some of the friends of Mrs [Jean] Stannard attained the Master's presence. He said:

> Mrs Stannard is truly a diligent person, ever searching for ways to be of service to humanity.

Then, with exceeding gladness, He made mention of the German friends and spoke of the gatherings that had been held in Stuttgart, saying:[879]

> The Bahá'ís of Germany are radiant. So long as no one leads them astray, they will make great strides.

A group of people from Scotland then attained the Master's presence. He related anecdotes from His sojourn in Edinburgh, and expressed His delight as He discussed the societies of that place.[880] This was especially the case with the president of the Theosophical Society of Edinburgh [Major David Graham Pole]. He said:

> There are those who, after drinking from the cup of true knowledge, say, 'Is there yet any more?'* Conversely, there are others who, upon seeing a mirage, deem their thirst to be quenched, and assert that they are without need, just as the people of Israel reacted to the advent of Christ. The sphere of a person's knowledge must be wide, and he must seek to learn under every circumstance. However much he drinks, he must grow only thirstier; he should not content himself with the drinking of a single draught.

The Master then discussed the parables in the Gospel and the sayings of Christ with regard to that king and the excuses made by those whom he had invited [to attend his banquet],[881] the farmer's sowing of seeds,[882] and [Christ's] fleeing from the fools.[883] One of those present asked about the biblical verses that describe how a number of people ate from a few loaves of bread, and how some of that bread was still left over.[884] The Master said:

> Jesus Christ Himself declared: 'I am the bread of life.'† Thus, the banquet represents heavenly perfections and bestowals, and the [twelve] baskets symbolize those well-assured souls, the Apostles of Christ. It is for this reason that Christ turned a mere fisherman into the great Peter, and made him into a channel for spiritual life to humankind. It is with respect to those heavenly bestowals, moreover, that Christ proclaimed: 'The Father is in me, and I am in you.'‡ Even as the reflection of the sun in stainless mirrors, the Apostles conferred that celestial feast upon all humanity through

* Qur'án 50:30.
† John 6:35.
‡ See John 14:10, and also verse 20 of that chapter.

> the purity of their minds and souls, the spirit of prophethood, and the Holy Spirit.

A question was then raised concerning the changing of water into wine.[885] The Master said:

> By this is meant that Christ imbued the meanings of the ancient law with new life and invested them with a fresh effect . . .

At the gathering that afternoon, the Master exhorted Mrs Richard and some of the believers to give talks at gatherings and impart guidance to the people. He said:

> The power of the Holy Spirit makes every weak one strong. Observe how it exalted the abased people of Israel! It is this power which made a humble fisherman famed throughout the world, and turned the primitive tribes of the Arabian desert into the caliphs of the earth. Focus not, then, on your own abilities. Arise and cry out: 'Awaken, O people of Paris, for the Sun of Truth is shining! Be vigilant, for the breeze of bounty is blowing! Bestir yourselves, for the world of humanity is roused to movement! Rise up, for the Kingdom of God is manifest! Be apprised, for the breaths of the Holy Spirit are pervading!' . . .

Following this, Ras͟híd Pás͟há and the envoy of Persia attained the presence of the Master, Who recounted for them extensive episodes from the history of the Cause of God, as well as anecdotes from His own travels throughout America and Europe.

Tuesday, 13 May 1913
[Paris]

Before the believers attained His presence that day, the Master told a story about the Apostles following the martyrdom of Jesus Christ that can be summarized as follows:[886]

> They gathered on top of a mountain, and made a pact whereby they would consent to bear tribulations, renounce their comfort, and spread guidance. When they came down from the mountain, each of them went in a different direction and never returned. In various regions, they all arose and summoned the people to the Kingdom of God. All these powerful effects proceeded from that gathering.

A number of letters from America were translated and presented to the Master. Once He had read them, He said:

> There should not be any secret societies in the Cause of God. Even if people who are pure and impartial should establish such a society today, in the future it would create a breach in the Cause of God, and become a pretext on which one might promote one's own personal interests. Similar to the dispensation of Islam, such people would make distinctions between the 'outer' and 'inner' meanings [of words];[887] in these terms would they speak accordingly, and on that basis would they create division and dissension among the people of Bahá.

The Master did not give talks at any gatherings that day. Instead, He summoned the people and spoke with them, one by one and two by two. Each of them was privileged to ask Him questions and hear His answers, and honoured to have a private audience with Him. He addressed these closing remarks to some of His visitors as they were being dismissed:

> The first duty which humanity is bidden to carry out is to investigate the realities of things. It is incumbent upon the people to seek to unravel every truth, that thereby they might unveil every mystery and turn every difficulty into ease. The world of creation is a boundless ocean, and in its depths lie hid precious pearls and gems. When a person deepens himself and investigates, he will acquire useful knowledge of the realities and subtleties of things, and prodigious results will be seen from his efforts.

After going for a stroll, having His lunch, and relaxing His nerves, the Master went to the reception room of the hotel. As He was drinking His tea, a number of respected Persians, who were accompanying [——],[888] attained His presence. They were immensely delighted to hear Him speak on spiritual matters. When the topic of Persia was raised, the Master spoke most fondly of the late Qá'im-Maqám. Among the remarks He made on that subject were as follows:

> If the Qá'im-Maqám were still with us, he would revive the whole of Persia.

The hearts of the Master's visitors were stirred and gladdened as they listened to His words, and when they were dismissed, they showed perfect humility and deference as they departed His presence. The Master then went outside to pay visits to certain respected friends.[889]

For His dinner that night, He had only a bit of bread and milk, and nothing else.

Wednesday, 14 May 1913
[Paris]

After prayers and meditations, the Master went to the reception room of the hotel and said the following as He had His tea:

> Bread and milk are more healthful than any other kind of food. The Blessed Beauty used to say: 'During My days in Sulaymáníyyih, My food on most occasions consisted of milk and sometimes rice pudding.'

He then set Himself to composing wondrous Tablets in response to letters from the believers of America. Sometime thereafter, a group of the friends came to visit,[890] and the Master exhorted them to diffuse the divine fragrances:

> Arise to guide the people aright – to give sight to the blind, hearing to the deaf, life to the dead, and speech to the mute. Should you rise up to perform this important task, you would receive such confirmations as would leave you utterly astounded . . .

Once the friends had all departed His presence with the utmost ecstasy and excitement, the Master decided to go out on an excursion by carriage;[891] Qá'im-Maqám[í], as well as some other believers and Persian attendants,[892] rode with Him. Along the way, the Master said:

> When I was in Germany, Austria, and Hungary, I was sick and exceedingly busy, but my heart was still very much cheered. Now that I am in Paris, however, despite the fact that my health is good and there are fewer demands on my time, my heart is heavy nonetheless.

When the Master's carriage reached the Bois de Boulogne, He told stories from the days when He was in Mazandaran and Tehran.[893] He then alighted the carriage and walked about the area, as it was a most beautiful sight. The weather was mild and the trees were in full bloom; the grass was green and the vegetation was verdant. Even as a spotless and sparkling mirror, the lake shimmered in the sunlight, and the boats sailed on its water. It was indeed a pleasant scene to behold. The Master remarked:

> All things in this place can be seen in their utmost degree of beauty and elegance, and it is evident that they have fulfilled the purpose of their creation – except for the people, who are far removed from achieving the fruit of their existence and resemble a gathering of beasts. One receives the impression that they have been created to serve the material world, not that material things exist to serve humanity and help their perfections to be made manifest.

People from all walks of life attained the Master's presence that evening.[894] In response to questions raised by some of the members of His audience, He spoke mostly on the differences between the beliefs of the Sufis and the aims of the divine prophets, the sanctification of the Essence of God from all likeness and comparison, the proof of His existence as the Necessary Being, the composition of elements and constituent parts through His Will, and the inabilities and imperfections of the world of nature:

> The philosophers, too, each maintain that a power or Universal Reality is the source of all beings. Their only difference with the prophets is that the prophets say that Universal Reality and all-unifying agency is without need, absolute, sentient, and free to do as it wills, while the philosophers deem it to be insentient, in need, and devoid of volition. They disagree on its attributes and perfections, since the philosophers do not believe it possesses that spiritual power or absolute perfection, whereas the prophets have explained that the powerlessness of every creature consists in its inability to comprehend the essential reality of any thing – this so that God, that Ancient Being, will not be confined to the perceptive powers of this contingent world. The prophets do not believe that a person's inability to perceive that Necessary Being proves the absence of His supreme perfections.

To summarize, that gathering went on for some time and the Master spoke at considerable length. As a result, His audience was made thoroughly vigilant, and those seeking souls evinced their heedfulness and humility.

Thursday, 15 May 1913
[Paris]

The talk the Master gave at the public gathering that morning dealt with the permanence of the signs of spiritual people and the transience of worldly affairs. Among His remarks to that effect were the following:

What happened to Napoleon? Where are the many king Louises, the emperor Aurelian, and the like? Their endeavours, their stations, their very lives can all be likened to a mirage. 'Take ye good heed, O people of insight!'*

As He was concluding the gathering, the Master caressed the children tenderly and gave these instructions regarding their education:

Children must be reared with a spiritual education. Their training must not resemble the practice prevalent among the mothers of today, who tell their children, from the very beginning of their lives, 'You must seek to accumulate wealth and become a millionaire.' Apart from such talk as this, they say nothing else. These mothers never say to their children, 'Be honest and trustworthy; render service to the world of humanity.' Spiritual education conduces to the preservation of one's existence, and causes one to observe moderation in one's affairs. It is possible to train a child in a way that will lead him to exercise moderation in all things and feel love for humanity with all his heart. Yet by the same token, it is possible to treat a child with a neglect that will turn him into the basest of all creatures.

You all are my children. I wish for you to receive a spiritual education and become radiant . . .

He repeatedly caressed the children and showed them effusive loving-kindness – in particular the little daughter of Mr Holley, who seemed very close with the Master and made Him beam with joy on most days.

The Master was invited to have lunch at the home of Mr and Mrs Dreyfus-Barney.[895]

In the afternoon, after receiving a number of visitors and composing Tablets for the American friends,[896] the Master went outside for a stroll.[897] In one of the shops, He saw some white tea that was of good quality; He bought some of it, brewed it in His residence, and served it to His attendants.

* Qur'án 59:2.

Friday, 16 May 1913
[Paris]

As the Master was walking in the reception room of the hotel early that morning, He looked out at some of the city's buildings from behind the glass door, and spoke these exalted words:

> Should the loved ones of God arise as they must; should they come to exemplify these ideals: 'Keep all my words of prayer and praise confined to one refrain; make all my life but servitude to Thee';* and should they be totally annihilated in the Cause of God, they would transform all the peoples of the earth in no time at all. Even if just two devoted believers were to be found in every city who will consign their own selves to oblivion, this would suffice.

After seating Himself, the Master told stories about the services rendered by the King of Martyrs, the Beloved of Martyrs, and the honourable Fatḥ-i-A'ẓam,[898] and spoke of their self-effacing devotion to the Cause of God. He also mentioned the purity of Mullá Ḥusayn:[899]

> One night in Mazandaran, when Mullá Ḥusayn saw Quddús and heard his utterances of wisdom and knowledge, he arose at once to serve Him like a lowly thrall. As morning approached, the companions of Mullá Ḥusayn noticed that, although he was the chief authority to whom they turned and the leader of the believers, he was standing in the presence of Quddús with the utmost reverence; his arms were folded across his chest, and he was showing a degree of humility that astonished them all.

Following this,[900] one of the friends came to see the Master, and asked Him to permit a Persian youth, who identified himself as a Bahá'í, to also attain His presence. The Master replied:

---

* A passage from the *Du'áy-i-Kumayl*, a prayer attributed to Khiḍr by the Imám 'Alí, who famously recited it to his close companion, Kumayl ibn Zíyád.

> Now see here! If someone were to commit a hundred offences whose harm reverts only to me, I would shut my eyes to the matter. I would treat him with such love that he would mistake it [for unmindfulness]. Should he perpetrate the most grievous treachery against me, such would be my behaviour towards him that he would think himself to be the most trustworthy of all people. Yet if any harm comes to the Cause of God, I will not ignore it. Imagine that a person has begun to destroy the house of the Cause of God, and as I stand and watch him, he grows angry with me and asks me, 'Why do you not lend me a hand in this destruction?' You contemptible man! You have set yourself to destroying the house of the Cause of God and expect the hearts to take no offence whatsoever to your doings? [901]
>
> I wish you to walk in my footsteps. Cause no offence to any heart, and be at peace with everyone. Overlook the wrongs and shortcomings of others, and bring joy to the human race. Look at what I do. If others do not know the extent of my patience, surely you are aware of it. You have been with me; you see and you hear.
>
> The things which destroy people are self and passion; always pray that you may be kept far from them. Had that person killed me, it would have been preferable to his defrauding the people, for in the former case harm would have come only to me, while in that of the latter it has reached the Cause . . .

A large crowd of people then attained the Master's presence. Their meeting ended with an exchange of questions and answers, and their hearts brimmed with joy and delight as they listened to His tender counsels and blessed exhortations. One of their questions concerned the eating of meat and killing of animals for this purpose. The Master replied:

> When the Blessed Beauty said that it would certainly be preferable for a person to refrain from slaughtering animals and instead content himself with vegetables, He did not forbid this slaughter because it is impossible for one not to eat animals, for within every drop of water, every vegetable, and every piece of fruit are animals

that one cannot avoid consuming. Ultimately, some of these things have fewer animals while others have more.

A question was then raised about how one should deal and associate with people who are impolite and immoral. The Master replied:

Such people are of several kinds. There are those who are so defiled that to associate with them would not only be devoid of benefit, but in fact prove harmful. One must certainly avoid the company of such people. There are also those who are prone to immorality and misbehaviour but can be reformed. Such people should not be overly shunned, but one's association with them must be limited strictly to making them vigilant and heedful. Lastly, there are those who are impatient or unforgiving; they are well-intentioned, but this is not evident in their demeanour. Such people are not to be abhorred, for they are truthful, not dishonest, and they are trustworthy, not treacherous. Infer the rest from this.

Let us now speak of good-natured people, who are radiant and spiritual, sincere and humble, faithful and firm, affable and kind – people who are the cause of heartfelt joy. In the East, there are Bahá'ís who are the embodiments of existence. They are bright candles in every gathering; they are promoters of the peace and well-being of all the world's peoples, and well-wishers of all the kindreds of the earth. God has created people in human form so that they might possess heavenly qualities and attributes, not move and behave like ferocious animals.

That afternoon, the Master smiled as He made humorous remarks about the people of Paris, among them the following:

With the denizens of Paris, even when you wish to guide them to spiritual matters, you must first start by singing songs, playing instruments, and making merry. Afterwards, begin with the melodies of the Kingdom; otherwise, they will not listen to you.

Since it was raining that day, the Master did not leave His residence at all. Well into the night, He walked in the reception room, where He spoke of Bahá'u'lláh and reminisced about His loved ones [the Bahá'ís].

Saturday, 17 May 1913[902]
[Paris]

A crowd was present for the public gathering held that morning. The Master went to the reception room of the hotel and gave a talk on how the peoples of the world have been heedless and shut out as by a veil at the advent of every Manifestation of ancient bounty. At the end of that gathering, one of the attendees asked whether people who perform good deeds will be totally deprived of divine mercy if they do not believe in the Cause. The Master replied:

> As this is the dispensation of grace, those who perform good deeds and exhibit goodly conduct but do not believe in the Cause will not be deprived of God's bounty and favour. A person who does not believe but still performs good deeds is certainly better than the one who makes pretensions to love and belief while his actions reflect the influence of Satan. Perfection, however, will only be attained when good deeds are conjoined with belief – and should a person perform good deeds, strive to promulgate the oneness of humankind, and promote peace and unity among the peoples and kindreds of the earth, he will assuredly have attained to the more glorious station.
>
> Even if one does believe, one would still be in need of a subduing power and a penetrating Word that promotes the various degrees of loyalty and faithfulness, and develops other human stations and perfections, across the classes that compose the many groups and peoples of the world. A power is needed whose effect will be extraordinary; a blessed Word is required whose influence will be mighty. This power, this Word, must create humanity anew and revolutionize their very natures.
>
> Every thing inevitably needs a centre. The centre of this

> irresistible force is the Manifestation of the all-compelling Word of God and the Embodiment of His all-subduing Cause, He Who is able to free the people from the shackles of cruelty and treachery without subjecting them to imprisonment or punishment. Whoever enters beneath the shade of this blessed Word will feel genuine love for humankind and wish them well from the bottom of his heart, not from fear of harm or retribution. Should he be ignorant, in the realm of action he would be equal to the learned one, and his deeds would prove more beneficial to the ordering of the world and the refinement of people's characters than the results that proceed from the behaviour of most people of great intellect. This transformation of the hearts cannot occur through any power but belief in divine religion and adherence to the spiritual teachings.

A great number of people attained the Master's presence at various times that afternoon. His most extensive remarks to them concerned the subject of economics, along the same lines as His discussion of the blessed teachings on that topic while He was in Dublin [New Hampshire], which is recorded at length in the first volume of this chronicle.[903]

At the approach of sunset, the Master went out for a stroll to dispel His fatigue.

Sunday, 18 May 1913
[Paris]

The Master humorously said:

> Light the samovar! Lay out the tea set on the table! Come now, be sensible!

Such were the jocose remarks He made to His attendants. He also said:

> Tea prepared in a samovar grants a matchless kind of delight.

The Master then made mention of Muḥammad Muṣṭafá Baghdádí; He recounted his steadfastness and sincerity and spoke of his precious children in a way that stirred us all to joy.[904]

As it was Sunday, a crowd larger than ever before gathered in the (apartment)[905] reception room of the Master's residence. When the Master joined the gathering, He first showed loving-kindness to the children of Mrs Moreau and said:

> Should one ponder carefully, one would realize how important it is to give children a spiritual education from their earliest years. That which is firmly established in the mind of a child, and the lines along which he grows and develops throughout his childhood, will take such deep root in his heart as to become second nature to him. This will especially apply after his adolescence, when he will persist in that way of life, and make a mighty effort to continue his spiritual training and acquire divine perfections.
>
> But God forbid that that child grow and develop with a harmful character, or illaudable thoughts and intentions, for if he persists along those lines for long enough, he will remain in irredeemable error and misfortune for the rest of his life. Such a one would, in his indulgence of harmful thoughts and deeds, resemble a person addicted to opium, who would prefer every lethal poison to delectable feasts, and deem bitterness to be better than every kind of sweet. It is for this reason that, in the estimation of such people, the sweetness of divine guidance is worthy of reproach, just as the radiance of the world-illumining sun is ominous to the bat, and the fragrance of the rose-garden is imperceptible to one whose head is filled with rheum. The life-giving breath will not revive the dead ones of this sort, nor can the vernal shower of God cause the salty soil of their hearts to yield any fruit.

Then, in response to a question by Mrs [Lucy] Moore (who had recently arrived from America) on the subject of willpower, the Master gave an extensive talk that roused His listeners to such irrepressible ecstasy that their faces could be likened to blooming flowers.[906] It was evident that their hearts had been filled with boundless joy.

Following this, as the Master was walking and talking with some of the respected Persian friends that afternoon, they expressed their desire to visit a racetrack, so there He went.[907] After stopping there for a few minutes, the Master entered the car once again, returned to the hotel, and said:

> These excursions by car are inadequate. It is better to walk. There is no kind of stroll like the one taken on foot. Travelling by car is good when time is short and there is no opportunity for anything more, but it is not suitable if one wishes to exercise and strengthen oneself. If I do not take walks, I will have no appetite for food.

Consequently, the Master went outside and walked a great deal with Dr Muḥammad Khán.

He was with Mr [Paul Antoine] and Mrs Richard until midnight.[908] He spoke with them at length on a variety of subjects pertaining to Sufism, delivering exalted utterances and adducing sufficient proofs in response to each and every one of their questions.

Monday, 19 May 1913
[Paris]

Before having His tea that morning, the Master read some letters from Tehran that described the corruptive actions of the seditious Azalís, whose mischievous provocations prevented the friends in Tehran from holding gatherings in the days of Riḍván. Most of this mischief had been made in Tehran by the Ṣadru'l-'Ulamá,[909] an Azalí who meddled in political affairs and caused a fresh tumult every day and night. Accordingly, the Master remarked:

> Soon will the root of that deceitful antagonist be pulled up from the ground. These makers of mischief imagine that they can oppose the Cause of God!

This blessed utterance was conveyed in writing to Tehran. No sooner had the message arrived, at a time when it had yet to be circulated among all the believers there, than the seditious meddling of the Ṣadru'l-'Ulamá in political affairs prompted the Ministry of the Interior to order that that evil-doer be expelled from the city, from which he began making his way towards Khurasan and Mashhad.

Once the Master had had His tea, Mrs Moore attained His presence.[910] She spoke of the gatherings that the believers were holding in New York, and described how Bahá'í representatives from the various states of America had come from far and wide to discuss matters related to the Mashriqu'l-Adhkár. The Master said:

> The divine call is raised in the cities of America. The future of that place will be bright indeed; the whole of America will be illumined.

The Master's address to the gathering that day was occasioned by a question from a female seeker.[911] He spoke of spiritual feasts and humanity's establishment in spiritual perfections, observing that these perfections must take firm hold in one's existence. The hearts of His listeners were deeply affected by the profound meaning of His words, so much so that the aforementioned woman began to weep.

Since the Master was visibly tired when that gathering was concluded, He went outside for a stroll.[912] Eventually, He entered one of the parks of the city, leaned against a bench, and said:

> How mindful one becomes when one meditates on the bounties of God! This mindfulness is a means to the acquisition of insight. What lovely weather, what a pleasant breeze! What remarkable powers and abilities [we have]! How good it is for people to appreciate the value of these bounties! It behooves them to arise with thankfulness to carry out their duties to the world of humanity – to promote the peace, welfare, prosperity, and salvation of all God's servants.

In the afternoon, respected Persians attained the Master's presence, one after the other, and each of them was roused to a special degree of vigilance as they listened to Him speak on spiritual subjects.[913] When they were eventually dismissed,[914] they departed His presence with the utmost gratitude. Some of those visitors, however, were still with Him when He sent the members of His retinue to the home of Mr and Mrs Scott – as that was the day of the week when the gathering of Bahá'ís was regularly held there – and said:

> I have neither the time nor the strength to go there.

When the Master's attendants returned from that gathering, they told Him how attracted the believers there were, and mentioned the talk which a certain professor – one of the friends living in Paris – had given. This news gladdened the Master's heart immensely, and He said:

> You must always be the bearers of good news. Spread such news quickly, and become the means through which the hearts are made cheerful and vigilant. If, however, you have bad news to give someone, do not mention it to him in haste and become the cause of his sadness. When I have bad news for someone, I do not convey it to him outright. Rather, I speak with him in such a way that my words will bring him solace when he hears that news.

Shortly after nightfall, the Master went to the home of that handmaid of God, Miss Sanderson. He showed her great loving-kindness and commended the way she conversed with Him in Persian. He instructed that she read the poems of the Blessed Beauty and commit them to memory. After promising her that she would be confirmed and aided to progress, He said:

> I have not studied Arabic. When I was a child, I had a book of the Báb's prayers in the handwriting of the Blessed Beauty, and I very much yearned to read it. At night, I would waken, get out of bed, and peruse this book – and the fervour of my quest, the intensity of

> my longing, would move me to tears. Eventually, I saw that I understood Arabic well. My old friends know well that I have not studied Arabic, and yet I speak and write it better than the most eloquent of Arabs. I hope that you make great progress in learning the Persian language.

For the Master's dinner that night, Mr and Mrs Dreyfus-Barney cooked a Persian meal consisting of chicken and rice and sent it over to Him.

Tuesday, 20 May 1913
[Paris]

After some prayers by Bahá'u'lláh were chanted that morning, the Master said:

> There is no state like the state of prayer. It attracts the pure hearts, awakens the holy souls, and confers remarkable spirituality.

After this, once the public gathering had been convened, the Master delivered – in response to a question from one of those present – a talk in which He spoke of the resurrection and descent of Christ from heaven; interpreted certain verses from the Gospel of John; and explained the language used in the Gospel to the effect that, although Christ issued from the womb of Mary, He declared: 'I have come from heaven'.[915]

Miss [Fanny] Knobloch attained the presence of the Master, Who showed her great loving-kindness and spoke fondly of both her and her sister [Alma Knobloch]:[916]

> God raised you up from America, and through you the Cause of God has been spread in Germany. You have rendered a great deal of service. I wrote to your sister to travel from Stuttgart to the other cities of Germany to teach the Cause; God will confirm her.

She was truly showered with the Master's loving-kindness, and felt proud that her sister had been aided to teach the Cause of God. She herself had extended financial assistance [to her sister] and paid the expenses of her travels.

A gathering was held once again that afternoon at the residence of the Master, Who began His talk with these words:[917]

> Most of the people are like children. They are made happy or sad by trivial affairs, but attach no importance to matters of great significance.

He then launched into an extensive discussion of the inception of the dispensation of Christ and the negligence showed by the people of His time.[918] At the end of that gathering, He encouraged Rúḥíyyih K͟hánum (Miss Sanderson) once again to read the Persian Tablets and verses.

Following this, a number of respected Persians attained the Master's presence.[919] They listened to Him speak at length on numerous subjects and spiritual matters, and they grew enamoured of His captivating utterance and soul-stirring temperament. As that visit was drawing to a close, mention was made of Persian students who were studying various disciplines in Europe, and the Master made these remarks accordingly:

> When the people of Israel taught both material and spiritual subjects at their schools, this resulted in the education of people who were versed in many arts and sciences. Yet afterwards, the people of religion, in particular the Muslims, confined the instruction they gave in their schools to the members of their own communities to religious topics, and this instruction ended with mere words.

The Master then spoke of the Niẓámíyyih in Baghdad,[920] and gave an explanation concerning the teacher, the expert, and the scholar, which can be summarized as follows:

> The teacher was regarded as one who had comprehensive proficiency in all the disciplines of his day, and had no peer to rival him; the expert was one who was skilled in the disciplines of his time, regardless of whether or not he had a peer; and the scholar was one who was well-versed in one or two disciplines.

After His visitors expressed their humble gratitude and were dismissed from His presence, the Master went to the home of Mr and Mrs Dreyfus-Barney. From there, He was driven to the Bois de Boulogne – and as He was returning in the carriage that day, He chanted prayers in a sweet and wondrous tone, and rendered thankful praise to God, the Ruler of the Kingdom of Names and Attributes.

Wednesday, 21 May 1913
[Paris]

The Master did not give a talk at the public gathering that day; instead, He summoned people to His room and expounded the Writings and teachings of Bahá'u'lláh. The friends and others alike were moved to matchless delight that day as they received the Master's special kindnesses and exchanged questions and answers in their private audiences with Him. They all rendered thanks for His abundant bounties and yielded praise to Him Who was the ample source of imperishable grace.

One of the Master's visitors that day was an American,[921] who had been roused to ecstasy in attaining His presence and asked Him this question:

> What can I do to put these blessed teachings into practice? How might I overlook the faults of others and adopt an attitude of forbearance?

The Master replied:[922]

> Always be mindful of your own state. Determine what shortcoming you yourself have, and then strive to rectify it. The human

eye is blind, but at the same time it can see with microscopic precision – it is blind to one's own deficiencies, but sighted and far-seeing when it comes to the faults of others.

The Master also made these remarks to some others:

Centre your thoughts on becoming spiritual and receiving your share of the bounties of Bahá'u'lláh. Yield thanks to God that you are living in the age of Bahá'u'lláh and are being blessed with the outpourings of His grace.

And to still others He said:[923]

Yours is a lofty station because you have set your faces towards the horizon of truth in these days. Many will profess their belief in the years to come, but those who have recognized the truth at the beginning of this dispensation know eternal happiness, for in the day of their test they have attained to faith and assurance. In the time of Christ, they placed a crown of thorns on His head, but today millions build statues depicting Him with a crown of gold and glorify these representations, notwithstanding that in the days of His life they paid Him no mind whatsoever.

The Master had lunch at the home of Mr and Mrs Dreyfus-Barney. From there, He paid a visit to His daughter at the Maison de Santé, and then went – at the request of the friends – to a certain facility where His voice was recorded on a number of phonographic records.[924]

Thursday, 22 May 1913
[Paris]

After having His tea, the Master went to the home of [——].[925] That respected individual showed the utmost reverence and humility in His presence. Even as he entered, that gentleman kissed the Master's hand and mentioned how proud he was to know that such a glorious Cause – which has exalted the Easterners, especially the Persians – has appeared from Persia. He related anecdotes in that vein to the Master, among them the following:

> I was once at an important gathering in London where all the attendees were among the grandees and lords of England. A highly distinguished woman was seated near me, and I noticed she was wearing a ring set with carnelian. This surprised me considerably; why should this lady of so lofty a rank – bedecked as she was with an abundance of gold, jewellery, and other ornaments – choose to wear a ring with a stone of such little value? When I finally asked for the reason, she looked me in the eye, laughed, and said, 'To me, this stone is the most precious of all gems and the dearest of all the world's adornments.' This remark only added to my surprise. 'Why is that?' I asked. 'Are you not a Persian?' she replied, and further inquired, 'Do you not recognize the name of Bahá'u'lláh which is engraved on this stone, or realize that I consider it an honour to possess this ring?' It moved me profoundly to see that esteemed woman in such a state, at once priding and humbling herself in this way at the very mention of Bahá'u'lláh's name, yet at the same time I was filled with shame. How could I have been unaware of this weighty Cause, which is a credit to the people and the nation of Persia, while such significant people as this speak of it with great admiration? Why should I harbour feelings of jealousy and animosity in my heart?
>
> Thy watchful keeper circled thee
> And this myself I failed to do
> My piety prevented me
> Do let me now adore thee too

In brief, this illustrious man was visibly humble and reverent, and the Master showered him with benevolence and loving-kindness as a result.

At that meeting, the Master first spoke of the oneness of the principles of the divine religions, as well as the spread of the Cause of God in the states of America. He was asked about the Bahá'ís of America, and replied:

> They are people of every stripe. There are those pure Bahá'ís who believe in all the divine religions and subscribe to the truth of Islam. There are also those who consider this Cause to be the focal point of peace and welfare, and regard Bahá'u'lláh as a perfect Man. Beyond them, there are still a great many more who simply feel love and affection for the people of Bahá. There are many of them, and they fall into a variety of categories.

Following this, He gave a detailed explanation of the history of this wondrous Cause, recounted the martyrdoms of those who gave up their lives for the Faith, and responded to the objections of the cavillers:

> Such people say that the goal of the prophets has been to claim a position of earthly sovereignty and leadership for themselves, notwithstanding that the foundation of the Cause of God and the claims of the divine Manifestations have been entirely incompatible with comfort, tranquillity, and enjoyment, let alone the thought of worldly leadership. Bahá'u'lláh addressed these words to Náṣiri'd-Dín Sháh:
>
> > Amongst the people are those who allege that this Youth hath had no purpose but to perpetuate His name, whilst others claim that He hath sought for Himself the vanities of the world – this, notwithstanding that never, throughout all My days, have I found a place of safety, be it to the extent of a single foothold. At all times have I been immersed in an ocean of tribulations, whose full measure none can fathom but God. He, truly, is aware of what I say . . . Is it conceivable that He Who expecteth to lose His life at any moment should seek after worldly vanities? How very strange the imaginings of those who speak as prompted by their own caprices, and who wander distractedly in the wilderness of self and passion!

> Erelong shall they be called upon to account for their words, and on that day they shall find none to befriend or help them.*

Beyond these perils and afflictions, the effects and results produced by the Cause of them Who are the Dawning-places of God's Word bear still further testimony to the truth of their claim. Moreover, the purpose of the sacrifices made by those Holy Beings has ever been to educate humanity. Christ declared, 'Ye shall know them by their fruits.'† No bitter tree will ever bear sweet fruit, neither will a tree that is sweet ever yield fruit that is bitter.

> That soul which hath itself not come alive,
> Can it then hope another to revive?‡

How could one who is himself dishonest – a person who thinks of nothing but himself and his own interests, and is entirely unconcerned with the education and progress of humanity or sacrifice in the path of God – ever exalt a people from the depths of degradation to the heights of glory and prosperity? How can the influence of their goodly words possibly conduce, across numerous ages and centuries, to the transformation of people's characters, or the refinement of their attributes, or the moderation of their conduct, or the unification of the various kindreds to which they belong? When a person who has made his claim on the world and seeks to acquire its vanities is subdued to the utmost by the calamities and cruelties heaped upon him by aggressive peoples, his ambitions will vanish altogether. In the face of death, all his desires will disappear, and the tree of the hopes he once cherished will be uprooted from its foundation.

By contrast, one of the miraculous things about the Word of God and the perspicuous signs of the divine Claimants is that, in spite of the oppression and martyrdom meted out to them by their foes and the afflictive hardship they suffered, their Cause grew

---

* Bahá'u'lláh, *Summons*, p. 100.

† Matt. 7:16.

‡ From the *Haft Awrang* of Jámí; translation by Marzieh Gail, taken from *Selections from the Writings of 'Abdu'l-Bahá*, no. 221.

> increasingly pervasive with every passing day. Their abasement is the cause of their glory; their captivity and imprisonment are tantamount to their freedom and deliverance. You have seen the dire calamities and adversities that befell this Cause in Persia. The Persian people and their government mistakenly believed this Cause to have a human basis, and imagined that the memory thereof would be forever effaced from every heart the very instant it was made the target of their persecution. They failed to realize that grievous hostility, calamity, murder, and martyrdom will only enhance the influence of God's Cause and further exalt His Word. It is for this reason that, however much they wished to extinguish this divine lamp, it grew only brighter. Had they acted with this aggression in America or Europe, or imprisoned me or crucified me there, the influence of this Cause would surely have been more intense. Thus, the circumstances attending the advent of the Holy Manifestations are diametrically opposed to those of such people as have set their ambitions on earthly leadership; there is no similarity between them whatsoever. Indeed, the pervading influence of the Cause of God, as well as the penetrating power of His Word, are without rival or peer in the world of existence.

The Master was tired that morning, so He did not give a talk at the gathering upon His return.[926] Instead, seekers and others well-disposed to the Faith were gradually admitted into His room, where they were showered with His tender kindnesses, exhorted to acquire the virtues that define the world of humanity, and encouraged to arise and spread the divine fragrances.[927]

A number of illustrious individuals attained the Master's presence in the afternoon.[928] After extending His loving-kindness to them, He said:

> I have promised to go somewhere. Consider this place your own home; stay and converse with the others. I must go.

The Master then departed, and in keeping with His prior commitment, He went to see that respected lady, Miss [Mary 'Edith']

Jackson, whom He treated with great kindness. Sick though she was, that handmaid of God was stirred to fresh delight by the Master's visit.

Following His return, a reporter who wrote for *The Christian Commonwealth* attained the Master's presence and remained there until nighttime. It filled him with great pride and joy to have the privilege of listening to the Master's utterances and recording them for publication.

Friday, 23 May 1913
[Paris]

According to solar reckoning and European calendars, this day marked the birth of 'Abdu'l-Bahá and the Declaration of the Báb – may the spirits of all living things be a sacrifice for their beneficence!

From early in the morning until nighttime, the believers and other friends attained the Master's presence with bouquets of flowers to extend their felicitations.[929] They expressed their utter joy and delight, saying, 'Today is a great day; it is the day of Your birth, and also the day on which the Báb declared His mission!' The Master said:

> Indeed, as this day marks the Declaration of the Báb – the day when that Sun dawned forth and announced the greatest of glad-tidings – it is an exceedingly blessed day. By chance, it also happens that I was born on this day.

The talk the Master gave to the gathering dealt with the days of exile in Baghdad,[930] the utterances of the Abhá Beauty regarding the 'City of God',[931] and those divine teachings that pertain to matters of economics.[932]

In the afternoon,[933] the Master spoke with Mr and Mrs Richard about parables of Christ that are not found in the Gospel. Occasioned by a visit from the children, He also made these remarks on the subject of their education:[934]

A person's perfection lies in this – that he also rear, to the extent that he is able, the offspring of the poor and other children, regarding them even as his own progeny, and seeing no difference whatever between them. Indeed, whichever child demonstrates the greater degree of vigilance, that child should receive the larger share of attention and training, that thereby he may become the wellspring of perfections and the promulgator of the virtues of humanity.

Were one to raise only one's own child, this would be a commendable act and an attractor of the bounties of the Ever-Forgiving, but it is an act which every person is naturally inclined to perform. Therefore, the merit, the honour, and the goodwill of the world of humanity consist in the rearing of those children who have no one, and the offspring of the poor and the weak. Such children will, as a result, be forever thankful to their benevolent guardians, and generally exhibit a more grateful and appreciative attitude. They will, moreover, stand in stark contrast to those children who deem themselves deserving and entitled, and consider their parents obligated to train and educate them. Children of this sort hardly value such efforts; they do not crave their education – nor do they show gratitude to their nurturers – the way the other children, bereft as they are of someone to care for them, most certainly would. This attitude can, at present, be seen in the majority of children.

Well is it with those blessed souls who have been graciously aided to render this service, and have carried out this duty in the world of humanity.

Some of the friends expressed their desire to go to a flower show,[935] so there the Master went. This was an event held every year in most of the countries of Europe, especially France, in which an exhibition (or a festival) of flowers was held. There were many flowers of all kinds that had been arranged most neatly and exquisitely. Their appearance from every side filled all those present with vigour and gladness. In every corner of that space, there was some colour or freshness, some fragrance or delicacy, that stirred a crowd to great delight. As it was the anniversary of the Báb's Declaration and that of the Master's birth, the fact that this event was, by some happy coincidence, also being held on the same day rejoiced the eager Bahá'ís in attendance, and added to the attraction and excitement that those lovers of the Master were exhibiting. It was as if that festival had been held specifically to commemorate this auspicious anniversary, and it seemed that all the things of that place had been moved, in their ecstasy from beholding the Master, to sing songs of congratulations.

A lively and delightful gathering was held at the home of Mr and Mrs Dreyfus-Barney that night to celebrate the aforementioned anniversary. Following the chanting of divine verses that are traditionally recited on this day, and after Mr Dreyfus and Mrs Bernard each gave a speech, the Master delivered an eloquent talk on the dawning of that Sun [the Báb] Who bore the greatest of glad-tidings, as well as the rising of the Most Exalted Beauty [Bahá'u'lláh] Who would succeed Him.[936]

After having ice cream, *sharbat*, and sweets, that gathering was brought to a close with the utmost spiritual gladness.

Saturday, 24 May 1913
[Paris]

Telegrams from groups of Bahá'ís in America and Europe poured in,[937] one after the other, expressing their good wishes to the Master, and this brought great joy to the hearts of the friends.

On that day, too, visitors entered the Master's room – one by one and two by two – where they had private audiences with Him and received a special share of His tender kindnesses. When some Americans attained His presence, the Master spoke happily and approvingly of the American government and the gentleness of its people, stating that they were all receptive to peace and unity.[938] Yet to a group of Persians He said:

> The people of Persia have remained heedless of the greatness and nobility of this Cause and have failed to appreciate its significance. Although it had been demonstrated that even the dry ground and

> the infertile soil of the Arabian desert could become a spot worthy of circumambulation by virtue of the fact that the Cause of God appeared there, they still paid no heed.

Such were the remarks with which the Master counselled each group and person who visited Him.

In the afternoon, He went to the home of Ras͟híd Pás͟há, and then paid visits to some respected Persians.

Unexpectedly, [——][939] telephoned that night to ask the Master's permission to see Him and fix a time for this visit. A number of others accompanied that person to the Master's presence,[940] and among the questions posed by these companions was the following:

> People say that Muhammad, the Apostle of God, killed people and plundered their possessions, and also that He waylaid caravans. How should we respond to these objections?

The Master then adduced comprehensive proofs, gave extensive explanations, and elaborated on historical episodes, all of which left His listeners satisfied and thankful. Here is a summary of certain remarks which the Master made along these lines:

> One must understand the truth of such matters. Are you at all aware of the age in which Muhammad lived, or the clans and peoples in whose midst He was raised up? It was a time when the tribes of Arabia took the utmost pride in murdering and pillaging, as well as damaging each other's reputation and sullying their honour. Since Muhammad was raised up to edify those barbarous people, moderate their characters, and refine their primitive behaviours and customs, from the inception of His ministry to the time of the *hijrat* . . .

The Master then proceeded to speak at length on the history of Islam:

> Even after He had endured those hardships and sustained those heavy blows, those brutal people deemed it lawful nevertheless to rob Muhammad and His companions of their possessions, and considered it an obligation to slay them. Abú Sufyán plundered all their belongings and set himself to wiping out Islam and the Muslims altogether. So agitated had the companions of Muhammad become that, while they were in Medina, they subsisted only on the pits of dates. In another respect – one still worse than this adversity and captivity – the foundation of Islam itself was in grave danger. It was at such a time as this when a caravan belonging to Abú Sufyán was passing by, and Muhammad's companions, out of necessity and having no other recourse, retaliated by stopping the caravan.
>
> Let us now disregard the circumstances of that time. If such acts of hostility were to be perpetrated against you in this day and age as would reduce you to needing the most basic of provisions to sustain yourselves – and if, in addition to this, you should see that so precious a goal, which is itself the indispensable foundation for the elimination of all such hostilities, and the means through which the characters and qualities of humankind will be improved, is being completely trampled underfoot – what would you do in this situation?

Everyone replied that there would be no choice but to resist and confront the aggressors.

The Master then gave a preliminary account of the digging of the trench, the breaking of the pact,[941] the alliance of various tribes in their common goal to utterly annihilate Muhammad, and the measures taken to defend and protect the religion of Islam:

> It would not have been possible to protect the Cause by any other means than the ones that transpired. Suppose today you were to ask those same civilized people and those intellectuals of Europe – from whom these sorts of objections have now proceeded and taken root in the minds of the Easterners – the following question: 'If in this age, which is the age of civilization, you were to find

within your country, or in a neighbouring nation, such barbaric tribes and atrocious hostilities as the kind just described, in what way would you deal with them?' How do you think they would respond to this question? Will they say, 'Given the need to educate and chasten them, it is our duty to stamp out, by whatever means necessary, the malice and aggression they show one another'? Or will they deem it preferable to hold their peace and leave those people to their own devices?

Bear in mind that the pretext cited most often today by domineering and well-developed governments for meddling in the affairs of other countries is none other than this: that in spite of the civilization and capability which those other countries and their peoples already possess, these governments perceive those people to be living in a state of disorder, and regard it as both an affront to justice and a dereliction of their duty as civilized and educated people to leave the inhabitants of those places to themselves. It is for this reason that they feel compelled to stretch out the hand of their chastisement and mount an attack that will demonstrate their power and might. Yet all this notwithstanding, when the name of the religion of Muhammad is mentioned, they speak with the utmost prejudice, prompted by the vehemence of their bigotry to express such rueful wishes as these: 'If only a Messenger like this had never been raised up in the midst of these Arab tribes, and never stayed the encroaching hand of wild and primitive peoples! Would that he had never laid the foundation of felicity, and that the enlightening and sufficing hallmarks of its civilization had never travelled from Asia and reached the frontiers of Europe!'

The Master spoke for more than an hour; all His remarks were in this vein, and He made them with such consummate power and majesty as to profoundly affect the hearts of His listeners and move them to sing His praises. They had all been humbled – even Jináb-i-Mu'ín, considered by some to be a difficult person to satisfy – and they all attested to the force of the Master's utterance and the decisiveness of His argument.[942]

Sunday, 25 May 1913
[Paris]

The first thing to happen that morning was that the friends and seekers came in groups to visit the Master in His room.[943] They raised topics and subjects for His consideration, and their attraction and delight only grew as they listened to His responses.

The Master then went to a gathering of believers and gave a brief talk that began with these words:[944]

> The weather in Paris today is good, but my hope is that an entirely different kind of pleasantness will appear in Paris – that it will acquire a spirituality that will stir the hearts and souls. I hope it will make spiritual discoveries and deliver the people to true liberty and freedom from selfish defilements. May the star of the East so shine upon these lands that it will illumine the skies of these countries, and turn the gardens of the hearts into the envy of flowers and roses. May every nostril be perfumed; may every face be illumined. This is my hope.

At the end of that gathering, one of the respected attendees, who had also been in the Master's presence the previous night, mentioned to Him how moved and enraptured he and his companions had become:

> In Your absence last night, everyone expressed their devotion and remarked that they had grown enamoured of You.

The Master replied:

> How very interesting that we are the ones who must prove the legitimacy of the Apostle of God for the Muslims! And yet, even in spite of this, the Muslims are still not satisfied with us, and they spare nothing in expressing their enmity and hatred towards us.

In the afternoon,[945] a splendid gathering was held at the home of Mr and Mrs Richard,[946] where the Master gave a talk on serving the world of humanity, turning towards the Pivot of divine perfections, and receiving bestowals from the Centre of heavenly grace. He expounded, moreover, on some of the sacred teachings and also *The Hidden Words*. In unison, all those in attendance voiced their praise and gratitude, and expressed their astonishment at how remarkably the Master had arisen to spread the signs of God. He then unloosed His bountiful tongue once more, and looked at each and every one of those present with the tender glances of His generous compassion. When it was time to depart, the attendees approached the Master one by one to shake His hand. Out of their overwhelming ecstasy and rapture, they formed a circle around Him and supplicated His blessings and confirmations.

From there, the Master went to the home of Munír Pá<u>sh</u>á.[947]

After returning to the hotel, He recounted the remarks He made to the aforementioned pá<u>sh</u>á and the members of his household, and described the attraction and sincerity they evinced.

Monday, 26 May 1913
[Paris]

Early that morning, Miss [Fanny] Knobloch, who was about to leave for America, attained the Master's presence. He extended His loving-kindness to – and spoke fondly of the faithfulness of – her, her sisters [Alma Knobloch and Pauline Knobloch Hannen], Mr [Joseph] Hannen,[948] and the other friends of America. He addressed her most graciously, assuring her that confirmations and blessings would be forthcoming, and exhorting them all to promote the Word of God and serve His Cause.[949]

A crowd of people attained the Master's presence, and some of these visitors were teachers of music.[950] Accordingly, after expressing His praise and encouragement, the Master told this story:

> When we were travelling from New York to London, an orchestra played music on the ship every morning and afternoon, and the

> passengers would listen simply to pass the time. At most, when the orchestra would sometimes play better than usual, the passengers would be roused to ecstasy for a few minutes, and then applaud when the orchestra had finished playing. This was the fruit of their merriment and music; it was temporary, not everlasting. Thus, a melody must be played that will stir the Concourse on High to exceeding rapture, and produce effects and results that shall prove enduring. Ultimately, these physical circumstances are only reliable and present for as long as the body exists; afterwards, they will disappear and be forgotten. Spiritual perfections and excellences, on the other hand, will persist into perpetuity; that is where true significance lies. Strive to attain such a station as this – to discover eternal happiness, convene a divine celebration, hold a celestial feast, lay out the banquet of heavenly existence, and grant everlasting life to the peoples of the earth. This is what befits the world of humanity.

Following this, the Master went to the home of Aḥmad Pá<u>sh</u>á. He spoke with him at length on many subjects, and their conversation went on for so long that the Master grew tired in the end. His heart, however, had been thoroughly cheered by the devotion and humility demonstrated by the pá<u>sh</u>á and his family, and His tender kindnesses towards those illustrious individuals only increased as a result.[951]

A lively gathering was held at the home of Mr and Mrs Scott that evening. Every soul in attendance[952] was magnetized by the Most Glorious Kingdom, and every heart enamoured as it voiced its praise of the Master. Prayers were chanted at the beginning of the gathering, and once Miss [Beatrice] Irwin had recited some of the Writings in translation,[953] the Master joined that assemblage of yearning friends. He gave an extensive talk that dealt with the progress of the soul, traversing the various stages of the world of being, and the inability of the occupants of a lower plane of existence to comprehend the realms above it. With His mention of the Ancient Beauty, He imbued the bodies of all those present with new life.[954]

Tuesday, 27 May 1913
[Paris]

The Master moved into the Pension Hotel (on Lauriston street),[955] where He had also stayed previously for a time. Before He did this, however, a group of friends,[956] along with some respected Ottomans,[957] attained His presence. He related extensive anecdotes from His journeys to America and Europe, and as He did this, the spirit of knowledge and assurance that was born of His utterance seemed to flow through the veins and limbs of His visitors.

When the Master arrived at the [Pension] hotel, He said:

> I feel very weak and fatigued. For the time being, while the people have not yet learned of this new residence, we will have a few days to rest.

He then said the following with regard to the people of Paris:

> So immersed are they in self and passion that even when they become enraptured and transformed, they revert to their initial state the very next day. We have remained here to tend to other matters and occupations. At least our meetings with the Ottomans have proven more useful and yielded better results.

Such were the remarks He made time and again.

In the afternoon, the Master went to visit Rúḥá Khánum at the Maison de Santé. After returning,[958] He went with Dr Muḥammad Khán and walked throughout some of the streets of Paris until well into the night.

Wednesday, 28 May 1913
[Paris]

A group of the friends had learned of the Master's new residence, and they came to attain His presence. For His talk, He expounded the station of divinity and spoke of the wholly sanctified nature of the Essence of God. He observed that every people has ascribed certain limits and qualities to God – glorified and exalted be He – notwithstanding that the habitation of His transcendent glory is sanctified from all restrictions, and that His gracious outpourings and divine perfections are without limit. He then discussed the beliefs of the ancient philosophers – their vain imaginings, their attachment to the stars, and their worship of statues built to depict those celestial bodies.

In the afternoon, too, another group of people, including some respected Ottomans,[959] attained the Master's presence. To them He gave an extensive address on invisible powers that exercise only spiritual influence without any physical action.[960]

Most of the time, Mr and Mrs Dreyfus-Barney, or Aḥmad Pá<u>sh</u>á, or still yet others, would cook a special meal in their own homes for the Master's lunch and dinner, which they would then send to the hotel. As they knew that the food at the hotel did not agree with the Master, and that He was having a difficult time as a result, they would send Him these meals on most occasions even though He had emphatically forbidden it. Furthermore, whenever He had guests at the hotel, He would usually sit at the dining table with them.

The Master paid a visit to Miss Jackson that afternoon. After returning, He remarked:

> Until I walk a great deal, I will not have any appetite for food. It is not enough to go on an excursion by car.

Consequently, He went outside once again, walked for a long time, and then returned.[961]

Thursday, 29 May 1913
[Paris]

That morning, the Master spoke to the Bahá'ís about the need to gather and associate with one another, and discussed the fruits that come from this intimacy and fellowship. He also exhorted some of them to study the Persian language.[962]

The Master and some of His attendants were invited to the home of [——][963] for lunch that day. Before having their meal, the Master told stories about the exile [of His family] from Tehran and the fierce blizzards they encountered as they passed through Hamadan and Kermanshah. He likewise gave a brief account of their days in Baghdad and Adrianople, eventually leading up to the prison of 'Akká. He also told stories from recent times, discussing the reign of Sulṭán 'Abdu'l-Ḥamíd; mentioning the movers of sedition, both from within [the Cause] and without; and commenting on their wickedness and the loss they faced in the end.

Once that esteemed individual had spoken to the Master about himself, everyone went over to the dining table. Persian dishes of all kinds had been prepared and laid out, and the Master partook of them with abundant joy and good humour. As He was having His meal, He spoke of those who were well-versed in Islamic jurisprudence and doctrine:

> How great the results that would have appeared if these people had practised that kind of hair-splitting on matters of actual importance! To what avail did they spend all the days of their lives on sciences and subjects that begin with words and end with words? Their endeavours bore no other fruit but this.

After lunch, the Master gave a talk in which He praised the late Shaykh Murtaḍá [Anṣárí],[964] may God exalt His station! He recounted the extent of the Shaykh's piety and detachment from dogma, remarking that the courtesy and deference with which he treated this Cause during the days of banishment in Baghdad reached the highest possible degree. The decorum that attended the hospitality of that luncheon, the genuine devotion and heartfelt love that had been extended by its respected host, and the reverence and humility shown by those present rejoiced the hearts of the Master's servants immeasurably.

Upon His return that afternoon, the Master went to rest, and it was at this time that Munír Páshá came to His residence to pay Him a visit. As soon as he learned that the Master was resting, he expressed his submissive devotion and said, 'I will leave now and come back another time.' When it was later mentioned to the Master that Munír Pá<u>sh</u>á had come to see Him and then demonstrated his servitude, He said:

> You must inform me of these things! In cases like this, you should completely disregard my comfort. My repose consists in service to the Cause of God. As the Parisians are not all that receptive, one must devote one's attention to the people of the East. Perhaps some of them will take heed; perhaps they will be saved from that which leads to abasement and perdition, and awakened from the sleep of heedlessness.

Following a visit from a group of friends that afternoon, the Master went to see some of the believers who were sick.[965]

Friday, 30 May 1913
[Paris]

In response to a question from one of those present at the gathering that morning, the Master gave a talk on seclusion and rigorous austerities:[966]

> In the past, some would engage in mortification of the flesh with the aim of renouncing carnal delights and suppressing feelings of anger and passion. It is indeed the case that, because the body grows weaker when one practises this abstinence by eating and drinking very little, the manifestations of one's anger and passion will decrease as a result. But this soothing of anger and this diminishing of passion are accidental, not essential, for whenever one begins to eat and drink again, one will revert to one's initial state. If the culmination of a person's sanctification consists in his physical weakness, then whoever is the weaker person should be regarded as the more perfect one.
>
> One's goal, then, in living a rigorous life should be to renounce self and passion while still sustaining oneself with food, rather than

> depriving oneself of those gifts. God has created these bounties for humankind, and made good health and bodily vigour to be channels through which the power of the human spirit can be made manifest. Should the human self remain healthy in spite of one's physical strength, and if one is able to observe righteousness while also being powerful, this would constitute perfection. Otherwise:
>
> Your self's a serpent – how can it be dead?
> Through grief and lack of means it froze instead.*

Consul Schwarz and his respected wife came from Stuttgart to Paris that afternoon expressly to visit the Master. They spoke to Him of the servitude and attraction of the German Bahá'ís, recounting the gatherings held by the friends in Stuttgart and Esslingen, and describing the devotion and zeal of those eager souls. It cheered the Master's heart to hear these accounts – these joyful reports of the divine fragrances being spread in those regions – and He showered the consul and his wife with loving-kindness as a result.[967]

A gathering charged with gladness was held that night at the home of Mr and Mrs Dreyfus-Barney. It was attended by a large number of people, hailing from America, England, Paris, Persia, Germany, and the Ottoman territories. After some Arabic prayers were recited, and once Mr Dreyfus and Consul Schwarz had each given a talk,[968] the Master entered and joined that gathering of friends, filling the hearts of those lovers with such overwhelming joy, such exceeding bliss, as to make them the envy of the garden of paradise. The Master then delivered an address on the advent of the power of the Word of God and the influence of the Cause of Bahá'u'lláh:

> Behold how the diverse peoples of Germany, Persia, America, England, and France have come together in this gathering with the utmost genuine fellowship! The East and the West have taken one

* A couplet from the *Mat͟hnaví* of Rúmí, Book 3, sec. 37, p. 65, translated by Jawid Mojaddedi ('Story about the snake-catcher who thought a frozen snake was dead, tied it up, and brought it to Baghdad').

another in their embrace. It would have been impossible to establish this kind of connection, or bring about this sort of unity and intimacy, through any power but the power of God, or any effect but the one produced by the influence of His blessed and all-embracing Word . . .

Saturday, 31 May 1913
[Paris]

A certain person asked the Master for money that morning.[969] He gave him some, and then said:

> You must not, however, become a spendthrift, for extravagance always leads to one's sadness and distress. If you see that I make certain expenses, know that they are all made strictly for the fulfilment of religious obligations and in view of considerations pertaining to the Cause of God; their fruits will become known in the future. During my days in Baghdad and Adrianople, I had a hat and a garment that I owned for many years; they were coming apart at the seams, but I had no intention of borrowing anything. Now, too, had we chosen to disregard certain matters and considerations, we would have lodged at a smaller and less expensive place in this city.
>
> Every necessity has been designed to meet a certain need. This applies also to food, but to eat more than is necessary will lead to despondency and weariness, and ultimately culminate in illness. How base must one be to content oneself with these conditions and defile oneself with these excesses! One's merit lies in one's divine perfections, one's knowledge of God, and the domination of one's spiritual dimension over one's animalistic side.

A group of friends from Germany,[970] America, England, France, and Persia then attained the Master's presence, and to them He said:

> You all are the variegated flowers of the garden of the Most

> Glorious Paradise. These are flowers that will never wilt; they shall never dry up or droop to the ground. Through the gracious outpourings raining down from the Kingdom of Abhá, these flowers will always be lush and luxuriant, for their freshness and exquisiteness will stem solely from spiritual love and fellowship, and be wholly sanctified from physical impurities and all relationship to the material realm.

When that gathering was concluded, a highly spiritual Bahá'í – Mr [Henri] Boutaric, who had come from Toulouse – attained the presence of the Master, Who extended His loving-kindness to him, and counselled him to teach the Cause of God and diffuse the divine fragrances.[971]

Additionally, a grandee from Egypt [Prince Muḥammad-'Alí Bey] also attained the Master's presence.[972] While he was in His room, this gentleman was privileged to receive the Master's tender kindnesses and moved to boundless ecstasy as he listened to His wondrous utterances.

In the afternoon, He repaid visits to some of the friends and certain respected persons from the East.[973]

When He returned to His residence, the Master found a crowd of believers who were waiting to meet with Him, and they all derived a fresh measure of His bounty and grace. He encouraged Miss Irwin to speak at gatherings and promote the divine principles, and she replied:

> I had thought that the woman's place was to be silent, and that it becomes the man to arise and raise the call. For this reason, I had always shied away from speaking.

In response, the Master said:

> In the Kingdom of God, women and men are one and the same. It is incumbent on everyone to summon humanity to turn towards the Most Exalted Horizon and to spread the sweet savours of God.

After addressing His audience with a talk on exhibiting goodly behaviour and disseminating the divine signs, the Master went outside to go for a stroll.[974]

That night, He spoke at length on subjects related to Sufism with Mr and Mrs Richard, who brimmed with abundant gladness from the bounty of being in His presence.

Sunday, 1 June 1913
[Paris]

Áqá Mírzá Jalál, who was the Master's son-in-law, and Mírzá 'Alí-Akbar Nakhjavání both returned from the Holy Land and attained the Master's presence.[975] They conveyed to Him the sentiments of longing and affection that had been expressed by His ardent lovers, and relayed messages of great yearning and devoted servitude from the Greatest Holy Leaf, the Exalted Consort,[976] the ladies of the Holy Family, and some of His specially favoured friends. It was mentioned in a myriad ways that restless souls were anticipating His return, and that a great number of travellers and other people were waiting to attain His presence.[977] Eventually, the Master unloosed His bountiful tongue to speak of the friends of the East:

> Though I have been in the West during this time, my heart has always remained inclined to the East, and my thoughts have ever been fixed on the remembrance of Eastern Bahá'ís. This applies in particular to those special souls residing in the Holy Land. The devotion and services of those friends are always on my mind; I remember them most fondly, and this remembrance fills me with joy.

The Master then proceeded to inquire after each and every one of the believers, asking how His companions in the Holy Land, Syria, Egypt, the Caucasus, Russia, and Persia were faring. When some mail arrived, it was mentioned to Him that several people had fervently hoped He would confirm them in their services to the Cause of God and crown their efforts with success. Supplications to be aided and assisted, as well as prayers to be protected and preserved, were conveyed to the Master on behalf of the following people:

- Ḥájí Mírzá Ḥaydar-'Alí and the other friends of the Holy Land
- Mírzá Abu'l-Faḍl and the other loved ones of Egypt
- Ba<u>sh</u>ír-i-Iláhí[978] and the other believers of Fars
- The Muḥibbu's-Sulṭán, Áqá Mírzá <u>Gh</u>ulám-'Alí, and the other spreaders of the heavenly fragrances
- [——],[979] Ibn-i-Abhar, Adíb, and the other Hands of this Holy Cause
- Ḥájí Mírzá Abu'l-Ḥasan Amín, Ḥájí <u>Gh</u>ulám-Riḍá Amín,[980] and all the other Trustees of the Merciful
- Síná[981] and all the other teachers of the Cause of God
- Samandar,[982] Ḥakím-i-Iláhí, and the other Bahá'ís of Qazvin
- The Ibtiháju'l-Mulk and the other lovers of Rasht
- The Aḥmadov brothers[983] and the other friends of Azerbaijan
- Mullá Bahrám[984] and the other friends of Zoroastrian background
- Ḥájí Mihdí Rifú'á[985] and the other Bahá'ís of Jewish extraction in Hamadan
- The sons of the late Muḥammad Muṣṭafá[986] and the other Arab Bahá'ís
- Ḥájí Siyyid Mihdí,[987] Áqá Siyyid Muṣṭafá,[988] Áqá Mírzá Maḥram,[989] and the other loved ones of India[990]
- Áqá Mírzá Ismá'íl[991] and the other companions of Bádkúbih [Baku]
- The servants at the threshold of God and other friends in 'I<u>sh</u>qábád
- Those who have survived their martyred kin,[992] as well as the other friends of Yazd
- The special friends and other Bahá'ís of Kerman
- Those residing in other countries, cities, villages, and hamlets

The Master implored that all these souls may be confirmed, and expressed the hope that they would be aided to keep the Covenant, promote unity, and consecrate themselves to the all-pervading Word of Bahá'u'lláh. He promised, moreover, that He would soon make His speedy return to the East.

Once the anticipation of those righteous believers and the messages of devotion from those friends had been communicated to Him, the Master went to the reception room of the hotel. In response to questions raised by some of those present at the public gathering, He gave a talk in which He expounded the meaning of the statement 'the explication of everything is in everything', gave proofs of the return of Christ according to the explicit text of the Gospel,[993] discussed the influence of the Cause of God, and described the effects of the Word of God on the hearts of the peoples and kindreds of the earth. The Master's remarks that day magnetized the hearts and attracted the souls more than on any other.

Additionally, a number of odes and other poems, which had been composed by some of the friends of Persia in praise of the Master and had been sent to Him, arrived that day. At the request of those ardent lovers, their poems were recited in His presence. Among them was a most sweet poem from Bíni<u>sh</u>-i-<u>Sh</u>írází ('Imád-Ábádí)[994] which had been sent by Áqá Mírzá Hádí,[995] an Afnán and son-in-law of the Master, with the intention that it be presented to Him – and He found it highly commendable. There was also an ode from Mas'úd Qazvíní;[996] this was a wonderfully mellifluous poem which lauded the Master and concluded with a humorous remark that concerned a conversation between the poet and Áqá Siyyid Naṣru'lláh Báqiroff to this effect:

> As he* is a man of reason, he has forbidden me from expressing sentiments of love. He dislikes anything I might say in my praises of the Master unless it is to recount His servitude.

Once those eloquent poems had been read for the Master, He said:

---

* Áqá Siyyid Naṣru'lláh Báqiroff.

> That which Siyyid Naṣru'lláh has said with regard to the servitude of 'Abdu'l-Bahá is correct.

He then discussed the degrees of love and longing demonstrated by the favoured ones of God:

> This kind of love is the fruit of consummate reason, for the firmer the foundation of reason and knowledge, the greater the heights that the lofty palace of love will reach:
>
> Should he of reason not lay eyes
> Upon that fair and charming face,
> How could he turn toward the prize
> And look upon the lover's place?
> For them who are to God resigned
> Both love and reason well accord,
> Unlike that earthly heart and mind
> Which in this nether world are stored.

He proceeded to tell stories on this topic that were extensive indeed.[997]

Monday, 2 June 1913
[Paris]

While the Master was walking to and fro in the reception room of the hotel that morning, He expressed great joy and delight as He mentioned the Holy Land, remarking that, because that blessed place is the centre of the Cause of God, all the institutions in its vicinity will be kept safe by virtue of the protection it enjoys.

It was noted several times that no less than forty travellers were in Haifa and were waiting to see the Master. He replied:

> We will certainly depart this week. The Bahá'ís of Persia have truly endured dire adversities and offered themselves up as shields against the darts of the enemies in this path.

He then mentioned some of the exiles:

> As we travelled from Baghdad to Adrianople, some of the believers such as Áqá Riḍá,[998] Áqá Mírzá Maḥmúd,[999] and Áqá Mírzá Ja'far[1000] took great pains indeed. They were truly blessed souls. Both while travelling and at every stop, they rendered service to the entire company of exiles. They would always run ahead of Bahá'u'lláh's litter and prepare food whenever we reached a stopping-place on that journey, notwithstanding our lack of adequate provisions. Most of the time, I would go with one of them to the local villages to look for hay, barley, or other animal fodder until midnight, after which the caravan would move onward once again just as they were beginning to try and get some rest. Their nights and their days passed by in this way, and they never enjoyed a moment's peace.

The Master then gave a talk that dealt with the all-encompassing nature of the Cause of God in every day and age, observing that divine religion has always embodied the virtues and perfections of the world of humanity – that every token of bounty and grace has ever derived from it and existed beneath its shade. He remarked, moreover, that divine religion, as well as the all-unifying power which it holds, can be likened to an excellent body that possesses every limb, thus enabling it to meet all the needs of humanity.

Following this, the Master transitioned to a discussion of divine philosophy and natural philosophy. This included an explication of the journey of individual essences throughout the limitless forms of the world of existence, and the appearance of their perfections in the frames of every one of those beings. His talk drew an even greater measure of His audience's attention and only further captivated their minds.

Some of the grandees and princes of the East visited the Master that afternoon.[1001] It so happened that a Persian who had not met with Him before requested permission to see Him.[1002] When he attained the Master's presence, it astonished and affected him profoundly to witness the humility and reverence the other dignitaries of Persia were showing Him, and he made these comments:

> For me, this is the greatest vindication of the truth: to behold these illustrious people, once the enemies of this Cause who sedulously strove day and night to utterly exterminate this group, now humbled and laid low, to this degree and in such a city as this one, by the power and influence of that same Cause.

The Master addressed each of His visitors with extensive remarks, and He magnetized their hearts and souls through His incisive utterances on numerous subjects.[1003]

At five o'clock, He went to the gathering of believers at the home of Mr and Mrs Scott. Once prayers had been chanted, some of the Arabic verses were read out loud and then recited in French translation. A few Bahá'ís then gave talks,[1004] and eventually the Master came out from a separate room and joined that gathering of yearning souls. He delivered a specific and emphatic address on the Covenant, which was rooted in the Writings and can be summarized as follows:[1005, 1006]

> The protection of the Cause of God and the unity of the people of Bahá are dependent on firmness in the Covenant of God and adherence to the writings of the Expounder of the divine verses. Apart from this, every hope will end in despair, and every remark will lead to toil and abasement. He who searches for any path but this one will fall into a darksome abyss, and every seeker of rank and glory who fails to promote this servitude shall find himself wailing and sighing in the end.

Tuesday, 3 June 1913
[Paris]

After praise and remembrance of the One True God that morning, and also prayers and meditations devoted to Him Who is the Unconstrained King, the Master made these remarks on the power of the Cause of God and the influence of His Word:

Observe how the Cause of God has encompassed the world! The call of God has been spread to every corner of the earth; it has abased every other sound and voice, and humbled every worldly head and leader. Now that the shrill voice of the Supreme Pen has been lifted up, it is certain that no trace of the droning of the gnat will remain.

After having His tea, He also said:

In this day, the hosts of success and confirmation are the supporters of those who arise to promote the Most Sublime Word and busy themselves with exalting the Cause of God. Heavenly forces shall aid those blessed souls to prevail over all the world's powers. Were people to ponder and reflect even briefly, they would soon be awakened, and come to realize that no serenity can be found outside the shadow of God's Word, nor is there anything that will gladden the soul, solace the mind, or assure the heart except setting one's face towards spiritual power and cleaving tenaciously to the divine teachings.

Free from wild beasts and traps there is no place
No peace but in retreat with God's pure grace.*

Soon you will see that the civilization of the Europeans will also give rise to a world-consuming war, and culminate in tumult and pandemonium. What blows and calamities the Blessed Beauty sustained! What holy souls were sacrificed so that this foundation of eternal prosperity and glory could be laid, and this pavilion of the oneness of humanity be upraised! Now must the loved ones of the Blessed Beauty engage themselves in service day and night, and centre their thoughts on preserving and guarding the foundation of the Cause of God. They should not be preoccupied with their own selves; they must shut their eyes to their personal

* A couplet from the *Mat͟hnaví* of Rúmí, Book 2, sec. 16, p. 37, translated by Jawid Mojaddedi ('How the announcers serving the judge spread news around town about a bankrupt').

thoughts and circumstances, and not allow all this toil and suffering to go to waste.

Once the crowd had gathered, the Master gave a talk on the return and descent of Christ in response to a question from a female leader of the Theosophical Society.[1007]

Following this, Consul Schwarz and his esteemed wife attained the Master's presence. Since they were departing for Stuttgart that day,[1008] He spoke these words addressed to the Bahá'ís of Germany:[1009]

> Jesus Christ proclaimed: 'People shall come from the East and the West and enter the Kingdom of God, but the children of the Kingdom shall be cast out.'* This is why many of the compatriots and kindreds of the Blessed Beauty have remained debarred from the Most Glorious Kingdom, and it is the reason that you, who outwardly seemed to be far from it, have enjoyed its benefits and attained to heavenly life . . .

When a number of respected women attained the Master's presence that afternoon, He told this story about Mary Magdalene:[1010]

> Through her faith and service to the Cause of Jesus Christ, she has become the pride of all men, and her fame is celebrated throughout the world. What queens and princesses once lived whose names have been lost to history! How many the sons and daughters of the world's rulers and dignitaries who have vanished without a trace! Yet Mary Magdalene, a woman from a village though she was, achieved nonetheless this kind of immortal life. Thus, imperishable glory and perpetual existence consist in the renouncement of

* As mentioned in a previous note, this may be a paraphrase of Matthew 8:11–12, 'And I say unto you, that many shall come from the east and west, and shall sit down with Abraham, and Isaac, and Jacob, in the kingdom of heaven. But the children of the kingdom shall be cast out into outer darkness: there shall be weeping and gnashing of teeth,' or Luke 13:29: 'And they shall come from the east, and from the west, and from the north, and from the south, and shall sit down in the kingdom of God.'

selfish concerns and service to the divine threshold. I hope that you shall attain to such a station as this – that you will arise to spread the sweet savours of God and teach His Cause. My hope is that you will promote the single foundation underlying all the divine religions, and promulgate the oneness of the races and nations. May you pitch the tabernacle of universal peace and the unity of all humanity, that thereby you may be exalted in both this world and in the world to come.

Afterwards, the Master went to visit Rúḥá Khánum,[1011] and from there He paid visits to some of the grandees of the East.[1012]

His lunch and dinner that day were prepared by ibn-i-Adíb at the home of Mírzá 'Abdu'l-Karím,[1013] and these meals were brought to the hotel, but in keeping with the Master's instruction, and according to a prior arrangement, the members of His retinue and His esteemed guests had their food in the dining hall of the hotel.

Wednesday, 4 June 1913
[Paris]

In the morning, the Master spoke of subjects pertaining to the Tarbíyat school. Eventually, He said:

In order to do good things, one must have good intentions. So long as good intentions, which are even as a firmly planted root, are not present, the tree of action will bear no blessing, neither will it yield any goodly fruit. The most vital foundation needed for the world of humanity to produce good results is good intent, inasmuch as it prohibits all duplicity and hypocrisy. How often does a person perform a good deed while his intent is impure, striving for fame or glory, or seeking to vaunt himself with pride, or deceptively cherishing the goal of leadership! Deeds of this sort do not have lasting results, and will be of no benefit to the common weal; they will never illumine the world of humanity, nor will they ever grant eternal peace and prosperity, firm though their foundation may appear to be.

If, however, those deeds are conjoined with good intentions, they will vivify humankind. Such deeds will turn this nether world into a reflection of the celestial Kingdom, and transform the earth into the mirror-image of the all-highest Paradise. Should you observe correctly, you would know of a certainty that these genuine hopes, these pure intentions, stem from the power of the Word of God and the influence of His religion. You would, moreover, rest assured that sincere love, heartfelt devotion, and service to humanity are manifested in people through spirituality, faith, and the knowledge of God, for it is the spiritual force of godliness which governs the hearts and souls. It is the love of God and also the fear of Him which pervade the veins of the people and permeate their nerves, and protect their inner faculties and preserve their inmost selves. Through this holy power, the children of humanity will come to serve and love one another, and the basis of the world's order – the foundation on which the welfare of all its peoples will rest – shall be strengthened and fortified.

In the *Tablet of the World*, Bahá'u'lláh states: 'The system of government which the British people have adopted in London appeareth to be good . . . while that which guardeth and restraineth man both outwardly and inwardly hath been and still is the fear of God.'*

When a group of believers attained the Master's presence, He gave a talk on divine happiness and spiritual gladness:[1014]

This happiness is perpetual and results in heartfelt gladness throughout all the realms of God. When a person rejoices at the outpourings of heavenly grace, he will not be saddened under any circumstance, even if the changes and chances of this world should be contrary to his wishes, and earthly vicissitudes fail to further his hopes and dreams. Rather, such will be his trust and reliance in the Will of God that, in spite of all the effort he may devote to his endeavours, he will have no other desire but for what shall ultimately come to pass, nor any wish save for what will eventually

* Bahá'u'lláh, *Tablets of Bahá'u'lláh Revealed after the Kitáb-i-Aqdas*, p. 93.

unfold. In such a state as this, he will consider every affair to be in perfect alignment with his own volition and desire, and account it a promoter of his own glory and welfare. He will feel no agitation, only assurance, and no quarrel or cruelty will he seek, only peace and tranquillity. Such happiness is perpetual, and such a station yields eternal life. This is the station I desire for you. Through this station, success and prosperity are achieved, but not the sort of happiness that is subject to change. Happiness that comes from material matters will inevitably be altered, for a person is healthy one day and sick the next; at one moment he is rich, and at another he is needy; at one time he lives in comfort, and at another he is afflicted with toil. His mind is never at ease, and at every moment his spirit is agitated by some vexation or another. Yet if his heart is turned towards the Kingdom of God, and if he is gladdened by the divine outpourings vouchsafed from the Most Exalted Horizon, he will be freed from every sadness. He will set his affections on the realm of God, becoming a consoler to the world of humanity and a promulgator of heavenly signs and mysteries.

In the afternoon, the Master went to the homes of certain páshás to bid them farewell, and He made extensive remarks at each of these places.[1015]

He passed through a few streets as He was returning, and as soon as some children saw Him from afar, they came running towards Him. In such cases as this, He would always give each of the children some money and say:[1016]

The children are my friends. I love them very much.

He spoke to those children most tenderly.

On the way back, the Master told this story:

Yesterday, I went to a fruit stand and noticed that people were looking at my clothing and overall appearance. They expressed their surprise, and some of them grinned. It so happened that a portrait of Jesus Christ – dressed in a long, flowing garment – had been put up on the wall. I called their attention to that image and said, 'Look! This clothing of mine is like the clothing of Christ; there is no difference between them.' They were deeply humbled and showed great respect.

Thursday, 5 June 1913
[Paris]

A report on the national Bahá'í convention, which was being held in New York, was presented to the Master that morning. This cheered His heart immensely; copies of both the original text and its translation [into Persian] were sent to the grandees of the East, and one copy was mailed to Tehran.[1017]

When some believers attained His presence, the Master exhorted them to render services, and also encouraged them to arise and fulfil the requirements of servitude and righteousness.

The public gathering was convened sometime thereafter, and the Master gave a talk on inborn disposition and spiritual education:

> This is the most important of the acquired perfections, inasmuch as acquired knowledge and material education aid one's inborn disposition, and serve as an instrument through which one's aims are furthered and one's innermost hopes are realized. Should material sciences be coupled with good intentions and a virtuous character, this would be light upon light. The world of the spirit would be illumined; one's life, one's very being, would mirror forth a divine likeness, and resemble the reflections of the realm above.
>
> Conversely, if a person is deprived of a heavenly character and bereft of spiritual education, his worldly knowledge will become an instrument for oppression, and his material education both a vehicle and a pretext for encroachment and aggression. In every domain, he would inflict some injury or other, and be the cause of harm and toil. In the realm of politics, he would gleefully prepare the means for war and destroy the foundation of welfare. In the realm of religion, he would promote his perverse opinions and idle imitations, and provoke enmity and dissension in the midst of

humankind, for in every age whenever the common people have placed their trust in their leaders and divines, they have consequently arisen to reject and persecute the Manifestation of God and His chosen ones. They have deemed the behaviour of every celebrated one to be the standard, and believed that blind imitation of every learned one will secure the good-pleasure of God. They have even accounted the clothing donned by the men of knowledge as a sign of piety, construing their outward forms to be indicative of their righteous characters, and allowing themselves to become the cause of corruption and sedition.

This is why the Blessed Beauty stated that not every cap is necessarily a mark of ignorance, nor is every turban a sign of knowledge. How many have worn the layman's cap and hoisted the standard of knowledge, and how numerous are the beturbaned who have abolished the laws of religion! If the merit of humanity consists in the turban, then the camel that is made to carry the equivalent of a thousand turbans should be considered more learned than the greatest of scholars![1018]

Strive always, therefore, to be the means through which people's characters are improved, and a channel whereby spiritual perfections are acquired and promoted.

The Master concluded with an account of the virtuous characters of the Bahá'í men and women of Persia. He then departed, and once His visitors had been dismissed, a telegram from the Master was sent to America stating that any future correspondence with Him should be mailed to Port Said.

In the afternoon, after some of the friends had come to see Him, the Master paid a visit to Rúḥá Khánum.

He had dinner at the home of Mr and Mrs Dreyfus-Barney that evening. All His attendants were likewise invited to that joyous occasion,[1019] and they expressed their gratitude for the blessed bounties and favours that had been granted them.[1020]

Friday, 6 June 1913
[Paris]

After leaving His room that morning and having a seat in the reception room, the Master told a story from His days in Baghdad which demonstrated the power of Bahá'u'lláh and His exaltation of the Word of God. He spoke of Kayván Mírzá in this way:[1021]

> He wished to attain the presence of Bahá'u'lláh at midnight, through the intermediation of Mírzá Muḥíṭ* and in the utmost secrecy. Since this request had been made out of amusement, and not spiritual insight or religious conviction, Bahá'u'lláh replied:
>
>> During My retirement in Kurdistan, I composed an ode that included these two verses: 'If thine aim be to cherish thy life, approach not our court; but if sacrifice be thy heart's desire, come and let others come with thee. For such is the way of Faith, if in thy heart thou seekest reunion with Bahá; shouldst thou refuse to tread this path, why trouble us? Begone!' Should he be willing to meet these conditions, very good! Otherwise, he should abandon the idea altogether.

Mírzá Muḥíṭ conveyed these blessed utterances to him word for word, and he was so overcome with fear that he did not dare attain the presence of Bahá'u'lláh. Before long, word was received that, owing to a severe bout of typhus, he had bidden farewell to this world and gone to the realm beyond.

From the earliest days of the Cause, all were astonished at the independence and self-sufficiency of the Blessed Beauty, and His endeavours to refine people's characters by rendering them sanctified and detached set every mind at ease, whether near or far. Day after day, the blessed verses and teachings humbled every neck, and the light of the Sun of Truth illumined the skies. Eventually, the banner of the Cause of God was raised up, and it became undoubtedly clear to the governments of the world that this group

---

* Mírzá Muḥíṭ Kirmání.

has no intention or purpose but the peace and well-being of all humanity, that they have no desire to meddle in political affairs or involve themselves in acts of corruption, and that they would sooner give up their own lives than take the life of another. How unfair are those people who shut their eyes to these perspicuous signs and rebuff this gracious bounty!

By God, besides Whom there is none other God! Were it not for the striving of the Abhá Beauty and the shrill voice of the Supreme Pen, naught would be left of the Revelation of the Primal Point but the chaos and confusion fomented by the followers of Mírzá Yaḥyá. The jumbled mixtures of erroneous locutions strung together by that utter fool, as well as his unseemly actions and those of his ilk, brought matters to such a pass that the people would ascribe every hideous and seditious thing to the very root of the Cause, and every conceivable excuse to oppose it had fallen into the hands of its enemies. How, then, could the common people have possibly known that the root of this Cause is sanctified from the defilements of them that are sullied with self and passion? Every trace of security had vanished. All the people were certain that the Bábís were hostile to their substance, their reputations, and their very lives. With regard to the attempt on the life of Náṣiri'd-Dín Sháh in Tehran, I recall that a cleric could be found shouting these words on every street: 'O people! If you love God and revere His Prophet* – if you seek to protect your lives, safeguard your possessions, and preserve your honour – then kill the Bábís! These people are the enemies of divine religion, the opposers of God's creed,' and so on and so forth. These incidents and occurrences would never have come to pass had it not been for the lustful appetites of Mírzá Yaḥyá, Siyyid Muḥammad Iṣfahání, and Mullá Ja'far Naráqí,[1022] who blackened the annals of those days and smirched the hem of that most pure garment, the Cause of God itself.

Behold the might with which the Blessed Beauty arose, and observe how He aided and protected the Cause of God – that in spite of those who have deemed this Cause contrary to their

* Muhammad.

religious law, and others who have refused to accept the truth of Bahá'u'lláh's claim, they have testified nonetheless to the power and greatness of this religion, and have borne witness to the sanctity and purity of the Bahá'ís, insofar as they are renowned all over the world for their lack of involvement in sedition and corruption. The Azalís, on the other hand, are present in every wicked affair; the iniquity of their desires and deeds can still be witnessed to this day, both within Persia and without, and their meddling and mischief are clear and apparent to every political office of that country. But praised be God, the people of Bahá have distanced themselves from these acts of corruption; they have set their faces towards the Kingdom of Light, and cleaved tenaciously to the counsels of Bahá'u'lláh, Who has declared that they 'will refuse, though they be dying of hunger, to stretch their hands and seize unlawfully the property of their neighbour, however vile and worthless he may be',* and likewise stated: 'Know ye that to be killed in the path of His good pleasure is better for you than to kill,'† and furthermore: 'O ye the loved ones and the trustees of God! Kings are the manifestations of the power, and the daysprings of the might and riches, of God. Pray ye on their behalf. He hath invested them with the rulership of the earth and hath singled out the hearts of men as His Own domain. Conflict and contention are categorically forbidden in His Book. This is a decree of God in this Most Great Revelation. It is divinely preserved from annulment and is invested by Him with the splendour of His confirmation. Verily He is the All-Knowing, the All-Wise.'‡

Such were the remarks which the Master made repeatedly and extensively until it was time to hold the public gathering, where He spoke of intentions and the purity of one's disposition, both of which are needed to further one's affairs and attract the confirmations of God. His talk gladdened every heart in attendance, and at

* Bahá'u'lláh, *Gleanings*, CXXXVII.

† Bahá'u'lláh, *Summons*, p. 110.

‡ Bahá'u'lláh, *Tablets of Bahá'u'lláh Revealed after the Kitáb-i-Aqdas*, pp. 220–21.

the end of that gathering, one of the attendees who was clearly enamoured of Him asked about the state of those who perform good deeds and possess a commendable character, but do not believe [in the Cause]. He replied:

> As this dispensation is one of grace, those who perform goodly deeds and possess a righteous character will not be deprived of divine mercy, even if they do not believe. There are, however, degrees to one's deeds and virtues. There is the sort of deed that redounds only to the benefit of the doer himself. There is another sort of deed that redounds to the benefit of a person's family, or to his people or tribe. Yet there is still another sort of deed that redounds to the benefit of all the peoples of the earth – a sort of deed whose results are without limit, and whose effects will last for as long as the world of being will endure. To have succeeded in performing deeds of this sort is to have attained the consummation of human existence – a consummation that is achieved through adherence to the divine teachings and the aid of spiritual power. It is for this reason that, in the divine religions, the acceptance of one's deeds is conditioned on the recognition of Him Who is the Day-spring of the Cause of God, and it is why knowledge and recognition [of the Manifestation] have been made contingent on one's fulfilment of the counsels imparted by Him Who is the Beneficent King. If action is coupled with knowledge, and obedience is practised in tandem with spiritual understanding, the fruit of the world of existence will emerge into view, and the mystery of the bounty bestowed by the Loving Lord on the visible realm will be unravelled.

That night, the Master was invited to the home of Aḥmad 'Izzat Páshá, where a few respected persons from the East attained imperishable honour and derived eternal happiness by being in His radiant presence.[1023] Most of the remarks He made in the gathering at that residence dealt with the fruits of faith and spiritual understanding, and He also told stories of the calamities and hardships which the Manifestations of God always endure when they first declare their Mission and lay the foundation of true religion.

Saturday, 7 June 1913
[Paris]

As He was having His tea that morning, the Master mentioned the services and the devotion of some of the servants at the divine threshold.[1024] He concluded His remarks by recounting episodes from the lives of a few companions from the earliest days of the Cause, which included the sincerity and purity of Shaykh Salmán, the courier of the divine verses,[1025] as well as an account of the steadfastness and spiritual understanding of 'Alavíyyih Khánum, the wife of the martyred Mullá 'Alí Ján,[1026] and also Rawḥání Bushrúyi'í.[1027] He stated that, in this most great dispensation, these women were the pride of all men, and observed that their true rank is not known at present.[1028]

The Master then spoke of the previous night's gathering at the home of Aḥmad 'Izzat Páshá and mentioned what a good time He had had there.

The believers then attained His presence, and their meeting concluded with an exchange of questions and answers. Among the Master's remarks were these, which He made in response to a query about the tree that bore the fruit Adam ate, for which He was expelled from the Garden of Eden:

> What is meant is the tree of human life. A person will be held accountable for his unlawful acts – that is, his transgressions and the desires that drove him to commit them – and he will be deprived of the bounties of spiritual paradise as a result. This can only be avoided if he treads the path of moderation, walks in the way of the divine teachings, and takes care not to exceed his limits or transgress his own station, for in this contingent realm, the life and salvation of every thing consist in moderation and timely action, while its death and perdition lie in the transgression of the bounds of moderation and the doing of deeds which are ill-timed. When any praiseworthy thing, such as a valuable remark or a useful deed, exceeds the bounds of moderation and timeliness, it becomes hideous and harmful. Bahá'u'lláh has stated: 'In all matters

moderation is desirable. If a thing is carried to excess, it will prove a source of evil. Consider the civilization of the West, how it hath agitated and alarmed the peoples of the world. An infernal engine hath been devised, and hath proved so cruel a weapon of destruction that its like none hath ever witnessed or heard."*

A question was then asked about predestination and free will. The Master replied:

In matters that pertain to the improvement of one's qualities and the moderation of one's character, or such things as will elevate one to lofty and exalted stations, people have free will. It is for this reason that when one's inborn capacities and divinely ordained gifts reach their consummation through proper training, the thorny thicket of ignorance and cruelty is changed into the rose-garden of knowledge and purity, and the gloomy edifice of enmity and hatred is turned into the illumined temple of love and faithfulness. But where universal affairs and divine law are concerned, one is unable to interfere and has no choice in the matter. For example, one cannot say, 'Why have I grown old?' Similarly, it is not within one's power to remain alive forever and never die. One is certainly constrained in such matters as these. A person is free, however, when it comes to the development of human virtues and the acquisition of spiritual perfections, and he is capable of changing his behaviour, consenting to be educated, and obtaining knowledge. It is the divine teachings and ordinances, moreover, which constitute the greatest foundation for the education of humankind on this earthly plane. Should you wish to train someone with a view to improving their character, you would need to toil for years and endure a myriad unpleasant trials – and even so, what would happen in the end? To what extent would your training have an effect on him? How long would that effect last, and what results would it yield? But when that person enters beneath the shade of divine religion, no sooner will he profess his belief than he will be entirely transformed, and come to love all

* Bahá'u'lláh, *Tablets of Bahá'u'lláh Revealed after the Kitáb-i-Aqdas*, p. 69.

> humanity from the bottom of his heart. His conduct and manners will continually improve, and he will become a new creation altogether, for the demeanour and the deeds of a devout commoner are more effective in establishing order in the world – as well as peace and tranquillity among its peoples – than the actions of a scholar who is irreligious. This is especially true of those cases in which neither the rule of law nor the force of punishment exert their pervasive and prohibitive influence, and thoughts of honour, fear, and fame are not considered. Only then will the value of the station of divine education, and also the influence and fruit of the spiritual teachings, become known.

On that afternoon,[1029] too, the Master's reception of His visitors was a sign of the power of God's covenant and an indication of the all-encompassing nature of the divine Word. The first to attain His presence after He had seated Himself in the reception room[1030] was one of the princes of Persia.[1031] Although he showed heartfelt humility and genuine deference before the Master, this prince still displayed a pompous attitude that stemmed from his youthful age. Almost immediately thereafter, Aḥmad 'Izzat Pá<u>sh</u>á – formerly a man of high rank in the government of [Sulṭán] 'Abdu'l-Ḥamíd – entered the presence of the Master with the utmost courtesy and reverence, and began to express His sincere devotion to Him.[1032] There were also respected men and women from England, America, and France, who entered the room and attained the Master's presence with great attraction and humility; one of them kissed His hand, another took hold of the hem of His garment. They were visibly honoured to have had the privilege of meeting with the Master; they implored Him to crown their services with success, and He, in turn, unloosed His tongue to confirm their efforts to exalt the Word of God. When the esteemed prince mentioned above saw the excitement and ecstasy of those people – as well as the humility and deference that such illustrious individuals were showing in the Master's presence – he was rendered speechless. At the end of that gathering, he expressed his astonishment at the influence of the Word of God and the grandeur of His Cause, saying:

> What greater honour could there be for the people of the East, especially those of us from Persia, than for us to behold the highly respected persons of both the East and the West humbling themselves to such a degree before this Cause, and to see the Westerners prostrating themselves in the presence of so glorious an Eastern Personage?

The Master and some of His attendants[1033] were invited to the home of [——][1034] that night. Both before and after having dinner, He gave a talk that dealt with the circumstances attending the advents of the Manifestations of God, the detriments of the blind imitations and prejudices propagated by leaders of religion, and the wrongs which the Manifestations and their chosen ones were made to suffer. The remarks of the Master made so profound an impression that the heart of the esteemed host of that gathering had been moved to exceeding tenderness, with tears streaming down his face.

Sunday, 8 June 1913
[Paris]

When the believers and other friends learned that morning that the Master would soon be leaving Paris, they expressed great sorrow and regret. To console and counsel them, He spoke these blessed words:[1035]

He is God

> There exists between us a spiritual bond and closeness that will never be followed by remoteness and separation. Praised be God, the light of guidance is shining brightly, and the Sun of Truth is shedding its splendour. The morn of grace is radiant, and the star of bounty is resplendently brilliant. Hidden though we may appear to outward seeming, yet in the realm of the heart and soul we are clearly manifest. However distant the body may be, the spirit remains ever intimate with the bounty of meeting, and the hearts are always close and connected to one another. A pure heart is like

a mirror; however far away from the sun the mirror may be, it will still reflect the radiant splendours and mysterious effulgences more than any other thing. It is, therefore, not physical proximity which is a prerequisite, but the receptivity and purity of the heart.

I hope that we will be together in all the realms of God – that we will gather in worlds that are sanctified from time and space. It is certainly the case that we have been and are still together throughout every realm; now, too, in the world of humanity – which is the culmination of the kingdoms of the mineral, the vegetable, and the animal – we enjoy intimate closeness with one another. This world, however, is dark, but the bounty and immensity of the world of God are without limit.

Show love to all the people of Paris. It is my hope that you shall act in a way that will spread the sweet savours of God, and promote His holiness and love. Praised be God, the greatest of ties have been formed among the hearts, and these are none other than the love of God and the oneness of humanity. In the Bahá'í Cause, this bond, this most significant of blessings, has no end and knows no severance. Thus, I shall never forget you. It is this most great bounty which has instilled such fellowship as this among our hearts; it is love which has brought us together and united us. How dark and narrow is the heart bereft of the love of God! Dead are the body and soul deprived of the grace of the Holy Spirit!

Give thanks to God, then, that you all feel the utmost love and fellowship towards one another – that in such a city as this, where all are immersed in self and passion, your faces are set towards the Kingdom of Holiness. It is due to the influence of God's Word that our hearts enjoy this degree of connection and amity. Otherwise, consider us, a group of Persians, and you, who come from Paris, England, and America, and reflect: What could we possibly have in common with one another? Praised be God, for the pervasiveness of His Word and the influence of His Cause have so united and harmonized us that we are now even as one spirit and one soul.

My hope is that, just as we enjoy this intimacy and fellowship with one another in this nether world, we may likewise be together in the realm of the Kingdom. Outwardly, it will seem that I am leaving Paris, but my heart and soul are with you. God grant that after my departure, your intimacy and fellowship may wax greater – that with every passing day, you may grow increasingly radiant.

Once He had made these remarks, He stated the following in response to a comment from one of those present regarding orphans:[1036]

God is the sustainer and the protector of the orphans. How many are the children of the wealthy who went on to wander this world as lost souls, and how numerous are the orphans and children of the poor who have attained to lofty stations! Were it not for the protection and assistance of God, the orphans should always be trampled underfoot, and only the children of the wealthy should remain. Thus, divine support and protection are extended to all humankind. Whoever strives harder to acquire the perfections of the world of humanity and demonstrates the more virtuous character will be nearer to the threshold of God and make the greater degree of progress.

When a group of believers attained His presence that afternoon, the Master instructed them, repeatedly and emphatically, to recite the Writings of the Abhá Beauty and observe His admonitions:

You must act on the divine counsels, inasmuch as they are the remedy for every ailment. Make use of this cure. Be mindful of God. Have discussions on spiritual subjects. Do not immerse yourselves in material things. The purpose of faith is to refine the souls, and the fruit of spiritual knowledge is the purification of the hearts. The Cause of God is founded on love and the oneness of humanity, and it is the means through which the corrupt aspects of one's character, and the harmful manifestations of the world of nature, will dwindle away into nothingness. Through the power of faith, a person can be saved from these harmful forces, and promote love and fellowship among the hearts. He can spread the signs of oneness and unity, promulgate the brotherhood of all

> people, and become a servant to the human race. Therefore, you must show the utmost truthfulness and sincerity to all people, and invoke the names of the Founders of every religion with honour and reverence. Focus on the basis of the divine religions, which represents a single truth, as well as the principles propounded by the Daysprings of God, which are one and the same – not the secondary teachings that were given according to the exigencies of the time, or the blind imitations which have caused dissension and discord among humankind – that you may raise up the banner of tranquillity and become the signs of the Greatest Name amidst the peoples of the earth.

Since there were believers who had travelled from England,[1037] the Master spoke most fondly of the Bahá'ís of London.[1038]

Monday, 9 June 1913
[Paris]

That morning, the Master spoke to His servants once again about the severe hardships of the days in Persia, as well as the imprisonment and suffering which Bahá'u'lláh endured. He related these episodes with a rueful sorrow that would have melted a heart of stone, and moved anyone with a hearing ear to wail with sadness. Tears rained down from the eyes of His attendants, and as they listened to the adversities which the Blessed Beauty was made to suffer, their hearts seemed to cry out with grief. We were, however, solaced to our very cores when we saw that radiant face [of the Master], witnessed the assistance from the Kingdom of the Covenant, and beheld those promised confirmations descending from the horizon of grace and bounty.

When a group of believers and seekers attained the Master's presence, He gave a talk on confirming and encouraging the Bahá'ís to exalt the Word of God:

> When you turn towards the Abhá Kingdom and arise to serve the Cause of God, you will be granted a fresh confirmation day after

> day, and graciously aided to conquer the cities of people's hearts. Because the [Bahá'í] men and women of Persia had set their faces toward the Most Glorious Kingdom, they remained as firm in the Cause as an immovable mountain, and became the bearers of the signs of God. Similarly, there are people in America who have been raised up with the utmost firmness. My hope is that you, too, may remain firm and steadfast, and serve as channels through which the divine fragrances are spread . . .

When that gathering was concluded, the Master sent some of His attendants to visit certain grandees from the East,[1039] and in the afternoon He had them go to the gathering of Bahá'ís at the home of Mr and Mrs Scott. He Himself went to the residence of Munír Pá<u>sh</u>á, where He spoke on the advancements of this age; the renewal of industries, laws, and sciences; and the need for the religion of God to be renewed.[1040]

Well into the night, the Master answered the questions of Mr and Mrs Richard,[1041] and discussed topics pertaining to the Sufis, including their aims and aspirations. The Richards were immensely pleased and satisfied with His explanations.

Tuesday, 10 June 1913
[Paris]

That morning, the Master instructed us to prepare for our departure from Paris and return to the East, as we would be setting off in just two days. Accordingly, His address to all the believers and seekers dealt with steadfastness and firmness in the Cause of God, arising to spread His fragrances, and rendering service to His Kingdom. He observed that these confirmations are obtained through detachment and sanctification from the forces of self and passion. Among the remarks He made that day, which caused one of His compatriots to fall in love with His valuable aphorisms, was the following:

> Paris is, in every sense, a symbol of the world of nature.

Here is another one of those pithy statements:

> The denizens of the Most Glorious Kingdom bestow life; they do not take it.

When His listeners heard these concise and useful remarks, they would say time and again:

> Not everyone is capable of speaking in this way, let alone with a majesty and potency that attracts people's hearts and conduces to the advancement of their minds.

In the afternoon,[1042] a group of travelling Persian Jews attained the Master's presence.[1043] They first implored Him to aid and confirm the guards who kept watch over the roads to Tehran and Qazvin,[1044] and then asked Him to recommend a course of action on certain matters between the Jews of that place[1045] and the believers of Jewish background residing in Tehran and Hamadan.[1046] The Master acceded to their first request, but did not comment on the second matter, referring them to a Bahá'í Assembly instead.

That night, a number of believers had the honour of visiting the Master, Who spoke on teaching the Cause of God, and also on love and fellowship with all the peoples of the world.[1047] Among His remarks were the following:

> In every age, the act of arising to teach the Cause of God and exalt His Word has enabled humanity to achieve eternal life. Through this service, such lowly people as Simon* and Peter have reached the pinnacle of imperishable glory. Though no one paid them any mind at first, in the end the kings and rulers of the earth humbled themselves at the very mention of their names. Thus, the thing that attracts the confirmations of God is the act of teaching and exalting His Word. We must all spread the divine fragrances and consort with all the peoples and kindreds of the earth in a spirit of utmost love and unity, inasmuch as the Blessed Beauty has stated:

* Presumably Simon the Zealot, one of the Twelve Apostles of Jesus Christ.

'O people of Bahá! Ye are the dawning-places of the love of God and the daysprings of His loving-kindness. Defile not your tongues with the cursing and reviling of any soul, and guard your eyes against that which is not seemly. Consort with all men in a spirit of friendliness and fellowship.* Set forth that which ye possess. If it be favourably received, your end is attained; if not, to protest is vain. Leave that soul to himself and turn unto the Lord, the Protector, the Self-Subsisting. Be not the cause of grief, much less of discord and strife.'†

Wednesday, 11 June 1913
[Paris]

The first person to attain the Master's presence that morning was the respected woman who served as the president of the Theosophical Society. Following this, a crowd of people, believers and others, were acquainted with the mysteries of God's religion as a result of hearing the Master's utterance, and they expressed the utmost pride and joy as they listened.

In response to the aforementioned woman, the Master began His addresses that day with a talk in which He spoke of the oneness of God and the wholly sanctified nature of His Essence, and gave accounts of the lives of the Manifestations of His Names and Attributes. He then discussed the signs and prophecies of the advent of the Promised One.

Sometime thereafter, a few Persian Jews attained the Master's presence.[1048] Although He was about to leave, He sat with them awhile nonetheless, strictly for their sake and despite His lack of time. In response to a question one of them had asked, the Master interpreted his dream and what it augured for him, and the inquirer expressed his satisfaction and happiness with His explanation. The Master then said:

---

* Although this sentence appears in Zarqání's chronicle, it does not actually occur in the Tablet of Bahá'u'lláh quoted here; it belongs to a different Tablet partially translated in *Gleanings*, CXXXII.

† Bahá'u'lláh, *Tablets of Bahá'u'lláh Revealed after the Kitáb-i-Aqdas*, p. 129.

> This is my last day; I am about to leave and prepare for my departure. In addition to this, I must pay visits to certain respected individuals. Hence, I cannot devote any more time than this to answering your questions. Come back tonight, if you wish.

With that, He took His leave.

That afternoon, [——][1049] and a number of respected Persians were roused to exceeding gladness and ecstasy after attaining the Master's presence. Until sunset, several illustrious individuals, the majority of them Persian, had the immense bounty of meeting with Him. He mostly imparted extensive counsels and admonitions that He had previously given early on – even before the [Constitutional] revolution – to the government and people of Persia. Among them were these most sweet utterances:

> Until the government [of Persia] and its people become commingled, even as milk and honey, their success and prosperity will remain entirely unattainable. Persia shall fall into ruin, and the governments of its neighbouring realms will ultimately meddle in its affairs. Then strive, O loved ones of God, to foster perfect harmony [between the government and the people], and should you find yourselves unable to achieve this, then withdraw from the matter entirely. Beware, beware, lest you involve yourselves in shedding the blood of a single Persian. Though others have failed to heed these words, praised be God, for the Bahá'ís have carried out their duties; they have not, in the least, been a party to corruption, nor have they interfered in matters of politics.

It was asked, 'If some of the Bahá'ís are employed at governmental offices, what should they do?' The Master replied:

> The responsibility of religion is one thing, while the responsibilities entailed by one's obligation to and membership in that office is another. A high officer or soldier must certainly perform his duty, and act with the utmost truthfulness and obedience towards his government. The people of Bahá are charged with obedience to the

> government of the country in which they reside. Had the people of Persia been apprised of this fact, and had they appreciated the value of these divine teachings, they would have been freed from every calamity. Among the statements which Bahá’u’lláh made in several of His Tablets are the following: ‘Certain laws and principles are necessary and indispensable for Persia. However, it is fitting that these measures should be adopted in conformity with the considered views of . . . the learned divines and of the high-ranking rulers.’*

The Master then spoke with some of the Parisian believers about certain material phenomena – such as complementary colours, the purity inherent in cleanliness, consummate exquisiteness, and even ordinary sounds and melodies – observing that, although these are physical phenomena, in reality they exert an influence on the spirit.

The Master concluded by bidding farewell to the believers with these words:

> I was in your midst for some time. I have felt and still feel the utmost love towards you. My heart constantly swelled with your love. I have lit the candle of God’s love in the niche of your hearts, and expounded the divine admonitions for you. My hope is such that you may strive so that, with every passing day, the light of God will make you ever more luminous, and the splendours of the Most Glorious Kingdom will shine with increasing resplendence. Rest not at all as you guide the people aright. Revive these dead ones! Alert the uninformed! Enkindle the despondent and dispirited with the fire of the love of God! I will ever be waiting to hear good news from you.

The hearts of the friends were moved to exceeding tenderness as they listened to these blessed utterances. They promised to serve the Cause of God, and implored to be confirmed in their thraldom to the divine threshold.

* Bahá’u’lláh, *Tablets of Bahá’u’lláh Revealed after the Kitáb-i-Aqdas*, p. 92.

Thursday, 12 June 1913
[Paris → Marseilles]

Early in the morning, after prayers and meditations, the Master instructed us to gather our belongings and depart. At eight o'clock that morning,[1050] we left the hotel and went to the train station [the Gare de Lyon]. All the believers had gathered there ahead of time and were waiting for the Master to arrive.[1051] Once He had embarked the train, they all gazed upon that beautiful face of His with the utmost sorrow and regret as they stood before the car in which He was riding. They approached the car, one by one, to express their despondency and implore His aid and bounty. He, in turn, assured each and every one of them that they would be confirmed, and exhorted those eager souls, with these words, to spread the teachings of Bahá'u'lláh:

> Do not be silent! Be gracious to others! Always be united even as a single assemblage! Make mention of God at your gatherings, and exert yourselves as you endeavour to spread His signs. I am always thinking of you, and am ever supplicating that you be granted invisible confirmations.

At nine o'clock,[1052] the Master's train departed for Marseilles. The verdant meadows and trees we saw on the way, along with the scenic hills and rivers, made for a truly majestic sight, and the mountain slopes on either side of the tracks were covered with flowers. As the Master looked out at all this natural beauty, He said:

> The environs of Paris are most pleasant to behold.

Once He had mentioned some of the friends who had been disloyal, the Master had His lunch in the train car and then rested for a bit.

After having His tea that afternoon, the Master was reading letters from the believers when a number of French people requested permission to attain His presence. They were humbled and filled with gladness as they listened to Him speak on spiritual subjects, the need for religious belief, the oneness of humanity, and universal peace.[1053]

At twelve o'clock midnight,[1054] the Master's train arrived at Marseilles, and He lodged at a hotel adjoining the station.[1055]

Friday, 13 June 1913

[Marseilles → En route to Port Said, on board the *Himalaya*]

The Master was slightly ill in the morning, but once He boarded the ship, His health continually improved and His heart increasingly rejoiced with every passing hour – no, every minute!

At nine o'clock that morning,[1056] He embarked the *Himalaya*, which was owned by the P&O Company.[1057] He looked at a few of the first-class rooms and eventually chose a private cabin for Himself (no. 250) that was on the upper deck and had spacious surroundings.[1058]

The Master then went to examine the second-class cabins, where the members of His retinue were staying.[1059]

Four attendants accompanied the Master on that journey from Paris to Port Said: Mírzá 'Alí-Akbar Nakhjavání, Mirza Ahmad Sohrab, Siyyid Asadu'lláh Qumí, and this lowly servant.

Once the Master had seated Himself on a bench, two French travellers attained His presence.[1060] They said:[1061]

> Following Your departure, the believers of France sent us to convey their sentiments of servitude to You, and to implore Your assistance and bounty on behalf of the friends, in particular Mr and Mrs Richard.

The Master extended His loving-kindness to those travellers, spoke fondly of the friends of Paris, and counselled them to remain firm and steadfast in the Cause of God. When it was almost time to set sail, those visitors were dismissed, and they disembarked the ship shortly thereafter.

Once the voyage had begun, the Master read a telegram[1062]

from Mr and Mrs Dreyfus-Barney, who had written to inquire after His health and bid Him farewell.[1063] He prayed for them and the other friends in Paris, and expressed His happiness with the services they had rendered.

Afterwards, the Master instructed the members of His retinue to teach the Cause to the passengers on the ship, remarking, 'We must get to work!'[1064] He Himself first began to converse amiably with an Indian man who was staying in a first-class cabin adjacent to His stateroom.[1065] He asked this gentleman how he was faring and inquired about his country. When the man told Him about the various groups and peoples of India, the Master discussed the need for a pervasive power, as well as an all-embracing and all-subduing Cause, that will draw all the peoples and kindreds of the earth to gather beneath the shade of a single Word:

> In this day, all the world, especially the peoples of the East, stand in need of such a pervasive power as this, that through it they may be freed and delivered into repose from the afflictions of dissension, strife, war, and murder.

He concluded His remarks with these words:

> Apart from the power of God and that of the spiritual teachings, no other power can accomplish this important task. The splendour of the spiritual teachings has always shone from the horizon of the East; the focal point of mystic power and divine religion has ever lain in Eastern lands, and the Sun of Truth has ever cast its rays from the Eastern sky upon the climes of the West.

The Indian gentleman was roused to blissful joy as he listened to the Master's words, and on every day thereafter, he rejoiced with exceeding gladness whenever he attained the Master's presence while on board the *Himalaya*.

As He was walking after having lunch and a bit of rest, the Master noticed the labourers on the ship and said:

> How poor are they, and how hard they toil! The presidents of factories and other operations must allocate a share [of the profits] for the workers in their companies, so that these poor souls may know some comfort. Perchance they may serve with all their heart and soul as a result and not go on strike.

An[other] Indian person then attained the presence of the Master, Who spoke to him extensively on the rising of the Sun of Truth over the horizon of the East, and also on the new and wondrous teachings. This person was immensely gladdened by the Master's words, and amply demonstrated his devotion to Him.

After having dinner that night, the Master's attendants went, with His permission, to sit on the benches outside His room and attain His presence in so doing. He commented on the pleasant sea, the gentle breeze, the exquisite weather, the radiant moonlight, the sound of the water, and the rising and falling of the ship, remarking, 'This is a good night.'

The Master was happy as could be, and His ardent lovers gave thanks and praise to God.

Voyage to Egypt

Saturday, 14 June 1913

[En route to Port Said, on board the *Himalaya*]

The Master's attendants were in His presence that morning, in front of His room on the first-class deck. They drank tea that He served with His own two hands, and they read Him telegrams that wirelessly conveyed news about the Ottomans.

Sometime thereafter, a person from India attained the presence of the Master, Who said:[1066]

> So long as the East fails to overcome these prejudices, it will never be saved.

Following this, He discussed the unification of the various peoples beneath the shade of a single Word through the power of Bahá'u'lláh, and then went to the lunch table.

In the afternoon, once He had had His tea, the Master went to the second-class deck and seated Himself on one of the benches in the upper part of that level. A few Indians who very much wished to see Him attained His presence, and were stirred to abundant vigilance as they listened to His most sweet and sublime utterances on the single set of principles underlying all the divine religions, as well as the kinds of dissension and other harmful effects that result from blind imitation and bigotry.[1067]

The Master then rose from His seat and went for a stroll on the second-class deck. Among the people with whom He discussed the Cause of God, and who rejoiced at having had the honour of meeting with Him, was a Jew who lived in Jerusalem. After this encounter, he asked the Master for permission to visit Him in His room, where he listened to Him speak extensively on the prophecies of the prophets, the gathering of the Jews in the Holy Land, and the glory and salvation of those learned ones whose names are mentioned in the Book of Life.[1068] He was so delighted by the

Master's words that he remarked:

> For some time now, I have heard about how famously glorious and perfect You are, and I have wanted to attain Your presence. I now give thanks to God that I have been honoured with such a blessing as this.

The Master had His dinner in the dining hall that night.

Afterwards, during the few minutes He was seated on the bench in front of His room, He remarked:

> The weather is good tonight, too, and the sea is calm. How pleasant it is! These waves look so radiant in the moonlight.

Sunday, 15 June 1913

[En route to Port Said, on board the *Himalaya*]

The English consul, Sir William Meyer, and his daughter [Cicely Meyer] attained the Master's presence as He was having His tea that morning.[1069] This gentleman presented the Master with a copy of an Eastern magazine that included a transcript of a talk He gave at a mosque in London, along with a photograph of that occasion, which He had permitted to be published.[1070] The Master discussed the history and teachings of this blessed religion, and the remarks He made in response to his questions moved him to sing the praises of this wondrous Cause.[1071]

In the afternoon, some of the Indians on board requested permission to attain the Master's presence, and He granted their request.[1072] His address to them dealt with the perfection and permanence of the spiritual realms, and the imperfection and corruption of the world of nature. He concluded His remarks by expounding on the prophecies concerning this Most Great Revelation and explaining the holy teachings:

> These teachings are what the world needs in this luminous age, for this is not an age of blind imitation; it is the age of light, and the

> century in which mysteries will be made manifest. It is the time for the oneness of the world of humanity, and the day wherein universal peace must be promoted.

Such were the extensive remarks which the Master made, and through them His listeners reached the height of their devotion, their attraction, and their delight.

Another Englishman and his French wife attained the Master's presence that night. When they told Him about the death of their dear child, the Master spoke of the ephemerality of material things and the immortality of spiritual excellences, and encouraged them to acquire heavenly perfections. He did all this in a way that turned their grief into joy; their anguish and sadness had vanished altogether, and their sorrowful hearts had been consoled to the utmost.

After them, a few of the other passengers on board were intoxicated with the wine of inner meaning as they listened to the Master's words. When the first dinner bell was eventually rung, these visitors were dismissed from His presence, with songs of praise and gratitude on their lips as they left.

Once He had had His dinner, the Master took a seat in the moonlight, and His attendants described for Him the attraction and happiness that some of the passengers had shown, remarking, 'They were most ecstatic and deeply honoured to have had the privilege of attaining Your presence.' He replied:

> Efforts must be made to sow seeds in the soil of people's hearts, that perchance the hyacinths of love and knowledge may grow therefrom, and the flowers of fellowship and oneness may transform the realm of human souls into the likeness of Paradise itself. It is for this reason that, in spite of my weariness, which leaves me entirely bereft of the strength to speak, I converse nonetheless with the utmost happiness and strive to spread the sweet savours of God.

Monday, 16 June 1913

[En route to Port Said, on board the *Himalaya*]

When we attained the Master's presence that morning, we found that He was rather weak and tired, but His heart was cheered to the utmost, and He said the following:[1073]

> The most important of all affairs is to teach the Cause of God. This work attracts confirmations. Of all the people in this world, I am most deserving of ease and comfort. Notwithstanding my weak constitution and my advanced age, I must remain at the centre, so that from every corner of the earth I may be kept abreast of how the work is proceeding and tend to various matters. Yet in spite of all this, I am restlessly eager to teach the Cause of God and exalt His Word; perchance I may render some service to the divine threshold, and this may serve as an example to the believers.

The Master made remarks of this sort repeatedly and emphatically.

At that moment, I recalled something that happened toward the end of our sojourn in Paris. One day, two of the Master's attendants were having a conversation that involved a suggestion to write to some of the eminent Bahá'ís in the cities of Persia and encourage them to strive, with consummate holiness and detachment, to teach spiritual principles to certain important persons. The hope was that, as a result of this effort, those persons would go on to do things that would redound to their glory in both this world and in the world to come, and devote themselves to the promotion of perpetual happiness. In the course of this conversation, the Master came onto the scene and asked, 'What are you discussing?' They apprised Him of the topic under discussion and said:

> Should this idea meet Your approval, perhaps You could issue a directive to that effect, so that the believers may begin to think about reinforcing these important persons, and arise to lend their diligent support to the vitality of the Cause of God.

The Master replied:

> An injunction from me is not necessary. The believers must rise up, on their own, to make firm the steps and hoist the banners of guidance. They must labour ceaselessly, by day and by night, and ever fix their thoughts, with the utmost devotion and detachment, on teaching the Cause of God. Should this come to pass, they will certainly be assisted to do what befits them. I swear by God, besides Whom there is none other God, that if one rises up as he ought to, the gates of heaven will be opened before him, and the hosts of the Concourse on High will come to His aid. His will be ancient glory; his will be life everlasting.

When one of our Indian friends called on the Master that afternoon, he seemed utterly enamoured as he enjoyed the blessing of being in His presence.[1074] The Master showed him some photographs of the German friends that had been taken at their gatherings, and said:

> I hope that you will hold these kinds of gatherings in Allahabad, and that you may be aided with divine confirmations. Focus not on your own self; rather, direct your attention to the power of God's Kingdom, which can change a drop into an ocean, transform a gnat into a phoenix, turn a nameless one into a centre of attraction whose fame will endure for ages and centuries, invest an indigent one with everlasting sovereignty, and grant a dead one with eternal life. These are the things which the confirmations from the Kingdom of God can bring about.

Following this, a Jew attained the presence of the Master, Who spoke to him at length on divine philosophy, the advancements of the world of being, the prophecies of the prophets, and the teachings of Bahá'u'lláh. As a result, this man showed his humble devotion to the Master more than ever before.[1075]

Sometime thereafter, a French woman entered the Master's presence. He gave her tender counsels, exhorting her to acquire spiritual excellences and obtain the perfections of the world of humanity.

That night, too, was a blessed night. Although the wind was blowing fiercely, the sea was calm and the weather was clear. In the radiance of the moonlight, the water shimmered like a spotless and sparkling mirror. The sound of the surging waves, lapping the ship on either side, resembled the billowing and babbling of two flowing rivers, and the ship itself seemed to whine like a young fatling, priding itself in the Most Great Mystery it was carrying. The hearts of His devoted attendants throbbed constantly with this heavenly anthem:

This is the mighty Mystery
None other than the Branch of old
That great Secret in Whom do we
The mercy of the Lord behold.

And afterwards, they would gently murmur these words:[1076]

How great indeed this blessed night
Which far outranks the best of days
'Tis on this night our Sun so bright
Will cease to shed His Western rays
His trips through Europe's land and seas
Upon this night have reached their end
His beaut'ous light, if God should please,
Will soon to Eastern skies extend
That precious Friend will disembark
To lay His steps on Eastern ground
And thereupon will all remark:
'It's here alone that heaven's found!'

It was around that time that we suddenly heard the sweet voice of the Master, Who was saying these words as He walked with His graceful gait:

We will arrive at Port Said tomorrow night. When I was on my way to America, I had no hope that I would return in good health, for I was quite ill and my constitution was very weak. In the course of that journey, moreover, my sickness and weakness grew more severe several times. Yet on every one of those occasions, through the aid and bounty of the Blessed Beauty, as well as my preoccupation with serving the divine threshold and the happiness that resulted therefrom, my sickness was turned into good health, and my weakness was changed into strength. His assistance and protection reached me at every turn, and the succor and support of the Most Glorious Kingdom were always at my side. This has remained the case to this very moment, at which we are now returning to Port Said with the utmost gladness.

Tuesday, 17 June 1913

[En route to Port Said, on board the *Himalaya* → Port Said]

Before having His tea, the Master went for a stroll outside His room early that morning. The evidences of supreme joy were apparent on His beautiful face.

Once He had had His tea, some men and women from India and Europe came to bid the Master farewell and implore His assistance and confirmation. They showed great devotion and submissiveness before Him, and received His loving-kindness accordingly, as well as His repeated exhortations to promote universal peace and oneness and to promulgate the unity of humanity.

After they were dismissed, the outskirts of Port Said came into view from a distance.[1077] The Master used His binoculars to watch the other ships go by and look at the city of Port Said itself.

The lunch bell was rung sometime thereafter, and the Master said, 'I will not be coming to the table.' A bit of bread, cheese, and fruit[1078] were prepared for Him in His room.

He had not yet finished all of His lunch when the ship reached the harbour.[1079] Without a moment's delay, Áqá Mírzá Muḥsin, the Master's son-in-law; Aḥmad Effendí Yazdí; Ḥájí Áqá Muḥammad;[1080] Áqá Muḥammad-Taqí Iṣfahání; Áqá Mírzá Munír;[1081] and Áqá

Khusraw[1082] came onto the ship and threw themselves at His feet.[1083] In attaining His presence and prostrating themselves before Him, their eyes and hearts were illumined, and they were recompensed at last for all those days of separation from their Beloved. They spent the next few minutes gathering His belongings.

After tipping the servants and other attendants who worked on the ship, the Master was taken from the ship to the pier with a special motor launch. A group of believers were waiting for Him on the shore, and their most dearly cherished hope was fulfilled as they reached the Paradise of His presence.[1084]

Once He had extended His loving-kindness to each and every one of those friends, He called on Áqá Aḥmad [Effendí Yazdí], while seated in a special carriage, to take Him to his residence at once. The Master's daughter, Ṭúbá Khánum, and her husband, Áqá Mírzá Muḥsin Afnán (the Master's son-in-law), had come from the Holy Land to welcome and salute Him on His arrival, and they, too, were present at that residence. Consequently, He made arrangements for His attendants and the other travellers who had come to see Him to lodge at the Hotel Sulṭání.[1085]

Egypt

At the request of some of the friends, the Master decided to stay in Egypt for a while to regain His strength and maintain His health. It was hoped that this sojourn would somewhat allay the fatigues of His travels, such that He would not lapse into sickness when He returned to the Holy Land, where He would be tending to the coming and going of His visitors from near and far, and devoting Himself to the other affairs that would be demanding His attention. It was for this reason that the Master instructed that a two-story house be rented[1086] and sent a telegram summoning those who had travelled to the Holy Land.

At one of the meetings,[1087] He made these remarks concerning His travels:

> We had crossed half the globe in the span of twelve hours when we arrived at Los Angeles on this journey. Had we returned by way of China, Japan, and India, we would have made a full trip around the world!
>
> The call of God must be raised in every country. Although it may take longer for certain countries to be stirred to movement, the influence of God's Word will ultimately be more intense when it is spread in such countries as those. The Cause of God will become prevalent; His Word cannot be prevented from exerting its influence. When it is imparted to the rock, it will be split; and when to the dead, they will rise up; and when to the mountain, it will be cleft; and when to the deaf, they will hear; and when to the dumb, they will speak. The Word of God has begun to flow, and it will only continue to do so.
>
> We, however, must be thinking of how we can derive our share of this most glorious bounty – how we can obtain a spiritual radiance whose light will shine brilliantly throughout all the divine realms, and whose signs will remain enduring and perspicuous – for there can be no doubt that the blessed Word is so pervasive that it can be likened to the heat of the sun, which has an effect

> on all things. Ultimately, its effects may simply take longer to be made manifest in certain things, while in others they will appear more quickly . . .

Were I to write a detailed account of the Master's sojourn in Egypt following His return from His journey to America and Europe, it would prove overly lengthy. Hence, I will cover, as concisely as I can, the events leading up to His arrival in the Holy Land – a period spanning nearly six months, during which the city of Port Said, as well as Alexandria and its suburbs, were graced with His holy footsteps.

When the Master had just arrived [in Egypt], more than forty people in the Holy Land were waiting to visit Him.[1088] Along with a number of Bahá'ís from Egypt and the surrounding areas, they received permission to do this, and in attaining His presence, they were compensated for all those days of separation from the Centre of the Covenant. They were filled with a fervent excitement that roused the people to commotion and raised a clamour in the city, for with every day a new crowd would arrive, each dressed in its own garb. Some of these people came from India, while another group consisted of friends from Tabriz, Saysan, and Mamaqan. Some had come from Tehran and Mazandaran, while still other visitors included the Arab Bahá'ís and friends from that region. Whenever these people entered and met the other seekers, and also the Master's attendants, they would shake hands, take each other in their embrace, and come to feel mutual fondness. Some of them laughed out of the abundance of their delight, while others cried from the intensity of their ecstasy. The people in the streets and bazaars nearby watched these scenes with astonishment as they wondered to themselves:

> What is the meaning of this? What has caused these people, who hail from various countries and belong to diverse kindreds, to grow this enamoured of one another and become so taken with their temperaments?

The crowd eventually swelled to such great proportions that the hotel could not accommodate everyone. As a result, a wonderfully majestic tent, the kind that the Egyptians use specifically to hold public gatherings, was pitched on the roof of that building, which was wide and flat, and a flag bearing the emblem of the lion and the sun[1089] was affixed to the top of that glorious tent.

The Master would receive His private audiences, believers and others, at His residence (the home of Consul Aḥmad Effendí Yazdí). For the most part, people went there in groups and were granted permission to attain His presence. The public gatherings and banquets, however, would be held with the utmost ascendancy beneath that glorious tent mentioned above. On most days, and also some nights, the hearts of his ardent lovers would, through His most holy presence and soul-stirring utterance, be transformed into the envy of Paradise itself on those joyous and radiant occasions.

Thursday, 19 June 1913
[Port Said]

A gathering was held in the aforementioned tent that night, and the Master gave a talk that began with these words:[1090]

He is God

> It is wondrous indeed that a gathering as grand as this one has been convened in Port Said. It would be good if the kings [of ages past] were to lift up their heads from beneath the dust to behold how the ensigns of truth have been hoisted high and the banners of oppression hauled down! . . .

Friday, 20 June 1913
[Port Said]

On that afternoon, the Master seated Himself underneath that same tent for another gathering that was to be held there; He showed the tenderest loving-kindness to each and every one of the believers and permitted them to take their seats. He then spoke these blessed words:

He is God

'It is the prerogative of God to contravene the rules of humanity.'* Indeed, it befits the power and purpose of God to violate the customs and practices of humankind. In these days when all are going to Paris, we have just come from that city! This is how things have come to pass.

It is similar to the time when the Ascension of the Blessed Beauty took place at the Mansion.† All the inhabitants of 'Akká bear witness to the fact that, while He was still alive, cholera broke out on four occasions. The disease swept throughout the entire vicinity, but did not penetrate the city of 'Akká itself. It even travelled to places with a favourable climate, such as Mount Lebanon, and it reached the gates of 'Akká – but again, it did not enter the city itself. Yet on the day of Bahá'u'lláh's passing, 'Akká was suddenly thrown into dire straits; the cholera permeated the city and everyone ran away. I was in the Mansion at the time; I saw that some of the believers in 'Akká were in danger, and that it would be unacceptable for me to be outside [the city]. Thus, at a time when all were fleeing from 'Akká, we left the Mansion and entered that city. Everyone was astonished. They evacuated their houses and committed them to our care. We, for our part, appointed a number of people to guard those homes. Some group or other would die with every day that went by, but the Bahá'ís all remained safe and healthy. In the end, the cholera spread out to the surrounding areas, and its severity within the city itself died down. As a result, everyone went to 'Akká to take refuge!

Now, too, at a time when all are fleeing the heat of Egypt for the city of Paris, we have chosen to come to Egypt. Praised be God, for wherever we may be, we are beneath the shade of the

* An Arabic saying.

† The Mansion of Bahjí.

Blessed Beauty. We busy ourselves with diffusing the divine fragrances, happy and well-assured in every respect . . .

Saturday, 21 June 1913
[Port Said]

The Master summoned the travellers to His residence in groups, and to each crowd He remarked on the greatness of the Cause of God and the gifts granted by the Abhá Beauty. Among the Bahá'ís who were in His presence was Áqá Mírzá 'Ináyatu'lláh [Aḥmadov], the son of Ḥájí Aḥmad Áqá Mílání, one of the veteran believers who was self-sacrificing in his services to the Cause of God.[1091]

On that day,[1092] the Master addressed the following words to some Bahá'ís who had come from Azerbaijan:[1093]

> Praised be God that you have come, and that you had the privilege of making pilgrimage to the Shrine of Bahá'u'lláh, where you perfumed your heads with the dust of its sacred threshold! It is as if you attained the presence of Bahá'u'lláh Himself, inasmuch as all the holy souls circle around that resplendent Spot, and both the Supreme Concourse and the inmates of eternal Paradise fix their gaze on the Shrines of the Báb and Bahá'u'lláh. Praise be to God that you have attained this station!
>
> Now that you are returning, guide your compatriots and say to them: 'Do you know what land you come from? Do you know what a bounty has been granted you? Do you know how esteemed is the crown that rests on your heads, or what gifts and favours have been bestowed on you?' The value of these bounties is not yet known; only later will it be made abundantly clear. Were the Persians to appreciate that value, they would soar with fervent delight.
>
> Observe how, when Jesus Christ appeared, His countrymen detested Him, and deemed it shameful to mention that they hailed from the same land or bore any other relationship to Him. With time, however, they came to realize what a bounty they had lost. Now, too, the Persians are oblivious of the gift they have been given and the bestowal that has appeared in their midst.

> Praised be God that you have lived in the Day of the Blessed Beauty and beheld the splendours of the Most Great Light. Give thanks to God and bend every effort to awaken the people of Persia. Say to them: 'O Persians, O Persians! Are you at all aware of what a Sun of Truth has shed its light from the horizon of the East? Are you at all aware of what a blessed Tree has sprung up from that land, or what an Ocean has surged forth? Arise, arise from your slumber! How long will you persist in your heedlessness and remain occupied with your own selves?' . . .

Some Bahá'ís from Mazandaran then attained the Master's presence with a great many letters in hand. When these were presented to Him, He said:

> You have brought very many letters. How challenging!
>
> You must each become even as a talking book. Indeed, my hope is such that you will all become lucid books. Whoever turns toward the Most Glorious Kingdom in this day, and purifies his heart from every defilement, will himself be like a talking book. Without this, nothing whatever will bear any fruit, and anything that fails to yield a result is unworthy of mention.

When Darvísh Karam-'Alí and Darvísh Khandán attained the Master's presence, He composed a number of sublime Tablets for the Bahá'ís of Fars, which they were to have the privilege of delivering, and this brought them abundant joy.[1094] They told Him about the Bahá'ís of Hindijan, the native land of Shaykh Salmán, and this prompted Him to speak of that heavenly courier with ample fondness and benevolence. He gave an account of the steadfastness of Shaykh Salmán – along with his sincerity, his devotion, and the toils of his travels – and eventually made these remarks:

> He was a blessed soul, very much pure and holy. Just as Persians prided themselves on the belief which Salmán* professed in the

* Salman the Persian, the first Muslim convert from Persia and a companion of the Prophet Muhammad.

> dispensation of Islam, so too will the people of that land* soon take pride in the name of <u>Sh</u>ay<u>kh</u> Salmán.

In those days, all the Master's Tablets were written in His own hand. He was either busy with writing, or, when people came to see Him, He would spend His time talking with them. This would leave Him very tired, but He would still go out on brief excursions in the mornings and at sunset, sometimes on foot and sometimes in a vehicle. However much His friends and attendants told Him that excessive occupation would be harmful to His health, He would say:

> I wish to see how much my health will support me as I go about my business. I have made a promise to the Bahá'ís of the East; therefore, I must stay busy with work and tend to my affairs.

Telegrams from [Bahá'í] communities in both the East and the West, saluting the Master on His arrival [in Egypt], were received every day, and He would respond either telegraphically or in writing.

Monday, 23 June 1913
[Port Said]

The Master summoned the believers to His residence in groups. Each of them expressed some hope or other to the Master and made their own requests of Him, and He, in turn, would treat them each with a special loving-kindness. At one point in that day, He gave a sweet talk on conversing through the language of the spirit, as well as the detachment of spiritual people despite their occupation with physical matters. Here are some of the blessed words He spoke to that effect:

> Thoughts of wealth and riches, as well as hopes of rank and glory, are sheer illusion. God has cast these thoughts into our minds only

---

* Hindijan.

so that this world might prosper; apart from this, they are of no importance.

He also said:[1095]

I was intent on travelling to other countries – for instance, I wished to go to the principal seat of the Christian priests – but I returned to the East strictly for your sakes because the friends of the East are very dear to me.

Tuesday, 24 June 1913
[Port Said]

The Master was made intensely weak and weary by all the people who had come to visit Him, believers and others alike, and also as a result of excessive writing and tending to the other claims on His attention. He made the following remarks:

I have grown very tired today. In spite of the many demands on my time, I have set myself to writing – and beyond all this, you have no idea how preoccupied my mind is. It is these constant blows which prevent my fever from healing the instant there is an increase in my occupation. Additionally, the weather has been humid these past few days, and this has caused my fever to recrudesce.

His weak condition notwithstanding, the Master wanted to go outside that afternoon to dispel His fatigue. Just then, however, a few Christian preachers and missionaries – men and women, all highly prejudiced, who had learned of the Master's arrival [in Egypt] and heard that people of all creeds and kindreds were visiting Him – came to the door of His residence and requested permission to attain His presence.[1096] They were summoned right away, and He showered them with immeasurable kindness and love. This display of supremely tender affection emboldened these visitors, and they brazenly began to denounce the Muslims as liars and raise objections to Islam itself. The Master said to them:

> That which you have heard about Islam bears no relationship whatsoever to the foundation of that religion. Even the majority of what you hear from some of the Muslims themselves either consists of blind imitation or pertains to matters that are minor and trivial; it neither explains the truth of Islam nor expounds its foundation. Thus, you should refer to the Qur'án itself. Among the explicit verses of that Text is the following: 'Verily, they who believe,* and they who follow the Jewish religion, and the Christians, and the Sabeans – whoever of these believeth in God and the last day, and doeth that which is right, shall have their reward with their Lord: fear shall not come upon them, neither shall they be grieved.'† The veracity of both the Old and New Testaments, as well as the greatness of the divine prophets, are mentioned repeatedly in the Qur'án. Even where Jesus Christ is concerned, there are descriptions of Him in the Qur'án that have no peer in the Gospel. It is said in the Qur'án that Christ spoke in the cradle and that He laid claim to prophethood.‡ Hence, if your goal is to guide the Muslims, it is already achieved, inasmuch as their beliefs about Christ transcend your own.

One of these visitors then said the following with the utmost courtesy:

> It is said in the Gospel that Christ is the Son of God. This is the greatest description of Him in the New Testament, but it is not mentioned in the Qur'án.

The Master replied:

> In the dispensations of Moses and Christ, 'the Son of God' was a term that was applied even to the people of Israel, just as they are called 'the sons of God' in the Torah. Towards the end of the fourth chapter of [the Book of] Exodus, God says to Moses: 'And

* Muslims.

† Qur'án 2:62.

‡ Qur'án 19:29–30.

> thou shalt say unto Pharaoh, Thus saith the Lord, Israel is my son, even my firstborn . . . and if thou refuse to let him go, behold, I will slay thy son, even thy firstborn."* Thus, if the people of Israel are referred to in the Torah as 'the sons of God', then what rank or distinction is there in Christ being called 'the Son of God'?

The Master's visitors were rendered speechless and totally astounded by the power of His utterance and the strength of His proofs. He then began to speak extensively – imparting counsels, discussing various subjects, interpreting the prophecies alluding to this Most Great Revelation, and explaining some of the new and wondrous teachings – and He did this in such a way that His visitors arose to render Him thanks and praise for the admonitions and tenets He had shared with them. They were eventually dismissed, and they showed humility and submissiveness as they departed His presence.[1097]

There was a quality to that force inherent in the Master's speech, that power imbued in His address, and that profound transformation which He effected in the attitudes of those prejudiced people that day that would have compelled anyone who witnessed it to testify to the consummate might and grandeur of the Covenant of God, as well as the overwhelming majesty and influence of His Cause.

Friday, 27 June 1913
[Port Said]

A most exquisite banquet was held that night[1098] by Mírzá Ja'far Shírází [Hádíoff],[1099] the builder of the pilgrim house in Haifa. When the Master seated Himself beneath that glorious tent, the hearts of His friends circled around that face which shone brightly as a candle – each of them a fearless moth, all frenzied with the ecstasy of their love for Him. These are some of the remarks He made at the beginning of His talk:[1100]

---

* Exodus 4:22–23.

> They call this 'the place where the two seas meet',* and in the Qur'án there is mention of the letting loose of the two seas.† This refers to the place where Moses and Joshua met a great personage,‡ of whom God says 'We had instructed [him] with Our knowledge'§ when the dead fish came back to life,¶ and this has a new and wondrous meaning . . .

When dinner was ready, the Master served the rice and *khoresh* to each and every one of the guests with His own blessed hands. Eating in two turns, more than seventy believers in all had their meal at the table.[1101]

After dinner, the Master served sweets to everyone,[1102] and rendered thanks for the gifts and bounties of the Abhá Beauty.

He dismissed most of the travellers the following day[1103] – but at the time of their dismissal and farewell, those restless lovers wept with such a weeping that tears began to fall from His own dark blue eyes. They bewailed and bemoaned their impending separation from Him. His adoring admirers would always be overcome with this state at that dreaded moment of imminent remoteness, regardless of where they were. At every pier, every train station, every house, and every marketplace, the bitter cries those righteous friends would raise when it was time to say goodbye were enough to deeply astonish and profoundly affect the people in their midst, friends and others alike.

It was in those days that word of the poor health of Mírzá Abu'l-Faḍl was received. As a result, the Master sent someone from Port Said to Alexandria to assess his condition on two separate occasions: the first, Áqá Mírzá Muḥsin Afnán; the second, Siyyid Jalál, the son of Síná.

It was also in those days that I attained the presence of the

* Qur'án 18:60.

† Qur'án 25:53 and 55:19.

‡ Typically believed to be the prophet-like figure Khiḍr, as discussed in endnote 105. There are passages from the Writings of Bahá'u'lláh and 'Abdu'l-Bahá which state that Khiḍr was the 'higher reality' of Moses, or the personification of the 'station of unity' common to all the Manifestations of God; see Mázandarání, *Amr va Khalq*, vol. 2, pp. 201–05.

§ Qur'án 18:65.

¶ Qur'án 18:61.

Master one morning after being summoned there, and found Him beaming with joy as He was holding a number of letters from some of the respected people of Constantinople. Several times He read from a few of those letters, which had been written in Turkish, and He praised the fluidity of their prose and the excellence of their themes, as well as the attraction and devotion their authors had shown. He said:

> The effects of this journey have stirred the people to motion. Were it not for the Holy Land, I would have gone to Constantinople right away and raised the call of God there. Many individuals of high repute would have embraced this blessed Cause, and some of those who are prejudiced against us would have cried out in protest and encroached on the Shrines of the Báb and Bahá'u'lláh. It is for this reason that I cannot go there.

Sunday, 29 June 1913
[Port Said]

The Master relocated from the home of Consul Aḥmad Effendí Yazdí to a house that had been specially rented for Him.[1104] Gatherings would be held there every morning, and the outpourings of the Master's grace and bounty would frenzy the hearts and minds of His dearest friends. He Himself, however, was exceedingly busy, and the heat and humidity hindered His recovery and interfered with His comfort.

Tuesday, 1 July 1913
[Port Said]

The Master left His residence that morning and went for a stroll up to the seashore near the statue of [Ferdinand de] Lesseps.[1105] A number of believers accompanied Him on that walk.

Once He had seated Himself outside the hotel,[1106] He asked for some coffee to be brought for the friends. He then looked at the waves of the sea and said:[1107]

> The Cause of God is like a shoreless sea, whose surging and billowing no power can stop.

He concluded that talk with these remarks:

> It is pride and dissension that have always led to the abasement of every people, while the best vehicles for their progress are cognizance and harmony. The greatest means for the advancement of the world's peoples are knowledge and concord, whereas moral corruption and primitive prejudices will impede their development.

The respected people who came from outside [the city] to visit Him during the few weeks He stayed in Port Said included some of the grandees of Egypt; the editor of the *Paisa Akhbár* newspaper from the Punjab;[1108] and the Governor of Jerusalem, the account of whose meeting with the Master, as well as the humility and transformation he showed in His presence, is too extensive to write here. Additionally, some reporters who wrote for Egyptian newspapers composed several articles in praise of the Master after they had met with Him.

As to the latter days of His sojourn in Port Said, it can be said in short that, owing to the humidity of the climate, along with the great number of things that preoccupied His mind and demanded His attention, the Master became increasingly sick and His fever grew more severe with every passing day.

Friday, 11 July 1913

[Port Said → Ismailia]

At the request of some of the friends, the Master relocated to Ismailia[1109] and stayed there for a few days[1110] – but although it was less humid in that city, the Master's fever worsened nevertheless. As a result, He moved to the suburb of Ramleh in Alexandria [on 17 July], since the climate of that place was agreeable to His health.

His ardent devotion to matters of the Cause was such that, up until He left Ismailia – even though His face had become visibly flushed with the heat of His fever, and that this sight had anguished the hearts of His friends – yet despite such severe sickness, He continued to busy Himself with reading the correspondence that the believers would send Him. Once, toward the end of His time there, He said the following when He had finished reading a particularly lengthy letter:

> Observe how a piece of paper this large has been completely covered with such small writing – and yet I, with this condition of mine, have perused its contents anyway, only to find that the entirety of this letter lacked a single thing of substance to say! The purpose of composition should be to convey one's points and state one's aims; it should not be done merely to express ceremonial courtesies or string words together.

Thursday, 17 July 1913[1111]
[Ismailia → Ramleh, Alexandria]

When the land of Ramleh was graced with the Master's footsteps,[1112] He first lodged at the Hotel Victoria for two weeks. Following this, two houses near the Maẓlúm Pá<u>sh</u>á train station were rented at His behest: one was used as the Master's special residence, where He would summon the friends and other respected people to attain His presence most of the time, and the other was reserved for His attendants and other travellers who had come expressly to see Him. On most days, He would be seated on the veranda in front of His residence, where the eager believers would feel the utmost joy and attain to perpetual grace as they basked in the majesty of His person.

The Master's health improved day by day. This was especially the case a few weeks into His sojourn, when that most glorious fruit of the divine Lote-Tree, the Greatest Holy Leaf, along with Ḍíyá <u>Kh</u>ánum (the sister and daughter of the Master, respectively) – may my life be a sacrifice for those who serve them both – arrived from the Holy Land [on 1 August].[1113] They looked after the

The tent at 'Abdu'l-Bahá's guest house, Port Said.
Mírzá Maḥmúd Zarqání is seated on the right, front row

Muḥámmad Taqí Iṣfahání

'Abbás Ḥilmí Páshá, Khedive of Egypt

Mírzá Ja'far Shírází (Hádíoff), builder of the Pilgrim House in Haifa

Master, rendering Him various services, ensuring that He had what He needed to stay healthy, and providing the essential means for His happiness.

Beyond this, at the outset of the Master's arrival [in Ramleh], He took it upon Himself to personally see to the recovery of Mírzá Abu'l-Faḍl, instructing him to consult a competent physician and insisting that he seek treatment. Furthermore, He took special measures to rent him a house that was near His own residence and had a beautiful view with fine weather to boot.[1114] Consequently, he moved from Alexandria to Ramleh to repose in the sheltering shade of the Master's bounty.[1115] With every day, week, and month that went by, the infirmity of Mírzá Abu'l-Faḍl became less severe and he gradually began to regain his health. About two or three weeks before the Master travelled to the Holy Land [on 2 December], he returned to Cairo[1116] with the Master's permission, never to attain His presence again. Eventually [on 21 January 1914], Mírzá Abu'l-Faḍl ascended to the Kingdom of glory, and the people of Bahá held services in the East and the West alike to honour his memory,[1117] for they had learned of his passing through cables which the Master Himself had sent to the Bahá'ís of various regions to announce the news. Telegrams and letters of condolence from many countries were presented to Him. At every place and gathering He visited, He mentioned how tragic it was that Mírzá Abu'l-Faḍl had died,[1118] and spoke of his knowledge, his detachment, his firmness in the divine Covenant, and his steadfastness and sanctification in the Cause of God – all this because that pure soul had constantly bent the greatest of efforts to serve the Faith and refute the calumnies of its rejecters, and because he had sacrificed himself to the Word of God in every possible way.

* * *

The Master sojourned in Ramleh for five months.[1119] In addition to the Bahá'ís who came from the East and West to attain His presence,[1120] travellers from America and Europe; Jewish teachers from the [Syrian Protestant] college of Beirut;[1121] deputies of the parliament of Constantinople;[1122] and some of the grandees of Egypt, including even the Khedive ['Abbás Ḥilmí Pá<u>sh</u>á],[1123] attained His presence and benefited from the gracious outpourings of the Abhá Kingdom on several occasions. They expressed their praise and gratitude for having met 'Him round Whom all names revolve,' and all those blessed souls received His bounty and favour.

More generally, however, the people of Egypt did not have much receptivity or perceptiveness to speak of. The Master Himself mentioned this very thing in a story He told during the first day of His voyage to America, which concerns His travels to Tanta and Mansurih and is discussed in the first volume of this chronicle.[1124] Here is one of the anecdotes He related many times about the people of Egypt:

> When I was present at an important gathering in Alexandria, a certain patriot arose to voice his praise and support for his country. He recited a poem and then, with the utmost pride, he repeatedly made the following remark, which stirred those in attendance to more excitement than any of the other addresses had: 'We belong to the people who built the pyramids.' I said to the pá<u>sh</u>á sitting near me, 'How strange! The Muslims of Egypt are not the Copts, that they should pride themselves in this way on having built the pyramids (the tomb of Pharaoh). And they wish to promote love for their country with this pride? If this act of building is a source of pride, then it is the people of Pharaoh who should boast, not the people of Islam, for it was Pharaoh who built the pyramids – and what is more, those buildings were constructed through oppression. For fifteen years, Pharaoh made sixteen thousand of his hapless subjects to work every day. With excruciating toil and hardship, they built the pyramids so that Pharaoh might conceal his own corpse there. Here is the pivot around which the pride of this people revolves! Observe what things men vaunt themselves over!'

Such was the state of those people for the most part, and this applied especially to the prejudiced Muslims of Egypt.

Yet the Master's heart was most happy and pleased with the

distinguished people of that land. The first esteemed person who belonged to the class of Egyptian scholars and grandees, had the honour of attaining the Master's presence, and grew enamoured of Him as he beheld His beauty and perfection was the late Shaykh 'Alí Yúsuf, editor of the *al-Mu'ayyad* newspaper. When this man met the Master during His first journey [to the West], he was so profoundly affected that he took up his pen and let loose his tongue to make mention of Him and render Him praise, winning everlasting honour in so doing. Although he was not a Bahá'í – on the contrary, he was opposed to the Cause before he met the Master – the first article which that celebrated person wrote and published in his newspaper [after meeting Him] was the following:[1125]

al-Mu'ayyad
No. 6194
Sunday, 16 October 1910

> The honourable Mírzá 'Abbás Effendí – a scholar of religion, the head of Bahaism[1126] in 'Akká, and also its chief authority in the entire world – arrived in Alexandria, where he stayed first at the Hotel Victoria in al-Raml [Ramleh] for a few days, after which he occupied a house near Schutz.[1127]
>
> He is a venerable person, dignified, possessed of profound knowledge, deeply versed in theology, master of the history of Islam, and of its denominations and developments. He is seventy years of age or more.
>
> Although he has taken 'Akká to be his place of residence, he has followers, which number in the millions, in Persia, India, and even Europe and America. The esteem in which his followers hold him reaches the level of worship and sanctification, so much so that it has led his foes to spread rumours about him. Yet whosoever has consorted with him has seen in him a man exceedingly well-informed, whose speech is captivating, who attracts minds and souls, and who is wholly dedicated to belief in the oneness of humankind, which in political terms is a doctrine similar to that of the oneness of existence in theological belief.
>
> His teachings and guidance revolve round the axis of

> relinquishing prejudices: religious, racial, patriotic, or any other bias attending worldly life.
>
> We sat down with him on two occasions. His remarks and his views reminded us of the characteristics of the late Siyyid Jamál al-Dín al-Afghání, in terms of his vast knowledge of the subjects whereof he speaks and his ability to attract the souls of those who converse with him. He surpasses him, however, in his patience; he receives the words of his addressers with tenderness, and listens to them more attentively than Siyyid Jamál al-Dín . . .

Important people of this sort praised the Master in numerous articles. From the very beginning of His journey, the fame of His perfection and the force of His glory had been so widely spread, and had pervaded the hearts of humanity to such a degree, that even the enemies of this Cause would attain His presence with the utmost deference and submissiveness.

Among the opponents of this Cause was Mírzá Mihdí Írání[1128] of Egypt, who, in an effort to disprove the Faith and stir up trouble, had written *Bábu'l-Abváb*[1129] in the days when despotism reigned before the Persian and Ottoman revolutions took place.[1130] He visited the Master many times in the Egyptian city of Zaytun with an air of perfect reverence and humility. Although he did this with duplicity – and notwithstanding that the intentions he harboured in the presence of the Master were clear and apparent – he still seemed little more than a lowly servant before the magnetism of His radiant beauty, the tremendous power of His utterance, and the almost overwhelming force of His pardon and beneficence.

I will now recount an astonishing thing that would come to be seen in the speech and writing of Mírzá Mihdí Írání – a thing which will serve as proof of the influence and might of this great Cause. In his book, *Bábu'l-Abváb*, this man published the exact verses of Bahá'u'lláh concerning the tyranny and oppression that prevailed in the Ottoman Empire[1131] – along with those prophecies that predicted the disordering of its affairs,[1132] and foreshadowed the agitation and opposition of its masses[1133] – with the hope that this would incite a great sedition and provoke the Sultan to wipe out the Bahá'ís once and for all. He had circulated his book among the Muslims, and shared it in particular with supporters of despotism. Similarly, he included translations of the prophecies about the upheaval of the people of Berlin,[1134] the war that would be fought on the banks of the Rhine,[1135] and the defeat of Germany. He had presented all this in that book in such a way that anyone who read these verses and prophecies of Bahá'u'lláh alongside the other incendiary calumnies he had written which pertained to the history of this Cause would have had no doubt that all the Muslims, especially Sulṭán 'Abdu'l-Ḥamíd Khán, would certainly take steps to obliterate the foundation of this Faith. But following the publication of that book, the tables were turned in no time at all. The conditions of Persia and the Ottoman Empire were altered; despotism was changed into constitutionalism, and the Master, the Centre of the Cause of God, was freed from the prison of 'Akká. It was then that the promises enshrined in those perspicuous verses were realized. Accordingly, the things which that author had written yielded an outcome contrary to his cherished goal – especially where Berlin and Germany were concerned[1136] – for his intention had been to agitate the despots and induce them to exterminate the Bahá'ís, but the hand of divine power turned his machinations into a means for advancing the influence of the Word of God and spreading the glory of His Cause, and made it a testimony to His all-encompassing knowledge and a sign of the all-subduing power of the Manifestation of heavenly grace. So true did this prove that even the author of *Bábu'l-Abváb* himself made these remarks to the Bahá'ís in Egypt on numerous occasions:

> I have rendered a great service to this Cause, inasmuch as I published the original verses from the *Kitáb-i-Aqdas*, as well as the Tablets to various kings and rulers, exactly as they were written, and spread them throughout the world when they had yet to be fulfilled . . .

The history of this blessed Cause abounds with episodes like this one, through which the plotting of our foes has always added to the support and confirmation this Cause has received, and the cruelty and aggression of our enemies have invariably caused the Word of God to be only further exalted and noised abroad. Nowhere is this more evident than in the imprisonment of Bahá'u'lláh in the citadel of 'Akká, insofar as two tyrannical governments, Persian and Ottoman, had considered His remote confinement in that prison to be their last resort for destroying the foundation that God had laid. It was, however, through that same banishment and imprisonment – and at that very moment when the Lord of creation ennobled this hallowed Land with His footsteps – that the prophecies mentioned in the Books of God were realized, and the promises of the divine Manifestations concerning the appearance of the Promised One in this holy vale, none other than the Speaker on Sinai Himself, were conspicuously fulfilled, to such a degree that the various peoples who had expected and awaited the advent of God in these sanctified spots set their faces toward the Dayspring of celestial tokens. Now have they been led aright by the guidance of God; now have they beheld, from that blessed Tree, the blazing fire He has kindled. None of these manifest signs would have appeared had it not been for the cruelty of His enemies, nor would the wine of divine guidance stored in this vault of intoxicating love have reached the point of boiling without the sweltering heat of the calamities He sustained in the path of God.

It was for this reason that, after He had entered the Most Great Prison, the Ancient Beauty – magnified be His mention, glorified be His praise – acquainted the rulers of the earth with the Cause of God, and summoned all the world's peoples and kindreds to recognize the fulfilment of the predictions of the prophets of God, as well as the promises of His chosen ones. Among the utterances revealed by the Supreme Pen of Bahá'u'lláh before He arrived in 'Akká are these words addressed to Náṣiri'd-Dín Sháh:

> Verily God hath made adversity as a morning dew upon His green pasture, and a wick for His lamp which lighteth earth and heaven.*

* Bahá'u'lláh, *Summons of the Lord of Hosts*, p. 129.

Having made mention of His imprisonment and hardship in 'Akká, He then stated the following:

> Erelong shall . . . God . . . unlock a mighty portal unto His City. On that Day shall the people enter therein by troops . . .*

* * *

Following His return from His journey to America and Europe, while He was seated in the pilgrim house near the Shrine of the Báb on Mount Carmel, 'Abdu'l-Bahá spoke these words as He looked outside at the city of 'Akká and its surrounding areas through the door of the main hall:

> One will find it most strange when he reflects on where this Cause once was and where it has now reached. Consider the cities of Shiraz and Tehran, and then how far away from them are Baghdad and Rumelia, or Haifa and 'Akká! These occurrences transpired solely through the fulfilment of those prophecies that are recorded in the Holy Scriptures of the Prophets. The plan of God is a wondrous thing. Over the course of many long years, He has taken this Cause here and there, and drawn it in the end to such a spot as this, all to fulfil the prophecies of ages past. It is inevitable that God will clearly manifest the highway He has predicted through His Prophets; He will not allow a single word of those prophecies to go unrealized.

I will relate here an anecdote from the time when I was living in Tehran. One day, when I was at a gathering of Bahá'ís of Jewish background, a bigoted Jew found his way into our company. The Bahá'ís attempted to guide him to the dawning of the Most Great Light, but he began to quarrel and dispute with them a great deal. Eventually, they cited for him those predictions in the Books of the Prophets concerning the appearance of the Promised One in the Holy Land, and adduced the presence of Bahá'u'lláh at that blessed Spot as proof of the fulfilment of those divine pledges. Out of his

---

* ibid. p. 135.

ignorance, that fellow became upset and made this reply to the Bahá'ís: 'Bahá'u'lláh had read these promises mentioned in the Books of the Prophets, and travelled to that part of the world accordingly, so that by this means He might apply those scriptural prophecies to Himself.' The Bahá'ís then proceeded to tell him about the history of the Cause, informing him of the circumstances attending the banishment and imprisonment of the Ancient Beauty (at the behest of two tyrannical governments, Persian and Ottoman), and describing for him the divine aid and confirmation that was rendered. The fellow was utterly astonished, so deeply affected by what he had heard that he seemed to have been struck dumb. The state into which he had been thrust led him to embrace the Faith, and account the realization of those prophecies – fulfilled only through unseen power and assistance – as the greatest vindication of the truth of this Cause.

* * *

One of the important cables the Master sent during His sojourn in Ramleh was a telegram written in reply to some believers of Tehran, who had sent Him several letters regarding the election of members of the Persian parliament. In all these communications, they had requested the Master's permission to serve as members of parliament themselves, so that the Bahá'ís, too, could begin to elect people to political office, but He categorically forbade the believers to do this. The exact words of the telegram which He sent them in response, through Mírzá Ghulám-'Alí Daváfurúsh, are as follows:

> Wish for the good-pleasure of God, not membership in the parliament.

He likewise made these remarks in this vein:

> Following the revolution* up to the present time, the people of Persia have made repeated attempts to elect people and form con-

* The Persian Constitutional Revolution (1905–1911).

> sultative assemblies, but these efforts have borne no fruit. They have only thrown the nation's affairs into greater disarray and further agitated the tumult of the masses. This time is no different from the past. In such a case as this, however much the Bahá'ís keep their distance from this unrest, busying themselves instead with serving the Cause of God and spreading His sweet savours, it will leave them that much more untroubled. One must devote one's precious time to matters that will yield a result. One must render a service to the world of humanity and be the means through which the various peoples make progress and become united, rather than the cause of disordered affairs and the promoter of the interests of others.

It was also in those days that certain spreaders of corruption had created estrangement and incited open dissension among the believers of Tehran, so much so that people feared every conceivable sort of sedition would break out. In the end, when matters came to a dire pass, God laid bare the true colours of one of those conceited troublemakers, and apprised the friends of his corruptive machinations. The Master sent a cable addressed to the believers of Tehran which stated the following:

> 'Tamaddun'[1137] is an Azalí, and it is forbidden to associate with him.

The instant the Master's telegram was received, the flame of sedition was extinguished. All the friends came to realize that Mírzá 'Abdu'l-Ḥusayn Qalátí, who had gained fame for himself with the title of 'Tamaddun', was promoting fear and corruption at the instigation of the enemies of the Cause. His face, much like his stature,[1138] was exceedingly small and lacking, and his temperament, not unlike his visage, was riddled with abhorrent blemishes. Although he was notorious everywhere for his wicked deeds and wayward character, yet amidst some who are thoughtless, he had gained so strong a reputation for his 'noble service' that, even when there was a perceptive and thoughtful person among the believers,

Tamaddun would use him, too, to advance his selfish interests and assert his so-called superiority over his peers. Whenever such motives as these – which have invariably dissolved the oneness and unity of every nation, and conduced to the distress and abasement of every people – have appeared in humanity's midst, it has allowed people like that ill-natured person to seize their chance in a way that leaves all the friends oblivious to how gravely those actions affect the future of the Cause. People of this sort strive day and night, sparing nothing in their efforts to fulfil their imaginings and prove the purported validity of their opinions. Had it not been for divine confirmations, as well as the advent of that justice which proceeds from the Centre of the celestial Covenant, God only knows what an agonizing affliction that critical affair would have yielded. It truly behooves the people of Bahá to record these kinds of accounts and episodes with the utmost precision – and always converse with one another in a manner that instils vigilance and heedfulness – so that in the future they may be protected from this sort of peril, enabled to recognize every selfish seeker of rank and glory in their midst, and averse to unrest in whatever form it may appear.

As a result of some of the painful occurrences that transpired in those days, marked by distressing matters that unfolded in a way of which only God is truly aware, the Master's health suffered so badly that He was not even able to eat or sleep during the last days and nights of His stay in Ramleh. The behaviour of those heedless people had stricken Him with constant sadness. As it was hoped that a change of climate might improve His condition, the Master relocated [on 13 October] to Aboukir for a few days.[1139] The move, however, had no effect on His health; His weakness, fever, and sleeplessness remained the same. Eventually, the friends in the Holy Land began to raise their cries of longing more than ever before, imploring the Master to come back to Haifa and 'Akká and grace them with His lordly presence. In addition to this, a number of the believers came to convey to Him – on behalf of the members of the Holy Family, the Afnáns,[1140] and other dear souls in that hallowed land – their earnest wish for Him to return. At one point, when the severity of His weariness and sleeplessness had completely sapped Him of the strength to speak, He dismissed all His travelling visitors and said, 'We will leave this very week.'

And so it was that, with that same infirmity and lack of sleep, the Master set off for the Holy Land.

Tuesday, 2 December 1913

[Alexandria → En route to Haifa, on board the *Baron Call*]

That afternoon, the Master boarded an Austrian ship called the *Baron Call*,[1141] which set sail from Alexandria shortly after nightfall.

The ship arrived at Port Said on the morning[1142] of the fifth of Muḥarram [Wednesday, 3 December], and up until the afternoon, various people hailing both from Persia and from the Arab world – including the honourable Áqá Aḥmad [Effendí Yazdí], Ḥájí Siyyid Javád,[1143] and the other friends of that city – attained the Master's presence.

The attendants who accompanied Him on that voyage were four: the esteemed Áqá Mírzá Jalál, the Master's son-in-law (and the son of the King of Martyrs); Mirza Ahmad Sohrab; sweet Khusraw; and this lowly servant.

The Master's ship left the pier of Port Said that night and docked[1144] at Jaffa the following morning [Thursday, 4 December]. Although the waters were somewhat rough, which made it rather difficult to travel, Áqá 'Abdu'ṣ-Ṣamad, Áqá Raḥmatu'lláh and 'Alí Effendí nevertheless betook themselves to the Master's ship as soon as they learned of His arrival.[1145] Their hearts and eyes were illumined with the light of their meeting, and they rendered thanks for the confirmations that had been granted from the Most Glorious Kingdom.

As the turbulence of the sea had reached a point that made it impossible to continue travelling, the ship stopped at that place [Jaffa] for the rest of that day and night.

Friday, 5 December 1913

[Jaffa → En route to Haifa, on board the *Baron Call* → Haifa]

The Master's retinue set sail from Jaffa.[1146] The weather was mild, the waters were calm, and our restless hearts and souls found solace and peace in the elegance of His gait.

The seashore and other environs of the Holy Land came into the Master's view from a distance, and by that afternoon the ship was directly opposite the hallowed Mount Carmel.[1147] He walked to and fro, observing the holy cities of Haifa and 'Akká and their surroundings with His binoculars. The further His ship sailed, the more His radiant heart rejoiced with exceeding gladness. Indeed, the signs of delight would grow increasingly apparent on His beautiful face, which only continued to beam with ever more joy.

As His ship was approaching the shore, the Master instructed the members of His retinue to disembark, and then said the following to Áqá Mírzá Jalál:[1148]

> Do not allow a single person to go to any trouble, and do not let anyone come to the seashore or enter the ship. All the Bahá'ís, whether they have travelled from afar or live in the vicinity, should gather at my home.[1149] I will meet with all of them once I have entered the city.

When the Greatest Holy Leaf, the Exalted Consort,[1150] the ladies of the Holy Family, the Afnáns, and the other favoured friends of God received the good news that the Master and His retinue had arrived, they worked with great ecstasy and commotion to hold a jubilant celebration. They flung open the doors to abundant bliss, spread out magnificent rugs on the floor of His house, and prompted every heart to turn toward the Covenant of God.

When the Master came onto that scene,[1151] the first to attain His presence in the women's quarters and listen to His most sweet voice were the members of His household, the ladies of the Holy Family, and other female believers hailing from both the East and the West.

When He then went to meet the gathering of His ardent lovers,[1152] they all turned towards Him and fell at His feet, notwithstanding that He emphatically forbade them to do this.[1153] Their ecstasy moved them to tears, and they rendered thanks and praise to the Most Glorious Kingdom.

Once He had seated Himself,[1154] the Master gave a brief talk on expressing gratitude for the confirmations of the Ancient Beauty, as well as the aid and support of the Most Great Name. He then spoke of the pleasantness of the Holy Land and the weather of Mount Carmel:

> In other countries, there are many well-known places which are pleasant, but the freshness and pleasantness of those places are all artificial. The exquisiteness and freshness of this place are spiritual, and the vitality of this blessed spot is divine.

Following the chanting of prayers,[1155] and after the Master had extended His tender kindnesses, He took His leave. The believers were dismissed, and they showed the utmost joy and delight as they departed His presence, each of them receiving a confection as they left. Having attained to this sweet end, they came out of the Master's house with words of praise and gratitude on their lips.[1156]

The Holy Land

Saturday, 6 December 1913
[Haifa]

As the Master was heading for the Shrine of the Báb that morning, He found that all the believers, locals and travellers alike, had gathered on Mount Carmel and formed a line in the road He was crossing. When they reached the Shrine of the Báb, the Master motioned to the friends to enter through the first set of doors. He Himself entered through a different door and rested His brow on the sacred threshold.

Apart from that particular day, whenever the believers were in His presence as they were making pilgrimage to the Shrine of the Báb or Bahá'u'lláh at other times, the Master would first anoint them with fragrant rosewater, beckon them to enter, and then perform His own pilgrimage while standing behind everyone else.

When the Master went to the large [reception] room[1157] in the Shrine of the Báb after making His pilgrimage that day, some of the friends threw themselves at His feet, and this prompted Him to make these remarks again and again:

> This is not permitted by any means. According to the Holy Writ,* one should prostrate oneself only before the Shrines of the Báb

* Perhaps a reference to the following excerpts from a Tablet of Bahá'u'lláh: 'He, verily, hath forbidden you from bowing down and falling at My feet or at the feet of any other. This is that which We have revealed in the Book as bidden by Him Who is the All-Knowing, the All-Wise . . . Kiss not the hands of anyone, nor bow down upon entering the presence of another. To none is it allowed to abase himself before another soul. Such is the command of God . . . Prostration, bowing down, falling to the ground, and the kissing of hands have been forbidden unto you . . . Prostration is befitting only before Him Who is the Unknowable, the Unseen . . . It is not for anyone to prostrate himself before another, and he who hath done so must needs repent and repair unto God, the Ever-Forgiving, the Most Compassionate' (Bahá'u'lláh, *Áthár-i-Qalam-i-A'lá*, vol. 2, pp. 77–8; authorized translation provided by the Bahá'í World Centre).

> and Bahá'u'lláh and also the Blessed House.* Beyond this, it is forbidden to prostrate oneself in any other direction. Beware lest you transgress what has been revealed in the Scriptures of God!

A most lively gathering was held at His home that night, and a number of the distinguished men of 'Akká and Haifa were also present on that sublime occasion,[1158] where He gave a talk on His journey to America in which He mentioned His raising the Call of God and spreading the divine teachings at various churches, synagogues, and other large assemblages.

Sunday, 7 December 1913

[Haifa → 'Akká → The Shrine of Bahá'u'lláh, on the outskirts of 'Akká]

In the morning, the Master instructed the believers to take a special trip to 'Akká to make pilgrimage to the Shrine of Bahá'u'lláh.[1159] Accordingly, the friends who lived in the vicinity and those who had travelled from afar – nearly a hundred people in all – gathered at the train station. The Master took a separate railway carriage for Himself.[1160]

When everyone had boarded the train, they found the cars filled to the brim with Bahá'ís and entirely empty of anyone else.[1161] The songs and melodies they lifted up seemed to reach the clouds of the heavens. With all the jubilation that attended the Master's arrival, one might have thought that the believers were celebrating the Birth of the Abhá Beauty all over again,[1162] and the radiance that blossomed from their faces could have put the stars and the moon themselves to shame. The joyful congratulations they offered on His arrival were enough to shake every limb and reveal the mysteries of the Kingdom to every heart. All His ardent lovers intoned, in unison, the odes and other poems of the revered Varqá, the esteemed 'Andalíb,[1163] Jináb-i-Baṣṣár,[1164] and others – clapping and dancing as they sang – and they continued to sing anthems that saluted the Master on His arrival up until they reached 'Akká.[1165]

* This could refer either to the House of the Báb or the House of Bahá'u'lláh.

Everyone gathered at the house of the Master before having their lunch. With the utmost ecstasy and delight, they spoke of the confirmations of the Most Glorious Kingdom and expressed their praise of 'Him round Whom all names revolve'. Once they had had their meal, they left 'Akká to make pilgrimage to their holy destination.

Tears fell from their eyes as they humbled themselves in fervent supplication at the threshold of the Shrine of Bahá'u'lláh. They entreated the Abhá Kingdom to confirm all the Bahá'ís, and implored the aid and bounty of God. When they concluded their pilgrimage, they commenced festivities of heavenly communion in the pilgrim-house at [the Mansion of] Bahjí.

This went on until the afternoon, when it was time to return. Consequently, all those who had come on this trip – local residents and distant travellers alike – gathered at the train station, where many of the inhabitants of 'Akká itself were also present. The train arrived from Haifa, and suddenly 'Abdu'l-Bahá – may the spirits of all living things be offered up for His munificence – alighted the vehicle. Some of the leading men of 'Akká had gone to Haifa to attain His presence and were now on board the returning train with Him. When the eyes of those around Him, friends and others, fell on His luminous person, they all brought one of their hands up to their chests as a show of reverence. Each and every one of their necks was bowed in humility before the force of His glory and the magnetism of His matchless beauty, and the elegance of His gait would have aroused the obvious envy of the kings of the earth.

It was at that moment that the friends recalled the confinement of the Ancient Beauty in the Most Great Prison and the calamities He endured. Having been reminded of the pervasive influence of the Cause of God, as well as the fulfilment of the promises of the Abhá Beauty, they said to themselves:

> No one could have imagined that a time would come so quickly when the spinning wheel of fate would turn in a way that aligned with the hopes and desires of the righteous believers – that the Most Great Branch would be freed from the Prison of 'Akká, travel

> from the climes of the East to the farthest countries of the West to raise the Call of God and exalt His Word, and then return from America and Europe to the Holy Land with the hosts of victorious conquest at His side, or that He would alight here, at the train station by the city gate of 'Akká, with such power and majesty, and that people from both near and far, belonging to every walk of life, would treat Him with such profound reverence and show this degree of submissiveness before His luminous face.

Were the fair-minded ones to reflect even briefly on the momentousness of the things just recounted, they would see the extraordinary power of the Word of God before their very eyes, and clearly behold the invisible aid which at every moment supports this perspicuous Cause. This confirmation and assistance, this glory and grandeur, are themselves the realization of the promises of the Abhá Beauty and the fulfilment of the prophecies He recorded. Among them are the following statements revealed in His wondrous and sublime Tablet to Náṣiri'd-Dín Shāh that pertain to the Most Great Prison, as well as the triumph of the Cause of God and the influence of His Word:

> Erelong shall the exponents of wealth and power banish Us from the land of Adrianople to the city of 'Akká. According to what they say, it is the most desolate of the cities of the world, the most unsightly of them in appearance, the most detestable in climate, and the foulest in water. It is as though it were the metropolis of the owl, within whose precincts naught can be heard save the echo of its cry. Therein have they resolved to imprison this Youth, to shut against our faces the doors of ease and comfort, and to deprive us of every worldly benefit throughout the remainder of our days.
>
> By God! Though weariness lay Me low, and hunger consume Me, and the bare rock be My bed, and My fellows the beasts of the field, I will not complain, but will endure patiently as those endued with constancy and firmness have endured patiently, through the power of God, the Eternal King and Creator of the

nations, and will render thanks unto God under all conditions. We pray that, out of His bounty – exalted be He – He may release, through this imprisonment, the necks of men from chains and fetters, and cause them to turn, with sincere faces, towards His face, Who is the Mighty, the Bounteous. Ready is He to answer whosoever calleth upon Him, and nigh is He unto such as commune with Him . . .

Erelong shall the snow-white hand of God rend an opening through the darkness of this night and unlock a mighty portal unto His City. On that Day shall the people enter therein by troops, uttering what the blamers aforetime exclaimed, that there shall be made manifest in the end that which appeared in the beginning.[1166]

* * *

Praise be to God, the immeasurably glorious, that through the confirmations of the Abhá Kingdom and the Most Exalted Horizon, and also the assistance and bounty of 'Abdu'l-Bahá – may my soul and my very being be offered up for such of His loved ones as are firm in His most perfect Covenant – this lowly servant has successfully completed his composition of the first and second volumes of this chronicle. I was graciously aided to record episodes from the Master's journey with my own pen and then present Him with my account.[1167] The manifest traces of His travels have only been chronicled to the extent that my comprehension and capacity have allowed me, not in the plenitude of their peerless glory and grandeur. How well has it been said:

As thou art truly in thyself
What eye beholdeth thee?
All understand no further than
Their limited degree.[1168]

I appeal, therefore, to the bounty and beneficence of the heavenly threshold to forgive and pardon me, and I cherish the hope that the readers of these pages may overlook my shortcomings. Through this humble drop, may they apprehend that Sea of divine grace, and regard this insignificant atom as having portrayed the dazzling rays of the Sun of celestial favour. Every good thing is of God, and every evil thing is from ourselves.[1169]

I, the lowly servant Maḥmúd ibn-i-Ismá'íl Zarqání, do hereby conclude the first and second volumes of this chronicle on the hallowed Mount Carmel, in the vicinity of the Shrine of the Báb, and beneath the bountiful shade of 'Abdu'l-Bahá, may my soul be offered up for the ground which the footsteps of them who are firm in His most perfect Covenant have trodden.

Maḥmúd ibn-i-Ismá'íl Zarqání
Sunday, 19 July 1914

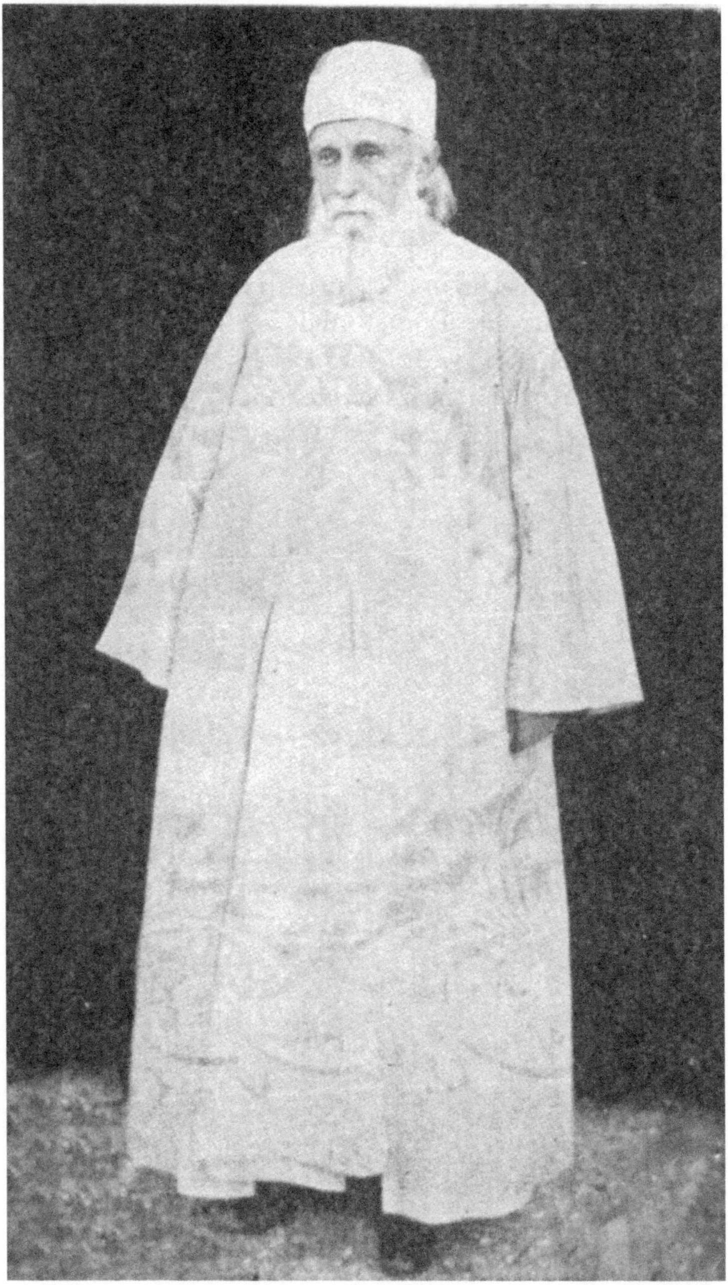

'Abdu'l-Bahá. A photograph taken in Haifa after His return from Europe

Appendix
Selected Biographical Notes

Most of the entries below have been taken verbatim from *'Abdu'l-Bahá in the West*, all with the kind permission of its author, Jan Jasion, and adapted for inclusion in this biographical index.

Adíb, Áqá Mírzá 'Alí Khán (Mírzá 'Alí ibn Adíb)
Persian Bahá'í
Met 'Abdu'l-Bahá in Paris, 1913.
Son of the Hand of the Cause Mírzá Ḥasan-i-Adíb (1848–1919).

Afnán, Mírzá Nayyir (d. Apr. 1952 Haifa)
Persian Bahá'í
Met 'Abdu'l-Bahá in London, 1911 and on 28 Dec. 1912, at the home of Lady Blomfield.
Nephew of 'Abdu'l-Bahá; son of Ḥájí Siyyid 'Alí Afnán and Furúghíyyih (a daughter of Bahá'u'lláh). Expelled from the Faith around 1941. After 1948 he was in Lebanon. Married to Rúḥangíz Rabbání.

Aguilar, Alejo (b. 1880 Cartago, Costa Rica)
Costa Rican coffee planter and merchant
It is likely that he is one of the Costa Rican coffee merchants who met 'Abdu'l-Bahá in Paris on 22 Feb. 1913, along with Ricardo Montealegre.

Akbar, Fatḥu'lláh Khán (Sardár-i-Manṣúr or Sipahdár-i-Rashtí) (c. 1866–c. 1947)
Persian statesman and wealthy landowner
Met 'Abdu'l-Bahá many times in Paris either at his residence at 42 ave. de La Bourdonnais or at one of the residences of 'Abdu'l-Bahá, 15, 16 Mar.; 31 May; 2, 3, 4, and 7 Jun. 1913.
Minister of the Interior, 1916. Prime Minister of Persia, 1920–21.

Alfassa, Mirra ('The Mother' and Mirra Richard) (21 Feb. 1878 Paris–17 Nov. 1973 Pondicherry [now Puducherry], India)
French Hindu leader
Met 'Abdu'l-Bahá in Paris: 11, 14, 17, 24 Feb.; 5, 10, 17, 20 Mar.; 1, 12, 14, 18, 23, 25, 26, 27, 31 May; 4, 9 Jun. 1913.
She was born Blanche Rachel Mirra Alfassa and was the daughter of Sephardic Jews from Turkey and Egypt, respectively. She studied art at the Académie des Beaux Arts in Paris. In 1897, she married the French painter Henri François Morisset and divorced in 1908. They had one son, André Morisset In 1911, she married the French lawyer Paul Antoine Richard. Around 1905 she started to become involved with the occult movement, first in France and from 1906–07 in Algeria. In 1914 she and Paul left France for India and met the Indian mystic Sri Aurobindo (1870–1950) at Pondicherry. They returned to France briefly, 1915–16. From 1916–20 she and Paul Richard were in Japan. In 1920 they arrived in Pondicherry and from then on she was permanently associated with the ashram of Sri Aurobindo and after his death, its head. She is buried in the Sri Aurobindo Ashram.
Publications: *Collected Works* (1972).

Ali, Sir Syed Ameer (Judge Amír-'Alí Ṣáḥib) (6 Apr. 1849 Cuttack, Bengal [now in Orissa], India–4 Aug. 1928 Rudgwick, Sussex)
Indian political leader and lawyer
Met 'Abdu'l-Bahá at the Shah Jahan Mosque, Woking, England, 18 Jan. 1913.
He was educated at Muhsiniyya ('Hooghly') College, near Calcutta. He went to England to study in 1869. He was called to the Bar in 1873. In 1904 upon retirement from the Bengal High Court he settled in England with his English wife, Isabelle Ida Konstam. In 1883 he became one of the three Indian members (and the only Muslim) on the Viceroy's Council, and in 1909 he was appointed the first Indian member of the Judicial Committee of the Privy Council in London. He founded in 1877 a 'National Mahommedan [sic] Association'. He was instrumental in setting up the London branch of the Muslim League. In 1913 he was a member of the council of the Persia Society, along with Edward G. Browne, and others. His loyalty to

Britain led him to resign in 1913 when the League joined with the Indian National Congress in talk of 'Home Rule'. After the First World War he came into prominence as the London champion of the Khilafat movement.
Publications: *Spirit of Islam* (1891).

Allard, Henri
French advocate
Most likely met 'Abdu'l-Bahá on one of His visits to the Persian legation.
Chancellor at the Persian legation in Paris, 1909–13.

Allen, Mary Sophia (12 Mar. 1878 Cardiff, Wales–16 Dec. 1964 Croydon, England)
British suffragette and policewoman
She met 'Abdu'l-Bahá in London 12 Jan. 1913, probably at Lady Blomfield's.
She was a leading pioneer in establishing women policing in England.
Her sister Christine Allen married John Duncan.

Amín, Ḥájí
See **Ardakání, Ḥájí Abu'l-Ḥasan (Ḥájí Amín or 'Amín-i-Iláhí')**

Amín-i-Iláhí
See **Ardakání, Ḥájí Abu'l-Ḥasan (Ḥájí Amín or 'Amín-i-Iláhí')**

Áqá, 'Alí 'Abbás
See **Tabrízí, 'Alí 'Abbás Áqá**

Ardakání, Ḥájí Abu'l-Ḥasan (Ḥájí Amín or 'Amín-i-Iláhí') (1831 Ardakan, Persia–27 May 1928 Tehran)
Persian Bábí (1851) and Bahá'í (c. 1867), merchant and trustee of Ḥuqúqu'lláh
Met 'Abdu'l-Bahá at 97 Cadogan Gardens, London, 19 Dec. 1912. In Paris with 'Abdu'l-Bahá, 22 Jan. 1913.
He met Bahá'u'lláh in 'Akká in the 1870s. Around 1880 he was

appointed by Bahá'u'lláh as the Trustee of the Ḥuqúqu'lláh, a special Bahá'í fund. He was imprisoned for a few years around 1891 on the orders of the Shah. He was a member of 'Abdu'l-Bahá's entourage in 1911 in England. He was posthumously appointed Hand of the Cause (1928) by Shoghi Effendi and is mentioned as one of the Apostles of Bahá'u'lláh. He was buried in the Bahá'í cemetery in Tehran.

'Árif, Mírzá Ḥusayn
Persian Bahá'í poet
Met 'Abdu'l-Bahá in Paris, on 7, 10, and 17 Feb. at His apartment, 30 rue Saint-Didier, and on 21 Mar. 1913 at the Martha-Pension.
He had been residing in Paris since about 1898. Possibly related to the Azeri poet Huseyn Arif (1924–1992).

Arundel, Sir Arundel Tagg (1 Jul. 1843 New Barnet, England–8 Nov. 1929 Guildford, Surrey, England)
British colonial civil servant in India
Met 'Abdu'l-Bahá at the Shah Jahan Mosque, Woking, England, 17 Jan. 1913.
He was educated at the University of London. In 1864 he was appointed to the Indian Civil Service. He held a variety of judicial and fiscal appointments. Member of Lord Curzon's staff. In 1901–06 member of Viceroy's and Governor-General's Council. Married to Catherine Helen Sim Arundel in 1875. He and his wife are buried at St James' Church, Abinger Common, Surrey.

Arundel (née Sim), Dame Catherine Helen (1853 Madras [today Chennai, Tamil Nadu], India–23 May 1933 Camberley, Surrey, England)
British
Met 'Abdu'l-Bahá at the Shah Jahan Mosque, Woking, England, 17 Jan. 1913.
Daughter of James Duncan Sim. In 1875, she married Sir Arundel Tagg Arundel. In 1891 she converted to the Roman Catholic faith. She is buried in St James' Churchyard, Abinger Common, Surrey.

Ashraf, Mírzá Ashraf (Jul. 1893 Tehran, Persia–5 Mar. 1991 Geneva)
Persian Bahá'í, student, educator and administrator
Met 'Abdu'l-Bahá in Paris on several occasions at 4 avenue de Camoëns in 1911 and 1913.
He studied in France from 1911 to 1915. He apparently held several government positions in Persia. He immigrated to Switzerland in 1953. Brother of Ghodsieh (Qudsíyyih) Khánum-i-Ashraf. Married (1918) Azizeh Attar (d. 1969).

Atta Ullah, Sheik
Indian law student
Met 'Abdu'l-Bahá at the Shah Jahan Mosque, Woking, England, 17 Jan. 1913.

Back de Surany, Hermann (24 Sept. 1848 Galgóc, Austrian Empire [today Hlohovec, Slovakia]–24 Mar. 1925 Nice, France)
French diplomat and entrepreneur
Persian consul-general in Paris, 1911–13. He married Mathilde Orosdi in 1877. Member of the Back-Orosdi family of entrepreneurs from Austria-Hungary who developed businesses in Cairo, Vienna, and Paris. He served on the board of managers of the firm Établissements Orosdi-Back. Converted from Judaism to Roman Catholicism. He was awarded the Légion d'Honneur. In 1913, listed as a member of the Comité de l'Orient.

Bacon, Francis Herbert (b. c. 1858 Canada)
English clergyman
Met 'Abdu'l-Bahá in London, 11 Jan. 1913 at Caxton Hall, Westminster, where he also spoke.
The Rt. Rev. Francis Herbert Bacon, was consecrated in 7 Jan. 1911 in England as a bishop of Durham in the British Old Catholic Church. From 1914 to 1920, Bishop Bacon lived in Canada and the United States, where he ordained Anglican priests in Old Catholic holy orders.

Bahárlú, Amír Khán (Emir Khan de Beharlou)
Persian diplomat; doctor
Met ʻAbduʼl-Bahá when He attended the Naw-Rúz celebrations at the Persian legation in Paris on 21 Mar. 1913. In 1907, he was a member of the Persian delegation to the second Hague Peace Conference. In 1911–13, he was at the Persian legation in Paris as the third secretary.

Bahnmüller, Berta
See **Bopp (née Bahnmüller), Berta**

Balogh, Vilma (Bánoczi Lászlóné) (23 Nov. 1873 Budapest–12 Jun. 1945 Budapest)
Hungarian journalist and photographer
She met and wrote about ʻAbduʼl-Bahá in a Budapest newspaper.

Báqiroff, Siyyid Aḥmad [Russian: Саид Ахмад Багиров (**Said Akhmad Bagirov**)]
Persian Baháʼí
Met ʻAbduʼl-Bahá in Paris, 22 Jan. and 4 Mar. 1913.
Member of ʻAbduʼl-Baháʼs entourage in 1913. His uncle, Siyyid Naṣruʼlláh Báqiroff (1857–1921), offered the major share of the expenses of ʻAbduʼl-Baháʼs travels in Europe and America. In 1901, he was residing in Baku, Azerbaijan.

Barclay, Sir Thomas (20 Feb. 1853 Dunfermline, Scotland–20 Jan. 1941 Versailles, France)
British journalist, jurist and proponent of international law
Chaired a meeting at which ʻAbduʼl-Bahá spoke at the Westminster Palace Hotel in London, 20 Dec. 1911.
Member of Parliament for Blackburn, 1910. In 1911 he was one of the original members of the Persia Society. He was nominated for the Nobel Peace Prize. He was president d'honneur of Amis de la Paix, Paris; chairman of the council of the Persia Society, and president of the British Chamber of Commerce in Paris, 1899–1900 and a member of Amities Internationales. He was appointed Commander of the Legion of Honour and Grand Officer of the Order of the Lion

and Sun. In 1877 he married Marie-Thérèse Teuscher. They made their home in Versailles, France. Their son, Captain George Reinhold Barclay (1882–1918), an intelligence officer in the British Army, was killed in an air raid in Kortrijk, Belgium on 30 Oct. 1918.

Barnes, Rev. Isaac Edmestone (2 Jun. 1857 Kingston, Jamaica–c. 1930)
Jamaican black clergyman and surveyor
Met 'Abdu'l-Bahá in London at Lady Blomfield's, Dec. 1912.
He entered the ministry in Jamaica in the Christadelphian Brotherhood. For some time he served his church in New York City. After leaving the church he worked as a land surveyor and civil engineer. He was appointed Surveyor General to the Republic of Liberia. He also worked in the mining areas of South Africa, Brazil and Sierra Leone.

Barney, Laura Clifford
See **Dreyfus-Barney, Laura Alice Clifford**

Barney, Natalie Clifford (31 Oct. 1876 Dayton, Ohio–1 Feb. 1972 Paris)
American feminist writer and salon hostess in Paris
She met 'Abdu'l-Bahá in London at Lady Blomfield's on 19, 27, and 28 Dec. 1912 and invited Him to dine with her in Paris 23 Jan. 1913.
Sister of Laura Dreyfus Barney and daughter of Alice Pike Barney. Noted for her poems and her alternative lifestyle. For over fifty years her salon at 20 rue Jacob was frequented by the famous literati of Europe and America. Of the writers who visited her salon over the years, some were inclined to make reference to the Bahá'í Faith in their works, and they included Ezra Pound, Remy de Gourmont, Rainer-Maria Rilke (1875–1926), Sinclair Lewis (1885–1951), Salomon Reinach (1858–1932), Édouard Herriot (1872–1957), Guillaume Appolinaire (1880–1918), etc. She is buried in the Cimetiere de Passy, Paris with her sister.
Biography: Suzanne Rodriquez, *Wild Heart: A Life* (2002), among others.

Bashir Uddin, Shah
Indian law student
Met 'Abdu'l-Bahá at the Shah Jahan Mosque, Woking, England, 17 Jan. 1913.
He was studying law at Middle Temple, London.

Baudry (née Sacy), Mercedes (18 Jun. 1895 Cairo, Egypt–1988)
Met 'Abdu'l-Bahá in Paris at 4 avenue de Camoëns, with her mother, Madeleine Jenny Sacy, in 1911, and again on 9 and 23 Feb., and 29 May 1913.

Beauchamp, Jeanne
French spiritualist
Welcomed 'Abdu'l-Bahá with opening remarks at the meeting of the Alliance Spiritualiste in Paris, 9 Nov. 1911 and in the Salle de Troyes, Paris, 21 Feb. 1913.
She also met Him at His residence on 26 Feb. 1913.
President and founder (1910) of Alliance Spiritualiste. In 1912 she wrote *Étude comparée de la Doctrine Esotérique des Religions et Philosophies religieuses* (Paris). She resided in Amien, Somme.

Beede, Alice R. (23 Dec. 1860 New York City–1929 New York City)
American Bahá'í
She first met 'Abdu'l-Bahá at 4 avenue de Camoëns in Paris, 15 Oct. 1911. She sailed from Cherbourg on 21 Oct. 1911 for New York City. She saw 'Abdu'l-Bahá again at the Fourth Annual Convention of Bahai Temple Unity, 30 Apr. which she attended as a delegate from Montclair, New Jersey, and also at the Hotel Ansonia, New York City, 12 Apr. 1912, and at the ground-breaking ceremony for the Bahá'í Temple, 1 May 1912 and during the period 1–23 May 1913 in Paris. In 1910 elected to the Bahá'í New York City Women's Board of Council. Married to William H. Beede (b. 1850), a stockbroker.

Benjamin, Ida A. M. (8 Aug. 1858 Afton, Iowa–4 Apr. 1952 Santa Clara, California)
Scottish-American Bahá'í, nurse, astrologer

Met 'Abdu'l-Bahá in Paris, 8 Jun. 1913.
She resided in London, 1912–14. After returning to America she lived in Alameda and Santa Barbara, California. Buried in Saratoga I.O.O.F. Cemetery, Saratoga, California.

Bernard, Claire
French Bahá'í
Met 'Abdu'l-Bahá in Paris at 30 rue Saint-Didier, 23 Jan. 1913 and on subsequent days.
She was originally English. She had travelled to India and had adopted two Indian [Hindu] boys. Wife of Alfred Auguste Marie Bernard.

Bernard, Alfred Auguste Marie (14 Feb. 1887 Laneuville-au-Raupt, Meuse, France–22 Aug. 1914 Audun-le-Roman, Meuse, France)
French Bahá'í
Met 'Abdu'l-Bahá in Paris on many occasions in 1911 and 1913.
He was an active member of the Paris Bahá'í community. During World War I he was a soldier in the 29eme Bn. de Chasseurs à Pied of the French army and was killed during the first weeks of the war. Married to Claire Bernard.

Bey, Prince Muḥammad-'Alí (9 Nov. 1875 Cairo–18 Mar. 1955 Lausanne, Switzerland)
Egyptian prince; sometime regent
'Abdu'l-Bahá visited him at the Belmont Hotel, Fifth Avenue, New York City, 22 Jul. 1912, and then he met Him 31 May; 1, 3 and 4 Jun. in Paris and in Marseilles; 13 Jun. 1913 on board the *SS Himalaya*, on which they sailed to Egypt.
Son of Khedive Muhammad Tewfik Pasha (1852–92) and Princess Emine Ibrahim (1858–1931). He was the younger brother of Khedive Abbas Hilmi II (1874–1944), whom 'Abdu'l-Bahá had met in Alexandria in 1910. He was educated at the Ali School, Cairo; the Victoria College, Alexandria; and at Château de Lancy, Geneva. Raised to the rank of an Ottoman vizier in 1910. Heir presumptive 1892–99, 1917–20, 1936–52, and 1952–53. President of the Council of Regency during the minority of King Faruk 1936–37, and of the

Council of the Court 1937–38. Received the GC of the Orders of the Legion of Honour of France, 1936. Married at Cairo (1941) Suzanne, née Hémon, a former French actress. Buried at the Khedive Tawfik Mausoleum, Kait Bey, Cairo.

He mentioned meeting 'Abdu'l-Bahá in his *Riḥlat sumuww al-amír Muḥammad 'Alí Búshá shaqíq al-janáb al-'alí al-kidawí il'a al-jiha al-shamálíyyah al-Amríká* (Cairo: al-Maṭba'ah al-Amíríyyah, 1913).

Biography: For a pictorial history of the Egyptian royal family see: Osman Ibrahim, *Méhémet Ali le grand: Mémoires intimes d'une dynastie (1805–2005)* (2005).

Bhawani Singh Bahadur, *Raj Rana of Jhalawar* (3 Sept. 1874 Fatehpur, Jhalawar State [now in Rajasthan], India–13 Apr. 1929 at sea near Aden Settlement [now in Yemen])

Maharaja of Jhalawar

Visited 'Abdu'l-Bahá at 97 Cadogan Gardens, London, 29 Dec. 1912. In 1898 he was appointed by the government as the Maharaja of Jhalawar, India. He was educated at Mayo College, Ajmer, and at New College, Oxford 1921–22. Member of the Royal Society of Great Britain. He built Kemball Public Library, Colvin Girl's School and Parmanand Hostel, and established the Rajendra Literary Institute. Married 1894, HH Maharani Brij Kunwar. He died 13th Apr. 1929 at sea and was cremated in Aden.

See: Lua Moore Getsinger, 'What Constitutes a Prince: A Heretofore Unpublished Account of a Visit to the Maharaja of Jhalawar', in *Star of the West: The Bahá'í Magazine*, vol. 15, no. 4 (Jul. 1924), pp. 102–06.

Blomfield, Lady Sara Louisa Ryan ('Sitárih Khánum') (1859 Dublin, Ireland–31 Dec. 1939 London)

British Bahá'í (1907)

Hosted 'Abdu'l-Bahá at her home, 97 Cadogan Gardens, London, Sept. 1911. She was the prime mover behind recording and publishing 'Abdu'l-Bahá's Paris talks in 1911. She was sent by Him with others to Stuttgart for a three-day visit 4–7 Dec. 1911. On His second trip to England she accompanied 'Abdu'l-Bahá to the Shah Jahan Mosque in Woking, England, 17 Jan. 1913. During WWI, she served

in military hospitals in France and was involved with the beginning of the Save the Children Fund. In 1922 elected to the All-England Bahá'í Council. She was married (1887) to Sir Arthur William Blomfield (1829–99). She is buried in the Hampstead Municipal Cemetery, London.
Author: *The Chosen Highway* (1940); co-author *The First Obligation* (1921); compiled *Mornings Spent with Abdul Baha Abbas in London and Paris* (1911); *Talks of Abdul Baha Given in Paris* (1912).
Biography: Robert Weinberg, *Lady Blomfield* (2012).

Bopp (née Bahnmüller), Berta
German Bahá'í
Met 'Abdu'l-Bahá in Stuttgart, Apr. 1913.

Bourlet, Carlo (25 Apr. 1866 Strasbourg, France–12 Aug. 1913 Annecy, Haute-Savoie, France)
French Esperantist and mathematician
Met 'Abdu'l-Bahá in Paris, 12 Feb. 1913 and introduced Him at the annual Esperanto banquet at the Hôtel Moderne, Place de la Republique.
President of the Paris Esperanto Group. He was the founder of the journal *La Revuo*. He died in an accident.

Boutaric, Henri (1860–20 Jul. 1924 Toulouse, France)
French Bahá'í from Toulouse
Met 'Abdu'l-Bahá in Paris, 31 May 1913.
Commercial representative of the company Sels de Bayonne. Married Anne Jeanne Renaud.

Browne, Edward Granville (7 Feb. 1862 Uley, Gloucestershire, England–5 Jan. 1926 Cambridge, England)
English Orientalist and scholar of Persian
Met 'Abdu'l-Bahá in London at 97 Cadogan Gardens, 18 and 19 Dec.1912; and in Paris 9 Mar. 1913.
He was educated at Eton, Cambridge College and St Bartholomew's Hospital. Travelled in Persia and the Middle East. He was Professor of

Arabic at Pembroke College from 1902 and also a lecturer in Persian, from 1888–1902. In 1911 he was one of the original members of the Persia Society. He is buried in Elswick Cemetery, Newcastle-upon-Tyne.
Publications: *A Year Among the Persians* (1927); *A Traveller's Narrative* (1891); others.

Buckton, Alice Mary (9 Mar. 1867 Haslemere, Surrey, England–10 Dec. 1944 Wells, Somerset, England)
English Bahá'í and mystic, educationalist and writer
Met 'Abdu'l-Bahá at Lady Blomfield's on several occasions and He visited her home at Vaneer's in Byfleet, Surrey 9 Sept. 1911; she was present at the Tudor Pole home in Bristol in Sept. 1911 and also present at a meeting at which 'Abdu'l-Bahá spoke at the Westminster Palace Hotel in London, 20 Dec. 1911; she again met him in New York City, 5 Jun.; Dublin, New Hampshire, 8 Aug. 1912; and at the Shah Jahan Mosque, Woking, England, 17 Jan. 1913.
She wrote and produced the play *Eager Heart* at Church House, Westminster, which was viewed by 'Abdu'l-Bahá. In 1910 she visited the United States, where she presented her play *Eager Heart*. In 1911 she presented a lecture at Wellesley College. She resided (1914) at Chalice Well House, Chilkwell Street, Glastonbury. Memorial plague in the Church of St. John the Baptist, Glastonbury.
Publications: *Eager Heart* (1904).
Biography: Tracy Cutting, *Beneath the Silent Tor* (2004).

Campbell, Hilda May (1891–1935)
English
Met 'Abdu'l-Bahá in London at Lady Blomfield's.
Daughter of Rev. Reginald John Campbell.

Campbell, Mary Elizabeth Slack (1861–1924)
English
Met 'Abdu'l-Bahá in London at Lady Blomfield's.
Wife of Rev. Reginald John Campbell.

Campbell, Rev. Reginald John (29 Jan. 1867 London–1 Mar. 1956 Fairwarp, near Uckfield, Sussex, England)
English clergyman
Met 'Abdu'l-Bahá in London at Lady Blomfield's, then invited Him to speak at his church, the City Temple, Holborn, London, 10 Sept. 1911, the first clergyman in the West to do so.
He was educated at University College, Nottingham and Christ Church, Oxford. From 1902 to 1903 he was minister of the Congregational Union Street Chapel, Brighton and from 1903 to 1915 minister of City Temple 'the cathedral of nonconformity', in London. He was involved with the New Theology controversy which erupted in 1907. In 1908 he was elected to the Fabian Society. In 1913 he was the president of the Liberal-Christian League. In 1915 he resigned from the City Temple and the same year was ordained in the Church of England and joined Birmingham Cathedral. He was also vicar of Christ Church, Westminster. In the period 1924–30 he was at Trinity Chapel, Brighton and from 1930 to 1936 resident canon at Chichester. In 1889 he married Mary Elizabeth Slack (1861–1924) of Nottingham.

Carpenter, Dr Joseph Estlin (5 Oct. 1844 Ripley, Surrey, England–2 Jun. 1927 Oxford, England)
English Unitarian Biblical scholar
Presided at a meeting with 'Abdu'l-Bahá at Manchester College in Oxford, 31 Dec. 1912.
Principal of Manchester College, Oxford 1906–15. He is buried in Wolvercote Cemetery, Oxford.
Publications: *Comparative Religion* (1913); *Studies In Theology* (1903).

Cart, Théophile (31 Mar. 1855 Saint-Antoine-de-Breuilh, France–21 May 1931 Paris)
French Esperantist and linguist
Met 'Abdu'l-Bahá at the Hôtel Moderne, Paris on 12 Feb., and again on 14 Feb. 1913.
From 1891 to 1892 he lectured in French at the university in Uppsala, Sweden. He was a professor at the Lycée Henri-IV in Paris

(1892–1921), and a professor at the École libre des sciences politiques in Paris (1893–1931). As an ardent Esperantist, he held many posts in Esperanto organizations including president of the Société française pour la propagation de l'espéranto (1909–12). He was also the director of the journal *Lingvo internacia* (Paris). He is buried in Cimetière du Père Lachaise, Paris.
Publications: *Vortoj de Profesoro Th. Cart* (1927).

Chamberlain, Isabel Fraser (7 Mar. 1871 San Francisco–12 Feb. 1939 Los Angeles)
Scottish-American Bahá'í (1909) and writer
Met 'Abdu'l-Bahá in Liverpool at the dock, 13 Dec. 1912; also in Paris 1913.
She was the daughter of Daniel Fraser and Isabella Ross Fraser from Scotland. She was buried in Cypress Lawn Memorial Park, Colma, California. She was married to Samuel Selwyn Chamberlain. She travelled to Palestine in 1922. This trip also took her to Portugal, Great Britain, France, Italy, Switzerland, and Egypt.
Publications: *Abdul-Baha on Divine Philosophy* (1916) and articles in *Star of the West* and *The Christian Commonwealth.*

Chamberlain, Samuel Selwyn (25 Sept. 1850 Walworth, New York–26 Jan. 1916 San Francisco)
American journalist
Met 'Abdu'l-Bahá in Paris, Jun. 1913 and interviewed Him for *The London Budget.*
Editor of *The London Budget* (a Hearst newspaper) and *The Boston American.* He was also the founder and editor of the Paris newspaper *Le Matin.* He married Isabel Fraser Chamberlain. He is buried in Kensico Cemetery, Valhalla, New York.

Chevallier, Faith (1851 Nacogdoches, Texas–26 Apr. 1935 Los Angeles)
French-American Bahá'í
Met 'Abdu'l-Bahá at the Unity Feast in Oakland, California on 16 Oct. 1912 and in Paris, 14 May 1913.

Her father was born in France. She was known for her welfare work among prison inmates. She resided in Los Angeles, California.

Cheyne, Elizabeth Gibson (2 Jan. 1869 Hexham, Northumberland, England–24 Apr. 1931 London)
English poet and suffragist
'Abdu'l-Bahá visited her and her husband at their home in Oxford, at 17 Parks Road, 31 Dec. 1912.
She was educated at Gateshead High School. Wife (1911) of Thomas Kelly Cheyne. She is buried in the Holywell Cemetery, Oxford.
Biography: Judy Greenway, *From the Wilderness to the Beloved City: Elizabeth Gibson Cheyne.*

Cheyne, Thomas Kelly (18 Sept. 1841 London–16 Feb. 1915 Oxford)
British Biblical scholar; Bahá'í (1914)
'Abdu'l-Bahá visited him and his wife at their home in Oxford, at 17 Parks Road, 31 Dec. 1912.
In 1864–68 he was vice-principal of St Edmund Hall; in 1868–82 fellow at Balliol College; in 1880–85 rector of Tendring, Essex; and in 1885–1908 Oriel Professor of the interpretation of scripture at Oxford. Author of many works on biblical interpretation; initiated the critical movement of biblical studies in Britain. He married (1911) Elizabeth Gibson Cheyne. He is buried in the Holywell Cemetery, Oxford.
Publications: *The Reconciliation of Races and Religions* (1914), etc.

Child, C. W.
English palmist
Met 'Abdu'l-Bahá in London, 1912.
He read 'Abdu'l-Bahá's palms and published the results with photographs. In 1925, he resided at 6, Netherford Road, Larkhall Rise, Clapham, London, S.W.4.
Publications: "The Hands of Abdul Baha", in *The International Psychic Gazette* (London) vol. 1, no. 7 (Feb. 1913), pp. 199–200; also R. Jackson Armstrong-Ingram, *Written in Light: 'Abdu'l-Bahá and the American Bahá'í Community, 1898–1921* (1998), pp. 32–3.

Clark, Sir John Maurice (17 Mar. 1859 Edinburgh–27 May 1924 Edinburgh)
Scottish publisher
Met ʿAbdu'l-Bahá in Edinburgh 8 Jan. 1913.
He was the owner and manager of the well-known publisher T. & T. Clark. They published *The Encyclopaedia of Religion and Ethics* (1908–).

Clayton, Margaret Honor Blomfield (1907 Kensington, London–23 Apr. 1948 Chetnole, Dorset, England)
English
Met ʿAbdu'l-Bahá with her mother in London at Lady Blomfield's on 22 Dec. 1912.
She married (1931) Colonel Valentine Gardiner Clayton (1898–1975).

Cobb, Stanwood (6 Nov. 1881 Newton, Massachusetts–29 Dec. 1982 Chevy Chase, Maryland)
American Baháʾí; educator
Met ʿAbdu'l-Bahá in Boston, 1912 and Paris on 23 and 28 Mar. 1913.
During 1907–10 he taught history and Latin at Robert College, Istanbul. In 1910 he graduated from Harvard Divinity College. In 1910 member of the Central Executive Board of the Persian-American Educational Society. In the years 1912–13 he was a teacher with Sargent's Travel School for Boys. During 1914–15 he was the head of English department at St John's College, Annapolis, Maryland. In 1915–16 he was a teacher at Asheville School for Boys, Asheville, North Carolina. During 1916–19 he served as instructor in English and history at the United States Naval Academy, Annapolis, Maryland. In 1919 founder and principal of the Chevy Chase Country Day School, also in 1919 founder of the Progressive Education Association and its president in 1927–30. In 1922 he was a member of the national Baháʾí Children's Education Work Committee. He served as one of the editors of the *Baháʾí Magazine*, 1934. He married Ida Nayan Whitland Cobb (1878–1967) in 1919. He is buried in Rock Creek Church Yard, Washington, D.C.

Author: *The Real Turk* (1914), *Ayesha of the Bosphorus* (1915), *Essential Mysticism* (1918), *New Horizons for the Child* (1934), etc.

Cobden-Sanderson, Annie (20 Mar. 1853 Paddington, City of Westminster–2 Nov. 1926 Hammersmith, London)
English artist; suffragette
Met 'Abdu'l-Bahá in London at Caxton Hall, 11 Jan. 1913.
She was a founding member of the Women's Freedom League. She was the wife (1882) of Thomas James Cobden-Sanderson (1840–1922), a bookbinder and printer associated with the Arts and Crafts movement.

Cochrane-Baille, Charles Wallace Alexander Napier, 2nd Baron Lamington (Lord Lamington) (29 Jul. 1860 London–16 Sept. 1940 Lamington, Lanarkshire, Scotland)
British statesman and colonial administrator
Hosted 'Abdu'l-Bahá at his home, Wilton Crescent, London, 25 Dec. 1912. He met Him again at the Shah Jahan Mosque, Woking, England.
He was governor of Queensland (1896–1901) and governor of Bombay (1903–07) and an officer of the East India Association. He also served in Syria and Palestine. In 1911 he was one of the original members of the Persia Society and served as its president. He was married (1895) to Mary Haughton Hozier Cochrane-Baille.

Cooper, 'Ella' Eleanor Frances Goodall (12 Jan. 1870 San Francisco–12 Jul. 1951 San Francisco)
American Bahá'í (1898) in Oakland, California
She was the daughter of Helen Mirrell Goodall and a member of the first pilgrimage by Westerners to the Holy Land in 1898–99, organized by Phoebe Hearst (see Kathryn Jewett Hogenson, *Lighting the Western Sky*). She saw 'Abdu'l-Bahá at the ground-breaking ceremony for the Bahá'í Temple, 1 May 1912 and she met him again at the train station in San Francisco, 1 Oct. 1912. She, along with her mother were the main organizers of His California visit. Member of Bahai Temple Unity 1915 and, 1916. She was the alternate delegate to the

1918 and 1919 national Bahá'í Conventions. Attended the 1944 US Bahá'í National Convention in Wilmette. She was a member of the California Club in 1911–12. She married (1904) Dr Charles Minor Cooper. Buried in Cypress Lawn Memorial Park, Colma.
Co-author: *Daily Lessons Received at Acca, January, 1908* (1908).

Coppin (née Richert), Marie Elénore
French
Met 'Abdu'l-Bahá at 30 rue Saint-Didier in Paris with her daughter and granddaughters, 23 Feb. 1913.
Mother of Madeleine Jenny Sacy, the widow of Gabriel Sacy. She was married to Émilien Auguste Coppin.

Cordes, Johann
See **Kreuz (or Cordes), Johann**

Cropper, Mary Thornburgh
See **Thornburgh-Cropper, Mary 'Minnie' Virginia Shepherd**.

Crookes, Sir William (17 Jun. 1832 London–4 Apr. 1919 London)
British chemist and science journalist
Met 'Abdu'l-Bahá in London, Jan. 1913.
He studied chemistry at the Royal College of Chemistry, London. He patented numerous discoveries of industrial use and published several scientific journals. He was a spiritualist interested in psychic phenomena. He was married in 1856 to Ellen Humphrey Crookes (d. 1916). He is buried in Brompton Cemetery, West Brompton, Greater London.

Cruttwell, Maud Alice Wilson (1860 Frome, Somerset, England–21 Aug. 1939 Paris)
English author and art historian
Met 'Abdu'l-Bahá at the Martha-Pension in Paris on 27 May 1913.
She was a historian and author of studies on many of the Italian Renaissance artists.

Cuthbert, Arthur
Scottish Bahá'í (1906)
Met 'Abdu'l-Bahá at the railway station in London, 16 Dec. 1912 and also at Lady Blomfield's.
He lived in London and in Stranraer, Scotland. In 1914 he was the general secretary of the Bahá'í Committee in London.

d'Astre, Baroness Georgine d'Ange (b. Oct. 1864 France)
French Bahá'í; actress, seamstress, and nurse
Met 'Abdu'l-Bahá in Paris, 1911 and 1913.
In 1900 resided in Fruithurst, Alabama. While living in Washington, D.C., she sewed and embroidered the curtain for the Shrine of Bahá'u'lláh, which was designed by Mason Remey (c. 1904). She went on pilgrimage in Jan. 1905. In the pre-war years, she was in Paris, where she worked as an actress, playing, among other roles, Ariel in William Shakespeare's *La Tempête* produced by Camille de Sainte-Croix. As a Red Cross nurse she worked in a French military hospital at Chichli, Istanbul in 1913 and in 1914–16 in Thessaloníki, Greece. She attained the rank of infirmière major [principal matron]. She also commanded a military hospital in Serbia and was decorated by the Serbian government. After the war she resumed her interest in the arts and in 1928 was the secretary of the society l'Aide à la Musique. Married (1884) Frédéric d'Astre (b. 1860 France). Her daughter, Odette M. d'Astre (b. Apr. 1889 Dinard, France) was also active in the Faith and contributed to various Bahá'í funds, including the Orient-Occident Unity. She was residing in Paris in 1911.
Biography: 'A Persian Prophecy and How it Made a French Nurse', *Marlborough Express* (Blenheim, New Zealand) vol. L, issue 109 (May 10, 1916), p. 2.

Dawson, Albert (15 Jul. 1866 Clerkenwell, London–6 Feb. 1930 London)
English editor
Interviewed 'Abdu'l-Bahá in London at Lady Blomfield's, 5 Sept. 1911 and in Paris, 22 May 1913.

Corresponding journalist for American newspapers. He was the principal proprietor and editor of *The Christian Commonwealth*, 1901–1919. In 1892 he married Annie Hutchison and had three children (Elizabeth Bowe, Graham George and Albert Walter). In 1911 he resided in Hornsey, Middlesex.

Dáwúd, Mírzá Yuḥanná (1885 Kermanshah, Persia–1969 Highgate, London)
Persian Bahá'í of Jewish background, noted collector of Islamic art
Met 'Abdu'l-Bahá in Paris, and in London on 1 Oct. 1911. Married by 'Abdu'l-Bahá to Regina Núr Mahal Khánum [Dáwúd] in Islington, London.
His notable art collection is now in Jerusalem.
Translations into English: *The Mysterious Forces of Civilization* [by 'Abdu'l-Bahá] (1910); *The River of Life: A Selection from the Teachings of Baha Ullah and Abdul Baha* (1914).

de Néry, Amélie
See **Markovitch, Marylie (pseudonymously 'Amélie de Néry')**

Despard (née French), Charlotte (15 Jun. 1844 Ripple Vale, Kent, England–10 Nov. 1939 Whitehead, near Belfast, Northern Ireland)
English suffragist, writer and social worker
Present at a meeting at which 'Abdu'l-Bahá spoke at the Westminster Palace Hotel in London, 22 Dec. 1912.
In 1906 she joined the National Union of Women's Suffrage Societies. Later she joined the Women's Social and Political Union; in 1907 she co-founded the Women's Freedom League. She moved to Ireland and there, in 1908, she co-founded the Irish Women's Freedom League and was involved first with organizations supporting Sinn Fein and later became a member of the Communist Party. Member of the executive committee of the Theosophical Society. Married Maximilian Carden Despard (d. 1890). Buried in Glasnevin Cemetery, Dublin, Ireland.
Publication: 'Towards Unity', in *The Vote* (London) vol. 7, no. 168 (10 Jan. 1913).

Dickinson (née Sacy), Giselle (18 Feb. 1897 Cairo–21 Jan. 1987)
French
Met 'Abdu'l-Bahá in Paris at 4 avenue de Camoëns, with her mother, Madeleine Jenny Sacy, in 1911, and again on 9 and 23 Feb., and 29 May 1913.
Married (before 1919) John B. Dickinson, a dental surgeon from Bermuda. She and her husband resided in Hamilton, Bermuda. In 1943 she immigrated to Mexico City.

Döring, Margarethe
German Bahá'í (1907)
Met 'Abdu'l-Bahá in Paris, 13 Oct. 1911; also in Stuttgart where she invited Him to dinner at her home on 6 Apr. 1913.
Librarian of the Stuttgart Bahá'í community.

Dreyfus, Léa Marie Sophie Inès Cardozo (14 Nov. 1848 Bordeaux, France–2 Oct. 1913 Paris)
French Bahá'í
Met 'Abdu'l-Bahá in Paris, 1911 and on 10 May and 2 Jun. 1913 at her home.
She was a descendant of one of the Jewish families that left Portugal to settle in southern France. Her parents were Hippolyte Cardozo (1818–1860) and Sarah Aline Cerf (b. c. 1828). In 1872 she married Georges Arthur Lucien Dreyfus (1840–1911). They had two children, Hippolyte Isidore and Yvonne Dreyfus Meyer May. She and her husband became Bahá'ís in the early 1900s. She is buried in the family vault in the Cimetière de Montmartre, Paris.

Dreyfus-Barney, Hippolyte Isidore (2 Apr. 1873 Paris–20 Dec. 1928 Paris)
French Bahá'í (1900); lawyer and translator
Met 'Abdu'l-Bahá in Marseilles and Thonon-les-Bains, France, Aug. 1911; London, Sept. 1911; Paris, 1911 and 1913 and New York City, 21 Jul. 1912.
He was designated a Disciple of 'Abdu'l-Bahá. Lawyer at the Cour d'Appel. He translated a number of works on the Bahá'í Faith from

Persian into French. Married (1911) Laura Alice Clifford Barney. He is buried in the family vault in the Cimetière de Montmartre, Paris.
Publications: *The Universal Religion, Bahaism* (1909), etc.
Biography: Armindo Pedro (ed.), *Hippolyte Dreyfus: Apôtre d'Abdu'l-Bahá* (1996).

Dreyfus-Barney, Laura Alice Clifford (30 Nov. 1879 Cincinnati, Ohio–19 Aug. 1974 Paris)
American Bahá'í (1900) in France; writer; social activist and artist
Met 'Abdu'l-Bahá in Thonon-les-Bains, France, Aug. 1911; London, Sept. 1911; Paris 1911 and 1913, and Washington, D.C., 10 May 1912.
She was an accomplished painter and sculptor. In 1907 she went on pilgrimage to 'Akká and was the interlocutor with 'Abdu'l-Bahá that resulted in the profound exposition *Some Answered Questions.* According to Ezra Pound, she was acquainted with several writers living in London, namely the English novelist May Sinclair (1865–1946) and the American poet and prose writer Hilda Doolittle (1886–1961). She was very involved in the international women's movement and with the representation of non-governmental agencies at the League of Nations and later the United Nations. During World War I, she worked as a nurse with the Red Cross and with the American Ambulance Corps in Paris, was involved with a children's hospital in Avignon and worked in Marseilles to re-educate the war's handicapped. She was a delegate of the American Red Cross Comité de Patronage des Rapartriés. For her humanitarian services, she was twice awarded the Legion of Honour and later made a Chevalier. After the war, she was heavily involved with the International Council of Women. Married Hippolyte Dreyfus in 1911. She is buried in the Cimetière de Passy, Paris.
Publications: *Some Answered Questions*, by 'Abdu'l-Bahá (1908); *God's Heroes* (1910); 'Consultation and Conciliation versus Conflict', in *Bulletin of the American Women's Club of Paris* (Paris) (1926?); 'A Practical Effort Towards World Peace', in *Bulletin of the International Council of Women* (London) (1926?).
Biography: Mona Khademi, *The Life of Laura Barney* (2022); 'A

Glimpse into the Life of Laura Dreyfus-Barney', in *Lights of 'Irfán* (2009).

Drower (née Stevens), Lady Ethel May Stefana (1 Dec. 1879 Highgate, London–27 Jan. 1972 New Barnet, London)
English writer and lecturer
Met 'Abdu'l-Bahá at 97 Cadogan Gardens, London, 20 Dec. 1912.
Student of the religions, languages, and folklore of the Middle East, particularly of the Mandaeans. Married (1911) Edwin Mortimer Drower (d. 1951).
Publications: *The Mountain of God* (1910); etc.

Drummond, Rev. Robert Blackley (9 Feb. 1833 Dublin, Ireland–30 Dec. 1920 Edinburgh)
Scottish clergyman
Spoke words of thanks at a meeting where 'Abdu'l-Bahá spoke in Edinburgh, 8 Jan. 1913.
He was at St Mark's Unitarian Church, Edinburgh, 1859–1912.

Dunlop, Daniel Nicol (28 Dec. 1868 Kilmarnock, Scotland–30 May 1935 London)
Scottish theosophist and electrical industry executive.
In Aug. 1911, he sent a telegram to 'Abdu'l-Bahá on behalf of the Theosophical Summer School, welcoming Him to Europe.
He started his professional career as an employee of the Westinghouse Electrical Company in the United States, moving back to Britain in 1899. In 1910, he established the magazine *The Path*. He co-founded the British Electrical and Allied Manufacturers Association (1911). He wrote several articles on theosophy and he also founded various Theosophical lodges and was the promoter of the summer schools held by British theosophists. In 1924, he served as the co-founder and chairman of the World Power Conference (today the World Energy Council). He later went on to play a major part in the introduction of Anthroposophy (Rudolf Steiner) to Britain (see Momen et al,, *Community*, pp. 205–06). He was married to Eleanor Ossary Fitzpatrick ca. 1867–1932).

Eckstein, Adolf (d. 1926 Stuttgart, Germany)
German Bahá'í
In 1908 he was the chairman of the Bahá'í assembly in Stuttgart.
Met 'Abdu'l-Bahá in Paris, Oct. 1911 and again sometime in 1913.
Translated at a meeting with 'Abdu'l-Bahá in Stuttgart, 3 Apr. 1913.
In 1919, he and his wife co-founded the German Bahá'í Publishing Trust, which they owned jointly. He also ran the library.

Eckstein, Agatha
German Bahá'í
She met 'Abdu'l-Bahá in Paris in Oct. 1911, and again sometime in 1913 and in Stuttgart in Apr. 1913. Wife of Adolf Eckstein.

Effendi, Rev. Abdul Latif
Ottoman diplomat
In Apr. 1913 he met 'Abdu'l-Bahá in Budapest.
He was the Ottoman consul in Budapest in 1913. He also served as an Ottoman diplomat in Albania in 1880.

Effendí, Ríyáḍ Salím
Bahá'í from Cairo
Met 'Abdu'l-Bahá in Thonon-les-Bains, France, Aug. 1911; and in Paris, Feb. 1913.
He was living in Lausanne, Switzerland during the period 1911–13.

Effendí, Dr Ṣáliḥ Muḥammad (1884–12 Nov. 1943 Cairo)
Egyptian Bahá'í (1900); doctor
He was with 'Abdu'l-Bahá at 4 avenue de Camoëns in Paris, 1911 and 1913 and occasionally served as His translator.
Studied medicine at the University of Beirut and in Paris, also at the Université de Lyon. In 1913 he was in Lucerne, Switzerland. Chairman of the National Spiritual Assembly of the Bahá'ís of Egypt and of the Bahá'í Spiritual Assembly of Alexandria.
Published: Étude critique des états dits pseudo-tumeurs cérébrales (1912).

Eger, Gustav
German Bahá'í
Met 'Abdu'l-Bahá in Paris, 12 Feb. 1913 at 30 rue Saint-Didier and with his wife and daughter in Stuttgart.
Resided in Esslingen am Neckar, Germany.

Eigel, Nándor (or Ferdinand)
Hungarian diplomat
Served as a secretary at the Ottoman consulate. Visited 'Abdu'l-Bahá in Budapest at His room in the Hotel Ritz on 10 Apr. 1913.

Enthoven, (Augusta) Gabrielle Eden (Romaine) (12 Jan. 1868 London–18 Aug. 1950 London)
English Bahá'í and theatre archivist
Met 'Abdu'l-Bahá in Paris 26 Nov. 1911 and at the home of Lady Blomfield in London, 17 Jan. 1913.
Noted collector of theatre memorabilia. She was heavily involved with Red Cross work during World War I. President of the Society for Theatre Research, 1948–50. Married (1893) C. H. Enthoven (d. 1910). Author of the play *Quest of Life* (1916). She requested that her remains be cremated.
Biography: Eve Smith, *The Private Life of Gabrielle Enthoven* (London: Victoria and Albert Museum, 2015). Internet document. http://www.vam.ac.uk/blog/theatre-and-performance-2/the-private-life-of-gabrielle-enthoven.

Farmánfarmá'íyán, Muḥammad-'Alí Mírzá (1891–1983 Persia)
Persian economist and politician
Met 'Abdu'l-Bahá at 30 rue Saint-Didier in Paris in 23 Feb. 1913.
Son of 'Abdu'l-Ḥusayn Mírzá, the Farmán-Farmá (1859–1939), and the princess 'Izzatu'd-Dawlih. He was educated in Beirut and in Paris he studied economics at the Lycée Janson de Sailly and at a university. He returned to Persia at the onset of World War I. He held various administrative posts in Tabriz. He was elected to the Majlis (parliament) for five terms between 1917 and 1947. In 1946, he was

appointed minister of labour and propaganda. His brother was Fírúz Mírzá Fírúz, the Nuṣratu'd-Dawlih.

Fírúz, Fírúz Mírzá (the Nuşratu'd-Dawlih) (1889–Jan. 1938 Semnan, Persia)
Persian diplomat; attaché at the Persian embassy in Paris
Met 'Abdu'l-Bahá in Paris, in 1911 at 4 avenue de Camoens and in Jan., and on 21 and 23 Feb. 1913 at 30 rue Saint-Didier.
Son of 'Abdu'l-Ḥusayn Mírzá, the Farmán-Farmá (1859–1939), and the princess 'Izzatu'd-Dawlih. He was educated at the Lycée Janson de Sailly, Paris, the Syrian Protestant College of Beirut and the Sorbonne, Paris. He was appointed Governor of Kerman in 1907, under-secretary for justice in 1915–16, Minister for justice in 1916–17 and again in 1918–19 and in 1925, Governor of Hamadan and Kermanshah in 1918; Minister of Foreign Affairs in 1919–21, Governor-general of Fars in 1923–24, and Minister of Finance in 1927–29. He was imprisoned in 1921 and 1929–30. He was elected a Deputy for Kermanshah to the fourth, fifth and sixth Majlis. Married first (1905, divorced 1908) his first cousin, Daftaru'l-Mulk; second (1908) 'Aḍudu's-Sulṭán. He died in Semnan, Jan. 1938 (it is presumed that he was killed on the orders of Reza Shah Pahlavi).
His brother was Muḥammad-'Alí Mírzá Farmánfarmá'íyán.

Fisher (originally Fischer), Edwin Karl (10 Jun. 1861 Ludwigsburg, Württemberg [now in Baden-Württemberg, Germany]–6 May 1936 Los Angeles)
German-American Bahá'í (1905); dentist
Met 'Abdu'l-Bahá in Paris, 11 Feb. 1913; and in Stuttgart, 1913.
In 1878 he immigrated to the United States. In 1884 he became a US citizen. He became a Bahá'í in New York City. He was the first Bahá'í pioneer to Germany in 1905. Married to Josephine Dickinson. Buried in Inglewood Park Cemetery, Inglewood, California.

Fraser, Isabel
See **Chamberlain, Isabel Fraser**

Fraser, Ethel Patterson (b. c. 1872 California)
American Bahá'í (1901) in South Africa
Met 'Abdu'l-Bahá at the Baltimore Hotel, Paris, 4 May 1913. She was invited to the Unity Feast in Oakland, California, so it is possible she met Him there as well.
She was originally from California. She met Martha Root sometime between Jan. and Feb. 1925 in South Africa. Her address was 'Bywoods', Third Ave., Johannesburg. Her husband was Sir Henry Paterson Fraser (b. 1869) from England, who represented the Chamber of Mines in Parliament and was knighted in 1920 for services in connection with the East Rand Mines War Fund and the Governor-General's' Fund.

Gamble, Annie Eliza (1848–1947)
English Bahá'í
Met 'Abdu'l-Bahá at the railway station in London, 16 Dec., at the home of Lady Blomfield, and at a meeting at her home on 29 Dec. 1912 in the London district of Putney.

Geddes, Sir Patrick (2 Oct. 1854 Ballater, Scotland–12 Apr. 1932 Montpellier, France)
Scottish town planner; social reformer and educator
Met 'Abdu'l-Bahá at the Outlook Tower, Edinburgh, 7 Jan. 1913.
Studied at the Royal College of Mines, London. He held the Chair of Botany at University College, Dundee, 1888–1919 and the Chair of Sociology at the University of Bombay, 1919–24. In Montpellier he established the Collège des Écossais. He was knighted in 1932. As a town planner he drew up the master plan for Jerusalem in 1919 and for Tel Aviv in 1925. In India he worked on the urban plans for Bombay and Madras. In Haifa, he consulted with 'Abdu'l-Bahá on the first concept of the terraces leading to the Shrine of the Báb on the slopes of Mount Carmel. In 1921 he was one of the speakers at the national Convention of the Bahá'ís of India in Bombay. He was also the founder of the journal *Theosophy in Scotland.*

Germanus, Gyula (or Julius) (6 Nov. 1884 Budapest, Austria-Hungary–8 Nov. 1979 Budapest)
Hungarian Orientalist and Islamist
Met 'Abdu'l-Bahá in Budapest, Apr. 1913.
Studied at the University of Sciences, Budapest. His mentor was Ármin Vámbéry. He also studied under the Hungarian Orientalists Ignác Goldziher and Ignác Kúnos. Travelled widely in the Middle East, especially Turkey and Saudi Arabia, and also India. Taught at universities in Hungary, India and Egypt. Wrote extensively on Turkey, the Balkans, Indian languages, and Islam. Married Rózsa Hajnóczy (1892–1944). Buried as a Muslim at the Farkasréti cemetery in Budapest.

Ghani, Abdul (b. 1887 Gujrat, Punjab, India (now in Pakistan)
Indian law student
Met 'Abdu'l-Bahá at the Shah Jahan Mosque, Woking, England, 17 Jan. 1913.
He was admitted to Lincoln's Inn of the Inns of Court, London, to study law in 1910. Called to the bar in Jun. 1913.

G͟haffárí, Mírzá Mihdí K͟hán (d. 1917)
Persian courtier at the palace of the Shah and a Bahá'í
Met 'Abdu'l-Bahá at 30 rue Saint-Didier in Paris on multiple occasions in late January 1913.
His titles were Vazír-Humáyún, Ajúdán-i-Mak͟hṣúṣ, and Qá'im-Maqám. He held a number of governorships. He was the son of Farruk͟h K͟hán, the Amínu'd-Dawlih (d. 1868).

Giesswein, Sándor (or Alexander) (4 Feb. 1856 Tata, Austrian Empire, today Hungary–15 Nov. 1923 Budapest)
Hungarian prelate, editor, Christian-Socialist politician
Met 'Abdu'l-Bahá in Budapest, Apr. 1913.
President of the Hungarian Esperanto Society. Member, Executive Committee of the Central Organization for a Durable Peace (The Hague) (1920).

Goldziher, Ignác (22 Jun. 1850 Székesfehérvár, Austrian Empire, now in Hungary–13 Nov. 1921 Budapest)
Hungarian orientalist
Met 'Abdu'l-Bahá in Budapest, Apr. 1913.
Professor of Islamic Studies at Budapest University.
Publications: *Introduction to Islamic Theology and Law* (1981).

Goodall, Helen Mirrell Sturtevant (13 Mar. 1847 Winterport, Maine–19 Feb. 1922 San Francisco)
American Bahá'í in Oakland, California
She saw 'Abdu'l-Bahá at the Fourth Annual Convention of Bahai Temple Unity, 30 Apr. and at the ground-breaking ceremony for the Bahá'í Temple, 1 May 1912. Met 'Abdu'l-Bahá at the railway station in San Francisco, 1 Oct. 1912.
She was designated a Disciple of 'Abdu'l-Bahá. Member of the Bahai Temple Unity 1909. In 1912 she was elected as one of the vice-presidents of the Persian-American Education Society. In 1913 she was the treasurer of the San Francisco and Oakland Bahá'í community. In 1917 she attended the annual Convention of the Bahai Temple Unity as a delegate from Los Angeles and was an alternate delegate to the 1919 Convention. In 1920 she again went on pilgrimage to Haifa. Married (1868) Edwin Goodall (1843–1909). Mother of Ella Frances Goodall Cooper. She is buried in the Cyprus Lawn Memorial Park, Colma, California.
Co-author: *Daily Lessons Received at Acca: January 1908* (1908).

Gottesmann-Baktay, Antónia (or Marie Antoinette) (1882–1948)
Hungarian musician and socialite
Met 'Abdu'l-Bahá in Budapest, Apr. 1913. She was married (1912) to Umrao Singh Sher-Gil.

Hagara, Viktor (or Victor) (1848 Magosliget, Hungary–1923)
Hungarian jurist, politician, and parliamentarian
He met 'Abdu'l-Bahá in Budapest, Apr. 1913.

Ḥákím-i-Iláhí
See **Ḥakím-Bá<u>sh</u>í, Mírzá Músá ('Ḥakím-i-Iláhí')**

Ḥakím, Luṭfu'lláh S. (1888 Persia–10 Aug. 1968 Haifa, Israel)
Persian Bahá'í in England; physiotherapist
Met 'Abdu'l-Bahá at the railway station in London, 16 Dec. 1912; he accompanied Him to Edinburgh in 1913 and met Him again at the Martha-Pension in Paris 23 Mar. and 8 Jun. 1913.
He was the brother of Arastú <u>Kh</u>án Ḥakím. In Jul. 1913 he went to Stuttgart on the instructions of 'Abdu'l-Bahá. While in England resided at 13 Wood Lane, Shepherd's Bush, London W. From 1924 to 1948 he was in Persia and while there assisted Dr Susan I. Moody. Returned to Britain in 1948, first to Edinburgh for studies, where he served on the Bahá'í assembly for two years. Appointed in 1952 to the International Bahá'í Council. In 1963 elected to the Universal House of Justice, and resigned in 1967 due to poor health. He was married to Bahíyyih Ḥakím. He is buried in the Bahá'í Cemetery, Haifa.

Ḥakím-Bá<u>sh</u>í, Mírzá Músá ('Ḥakím-i-Iláhí') (d. 12 Sept. 1925)
Persian Bahá'í physician
Met 'Abdu'l-Bahá at 4 avenue de Camoëns in Paris, 17 Oct. 1911.
Around 1898 he was residing in Qazvin, Persia.
<u>Biography</u>: 'Azízu'llah Sulaymání, *Maṣábíḥ-i-Hidáyat*, vol. 4, pp. 468–98 (in Persian).

Hall (née Blomfield), Mary Esther 'Parvine' (1888 London–28 Apr. 1950 London)
British Bahá'í (1907)
Met 'Abdu'l-Bahá in London, Paris 1911.
Daughter of Lady Blomfield. Served on the National Spiritual Assembly of the Bahá'ís of the British Isles for five years. She married (1920) Captain Basil Hall.
<u>Publications</u>: *Talks of Abdul Baha Given in Paris* (1912); *The Drama of the Kingdom* (1933).

Hammond, Eric (Joseph Oliver Eric Hammond) (1852 Gosport, Hampshire, England–1936 Wimbledon, London)
English Bahá'í; writer
He and his wife met 'Abdu'l-Bahá in London on several occasions at Lady Blomfield's, 1911 and 1912.
Publications: *The Splendour of God* (1909), etc.

Hannen, Pauline Knobloch (29 Aug. 1874 Washington, D.C.–4 Oct. 1939 Cabin John, Maryland)
German-American Bahá'í (1902)
She saw 'Abdu'l-Bahá at the Fourth Annual Convention of Bahai Temple Unity, 30 Apr. which she attended as a delegate from Washington, D.C., and also at the ground-breaking ceremony for the Bahá'í Temple, 1 May 1912. 'Abdu'l-Bahá spoke at her home at 1252 Eighth Street, N.W., Washington, D.C., 10 Nov. 1912.
Wife (1893) of Joseph H. Hannen, sister of Alma Knobloch and Fanny A. Knobloch. She had two sons, Carl Anthony Hannen and Paul Hannen. In 1911, she was the assistant librarian of the Persian-American Educational Society. She is buried in Prospect Hill Cemetery, Washington, D.C.

Heron, Louise (b. 12 Nov. 1886 Vallejo, California)
English Bahá'í; writer
Met 'Abdu'l-Bahá in London at Lady Blomfield's.
In London she resided at the home of Mary Thornburgh-Cropper at 31 Evelyn Mansions, Carlyle Place, London. She was the daughter of Mary E. Heron. She returned to the United States in Aug. 1914, arriving at Philadelphia on 25 Nov. 1914 on board the *SS Haverford* from Liverpool.

Herrick, Elizabeth Skinner (1864 Norwick, Lincolnshire, England–20 Oct. 1929 Wandsworth, London)
English Bahá'í; milliner; suffragist
Arranged a meeting for 'Abdu'l-Bahá at 10 Cheniston Gardens, Wright's Lane (sometimes given as 137a Kensington High Street) with Marion Jack in London, 22 Sept. 1911. She also met Him at Lady Blomfield's.

Formerly lived in Liverpool. In London she owned a hat shop and participated in militant suffragette campaigns.
Publications: *Unity Triumphant* (1923).

Herrigel, Wilhelm (1865–1932)
German Bahá'í (1909); translator, publisher
Met 'Abdu'l-Bahá in London 1911; Paris in Mar. 1913; and in their home in Stuttgart, Apr. 1913. He travelled with Him to Vienna and Budapest.
One of the founders of the Bahá'í publishing enterprise in Germany. In 1914 he translated *Talks by Abdul Baha Given in Paris* (1912) into German as *Evangelium der Liebe und des Friedens für unsere Zeit* (Stuttgart, 1914). He also translated several other Bahá'í books into German. In 1930, largely due to misunderstandings and personal differences, he withdrew from the German Bahá'í community.

Herrigel, Marie
German Bahá'í
Met 'Abdu'l-Bahá in London, 1911; in Paris, Mar. 1913; and at their home in Stuttgart, Apr. 1913.
Wife of Wilhelm Herrigel and daughter of Gottlieb Pfund.

Hieston, Annie Lilian Gertrude Hayden (16 Jun. 1863 Dorchester, Massachusetts–1940)
American Bahá'í in Paris; teacher and journalist
Hosted a meeting with 'Abdu'l-Bahá on 17 Feb. 1913 in Paris at 170 Bld. Montparnasse. She was the sister of US Rear Admiral Edward Everett Hayden (1858–1932). She married Walter Hieston, and they were divorced in 1907. She resided in France from 1907 to 1914. In 1919 she was a member of the Austrian section of the Inter-Allied Reparations Commission. She is buried at Arlington National Cemetery.

Hodgson, Dorothy Mary (2 Sept. 1884 Sydenham, England–2 Jul. 1949 Pondicherry, French India [now Puducherry, India])
English Bahá'í and later Hindu from Kent, England

Met 'Abdu'l-Bahá in London, 1911; and in Paris from 25 Feb. 1913. In 1913 she was living in Paris. In 1916 she travelled to Japan and India and became a follower of 'The Mother' (Mirra Alfassa) and took the name 'Datta'. She is buried at Pondicherry.

Hohl, Louis
French diplomat
Chancellor at the Persian consulate in Paris, 1911–13. He was also a member of the *conseil d'administration* of the firm Établissements Orosdi-Back.

Holbach, Augusta Maude Margaret (Jan. 1868 Grantham, Lincolnshire, England–8 Apr. 1934 Falmouth, Cornwall, England)
English travel writer
Met 'Abdu'l-Bahá in New York City, 1912; Paris, 21 and 23 May 1913.
In 1913 she resided in Brittany, France. She married the German photographer Otto Holbach (b. 1861).
Publications: *Bible Ways in Bible Lands: An Impression of Palestine* (1912); 'The Bahai Movement, with Some Recollections of Meeting with Abdul Baha', in *The Nineteenth Century Review* (London) (1915).

Holley, Bertha D. Herbert (4 Apr. 1879 Bayfield, Wisconsin–Sept. 1969 Harrison, New York)
American Bahá'í in Paris; artist, fashion designer
She had studied art in Paris. In 1919 she was living in New York City; in 1932 in Westport, Connecticut; and in 1946 in Greenwich, Connecticut. Married (1909) Horace Holley, divorced before 1919.

Holley, Hertha (8 Jun. 1910 Florence, Italy–9 Mar. 1936)
American
Daughter of Bertha Holley and Horace Holley. After her parents divorced, she lived with her mother in New York City.

Holley, Horace Hotchkiss (7 Apr. 1887 Torrington, Connecticut–12 Jul. 1960 Haifa, Israel)
American Bahá'í; editor and Bahá'í administrator
He and his wife, Bertha, and daughter, Hertha, met 'Abdu'l-Bahá at the Grand Hôtel du Parc in Thonon-les-Bains, France, 29 Aug.1911 and in Paris on many occasions in 1911 and 1913.
He was first introduced to the Bahá'í Faith in 1909. From about 1909 to 1912 he lived in Siena, Italy. In 1912 he moved to Paris, where he operated the Ashur Art Gallery. In Oct. 1914 the Holleys left France, eventually settling in Greenwich Village, New York City. He worked as an advertising copy editor. In 1923 he was elected to the National Spiritual Assembly of the Bahá'ís of the United States and Canada, and served till 1959 and for many years as full-time secretary. During these years he was also editor of *World Unity*, *Bahá'í News*, and *World Order*. Shoghi Effendi appointed him Hand of the Cause of God in 1951. In Dec. 1959 he moved to Haifa with his wife. Married first (1909) Bertha Herbert, divorced (1919); second (1919) Doris Pascal. He had two daughters by his first marriage: Hertha and Marcia (b. 1916). He is buried in the Bahá'í Cemetery, Haifa.
Publications: *Bahaism, the Modern Social Religion* (1913), *The Social Principle* (1915), *Bahai, the Spirit of the Age* (1921), *Religion for humankind* (1956), etc.
Biography: Kathryn Jewett Hogenson, *Infinite Horizons: The Life and Times of Horace Holley* (2022)

Huguenin (née Sacy), Edmée (28 Dec. 1898 Cairo–4 Aug. 1959)
French
Met 'Abdu'l-Bahá in Paris at 4, avenue de Camoëns, with her mother, Madeleine Jenny Sacy, in 1911, and again on 9 and 23 Feb., and 29 May 1913.
Married Robert Huguenin and resided in Paris.

Humáyún, Mírzá 'Alí Khán Iḥtishám (Humayoun Ehtecham)
Persian diplomat
Met 'Abdu'l-Bahá in London on 14 Jan. 1913 at the Persian legation. He was the first secretary at the Persian legation in London, 1911–14.

ibn-i-Adíb
See **Adíb, Áqá Mírzá 'Alí Khán (Mírzá 'Alí ibn Adíb)**

Intiẓámu's-Salṭanih
See **Muḥammad, Mír Siyyid (the Intiẓámu's-Salṭanih)**

Irwin, Beatrice (16 Jul. 1877 Dagshai, India–20 Mar. 1956 San Diego, California)
British-American Bahá'í (1913) of Irish origin, illuminating engineer
Met 'Abdu'l-Bahá in London on 20 Jan. 1913 and was almost constantly in His presence while He was in Paris that year.
Shoghi Effendi called her a 'steadfast, devoted, indefatigable promoter of the Faith'.
Studied at Cheltenham Ladies' College in her adolescence. Acted professionally from 1898 to 1912 in the United States (where she spent many years and ultimately immigrated to), Britain, South Africa, and Australia.
Publications: *The Pagan Trinity* (1912); 'The Bahai Movement', *The Occult Review* (London) vol. 18 (Dec. 1913), pp. 280–86, a notice about which appeared in Soudbo, 'Revues et journaux', in *La Voile d'Isis* (Paris), no. 48 (Dec. 1913), p. 493; *The New Science of Color* (1915); *The Gates of Light* (1930); *Heralds of Peace* (1938); many articles and poems.
Biographical notes: Janet Fleming Rose, in Moojan Momen et al., *The Bahá'í Community of the British Isles* (2023), pp. 224–25 and 455–58.

Jack, Marion Elizabeth ('General Jack') (1 Dec. 1866 Saint John, New Brunswick–25 Mar. 1954 Sofia, Bulgaria)
Canadian Bahá'í (1900) painter
Arranged a meeting for 'Abdu'l-Bahá at 10 Cheniston Gardens, Wright's Lane (sometimes given as 137a Kensington High Street) London, 22 Sept. 1911, with Elizabeth Herrick; also met Him in London in 1912 and in Paris.
Studied art in Saint John, London and Paris. She attended the Bahai Temple Unity Convention in 1914. Resided in Maine, Florida, Haifa, Chicago and after 1930 in Bulgaria. Exhibited in major art exhibitions

in London, Paris, Montreal, Toronto, and Birmingham. She was active in the Bahá'í communities in Canada, United States, Great Britain, France, Germany and Bulgaria. In 1911 she lived at 58 Gloucester Gardens, London. She is buried in the British Sofia War Cemetery, Sofia.
Publication: 'Qurrat'ul-'Ain', in *The Christian Commonwealth* (London) (Sept. 13, 1911), p. 660.
Biography: Jan Teofil Jasion, *Never be Afraid to Dare* (2001).

Jackson, Mary 'Edith' Tewkesbury (19 Mar. 1849 Hampstead, New Hampshire–15 Mar. 1914 Nice, France)
American Bahá'í in Paris
Met 'Abdu'l-Bahá in Paris, 22, 31 May and 2 Jun. 1913.
Contributed financially to building 'Abdu'l-Bahá's house in Haifa. She arrived in Paris Nov. 1903. On 26 Mar. 1910 she sailed from New York on route to Haifa. In Paris she resided at 15 Ave. d'Antin (today Avenue Franklin-Roosevelt). She was the wife of James Jackson (1843–1895 Paris) and the sister of Mrs Ellen White. Buried in the British Cemetery in Nice.

Jalál, Áqá Mírzá
See **Shahíd, Áqá Mírzá Jalál**

Jenkyn, Daniel (Apr. 1884 Penzance, Cornwall, England–31 Dec. 1914 St Ives, Cornwall)
English Bahá'í; clerk
Met 'Abdu'l-Bahá in London on several occasions.
Resided at 3 Bowling Green, St Ives. Travelled to Holland with the express purpose of promoting the Faith in 1913. He contributed to the scholarship fund of the Persian-American Educational Society in 1913. Buried in the Barnoon Cemetery, St Ives.

Johnson, Rev. Henry Harrold (14 Dec. 1869 Leicester, England–9 Aug. 1940 Burbage, near Buxton, England)
English Unitarian clergyman
Met 'Abdu'l-Bahá in London, Sept. 1911.

Studied at Cambridge, Sorbonne and Leipzig. Minister, 1897–1939. Secretary of the Moral Education League, 1903–13. In 1912 at the International Congress of Moral Education at the Hague, he expanded on the theme of moral education as outlined by 'Abdu'l-Bahá. In 1919 he was called to the College Street Chapel, Manchester. In 1920 he met Shoghi Effendi in Cheetham Hills, near Manchester. From 1929 he was in Buxton.
Author: 'Bahaism, the Birth of a World Religion', in *Contemporary Review* (London), vol. 101 (Mar. 1912); and 'The Travail of the World', in *'Abdu'l-Bahá in London* (1912).

Jones, Sir Tracey French Gavin (c. 1872 India–14 May 1953 Tunbridge Wells, England)
British industrialist
Met 'Abdu'l-Bahá in London, Dec. 1912.
Publication: *The Origin of the Crisis and Britain's Task* (1941).

Kamal-ud-Din, Khwaja (1870 Lahore, India [today in Pakistan]–28 Dec. 1932 Woking, England)
Imam of the Woking Shah Jahan Mosque (Ahmadiyyah)
Met 'Abdu'l-Bahá at the Shah Jahan Mosque, Woking, 17 Jan. 1913.
Professor of history and economics, Islamia College, Lahore; admitted to the bar in 1898; came to England in 1912; founded the Muslim Mission in Woking in 1913; started a monthly journal, *Islamic Review*.

Káshání, Mírzá Faraju'lláh Khabbáz
Persian Bahá'í; baker
Met 'Abdu'l-Bahá in Paris, in Jan. and Feb. 1913.
In Tehran, he owned two large bakery shops with his brother, Mírzá Mihdí Khán (not to be confused with the Mushíru'l-Mulk of the same name).

Kelman, Rev. John (20 Jun. 1864 Dundonald, Ayrshire, Scotland–3 May 1929 Edinburgh)
Scottish Presbyterian clergyman

Chaired a meeting at which 'Abdu'l-Bahá spoke in Edinburgh, 7 Jan. 1913.
He was a minister of the United Free Church in Aberdeen. Later he was appointed minister at St George's United Free Church, and assistant to Alexander Whyte. He married Ellin Runcorn Bell (1864–1935) and they resided in Edinburgh.
Publication: 'Dr. Kelman on Bahai Teaching', in *The Christian Commonwealth* (London) (Jan. 22, 1913).

Kendirdjy, Dr Georges
French diplomat
Very likely met 'Abdu'l-Bahá at the Persian legation on 21 Mar. 1913, as well as on other occasions.
Secretary at the Persian consulate in Paris, 1911–13. Member of the Comité de l'Orient, 1913.

Khamsí-Báqiroff, Siyyid Mihdí Riḍá (d. 1932 Vienna)
Persian Bahá'í
He and his wife and three children met 'Abdu'l-Bahá in Vienna in May 1913.
He settled in Vienna in 1911. He was the brother of Siyyid Aḥmad Báqiroff.

Khamsí-Báqiroff, Khánumgol
Persian Bahá'í
Met 'Abdu'l-Bahá in Vienna in May 1913.
She returned to Persia at the beginning of the Second World War. Wife of Siyyid Mihdí Riḍá Khamsí-Báqiroff.

Khamsí-Báqiroff, Roghi (1903–2 Jul. 1931 Vienna)
Persian-Austrian Bahá'í
Met 'Abdu'l-Bahá in Vienna in May 1913. Daughter of Siyyid Mihdí Riḍá Khamsí-Báqiroff.

Khán, Mírzá 'Abdu'l-Ghaffár
Persian diplomat

Met 'Abdu'l-Bahá in London at 97 Cadogan Gardens on 18 Dec. 1912 and at the Persian legation on 14 Jan. 1913.
Councillor at the Persian legation, London in 1911 and 1914. In 1913 he was the honorary vice-president of the Persia Society.

Khán, Áqá Aḥmad ('Aga Ahmad Khan')
Persian student
Met 'Abdu'l-Bahá at Caxton Hall, London, 11 Jan. 1913
Friend of Mirza Ahmad Sohrab from Tehran. Sailed to America around 25 Jan. 1913.

Khán, Dr Aḥmad
Persian Bahá'í; writer
'Abdu'l-Bahá invited him to dine with Him in Paris, 26 Mar. 1913. He also met Him numerous times in London.
Educated in Paris and London. Resided in London.

Khán, Dúst Muḥammad (the Mu'ayyiru'l-Mamálik) (c. 1856–1913)
Persian nobleman, architect
Met 'Abdu'l-Bahá at the home of Lady Blomfield in London, Dec. 1912 and several times in Paris in 1913.
Master builder of palaces and an amphitheatre. He designed the Shamsu'l-'Imárat in the Gulistán palace complex in Tehran. In 1873, married Fáṭimih Khánum, the 'Iṣmatu'd-Dawlih (1856–1905), daughter of Náṣiri'd-Dín Sháh.

Khán, Ḥájí 'Alí-Qulí (the Sardár-i-As'ad) (1857–1918 Tehran)
Persian politician and Bakhtíyárí leader
Called upon 'Abdu'l-Bahá at the Martha-Pension in Paris on 21 Mar. 1913.
Appointed minister of the interior in 1908. Member of the Directory, 1909. He was the brother of the Ṣamṣámu's-Salṭanih; Najaf-Qulí Khán; and Ḥájí Khusraw Khán, the Sardár-i-Ẓafar.

Kh̲án, Ḥájí Khusraw (the Sardár-i-Ẓafar) (1858–1933)
Persian politician and Bak̲h̲tíyárí leader
Called upon 'Abdu'l-Bahá at the Martha-Pension in Paris on 2 Jun. 1913.
In 1912, he was the governor of Isfahan. He was the brother of the Ṣamṣámu's-Salṭanih; Najaf-Qulí Kh̲án; and Ḥájí 'Alí-Qulí Kh̲án, the Sardár-i-As'ad.

Khan, Inayat (or 'Ináyatu'lláh Kh̲án) (5 Jul. 1882 Baroda [today Vadodara, Gujarat], India–5 Feb. 1927 Delhi, India)
Indian Sufi leader and musician
Met 'Abdu'l-Bahá in Paris, 7 Feb. 1913 at 30 rue Saint-Didier when he sang and played his musical instrument for Him. On 29 May he again called on Him at the Martha-Pension, in Paris.
He was initiated in the Chishti order of Sufism. He travelled to Europe and America in 1910 as a touring musician and teacher of Sufism. He established the Western Sufi movement now called the Sufi Order International. He married Ora Ray Baker and they settled in Suresnes, near Paris with their four children. In 1926, he returned to India where he died. He is buried in the Nizamuddin Dargah, Delhi, India. His daughter, Noor Inayat Khan (1914–44), was a famous British SOE agent who served with the French resistance.
Publication: *Biography of Pir-o-Murshid Inayat Khan* (1979).

Kh̲án, Mírzá Mihdí
Persian Bahá'í, baker
Met 'Abdu'l-Bahá in Paris at 30 rue Saint-Didier, 31 Jan. 1913.
Brother of Mírzá Faraju'lláh Kh̲abbáz Kás̲h̲ání.
Not to be confused with the Mus̲h̲íru'l-Mulk of the same name.

Kh̲án, Mírzá Mihdí (the Mus̲h̲íru'l-Mulk)
Persian diplomat
Met 'Abdu'l-Bahá in London, 20 Dec. 1912.
He was the Minister to St Petersburg, 1902; Minister plenipotentiary in London 1911–20; in Nov. 1911 together with Lord Lamington, the Earl of Ronaldshay, E. G. Browne, and Mr. H. F. B. Lynch formed

the Persia Society, the forerunner of the Persia Society. His residence in London was 22 Queen's Gate Gardens, SW.
Not to be confused with the Persian Bahá'í baker and brother of Mírzá Faraju'lláh Khabbáz Káshání of the same name.

Khán [Maḥallátí], Dr Muḥammad
Persian Bahá'í in Paris; doctor
Met 'Abdu'l-Bahá at 30 rue Saint-Didier in Paris, 23 Jan. 1913 and many times later with his wife.
He resided in Paris with his wife.

Khán, Najaf-Qulí (the Ṣamṣámu's-Salṭanih) (1852–1930 Isfahan)
Persian politician and Bakhtíyárí leader
He called on 'Abdu'l-Bahá in Paris 31 Mar. at the Martha-Pension and on 22 May 1913 'Abdu'l-Bahá paid him a visit at his residence at 4 avenue de Camoëns.
He was one of leaders of the Constitutional Revolution. He was Governor of Isfahan in 1909 and 1913–14 and twice Prime Minister: in 1911–12 and in 1918. While in Paris in 1913, he rented 'Abdu'l-Bahá's former apartment at 4 avenue de Camöens.

Khánum, Parvine (or Parveen, Parvín, etc.)
See **Hall (née Blomfield), Mary Esther 'Parvine'**

Khánum, Riḍváníyyih
Persian Bahá'í; servant
Met 'Abdu'l-Bahá in Paris, Mar.–May 1913, when she accompanied Rúḥá Khánum.
She was the daughter of Ḥájí Siyyid Javád and the wife of Mírzá Ḥusayn Ḥájí, the brother of Aḥmad Yazdí. She was also the niece of Munírih Khánum, the wife of 'Abdu'l-Bahá. It is reported that she was fluent in French.

Khánum, Rúḥíyyih
See **Sanderson, Edith Lawrence ('Rúḥíyyih Khánum', or 'Roohie')**
Not to be confused with Mary Sutherland Maxwell, known to most

Baháʼís as Rúḥíyyih Khánum, who married Shoghi Effendi in 1937.

Khánum (Shahíd), Rúḥá (b. 1880 ʻAkká, Syria, Ottoman Empire (now in Israel))
Daughter of ʻAbduʼl-Bahá and Munírih Khánum
She was reunited with ʻAbduʼl-Bahá in Paris, 19 Mar. 1913, when she came for medical treatment for a throat ailment. She stayed in Paris for some time after ʻAbduʼl-Bahá left. She was hospitalized at the Maison de Santé, Paris. She was expelled from the Faith in the 1940s for causing serious dissension. Wife of Mírzá Jalál Shahíd.

Kinnaird, Baron Arthur Fitzgerald (16 Feb. 1847 Kensington, London–30 Jan. 1923 London)
British footballer, banker, and philanthropist
He met ʻAbduʼl-Bahá in London and the home of Lady Blomfield, on 24 Dec. 1912.
He was a keen footballer, president of the Football Association. He was involved with the YMCA and was the Lord High Commissioner of the General Assembly of the Church of Scotland. He was a partner in the banking firm of Barclay, Ransom and Co.

Knobloch, Alma Sedonia (9 Sept. 1863 Bautzen, Saxony–22 Dec. 1943 Cabin John, Maryland)
German-American Baháʼí (1903), teacher
Met ʻAbduʼl-Bahá in London, 1911; Paris, 12 Feb 1913; Esslingen, 4 Apr. 1913.
She moved to Germany in 1907 and lived first in Stuttgart and then Leipzig before returning to America in 1920. She became a naturalized American citizen in 1926. She was the sister of Pauline Knobloch Hannen and Fanny Almine Knobloch. She is buried in Prospect Hill Cemetery, Washington, D.C.
Biography: Jennifer Redson Wiebers, *Alma Sedonia Knobloch: Maidservant of the Divine Plan* (2023)

Knobloch, Fanny Almine (22 Dec. 1859 Bautzen, Saxony–9 Dec. 1949 Glenview, Illinois)

German-American Bahá'í (1904)
Met 'Abdu'l-Bahá in Dublin, New Hampshire, 4 Aug. 1912; Germany, Apr. 1913; and Paris 20, 21, 23 May 1913.
Member of the Spiritual Assembly of the Bahá'ís of Washington, D.C. 1910. She lived in Springfield, Massachusetts in 1919. In 1923–26 and 1928–30 pioneered to South Africa. Buried in the Prospect Hill Cemetery, Washington, D.C. Sister of Pauline Knobloch Hannen and Alma Knobloch.

Knobloch, Pauline
See **Hannen, Pauline Knobloch**

Köstlin, Anna (1884 Stuttgart, Württenberg, German Empire–27 May 1972)
German Bahá'í (1907); shopkeeper
Met 'Abdu'l-Bahá in Paris at 4 avenue de Camoëns, 1911 and 12 Feb. 1913. She organized a meeting on behalf of the children with 'Abdu'l-Bahá in Esslingen, Apr. 1913.
Member of the National Spiritual Assembly of the Bahá'ís of Germany and Austria.

Kreuz (or Cordes), Johann (Hamburg, Germany–1960 South Africa)
Austrian Theosophist
Met 'Abdu'l-Bahá in Vienna, 20 Apr. 1913.
Chairman of the Theosophical Society of Austria. In 1938 he immigrated to South Africa.

Kúnos, Ignác (22 Sept. 1860 Hajdúsámson, Austrian Empire (today in Hungary)–7 Jan. 1945 Budapest)
Hungarian Turcologist, folklorist
Met 'Abdu'l-Bahá in Budapest, Apr. 1913.
One of the foremost experts on Turkish folklore literature. Director of the Oriental College of Commerce in Budapest, 1899–1919. He was a pupil of Ármin Vámbéry.

Lacheny (Lachenay or Lashney), Emmanuelle
French Bahá'í (1900); governess
Met 'Abdu'l-Bahá in Paris 22 Mar. 1913 at 26, rue La Trémoille, the home of Ṣáliḥ Munír Páshá.
She was a governess to Natalie Barney until 1906. She had been to 'Akká with Laura Clifford Barney. In Jun. 1906, she accompanied Hippolyte Dreyfus and Laura Barney to Ashkabad.

Lagente (née Sacy), Gabrielle (5 Aug. 1903 Paris–23 Jan. 1998 Chartres, France)
French
Met 'Abdu'l-Bahá in Paris at 4 avenue de Camoëns, with her mother, Madeleine Jenny Sacy, in 1911, and again on 9 and 23 Feb., and 29 May 1913.

Lamington, Lord
See **Cochrane-Baille, Charles Wallace Alexander Napier, 2nd Baron Lamington**

Landor, Arnold Henry Savage (2 Jun. 1867 Florence, Italy–26 Dec. 1924 Florence)
English painter and world traveller
Met 'Abdu'l-Bahá in London 12 Jan. 1913.
He studied in Paris. He travelled in many countries: Latin America, Africa, India, China, Japan, Tibet, Persia, etc. He wrote several books about his travels, including *Across Coveted Lands* (1903), about his travels across Persia, in which he has a brief reference to the Bahá'ís of Yazd.

Leitner, Henry (1869 Lahore, India (today in Pakistan)–1945 Wandsworth, London)
British Muslim
Met 'Abdu'l-Bahá at the Shah Jahan Mosque, Woking, England, 17 Jan. 1913.
He was the son of Dr Gottlieb Wilhelm Leitner (1840–94), the founder of the Woking Shah Jahan Mosque. He was a managing

director of Electrical Manufacturing Corp. Married to Sapho Leitner (b. 1875).

Lewis, Alice (b. c. 1871 Esh, Cheshire)
English
She invited 'Abdu'l-Bahá to their home at 11 Lambolle Rd., Hampstead, London N.W., the day before He spoke.
Wife of Edward William Lewis.

Lewis, Rev. Edward William (b. c. 1872 Middleton, Cheshire, England)
English New Theology clergyman
Welcomed 'Abdu'l-Bahá to the King's Weigh House Chapel, 29 Dec. 1912.
Member of the editorial board of *The Christian Commonwealth*. Married to Alice Lewis. Resided in Hampstead, London.

Lewis, John (17 Jan. 1858 Toronto–18 May 1935 Toronto)
Welsh-Canadian, journalist, author, and politician
He and his wife met 'Abdu'l-Bahá at the Lake Mohonk Conference on International Arbitration, May 1912, and also at the Maxwell home in Montreal, 30 Aug. 1912.
He worked on several different Canadian newspapers, including *The Toronto World*, *The Winnipeg Tribune*, and *The Globe*. He was the editor of the Toronto daily newspaper *The Star* from 1905 to 1919. In 1925, Prime Minister William Lyon Mackenzie King appointed him a senator, and he served in this capacity until his death. He and his wife are buried in Saint John's Norway Cemetery, Toronto.

Lillienthal, Maud
See **von Behr (née Lillienthal), Maud**

Lukaneder, Paul
Austrian Theosophist
He and his family met 'Abdu'l-Bahá in Vienna on 21 and 22 Apr. 1913, and when 'Abdu'l-Bahá spoke to the Theosophischen Gesellschaft.

Their address is given as Johannesgasse 2, Wien I. His mother, in particular, is noted by both Mírzá Maḥmúd Zarqání and Mirza Ahmad Sohrab in their accounts as having been present on all these occasions, but her name is recorded only as 'Mrs. Lukaneder'.

MacDonald, James Ramsay (12 Oct. 1866 Lossiemouth, Morayshire, Scotland–9 Nov. 1937 at sea)
British politician and journalist
Met 'Abdu'l-Bahá at Lady Blomfield's on 2 Jan. 1913.
He was a Member of Parliament, 1906–18, and Prime Minister, 1924 and 1929–35. He was also a member of the Persia Committee.

Mann, William MacCarthy
British editor
He met 'Abdu'l-Bahá at the Shah Jahan Mosque, Woking, England.
He was co-editor along with Gilbert Lynn of *The Asiatic Quarterly Review.*

Margoliouth, David Samuel (17 Oct. 1858 London–22 Mar. 1940 London)
British Orientalist and translator
He and his wife met 'Abdu'l-Bahá at Caxton Hall, Westminster, London, 11 Jan. 1913.
Professor of Arabic at the University of Oxford, 1889–1937. In 1911 he presented a paper at the First Universal Races Congress in London.
He married (1896) Jessie Payne Smith Margoliouth.
Publications: *Mohammedanism* (1911).

Markovitch, Marylie (pseudonymously 'Amélie de Néry') (1866–Mar. 1926 France)
French Bahá'í (1904); dramatist, writer, and teacher
Met 'Abdu'l-Bahá on 24 Mar. 1913 at the Martha-Pension in Paris.
At one time, she was a teacher of literature at a girl's secondary school at Montélimar in the department of Drôme, in the south of France.
It is possible that she wrote a play about Ṭáhirih.

Publication: 'La vie des femmes en Perse', in *Revue pour les Français* (Paris), no. 2 (fév. 1909).

Mead, G. R. S. (George Robert Stowe) (22 Mar. 1863 Nuneaton, England–28 Sept. 1933 London)
English author, editor, translator
Met 'Abdu'l-Bahá at the Shah Jahan Mosque, Woking, England, 17 Jan. 1913.
He was an influential member of the Theosophical Society. He was educated at St John's College, Cambridge. Mead became a member of the Theosophical Society in 1884. He became Helena Petrovna Blavatsky's private secretary in 1889, a capacity in which he continued to serve until her death in 1891. During this time, he was also an assistant editor to her monthly magazine, *Lucifer*. When he finally took over as its editor, he renamed it *The Theosophical Review*. He also was associated with the *Quest* magazine. In 1899, he married another prominent theosophist, Laura Cooper. Residence: Saint-Maxime, Var, France.

Mészáros, Gyula (1883 Szakcz, Hungary–1957 New York City)
Hungarian ethnographer, orientalist and Turkologist
Met 'Abdu'l-Bahá in Budapest Apr. 1913.

Meyer, Cicelia Lila Evelyn (c. 1898 Madras (now Chennai), India–1914 India)
English
Met 'Abdu'l-Bahá on board the *SS Himalaya*, 15 Jun. 1913.
Daughter of Sir William Stevenson Meyer.

Meyer, Sir William Stevenson (13 Feb. 1860 Galați, Moldavia (now in Romania)–19 Oct. 1922 London)
British colonial administrator in India
He and his daughter met 'Abdu'l-Bahá on board the *SS Himalaya*, 15 Jun. 1913.
In 1912, he held the position of chief secretary of the Government of Madras; in 1920 and 1921, he represented India at the first and

second assemblies of the League of Nations; in 1921, he was High Commissioner for India in London. Married (1895) Mabel Henrietta Jackson (c. 1870–1914).

Mírzá, Sulṭán-Mas'úd (the Ẓillu's-Sulṭán) (5 Jan. 1850 Tehran–2 Jul. 1918 Isfahan)
Persian prince and politician
He and four of his sons met 'Abdu'l-Bahá at Le Grand Hôtel du Parc in Thonon-les-Bains, France, Aug. 1911; again in Paris, 1911, probably at 4 avenue de Camoëns; and on 2 Jun. 1913 at the Martha-Pension in Paris.
He held various governorates, including: Mazandaran, 1861–62; Fars, several times between 1862 and 1908; Isfahan, four times between 1865 and 1917; Yazd; Luristan; Kermanshah; and Khuzistan. He was incriminated in the martyrdom of several Bahá'ís. He was exiled to France with his sons. Son of Náṣiri'd-Dín Sháh Qájár (1831–96) and 'Iffatu's-Salṭanih (d. 1892). He had ten wives and twenty-five children. He was buried in Mashhad.
Biography: Heidei A. Walcher, *In the Shadow of the King: Zill al-Sultan and Isfahan under the Qajars* (2008).

Mírzá, Sulṭán-Ḥusayn, the Jalálu'd-Dawlih (1870 Isfahan–9 Dec. 1913)
Persian prince and provincial governor
Met 'Abdu'l-Bahá at Le Grand Hôtel du Parc in Thonon-les-Bains, France, Aug. 1911; at 97 Cadogan Gardens, London, Dec. 1912 and on 7 Jun. 1913 at the Martha-Pension in Paris.
Son of Sulṭán-Mas'úd Mírzá (the Ẓillu's-Sulṭán) and Hamdamu's-Salṭanih. He was appointed deputy Governor of Arabistan (Khuzistan) in 1879–80, Luristan in 1879–80, Yazd in 1890–91 and 1895–97; Governor-general of Fars in 1881–87; Governor of Burujird in 1894, Luristan in 1896–97, Yazd in 1903–04, and Kurdistan in 1906. He was also a major-general and chief of the Army Supply Dept. in 1905–06. He was castigated by Bahá'u'lláh for the Bahá'í martyrdoms in Yazd in 1891 and by 'Abdu'l-Bahá for those of 1903. He was exiled with his father in 1908.

Note: His first appointment was at the age of nine. The intricacies resulting from the multitude of royal spouses intermarrying can be illustrated by Sulṭán-Ḥusayn Mírzá, who could count among his immediate family the following shahs: Náṣiri'd-Dín Sháh, paternal grandfather; Muḥammad Sháh, paternal and maternal great-grandfather; Fatḥ-'Alí Sháh, paternal and maternal great-great-grandfather; Muẓaffari'd-Dín Sháh, uncle; and Muḥammad-'Alí Sháh, cousin.

Monnier, Henri (24 Apr. 1871 Saint-Quentin, France–16 Jul. 1941 Paris)
French Protestant theologian
He invited 'Abdu'l-Bahá to present a lecture at the Faculté de théologie protestante de Paris, 16 Feb. 1913.
He studied first in Germany and was ordained in 1895. In 1897 he was at the Église réformée de l'Étoile. The year 1933 saw him installed as the doyen professor at the Faculté de théologie protestante de Paris. In 1898 he married Suzanne du Pasquier (b. 1876).

Montealegre, Ricardo (b. 1873 San José, Costa Rica)
Costa Rican coffee planter and merchant
It is likely that he is one of the Costa Rican coffee merchants who met 'Abdu'l-Bahá in Paris on 22 Feb. 1913, along with Alejo Aguilar.
Married to Adelia Montealegre (b. 1875).

Moore, Edward William (18 Nov. 1873 Chicago–21 Feb. 1955 Chula Vista, California)
American Bahá'í; merchant
Met 'Abdu'l-Bahá in Paris, 28 Mar. 1913 and in Budapest.
He was a merchant in Budapest for the Ingersoll Rand Company from about 1908. On 28 Oct 1913 he attended the first Bahá'í meeting in Budapest. In 1901 he married Elcy Noble Boyd Moore and had three sons, James Edward Moore, Charles C. Moore, and Frank K. Moore. His cousin was Dr Susan I. Moody (1851–1934), the founder of the Tarbíyat School for girls in Tehran.

Moore, Lucy A. (b. 1857 Virginia)
American
Met 'Abdu'l-Bahá in Green Acre, 21 Aug. 1912 and at the Martha-Pension in Paris 17 May 1913.
Wife of Dr Millard Fillmore Moore.

Moreau (possibly Moro, Mareau, etc.), Mrs
French Bahá'í
Met 'Abdu'l-Bahá in Paris, first at the Baltimore Hotel on 2 May and then again on 6 Jun. 1913 at the Martha-Pension.
She stated that she was writing a pamphlet on the Bahá'í Faith in French.

Morrison, Mary B. (Oct. 1843 Massachusetts–c. 1929 Denver)
American Bahá'í; dressmaker
Met 'Abdu'l-Bahá in Denver, Colorado. He wrote to her from Paris, 10 May 1913.
She was a widow.

Moscheles, Felix Stone (8 Feb. 1833 London–22 Dec. 1917 Tunbridge Wells, England)
British painter and pacifist
He and his wife met 'Abdu'l-Bahá at their home, 80 Elm Park Road, London SW, 20 Jan. 1913, and also at the London home of Lady Blomfield.
Member of the International Peace and Arbitration Association; president of the London Esperanto Club at its founding, 1903; nominated for the Nobel Peace Prize. Moscheles edited Felix Mendelssohn's letters to his father.

Moser, (Georg Heinrich) Henri (13 May 1844 St Petersburg, Russia–15 Jul. 1923 Vevey, Switzerland)
Swiss watchmaker, traveller and art collector
He and his wife met 'Abdu'l-Bahá at the Martha-Pension in Paris 31 Mar. 1913.
Travelled in Central Asia, including Bokhara and Ashkabad.

Accumulated a priceless collection of Oriental weapons and artifacts. He donated his collection to the museum in Bern.

Moser, Sophie Margaritha Schloch (15 Jun. 1862–11 Sept. 1929 Schaffhausen)
Swiss
Met 'Abdu'l-Bahá at the Martha-Pension in Paris 31 Mar. 1913.
Wife (1887) of Henri Moser.

Mu'ayyiru'l-Mamálik
See **Khán, Dúst Muḥammad (the Mu'ayyiru'l-Mamálik)**

Muḥammad, Mír Siyyid (the Intiẓámu's-Salṭanih)
Persian nobleman; Bahá'í
Met 'Abdu'l-Bahá at 30 rue Saint-Didier in Paris, 19 Feb. and 17 Mar. 1913.
He has been described as being very devoted to 'Abdu'l-Bahá. His great-grandfather was Fatḥ-'Alí Sháh. His brother-in-law was the Hand of the Cause Ibn-i-Aṣdaq (d. 1928). His grandmother was the fourth wife of Mírzá Buzurg Núrí (d. 1839), the father of Bahá'u'lláh.

Mumtáz, 'Abdu'ṣ-Ṣamad Khán (the Mumtázu's-Salṭanih) (1869 Tabriz, Persia–1955 Paris)
Persian diplomat
Called upon 'Abdu'l-Bahá or met Him at His residences in Paris on many occasions between Jan. and May 1913.
Born in an Azerbaijani family in Tabriz. He was a professional diplomat who served in a variety of capacities in the years 1883 to 1951. Between 1883 and 1899 he served as secretary and then counsellor at the Persian legation in St Petersburg. In 1904 he is noted as being the ambassador to the Hague and then envoy extraordinary and Minister plenipotentiary at the Hague Conferences of 1899 and 1907. He was the Persian Minister in Paris Apr. 1905–Mar. 1926. Appointed member Comité International Olympique (IOC) 1924–27. In 1925 he was nominated by France for the Nobel Peace Prize for his services as a member of the International Court of Arbitration at the Hague.

He was counsellor to the Persian Embassy in Paris from 1946 to 1951. Buried in Père-Lachaise Cemetery, Paris. His son Abdullah Khan was attending the military college at St-Cyr in 1913, and possibly also met 'Abdu'l-Bahá in Paris.

Murshidzádih, Mírzá Maḥmúd
Persian student
Met 'Abdu'l-Bahá in Paris, Naw-Rúz 1913.
Student at the École de pédagogie [teachers' college], Versailles.

Nádler, Róbert A. (22 Apr. 1858 Pest, Austrian Empire (now part of Budapest, Hungary)–7 Jun. 1938 Budapest)
Hungarian painter
'Abdu'l-Bahá went to his studio in Budapest and sat for a portrait, 13 Apr. 1913.
Nádler was an established portrait painter in Hungarian society. In 1908 he was the president of the Apollo Theosophical Society in Budapest. On 28 Oct 1913, he attended the first Bahá'í meeting in Budapest.

Naimutullah, Shah Mohammad (b. 1890 Monghyr, Bengal (today Munger, Bihar), India)
Indian lawyer
Met 'Abdu'l-Bahá at the Shah Jahan Mosque, Woking, England, 17 Jan. 1913.
Enrolled in the Middle Temple of the Inns of Court, London in 1910. He wrote several articles on the problems of colonial India.

Nakhjavání, Mírzá 'Alí-Akbar [Russian: Мирза Алекпер Мамедханов **(Mirza Alekper Mamedkhanov)]** (1865 Baku, Russia (now in Azerbaijan)–31 Dec. 1920 Shualan, Azerbaijan)
Persian Bahá'í from Baku, executive secretary
Met 'Abdu'l-Bahá in New York City, 6 Jun. 1912; and in Paris, 1 Jun. 1913.
In Baku he was the executive secretary to the oil millionaire Áqá Músá Naqiov. Member of 'Abdu'l-Bahá's entourage in 1912–13. He arrived

in New York City on board the *RMS Mauretania* on 7 Jun. 1912. Married Fáṭimih Kh͟ánum Tabrízí. His son, 'Alí Nakh͟javání (1919–2019), served on the Universal House of Justice from 1963 to 2003. Biography: Ali Nakhjavani, *Mírzá 'Alí-Akbar-i-Nakh͟javání* (2018)

Naruse, Jinzō (23 Jun. 1858 Yamaguchi Prefecture, Japan–4 Mar. 1919 Tokyo)
Japanese educator
Met 'Abdu'l-Bahá in London, 30 Dec. 1912.
In 1875, he entered the Yamaguchi Prefectural Teachers' Training School and become a primary school principal. He became a Christian and devoted himself to the education of women. In 1888, he founded the Baika Girls' School in Osaka. He went to the United States in 1890 to study. He was the founder, with Shozo Aso, of the Nihon Women's College (1901) and served as its first president from 1901 to 1919. He also founded the Association Concordia for the better understanding between religions and cultures. Buried in Zoshigaya Cemetery, Tokyo.

Naẓar-Áqá, Ardish͟hír Kh͟án (Ardachir Khan Nazare-Aga, Léon Sylvestre Nazare-Aga)
Persian diplomat; medical doctor
Met 'Abdu'l-Bahá in Paris, 23 Jan. and 1 Feb., 1913.
In 1900 he was appointed first secretary at the Persian legation in Paris. Studied medicine at the Université de Paris, 1903–04. In 1945, he was one of the vice presidents of the Chambre de Commerce Franco-Iranienne. He was the son of General Lazare Nazare-Aga Yémin (1827–1912), the former ambassador to France, 1870–1905. Married (1896) Wanda Françoise Balbina Gałęzowska (1874–1906).

Naẓar-Áqá, Yúsuf Kh͟án (Etienne Lazare Nazare-Aga) (28 Aug. 1870 Paris–1942)
Persian diplomat; composer
Met 'Abdu'l-Bahá on 30 Jan. 1913.
Counsellor at the Persian legation in Paris. He was a lieutenant in the artillery in the Persian army, then in the French army in the Second

Regiment of Artillery. Later he served with distinction during World War I in the French Foreign Legion. He was the son of General Nazare-Aga Yémin (1827–1912), the former ambassador to France. Married Clothilde d'Oliveira in 1895.

Pagan, Jessie Hair
See **Pole, Jessie Hair Pagan**

Pagan, Jessie Osborne (1843 Glasgow–1938)
Scottish poet
She met 'Abdu'l-Bahá in Edinburgh at the Theosophical Headquarters, 9 Jan. 1913, along with her seven daughters.
She was the wife of George Hair Pagan, a banker from Cupar, Scotland.

Paikert, Alajos (31 May 1866 Nagyszombat, Austrian Empire (now Trnava, Slovakia)–30 Jul. 1948 Budapest)
Hungarian economist, editor
Met 'Abdu'l-Bahá in Budapest, Apr. 1913.
He was the organizer of the Budapest Museum of Agriculture. He served as the executive vice-president of the Turanian Society. Involved with the peace movement and the League of Nations.

Pankhurst, Emmeline Goulden (14 Jul. 1858 Manchester, England–14 Jun. 1928 London)
English suffragist
She had an interview with 'Abdu'l-Bahá at Lady Blomfield's in London, Dec. 1912.
In 1889 she founded the Women's Franchise League and in 1903 co-founded with her daughter Christabel Pankhurst, the Women's Social and Political Union. She was extremely militant in her actions for women's suffrage, was imprisoned several times and underwent hunger strikes. Attended one of Natalie Barney's salons in Paris. Married (1879) Richard Marsden Pankhurst (1834–1898). She is buried in Brompton Cemetery, London.

Pankhurst, Estelle Sylvia (5 May 1882 Manchester, England–27 Sept. 1960 Addis Ababa, Ethiopia)
English suffragist and socialist
Met 'Abdu'l-Bahá in London, Dec. 1912.
Founder of the East London Federation of the Suffragettes, 1914–24. Also involved with the Communist Party and other antifascist organizations. In 1956 moved to Ethiopia and became a friend and advisor to Emperor Haile Selassie. She was the daughter of Emmeline Goulden Pankhurst. She is buried at Trinity Cathedral, Addis Ababa.

Pá<u>sh</u>á, Aḥmad
Former Ottoman general in exile in Paris
Met 'Abdu'l-Bahá in Paris on numerous occasions between Jan. and Jun. 1913.
Not to be confused with Aḥmad 'Izzat Pá<u>sh</u>á (Furgaç).

Pá<u>sh</u>á, Mrs Aḥmad
Wife of the former Ottoman general, Aḥmad Pá<u>sh</u>á.
With her husband, she met 'Abdu'l-Bahá in Paris, 28 Jan. 1913.

Pá<u>sh</u>á, Ra<u>sh</u>íd Mumtáz (Oct. 1856 Istanbul–2 Apr. 1924)
Ottoman politician
Met 'Abdu'l-Bahá in Paris, 29 Jan.; 15, 16, 23 Feb.; 12 Mar.; 10, and, 12 May 1913.
He was Governor of the province of Beirut from Aug. 1897 to Sept. 1903, during the time that 'Abdu'l-Bahá was under house arrest in 'Akká. Later, he was a senator and minister for the interior. In 1912–13, he was the leader of the Ottoman delegation negotiating with the Balkan League in London to end the First Balkan War.

Pá<u>sh</u>á, Ṣáliḥ Munír (1857 Istanbul–27 Jan. 1939 Istanbul)
Ottoman diplomat
Met 'Abdu'l-Bahá at 30 rue Saint-Didier in Paris, 28 Jan. and 23 Feb.; and at the Martha-Pension, 8 Jun. 1913; and also at his residence at 26 rue de La Trémoille, Paris on 8 and 22 Mar., 24 and 26 May, and 9 Jun., 1913.

Between 1872 and 1879, he held various government functions, including master of ceremonies at the royal palace. In 1881 he was the Minister of commerce and forests; 1888 Minister of foreign affairs; and in 1897–1908 Minister to France. In 1912–13, he was a member of the Ottoman delegation negotiating with the Balkan League in London to end the First Balkan War.

Páshá, Mrs Ṣáliḥ Munír
Wife of Ṣáliḥ Munír Páshá
Met 'Abdu'l-Bahá in Paris, at her residence at 26 rue de La Trémoille, 26 May and at the Martha-Pension, 7 Jun. 1913.

Páshá (Furgaç), Aḥmad 'Izzat (1864 Naslie, Macedonia, Ottoman Empire (now Korçë, Albania)–31 Mar. 1937 Istanbul)
Ottoman army officer in exile in Paris
Met 'Abdu'l-Bahá in Paris, 7 Jun. 1913, and with his son on 9 Jun.
He graduated from the Army Staff School in 1887. In the 1890s he served in Palestine and Syria. Took part in the Greek and Balkan wars and in the rebellions in Yemen. After 1916, commander of the Caucasus front in World War I. Appointed Grand Vizier on 14 Oct. 1918, but only kept the position for one month. Later appointed Minister of foreign affairs in the early years of the Republic.
Not to be confused with Aḥmad Páshá.

Pekár, Gyula (8 Nov. 1867 Debrecen, Hungary–19 Aug. 1937 Budapest)
Hungarian writer, journalist, politician
He met 'Abdu'l-Bahá in Budapest, Apr. 1913.

Pfund, Gottlieb
German Bahá'í
Met 'Abdu'l-Bahá in Stuttgart, Apr. 1913.
Father of Marie Herrigel. Resided in Fellbach.

Platt, Beatrice Marion (b. Feb. 1878 Kilburn, London)
English Bahá'í; private secretary, governess

Met 'Abdu'l-Bahá in London and in Paris, 1911.
Friend of Lady Blomfield and one of the team who took down His talks stenographically and assisted in editing and compiling them. They were published as *Talks Given by Abdul Baha in Paris* (1912).

Pole, Major David Graham (11 Dec. 1877 Leith, Scotland–25 Nov. 1952 London?)
Scottish lawyer
Met 'Abdu'l-Bahá at Lady Blomfield's, London, in 1911. He introduced 'Abdu'l-Bahá at a meeting of the Theosophical Society in Edinburgh, 9 Jan. 1913.
Qualified and practised as a solicitor in Edinburgh, 1900–14. He was admitted as a member of the Society of Solicitors before the Supreme Courts of Scotland, 1901 and a Notary Public in 1903. He served as secretary of the Theosophical Society of Edinburgh. He joined the army (reserve 1899) and served in France. At the battle of Loos he was wounded and invalided home. He was elected a Member of Parliament, 1929–31 for South Derbyshire. Editor of *Theosophy in Scotland.* Married (1918) Jessie Hair Pagan.

Pole, Alexander Cecil Tudor (1887 Somerset–10 Jun. 1963 Mexico)
English, Theosophist, wireless engineer
Met 'Abdu'l-Bahá in London 4 Jan. 1913.
He was the brother of Wellesley Tudor Pole. He worked for the Marconi company in Latin America.

Pole, Jessie Hair Pagan (9 Aug. 1863 Cupar, Scotland–9 Jan. 1958 Farnham, Surrey/England
Scottish Theosophist
She met 'Abdu'l-Bahá in Edinburgh, 9 Jan. 1913, along with her mother and six sisters.
The daughter of the banker George Hair Pagan and Jessie Osborne of Cupar. In 1918, she married David Graham Pole.

Pole, Wellesley Tudor (23 Apr. 1884 Weston-super-Mare, England–13 Sept. 1968 Hurstpierpoint, Sussex, England)
English Baháʼí, mystic; merchant, soldier
ʻAbduʼl-Bahá stayed at his Clifton Guest House in Bristol, Sept. 1911 and again on 15 Jan. 1913. He also met Him in Egypt, 1910, Paris, 1911, London at Lady Blomfield's home in 1911 and 1913 and later in Palestine.
In 1915 he enlisted in the Royal Marine Light Infantry. Military officer in Egypt and Palestine during World War I with the Occupied Enemy Territory Administration. He rose to rank of Major. After the War he became the founder of the Chalice Well Trust, Glastonbury and The Silent Minute. Resided at 16–17 Royal York Crescent, Clifton, Bristol. Married on 17 Aug. 1912 Florence Snelling Pole.
Publications: *Private Dowding* (1917); *The Silent Road* (1960); *A Man See Afar* (1965); *Writing on the Ground* (1968); *My Dear Alexias* (1979), etc.
Biography: Fenge, Gerry. *The Two Worlds of Wellesley Tudor Pole* (2010).

Pollen, John (3 Jul. 1848 Kingstown, Ireland (now Dún Laoghaire, Rep. of Ireland)–18 Jun. 1923 Isle of Man)
Irish Orientalist and Esperantist
Met ʻAbduʼl-Bahá at the Shah Jahan Mosque, Woking, England, 17 Jan. 1913.
Educated at the University of Dublin. Member of the East India Association. He was also president (1904) and later vice-president of the British Esperanto Association. He held many government posts in British India. He translated some of the poetry of Omar Khayyam into English (1915). He married (1880) Mary Haggard.

Pool, Rev. John James (1857 Allonby, Cumberland, England–29 Oct. 1927 St Pancras, London)
English Congregational minister
ʻAbduʼl-Bahá accepted an invitation to speak at his church, at Woolwich, London on 12 Jan. 1913.
Educated at Rotherham College, Rotherham, Yorkshire. He served as minister for six years at Union Chapel, Calcutta and for ten years at

the English Congregational Church, Rheims. From 1901–06, he served as the minister at the Hanover Chapel in Peckham, London. Pastor of New Congregational Church, 18 Parson's Hill, Woolwich, London. Married Ann Ellen Pool (b. 1850).

Qá'im-Maqámí, Mírzá Áqá Khán (1868–1954)
Eminent and wealthy Persian Bahá'í
Met 'Abdu'l-Bahá in London 14 Jan. 1913 and at 30 rue Saint-Didier in Paris, 23 Jan.; 19 Feb. 1913.
He was occasionally a member of 'Abdu'l-Bahá's entourage in 1913.
Great-grandson of Mírzá Abu'l-Qásim Faráhání, the Qá'im-Maqám (c. 1779–26 Jun. 1835), who played an instrumental role in Muḥammad Sháh's accession to the throne, served as his first Prime Minister, and was eventually killed on the Shah's orders at the instigation of Ḥájí Mírzá Áqásí. Notably made a donation worth 'approximately ten thousand dollars' (*Bahá'í News*, no. 17, p. 8), which he earmarked for the construction of the Mashriqu'l-Adhkár in Wilmette, Illinois.
Biography: Ḥasan Núshábádí, 'Rajul-i-Rashíd', in *Áhang-i-Badí'* Azar/Dey 1352 (Dec. 1973/Jan. 1974), pp. 18–39. Translated into English by Adib Masumian under the title 'The Man of Courage'; available online at:
https://bahai-library.com/masumian_nushabadi_man_courage.

Qazvíní, Mírza Muḥammad Khán (Mar. 1877 Tehran–27 May 1949)
Persian writer, editor, critic, historian
Met 'Abdu'l-Bahá at 4 avenue de Camoëns in Paris, 15 Oct. 1911; 22 Jan. 1913.

Qumí, Siyyid Asadu'lláh (b. c. 1837 Qum, Persia)
Persian Bahá'í; attendant
Accompanied 'Abdu'l-Bahá on His second voyage to the West in 1912 sailing from Alexandria on the *RMS Cedric*.
Personal attendant (cook) to 'Abdu'l-Bahá during the entirety of His Western trips.

Qurayshí, Ḥishmatu'lláh
Indian Bahá'í
Met 'Abdu'l-Bahá in Paris on 1 Jun. 1913.
Resided in Agra, India. He contributed to the scholarship fund of the Persian–American Educational Society in 1913. He was a member of the National Spiritual Assembly of the Bahá'ís of India between 1923 and 1935. He assisted in the translation of *Bahá'u'lláh and the New Era* by John Esslemont into Urdu.

Rafsanjáni, Mírzá 'Alí-Akbar (1880–1921)
Persian Bahá'í; Bahá'í travelling teacher
Met 'Abdu'l-Bahá in Paris at 30 rue Saint-Didier, 31 Jan., 9 Feb. 1913.
He was an occasional member of 'Abdu'l-Bahá's entourage. He was sent by 'Abdu'l-Bahá to Germany, Switzerland (1913) and England (1914) to teach the Faith.

Rashtí, Ḥájí Khalílu'lláh Khán (Ḥájí Áqá Khalíl)
Persian Bahá'í from Rasht
Met 'Abdu'l-Bahá in Paris on 28 Jan. 1913. On 7 Mar. 1913, 'Abdu'l-Bahá visited his flat at 8 rue des Pavillons, Paris 20.

Rice, Alice
American music teacher
She and her sister Nellie Rice met 'Abdu'l-Bahá at the home of Lady Blomfield in London on 11 Jan. 1913.
She resided in Honolulu, Hawaii.

Rice, Nellie
American Theosophist
She and her sister Alice Rice met 'Abdu'l-Bahá at the home of Lady Blomfield in London on 11 Jan. 1913.
She resided in Honolulu, Hawaii. In 1920 she was living in San Francisco.

Richard, Mirra (Mrs Richard)
See **Alfassa, Mirra ('The Mother')**.

Richard, Paul Antoine (17 Jun. 1874 Marsillargues, France–Jun. 1967 Brooklyn, New York City)
French Hindu; lawyer
Met 'Abdu'l-Bahá in Paris on many occasions during May and Jun. 1913.
He was the husband of Mirra Richard, better known as 'The Mother'. He was a former Christian pastor and an advocate at the court of appeal in Paris with Hippolyte Dreyfus and a journalist (1907–14). He met Sri Aurobindo in 1910 in India. Editor of the monthly journal *Arya* in Pondicherry. Founder of the *Asian Review*.
Publications: Michael Paul Richard, *Without Passport: The Life and Work of Paul Richard* (1987).

Ridgway, Sarah Ann (20 Jan. 1849 Ashton-under-Lyne, England–11 May 1913 Salford, England)
English Bahá'í (1899); silk weaver
Met 'Abdu'l-Bahá in London, Sept. 1911 and in Liverpool, 15 Dec. 1912.
She was employed in a textile factory. She is buried in the Agecroft Cemetery, Salford, England.
Biography: Madeline Hellaby, *Sarah Ann Ridgway: First Bahá'í in the North of England* (2003).

Robb, Rev. Alexander Barrie (27 Apr. 1872 Armadale, West Lothian, Scotland–27 Jan. 1939 West Lothian)
Scottish Presbyterian clergyman from Falkirk
Spoke words of thanks at a meeting where 'Abdu'l-Bahá spoke in Edinburgh, 8 Jan. 1913.

Roohie
See **Sanderson, Edith Lawrence ('Rúḥíyyih Khánum', or 'Roohie')**
Not to be confused with Mary Sutherland Maxwell, known to most Bahá'ís as Rúḥíyyih Khánum, who married Shoghi Effendi in 1937.

Rosenberg, Ethel Jenner (6 Aug. 1858 Bath, England–17 Nov. 1930 London)
English Bahá'í (1899); miniature portrait painter
Invited 'Abdu'l-Bahá to her home at 74 Sinclair Rd., Kensington, London, 8 Sept. 1911. She organized a meeting at Passmore Edward's Settlement, Tavistock Place, London where 'Abdu'l-Bahá spoke on 29 Sept. 1911.
In 1915 she was the 'honourable secretary of the Bahai Society in London'. She is buried in Gap Road Cemetery, Wimbledon, London.
Publications: *A Brief Sketch of Behaism* (1905); *A Brief Account of the Bahá'í Movement* (1911).
Biography: Robert Weinberg, *Ethel Jenner Rosenberg* (1995).

Sacy, Edmée
See **Huguenin (née Sacy), Edmée**

Sacy, Gabriel (Jibrán Effendí) (d. 21 March 1903)
Syrian convert to the Bahá'í Faith and the brother of Ibrahim George Kheiralla. Of Sacy, Edward Browne has written, 'He was a Syrian Christian who had become a fervent Bahá'í with a very remarkable faculty for interpreting the prophecies of the Old and New Testaments, especially those of the Book of Daniel and Revelation, in support of the Bábí and Bahá'í claims' (*Materials for the Study of the Bábí Religion*, pp. 185–86).
Publication: *Du Règne de Dieu et de l'Agneau, connu sous le nom de Babysme* (1902).

Sacy, Gabrielle
See **Lagente (née Sacy), Gabrielle**

Sacy, Giselle
See **Dickinson (née Sacy), Giselle**

Sacy (née Coppin), Madeleine Jenny (22 Jul. 1874 Saint-Albain, France–24 Sept. 1940 Paris)
French Bahá'í

Met 'Abdu'l-Bahá in Paris at 4 avenue de Camoëns, with her four daughters in 1911; and again on 9 and 23 Feb., and 29 May 1913. She was the daughter of Émilien Auguste Coppin and Marie-Elénore Richert Coppin. In 1894, she married Gabriel de Sacy (1858–1903) in Douchy, France. She and her husband returned to Egypt. They had four daughters who were educated in a Catholic convent school.

Sacy, Mercedes
See **Baudry (née Sacy), Mercedes**

Ṣadíq, 'Ísá (b. 1895 Tehran)
Persian-Armenian Bahá'í, teacher
Met 'Abdu'l-Bahá at the Persian legation in Paris, 21 Mar. 1913.
Student at the École de Pédagogie, Versailles. In the 1930s he studied at the Teacher's College, Columbia University, New York City. He was the author of several works on Persian education, history, and culture, including *Modern Persia and Her Educational System* (1931).

Ṣáḥib, Amír-'Alí
See **Ali, Sir Syed Ameer (Judge Amír-'Alí ṣáḥib)**

Sanderson, Edith Lawrence ('Rúḥíyyih Kh̲ánum', or 'Roohie') (13 Dec. 1871 San Francisco–18 Sept. 1955 Paris)
American Bahá'í (1901) in France
Met 'Abdu'l-Bahá in Vevey, Switzerland, 27 Aug. 1911, and held meetings at her home, 46 avenue de Malakoff, Paris, with 'Abdu'l-Bahá, in 1911 and 1913. She and her mother also hosted Rúḥá Kh̲ánum and her husband in Paris.
She first arrived in Paris in 1902. During the years 1915 to 1924 she was residing in Vevey almost permanently for health reasons. She stayed at the Hotel Moser, and in 1924 at Villa Edelweiss, Bd. St-Martin, Vevey. Daughter of Silas Woodruff Sanderson (1823–1886) and Margaret Sanderson. Her ashes were interred at the Lakewood Cemetery, Minneapolis, Minnesota.
She was given the title 'Rúḥíyyih Kh̲ánum' (which she transliterated as 'Roohie') by 'Abdu'l-Bahá. Not to be confused with Mary

Sutherland Maxwell, known to most Bahá'ís as Rúḥíyyih Khánum, who married Shoghi Effendi in 1937.
Translated: Mohammed Ali Alkany, *Lessons in Religion* (1923).

Sanderson, Margaret Beaty Ormsby (1839 Westmoreland County, Pennsylvania–21 Oct. 1913 Paris)
American in Paris
Met 'Abdu'l-Bahá in Vevey, Switzerland, 27 Aug. 1911 and at her home in Paris in 1913.
Widow of Silas Woodruff Sanderson (1823–86), chief justice of the Supreme Court of California; mother of the opera singer Sibyl Sanderson (1865–1903) and of Edith Sanderson.

Sardár-i-As'ad
See **Khán, Ḥájí 'Alí-Qulí (the Sardár-i-As'ad)**

Sardár-i-Manṣúr
See **Akbar, Fatḥu'lláh Khán (Sardár-i-Manṣúr or Sipahdár-i-Rashtí)**

Sardár-i-Ẓafar
See **Khán, Ḥájí Khusraw (the Sardár-i-Ẓafar)**

Sargent, Porter Edward (6 Jun. 1872 Brooklyn, New York–27 Mar. 1951 Brookline, Massachusetts)
American educator and author
With Stanwood Cobb, he met 'Abdu'l-Bahá at the Martha-Pension in Paris, 25 Mar. 1913.
Founder and director of Sargent's Travel School for Boys, 1904–14.

Scatcherd, Felicia Rudolphina (1862 London–12 Mar. 1927 London)
English Bahá'í and editor
Met 'Abdu'l-Bahá at the home of Lady Blomfield, 97 Cadogan Gardens, London, 1911.
She was the editor of *The Asiatic Review*. She was also an active

member of the following: Council of the East India Association; the Sociological Society; the British Association for the Advancement of Science; vice-president of the (W.T.) Stead Bureau; the Society for Psychical Research; vice-president of the Greek Socialist Party and the Greek Labour League. She was acquainted with the Greek politician Platon E. Drakoules.
Publication: *A Wise Man from the East* (1912).

Schepel, Annette Hamminck (1844 The Hague, Netherlands–3 Mar. 1931 Glastonbury, England)
English Bahá'í; teacher
Met 'Abdu'l-Bahá in Vanners, Byfleet, England, 1911; and at the summer home of Agnes Parsons, Dublin, New Hampshire, 8 Aug. 1912.
Promoter of preschool education for children. She was a lifelong friend of Alice Buckton. Director of Pestalozzi-Froebel House Training College, Berlin, c. 1883. Principal of Sesame House [a training centre for teachers of preschool children], London, 1899–1907. In 1911, she was the honorary secretary of the Bahá'í Centre, London. She resided at Chalice Well, Glastonbury.

Schwarz, Consul Albert (14 Dec. 1871 Stuttgart, German Empire–13 Jan. 1931 Stuttgart)
German Bahá'í, diplomat and businessman
He and his wife met 'Abdu'l-Bahá when He visited their home in Stuttgart in Apr. 1913 and their hotel and spa in Bad Mergentheim, 7 Apr. 1913. They also met Him at the Martha-Pension in Paris, 30 May 1913.
He was appointed the commercial consul for Norway. He was the chairman of the National Spiritual Assembly of the Bahá'ís of Germany and Austria for many years in the 1930s. He was designated a Disciple of 'Abdu'l-Bahá. Husband of Alice Schwarz-Solivo. Buried in Pragfriedhof, Stuttgart.
Biography: Guido Ettlich, *Konsul Schwarz: Bankier, Bürger & Bahá'í in Stuttgart und Bad Mergentheim* (2019).

Schwarz-Solivo, Alice (12 Jul. 1875 Stuttgart, German Empire–7 Apr. 1965 Stuttgart)
German Bahá'í (1912); editor and publisher
Founder of the Bahá'í journal *Sonne der Wahrheit.* Member of the Spiritual Assembly of the Bahá'ís of Stuttgart. She was secretary in 1930 and the chairman in 1935 of the National Spiritual Assembly of the Bahá'ís of Germany and Austria. Wife of Consul Albert Schwarz. Buried in Pragfriedhof, Stuttgart.

Schweizer, Annemarie (1874?–23 Aug. 1957 Esslingen, Germany)
German Bahá'í
She and her husband Friedrich met 'Abdu'l-Bahá at 4 avenue de Camoëns in Paris, 1911 and on 12 Feb. 1913. 'Abdu'l-Bahá visited their home in Stuttgart on Apr. 1913.
They resided at Karlstrasse 26, Zuffenhausen. She was arrested and imprisoned by the Gestapo during World War II for her religious beliefs.

Schweizer, Friedrich R. (12 Sept. 1884 Esslingen, Württemberg–13 Jul. 1946 Stuttgart)
German Bahá'í (1910); topographer
Met 'Abdu'l-Bahá at 4 avenue de Camoëns in Paris, 1911 and on 12 Feb. 1913.
Treasurer of the National Spiritual Assembly of the Bahá'ís of Germany and Austria from 1930 to 1935. Married to Annemarie Schweizer.

Scott, Frank Edwin (21 Oct. 1862 Buffalo, New York–23 Dec. 1929 Paris)
American Bahá'í and painter in France
He and his wife held meetings at their home, 17 rue Boissonade, Paris, with 'Abdu'l-Bahá in 1911 and 1913.
He enrolled in the Art Students League, New York City in 1881. His first trip to Paris was in 1882 to study at the École des Beaux-Arts. In 1886 he returned to France permanently. His first exhibit was in 1888 at the Salon des Artistes Français. From 1906–29, he exhibited annually with the Societé National des Beaux-Arts and with the International

Society of Artists. Exhibited primarily in France but also in Belgium and the United States. The French government awarded him the Légion d'Honneur in 1927. He is buried in the historical cemetery of Sceaux in the Parisian suburbs with his wife, Josephine Sanford Scott. Married first (1888) Winnogene Ramsdell (1864–1953); second (1908) Josephine Sanford Scott.
Biography: Donald McClelland, *Paintings by Edwin Scott from the Alice Pike Barney Memorial Collection, Smithsonian Institution* (1970).

Scott, Josephine Sanford (2 Sept. 1863 Cleveland, Ohio–3 Dec. 1955 Versailles, France)
American painter and Bahá'í in France
She and her husband held meetings at their home, 17 rue Boissonade, Paris, with 'Abdu'l-Bahá in 1911 and 1913.
Wife (1908) of Frank Edwin Scott, with whom she is buried in Sceaux, France.

Shahíd, Áqá Mírzá Jalál (b. c. 1879 Isfahan, Persia)
Persian Bahá'í
Met 'Abdu'l-Bahá at 4 avenue de Camoëns in Paris, Oct. 1911 and in 1913. He was an occasional member of 'Abdu'l-Bahá's entourage in Paris.
His father was Mírzá Muḥammad-Ḥasan ('King of the Martyrs') (1833–79). He married Rúḥá Khánum, the daughter of 'Abdu'l-Bahá. He later sided with the enemies of the Bahá'í Faith and was expelled by Shoghi Effendi.

Sher-Gil, Sardar Umrao Singh (Sirdar Omrah Singh) (1870 Majitha, Punjab, India–17 Dec. 1954 Delhi, India)
Indian Sikh aristocrat and scholar of Persian and Sanskrit literature
Met and hosted 'Abdu'l-Bahá in Budapest, Apr. 1913.
He was also known as a photographer. He married Antónia (or Marie Antoinette) Gottesmann-Baktay in 1912. They settled in Budapest in 1912 and lived there until 1921 when they moved to India. On 28 Oct. 1913, he attended the first Bahá'í meeting in Budapest. Their daughter was the famous painter, Amrita Sher-Gil (1913–1941).

Sipahdár-i-A'ẓam
See **Tunukábuní, Muḥammad-Valí Khán (the Sipahdár-i-A'ẓam and Naṣru's-Salṭanih)**

Sipahdár-i-Rashtí
See **Akbar, Fatḥu'lláh Khán (Sardár-i-Manṣúr or Sipahdár-i-Rashtí)**

Skrine, Francis Henry Bennett (23 Dec. 1847 Cahir, Co. Tipperary, Ireland–8 Dec. 1933 Les Bosquets, Aix-en-Provence, France)
British Orientalist and colonial administrator
Met 'Abdu'l-Bahá in London at Lady Blomfield's, 1911; and possibly in Paris, 1911.
Entered the Bengal Civil Service 1868. Fellow of the Royal Historical Society. He was married (1887) to Helen Lucy Stewart (b. 1867).
Publication: *Bahaism, the Religion of Brotherhood* (1912).

Sohrab, Mirza Ahmad (c. 1890* Sidih, Isfahan, Persia–20 Apr. 1958 New York City)
Persian Bahá'í in America; translator; writer
Met 'Abdu'l-Bahá in Marseilles, 7 Dec. 1911; interpreted for 'Abdu'l-Bahá in Dublin, New Hampshire, and at Green Acre, Aug. 1912, and was with Him throughout His entire stay in Europe in 1913.
In 1910, he co-founded the Persian-American Educational Society and served as its treasurer. He also worked as secretary of the Persian legation in Washington, D.C. He was an honorary member of the editorial staff of *Star of the West* in 1914. Around 1939, he was expelled from the Faith for causing a schism by setting up The New History Society. He married Juanita Marie Storch in 1920 (divorced 1923). In 1925–26, he was the chairman of the Spiritual Assembly of the Bahá'ís of Los Angeles. Buried in Saint Paul's Episcopal Church Cemetery, Glen Cove, New York.
Publications: *Abdul Baha in Egypt* (1929).

---

* This is according to his headstone. In his autobiography, Sohrab writes that he was born in approximately 1894 (*My Bahai Pilgrimage*, p. 21), but this appears to be an error, as he was translating Tablets under the name 'Ahmad Esphahani' as early as 1906.

Spencer, Col. John (d. 10 Nov. 1938 Palmers Green, North London)
English clergyman; Salvation Army officer
Met 'Abdu'l-Bahá when He visited a Salvation Army shelter in Westminster, London, 25 Dec. 1912.
Chief accountant and general secretary at the Salvation Army Men's Work Social Headquarters, London. In 1913, held the rank of Lieutenant Colonel; later attained rank of Colonel.

Stäbler, Elise (Lisa)
German Bahá'í
Met 'Abdu'l-Bahá in Stuttgart, Apr. 1913.
She was the sister of Julie Stäbler.

Stäbler, Julie (d. 1914 Stuttgart)
German Bahá'í
Met 'Abdu'l-Bahá at 4 avenue de Camoëns in Paris, 1911, 1913 and in Stuttgart 6 Apr. 1913.
She was the sister of Elise (Lisa) Stäbler.

Stannard, Jean E. (1865–Nov. 1944 Paris)
English Bahá'í
Met 'Abdu'l-Bahá at Passmore Edward's Settlement in London, 29 Sept. 1911 and in Paris.
She lived in Egypt from 1908 and in India, c. 1914. From 1925–28 she headed the International Bahá'í Bureau in Geneva. She is buried in the Cimetière parisien de Thiais.
Translated: *Hidden Words from the Supreme Pen of Baha'u'llah* (Cairo 1921).
Author: 'Letters from Count Leo Tolstoy to Eastern Correspondents', in *Le Messager Bahai de Geneve*, no. 1 (20 Jul. 1926), pp. 7–8; *Herald of the South* (Sydney), Dec. 1926/Jan. 1927; Tolstoi und der religiöse Einheit', in *The Bahá'í-Messenger* (Geneva), no. 1 (20 July 1926).

Stapley, Lady Annie (Elizabeth) Jenner (1839 Brighton, England–Mar. 1917 St Giles, London)
English

Met 'Abdu'l-Bahá at the Shah Jahan Mosque, Woking, England, 17 Jan. 1913. Invited 'Abdu'l-Bahá to dine at her home, 33 Bloomsbury Square, London, 12 Jan. 1913. They were frequent visitors to Lady Blomfield's when 'Abdu'l-Bahá was staying there.
Wife (1866) of Sir Richard Stapley.

Stapley, Sir Richard (28 Oct. 1842 Fletching, England–20 May 1920 died at sea)
British entrepreneur
One of the speakers at the meeting at Passmore Edward's Settlement when 'Abdu'l-Bahá spoke in London, 29 Sept. 1911. He met 'Abdu'l-Bahá at the home of Mr Sidley, 1 Jan. 1913; invited Him to dine at his own home, 33 Bloomsbury Square, London, 12 Jan. 1913; and accompanied Him to the Shah Jahan Mosque, Woking, England, 17 Jan. 1913.
Director of the clothing business Stapley and Smith, and philanthropist. Justice of the peace; member of the City of London Council; and Liberal politician. He was knighted in 1908. He established the Sir Richard Stapley Trust for students. Married (1866) Annie Jenner Stapley.

Stark, Karolina
Hungarian Bahá'í; peace activist
Met 'Abdu'l-Bahá at the Hotel Ritz in Budapest, 9 Apr. 1913, and again in Vienna on 23 Apr. 1913.
Wife of Lipót Stark.

Stark, Lipót (Leopold) (4 May 1866 Trencsén, Austrian Empire (today Trenčín, Slovakia)–17 Dec. 1932 Budapest)
Hungarian Bahá'í; electrical engineer
He and his wife met 'Abdu'l-Bahá at the Hotel Ritz in Budapest, 9 Apr. 1913.
Graduated from the Budapest Technical University in 1887. Supervised the construction of power stations in South America, 1891–93. He was the chief director of the electrical works in Istanbul, 1911 and in Budapest, 1911–19. He was president of the Theosophical Society

in Budapest, 1910–11. He and his wife, Karolina, held the first Bahá'í meeting in Budapest at their home on 28 Oct. 1913.

Sursock, Nicolas
French diplomat
Met 'Abdu'l-Bahá at the Persian legation, 21 Mar. 1913 and probably on other occasions.
Attaché at the Persian legation in Paris, 1911–13.

Suttner, Baroness Bertha von
See **von Suttner, Baroness Bertha**

Tabrízí, 'Alí 'Abbás Áqá
Persian carpet merchant from Tabriz, living in Budapest
Gave a dinner party for 'Abdu'l-Bahá in his own home in Budapest, 14 Apr. 1913.

Tennant, Edward Priaulx, 1st Baron Glenconner (31 May 1859 Innerleithen, Peebles, Scotland–21 Nov. 1920 London)
He married (1895) Pamela Adelaide Genevieve Wyndham.
He was educated at Eton College, Windsor, Berkshire, England and graduated from Trinity College, Cambridge University, in 1885 with a Master of Arts (M.A.) He was a Member of Parliament (Liberal) for Salisbury between 1906 and 1910. He succeeded to the title of 2nd Baronet Tennant [U.K., 1885] on 4 Jun. 1906. He held the offices of Lord-Lieutenant of Peeblesshire between 1908 and 1920, and of Lord High Commissioner of the General Assembly of the Church of Scotland between 1911 and 1914. He was created 1st Baron Glenconner, of Glen, co. Peebles [U.K.] on 3 Apr. 1911. He held the office of Justice of the Peace for Wiltshire. Buried in Traquir Kirkyard, Traquir, Scotland.

Tennant, Pamela Adelaide Genevieve Wyndham, Baroness Glenconner **(Pamela Genevieve Adelaide Grey, Viscountess Grey of Fallodon)** (14 Jan. 1871 Salisbury, England–18 Nov. 1928 Wilsford, Wiltshire, England)
English author

Met 'Abdu'l-Bahá in London at Lady Blomfield's and at her home, 1911; also on 16 Jan. 1913 with her husband and four of her children. She was the sister of Mary Constance Wyndham Charteris, Countess of Wemyss; married first (1895) the Scottish Labour politician, Edward Priaulx Tennant, first Baron Glenconner (1859–1920) with whom she had six children; second (1922) Sir Edward Grey, first Viscount Grey of Fallodon (1862–1933). She, along with her sisters, was a member of the social clique known as 'The Souls'. Buried in St Michael's Churchyard, Wilsford, Wiltshire.

Thaler, Baroness Marie
Austrian stage actress; formerly a Theosophist, later a Bahá'í
Met 'Abdu'l-Bahá in Vienna, 20 Apr. 1913.
Apparently served as secretary of the Austrian Theosophical Society and eventually became a Bahá'í. Wife of Willy Thaler. In Mírzá Maḥmúd Zarqání's original chronicle, her surname has been transliterated into the Persian alphabet as 'Tyler'.

Thern, Lajos (Louis) (18 Dec. 1848 Budapest–12 Mar. 1920 Vienna)
Hungarian pianist
Met 'Abdu'l-Bahá in Vienna, Apr. 1913.
He was the son of the famous musician, Károly Thern (1817–86).

Thern, Marguerite
Hungarian Theosophist and piano teacher
Met 'Abdu'l-Bahá in Vienna, Apr. 1913.
She wrote two books on Theosophy and was the wife of Lajos Thern.

Thornburgh-Cropper, Mary 'Minnie' Virginia Shepherd (1850 California–15 Mar. 1938 London)
British Bahá'í (1898)
Organized a meeting at the Passmore Edward's Settlement at which 'Abdu'l-Bahá spoke in London, 29 Sept. 1911; held a reception for 'Abdu'l-Bahá in London, 17 Dec. 1912, and also met Him at Lady Blomfield's.

She and her mother, Mrs Harriet Burtis Thornburgh (d. 1905), were members of one of the earliest Western pilgrimage groups in 1898. Married (1874) Edward Denman Cropper (1854–1902); divorced 1897.

Tunukábuní, Muḥammad-Valí Khán (the Sipahdár-i-A'ẓam and Naṣru's-Salṭanih) (1848 Tunukábun–Jan. 1926 Tehran)
Persian politician
Most likely met 'Abdu'l-Bahá at the Shah Jahan Mosque, Woking, England, 17 Jan. 1913, and again in Paris, 28 Feb.; and 6, 25, and 30 Mar. 1913.
His father was the Sa'ídu'd-Dawlih (the Sardár). He was the Governor of Tunukábun for many years. In 1885, he became the Brigadier General of the Tunukábun Regiment; in 1899, the Governor of Rasht; later, the leader of the Constitutional Movement in Persia. In 1909, as leader of the nationalist forces, he headed the march to Tehran, forcing the abdication of Muḥammad-'Alí Sháh, and was appointed Minister of War. In 1909, he was elected to the twenty-person Directory. Later, he served as Prime Minister during three short periods in 1909–10, 1911 and 1916–17, and also as the Governor of Tabriz in 1912.

Tyler, Marie
See **Thaler, Baroness Marie**
In Mírzá Maḥmúd Zarqání's original chronicle, Thaler's surname has been transliterated into the Persian alphabet as 'Tyler'.

Urusov, Prince Lev Pavlovich (1839 Warsaw, Russia (now Poland) –28 Jun. 1933 Paris)
Russian diplomat
He and his wife met 'Abdu'l-Bahá at the Shah Jahan Mosque, Woking, England 17 Jan. 1913.
Russian ambassador to Rome (1904) and later to Vienna (1913); member of the International Olympic Committee (IOC), 1910–33. After World War I lived in exile in Paris.

Urusova (née Abaza), Praskov'ia Aleksandrovna (1852–1928 Nice, France)
Russian
Met 'Abdu'l-Bahá at the Shah Jahan Mosque, Woking, England 17 Jan. 1913.
Her father was Aleksandr Abaza (1821–95), the Russian Minister of Finance. She was the wife of Prince Lev Pavlovich Urusov.

Vámbéry, Ármin (or Arminius) (19 Mar. 1832 Dunaszerdahely, Austrian Empire (now Dunajská Streda, Slovakia)–15 Sept. 1913 Budapest, Austria-Hungary)
Hungarian orientalist; Bahá'í
'Abdu'l-Bahá went to meet him in his home at 27 Francis Joseph Quai, in Budapest, 11 Apr. 1913.
Professor from 1865 to 1905 of Oriental Languages at the University of Budapest. Best known for his journey of 1863 through the countries of Central Asia through Bokhara and Samarqand as far as Hirat disguised as a dervish. He was fluent in over twenty languages of Central Asia. He is buried in the Kerepesi Cemetery, Budapest.
Publications: *Travels in Central Asia* (1864); *Western Culture in Eastern Lands* (1906).

Varqá, Mírza 'Azízu'lláh Khán (d. 1931 Persia)
Persian Bahá'í; merchant and farmer
Translated into French for 'Abdu'l-Bahá in Paris, on 29 Oct. 1911 at the home of Madeleine Jenny Sacy, and he was also with 'Abdu'l-Bahá in Paris in 1913.
He was the elder son of the celebrated martyr, Mírzá 'Alí-Muḥammad Varqá (d. 1896). Around 1899, he operated a shop on Lálihzár Avenue in Tehran selling merchandise imported from Europe. In 1925, he was a noted farmer in Persia. He was the brother of Mírzá Valíyu'lláh Khán Varqá.

Varqá, Mírzá Valíyu'lláh Khán (1883 Tabriz, Persia–12 Nov. 1955 Tübingen, Germany)
Persian Bahá'í; translator

Met 'Abdu'l-Bahá in New York City. Accompanied 'Abdu'l-Bahá at the ground-breaking ceremony for the Bahá'í Temple, 1 May 1912, and was also in Paris from 22 Jan. till 6 Feb. 1913 as a member of 'Abdu'l-Bahá's entourage.
He was the younger son of the celebrated martyr, 'Alí-Muḥammad Varqá (d. 1896). He studied at the Syrian Protestant College in Beirut. Secretary at the Russian Embassy in Tehran, 1909–12. He was employed as first secretary translator at the Ottoman Embassy in Tehran, 1913 till at least 1925. In 1938, he was appointed by Shoghi Effendi as the Trustee of the Ḥuqúqu'lláh. In 1935, he was elected to the National Spiritual Assembly of the Bahá'ís of Persia and continued to be elected in subsequent years until 1948. He was appointed a Hand of the Cause of God in 1951 by Shoghi Effendi. In 1953, he participated in the Intercontinental Conferences in Kampala, Chicago, Stockholm and New Delhi. He travelled widely in South America, Germany, Iraq, Egypt, and Turkey. In 1909, he married Bahíyyih Khánum, the daughter of the Ṣaní'u's-Sulṭán, surnamed Ṣaníy-i-Iláhí. He was the younger brother of Mírzá 'Azízu'lláh Khán Varqá. He is buried at the Steinhaldenfriedhof in Stuttgart.

Vesel, C. Jessie
British Spiritualist
In Jan. 1913, he wrote an article in defence of the Bahá'í Faith (C. Jessie Vesel, 'The Bahai Movement', in *Light* (London) vol. 33 (25 Jan. 1913), pp. 47–8).

Vikár, Béla (1 Apr. 1859 Hetes, Hungary–22 Sept. 1945 Dunavecse, Hungary)
Hungarian ethnographer
He met 'Abdu'l-Bahá in Budapest, Apr. 1913.
He is buried in the Budapesten Farkasréti.

Vikár, Dr Géza (d. 1949 Budapest)
Hungarian Jewish lawyer
He met 'Abdu'l-Bahá in Budapest, Apr. 1913, and later attended the first Bahá'í meeting in Budapest at the Stark residence on 28 Oct. 1913.

He was secretary of the ‘Altruismus’ branch of the Hungarian Theosophical Society. He was married to Helena Zipernowsky, the daughter of Károly Zipernowsky.

von Behr (née Lillienthal), Maud (1865 Yonkers, New York–20 Jan. 1931 Asheville, North Carolina)
German-American Bahá’í
Met ‘Abdu’l-Bahá in Paris, almost every day 1 May–2 Jun. 1913.
Visited ‘Abdu’l-Bahá in Ramleh, Egypt on 29 Oct. 1913 together with Alice R. Beede. In 1917, she was active in Green Acre. Her father was the wealthy tobacco manufacturer, Christian H. Lillienthal (b. c. 1821). Married Carl Behr (1853–1942) a well-known zither player.

von Suttner, Baroness Bertha (4 Jun. 1843 Prague, Bohemia, Austrian Empire (now Czech Republic)–21 Jun. 1914 Vienna, Austria-Hungary)
Austrian peace activist, Nobel laureate
Met ‘Abdu’l-Bahá in Chicago Sept. 1912 and in Vienna, 23 Apr. 1913.
Austrian novelist. She founded an Austrian pacifist organization in 1891 and was ceaselessly active in the movement. In 1905, she became a Nobel Peace Prize laureate. In 1876, she married Baron Arthur Gundaccar von Suttner (d. 1902).

Warneke, H. E. (b. c. 1885)
American importer
Met ‘Abdu’l-Bahá on the train returning to Paris from Stuttgart, 30 Apr. 1913.
Importer of chinaware and bronze statues. His address was 9 East 37th St., New York City. His showroom was on Fifth Avenue near Thirty-Seventh Street.

Weardale, Philip James Stanhope (8 Dec. 1847 Marylebone, London–1 Mar. 1923 Sevenoaks, Kent, England)
British politician
Met ‘Abdu’l-Bahá in London at the home of Lady Blomfield on 19 Dec. 1912.

He was a Member of Parliament and president of the Inter-Parliamentary Union, 1912–22. Member of the House of Lords from 1906. He was also president of the Save the Children Fund. He was the president of the First Universal Races Congress, 1911. He married Countess Alexandra Tolstoy (1886–1934). He is buried at Chevining House, Sevenoaks, England.

Woodcock, Percy Franklin (17 Aug. 1855 Athens, Canada West (now Ontario)–11 Feb. 1936 Montreal)
Canadian Bahá'í; painter
Met 'Abdu'l-Bahá several times in Paris, 1911. With his wife and daughter joined 'Abdu'l-Bahá on board the *RMS Cedric* at Naples, 25 Mar. 1912, and met Him again in New York at the Hotel Ansonia, 12 Apr., in Montreal in Aug./Sept. 1912, and London in Dec. 1912.
Studied in Paris and exhibited at the Paris Salon in 1883. He was a member of the Royal Canadian Academy. In 1910 he was elected to the New York City [Bahá'í] Board of Counsel and a member of Bahai Temple Unity in 1911. In 1911 he lectured at Green Acre. He married (17 Jun. 1878) Aloysia Pratt Woodcock from Montreal. Buried in Mount Royal Cemetery, Montreal.

Woodcock, Aloysia Pratt (20 May 1853 Canada East (now Québec)–1 Nov. 1941)
French-Canadian Bahá'í
Met 'Abdu'l-Bahá several times in Paris, 1911. With her husband and daughter she joined 'Abdu'l-Bahá on board the *RMS Cedric* at Naples, 25 Mar. 1912, and met Him again in New York at the Hotel Ansonia, 12 Apr., in Montreal in Aug./Sept. 1912, and London in Dec. 1912. On 17 Jun. 1878, she married Percy Franklin Woodcock. Buried in Mount Royal Cemetery, Montreal.

Whyte, Dr Alexander (13 Jan. 1836 Kirriemuir, Scotland–6 Jun. 1921 Hampstead, London)
Scottish clergyman
Invited 'Abdu'l-Bahá to their home in Edinburgh, 6 Jan. 1913.
In 1862, he graduated from King's College, Aberdeen; 1866–70,

colleague at St John's Free Church, Glasgow; 1870–1916, minister at St George's Free Church, Edinburgh (resigned 1916); 1898, elected moderator of the General Assembly of the United Free Church of Scotland; 1909–18, Principal of New College, Edinburgh. In 1910, he was presented with the freedom of the city of Edinburgh. He married Jane Elizabeth Barbour in 1881.
Biography: G. F. Barbour, *The Life of Alexander Whyte, D.D.* (1923).

Whyte (née Barbour), Jane Elizabeth (1857 Edinburgh–12 Nov. 1944 Beaconsfield, England)
Scottish Bahá'í
Met 'Abdu'l-Bahá in London at Lady Blomfield's; invited Him to her home in Edinburgh, 6 Jan. 1913. She visited 'Abdu'l-Bahá in 'Akká in 1906.
She held Bahá'í meetings at her home in Edinburgh at 7 Charlotte Square, and in later years was a member of the London Bahá'í community. Wife (1881) of Alexander Whyte.

Whyte, Lancelot Law (1896 Edinburgh–1972 Hampstead, London)
Scottish financier, scientific philosopher and industrial engineer
Son of Jane and Alexander Whyte. Met 'Abdu'l-Bahá in Edinburgh at the family home 6 Jan. 1913.
Married first (1921) Sylvia Margaret Sanderson; second (1926) Lotte Heller; third (1947) Eva Korner (d. 1988).

Yandell, Maud (4 Jun. 1871 Louisville, Kentucky–14 May 1962 Royal Cheadle, Cheshire, England)
American Bahá'í; psychologist
Met 'Abdu'l-Bahá at Lady Blomfield's in London, 1911.
She resided in London from 1910.

Yazdí, Aḥmad Effendí (Mírzá Aḥmad Yazdí)
Persian Bahá'í and diplomat
Met 'Abdu'l-Bahá in Thonon-les-Bains, France, 1911; and in Liverpool at the quayside, 13 Dec. 1912.
Lived in Paris for a short while. Became 'Abdu'l-Bahá's son-in-law

through his marriage with Munavvar Khánum (d. 1971). He was the Persian consul in Port Said, Egypt. Later expelled from the Faith by Shoghi Effendi for breaking the Covenant.

Yehya, Shah Mahomed (b. 1886 Monghyr, Bengal (now Munger, Bihar), India)
Indian lawyer
Met 'Abdu'l-Bahá at the Shah Jahan Mosque, Woking, England, 17 Jan. 1913.
Enrolled in 1909 in the Middle Temple of the Inns of Court, London. Called to the bar in 1913.

Zafar Ali Khan, Maulana (1873 Kot Mahrath, Sialkot, Punjab, India (now in Pakistan)–1956 Karamabad, Pakistan)
Pakistani (Urdu) writer and journalist
Met 'Abdu'l-Bahá at the Shah Jahan Mosque, Woking, England, 17 Jan. 1913.
Considered the father of Urdu journalism. Edited the Urdu newspaper *Zamindar*. He was also involved in political movements which advocated independence from Great Britain. In 1937–47 he was elected to the Punjab Legislative Assembly. He is buried in Karamabad.

Zarqání, Mírzá Maḥmúd (c. 1873 Zarqan, Persia–11 Oct. 1927 Rasht, Persia)
Persian Bahá'í; travel-teacher, most notably to India for several periods
Born to a Bahá'í family but came to believe in the Faith in his youth. Before this, he practised his father's profession of *gívih-dúzí* (making cotton summer shoes), but when the Bahá'í poets and brothers, Nayyir and Síná, passed through his village of Zarqan, he gave up this line of work to accompany them on their teaching trips throughout Persia. He then accompanied Ḥájí Mírzá Ḥaydar-'Alí Iṣfahání on his more extensive travels, after which he began to travel as a Bahá'í teacher throughout Persia independently.
Zarqání first went to India possibly as early as 1902 (but certainly by 1904), residing there for several lengths of time and becoming a

prominent member of the Indian Bahá'í community. Several eminent Bahá'ís from that region, such as Pritam Singh and Maḥfúzu'l-Ḥaqq 'Ilmí, became Bahá'ís through his efforts. Known to have met with Muḥammad Iqbál (1877–1938), often called 'the Spiritual Father of Pakistan', on many occasions, and several other renowned Pakistanis besides. Additional services rendered by Zarqání in India have been published in the memoirs of Siyyid Muṣṭafá Rúmí, translated by Irán Furútan Muhájir.

He left India for the Holy Land in 1908 and remained there until he set off for the West as one of the members of 'Abdu'l-Bahá's retinue. Following his return from the West in 1913, he was sent to India again in 1914, where he remained until 1919, when he went to the Holy Land. He then returned to India in 1920, remaining there until the end of 1921, when he was recalled to the Holy Land again by the Greatest Holy Leaf following the passing of 'Abdu'l-Bahá. He then returned to India in 1924 and sojourned there for the last time. Afterwards, he went back to the Holy Land and stayed there until early 1927, at which time he went to Persia and died of an unidentified illness in Rasht on 11 Oct. 1927. He was buried at the Mudíríyyih cemetery in Rasht, but his resting-place is reported to have been destroyed in the Iranian Revolution of 1979.

He was thrice married; the first marriage yielded one child who died (along with the mother) in childbirth, while the other two produced no children.

He is known to have been fluent in Persian, his native language, and also Urdu, which he learned during his extensive sojourns in India. Available evidence suggests he also knew Arabic and English.

Biography: 'Azízu'llah Sulaymání, *Maṣábíḥ-i-Hidáyat*, vol. 8 (1973), pp. 147–86; translated by Adib Masumian and included in the online supplement to this book.

Writings: (1) *Javáb-i-Nuṭq-i-Qádíyání*, published in *Paisa Akhbár* (and translated into Urdu by Siyyid Muṣṭafá Rúmí in 1908) in response to Mírzá Ghulám Aḥmad's *Lecture Lahore*; (2) *Iḥqáqu'l-Ḥaqq*, written, and published in an unidentified place, in response to an article on the Bahá'í Faith by the Lahore Ahmadiyya leader, Maulana Muhammad Ali, published in *Review of Religions*; (3) *Asráru'n-*

Nus̲h̲úr, a treatise on the Resurrection partially published in the Bahá'í magazine *Kawkab-i-Hind*; (4) *Badv-i-Ṭulú'-i-Amr*, a brief history of the Bahá'í Faith; (5) Several leading articles and other contributions in the Indian Bahá'í periodical *al-Bis̲h̲árat (Bahá'í News* (India)); (6) *Badáyi'u'l-Át̲h̲ár*, vol. 1 (India, 1914), translated into English under the title *Maḥmúd's Diary*; (7) *Badáyi'u'l-Át̲h̲ár*, vol. 2 (India, 1921), translated into English in the present volume.

Ẓillu's-Sulṭán
See **Mírzá, Sulṭán-Mas'úd (the Ẓillu's-Sulṭán)**

Zipernowsky, Károly (4 Apr. 1853 Vienna, Austrian Empire–29 Nov. 1942 Budapest, Hungary)
Hungarian electrical engineer
He met 'Abdu'l-Bahá at the Ritz Hotel in Budapest, 10 Apr. 1913. On 28 Oct. 1913, he and his wife, Anna Kline, attended the first Bahá'í meeting in Budapest. He studied at the Technical University in Budapest, where he eventually lectured (1892–1924). He was the co-inventor of the transformer and other AC electrical devices. He is buried in the Farkasréti cemetery in Budapest.

Bibliography

'Abdu'l-Bahá. *Majmú'iy-i-Khiṭábát-i-Ḥaḍrat-i-'Abdu'l-Bahá*. Hofheim-Langenhain: Bahá'í-Verlag, 1984.

—*Memorials of the Faithful*. Trans. Marzieh Gail. Wilmette, IL: Bahá'í Publishing Trust, 1971.

—*al-Núr al-Abhá fí Mufávaḍát-i 'Abdu'l-Bahá: Guftugú bar Sar-i-Nahár*. London: Kegan Paul, 1908. Translated into English as *Some Answered Questions*. Haifa: Bahá'í World Centre, 2014 (rev. ed.).

—*The Promulgation of Universal Peace: Talks Delivered by 'Abdu'l-Baha During His Visit to the United States and Canada in 1912* (1922, 1925). Comp. H. MacNutt. Wilmette, IL: Bahá'í Publishing Trust, 2nd ed. 1982.

—*Selections from the Writings of 'Abdu'l-Bahá*. Comp. Research Department of the Universal House of Justice. Haifa: Bahá'í World Centre, 1978.

—*The Will and Testament of 'Abdu'l-Bahá*. Wilmette, IL: Bahá'í Publishing Trust, 1990 reprint.

Afrúkhtih, Yúnis (Youness Afroukhteh). *Irtibáṭ-i-Sharq va Gharb*. N.P., 1931.

—*Kháṭirát-i-Nuh Sálih*. Iran: N.P., 1942. Translated into English by Riaz Masrour as *Memories of Nine Years in* 'Akká. Oxford: George Ronald, 2003.

Algar, Hamid. 'Atabāt', in *Encyclopedia Iranica*; available online at: https://www.iranicaonline.org/articles/atabat.

Amanat, Abbas. 'Sayyed Yaḥyā Dawlatābādī', in *Encyclopedia Iranica*; available online at: https://www.iranicaonline.org/articles/dawlatabadi-sayyed-yahya.

Amánat, Músá. *Bahá'íyán-i-Káshán*. Madrid: Fundación Nehal, 2012.

Amini, Tooraj. *Abu'l-Faḍá'il-i-Gulpáygání dar Áyniy-i-Asnád*. Madrid: Fundación Nehal, 2015.

Badiei, Amir. *Stories Told by 'Abdu'l-Bahá*. Oxford: George Ronald, RP 2007.

The Bahá'í World: An International Record. Vol. III (1928–1930), vol. V (1932–1934), and vol. XII (1950–1954), Wilmette, IL: Bahá'í Publishing Trust; vol. XIII (1954–1963), Haifa, The Universal House of Justice; vol. XVII (1976–1979), Haifa: Bahá'í World Centre, 1981; vol. XVIII (1979–1983), Haifa: Bahá'í World Centre, 1986.

Badí'u'lláh, Mírzá (trans. Ameen Ullah Fareed). *An Epistle to the Bahá'í World*. Chicago: Bahá'í Publishing Society, 1907.

Bahá'u'lláh. *Áthár-i-Qalam-i-A'lá*, vol. 2. Dundas, Ontario: Institute for Bahá'í Studies in Persian, 2002.

—*Epistle to the Son of the Wolf.* Trans. Shoghi Effendi. Wilmette, IL: Bahá'í Publishing Trust, rev. ed. 1976.
—*Gems of Divine Mysteries: Javáhiru'l-Asrár.* Haifa: Bahá'í World Centre, 2002.
—*Gleanings from the Writings of Bahá'u'lláh.* Trans. Shoghi Effendi. Wilmette, IL: Bahá'í Publishing Trust, 2nd ed. 1976.
—*The Hidden Words of Bahá'u'lláh.* Trans. Shoghi Effendi. Wilmette, IL: Bahá'í Publishing Trust, 1970; New Delhi: Bahá'í Publishing Trust, 1987.
—*The Kitáb-i-Aqdas: The Most Holy Book.* Haifa: Bahá'í World Centre, 1992.
—*Kitáb-i-Mubín* (Bombay, 1890). Dundas, Ontario: Institute for Bahá'í Studies in Persian, 1996.
—*La'áli'u'l-Ḥikmat,* vol. 2. A compilation of Tablets revealed by Bahá'u'lláh. Rio De Janeiro: Editoria Bahá'í Brasil, 2nd ed. 1996.
—*The Summons of the Lord of Hosts: Tablets of Bahá'u'lláh.* Haifa: Bahá'í World Centre, 2002.
—*Tablets of Bahá'u'lláh Revealed after the Kitáb-i-Aqdas.* Comp. Research Department of the Universal House of Justice. Haifa: Bahá'í World Centre, 1978.

Balyuzi, H. M. *'Abdu'l-Bahá.* Oxford: George Ronald, 1971.
—*Edward Granville Browne and the Bahá'í Faith.* George Ronald: Oxford, 1987.
—*Eminent Bahá'ís in the Time of Bahá'u'lláh.* Oxford: George Ronald, 1985.
—*Bahá'u'lláh, the King of Glory.* Oxford, George Ronald, 1980.

Bashirelahi, Nasir. *Alváḥ-i-Názilih bih I'záz-i-Mírzá Áqá Khán Bashíru's-Sulṭán, Mulaqqab bih Bashír-i-Iláhí.* Private publication, 2010.

Browne, E. G. (ed.). *Materials for the Study of the Bábí Religion.* Cambridge, UK: Cambridge University Press, 1918.

Bryan, William Jennings. *The Old World and Its Ways* (1907). Available at https://www.gutenberg.org/files/45376/45376-h/45376-h.htm.

Bushrú'í, Mírzá Badí'. *Dar Ẓill-i-Shajariy-i-Míthág.* Ed. Suheil Bushrui and Ashkan Monfared. Madrid: Fundación Nehal, 2016.

Bushrui, Suheil. *'Abbás Afandí fí al-dhikrá al-mi'awíyah li-ziyáratihi ilá Miṣr (1910–1913).* Beirut: Manshúrát al-Jamal, 2010.
—*'Abdu'l-Bahá 'Abbás: bih Yádbúd-i-Ṣadumín Sálgard-i-Dídár-i-Ḥaḍratash az Miṣr: 1910–1913.* Trans. Nahid Rouhani. Yárán, 2012.

Chamberlain, Isabel Fraser. *'Abdu'l-Bahá on Divine Philosophy.* Boston: The Tudor Press, 1918.

The Dawn-Breakers: Nabíl's Narrative of the Early Days of the Bahá'í Revelation. Trans. Shoghi Effendi. Wilmette, IL: Bahá'í Publishing Trust, 1932, 1999.

Dhuká'í Bayḍá'í, Ni'matu'lláh. *Tadhkariy-i-Shu'aráy-i-Qarn-i-Avval-i-Bahá'í*, vol. 1 (1964); vol. 2 (1968); vol. 3 (1969); vol. 4 (1974). Tehran: Mu'assisiy-i-Millíy-i-Maṭbú'át-i-Amrí.

Egea, Amín. *The Apostle of Peace: A Survey of References to 'Abdu'l-Bahá in the Western Press, 1871–1921. Volume Two: 1912–1921.* Oxford: George Ronald, 2018.

Esposito, John L. (ed.). *The Oxford Dictionary of Islam*. Oxford: Oxford University Press, 2004.

Ettlich, Guido. *Konsul Schwarz: Bankier, Bürger & Bahá'í in Stuttgart und Bad Mergentheim*. Berlin: Der Erzählverlag, 2019.

Fananapazir, Khazeh. ' 'Abdu'l-Bahá on Christ and Christianity: An interview with Pasteur Monnier on the relationship between the Bahá'í Faith and Christianity, Paris', in *Bahá'í Studies Review*, vol. 3, no. 1 (1993), pp. 7–10; available online at: https://bahai-library.com/abdulbaha_christ_christianity_monnier.

Furutan, 'Ali-Akbar. *Bahá'í Education for Children: A Teacher's Guide*, Book 1. New Delhi: Bahá'í Publishing Trust, 1999. Online edition by Iran Furutan Muhajir, 2004, at https://bahai-library.com/pdf/f/furutan_children_book1.pdf.

Furutan Muhajir, Iran. *Siyyid Muṣṭafá Rúmí: Hand of the Cause of God, Apostle of Bahá'u'lláh*. Wilmette, IL: U.S. Bahá'í Publishing Trust, 2020.

Geula, Arsalan. *Iranian Bahá'ís from Jewish Background: A Portrait of an Emerging Bahá'í Community.* Claremont, Calif.: Arsalan Geula, 2008.

Glassé, Cyril. *The Concise Encyclopedia of Islam*. San Francisco: Harper & Row, 1989.

Gollmer, Werner. *Mein Herz ist bei euch: 'Abdu'l-Bahá in Deutschland.* Hofheim-Langenhain: Bahá'í-Verlag, 1988.

Gulpáygání, Mírzá Abu'l-Faḍl (ed. Ruhollah Mehrabkhani). *Rasá'il va Raqá'im*. Tehran: Mu'assisiy-i-Millíy-i-Maṭbú'át-i-Amrí, 1977.

Handal, Boris. *The Khamsis: A Cradle of True Gold.* Boris Handal, 2020.

Hannen, Joseph. 'Abdul-Baha at Stuttgart and Esslingen, Germany', in *Star of the West*, vol. 4, no. 9 (20 August 1913).

Hatcher, John S. and Amrollah Hemmat. *Reunion with the Beloved: Poetry and Martyrdom*. Hong Kong: Juxta, 2004.

Hayyim, Sulayman. *The Larger Persian–English Dictionary: Complete and Modern: Designed to Give the English Meanings of over 50,000 Words*. Vol. 2. Tehran: Farhang Moaser, 1985.

In the Footsteps of 'Abdu'l-Bahá in Budapest 1913. Budapest, 2019. Digitally published at: https://tinyurl.com/AbdulBahaBudapestBooklet.

International Standard Bible Encyclopedia. Ed. James Orr (1915).

Iṣfahání, Ḥájí Mírzá Ḥaydar-'Alí. *Bihjatu'ṣ-Ṣudúr*. Bombay, 1913. Abridged English translation by Abu'l-Qasim Faizi as *Stories from the Delight of Hearts*, Los Angeles, 1980.
—(ed. Heshmat Moayyad) *Fereschteh Karmel [Firishtiy-i-Karmil]*. Luxembourg: Adel Publisher, N.D.

Ishráq-Khávarí, 'Abdu'l-Ḥamíd. *Núrayn-i-Nayyirayn*. Tehran: Mu'assisiy-i-Millíy-i-Maṭbú'át-i-Amrí, 1966.
—*Jannát-i-Na'ím*. Vol. 1. Tehran: Mu'assisiy-i-Millíy-i-Maṭbú'át-i-Amrí, 1973.
—*Jannát-i-Na'ím*. Vol. 2. Tehran: Mu'assisiy-i-Millíy-i-Maṭbú'át-i-Amrí, 1974.
—*Má'idiy-i-Ásmání*. Vol. 5. Tehran: Mu'assisiy-i-Millíy-i-Maṭbú'át-i-Amrí, 1972.
—*Má'idiy-i-Ásmání*. Vol. 9. Tehran: Mu'assisiy-i-Millíy-i-Maṭbú'át-i-Amrí, 1965.
—*Risáliy-i-Ayyám-i-Tis'ih*, 5th ed. Tehran: Mu'assisiy-i-Millíy-i-Maṭbú'át-i-Amrí, 1972.

Jasion, Jan. *'Abdu'l-Bahá in France*. Éditions bahá'íes France: Paris, 2016.
—*'Abdu'l-Bahá in the West*, 2nd ed. (forthcoming).

Käfer, Alexander. *Die Geschichte der Österreichischen Bahá'í-Gemeinde*. Berlin: Horizonte Verlag, 2005.

Lederer, György. "Abdu'l-Bahá in Budapest', in *Bahá'ís in the West: Studies in the Bábí and Bahá'í Religions*, vol. 14, pp. 108–26. Los Angeles: Kalimát Press, 2004.

Málmírí, Muḥammad Ṭáhir. *Kháṭirát-i-Málmírí*. Hofheim-Langenhain: Bahá'í-Verlag, 1992.
— *Táríkh-i-Shuhadáy-i-Yazd*. Cairo: Faraju'lláh Zakíyyu'l-Kurdí, 1923.

Masumian, Adib. *A Supplement to 'Abdu'l-Bahá in Europe, 1912–1913*. Digital resource at https://bahai-library.com/supplement_abdul-baha_europe_1912-1913.

Mázandarání, Fáḍil. *Amr va Khalq*. Vol. 2. Hofheim-Langenhain: Bahá'í-Verlag, 1985.
—*Táríkh-i-Ẓuhúru'l-Ḥaqq*. Vol. 4. Hofheim-Langenhain: Bahá'í-Verlag, 2011; vol. 8, part 2. N.P, N.D.

Mehrabkhani, Ruhollah. *Khándán-i-Sádát-i-Khams*. Darmstadt: 'Aṣr-i-Jadíd, 1994.

—*Zindigániy-i-Mírzá Abu'l-Faḍl-i-Gulpáygání*, 3rd ed. Madrid: Fundación Nehal, 2022.

Mihdí Khán, Mírzá (the Za'ímu'd-Dawlih). *Miftáḥ-i-Bábu'l-Abváb*. Cairo: Maṭba'at Majallat al-Manár, 1903. This polemical work was later translated into Persian by Ḥasan Faríd Gulpáygání under the title *Miftáḥ-i-Bábu'l-Abváb, Yá, Táríkh-i-Báb va Bahá* (Tehran: Kitábkhániy-i-Shams, 1961).

Merrick, David. *'Abdu'l-Bahá in Britain, 1913*. Digitally published at the Bahá'í Library Online, 2018. http://paintdrawer.co.uk/david/folders/spirituality/bahai/abdulbaha/sohrab-diary-uk-1913.pdf.

Momen, Moojan. 'Abu'l-Fażl Golpāyegānī', in *Encyclopedia Iranica*; available online at: https://www.iranicaonline.org/articles/abul-fazl-or-abul-fazael-golpayegani-mirza-mohammad-prominent-bahai-scholar-and-apologist.
—*The Bahá'í Communities of Iran, 1851–1921*, vol. 1. Oxford: George Ronald, 2015.
—*The Bahá'í Communities of Iran, 1851–1921*, vol. 2. Oxford: George Ronald, 2021.
—; Thorne, Adam; Rose, Janet Fleming; Redman, Earl. *The Bahá'í Community of the British Isles, 1844–1963*. Oxford: George Ronald, 2023.
—'Gulpáygání, Mirza Abu'l-Fadl'. Available online at: https://bahai-library.com/momen_encyclopedia_abul-fadl_gulpaygani.
—'Ḥaydar 'Ali Eṣfahāni, Ḥājji Mirzā', in *Encyclopedia Iranica*; available online at: https://www.iranicaonline.org/articles/haydar-ali-esfahani.

Muḥammad, Mírzá (Ná'ím). *Aḥsanu't-Taqvím Yá Gulzár-i-Na'ím*. Bahá'í Publishing Trust of India, 1961.
—*Kullíyyát-i-Na'ím*. Bombay: Maṭba'iy-i-Muṣṭafaví, 1927.

Nakhjavani, Ali. *Mírzá 'Alí-Akbar Nakhjavání*. Wilmette, IL: Bahá'í Publishing Trust, 2018.

National Spiritual Assembly of the Bahá'ís of France. *Payám-i-Bahá'í*. No. 122. Lyon, January 1990.

National Spiritual Assembly of the Bahá'ís of the United States. *World Order: A Bahá'í Magazine*, second series. Vol. 2, No. 2 (Winter 1967).

Rafati, Vahid. *Ma'ákhidh-i-Ash'ár dar Áthár-i-Bahá'í*. Vol. 3. Dundas, Ontario: Institute for Bahá'í Studies in Persian, 2000.
—'Qá'im-Maqám Faráhání dar Áthár-i-Bahá'í'. *Safíniy-i-'Irfán*. No. 18 (2015). Translated into English by Adib Masumian as 'Qá'im-Maqám Faráhání in the Bahá'í Writings.' *Lights of 'Irfán*, Book 20 (May 2019).

Research Department of the Universal House of Justice. *Bahíyyih Khánum, the Greatest Holy Leaf: A Compilation from Bahá'í Sacred Texts and Writings of the Guardian of the Faith and Bahíyyih Khánum's Own Letters*. Haifa: Bahá'í World Centre, 1982.

—'The Development of the Institution for the Ḥuqúqu'lláh', March 1987; included in a message addressed by the Department of the Secretariat to all National Spiritual Assemblies, 25 March 1987.

Rideout, Anise. 'Early History of the Bahá'í Community in Boston, Massachusetts,' Digitally published at the Bahá'í Library Online, 2013.

Rúmí, Jalál al-Dín. *The Masnavi*. Trans. Jawid Mojaddedi. Book Two (2008); Book Three (2014). Oxford: Oxford University Press.

Sárközy, Miklós. 'Arminius Vámbéry and the Baha'i Faith', in *Bahá'í Studies Review*, vol. 18, no. 1 (June 2012), pp. 55–81.

Shahvar, Soli et al., *The Bahá'ís of Persia, Transcaspia, and the Caucasus*. Vol. 2. London: I.B. Tauris, 2011.

Shoghi Effendi. *God Passes By* (1944). Wilmette, IL: Bahá'í Publishing Trust, rev. ed. 1974.

Society for Persian Arts and Letters. *Khúshih-há'í az Kharman-i-Adab va Hunar*. Vol. 8. Darmstadt: 'Aṣr-i-Jadíd, 1997.

—*Dánish va Bínish*. Vol. 5. London: Bahá'í Society for Persian Arts and Letters, 2004.

Sohrab, Ahmad. *Abdul Baha in Egypt*. New York: J. H. Sears & Co. Inc. for New History Foundation, 1929.

—Diaries and letters, facsimiles provided by the US Bahá'í National Archives.

Star of the West: The Bahai Magazine. Periodical, 25 vols. 1910–1935. Vols. 1–14 RP Oxford: George Ronald, 1978.

Sulaymání, 'Azízu'lláh. *Maṣábíḥ-i-Hidáyat*. Vol. 1, 2nd ed. (1964), vol. 3, 2nd ed. (1966), vol. 4 (1959), vol. 5 (1961), vol. 7 (1972): Tehran: Mu'assisiy-i-Millíy-i-Maṭbú'át-i-Amrí; vol. 10: East Lansing, Michigan: H-Bahai, 2007, at: https://www.h-net.org/~bahai/areprint/authors/sulayman/masabih10/Masabih_Hidayat_v10.pdf.

Taherzadeh, Adib. *The Covenant of Bahá'u'lláh*. Oxford: George Ronald, 1992.

—*The Revelation of Bahá'u'lláh*. 4 vols. Oxford: George Ronald, 1974–1987.

Thompson, Juliet. *The Diary of Juliet Thompson*. Los Angeles: Kalimát Press, 1983.

Wiebers, Jennifer Redson. *Alma Sedonia Knobloch: Maidservant of the Divine Plan*. George Ronald: Oxford, 2023.

Zarqání, Maḥmúd. *Kitáb-i-Badáyi'u'l-Áthár fí Asfár-i-Mawli'l-Akhyár ilá Mamáliki'l-Gharb bi'l-'Izzati va'l-Iqtidár* (A Book of the Wondrous Traces of the Master's Glorious Travels to the West). Vol. 1 (Bombay, 1914); vol.

2 (Bombay, 1921). Hofheim-Langenhain: Bahá'í-Verlag, 1982, 1987. Available at https://reference.bahai.org/fa/.

—*Maḥmúd's Diary: The Diary of Mírzá Maḥmúd-i-Zarqání Chronicling 'Abdu'l-Bahá's Journey to America.* Trans. Mohi Sobhani with the assistance of Shirley Macias. Oxford: George Ronald 1998.

Notes and References

Foreword by the Translator

1 Balyuzi, *'Abdu'l-Bahá*, pp. 343–404.

2 See nos. 28, 48, 61, 68, 86, 92, 93, 94, 96, 98, 111, 114, 117, 144, and 148.

3 *The Bahá'í World*, vol. 13, pp. 1186–88.

4 https://bahai-library.com/supplement_abdul-baha_europe_1912-1913.

5 Many of these come from the diary letters of Ahmad Sohrab and do not have readily available original texts.

6 All reviewed by the Research Department of the Universal House of Justice and approved for digital publication following the incorporation of some recommended revisions.

7 Zarqání himself speaks to these omissions at the end of his entry for 28 March 1913. Fortunately, the diary letters of Ahmad Sohrab were exempted from this circumspection since he was writing for a Western audience. Thus, for the most part, he was able to identify those individuals in his letters, and in these cases I have mentioned their names in accompanying endnotes, both for the benefit of historical completeness and because any sensitivity associated with retaining those names has faded in the more than hundred years that have passed since the chronicle was written.

8 To clarify: the Research Department did not review my translations of the words of Zarqání himself, only those which he attributed to 'Abdu'l-Bahá.

Preface by Mírzá Maḥmúd Zarqání

9 Zarqání appears to be paraphrasing this passage from the Writings of Bahá'u'lláh: 'Erelong will God raise up the treasures of the earth – men who will aid Thee through Thyself and through Thy Name, wherewith God hath revived the hearts of such as have recognized Him' (*Epistle to the Son of the Wolf*, p. 21).

10 Bahá'u'lláh, *Gleanings from the Writings of Bahá'u'lláh*, CXXIX.

11 Zarqání, *Maḥmúd's Diary: The Diary of Mírzá Maḥmúd-i-Zarqání Chronicling 'Abdu'l-Bahá's Journey to America.*

Voyage to England

12 In his diary letter dated 10 December 1912, Sohrab mentions that 'Abdu'l-Bahá stayed in a stateroom during this voyage.

13 Mírzá Yaḥyá (c. 1831–1912), also known by his title of Ṣubḥ-i-Azal ('Morn of Eternity'), was a half-brother of Bahá'u'lláh who rejected His

proclamation that He was a Manifestation of God, countering it with his own claim to divine revelation. He was stigmatized as 'the Arch-Breaker of the Covenant of the Báb' by Shoghi Effendi, who has discussed him in *God Passes By*. Extensive details on his seditious activities can be found in Adib Taherzadeh, *The Covenant of Bahá'u'lláh*, passim. The term 'Azalís' refers to the followers of Mírzá Yaḥyá.

14 A reference to Áqá (Muḥammad) Riḍá Shírází (d. 1912), also known as Áqá Riḍá Qannád ('confectioner'), 'one of the companions of Bahá'u'lláh who had come with Him from Baghdád' (Taherzadeh, *The Revelation of Bahá'u'lláh*, vol. 2, p. 403). Brief episodes from the life of Áqá Riḍá have been published in Taherzadeh, *The Revelation of Bahá'u'lláh*, vol. 1, pp. 288–89. A eulogy for him by 'Abdu'l-Bahá is also published in *Memorials of the Faithful*, pp. 39–41.

15 A reference to Ḥabíbu'lláh Huvaydá, the 'Aynu'l-Mulk. According to a letter from the Universal House of Justice addressed to National Spiritual Assemblies and dated 17 October 1979, he was later expelled from the Faith by Shoghi Effendi for refusing to cease his involvement in political activity.

16 Mírzá Abu'l-Faḍl Gulpáygání (1844–1914), also known by the title of Abu'l-Faḍá'il ('the father of virtues') that 'Abdu'l-Bahá gave him, was a Bahá'í author, scholar, and apologist who traveled extensively to teach the Faith. He was posthumously designated an Apostle of Bahá'u'lláh by Shoghi Effendi. Multiple biographies of Abu'l-Faḍl have been written in Persian, but the most thorough and systematic of these is Ruhollah Mehrabkhani, *Zindigáníy-i-Mírzá Abu'l-Faḍl-i-Gulpáygání*. Translated excerpts from the first edition of this biography and passages from other accounts of his life have been curated in Taherzadeh, *The Revelation of Bahá'u'lláh*, vol. 3, pp. 91–107 and 433–41, and idem., vol. 4, pp. 258–70. A large number of letters and other shorter writings of Abu'l-Faḍl in Arabic and Persian have been compiled by Mehrabkhani in *Rasá'il va Raqá'im* and Tooraj Amini in *Abu'l-Faḍá'il-i-Gulpáygání dar Áyniy-i-Asnád*. The proceedings of a conference held in honor of Abu'l-Faḍl by the Bahá'í Society for Persian Arts and Letters have been published in *Dánish va Bínish*, vol. 5, and a special issue of the Persian-language *Payám-i-Bahá'í* magazine (no. 122) was similarly devoted to him. For additional details and sources on his life in English, as well as a list of his publications (including those that have been translated into English), refer to Momen, 'ABU'L-FAŻL GOLPĀYEGĀNĪ', published in *Encyclopedia Iranica*, available online at: https://www.iranicaonline.org/articles/abul-fazl-or-abul-fazael-golpayegani-mirza-mohammad-prominent-bahai-scholar-and-apologist, and idem., 'Gulpáygání, Mirza Abu'l-Fadl' (*Bahá'í Library Online*, 1995: https://bahai-library.com/momen_encyclopedia_abul-fadl_gulpaygani).

17 A reference to Mullá Muḥammad Riḍáy-i-Muḥammad-Ábádí (d. c.

1896?), a Bábí who notably recognized the station of Bahá'u'lláh before He Himself had announced it. A biography of Mullá Muḥammad Riḍá has been published in Balyuzi, *Eminent Bahá'ís in the Time of Bahá'u'lláh*, pp. 98–111. Additional details on his life can be found in Moojan Momen, *The Bahá'í Communities of Iran*, vol. 2, pp. 358–9.

18 Sohrab refers to this person as 'the bath steward', and his account suggests that this interaction actually took place the previous morning (of 9 December).

19 Among the remarks 'Abdu'l-Bahá made on this subject, according to Sohrab, was this one: 'Trustworthiness is the most brilliant jewel in the diadem which crowns man's heavenly attributes.'

20 According to Sohrab, this was 'a musical concert for the Sailors' Fund'.

21 Dreyfus had come from Paris to see 'Abdu'l-Bahá.

22 This hotel still operates today and is now known as the Britannia Adelphi hotel.

23 Edward Granville Browne (1862–1926) was an eminent Iranologist who is best known to Bahá'ís for the memorable pen-portrait of Bahá'u'lláh that he wrote after visiting Him in 'Akká in April 1891, where he also met 'Abdu'l-Bahá for the first time. By the time the events in this chronicle were taking place, Browne had associated with both Bahá'ís and Azalís, and also risen to prominence in British and Iranian politics as a leading member of the Persia Committee, which he co-founded with H. F. B. Lynch in October 1908. Hence, he has been given special attention in this book.

24 Sohrab's account suggests that the following events actually took place on 15 December 1912.

England

25 Apparently the president of the local Liverpool Theosophical lodge, whom Sohrab calls 'Mrs. Armour'.

26 Identified by Sohrab as 'the Consul of Persia in Port Said.'

27 'Thanks to BAHA'O'LLAH, we arrived safely at Liverpool. Greeting to the friends. ABDUL-BAHA' (*Star of the West*, vol. 3, no. 16 (31 December 1912), p. 2).

28 Siyyid Yaḥyá Dawlatábádí (1863–1939) was a literary and political figure active in those spheres both during the Persian Constitutional Revolution and afterwards. His father, Siyyid Hádí Dawlatábádí, was a Bábí who had been appointed by the half-brother of Bahá'u'lláh, Mírzá Yaḥyá (Ṣubḥ-i-Azal), as the leader of the Azalís in Iran and his own successor. However, Siyyid Hádí died in 1908 a few years before Mírzá Yaḥyá's own death in 1912, so those positions were passed down to Siyyid Hádí's son, Siyyid Yaḥyá, but he showed little interest in pursuing them and strove to distance himself from any association with

Bábís or Azalís to further his other ambitions. Moojan Momen writes: 'When an interview with 'Abdu'l-Baha appeared in an Egyptian Persian-language periodical, *Chihrih-Nama*, in 1910, [Siyyid Yaḥyá Dawlatábádí] feared that he and another figure, Baha' ul-Va'izin, could be identified as Babis from the article, although no one had been named. He therefore wrote to the newspaper denying he was an Azali or a Babi and indeed saying that this religion was the greatest evil to befall Iran' (*The Bahá'í Communities of Iran*, vol. 1, p. 102). For more information, see Amanat, 'Sayyed Yaḥyā Dawlatābādī', in *Encyclopedia Iranica*; available online at:
https://www.iranicaonline.org/articles/dawlatabadi-sayyed-yahya.

29 An English translation of this talk appears in the online supplement to this book:
https://bahai-library.com/supplement_abdul-baha_europe_1912-1913.

30 The term *khoresh* refers to a class of dishes that consist of meat (often beef, lamb, chicken, or duck) braised with vegetables, herbs, spices, and other ingredients; they are invariably served with steamed rice. Examples include *ghormeh sabzi* (beef or lamb braised with an assortment of fresh herbs, dried limes, and several kinds of beans), *khoresh fesenjan* (duck or chicken braised in ground walnuts and pomegranate molasses), and *khoresh karafs* (beef or lamb braised with celery, parsley, mint, and dried limes). The present translator is grateful to Joshua D.T. Hall for kindly writing this description of *khoresh* for use in this book.

31 Sohrab writes: 'The Master had his tea and is praying for our confirmation. Every morning he prays for all the believers throughout the world, so that they may receive aid and assistance from the Divine Source. He stated that at all times he is supplicating and imploring at the Threshold of Bahaollah to encircle His faithful ones with spiritual powers, to illumine their hearts, and expand their thoughts, so that they may become enabled to raise the standard of International Peace, serve the world of humanity and attract the souls to the Kingdom of Abha.'

32 Sohrab notes that this was the 'President of the Theosophical Society of another city', whom he describes as 'a young, intelligent man' but does not name.

33 Sohrab notes that 'fifteen hundred people' were in attendance.

34 An English translation of this talk appears in the online supplement to this book:
https://bahai-library.com/supplement_abdul-baha_europe_1912-1913.

35 The vestry, according to Isabel Fraser.

36 Sohrab writes: 'At nine o'clock this morning we left the hotel in Liverpool, walking to the Lime street station, where we were to take the train for London, Monsieur Dreyfus-Barney going before to secure tickets. Arriving at the station we took our compartment, M. Dreyfus-Barney,

Ahmad Yazdi, Mrs. Fraser and Miss Herrick traveling with Abdul-Baha. On the way he spoke to Mrs. Fraser and Miss Herrick and said, "I am most pleased with you. You are the real servants of the Covenant." To Mrs. Fraser he said: "You have written excellent articles in the papers in regard to the Cause, I will never forget these services of yours. You must become like a burning torch so that you may be able to melt mountains of snow. Europe is filled with mountains which are snow-capped all the year around. May you attain to such a degree of heat that you may melt the snow. Europe is submerged in materialism. People are not thinking of God. All their attention is turned toward matter and nature. Like unto the cows they graze in the meadows which are overgrown with grass. They can see nothing beyond their noses. America is much better. People in that country are investigating the Reality. They are more susceptible to spiritual life"' (*Star of the West*, vol. 3, no. 19 (2 March 1913), p. 3).

37 At 1:40 p.m., according to Sohrab.

38 Sohrab writes: 'There were more than 50 Bahais ready to welcome our Beloved.'

39 Apparently to the nearby house (no. 62) of Mary Constance (Wyndham) Charteris, an English socialite then styled 'Lady Elcho'. For more on her, refer to Momen et al., *The Bahá'í Community of the British Isles, 1844–1963*, p. 190.

40 At approximately 4:20 p.m., according to Sohrab.

41 Sohrab writes: 'No sooner [had] we reached home than people began to come; especially a woman of high rank, whose name may not be wise to mention, but who goes to the English court a great deal[,] and an intelligent gentleman who has been for eleven years the Editor of one of the most influential paper[s] in India. With them the Master spoke about 3 hours and they had dinner with him.'

42 Sohrab notes that Browne spoke to 'Abdu'l-Bahá in Persian, which he spoke 'most fluently'. He goes on to write: 'Many subjects were discussed about Persia, history of the Bahai movement, education of women, inventions, etc. It is hoped the result of this meeting will be very good; for of late Prof Browne has not been very friendly to the Bahais and he [is] devoting more time to the literary, political and historical events of Persia than to the Bahai Cause. His wife was with him.' According to Sohrab, this meeting lasted 'for nearly one hour', and that 'all of us' (presumably, 'Abdu'l-Bahá's attendants) spoke with him afterwards.

43 Harold Mudie (1880–1916), who at the time served as both the president of the Esperanto Association of Britain and the first president of the World Esperanto Association.

44 Sohrab notes that the 'Counselor of the Iranian legation' was among these individuals.

45 According to Sohrab, this address – given sometime before noon on 'the suffragette question' – was 'an elaboration of ['Abdu'l-Bahá's] morning private talk with the woman who is a leader in that Cause', who was present herself on this occasion. Laura Dreyfus-Barney served as the interpreter. The suffragette leader referred to here may be the 'strong militant suffragist' who met with 'Abdu'l-Bahá that day and received these counsels from Him: 'The Master advised her that the women who are working for the interest of woman's enfranchisement should not commit unseemly acts and not resort to violent measures, such as window smashing, police-beating, train-wrecking, letter-box-destroying, etc., nay rather they should demand their rights with the power of intelligence, with scientific accomplishments, with artistic attainments. These destructive deeds would rather retard the realization of their cherished hope. In this age only a weak person resorts to frightful measures but an intelligent person uses the superior power of intelligence and wisdom.'

46 Which lasted for two hours, according to Sohrab.

47 Sohrab refers to Ḥájí Amín's three travel companions only as 'three other young Persian Bahais'. He writes that they had been staying in Paris 'for the last two weeks waiting for the arrival of the Master', and that they had 'recently arrived from Persia' before that.

48 Sohrab has recorded the following account of 'Abdu'l-Bahá's meeting with Ḥájí Amín: 'A most touching incident of the Cause was unfolded when Haji Ameen opened his handkerchief in which he had petitions from many believers in the East and what caught my eyes at first sight was two small loaves of bread and an apple presented by a Bahai from far off Russia. This was all this poor Bahai could send to our Beloved with his devotion and love. The Master looked at this love-offering with such tenderness, with such joy and kindness in his eyes that one can never forget. No doubt if millions had been lent to him they would not have made [Him] any happier. He ate a piece of the stale loaves and then gave them to Sayad Assadullah so that he may bring them to him at other meals.

'Haji Ameen spoke about a wonderful Bahai residing in Qazvin whose name is Hakim Bashi and who is the embodiment of hospitality, whose love is limitless and who is the "new Creation of this new dispensation". Then he told our Beloved, the general news of Persia; how the friends are united and happy, serving the Cause most faithfully, receiving most joyously the news of the Master's trip in America and holding divine Feasts of Peace and good fellowship.'

49 Ḥájí Mullá 'Alí-Akbar Shahmírzádí, known as Ḥájí Ákhund (1842–1910), appointed by Bahá'u'lláh as one of the Hands of His Cause and posthumously as one of His nineteen Apostles by Shoghi Effendi. The man to whom this question is addressed, Ḥájí Amín, was Ḥájí Abu'l-

Ḥasan Ardakání (1831–1928), a trustee of the Ḥuqúqu'lláh who would also go on to be named an Apostle of Bahá'u'lláh. For an account of the lives of both men, refer to Adib Taherzadeh, *The Revelation of Bahá'u'lláh*, vol. 3, pp. 76–86.

50 Bahá'u'lláh, *Kitáb-i-Aqdas*, para. 53.

51 According to Sohrab, one of these anecdotes focused on the Italian consul in 'Akká, who was refused divorce by the Pope and subsequently attempted to have his own wife killed.

52 Refer to the Kitáb-i-Aqdas, para. 68; its supplement titled *Questions & Answers*, nos. 12, 19, 31, 38, 73, and 98; and notes 100, 101, and 102.

53 Probably because 'many of the men and women callers were mourning for the deaths of their husbands, daughters or mothers', according to Sohrab.

54 Among them Ethel Stefana Drower, who according to Sohrab was 'smiling all the time' as he translated for 'Abdu'l-Bahá. Sohrab writes: 'When the Master finished speaking I found the smiling face was no other than Mrs. Dower [sic], the former Miss Stevens, author of the 'Mountain of God.' She had come from Southampton to meet the Beloved. Three years ago she stayed four months in Acca and Haifa and gathered the material for her book. The Master called her in his room and talked with her a great deal . . . the Master spoke with Mrs. Dower [sic] about the time she was living in Acca. She is going to Jerusalem for a sojourn of [a] few months and is planning to write a novel about the second coming of Christ. The plot consists of a number of Christians going to Mount Olivet expecting the descent of [the] Messiah from heaven but they start to quarrel amongst themselves and forget their object. Mrs. Dower [sic] is a very intelligent woman and has a well developed power of imagination. She can describe events and objects very minutely. The Master invited her to dinner and gladly she accepted. Then he went out with Ahmad Yazdi and Mirza Lotfollah for a walk in the Hyde Park. I was left home with other Persians and had a very interesting talk with Mrs. Dower [sic] about her work, America and other kindred subjects.'

Drower was present when 'Abdu'l-Bahá later met with a certain 'Mr. Lorge, a very prominent English educator'; Sohrab has summarized 'Abdu'l-Bahá's conversation with him as follows: 'The discussion was first turned upon America and our Beloved gave the utmost praise to that country for her freedom, her civilization, her spiritual susceptibilities, her readiness of advancing toward the Kingdom of God, her quenchless thirst for knowledge, her progressive ideals, and her future extraordinary illumination. In fact I had never seen our Beloved so enthusiastic about the wonderful possibilities of America. Europe is steeped in a sea of materialism. People are either agnostics or full of superstitions. In America it is all different; people are more spiritual, they seek the Knowledge of God, they hale [hail] the truth no matter from what quarter it comes – if they hear that there is a house in China whose architecture is novel they like to know all about it. They analyze everything, they dissect everything. In brief they are a nation of independent investigators.

'Then the question of spiritual communication was discussed. Yes, it is possible, for often people speak together without the means of tongue. There are two means of communication. One with the outward tongue, the other with the ideal tongue. When the spirit is in an abstract state, when the heart is in a subjective mood, then the ideal tongue can speak, but as long as the spirit is preoccupied and the heart is objective in its activity it is impossible to attain to that station. Is there not a wonderful ideal union between the loved one and the beloved? Often with a glance of an eye, with a handshake a whole world of thought is conveyed to others without uttering a word. Yes it is possible to attain to such a state of absolute concentration and revelation: if we are set aglow with the Fire of the Love [of] God, if we are attracted, if we are as burning torches, if we overlook material phenomena and objects.'

55 Mírzá Mihdí Khán, the Mushíru'l-Mulk, who at the time served as Persia's Envoy Extraordinary and Minister Plenipotentiary in Great Britain and would go on to serve in that same capacity in the United States (1914–18). Sohrab writes that 'Abdu'l-Bahá received the envoy 'very graciously and kindly', and that he 'stayed for nearly one hour and discussions shifted from one subject to another', including 'the political situation in Persia and Turkey' and 'the moral condition of Persian students in Europe'. During this visit by the envoy, 'Abdu'l-Bahá made complimentary remarks on America that Sohrab has summarized as follows: 'He praised the Republican form of government in America, its federal system, its independent and sovereign states, its liberal institutions, its educational system, its parliament, and its vast resources. He gave a great tribute to Washington D.C. – all the houses are built in lovely gardens, there are many parks, the avenues are shaded with trees. Likewise in Chicago and New York there are many large parks.'

56 Sohrab writes that he, 'Abdu'l-Bahá, Lady Blomfield, and Ḥájí Amín all drove to the Westminster Palace Hotel at 7:00 p.m.

57 Sohrab notes that 'more than 600 people' were in attendance, and that 'many writers, thinkers, literary men and distinguished personages were in the audience'.

58 At 8:00 p.m., according to Sohrab.

59 Isabel Fraser's transcript of Barclay's opening remarks, published in *Star of the West*, vol. 3, no. 17 (19 January 1913), pp. 5–6, is as follows:

'I am not here really to speak but to listen as a Western European deeply interested in Persia, in Persian thought and in Persian literature and glad of an opportunity to do honour to a venerated Persian. Abdul-Baha is known far beyond the immediate ranks of Bahais, known not only for his own sake, but also as the accredited Messenger of the Bahai teaching. Persia has been a fatherland of religions, but the Revelation of BAHA'O'LLAH is a system of thought and conduct.

'"All prejudices," said BAHA'O'LLAH, "whether prejudices of religion, prejudices of race, prejudices of politics or prejudices of nationality must be cast off, for they are a cause of the sickness of the world."

'Then again he says: "There is no contradiction between true Religion and Science. When a religion is opposed to Science, it is 'superstition.' Prejudice and superstition are the enemies of human development.

'"If a man would succeed in his quest for truth, let him first shut his mind to the traditional superstitions of the past." These traditional superstitions have grown over and disfigured true religion and the object of the Revelation of BAHA'O'LLAH is to get to the original truth and exclude no conscientious searches after undisfigured truth.

'I wonder if I have understood the Revelation of BAHA'O'LLAH. If I have, it has a singularly good Christian ring and I should interpret its meaning as "Be a real Christian and you will be a good Bahai."

'But I am merely presiding and not proselytising. I am proud to have been asked to preside at a meeting of those who have come together to do honour to one who deserves it so richly.'

60 An English translation of this talk appears in the online supplement to this book:
https://bahai-library.com/supplement_abdul-baha_europe_1912-1913.

61 At 9:00 p.m., according to Sohrab.

62 Isabel Fraser's summary of Alice Buckton's remarks, published in *Star of the West*, vol. 3, no. 17 (19 January 2013), p. 9, is as follows:

'Miss Buckton read the Hidden Words, commencing: "O Ye Discerning Ones of the People." She told how these "Hidden Words" had been written in prison and how they had come out of that prison and gone all over the world. She spoke of the significance of the Peace Conference being held in England and recalled Queen Victoria's answer to BAHA'O'LLAH's message proclaiming that war should cease and that the day of peace was at hand. Queen Victoria's reply was that if this proclamation was of God, it would stand.

'Miss Buckton emphasized the fact that this was no new religion, it sought the Unity of all Religions, shutting out none of them, but finding a common meeting place for all. She likened it to a garden of flowers where vast variety did away with monotony and made an interesting Unity.'

63 Isabel Fraser's record of Charlotte Despard's words, published in *Star of the West*, vol. 3, no. 17 (19 January 1913), pp. 9–10, is as follows:

'I am perfectly convinced that every one who has heard him, who so many today are calling the Master, one of the great Masters who has come to enlighten the world, are feeling how deeply privileged we are to have had the presence here in our western isle, of this eastern Master among us. I had the joy of seeing him when he was last over in this country. I have heard of the wonderful journeys that he has made. I know how he never falters. He believes that he is bringing a message to the world and we believe it too.

'I sometimes think that when in the future the story of the present generation comes to be summed up, we shall be shown it under two aspects. One aspect is that which is troubling us so much at the present moment – unrest. There is unrest everywhere, unrest in industry, unrest among the women of the country, unrest intellectually and unrest religiously, and some are frightened as they look out, and wonder if these days mean the disintegration of which we have been hearing, which is the very fruit of this. But some of us think that this unrest at the present moment is actually a healthy symptom. That it is on account of the unreality of things that people generally are troubled and anxious and longing for some settled thing.

'We have the mighty movements – the women's movement, the religious movement[,] the spiritual movement. At the basis of all the great religions that have moved the world there are the same great truths. This unrest at the moment, and of ancient times though in different words and different form are still the same. God is one. There is nothing but God anywhere. He is the one eternal life; because we are in Him therefore we are eternal; death is but the dropping of a garment.

'This is the principle of unity and we are thankful beyond measure that it has been brought to us today.'

64 Isabel Fraser's record of Hippolyte Dreyfus's words, published in *Star of the West*, vol. 3, no. 17 (19 January 1913), p. 10, is as follows:

'Ladies and Gentlemen: After the beautiful and interesting addresses you have heard, I have to make you a promise, it is, not to take up too much of your time, but I wish to say what a joy it is to me to see the wonderful interest that the movement has now awakened in London.

'Is it a religion, this movement? Some say no, looking only at the philosophical aspect of the teachings, looking only to its code of ethics; but I say yes, and you certainly will say so, too, after having heard what you have from this platform. It is a religion because it is founded upon the knowledge of God. The knowledge of God is the first thing we should try to acquire. It has, in former times, I think, been very difficult for, in the past, the esoteric part of religion was hidden from the people and the truth was only given in symbols. But in this day BAHA'O'LLAH appeals to our reason.

'Reason is the greatest gift of God to man, and it is through reason we can know God. How? BAHA'O'LLAH teaches us that we can know

Him best through His Manifestations. What does that mean? I think we should say, in order to make ourselves understood, through the greatest manifestation of God, because everything in the world manifests God to a greater or less degree. We can find the divine in the beautiful melodies that are sung by the birds in the forests, the divine in nature, but we find it specially in man, who is at the summit of creation, and especially in those supreme beings who are called the prophets. It is in understanding their teaching that we can reach the knowledge of God. But I said in the beginning I did not want to take up too much of your time. I think we can move in a high spirit in thanking the Chair for this wonderful gathering, which I hope will be the beginning of many similar ones in this city.'

65 An English translation of this prayer appears in the online supplement to this book:
https://bahai-library.com/supplement_abdul-baha_europe_1912-1913.

66 At approximately 11:45 a.m., according to Sohrab.

67 Sohrab's account indicates that the following events actually took place on 21 December 1912, and should therefore be read as a continuation of the previous entry.

68 This was a performance of *Eager Heart*, a play by Alice Buckton, which 'more than 1200 people' attended that night, according to Sohrab. 'Abdu'l-Bahá had a front-row seat; Mrs Thornburgh-Cropper sat to His left, and Sohrab to His right. Sohrab describes one notable scene from the play as follows: 'When Mary and Joseph came in with the child in her arms the Master was so deeply touched that he wept. I could not help myself but to weep. The story is so direct, so spiritual, so sincere, so holy and so above the sordid elements of life. The Master sat through the whole performance and was keenly interested in every act and move of the characters.'

69 Sohrab has this as 'the house of the Persian Ambassador', and writes: 'For more than two hours various subjects touching Balkans, the lives of the various Turkish ministers, the English rule in Cyprus and incidents in connection with it were discussed. At the door the Master put one English pound into the hands of the footman of the Embassy.'

70 According to Sohrab, the events in this entry actually took place on 22 December 1912.

71 A provisional English rendering of the full talk, produced by the present translator, appears in the online supplement to this book:
https://bahai-library.com/supplement_abdul-baha_europe_1912-1913.

72 According to Sohrab, these were 'Persian merchants who reside[d] in London'.

73 According to Sohrab, the following events actually took place on 23 December 1912.

74 According to Sohrab, 'Abdu'l-Bahá gave this talk to a small group of people in the hotel's salon at around noon.

75 Sohrab's account seems to suggest that 'Abdu'l-Bahá addressed these words to the Reverend Edward William Lewis and his wife, Alice Lewis, the following day (25 December).

76 Sohrab writes that these callers included 'the special correspondent of *The Christian Commonwealth* and the Editor of the Theosophical magazine'.

77 See http://www.thejourneywest.org/2012/05/15/peace-conference-at-lake-mohonk/.

78 Probably a reference to the London Conference of 1912–13, an international summit of the six Great Powers of that time (Great Britain, France, Germany, Austria-Hungary, Russia, and Italy).

79 Zarqání appears to have conflated 'Abdu'l-Bahá's remarks to two different people here. Sohrab writes that 'Abdu'l-Bahá said to a labourer, 'Every object in this world has the power of combustion. The objects by themselves and in themselves will not be ignited. A flame is necessary. I hope you will become that flame to enkindle the hearts,' and the following to a railroad man, 'You are paving the material roads. May you become able to straighten the pathway to heaven. That is more important. Straighten the path, for the Kingdom of God is nigh. Be a heavenly lineman.'

80 Zarqání's entry here, when compared with Sohrab's, seems to combine the events of 24 and 25 December 1912. Refer to endnote 82, indicating where the shift from 24 to 25 December occurs in this entry.

81 The present translator's provisional English rendering of lengthier remarks from 'Abdu'l-Bahá on this topic appears in the online supplement to this book:
https://bahai-library.com/supplement_abdul-baha_europe_1912-1913.

82 According to Sohrab's account, the remainder of this entry does, in fact, correspond with 25 December 1912.

83 An English translation of this talk appears in the online supplement to this book:
https://bahai-library.com/supplement_abdul-baha_europe_1912-1913.

84 At 3:00 p.m., according to Sohrab.

85 According to Sohrab, 'Abdu'l-Bahá actually went to the home of Mrs Thornburgh-Cropper (who took Him there herself), but as the purpose of the visit was for 'Abdu'l-Bahá to meet with the Lamingtons, Zarqání may have received the impression that the residence was theirs. Sohrab notes that the Lamingtons were both 'very respectful and called Abdul Baha the "Master" and listened very attentively to every word he said'.

86 Zarqání's estimate is actually the most conservative of the available figures. Sohrab notes that 'more than 700' people were in attendance, while Isabel Fraser states that a thousand were present.

87 An English translation of this talk appears in the online supplement to this book:
https://bahai-library.com/supplement_abdul-baha_europe_1912-1913.
Refer also to accounts in *The Christian Commonwealth* (documented in Egea, *Apostle of Peace*, vol. 2, pp. 35–37) and the *Social Gazette* (London), 11 Jan 1913, p. 2, col. 2–3.

88 Sohrab has this as twenty-five pounds, whereas Isabel Fraser has it as twenty pounds plus handfuls of silver coins.

89 Isabel Fraser notes that 'Abdu'l-Bahá ultimately gave this money to Colonel John Spencer of the Salvation Army Centre (whom Sohrab characterizes in his own account as 'the captain'), and Momen et al. have written that this was done 'so that the men could enjoy a similar meal on New Year's Day' (*Community*, p. 188 and n. 77 of that page), which ultimately did take place.

90 From *Farhang-i-Mu'ín*, a well-known dictionary of the Persian language: 'An Iranian coin equivalent to one-twentieth of a rial, which was in use during the Qájár era and the early years of the Pahlaví dynasty.'

91 Sohrab notes that 'Abdu'l-Bahá was too late and missed the children. As a result, He spoke to some others who were present before returning to His residence.

92 Sohrab has this as approximately noon.

93 Sohrab writes: '['Abdu'l-Bahá] spoke on the three kinds of baptism. Baptism with the water of life; baptism with the Fire of the Love of God[;] and baptism with the Spirit of God.'

94 English translations of 'Abdu'l-Bahá's remarks on this occasion appear in the online supplement to this book:
https://bahai-library.com/supplement_abdul-baha_europe_1912-1913.

95 According to Sohrab, the inquirer was 'Hon. Sir Tracy', likely a reference to Charles Hanbury-Tracy (1840–1922), who in fact posed questions about reincarnation and psychic abilities over the course of two hours.

96 Sohrab writes that Mrs Thornburgh-Cropper came at 7:45 p.m. to take 'Abdu'l-Bahá to Marion Jack's studio.

97 A term often used in the Persian and Arabic Bahá'í parlance of the time to refer to female Bahá'ís.

98 Sohrab writes: 'This morning the Master speaking with Haji Ameen about America stated that while in that country he was busy day and night. America is like another world. The meeting and gatherings were of another nature. One cannot compare them with anywhere else. The American people are very progressive. They are alive. They are active;

they are striving; their heads are full of modern ideas; they are all free. Praise be to God that in every city that he visited there were Bahais, except Salt Lake City. All the friends were attracted and enkindled, in some cities more than the others, but they were all good. They were all serving God and spreading the message of the Kingdom.'

99 Sohrab notes that this was 'a Duchess and her two daughters', but this would appear not to be correct: 'Duke is the highest title of peerage in the British aristocracy. If a Duchess had visited Cadogan Gardens, Lady Blomfield would certainly have mentioned this in *The Chosen Highway*. It seems likely that Sohrab merely used the term "duchess" to designate a member of the aristocracy. This probably refers to the visit of Lady Elcho. The "two daughters" would have been Lady Cynthia Asquith (who was married to the son of the prime minister) and Lady Mary Charteris' (Momen et al., *Community*, p. 204).

100 An alternative translation of the first two sentences in the following quotation reads: 'Children must first be trained in divine virtues and encouraged and urged to improve their character. Thereafter, efforts must be made to teach them sciences, crafts and knowledge to the extent possible, for without heavenly virtues and upright character, the mere acquisition of learning and arts will not suffice' (Furútan, *Bahá'í Education for Children: A Teacher's Guide*, Book 1, p. 1).

101 Sohrab writes: 'By this time many people had gathered in the hall and the Master spoke on the meaning of the "Word". Why Christ was called the "Word"? What was the reason? Because the "Word" comprehends all the significances, while a detached, single letter is meaningless.' (To clarify: 'comprehend' here is a synonym for 'encompass' or 'include'.) An English translation of this talk appears in the online supplement to this book:
https://bahai-library.com/supplement_abdul-baha_europe_1912-1913.

102 'Half a shilling' (also known as a sixpence), according to Sohrab.

103 Held at the Cedar Club House at 106A High Street, Battersea. According to Sohrab, this meeting consisted of some 200 poor women and children, whereas Louise Heron (see next endnote) states that it was about 60 mothers and over 100 children.

104 An account of 'Abdu'l-Bahá's visit to the Cedar Club, written by Louise Heron-Oliphant, is published in *Star of the West*, vol. 3, no. 18 (7 February 1913), pp. 9–10. Heron has recorded the words 'Abdu'l-Bahá spoke there as follows: 'I am very glad to be among you, who are blessed in God's name with children. They are the true signs of his spiritual love. The most divine gifts of God. These little ones will grow to be fruitful trees. We must look to them for the founders of many beautiful families. Let their education be directed in the ways of purity and useful service. Here are the seeds of the future race and upon them may be granted God's blessing.' Heron has also attributed these words

to 'Abdu'l-Bahá, spoken as He was leaving the Cedar Club: 'I am truly happy when among the gatherings of the poor. It brings full joy to my heart. I come in contact with those in high stations of life, and those rich in worldly possessions, but my joy is in being with those who are in material poverty, for their sufferings draw them nearer to God in spiritual gain.'

105 A prophet-like figure indirectly mentioned in the Qur'án (18:65–82), whom Zarqání appears to be equating with Santa Claus or Father Christmas.

106 A summary translation of this anecdote has been published in Balyuzi, *'Abdu'l-Bahá: The Centre of the Covenant*, pp. 351–2. Balyuzi concludes his presentation of the anecdote by noting that, 'Later, 'Abdu'l-Bahá compensated the grocer' (p. 352). Additionally, Sohrab writes: 'Afterwards the storekeeper was taken to the Master and when he left His Presence he was very glad that his store was ransacked.'

107 At 8.00 p.m., according to Sohrab, who states that this was a weekly gathering Lady Blomfield held at her home every Friday night.

108 Sohrab notes that several of these dignitaries (whom he does not name) later met with 'Abdu'l-Bahá privately.

109 Sohrab writes: 'The Master spoke on the Solidarity of humankind and incited them to work for the wellfare [sic] and progress of the people of the world.' An English translation of this talk appears in the online supplement to this book:
https://bahai-library.com/supplement_abdul-baha_europe_1912-1913.

110 Among them 'a correspondent from the "Standard",' according to Sohrab, who writes that he spoke with 'Abdu'l-Bahá for an hour and a half and 'asked many interesting questions'.

111 Bhawani Singh, Raj Rana Bahadur of Jhalawar (1874–1929). Sohrab writes that 'Abdu'l-Bahá spoke with him about 'India, its future developments and progress and the freedom of its people from blind dogmas and superstitions'.

112 Sohrab writes that he, 'Abdu'l-Bahá, Daniel Jenkyn, Mrs Thornburgh-Cropper, and Siyyid Asadu'lláh Qumí headed to the home of Annie Eliza Gamble (38 Santos Road, Putney, London) at 5:00 p.m. For more on her and the meetings she held, see Momen et al., *Community*, passim.

113 An English translation of this talk appears in the online supplement to this book:
https://bahai-library.com/supplement_abdul-baha_europe_1912-1913.

114 According to Sohrab, 'Abdu'l-Bahá arrived at the King's Weigh church at approximately 7:45 p.m. Reverend Lewis first gave his opening remarks, and then conducted 'Abdu'l-Bahá to the speaking platform at 8:02 p.m.

115 Sohrab's diary letters include these remarks by Reverend Lewis, which he had apparently asked Sohrab to convey to 'Abdu'l-Bahá: 'May I say on your behalf to 'Abdu'l Baha that we have heard with great pleasure his words so full of the wisdom of love, that our hearts have responded warmly to them, that our prayers follow him and that we pray that the joy of the Holy Spirit may abide in his heart always'. On the following day (30 December), Rev. Lewis wrote the following letter to Lady Blomfield:

Dear Lady Bloomfield [sic]!

Will you be good enough to present my loving compliments to Abdul Baha, and allow me to express to him, through you, my gratitude for his presence and his words at the King's Weigh House last evening. It was an exceeding kindness for him to come; his message was exhilarating and inspiring. I know that it was as seed sown in good ground and there will be much fruit of it. Particularly was his presence an encouragement to me, for, in my humble way, I have been preaching the gospel of unity and love for a good many years. I trust that he is not overtired with his most generously self-giving exertions. I do not presume to write to him directly, but I know that, through your mediumship, he will be willing to receive this expression of my sincere and loving respect.

I do not know what you do among yourselves when the Master has gone from you, how you arrange for your meetings and so forth, but there seemed to be so much in common between us from the beginning to the end of the service last evening that I am venturing to say how welcome any Bahai will always be at the King's Weigh House, and if any of our rooms would be likely to be of service to you at any time it would give me so much pleasure to think that we could make some return to you for the good you have done us.

With kind regards, and all good wishes for the New Year
Yours Most Sincerely
Ed. W. Lewis

116 An English translation of this talk appears in the online supplement to this book:
https://bahai-library.com/supplement_abdul-baha_europe_1912-1913.

117 Sohrab writes: 'So many people called on ['Abdu'l-Bahá] this morning that I do not know the number, neither can I clearly remember the context of Our Beloved's words to them.' He does note that the first person to visit 'Abdu'l-Bahá early that morning was an elderly gentleman who was 'working for the social and economic improvement of 20,000 Mohammadans who labor on the ships'; this gentleman remarked that the Christians felt he was wasting his time with such efforts, but 'Abdu'l-Bahá 'told him to go on with this noble work, to serve these helpless people, to spend as much time as he could and to strive to better their

conditions', assuring him that 'God is with him and will undoubtedly confirm him in the realization of his hopes'. This man was followed by another gentleman 'who ha[d] spent many years in India' and asked 'Abdu'l-Bahá 'by what means and what kind of organization did Abdul Baha intend to spread his teachings'. Sohrab's translation of 'Abdu'l-Bahá's response is as follows: 'Our organization is the Love of God, the Knowledge of the Almighty, the descent of the Breath of the Holy Spirit, and the outflow of the spiritual life. Our capital is good deeds, merciful attributes, heavenly characteristics and divine ethics.' After him came Jinzō Naruse, president of the Women's University in Tokyo, with whom 'Abdu'l-Bahá spoke on 'the principles of the Cause and how we are in need of a divine power to put these principles into practice. Just as the Sun is the source of all lights in the solar system, so today Baha-ollah is the center of the unity of the human race and of the Peace of the world'.

118 Sohrab relates the following anecdote from 'Abdu'l-Bahá's visit to Battersea Park that day: 'As we were walking behind Our Beloved in the Pattersee [sic] Park; on the edge of the distant lake, more than a hundred white-plumed birds were quietly basking under the sunshine. Looking at those birds which formed a lovely picture of peace and contentment, Abdul Baha pointed them [out] to us saying that his desire and fervent prayer was to see the believers all so united and so harmonious as to become as loving and as peaceful, as kind and as charitable towards each other as those happy birds. He watched the birds with such tender affection and such solicitation [solicitude] as though they were human beings, endowed with all the finer qualities of intelligence and ineffable grace. Perhaps he thought they were in a way better than all of us, because they were not aggressive.'

119 At 8:00 p.m., according to Sohrab.

120 According to Sohrab, this was the home of 'Mrs. Robinson and Mrs. Symonds', who lived at 166 Warrington Crescent, Maida Vale, London. Momen et al. have identified these women as Mrs Mary Letitia Robinson and Mrs Annie Symonds and observed that the address given is incorrect: 'Although Ahmad Sohrab's letter gives the address as 166 Warrington Crescent, Maida Vale, there was no such number at Warrington Crescent. According to the Kelly's Directory for *Paddington, Bayswater and Kensal Green*, for 1915, p. 243, these two ladies were living at 16 Warrington Crescent. They also appear in the Electoral Register for 1914. They were evidently Bahá'ís at this time but there is no further record of them as such' (*Community*, p. 205).

121 Sohrab writes that 'Abdu'l-Bahá spoke on 'the material and spiritual reciprocity and co-operation, explaining the real meaning of the nineteen day's Feasts'. An English translation of this talk was published in *Bahá'í News Letter*, or *Bahá'í News* for short (the bulletin of the National Spiritual Assembly of the Bahá'ís of the United States and

Canada), no. 33 (July 1929), pp. 1–2, where the date of 29 December 1912 has been assigned to it, which seems to be a mistake. Both Zarqání and Sohrab note that this talk was given on December 30th, and this is also corroborated by Momen et al. (*Community*, pp. 197 and 205). Accordingly, that translation of this talk has been reproduced in the online supplement to this book (https://bahai-library.com/supplement_abdul-baha_europe_1912-1913) with the date of 30 December 1912 rather than December 29th.

122 Sohrab writes: '. . . [Cheyne] is 70 yrs old and for the last 5 yrs he has been an invalid, his tongue is paralyzed, but he murmurs and through the motion of his lips his wife, who is an authoress and perfectly devoted to him tells us what he says. His mind is very clear and lucid and during the years of his affliction he has written 5 books.'

123 More specifically, at Manchester College (now Harris Manchester), one of the constituent colleges of the University of Oxford, at that time specializing in the study of theology.

124 17 Parks Road, Oxford.

125 At 3:00 p.m., according to Sohrab.

126 A summary of this talk in English appears in the online supplement to this book:
https://bahai-library.com/supplement_abdul-baha_europe_1912-1913.

127 Sohrab explicitly notes that no one had any questions to ask.

128 According to Sohrab, 'Abdu'l-Bahá departed Oxford by train at 5:50 p.m. and arrived in London at 7:30 p.m.

129 Taken from a reproduction published in Egea, *Apostle of Peace,* vol. 2, pp. 45–6. What Zarqání quotes in his chronicle is a translation of the article into Persian.

130 'Knight of the Theologian Spirit'.

131 Sohrab writes: 'About noon the Master came into the drawing room. All the people arose to welcome him. He bade them to be seated and he delivered a talk on the necessity of unity between the East and the West; a powerful appeal to those who were present to work for the co-operation of the Orient and the Occident.' A brief summary of a different address on civilization delivered that morning appears in the online supplement to this book:
https://bahai-library.com/supplement_abdul-baha_europe_1912-1913.

132 Sohrab writes: 'Today all the Persians, Lady Bloomfield [sic], and her daughters were invited to a New Year dinner in Mrs. T. Cropper's apartment and by the time we reached there, the Master and the rest of the party had already arrived. At 2 o'clock the dinner was served. There were exactly 19 guests at the two tables, very tastily [tastefully] decorated. Many courses of pigeon, chicken, etc. were served, all of which

were most delicious. The program of [the] Edinburgh meeting was presented to the Master. He told the friends that he had not reached that city yet, [but] they had already planned what he must do during every hour. Then he laughed and joked about these rigid customs, program-making, and date-fixing of the Western friends.' Sohrab's diary letter suggests that 'Abdu'l-Bahá and His retinue stayed there until sometime after 4:00 p.m.

133 Sohrab notes that over 300 people attended this gathering. His diary letter suggests that 'Abdu'l-Bahá had first wanted to go to the Salvation Army Centre, where 'many hundred[s] of the poor of London' were enjoying the meal to which He had treated them, but since they had stayed at Mrs Thornburgh-Cropper's apartment for too long and missed their chance to attend the dinner, He and His retinue went straight to the Cosmos Club instead.

134 Sohrab writes: '['Abdu'l-Bahá] spoke on the subject of the "spirit"; different kinds of "spirits"; [He] told the audience about the visible and invisible reality of man and of the rising and the setting of the Sun of Truth.' A translation of this talk appears in the online supplement to this book:
https://bahai-library.com/supplement_abdul-baha_europe_1912-1913.

135 According to Sohrab, Sidley had invited 'Abdu'l-Bahá and '16 other important personages' to this dinner.

136 A vegetarian restaurant with health facilities, then located on 40 Chandos Street, now the north side of William IV Street.

137 For biographical details on Moscheles, see Momen et al., *Community*, pp. 190–91. Although Zarqání goes on to describe Moscheles's ostensible conversion to the Faith, Momen et al. have written that 'there is no evidence that he took part in Bahá'í activities after 'Abdu'l-Bahá's departure, although he did not live long afterwards in any case' (ibid. p. 191).

138 Sohrab writes that 'Abdu'l-Bahá said the following that day in the course of an interview with a young Bahá'í woman 'from the country' who is identified only as a friend of Ethel Rosenberg's: 'The fragrance of the rose leads man to the garden and faith and assurance are the fragrance of the rose which attracts individual believing souls together. There are various attracting powers which unite people but they are more or less based upon definite or indefinite interests; just as there are many kinds of variegated flowers which are beautiful and the fragrances of which attract men of divergent temperaments; yet these flowers after awhile wither away and lose their scent, so also the numerous interests which are supposed to bind humankind together are temporary. Only the fragrance of the Rose of the Kingdom of Abha is ever-enduring and soul-refreshing, because it is imperishable. It is the never-fading flower of the garden of the heart and the soul which diffuses its sweet odor

throughout the expanse of the universe.' Others who visited 'Abdu'l-Bahá that day include a woman who was going to Los Angeles and had come 'to visit the Master and receive his blessings'; John Lewis, editor of *The International Psychic Gazette*, who elicited comments from 'Abdu'l-Bahá on reincarnation that appear in the online supplement to this book (https://bahai-library.com/supplement_abdul-baha_europe_1912-1913); C.W. Child, a palmist who took impressions of 'Abdu'l-Bahá's palms on this occasion for a piece that he later published ('The Hands of Abdul Baha', *The International Psychic Gazette* (London), vol. 1, no. 7 (Feb. 1913), pp. 199–200); Mr Arundel, a student of astrology; two women from 'a new town near London'; an unnamed Jewish rabbi; and Reverend Reginald John Campbell.

139 Sohrab calls this a talk 'on the necessity of universal peace (entirely from a new standpoint)'.

140 According to Sohrab, these distinguished guests included James Ramsay MacDonald, a Member of Parliament; the Iranian Envoy; and the Iranian chargé d'affaires.

141 According to Sohrab, Mrs Thornburgh-Cropper came at 7:55 p.m. to take 'Abdu'l-Bahá to this event.

142 Sohrab writes: 'As we arrived at the door we found there were hundreds of people clamoring to get in, for there were no more seats left inside. The large Hall and the gallery were crowded. More than one thousand people.'

143 According to Sohrab, Despard made this remark: 'I prefer to call ['Abdu'l-Bahá] a prophet than a teacher.'

144 An account of this occasion, which includes an English translation of 'Abdu'l-Bahá's remarks, appears in the online supplement to this book: https://bahai-library.com/supplement_abdul-baha_europe_1912-1913.

145 Held at the White Lodge, located at 8 Sunnyside, Wimbledon. Sohrab notes that Mrs Thornburgh-Cropper came by at 7:30 p.m. to take 'Abdu'l-Bahá to this meeting, which had been arranged by Eric Hammond, an early British Bahá'í who authored *The Splendour of God*. Sohrab summarizes the occasion in this way: 'There were many Theosophists present and the Master spoke from their standpoint: the evolution of the single atom through the various Kingdoms of being; in every stage going into the makeup of a certain composition and in every composition appearing with a distinctive virtue. Then he spoke on the eternal dominion of God, stating that it is not accidental or temporal but everlasting. Therefore His holy Divine Manifestations have always appeared and His Grace is never-suspended.' A translation of this talk appears in the online supplement to this book: https://bahai-library.com/supplement_abdul-baha_europe_1912-1913.

146 Daniel Nicol Dunlop (1868–1935) was a Scottish businessman who

spent time in the United States, where he became secretary of the Theosophical Society there; see 'Selected Biographical Notes'.

147 Sohrab's record of this day is completely different from Zarqání's account. While Zarqání writes that 'Abdu'l-Bahá did not leave Lady Blomfield's residence at all and received very few visitors, Sohrab's trajectory of events is as follows: 'Abdu'l-Bahá was first visited by Felix Moscheles, who had come to finish painting a portrait of Him that He had begun the day before; then a rabbi; and then an English captain who 'spoke a little Persian'. Following this, 'Abdu'l-Bahá came out of His room and went to the hall, where He gave an (apparently unrecorded) address based on a talk He had given at a synagogue in San Francisco. Afterwards, He went out with Mrs Thornburgh-Cropper, Luṭfu'lláh Ḥakím, and 'a new friend' for a drive. Upon His return, He received Wellesley Tudor Pole and his brother, Alexander Cecil Tudor Pole, who had both come from Bristol to meet with Him; then a 'vagrant tramp' who had walked thirty-five miles to see Him; then 'a celebrated actress and teacher of elocution' who was staunchly opposed to the suffragist movement; and then J.W. Sidley. At 8:30 p.m., 'Abdu'l-Bahá came out to Lady Blomfield's drawing room and gave a talk on the four kinds of love. (Sohrab's record of 'Abdu'l-Bahá's conversation with the anti-suffragist, as well as the transcript of His address on the four kinds of love that was originally published in *Paris Talks*, both appear in the online supplement to this book: https://bahai-library.com/supplement_abdul-baha_europe_1912-1913.) Furthermore, Sohrab does write that 'Abdu'l-Bahá 'was not feeling well' that day, but unlike Zarqání, he does not attribute this condition to a lack of sleep, but rather to the climate, which he characterizes as 'mild and temperate' for an Englishman, but 'rigorous' for 'Abdu'l-Bahá, writing that He was 'not accustomed' to it, that it was 'hard on his constitution', and that His condition was only compounded by all of 'the meetings and the interviews' He had, which Sohrab says were 'too exacting and too numerous'.

148 *Áb-gúsht* is an Iranian stew generally consisting of beef or lamb shanks, chickpeas, potatoes, tomato paste, and spices. The solid portion of the stew, after a long cooking period, is mashed and served with bread alongside the rich, flavourful broth. The present translator is grateful to Joshua D.T. Hall for kindly writing up this description of *áb-gúsht* for use in this book.

149 At 10:00 a.m., according to Sohrab.

150 At 12:00 p.m., according to Sohrab.

151 Muḥammad-'Alí Ṭabasí, known as Núr-'Alí Sháh I (c. 1757/58–1796/97), was a Persian poet and leader of the Ni'matu'lláhí Sufi order.

152 Literally 'thresholds', *'atabát* is a term that refers to the Shí'ih shrine cities of Iraq – Najaf, Karbala, Kazimayn, and Samarra – containing the

tombs of six of the Imams as well as secondary sites of pilgrimage. For more information, see Algar, 'Atabāt', in *Encyclopedia Iranica*; available online at:
https://www.iranicaonline.org/articles/atabat.

153 Sohrab has this as 6:15 p.m. – the more accurate record, as the timetable indicates an arrival time of 6:14 p.m.

154 To be more precise, Dr Whyte had served as Moderator of the Free Church General Assembly for a year in 1898.

155 Probably the Roxburghe Hotel, 38 Charlotte Square.

156 According to Sohrab, this audience consisted of members of the Committee of Arrangement, the Secretary of the Esperanto Society, the General Secretary of the Theosophical Society for Scotland, several professors, and many clergymen with their wives.

157 Sohrab's account reverses the order of the latter two events of the day, in that 'Abdu'l-Bahá first had dinner at 7:30 p.m. and then received His distinguished audience at 8:00 p.m.

Scotland

158 While Zarqání repeats the heading of the previous day for this entry, Sohrab's account indicates that the following events actually took place on 7 January 1913.

159 Sohrab writes: 'It was about half past eight when I heard the bell calling us as I found later to prayer. When I went down to the Library I saw principal Whyte with the members of the family standing on one side and all the maids which were seven, I think, standing on the other side, each having a hymn book in her hand. Mrs. Whyte gave me one of these books and she went to the organ. All of us sung the songs and afterwards Rev. Whyte prayed while all of them knelt down. It was a very new experience to me. Of course this is their daily custom for the Master and the servants to pray to God every morning before starting their daily labors. This is a very lovely custom and affords one a few moments whereby to commune with his Creator. After the prayer we had breakfast and I carried up Our Beloved's tea to His room.'

160 Sohrab writes: 'About 10:30 [a.m.] a number of people came to see Our Beloved, some with their children; others to receive His Blessings. The children of one of the callers were dressed à la Highlanders which looked very pretty.'

161 More specifically, Sohrab writes that a car had been sent by Sir William Stowell Haldane, whom he describes as 'the brother of Lord [Richard Burdon] Haldane the Chancellor or Secretary of the Navy of Great Britain'.

162 Sohrab writes: 'The Outlook Tower is an educational institution which attempts to teach astronomy, natural geography, oceanography maps etc.'

163 Zarqání is describing the historical camera obscura located in Edinburgh's Outlook Tower. This still exists today and is now a popular tourist attraction.

164 Zarqání is describing a kind of pinhole projection.

165 Sohrab writes: 'Prof. Geddes with great interest took us through these rooms, floor after floor till we reached to the highest room in the Tower. Here the room was made dark, in the center there was a round revolving canvass and in the ceiling a hole. I suppose over the roof our Prof. has installed certain mechanical devices and sun-cameras which are connected with wires to this room. Now by the manipulation of these wires the most marvellous thing becomes visible before your eyes. The Master and all of us are gathered around this round revolving canvass. Suddenly we see the city with its streets with its smoking chimneys with people walking to and fro, cars running hither and thither, even women dusting rugs from the windows. You must know this is not a moving-picture but just at that very moment that we were looking at the canvass these things were going on in the outside world. Most amazingly, every part of the city was shown, the scene constantly changing, giving us the most kaleidoscopic pictures of the real life of Edinburgh. Coming out of the Tower we had a most charming view of the whole city. The Master praised his energy and patience for Prof. Geddes has devoted 25 years of his life to this.'

166 Apparently a reference to Queen's Drive, which went around Holyrood Park (also called Queen's Park or King's Park).

167 Sohrab writes: 'At five o'clock the Oriental students began to come. First the Master met some of them in the small private room, then at 5:30 [p.m.] He entered in the large Library where all of them were sitting. There were almost 200, more than fifteen nationalities from Asia, all gathered under one roof, the most potent evidence of the power of the Word of God. First Rev. Whyte expressed his pleasure at having "our great Master amongst us" and talked several minutes; then a gentleman from India spoke very beautifully about the wonderful effect of the Bahai Cause and on behalf of the students thanked "Our Master" for His Presence. Then a very eloquent student from Damascus spoke. His speech was on peace, brotherhood[,] and a warm welcome to the Master. Then Our Beloved arose from His seat and spoke on Medicine, how the doctors must ever be the means of physical and spiritual healing. He spoke also on a few Bahai principles and advised them when they return to their respective countries they must be like shining stars. After Our Master's talk which was quite long a student from Persia spoke and on the part of the students he tendered a rising vote of thanks which was carried amidst loud clapping of hands. Then the Master called 3 of the Egyptian students and talked with them for some time.'

168 'Abdu'l-Bahá was taken to the Esperanto Society at 8 p.m., according to Sohrab.

169 96 George Street.

170 Sohrab likewise states that 300 people remained outside and estimates that 1,000 were seated inside. A report in *The Dundee Courier* dated 9 January 1913 and entitled 'Universal Brotherhood of Man' notes that 'The audience . . . consisted almost entirely of women, fashionably dressed for the most part, who accorded to the saintly-looking Abdul the most sympathetic of hearings . . .'

171 An English translation of this talk appears in the online supplement to this book:
https://bahai-library.com/supplement_abdul-baha_europe_1912-1913.

172 Sohrab's account indicates that the following events actually took place on 8 January 1913.

173 The articles '. . . detailing the Esperanto Society talk in the *Scotsman* and a long article in the *Edinburgh Evening Dispatch* devoted to Abdu'l-Baha, the Baha'i principles and its history, ending with some of the Hidden Words':
http://www.edin-bahai.org.uk/history/visit-abdul-baha.htm?12.

174 Sohrab notes that one of these visitors was Sir John Maurice Clark, who by that time had published the twelve-volume *Encyclopedia of Religion and Ethics*, which contained an article on the Bahá'í Faith by E.G. Browne. He also served as the superintendent of the four largest schools in Edinburgh with a combined body of more than 4,000 students: Merchant Maiden Hospital (now Mary Erskine School), George Watson's Hospital (now George Watson's College), Daniel Stewart's Hospital (now part of Stewart's Melville College), and James Gillespie's Hospital and Free School (now James Gillespie's High School). Sohrab adds that, during this visit with Clark, 'there was a woman sitting in a corner of the room making a miniature of the Master which was not finished'.

175 Sohrab writes that Sir William Haldane's car arrived at approximately 11:30 a.m. to take 'Abdu'l-Bahá to the Edinburgh College of Art.

176 The Edinburgh College of Art (east of Lady Lawson Street):
http://www.edin-bahai.org.uk/history/visit-abdul-baha.htm?13.

177 This was apparently the North Canongate School (5 New Street, Canongate):
http://www.edin-bahai.org.uk/history/visit-abdul-baha.htm?14.

Nearly two months later, Sohrab wrote, in his diary letter to Harriet Magee dated 27 February 1913, that 'Abdu'l-Bahá had delivered the following prayer while at this school: 'He is God! O Thou Kind Lord! These beloved children are created by Thy Mighty Hand. They are the signs of Thy Omnipotence. Confirm them in their lessons. Make them successful in their studies so that when they reach the age of maturity they may arise in the service of the world of humanity. O God! These children are like unto pearls. Rear them in the shells of Thy Providence. Verily Thou art the Generous, the Clement.'

178 The original Persian word used here, *ḥajjárí*, can alternatively be translated as 'stonecutting'.

179 In reality, this might have been a school for poor children, rather than an actual orphanage.

180 New College, the Mound, EH1 2LU.

181 An account of this occasion, which includes an English translation of 'Abdu'l-Bahá's remarks, appears in the online supplement to this book: https://bahai-library.com/supplement_abdul-baha_europe_1912-1913.

182 Both Sohrab's account and a report in *The Scotsman* state that the gentleman who did this was actually not Patrick Geddes, but Dr Alexander Hugh Freeland Barbour (1856–1927), a Scottish gynecologist.

183 According to Sohrab, this particular gathering was actually held the day before (7 January 1913) at 5:00 p.m. There were apparently some 200 people in attendance.

184 Possibly a reference to Acts 17:26: 'And hath made of one blood all nations of men for to dwell on all the face of the earth . . .', in which case Dr Whyte's attribution to Peter would be incorrect, as these are actually the words of Paul.

185 Possibly a reference to Luke 13:29: 'And they shall come from the East, and from the West, and from the North, and from the South, and shall sit down in the kingdom of God.'

186 Bahá'ís would refer to these as the 'social teachings' of divine religions, which deal with such things as dietary restrictions and other prohibitions subject to change, in contrast to the 'spiritual teachings', which remain fundamentally the same across all these religions.

187 According to Sohrab, 'Abdu'l-Bahá was taken to the cathedral at approximately 8:00 p.m. and 'thousands of people were present'.

188 At 4:00 p.m., according to Sohrab.

189 28 Great King Street. 'Abdu'l-Bahá arrived there at 6:45 p.m. and returned at 11:30 p.m.

190 One account gives an estimate of about 120 people in the main hall.

191 According to Sohrab, Pole made these remarks at approximately 8:00 p.m.

192 An English translation of this talk appears in the online supplement to this book:
https://bahai-library.com/supplement_abdul-baha_europe_1912-1913.
Regarding the meaning of humanity's 'second reality', 'Abdu'l-Bahá

states the following in His address at the White Lodge in Wimbledon, England on 3 January 1913: 'Man, however, enjoys a second or higher reality which is the intellectual reality that comprehends all phenomena, or is infinite as regards the phenomena. It is a governor, victorious over the world of matter. It discovers and unfolds the realities of sentient beings; it "explodes" the laws of nature, because from a physical standpoint it is superior, above and beyond the laws of nature' (*Star of the West*, vol. 7, no. 13, p. 117).

193 Sohrab writes: 'I suppose there were about 15 of the Theosophical Leaders who were invited for dinner. They had some Persian and Turkish dishes which were immensely enjoyed.'

194 The rendering of this prayer is authorized and was kindly supplied to the present translator by the Bahá'í World Centre.

195 A reference to the previous night, when Sohrab notes that 'Abdu'l-Bahá gave £10 for the wounded and sick in a Bulgarian hospital known for treating all nationalities equally.

196 Sohrab writes: 'Our Beloved asked for all the maids. When they all gathered He said: "You have a very good lady. For the last few days you have served me. I am very pleased with you. I will never forget you. I will pray for you that you may become confirmed and assisted and that your head be crowned with the diadem of eternal glory." Then in the palm of each hand He puts a £1.'

197 Sohrab has the following people at the train station: 'Mr. Page, the active and energetic Secretary of the Esperanto Society; Mr. Pole, the kind and hospital [hospitable] Theosophical General Secretary; one of the Persian students; and two Ministers with several ladies and gentlemen who have come to say farewell to Our Beloved.' Luṭfu'lláh Ḥakím adds Alexander Whyte and Jane Elizabeth Whyte to this list (Letter by Luṭfu'lláh Ḥakím dated 1948 describing 'Abdu'l-Bahá's visit; copy held at the Edinburgh Bahá'í Archives).

198 At 10:05 a.m., according both to Sohrab and also the timetable for the train that day.

199 Sohrab chronicles the events of the train ride as follows: 'At 1:30 p.m. all of us took lunch in the dining car with Our Beloved. He said: The most important food is the spiritual food. This material food must be eaten three times a day but whosoever eats of the spiritual food shall never hunger. The Spiritual food is the love of God, the Knowledge of God, attraction with the Breaths of the Holy Spirit and abstraction from material desires. These very conversations of ours today consisted of the spiritual food. God had so destined that you (Mrs. Fraser) be here with us in this train so that undisturbed we may talk together on these ideal subjects. There must be a wisdom in this. I hope that thou mayst become a great teacher of this Cause and be my daughter. Later

on the Master told her a story of a competition between the Chinese and Roman artists. The king appointed a large hall where both of them could paint. The Chinese asked for a curtain to be hung in the middle of the Hall so that their competitors may not see what they are doing. The Chinese Artists worked for 6 months day and night but the Roman Artists did not work and everybody thought they are going to lose. Just one day before the King's coming to give the award, the Roman Artists set to work and polished the wall like a mirror. The King's Ministers and courtiers came. First they saw the Chinese paintings. They were marvellous and beautiful. The curtain then was put aside so that they see also the Roman works. The wall polished by the Roman Artists was so transparent that the Chinese paintings on the opposite wall were entirely reflected therein. The award went to the Romans. Now, may your heart be as pure and as transparent so that the pictures and images of the Kingdom of Abha may be reflected therein.'

200 Sohrab has this as 7:00 p.m.

201 Sohrab identifies Marion Jack as one of these friends.

202 Sohrab writes: 'Lady Blomfield and her daughters and Miss [Beatrice Marion] Platt moaned and lamented and pleaded, the latter on her knees till the Master consented to stay.'

Return to England

203 More precisely, there were three of them, according to Sohrab, who writes: 'Then the three new Persians who have arrived during our absence went into the Presence of Our Beloved and He greeted them most affectionately. They would hardly speak or raise their heads.'

204 At 4:00 p.m., according to Sohrab.

205 In fact, Sohrab says this was a 'farewell meeting' for 'Abdu'l-Bahá. David Merrick writes of this: '11 Jan is quite early for a farewell meeting given that 'Abdu'l-Bahá stayed on until the 21 Jan, but originally the departure was expected 15th or 16th Jan' (*'Abdu'l-Bahá in Britain, 1913*, p. 142, n. 825; digitally published, rev. 11 June 2018; available online: http://paintdrawer.co.uk/david/folders/spirituality/bahai/abdulbaha/sohrab-diary-uk-1913.pdf). Sohrab notes, moreover, that 'the great big Hall, when we entered was filled to overflowing'.

206 Sohrab writes: 'Mrs. Cropper had requested the Master to speak on the life of Baha-ollah and similar incidents. Consequently while Our Beloved sat on the chair and the translator [Sohrab] stood behind His chair He began His eloquent address by quoting a verse from Isaiah chapter 45 verse 5th ["I am the LORD, and there is none else, there is no God beside me: I girded thee, though thou hast not known me"]. Then He spoke about the appearance of the Bab, Baha'u'llah, martyrs who have given up their lives, Qurratu'l-'Ayn and some of the Teachings. It created a profound impression for always the recital of the tragic stories of the friends

make me quite oblivious and the words are like hot volleys of rifles.'

207 Sohrab writes: 'While the Master was talking with people in the refreshment room, in the Hall speakers dispensed the sweet aroma of oratory.' Among them, he names Francis Herbert Bacon, a bishop; a certain 'Captain St. Jones' of the Salvation Army; Eric Hammond; Mrs Sidley, the wife of J.W. Sidley; Alice Buckton; and Lady Blomfield. A report in *The Christian Commonwealth*, entitled 'Joyous Gathering at the Caxton Hall' and dated 15 January 1913, also names Julia Sarah Anne Cobden-Sanderson, a socialist and suffragist; David Samuel Margoliouth, a professor and gifted Orientalist; and Bhawani Singh, the Maharaja of Jhalawar.

208 According to Sohrab, all the events recorded in the remainder of this entry actually took place the night before (11 January 1913), following the gathering at Caxton Hall.

209 33 Bloomsbury Square, London.

210 In the winter garden, according to Sohrab.

211 The reception room, according to Sohrab.

212 A pall of smog hung over London that day due to the large amounts of coal smoke that were being expelled from the city's chimneys. So thick and pervasive was this smog, according to Sohrab, that people in the same room could hardly see one another.

213 A reference to the Peace Society.

214 Sohrab writes that these were actually Turkish-speaking Armenians.

215 Sohrab has this as three taxi cabs, which is more feasible, as he also notes that about a dozen of them had gone to the rug store.

216 This group consisted of Mírzá Mihdí Khán (the Mushíru'l-Mulk), envoy; Mírzá 'Abdu'l-Ghaffár Khán, counsellor; Humáyún Iḥtishám, first secretary; and 'Alí Khán Ardaláni Qalam, attaché.

217 Among them Mírzá Áqá Khán Qá'im-Maqámí, according to Sohrab.

218 Among them Pamela Adelaide Genevieve Wyndham (Lady Glenconner), according to Sohrab.

219 According to Sohrab, the remainder of the events recorded in this entry actually took place on 12 January 1913.

220 Parson's Hill (northwest side). Sohrab writes that Mrs Thornburgh-Cropper came by at approximately 5:30 p.m. to take 'Abdu'l-Bahá to this event, and that they arrived at about 6:30 p.m.

221 Sohrab's summary of Reverend Pool's opening remarks is as follows: 'Abdul Baha calls Himself the Servant of God but I prefer to call Him My Master and myself His Servant. Abdul Baha is the King of Kings. He desires to be known as the servant of God, and, for this very reason we all call Him Our Master. I shall be proud to call myself His servant.

Accept the light from whatever place it may shine forth. Baha ollah was an Aristocrat of the Aristocrats but he gave up every thing so that he may be able to assist the poor. I desire you to arise when He enters the platform in order to show Him the sign of respect and love due to Him.'

222 Zarqání's timing differs from that of Sohrab, who writes: 'At about ten o'clock Mirza Mahmoud, Sayad Assadollah, Mirza Lotfollah and Mirza Afnan left the house for the station called Paddington. After a few minutes the Master also with Moair-al-Mamalek and Mrs. Cropper and Ahmad [a reference to himself] in the lovely automobile started for the station. At about 11 o'clock the train pulled out of the station. Miss Fraser was also with us.'

223 This was the Clifton Guest House at 17 Royal York Crescent. The Tudor Poles themselves lived next door at no. 16.

224 This excursion lasted for an hour, according to Sohrab, who has summarized it as follows: 'We passed through most enchanting parks and commons. Some of these places are known in History as the Camping Ground of the Roman soldiers. The river which winds through these lovely valleys and hills finally empties itself in the sea which is seen in the far off horizon. Wales is also visible in the distance.'

225 At 8:00 p.m., according to Sohrab and various other accounts.

226 Over 120 people, according to Sohrab.

227 At 8:30 p.m., according to Sohrab.

228 An English translation of this talk appears in the online supplement to this book:
https://bahai-library.com/supplement_abdul-baha_europe_1912-1913.

229 The title of Dúst Muḥammad Khán (c. 1856–1913).

230 Eight of them, according to Sohrab, who writes that they 'came in the Library and for nearly 30 minutes the Master spoke with them about things they were interested in'.

231 At 10:00 p.m., according to Sohrab, who writes that the dinner consisted of chicken and rice.

232 Sohrab writes that this excursion actually lasted for half an hour at most, noting that it began around 11:00 a.m. and that the train back to London departed an hour later at 12:00 p.m. Given that a photography session also took place in between returning from the excursion and boarding the train to London, Sohrab's estimate seems to be the more accurate one.

233 Sohrab writes that four individual photographs capturing two different poses were taken on this occasion. It may be the case, then, that Zarqání was referring to two poses, rather than two photographs.

234 Unique details on this visit 'Abdu'l-Bahá made to Woking can be found in Brendan McNamara, "Establishing Islam in Britain: The Founding

of Woking Mission", *Journal of Muslims in Europe*, vol. 7, no. 3 (11 Oct 2018), pp. 309–330.

235 In fact, these gatherings were held at the Oriental Institute, an educational establishment comprising various buildings, among them a building for *The Asiatic Quarterly Review*, where the first meeting (meal) of the day was held, and the Shah Jahan Mosque, where the second meeting was held.

236 Sohrab writes that he and Lady Blomfield also accompanied the group on this drive to Woking, while 'the rest of the Persians' went by train. The drive lasted an hour and a half, according to Sohrab.

237 See above, endnote 233, on the number of poses rather than individual photographs.

238 A provisional English rendering of the full talk, produced by the present translator, appears in the online supplement to this book: https://bahai-library.com/supplement_abdul-baha_europe_1912-1913.

239 Sohrab actually has this as heavy rain: 'While ['Abdu'l-Bahá] was speaking it started to rain hard. Umbrellas were raised. Not a soul left. Many people standing in the rain till the end of the lecture.'

240 According to William MacCarthy Mann, editor of *The Asiatic Quarterly Review*, Dr John Pollen actually made these remarks on behalf of 'Abdu'l-Bahá's host on this occasion, Henry Leitner, not Lord Lamington. Refer to *Bahá'í World*, vol. 3, p. 279.

241 A reference to Syed Ameer Ali (1849–1928).

242 According to Sohrab, these visitors included an unnamed 'representative of a newspaper which is published for the labouring class'; a gentleman from California who is described only as a poet and 'a great friend of Doctor [David Starr] Jordan'; Isabel Fraser; Sir William Crookes, a celebrated scientist (a record of 'Abdu'l-Bahá's interview with Crookes appears in the online supplement to this book: https://bahai-library.com/supplement_abdul-baha_europe_1912-1913); and Mírzá Aḥmad K͟hán (or Dr Aḥmad K͟hán), a Bahá'í living in London. Sohrab also writes that, before departing for Rev. Campbell's residence, 'Abdu'l-Bahá delivered a noonday address on the knowledge of God and the love of God, in which He remarked on 'how he hoped to see these ideas well spread in this country as a result of his trip'.

243 Sohrab offers the following trajectory of events, which seems to be the more accurate and precise account: 'Abdu'l-Bahá entered Campbell's residence, had lunch, and then delivered this address.

244 'In the beginning was the Word, and the Word was with God, and the Word was God.'

245 Enthoven actually visited 'Abdu'l-Bahá the night before (on 17 January).

246 A complete transcript of these words was later published as a play, *The Drama of the Kingdom*, published in a book by the same name prepared by Mary Basil Hall, one of the daughters of Lady Blomfield. The full text, taken from pp. 3–8 of that book, has been reproduced in the online supplement to this book: https://bahai-library.com/supplement_abdul-baha_europe_1912-1913.

247 According to Sohrab, 'Abdu'l-Bahá actually delivered this address on 18 January 1913.

248 According to Sohrab, these remarks were addressed to Ethel Rosenberg.

249 According to Sohrab, one of these visitors was a woman from Holland who had 'heard of the Cause' and was 'greatly interested'; she was 'received by the Master most cordially', and He then spoke to her the following words 'with power and authority':

When you return to Holland, summon the people to the Kingdom of God and cry out 'Glad tidings! Glad tidings! The Sun of Reality has dawned!

Glad tidings! Glad tidings! The doors of the Kingdom are opened!
Glad tidings! Glad tidings! The gates of heaven are flung wide!
Glad tidings! Glad tidings! The Beauty of Truth is revealed!
Glad tidings! Glad tidings! The hosts of heaven are descending!
Glad tidings! Glad tidings! The Fire of Moses has flamed forth!
Glad tidings! Glad tidings! The pillar of fire has become manifest!
Glad tidings! Glad tidings! The Clouds of Mercy are pouring!
Glad tidings! Glad tidings! The Effulgence of the Supreme Concourse has become visible!
Glad tidings! Glad tidings! The Call of the Kingdom is raised!
Awake! Awake! O ye people! Come and listen to this voice!
Awake! Awake! Gather ye together and hearken to this Celestial music!'

This is my message.

250 Sohrab's account indicates that the remainder of the events in this entry actually took place the night before (18 January).

251 At 59 Cromwell Road. This is a reference to the aforementioned Bhawani Singh, who was in fact not the Maharaja of Rajputana, but of Jhalawar, a state of Rajputana.

252 According to Sohrab, there were about twenty guests in attendance. This included Francis Henry Bennett Skrine (1847–1933), an English traveller, orientalist and official in British India, along with his wife, Helen Lucy Skrine (née Stewart).

253 According to Sohrab, 'Abdu'l-Bahá actually delivered this address on 19 January 1913.

254 Sohrab's account indicates that this encounter with the Bahá'ís from Honolulu actually took place several days earlier on 11 January 1913.

255 At 4:00 p.m. on the previous day (19 January 1913), according to Sohrab, not 20 January.

256 'The Grelix', located at 80 Elm Park, Chelsea.

257 An account of this occasion, which includes an English translation of 'Abdu'l-Bahá's remarks, appears in the online supplement to this book: https://bahai-library.com/supplement_abdul-baha_europe_1912-1913.

258 On 19 January 1913, according to Sohrab.

259 A reference to the Doré Art Gallery, then at 35 New Bond Street.

260 Sohrab has this as 'a wonderful address on the defects of nature'.

261 Published in the 1 January 1913 issue of *The Christian Commonwealth*, along with the Persian original.

262 This rendering has largely been taken from an authorized English translation published in *Selections from the Writings of 'Abdu'l-Bahá*, no. 220, but has been altered in certain places to more closely align with wording quoted by Zarqání that differs from the original text on which the authorized translation is based.

263 A reference to the London Peace Conference of 1912–1913.

264 According to Sohrab, the events recorded in this entry up until this point actually took place on 20 January 1913, while the remainder did happen on 21 January.

265 According to Sohrab, this included Bhawani Singh, who presented 'Abdu'l-Bahá with a wreath of flowers 'in the presence of the hundreds gathered to witness his departure'.

266 Jasion writes: 'Of the several possible crossings that day on the London to Paris route, it is supposed that ['Abdu'l-Bahá] used the London Brighton and South Coast Railway (LB & SCR) connection at 10.00 a.m. from Victoria Station to Newhaven, a small port on the Sussex coast, where He and His party boarded one of the cross-Channel steamers for Dieppe. There, they would have boarded a train of the Chemin du Fer du Nord and arrived at Gare Saint-Lazare in the centre of Paris early in the evening' (*'Abdu'l-Bahá in France*, p. 288).

267 30 Rue Saint-Didier, Paris 16.

France

268 Mírzá 'Alí-Muḥammad (d. 1896), one of the most eminent martyrs of the Bahá'í Faith, surnamed Varqá ('dove') by Bahá'u'lláh, referred to by 'Abdu'l-Bahá as a Hand of the Cause of God, and appointed by Shoghi Effendi as one of the nineteen Apostles of Bahá'u'lláh. A biography of Varqá that includes a small sample of his poetry in English translation has been published in Balyuzi, *Eminent Bahá'ís*, pp. 75–97. Additional poems translated into English can be found in John S. Hatcher and Amrollah Hemmat, *Reunion with the Beloved: Poetry and Martyrdom*,

items 2, 3, 4, and 7 (this one written by his son, Rúḥu'lláh, who was similarly martyred). Further details on Varqá's life can be found in Momen, *The Bahá'í Communities of Iran*, vol. 1, pp. 460–4 and passim. A more comprehensive Persian-language account of his life, and also that of Rúḥu'lláh, has been published in Sulaymání, *Maṣábíḥ-i-Hidáyat*, vol. 1 (2nd ed.), pp. 247–334. A more extensive selection of Varqá's poetry in Persian can be found in Bayḍá'í, *Tadhkariy-i-Shu'aráy-i-Qarn-i-Avval-i-Bahá'í*, vol. 4, pp. 353–91. 'Abdu'l-Bahá's eulogy for Varqá's father, Ḥájí Mullá Mihdí Yazdí, is published in *Memorials of the Faithful*, ch. 33.

269 Sohrab has this as 'every day from ten to twelve', and seems to suggest that this decision was made the following day (24 January).

270 Probably a reference to Ardishír Khán Naẓar-Áqá, 'a member of a distinguished Persian family of diplomats living in Paris' (Jasion, *'Abdu'l-Bahá in France*, p. 302, n. 705).

271 According to Sohrab, 'Abdu'l-Bahá also made the following remarks that day in a similar vein: 'The Parisian people are submerged in a sea of materialism. They are intoxicated with the wine of desire and selfish appetites. They think these material objects are permanent. They put their trust in them while all such things are subject to change. Today the palaces of the ancient kings are destroyed. The fishermen dry their nets on the ruined walls and the owls are making their nests in the cornices. It is my hope that you may enkindle such a lamp in Paris so as to make this city radiant. Man must lay the foundation of such a palace which may stand the encroachments of time, which day unto day may become newer and its imperial pinnacles may reach to the height of heaven.'

272 Mírzá Abu'l-Qásim Faráhání (c. 1779–1835), more commonly known by his title of Qa'ím-Maqám ('vicegerent'), was an enlightened and skillful politician who briefly served as prime minister of Persia under Muḥammad Sháh Qájár, who betrayed him by having him killed after he had played an instrumental role in his accession to the throne. The father of the Qá'im-Maqám, Mírzá 'Ísá Faráhání, was close friends with Mírzá 'Abbas Núrí, the father of Bahá'u'lláh – and coincidentally, both men were known by the same title of Mírzá Buzurg. Bahá'u'lláh notably lauded the Qá'im-Maqám as 'the Prince of the City of Statesmanship and Literary Accomplishment' in a Tablet of His titled *Kalimát-i-Firdawsíyyih* ('Words of Paradise'). Both Bahá'u'lláh and 'Abdu'l-Bahá have praised the Qá'im-Maqám in several other places. The most comprehensive survey has been done by Vahid Rafati in 'Qá'im-Maqám Faráhání dar Áthár-i-Bahá'í,' *Safíniy-i-'Irfán*, no. 18 (2015), pp. 268–293. The original Persian text of that article was rendered into English by the present translator and published as 'Qá'im-Maqám Faráhání in the Bahá'í Writings' (*Lights of 'Irfán*, Book

20, May 2019, pp. 161–196). Mírzá Áqá Khán Qá'im-Maqámí (1868–1954), mentioned in multiple places in this chronicle (and discussed in the 'Selected Biographical Notes'), was a Bahá'í and great-grandson of the Qá'im-Maqám.

273 In his diary letter dated 26 January 1913, Sohrab has recorded a very similar remark that 'Abdu'l-Bahá made to 'the Mu'ayyiru'l-Mamálik and a number of Persians in His apartment': 'If this Cause had appeared in America, today there would not have been a single soul in that country who would not be either a Bahá'í or a friend.'

274 An English translation of Persian notes from this talk appears in the online supplement to this book: https://bahai-library.com/supplement_abdul-baha_europe_1912-1913.

275 Sohrab's account of the words spoken by 'Abdu'l-Bahá on this occasion appears in the online supplement to this book: https://bahai-library.com/supplement_abdul-baha_europe_1912-1913.

276 Sohrab's translation of some excerpts from this talk is as follows: 'I hope that if I am permitted a third time to Paris I may obtain greater happiness. I may see [that] Paris is illumined, [that] Paris has become the Paradise of Abha, [that] from Paris the Summons of the Kingdom is heard, [that] in Paris the Stars of the Kingdom are shining . . . Bahaollah was a real physician. He diagnosed the sicknesses of the world of humanity. Therefore he hath prescribed [a] quick-healing remedy. There is no other medicine for the humankind except this course of treatment. If this medicine is taken, it is evident that the world of humanity will become luminous, the nether world will reflect the virtues of the divine world and all humanity will attain to the utmost of composure and peace' (Quoted in Jasion, *'Abdu'l-Bahá in France*, p. 309).

277 Sohrab's English translation of some excerpts from this talk appears in the online supplement to this book: https://bahai-library.com/supplement_abdul-baha_europe_1912-1913.

278 'Abdu'l-Bahá might be referring to the Adana massacre of 1909, in which thousands of Armenian residences in the Adana division of the Ottoman Empire were burned to the ground and some 30,000 Armenians were reported killed.

279 One of the first Bahá'ís to live in Egypt, taking up residence there in 1878. He was posthumously appointed a Hand of the Cause of God by Shoghi Effendi.

280 Ḥájí Mírzá Ḥaydar-'Alí Iṣfahání (c. 1830–1920) was an outstanding Bahá'í travel-teacher. He wrote a few works in Persian, perhaps the most well known being his memoirs, *Bihjatu'ṣ-Ṣudúr*, which has been published in abridged English translation by Abu'l-Qasim Faizi under the title *Stories from the Delight of Hearts*. An account of his life can be

found in Balyuzi, *Eminent Bahá'ís*, pp. 237–50. A more comprehensive biography of him, written in Persian, has been published in 'Azízu'lláh Sulaymání, *Maṣábíḥ-i-Hidáyat*, vol. 1 (2nd ed.), pp. 9–92. Twenty-eight letters he wrote to his wife, Nargis Khánum, along with twenty-three excerpts from *Bihjatu'ṣ-Ṣudúr*, have been compiled by Heshmat Moayyad and published, in Persian, as *Fereschteh Karmel* [*Firishtiy-i-Karmil*]. The proceedings of a conference held in honor of Ḥájí Mírzá Ḥaydar-'Alí by the Society of Persian Arts and Letters have been published in *Khúshih-Há'í az Kharman-i-Adab va Hunar*, vol. 8. For additional details and sources on his life in English, refer to Momen, 'ḤAYDAR 'ALI EṢFAHĀNI, Ḥājji Mirzā', published in *Encyclopedia Iranica*, available online at: https://www.iranicaonline.org/articles/haydar-ali-esfahani.

281 Very similarly, Sohrab has recorded, 'Mírzá Abu'l-Faḍl and Ḥájí Mírzá Ḥaydar-'Alí are peerless and unique. They are perfect Bahá'ís. They embody in themselves Bahá'í principles: their value is not now appreciated. It will become known later on.'

282 As Ḥájí Amín was trustee of the Ḥuqúq.

283 Likely a reference to Al-Ḥajjáj ibn Yúsuf (661–714), a notoriously ruthless governor of the Umayyad Caliphate.

284 At 17 rue Boissonade, Montparnasse, Paris 14.

285 See 'Abdu'l-Bahá, *Some Answered Questions*, ch. 83.

286 A partial English rendering of this talk, translated from the French notes of Hippolyte Dreyfus, appears in the online supplement to this book: https://bahai-library.com/supplement_abdul-baha_europe_1912-1913.

287 At the envoy's residence: Rue de Sontay, Paris 16.

288 Sohrab notes that 'Abdu'l-Bahá visited Edith Sanderson that day and made these similar remarks to her: 'Paris is like unto a green meadow. The people are like unto the sheep; they are grazing in this meadow, they drink of the flowing streams. The materialists, cow-like, graze also with the rest. They never raise their heads to see whether there is any heaven or any stars. They are submerged in the sea of materialism.'

289 Sohrab seems to suggest that 'Abdu'l-Bahá actually made these remarks on the following day (29 January). The present translator is grateful to Violetta Zein for bringing this possible discrepancy to his attention.

290 Ḥájí Amín and Dr Muḥammad Khán, according to Sohrab.

291 Sohrab offers this summary of 'Abdu'l-Bahá's remarks on this occasion: 'He ['Abdu'l-Bahá] has come to Paris striking the first note but he finds Paris is very cold. He was anticipating that in this trip he shall behold in this city the luminous torch of the Love of God [following His first trip there in 1911]. Now having arrived he finds that the inhabitants are steeped deeper in the darkness of materialism. Every mention is on

their lips excepts the mentions of God. They entertain every thought except the thought of the Kingdom of God. Every call is being heard in Paris except the call of the world of Light. As he pondered over this condition of the Parisians, he found that like unto the worms they are crawling in the dark strata of the earth. Day unto day they were going deeper and deeper, never desiring to extricate themselves from the gloom of these narrow labyrinths of the earth. Therefore it was his hope that the friends who were living in Paris may show an effort and make a move, that perchance its inhabitants may obtain a new tongue, may receive a new exhilaration, may take a goodly portion and a share from the heaven of illumination.'

292 A summary translation of this anecdote was previously published in Balyuzi, *'Abdu'l-Bahá: the Centre of the Covenant of Bahá'u'lláh*, pp. 375–6.

293 According to Sohrab, this was actually 'Abdu'l-Bahá's afternoon talk at His residence.

294 Sohrab's translation of Persian notes from this talk appears in the online supplement to this book: https://bahai-library.com/supplement_abdul-baha_europe_1912-1913.

295 Sohrab identifies this gentleman more fully as Mírzá Mihdí Khán Ghaffárí of Rasht. It may, however, be a reference to Mírzá Mihdí Khán, the baker and brother of Mírzá Faraju'lláh Khabbáz Káshání.

296 Sohrab writes that 'Abdu'l-Bahá 'received a favorable report' in response, which made Him very happy, and that He then told Mírzá Mihdí Khán that if he had brought Him 'the gift of a kingdom', he could not have made Him any happier, 'for He loved Mírzá Abu'l-Faḍl very much'.

297 According to Jasion, it is likely that one of these diplomats was Yúsuf Khán Naẓar-Áqá, the counsellor of the Iranian legation (*'Abdu'l-Bahá in France*, p. 331).

298 An English translation of French notes from this talk appears in the online supplement to this book: https://bahai-library.com/supplement_abdul-baha_europe_1912-1913.

299 Sohrab's translation of these remarks appears at the end of the talk cited in the preceding endnote.

300 Sohrab has this as two Russian women. A note by Jan Jasion (*'Abdu'l-Bahá in France*, p. 334, n. 794) appears to suggest that they could have been Vera de Blumenthal or Vanda K. Haack, two Russian-born Bahá'ís living in Paris, or possibly two women from among four Russian ladies who lived in Paris at the time and, while aware of the Faith, did not identify themselves as Bahá'ís: Véra Starkoff, Nina Halpérine-Kaminsky, Princess Praskov'ia Aleksandrovna Urusova, and Mrs Ra'fat Páshá.

301 15 Avenue Grueze.
302 The weekly gathering at the Dreyfus-Barney residence was held on Friday nights.
303 Sohrab has this as a dinner engagement that took place in the afternoon.
304 According to Sohrab, this was not Ḥájí Amín's associate, but in fact the identically-named diplomat Mírzá Mihdí K͟hán, the Mus͟híru'l-Mulk.
305 Qur'án 69:28–29.
306 Perhaps the 'one from an unspecified religious community' noted by Jasion ('Abdu'l-Bahá in France, p. 336).
307 Mírzá Muḥammad (1856–1916), who took the pen name Naʿím ('blessing'), was one of the most celebrated, skillful, and prolific Iranian Baháʾí poets. Although he is often associated with the village of Sidih in the province of Isfahan (as Zarqání has done here), Naʿím hailed more specifically from the hamlet of Furús͟hán in that village. An account of his life has been published in Balyuzi, *Eminent Baháʾís*, pp. 129–41. A shorter account that features translations of his poetry into English was written by Roy P. Mottahedeh and published as "Naʿím: A Baháʾí Poet" in *World Order*, second series, vol. 2, no. 2 (Winter 1967), pp. 47–53. Further details on Naʿím can be found in Momen, *The Baháʾí Communities of Iran*, vol. 2, pp. 51–4. A more comprehensive biography of Naʿím, written in Persian, has been published in Sulaymání, *Maṣábíḥ-i-Hidáyat*, vol. 3, pp. 114–171. His extensive output of poetry has been compiled in such anthologies as *Jannát-i-Naʿím* (2 vols.), *Kullíyyát-i-Naʿím*, *Aḥsanuʾt-Taqvím Yá Gulzár-i-Naʿím* (which begins with a selection of Tablets from Baháʾu'lláh and ʿAbdu'l-Bahá to Naʿím), and *Tad͟hkariy-i-S͟huʿaráy-i-Qarn-i-Avval-i-Baháʾí*, vol. 3, pp. 479–556. Additional English translations of poems by Naʿím have been published in Hatcher and Hemmat, *Reunion with the Beloved*, items 1, 11, 12, 15, and 16. Apart from his poetry, Naʿím is also well known for an *istidlálíyyih* (rational proof-treatise) that he wrote in defense of the Baháʾí Faith, which, as far as the present translator is aware, has not yet been translated into English.
308 Yúnis K͟hán Afrúk͟htih (1871–1948), or Youness Khan Afroukhteh, 'was educated in Persian and Arabic by Mirza Abu'l-Fadl Gulpaygani and learned French from various teachers including those at the French Lazarist school (later Collège St Louis). He also learned English. He was employed in the International Commercial Bank of Moscow. He visited ʿAbdu'l-Baha in 1897 and then from 1900 to 1909 served as ʿAbdu'l-Baha's secretary (probably because of his knowledge of European languages). During this time he studied medicine at Beirut for five years and spent the four months of the summer in ʿAkka and Haifa. He then returned to Tehran and set up a successful medical practice in

the city as well as teaching medicine and being appointed physician to various government departments and foreign embassies. He wrote an account of his time in 'Akka as well as an account of two subsequent journeys to Europe. He was a member of the Tehran Spiritual Assembly and later the National Spiritual Assembly' (Momen, *The Bahá'í Communities of Iran*, vol. 1, p. 74). The account of his time in 'Akka is titled *Kháṭirát-i-Nuh Sálih*, translated into English by Riaz Masrour as *Memories of Nine Years in 'Akká*; the one about his journeys to Europe is *Irtibáṭ-i-Sharq va Gharb* ('Union of the East and West') and, as far as the present translator is aware, has not yet been translated into English. An obituary of Afrúkhtih written by Habib Taherzadeh is published in *The Bahá'í World*, vol. 12, pp. 679–81, where it is notably mentioned that he served as the interpreter between 'Abdu'l-Bahá and Laura Barney at the historic luncheon talks whose transcripts would eventually be compiled and published as *Some Answered Questions*.

309 Sohrab's diary makes it clear that he was actually sent to Nice for this purpose the day before, 31 January; that he went from there to Monte Carlo on 4 February; and that he rejoined the Master and His retinue in Paris on the evening of 5 February.

310 This was at a 'settlement school founded by Victor Ponsonaille and his wife Fanny' (*'Abdu'l-Bahá in France*, p. 336), which ' 'Abdu'l-Bahá had previously visited . . . on 15 October 1911 during His first visit to Paris' (ibid. p. 339). An extensive eyewitness account of this particular visit was recorded by Isabel Fraser and is published in Jasion, *'Abdu'l-Bahá in France*, pp. 336–8.

311 Located at 46 Avenue de Malakoff, today Avenue Raymond Poincaré.

312 A reference to the Carnival of Paris.

313 A reference to Mirra Alfassa (1878–1973), who, according to Jasion, 'was so involved with the Bahá'í community that many took her to be a Bahá'í' (*'Abdu'l-Bahá in France*, p. 340, n. 815).

314 The weekly gathering at the Scott residence was held on Monday nights.

315 Zarqání appears to have redacted the names of these grandees and princes.

316 Zarqání appears to have redacted the names of these people from Rasht and Tabriz.

317 The present translator has not been able to locate the more detailed account referred to here; it seems not to be included in this volume.

318 A verse of poetry that some have attributed to Sa'dí.

319 Apparently at noontime, according to Sohrab.

320 An account of 'Abdu'l-Bahá's interview with Inayat Khan that day appears in the online supplement to this book: https://bahai-library.com/supplement_abdul-baha_europe_1912-1913. See also Jasion,

'Abdu'l-Bahá in France, pp. 344–5. Inayat Khan's own account of that meeting is published ibid. p. 343.

321 Jasion writes: 'To the delight of 'Abdu'l-Bahá, [Inayat Khan] played his vina and was accompanied on the tabla by an M. Ramakrishna' (*'Abdu'l-Bahá in France*, pp. 342–3).

322 Sohrab writes, 'Then the history of music and its origin was set forth by the Beloved, giving us the names of many instruments, singers too. He told us three stories of celebrated Persian musicians and how they graduated from the conservatories.'

323 Sohrab has this talk at noontime.

324 An English translation of Sohrab's Persian notes from this talk appears in the online supplement to this book:
https://bahai-library.com/supplement_abdul-baha_europe_1912-1913.

325 Sohrab writes, 'In the afternoon many prominent Persians who were formerly very influential in Persia came to see the Master. While he was talking to them suddenly the door burst open and in rushed a Persian, like a whirlwind, ran to the Master, kissed his hands, threw himself at his feet meanwhile talking. He asked his permission to read a poem and with a loud voice he recited a wonderful eulogy to the amazement of all those who were present. We were much impressed by his words.'

326 An Iranian student of law, according to Sohrab.

327 According to Sohrab, this actually happened the evening before (on 6 February at about 6:00 p.m.) at 'Abdu'l-Bahá's residence on 30 rue Saint-Didier.

328 Sohrab seems to suggest that this happened the following day (8 February) at 4:00 p.m.

329 According to Sohrab, this actually took place the day before (on 7 February).

330 Sohrab has recorded these remarks somewhat differently: 'How pitiful it is that man is satisfied with material things and so regulates his life as to gain more and more! He has made himself a "civilized animal," while the animals are uncivilized. The animals and birds from early morning till late in the evening are planning to gain food and grains; so also the people of this age are totally submerged in material affairs. It is strange that they are pleased with these trifling occupations. It is regrettable that the world of humanity is subjected to these afflictions; especially these countries that are so well built! The light of spirituality must shine from these regions and people become characterized with divine morals. They must become radiant beings, shining stars, luminous persons, and angels of heaven.'

331 An English translation of Persian notes from this talk appears in the online supplement to this book:

https://bahai-library.com/supplement_abdul-baha_europe_1912-1913.

332 See the entry on Gabriel Sacy in the 'Selected Biographical Notes'.

333 Zarqání's wording here seems to suggest that the widow and daughters of Gabriel Sacy were present during 'Abdu'l-Bahá's conversation with the Iranian envoy in Paris, 'Abdu'ṣ-Ṣamad Khán (the Mumtázu's-Salṭanih). According to Sohrab's chronology, however, 'Abdu'l-Bahá first met with the Sacys and then received the envoy privately later that day.

334 Jasion describes this as 'a long walk' (*'Abdu'l-Bahá in France*, p. 356) on which Sohrab accompanied 'Abdu'l-Bahá the entire time.

335 According to Sohrab, this was an excursion by carriage that lasted for about an hour.

336 Sohrab's account indicates that 'Abdu'l-Bahá went for a walk with Áqá Faraju'lláh Káshání at about 9:30 a.m. and returned at noon. Jasion writes that 'Sohrab does not indicate where they went' (*'Abdu'l-Bahá in France*, p. 357).

337 Jasion has this as 'an unknown journalist from the Netherlands' (*'Abdu'l-Bahá in France*, p. 359).

338 Sohrab's account makes no mention of a gathering at the Dreyfus residence that evening, but he does state that a meeting was held at the Scotts' studio at 5:00 p.m. (according to their weekly arrangement, this having been a Monday night). A summary of that meeting by Sohrab appears in the online supplement to this book:
https://bahai-library.com/supplement_abdul-baha_europe_1912-1913.

339 An English translation of French notes from this talk appears in the online supplement to this book:
https://bahai-library.com/supplement_abdul-baha_europe_1912-1913.

340 At 4:00 p.m., according to Sohrab.

341 According to Sohrab, this was Julie Siegfried (1848–1922), a French feminist then serving as chairperson of the National Council of French Women. Jasion writes that Siegfried 'had invited ['Abdu'l-Bahá] to meet Reverend Charles Wagner and to give a talk at her home [at 226 Boulevard Saint-Germain]' (*'Abdu'l-Bahá in France*, pp. 364–5).

342 At approximately 7:00 p.m., according to Sohrab.

343 Refer to *The Dawn-Breakers*, pp. 278 and 354, n. 3.

344 Sohrab's account suggests that 'Abdu'l-Bahá may have actually told this story the night before (10 February).

345 To the members of His retinue, according to Sohrab.

346 Sohrab's account suggests that this visit took place sometime in the morning (about 10:00 a.m.), rather than the afternoon, and that the visitors consisted of Alma Knobloch, Anna Köstlin, Annemarie Schweizer, and Gustav Eger.

347 According to Sohrab, 'Abdu'l-Bahá made these remarks after the Germans had left His presence.

348 According to Sohrab, this letter actually arrived two days earlier (on 10 February 1913), and enclosed with it were invitations from 'a number of societies in Budapest asking 'Abdu'l-Bahá to come there', including 'the Hungarian Peace Society, [the] Hungarian Esperanto Society, [the] Orientalist School, [the] Society of Scientists, and the British-American Society' (Jasion, *'Abdu'l-Bahá in France*, p. 361).

349 More precisely, Sohrab notes that Hippolyte Dreyfus took 'Abdu'l-Bahá to this banquet.

350 10 Place de la République.

351 This was at approximately 8:00 p.m., according to Sohrab.

352 Sohrab writes that 'two hundred guests' were in attendance.

353 Sohrab's English translation of Persian notes from this talk appears in the online supplement to this book:
https://bahai-library.com/supplement_abdul-baha_europe_1912-1913.

354 Sohrab's account seems to suggest that 'Abdu'l-Bahá's audience here consisted of the members of His retinue.

355 A fuller account of this episode appears in Balyuzi, *Bahá'u'lláh: The King of Glory*, pp. 125–6.

356 Zarqání seems to have conflated the London Library and the British Museum, which are two different institutions. The documents in question are indeed held at the British Museum, but in the area of it which is called the British Library.

357 Only a small sample from the much larger selection of these meaningless constructions quoted verbatim by Zarqání has been rendered into English here.

358 At 8:00 p.m., according to Sohrab.

359 According to Sohrab, this was actually the headquarters of the Theosophical Society of France, located at 59 Avenue de la Bourdonnais just past the Eiffel Tower.

360 An English translation of this talk appears in the online supplement to this book:
https://bahai-library.com/supplement_abdul-baha_europe_1912-1913.

361 Sohrab's translation of the closing prayer 'Abdu'l-Bahá chanted on this occasion is as follows:

O God, O God, O my Lord, O my Lord. I supplicate to Thee. I implore in Thy Presence, and invoke Thee with the tongue of my conscience; my soul my spirit and my mind, to shower down Thy merciful bestowals upon these holy souls, who have gathered in this great assembly.

I beg of Thee O my Lord, to favour them with the glances Thy mercifulness. I entreat of thee, O my Beloved to pour upon them the rain of Thy favour from the clouds of Thy mercy.

O Lord, O Lord, verily these are Thy servants, and Thy maid-servants, do not deprive them of the bounties of the rays of the Sun of Reality; do not make them portionless from the Ocean of Thy Generosity, and do not leave them in the darkness of them selves.

O Lord enlighten their hearts with the lights of unity, cheer their spirits with the mystic traces of Thy knowledge, illumine their eyes by beholding Thy signs, purify their souls with the wonders of Thy Majesty, inspire their consciences with the word of Thy Singleness, encircle them with Thy heavenly Graces.

Verily Thou art the Omnipotent and the Mighty.

O Lord O Lord, Thou seest the hearts humble before Thy Dominion, the soul rejoiced with Thy glad tidings, the spirits attracted by Thy holy fragrances.

O Lord confirm us in Thy good pleasure, assist us in Thy adoration, and cause us to become worthy servants, turning our faces toward the horizon of Singleness and illumined with the lights of the Sun of Thy Reality.

Verily Thou art the Clement, the Bounteous, and verily Thou art the Merciful of the most Merciful.

(Jasion, *'Abdu'l-Bahá in France*, p. 382; originally transcribed in Persian and translated by Mirza Ahmad Sohrab, carbon typescript held at the Bibliothèque Bahá'íe de France)

362 Sohrab's translation of Persian notes from this talk appears in the online supplement to this book: https://bahai-library.com/supplement_abdul-baha_europe_1912-1913. Furthermore, Sohrab's account suggests that 'Abdu'l-Bahá delivered this talk at noon.

363 An earlier translation of this telegram is as follows: 'I am Servant of Baha. His Holiness, Baha'o'llah is unique and peerless. All must turn to Baha'o'llah. This is the Religion of Abdul-Baha. Firmness in Covenant means love and obedience to the Command of Abdul-Baha. Announce this. (Signed) ABBAS' (*Star of the West*, vol. 3, no. 19 (2 March 1913), p. 8).

364 Mírzá 'Alí-Akbar Rawḥání Mílání, known as Muḥibbu's-Sulṭán, became a Bahá'í in 1890 or 1892 and spent much of his life reproducing Tablets, initially by transcribing them 'in his fine Naskh and Nasta'líq styles' (Momen, *The Bahá'í Communities of Iran*, vol. 1, p. 399), but eventually through photography, hectography (jellygraph), and lithography. He was also elected to the Spiritual Assembly of the Bahá'ís of Tehran in 1902 and became its secretary.

365 Sohrab's summary of 'Abdu'l-Bahá's portrayal of this anecdote appears in the online supplement to this book: https://bahai-library.com/supplement_abdul-baha_europe_1912-1913. Yet another version of the

same anecdote appears in Balyuzi, *Bahá'u'lláh: The King of Glory*, p. 22.

366 At 8:30 p.m., according to Sohrab.

367 According to Sohrab, Hippolyte Dreyfus was actually reciting passages from his translation of Bahá'u'lláh's *Epistle to the Son of the Wolf* into French, which had just been published.

368 Sohrab's chronology reverses the order of these two events: Mírzá 'Alí-Akbar Rafsanjání chanted the prayer first, and Mrs Richard then gave 'an introductory talk about the Faith' (Jasion, *'Abdu'l-Bahá in France*, p. 391).

369 An English translation of this talk appears in the online supplement to this book:
https://bahai-library.com/supplement_abdul-baha_europe_1912-1913.

370 Sohrab's translation of this prayer, originally in Arabic, is as follows:

I beg of Thee, O my God! My Lord! My hope, and my utmost desire! Verily Thou knowest my humility, my contrition, my poverty, my indigence, my agitation and my longing. I call upon thee with a heart overflowing with Thy love, a spirit stirred by the wafting of the graces of Thy Oneness and a soul assured by Thy commemoration and praise!

O Lord! O Lord! Verily these souls are attracted toward the Kingdom of Thy holiness and their hearts are enkindled with the fire of Thy love, and these spirits are soaring toward the apex of Thy Mercy.

O Lord! O Lord! Illumine the eyes with the lights of the Sun of Reality! Suffer the ears to hear the Voice of the Kingdom of Abha under all circumstances. Make us firm in Thy Cause, submissive before the Throne of Thy Majesty, acknowledging Thy Dominion, arising in Thy service, and engaged in Thy adoration. Verily Thou art the Merciful! Thou art the Omnipotent, and Thou art the Cleverest and the Wise.

(Jasion, *'Abdu'l-Bahá in France*, p. 396)

371 Sohrab has this as noon.

372 Sohrab has recorded some of the words 'Abdu'l-Bahá spoke on this occasion as follows: 'Man must enjoy these things but not be absorbed in them. Severance means the lack of attachment . . . There are certain souls who are very unhappy, if they lose anything to which to which they are attached. We must be attached only to God. We must praise Him for His Blessings. If we have plenty, we must be thankful; if we do not have anything we must not feel unhappy. We must attach our hearts to God and to those principles which will make possible for us to win life eternally. We must be attached to the Kingdom of God. Then in both worlds we shall obtain Everlasting Existence.'

373 More precisely, Sohrab writes that 'Abdu'l-Bahá was sending Mírzá 'Alí-Akbar Rafsanjání to the Swiss city of Lausanne to teach the Bahá'í Faith for one month, and that he departed at 7:00 p.m. accompanied by an

unnamed Arab Bahá'í. Jasion writes: "Abdu'l-Bahá was paying particular attention to the activities in Lausanne because of the actions of certain adherents of Mírzá Yaḥyá who were apparently causing confusion in the Persian and possibly Turkish and Egyptian communities there' (*'Abdu'l-Bahá in France*, p. 397). Refer also to the entry in this volume dated 14 December 1912, in which Zarqání mentions the indiscretions of Mírzá Yaḥyá Dawlatábádí, leader of the Azalís outside Iran, in Lausanne.

374 Siyyid Jamálu'd-Dín Burújirdí (d. 1907), whom Bahá'u'lláh honored with the title of Ismu'lláhu'l-Jamál ('the Name of God, the Beauteous'), was a *mujtahid* who became a Bábí and then a Bahá'í. Momen has described Burújirdí as 'probably the most prominent Baha'i in Tehran, and indeed in the whole country as far as the shah and government were concerned' (*The Bahá'í Communities of Iran*, vol. 1, p. 20), but his excessive ambition and disinclination to obey the leaders of the Faith made him a troublesome individual. After the passing of Bahá'u'lláh in 1892, Burújirdí began to demonstrate opposition to 'Abdu'l-Bahá and allegiance with His half-brother, Mírzá Muḥammad-'Alí, and this became public knowledge among the Bahá'ís when 'Abdu'l-Bahá expelled him from the community in 1897. From this point onward, Burújirdí was often stigmatized by the Bahá'ís as *pír-i-kaftár*, meaning 'the old hyena', and 'Abdu'l-Bahá Himself notably refers to Burújirdí with that epithet in Zarqání's entry in this volume dated 25 February 1913. Details on Burújirdí's life can be found in ibid. pp. 20–5 and passim, and idem., *The Bahá'í Communities of Iran*, vol. 2, pp. 17, 40, 87, 221, 227–8, 241, and 270.

375 At 4:00 p.m., according to Sohrab.

376 According to Sohrab, this was a 4:00 p.m. visit by Théophile Cart, an eminent Esperantist, with his Iranian students from the Free School of the Political Sciences in Paris.

377 An English translation of a report from this meeting (which includes remarks by 'Abdu'l-Bahá), originally written in Esperanto by Théophile Cart himself, appears in the online supplement to this book: https://bahai-library.com/supplement_abdul-baha_europe_1912-1913.

378 Sohrab's account makes it clear that this meeting actually took place the following night (of 16 February).

379 Jasion writes that this was actually the Faculté de théologie protestante de Paris (83 boulevard Arago, Paris 14), a seminary with mostly Lutheran faculty, and that 'Abdu'l-Bahá went there at 8:00 p.m. (*'Abdu'l-Bahá in France*, p. 403). An English translation of the dialogue that took place between 'Abdu'l-Bahá and Monnier appears in the online supplement to this book: https://bahai-library.com/supplement_abdul-baha_europe_1912-1913.

380 An authenticated Persian transcript of 'Abdu'l-Bahá's conversation with Monnier has been published in *Majmú'iy-i-Khiṭábát-i-Ḥaḍrat-i-'Abdu'l-Bahá*, pp. 737–43. An English translation was first published in Isabel Fraser Chamberlain, *'Abdu'l-Bahá on Divine Philosophy*, pp. 147–58. An annotated version of this early translation, prepared by Khazeh Fananapazir, has been published in ' 'Abdu'l-Bahá on Christ and Christianity: An interview with Pasteur Monnier on the relationship between the Bahá'í Faith and Christianity, Paris', in *Bahá'í Studies Review*, vol. 3, no. 1 (1993), pp. 7–10; available online at: https://bahai-library.com/abdulbaha_christ_christianity_monnier.

381 Sohrab writes, 'This Sunday morning the Master got up early, ordered Siyyid Asadu'lláh to prepare the tea and I to go out and bring a newspaper. It was six o'clock when I was drinking tea in His Presence.'

382 In the original Persian, *maṭrán*. Sohrab's account has this as 'a priest of an Orthodox sect'.

383 Mírzá Muḥammad-'Alí (1853–1937) was a half-brother of 'Abdu'l-Bahá who openly and actively opposed Him as head of the Bahá'í Faith after the passing of Bahá'u'lláh in 1892. Shoghi Effendi stigmatized him as 'the Arch-Breaker of Bahá'u'lláh's Covenant'. His many Covenant-breaking activities have been discussed in Taherzadeh, *The Covenant of Bahá'u'lláh*, passim.

384 The photographer was Valentin Vaucamps, who, according to Jasion (*'Abdu'l-Bahá in France*, p. 402), probably took the photograph(s) at the Lumina studio at 12 Avenue de la Grande-Armée.

385 Zarqání appears to have redacted this person's name. Sohrab's account seems to suggest that it was the Intiẓámu's-Salṭanih.

386 4:00 p.m., according to Sohrab.

387 170 Boulevard du Montparnasse. Of Hieston, Sohrab writes, 'She is a Bahá'í and only 3 weeks ago she arrived from America.'

388 'The King of Martyrs' is the title of Mírzá Muḥammad-Ḥasan, an eminent Bahá'í who was killed along with his brother, Mírzá Muḥammad-Ḥusayn ('the Beloved of Martyrs'), under circumstances described by Shoghi Effendi as follows: 'Their martyrdom was instigated by the wicked and dishonest Mír Muḥammad-Ḥusayn, the Imám-Jum'ih . . . who, in view of a large debt he had incurred in his transactions with them, schemed to nullify his obligations by denouncing them as Bábís, and thereby encompassing their death. Their richly-furnished houses were plundered, even to the trees and flowers in their gardens, all their remaining possessions were confiscated; Shaykh Muḥammad-Báqir . . . pronounced their death-sentence; the Ẓillu's-Sulṭán ratified the decision, after which they were put in chains, decapitated, dragged to the Maydán-i-Sháh, and there exposed to the indignities heaped upon them by a degraded and rapacious

populace' (*God Passes By*, pp. 200–01). A biographical account of both brothers, as well as English translations of Tablets revealed by Bahá'u'lláh in their honour, can be found in Balyuzi, *Eminent Bahá'ís*, pp. 33–51. A much more comprehensive biography in Persian featuring a more extensive selection of these Tablets can be found in 'Abdu'l-Ḥamíd Is͟hráq-K͟hávarí, *Núrayn-i-Nayyirayn*. The mother-in-law of the King of Martyrs was S͟hamsu'ḍ-Ḍuḥá, in whose honor 'Abdu'l-Bahá delivered a eulogy published in *Memorials of the Faithful*, ch. 68.

389 Sohrab's brief summary of this meeting, which includes his translation of some of 'Abdu'l-Bahá's remarks, appears in the online supplement to this book:
https://bahai-library.com/supplement_abdul-baha_europe_1912-1913.

390 According to Sohrab, this talk by 'Abdu'l-Bahá may have also included a discussion of 'the efficacy of the Holy Spirit':

Today our Beloved spoke on the efficacy of the Holy Spirit. Man cannot attain to the highest summit of human progress without the assistance of the breaths of the Holy Spirit. A man intellectually may become enabled to educate a few, but general education is imparted to the world of humanity through the prophets of God, because they are the real Instructors of the human race. The foundation of civilization is the amelioration of the conditions of morality; the basis of spirituality is the purity of morality. The Everlasting Glory of the world of humanity is in the readjustment of morality. The power and the potency of man is through the refinement of morality. And the beautification of morality is impossible except through the breaths of the Holy Spirit. Therefore whosoever is confirmed with the breaths of the Holy Spirit, will be assisted to confer a general education. This is the difference between the influence of religion and philosophy.

391 It seems this was Mírzá As͟hraf As͟hraf and three other students, all of whom were studying at various Parisian schools. Sohrab's translation of additional remarks from 'Abdu'l-Bahá to this group of students is as follows: 'I hope that you will study well; that you will acquire those sciences, which will be useful to Persia on your return. I trust you will fit yourselves to be the real pioneers of modern arts and sciences in Persia. The Persians in the past few ages have been only destroying, setting back that glorious nation in the scale of civilization, but I hope you will build. You will lay the solid foundation of true enlightenment. You are the young plants of the garden of hope, strive so that you may grow and develop and adorn the trees of your lives with delicious fruits' (Jasion, *'Abdu'l-Bahá in France*, p. 417). Sohrab further writes, quoting 'Abdu'l-Bahá's words in paraphrase, 'At six o'clock the students desired to leave for their school so the Master called them to His Presence and said: He was made very happy to meet them. He hoped the trees of

their existences may bring many fruits. Some of the young Persians who came to Paris learn only the vices of civilization. Now they must show them otherwise. May they study in such wise as to confer life upon Persia. May they be conducive to the promotion of the Cause of God! May they ameliorate the moral conditions of the nation! May they promote sanctity and holiness amongst the people! May they give impetus to progress, to agriculture, to commerce and arts.'

392 The first and second points are not included in Zarqání's account.

393 Sohrab quotes these remarks from 'Abdu'l-Bahá's talk: 'Now Europe in reality is in the utmost beauty and adornment. Material civilization has advanced greatly. It is a body in the utmost of comeliness, but regrettably it is not animated by the Spirit. How pitiful that it has not the heavenly illumination! How sad that it does not enjoy the Breaths of the Holy Spirit! It is a mirror in the utmost of transparency but a thousand times alas! that the rays of the Sun of Reality are not reflected thereon! It is a tree most verdant and elegant but alas! it produces no fruits. Come! Will you? Come ye together! Concentrate your spiritual forces! Arise with much fervor and enthusiasm! Show ye a united effort! Let a new attraction take possession of your hearts! Let a new spirit sweep over your temples, so that the Fire of the Love of God which is enkindled in your holy of holies may flame forth setting a spiritual conflagration to the whole of Europe. You must not rest day and night until you have breathed in this body a new spirit and ignited a light in this lamp.'

394 According to Sohrab, 'Abdu'l-Bahá apparently made these remarks on 19 February 1913.

395 According to Sohrab, this talk was actually delivered at noontime.

396 This was an address to the Alliance Spiritualiste, held at the hall of the Young Men's Christian Association (YMCA) at 2:30 p.m. that day.

397 An English translation of this talk appears in the online supplement to this book:
https://bahai-library.com/supplement_abdul-baha_europe_1912-1913.

398 Among them Louis Le Leu, secretary-general of the Alliance Spiritualiste, and Albert Jounet, the chairman-administrator. Sohrab's chronology, as portrayed by Jasion, seems to suggest that Beauchamp was the first to speak, then Le Leu, then 'Abdu'l-Bahá, and then Jounet. Sohrab's transcript of Le Leu's remarks is published in Jasion, *'Abdu'l-Bahá in France*, pp. 428–9. It seems that a transcript of Jounet's remarks is not available, but Jasion does characterize that talk as a lengthy one 'on the theme of the spiritual basis of peace' (ibid. p. 435).

399 These passages from Beauchamp's opening talk have been recorded in an untitled document held among Ahmad Sohrab's papers at the US Bahá'í National Archives, reproduced in Jasion, *'Abdu'l-Bahá in France*,

pp. 426–7. It is clear that this was a rather literal translation from the French. Only the remarks quoted by Zarqání in Persian translation are included here; see the citation just mentioned for a more complete transcript.

400 Humankind; possibly a literal translation of 'humanité', as the word in French takes the feminine form.

401 More correctly, 'that'.

402 Again, presumably humankind.

403 At 9:00 p.m., according to Sohrab.

404 Jasion writes that 'Abdu'l-Bahá 'did deliver a prayer for service and teaching' (*'Abdu'l-Bahá in France*, p. 436) on that occasion, but the text seems not to have been recorded by any of His attendants.

405 Khusraw Bimán was the first Zoroastrian to accept the Bahá'í Faith in India; he passed away in 1936 at the age of about 103 or 104 in Pune, where he is buried. In his autobiography, *Risáliy-i-Navíd-i-Jávíd*, Bimán describes his multiple attempts to obtain recordings of 'Abdu'l-Bahá's voice and the outcomes of each attempt:

As the means for capturing sound were at hand, repeated requests were made of the Master that He record His voice, and He consented to this strictly out of His grace. A number of records of His voice, as well as the voices of those who were with Him, were made. To transfer and produce those records, they were sent to Paris – since the necessary equipment was not available in Bombay – but in an unfortunate turn of events, on account of the hot summer heat, and owing to the fact that the records were not [adequately] protected, they all warped and the recorded voices were lost . . . Much later, my dear son, Sohrab . . . set off for the sanctuary of the Desired One. Humbly, bowing, he attained the Master's presence. As he had the equipment for capturing sound (a phonograph) with him, he implored the Master to record His voice once again. Sohrab captured the Master's voice on a few records, and after leaving His presence, he went at once to Paris and London, where he had those records produced. Some of the Master's words were in Persian, while some of them were in Turkish . . . As for the third time: When the Master returned from America to Europe, in Paris, Dr Muḥammad Khán – a friend of mine who treated me with great compassion and kindness – adjured the Master on behalf of this lowly servant once again, in view of the fact that He was in Paris and that all sorts of equipment were readily available in that city, to bestow a fresh bounty and have His voice be captured on a few [more] records. His request was accepted; the Master Himself went to that company [the recording studio], a few records of His voice were captured, and He Himself spoke of this joyful news in a sublime Tablet to this lowly servant . . .

(Quoted in Sulaymání, *Maṣábíḥ-i-Hidáyat*, vol. 10, pp. 35–7;

accessible online at:
https://www.h-net.org/~bahai/areprint/authors/sulayman/masabih10/Masabih_Hidayat_v10.pdf.

Rendered from the original Persian into English by the present translator. It should be noted that Sohrab, Bimán's son, was not the same person as Ahmad Sohrab.)

The Tablet of 'Abdu'l-Bahá to which Bimán refers is as follows:

He is God

O kind Khusraw! In Paris I went, for thy sake, to a phonographic recording studio. On two occasions were a talk and a chant of the Tablet of Visitation recorded, but the latter was left unfinished. I went a third time, but the studio failed to keep its promise. Although a time had been scheduled, the phonograph-recorder attended to other people, so I returned whence I had come. However, the first session, in which a talk was recorded, turned out well. The second session, devoted to the first portion of the Visitation, also turned out well. But as for the third session, since the studio did not keep its promise, the second portion of the Tablet of Visitation was not recorded. Hence, I offer my apologies . . .

(From a Tablet of 'Abdu'l-Bahá published in *Yárán-i-Pársí*, p. 447, selection no. 662. This provisional rendering by the present translator was approved at the Bahá'í World Centre for publication in this volume.)

For more on the recordings of 'Abdu'l-Bahá's voice produced in Paris, refer to Zarqání's entry dated 21 May 1913 in this book.

406 Probably at the recording studios of Pathé Frères at 98 Rue de Richelieu, Paris 2, according to Jasion (*'Abdu'l-Bahá in France*, p. 438). Sohrab notes that Dr. Muḥammad Khán accompanied 'Abdu'l-Bahá on this visit to the recording studio(s).

407 Sohrab has this talk in the morning, rather than the afternoon. His translation of it is published in the online supplement to this book: https://bahai-library.com/supplement_abdul-baha_europe_1912-1913.

408 At about 6:00 p.m., according to Sohrab.

409 Jasion writes that, on this occasion, 'Abdu'l-Bahá 'met a group of coffee merchants from Costa Rica. Apparently these devout Catholics were on their way back to New York from making a pilgrimage to the Holy Land. They enquired from 'Abdu'l-Bahá about His Faith. After hearing His explanation and short history, they declared their astonishment and indignation that for these teachings He should have been put in prison. Afterwards, He gave them some semi-precious ring stones as souvenirs' (*'Abdu'l-Bahá in France*, p. 439). Jasion adds that this group of coffee merchants probably consisted of Alejo Aguilar (b. 1880) and Ricardo Montealegre (b. 1873), who had both travelled from the Costa Rican capital of San José (ibid. p. 439, n. 1031).

410 At about 8:00 a.m., according to Sohrab.

411 According to Sohrab, the Dreyfuses were actually still asleep when 'Abdu'l-Bahá called on them, 'but they quickly rose' (Jasion, *'Abdu'l-Bahá in France*, p. 439).

412 Sohrab's account appears to suggest that this high-ranking Iranian, apparently from Azerbaijan, had been invited to attend a dinner engagement the evening after next (Tuesday, 25 February 1913), meaning the visit to which Zarqání alludes here had not actually happened yet. At any rate, it seems neither Sohrab nor Zarqání goes on to discuss this dignitary in their chronicles any further.

413 Sohrab's translation of some remarks from this talk is as follows: 'I hope that your intellectual powers may advance, your ideal knowledge may grow in proportion and the circle of your thoughts may expand, so that you may discover the divine worlds, worlds which are infinite. Just as there are phenomena infinite as regards to their forms and species, likewise the worlds of God are infinite. May you become informed everyday [sic] with a new mystery. Everyday [sic] may you obtain a new life. Everyday [sic] may you discover a new reality – so that you may find entrance to all the worlds of God' (Jasion, *'Abdu'l-Bahá in France*, p. 439).

414 Sohrab notes that Madeleine Sacy's mother, Marie-Elénore Coppin, was also present on this occasion.

415 Jasion has identified this daughter as Mercedes Sacy, who at eighteen was the eldest child of the family (*'Abdu'l-Bahá in France*, p. 439).

416 Sohrab writes: 'As the daughters are being educated in the Catholic Convent, they have become most devout and zealous in that front.'

417 According to Sohrab, it was 'Abdu'l-Bahá who had the last word in this discussion, stating: 'We follow Christ and not the priests. We give more importance to what Christ said than what the Popes and the cardinal[s] say. We are the followers of Christ. We love Him and we are always ready to sacrifice our lives for Him.'

418 Ra<u>sh</u>íd Pá<u>sh</u>á and Munír Pá<u>sh</u>á, according to Sohrab.

419 'For more than one hour', according to Sohrab.

420 Sohrab's account indicates that these two Persians were Fírúz Mírzá Fírúz (1889–1938), the Nuṣratu'd-Dawlih – an Iranian prince who was then serving as the attaché at the Iranian legation in Paris – and 'his younger brother', whom Jasion believes to have been Muḥammad-'Alí Mírzá Farmánfarmá'íyán (1891–1983), another Iranian prince who at the time was studying economics in Paris. Both men were the grandsons of Muẓaffari'd-Dín <u>Sh</u>áh (1853–1907; r. 1896–1907).

421 With regard to 'Abdu'l-Bahá's meeting with these two Persians, Fírúz Mírzá Fírúz (the Nuṣratu'd-Dawlih) and his younger brother, Sohrab

writes: 'Although ['Abdu'l-Bahá] was very tired, yet he spoke with them for a full hour.'

422 Sohrab's impression of this talk, which includes summary translations of 'Abdu'l-Bahá's remarks, appears in the online supplement to this book: https://bahai-library.com/supplement_abdul-baha_europe_1912-1913.

423 Sohrab's account seems to suggest that one of these people was Mírzá Mihdí Khán, the Mushíru'l-Mulk.

424 At 5:00 p.m., according to Sohrab.

425 A notable detail not mentioned here by Zarqání, but which Sohrab has recorded, is that, before 'Abdu'l-Bahá gave this address on Bahá'í martyrs (which, according to Sohrab, also included comments on 'the trials of Bahá'u'lláh'), He 'asked Mrs. Bernard and then Madame Richard to speak first'. Sohrab continues: '['Abdu'l-Bahá] is giving them wings with which they may fly when he leaves Paris and is training a few such men and women for public service. Both these women are able speakers and sincere Bahá'ís; so he has told them to speak in every meeting and rest assured that Bahá'u'lláh will inspire their hearts. He said, you must speak in every gathering. You must set the hearts aglow with the fire of the Love of God. You must shine like unto stars. You must illumine this city. If these conditions do not realize, there will be no fruits. Go out and speak. Speak with great determination. Turn your face to Bahá'u'lláh. Forget everything else. Forget yourselves.'

426 Manúchihr Khán Gurjí (d. 1847) served as governor of the province of Isfahan during the time of the Báb, in Whom he came to believe (see *The Dawn-Breakers*, passim). 'Abdu'l-Bahá's respect for Manúchihr Khán was immense, as evidenced not only by His favourable remarks on him in this chronicle, but also by the fact that He composed a Tablet of visitation in his honor (the original Arabic text of which is published in 'Abdu'l-Ḥamíd Ishráq-Khávarí, *Risáliy-i-Ayyám-i-Tis'ih*, pp. 195–6) and wrote, in a Tablet to the Bahá'ís of Qum – where Manúchihr Khán is buried – that they should visit his tomb from time to time on His behalf and light a few candles there, as this act will result in nearness to the threshold of divine grandeur (idem., *Má'idiy-i-Ásmání*, vol. 5, p. 227).

427 Another version of this account, recorded by Sohrab, appears in the online supplement to this book: https://bahai-library.com/supplement_abdul-baha_europe_1912-1913.

428 Sohrab has this as noon.

429 Sohrab offers a different account of the number of 'Abdu'l-Bahá's visitors that day: '['Abdu'l-Bahá's] voice was hoarse and he spoke with difficulty. Last night he slept very little and although he was not feeling well, while reclining in bed he received many visitors.' Quoting Sohrab, Jasion adds: 'Many Turks and Persians came to visit ['Abdu'l-Bahá] in

the afternoon. Edith Sanderson also called; to her, He spoke about teaching the Faith in Paris. The president of l'Alliance Spiritualiste, Albert Jounet, called with Georgine d'Ange d'Astre and had a lively discussion with 'Abdu'l-Bahá' (Jasion, *'Abdu'l-Bahá in France*, p. 446). The 'leader of the clergy' here, then, is a reference to Jounet. Also present during the dialogue that ensued between 'Abdu'l-Bahá and Jounet was Dr Muḥammad Khán, 'who sat on the edge of the bed massaging the feet of 'Abdu'l-Bahá' (ibid. p. 449).

430 Sohrab's more comprehensive transcript of the conversation between 'Abdu'l-Bahá and this gentleman, Albert Jounet, appears in the online supplement to this book:
https://bahai-library.com/supplement_abdul-baha_europe_1912-1913.

431 Sohrab writes that, despite 'Abdu'l-Bahá's illness, He paid a visit that morning to the Iranian envoy, 'Abdu'ṣ-Ṣamad Khán. When 'Abdu'l-Bahá returned, He received Edith Sanderson, Hippolyte and Laura Dreyfus, and the wife of 'Umar Páshá 'with two other ladies' (Jasion, *'Abdu'l-Bahá in France*, p. 450).

432 Sohrab notes that Rúḥá Khánum was suffering from an unspecified illness at this time; see Jasion, *'Abdu'l-Bahá in France*, p. 451.

433 According to Sohrab, 'Abdu'l-Bahá actually sent this telegram the following day (28 February 1913).

434 Sikkínih Sulṭán was 'a servant in the household of 'Abdu'l-Bahá' who 'frequently served as a nurse' and was 'for some unstated reason . . . not able to come to Paris' (Jasion, *'Abdu'l-Bahá in France*, p. 451). In his biography of 'Abdu'l-Bahá, Balyuzi writes: 'Sakínih Sulṭán was the widow of one of the martyrs of Yazd. She had a daughter named Fáṭimih, her only child, who died young, but left a baby, a solace for the stricken grandmother. Both because of her cruel bereavements and because of the services she had rendered (which included nursing both Mírzá Abu'l-Faḍl and Shoghi Effendi, during his first year at the university in Beirut), 'Abdu'l-Bahá always showed her a very generous measure of kindness. The tenderness of that kindness is shown in the many Tablets addressed to her' (*'Abdu'l-Bahá*, n. 233; see pp. 534–5).

435 Drawing on Sohrab's account, Jasion writes that "Abdu'l-Bahá's health showed great improvement after being ill for four days' (*'Abdu'l-Bahá in France*, p. 451). Thus, Zarqání's reckoning may have been off by a day at this point.

436 One notable visitor who stayed with 'Abdu'l-Bahá for more than an hour that afternoon, according to Sohrab, was Muḥammad-Valí Khán Tunukábuní (1846–1926), a prominent military leader of pro-Constitutionalist forces during the Iranian Constitutional Revolution and prime minister of Persia for three brief periods (1909–10, 1911, 1916). Jasion writes that Tunukábuní 'had met A.L.M. Nicolas in Persia and

was well acquainted with the teachings of the Báb' (*'Abdu'l-Bahá in France*, p. 452).

437 At about noon, according to Sohrab.

438 An English translation of some remarks from this talk appears in the online supplement to this book: https://bahai-library.com/supplement_abdul-baha_europe_1912-1913.

439 Sohrab has paraphrased the following remarks which 'Abdu'l-Bahá made to His German visitors on this occasion: '['Abdu'l-Bahá] had the greatest of love for the believers in Germany. They were the cause of the happiness of his heart. Although he has not yet visited Stuttgart yet his heart felt the susceptibilities of the Stuttgart friends. In reality they were firm and assured Bahá'ís. They were steadfast in the Covenant. God will confirm them. He told them last year and will repeat it this year that the Cause will be widely spread in Germany. After his return to the Orient, there will be a great awakening in Europe. When His Holiness the Báb declared his Cause, he would often state to his followers wait till the year nine, after his declaration. But after his martyrdom, the Bahá'ís were scattered and discouraged. When the year nine came around and at a time when even the name of the Báb was not mentioned and no one thought that the Cause will be rejuvenated, suddenly His Holiness Bahá'u'lláh appeared and all the horizons were illumined! Now, 'Abdu'l-Bahá likewise told them wait till nine years after this date and they will observe with their own eyes the spread of the Cause in Germany.'

440 Sohrab has this as 'a most prominent man from London' (Jasion, *'Abdu'l-Bahá in France*, p. 464). As with Zarqání's record, the gentleman is not identified.

441 An English translation of some remarks from this talk appears in the online supplement to this book: https://bahai-library.com/supplement_abdul-baha_europe_1912-1913.

442 Held at noontime, according to Sohrab.

443 Qur'án 39:68.

444 An English translation of some remarks from this talk appears in the online supplement to this book: https://bahai-library.com/supplement_abdul-baha_europe_1912-1913.

445 Zarqání had previously included the text of this article in his entry for 31 December 1912, but he reproduced it a second time in this entry. Accordingly, it has been repeated here in this translation.

446 'Knight of the Theologian Spirit'.

447 More precisely, Sohrab notes that Hippolyte Dreyfus was the one who took 'Abdu'l-Bahá for a drive and then returned Him to His residence.

448 Sohrab names Dorothy Hodgson (1884–1949), an Englishwoman who

identified as a Bahá'í at the time but would later leave the religion, as one of 'Abdu'l-Bahá's visitors on this occasion.

449 As Alma Knobloch herself makes clear in her response, 'Abdu'l-Bahá is speaking of these German Bahá'ís figuratively as her spiritual children. In reality, she never married or had children.

450 According to Sohrab's account, 'Abdu'l-Bahá actually addressed these words, as well as His additional remarks immediately thereafter regarding the Bahá'ís of Germany, to Wilhelm and Marie Herrigel the day before (4 March 1913) as they were about to leave Paris.

451 A fuller account of this brief talk, recorded by Sohrab, appears in the online supplement to this book:
https://bahai-library.com/supplement_abdul-baha_europe_1912-1913.

452 The title of Mírzá Ibráhím Khán, 'a well-known Bahá'í of Rasht' who 'died a martyr's death in 1921' (Jasion, *'Abdu'l-Bahá in France*, p. 507).

453 Sohrab is a bit more precise in calling it 'the early evening' (Jasion, *'Abdu'l-Bahá in France*, p. 469).

454 Sohrab has this as Abu'l-Qásim Khán Qaráquzlú (1856–1927), the Náṣiru'l-Mulk; brother of Mírzá Mihdí Khán, the Mushíru'l-Mulk; and regent of Persia from 1911 to 1914, who 'was in Paris on an official visit' (Jasion, *'Abdu'l-Bahá in France*, p. 469). Although Sohrab was in attendance and does note the length of 'Abdu'l-Bahá's visit with the Iranian envoy and regent ('an hour and a half' (ibid.)), it seems he 'did not transmit in his [daily] letter [to Harriet Magee] the notes he took of this meeting' (ibid.).

455 According to Sohrab, one of the Iranian grandees who visited 'Abdu'l-Bahá at about 6:00 p.m. and spent over an hour with Him that evening was Tunukábuní, who thrice served as Persia's prime minister.

456 On this day, 'Abdu'l-Bahá wrote a special Tablet for Áqá Faraju'lláh; Sohrab's translation of it is as follows:

To his honour Aga Faraj
Upon him be Baha-ollah El Abha!
He is the True One!

His Honour Aga Faraj like unto the wind sweeps across the deserts and like unto the birds soared over mountains and seas, till he arrived in Paris. Here he became the companion and the intimate friend of Abdul Baha. O God! Protect this rare soul from the evil influence of the erring ones and grant unto him a shelter and asylum under the shade of the Blessed Tree. Engage his tongue in sweet melody like unto the thankful birds, so that day and night he may spend his time in Thy glorification and praise!

(Sig) Abdul Baha Abbas.
(Jasion, *'Abdu'l-Bahá in France*, p. 470)

457 An English translation of this talk appears in the online supplement to this book: https://bahai-library.com/supplement_abdul-baha_europe_1912-1913.

458 Sohrab has this as two Indians and a young man from New York, but does not identify any of them.

459 Apparently of Iranian extraction, according to Sohrab.

460 Drawing on Sohrab's account, Jasion writes that 'Abdu'l-Bahá's remarks to these dignitaries were 'heavily laced with one humorous story after another' (*'Abdu'l-Bahá in France*, p. 472).

461 Sohrab has it as 'very cold, but sunny' (Jasion, *'Abdu'l-Bahá in France*, p. 474).

462 In the late afternoon, according to Sohrab.

463 Sohrab's translation of some praise which 'Abdu'l-Bahá expressed on that occasion for an unidentified Bahá'í woman in San Francisco is as follows: 'Truly I say, she is a real Bahai. See how the holy sanctified souls unconsciously express their sincerity and faithfulness in every word they say or write . . . While in America I strove day and night to prepare a few, holy sanctified souls to take up the burden of the Cause after my departure. A very few who have responded to this call have arisen to serve and to teach. As they were capable souls they forged ahead and advanced without much inaction on my part. In the middle of nights I constantly pray for them and beg of God to descend upon them His heavenly benediction! May they succeed in their noble task!' (Jasion, *'Abdu'l-Bahá in France*, p. 473).

464 A more comprehensive English translation of this talk appears in the online supplement to this book: https://bahai-library.com/supplement_abdul-baha_europe_1912-1913.

465 Drawing on Sohrab's account, Jasion's record of this stroll is slightly different; though it was apparently 'Abdu'l-Bahá's custom to 'walk along the banks of the Seine, cross the Pont d'Iéna, and walk by or under' the Eiffel Tower, on that particular day, He 'did not cross the bridge and contented Himself with sitting on a bench watching the children play' (*'Abdu'l-Bahá in France*, p. 475).

466 26 Rue de la Trémoille.

467 In addition to Zarqání, Sohrab also accompanied 'Abdu'l-Bahá on this visit to the home of Munír Pá<u>sh</u>á. Describing this meeting, as well as the character of Munír Pá<u>sh</u>á specifically, he writes: 'He was a wide awake man, well informed. His wife was a charming Turkish Lady who had called several times on the Master. They were beside themselves with joy. Both kissed the Beloved's hands. For two hours he stayed there talking on many subjects which were [of] interest to them. Both were very insistent that the Master should take a trip to Constantinople because his broad Teachings were much needed by the inhabitants of the near East.'

468 Sohrab's translation of these supplications, along with 'Abdu'l-Bahá's prefatory remarks, appear in the online supplement to this book: https://bahai-library.com/supplement_abdul-baha_europe_1912-1913. Sohrab, moreover, has this talk at noon rather than the morning.

469 According to Sohrab, these Persians were from Hamadan and had arrived the night before.

470 Sohrab has this as 'nearly three hours'.

471 'Abdu'l-Bahá gave Browne this pamphlet because 'Browne had stated more than once in his writings that he had not been able to find what the Bahá'í conception of life after death really was' (Balyuzi, *Edward Granville Browne and the Bahá'í Faith*, p. 110, n. 2), and in a Tablet written to Browne exactly one month earlier while in Paris on 9 February 1913 (the original text of which is published in *Má'idiy-i-Ásmání*, vol. 9, pp. 110–13), 'Abdu'l-Bahá had expressed His regret that 'their meetings in London were not more frequent because they had intended to talk about questions of metaphysics, including survival after death' (Balyuzi, *Browne*, p. 110).

472 Sohrab's more comprehensive translation of this talk – which, according to him, was given in the afternoon rather than the morning – appears in the online supplement to this book: https://bahai-library.com/supplement_abdul-baha_europe_1912-1913.

473 Delivered at noontime, according to Sohrab.

474 Sohrab writes, 'The day of our departure is in sight. The Master a few days ago cabled to Port Said to his daughter Rúḥá Khánum not to leave for Paris but wait in Port Said until his arrival. Yesterday he cabled to twelve countries of the Orient that he was on the eve of his departure for the Holy Land. He has written to several friends that the port of landing will be Port Said. All these are indications that erelong the Sun of the Covenant will shine from another horizon. Germany is destined to entertain the Beloved. The believers there are anxiously waiting to receive the King of Kings. They are very earnest, sincere Bahá'ís. Already much literature is spread throughout the whole German Empire through the indefatigable zeal of Mr. Herrigel and his co-workers. Miss Alma Knoblock [sic] in the last year has been teaching the Cause in Leipzig and other cities. There are a number of friends scattered here and there who expect to go to Stuttgart and visit the Beloved.'

475 Among them the Iranian envoy in Paris ('Abdu'ṣ-Ṣamad K͟hán), according to Sohrab, who writes that 'Abdu'l-Bahá did this 'toward the end of the afternoon' (Jasion, *'Abdu'l-Bahá in France*, p. 482).

476 After 9:00 p.m., according to Sohrab.

477 Sohrab's diary letter for this date seems to suggest that 'Abdu'l-Bahá addressed these words to a certain 'Mr. and Mrs. Wilkins', to whom he

refers in his letter dated 6 March 1913 as 'relatives of Mrs. Agnes Parsons of Washington D.C.'

478 Sohrab's account seems to suggest that not one, but three physicians examined 'Abdu'l-Bahá, and that this actually took place the following morning (13 March 1913).

479 On the subject of the Master's poor health at this time, Sohrab writes: 'The question of his departure from Paris was discussed and he intimated that in a few days he will depart for Stuttgart. He said that he must get a little stronger; that he did not have the tongue of complaint [i.e., that He was not disposed to complaining]. His sickness a few days ago was very serious. One night he got out of his bed to turn [on] the electric light; he was so weak that he fell on the floor and swooned. For a long time he was unconscious. Then when he came to himself, cold perspirations run all over his body. With the greatest of difficulty he arose and reached the bed. He went under the cover bed and was shaking with cold. Under such conditions he stayed in Paris, hoping that perchance the Fire of the Love of God will be ignited in the hearts; otherwise he had nothing to do in this city; if he was pursuing pleasures he could very easily go to Nice where the climate was most moderate. He lived for the Cause and not for his health. If he saw just now that his presence was needed in St. Petersburg or Siberia he would leave without delay; he would not wait one moment; he would not stop to think whether he was healthy or not. These considerations never came with the range of his thought.'

480 This banquet, held at 9:00 p.m. by Sohrab's account, was actually convened at the Petit Durand restaurant at 27 Avenue Victor Hugo (at the corner of Rue du Dome). Sohrab writes that eighteen guests were present, and that plans had been made to take a photograph, but this was ultimately not done as 'the photographer's flash did not work' (Jasion, *'Abdu'l-Bahá in France*, p. 484).

481 Sohrab's account seems to suggest that 'Abdu'l-Bahá met with Mírzá Mihdí Khán, the Mushíru'l-Mulk, not at the Iranian legation, but at the Hôtel Astoria (131 Avenue des Champs-Elysées), where they spent 'over an hour' discussing 'the striking differences between Western and Eastern civilizations', 'the customs and manners prevalent in each country', 'the status of the Persian students in Paris', and 'the American high cost of living' (Jasion, *'Abdu'l-Bahá in France*, pp. 484–5).

482 At 5:00 p.m., according to Sohrab.

483 According to Sohrab, this excursion lasted for about two hours. He writes: 'All the answers were illuminated; ['Abdu'l-Bahá] was most of the time quiet and when he talked it was about the complete heedlessness of all these crowds who were immersed in the sea of desire.'

484 Sohrab writes that this news was given through a cablegram delivered

by Hippolyte Dreyfus. Rúḥá Khánum, her husband Mírzá Jalál, and 'another lady' had already set sail and were to arrive in Marseilles around 18 March, and since 'Abdu'l-Bahá was planning to depart Paris for Stuttgart on that day, He decided to postpone the trip until after they had arrived.

485 Sohrab has summarized the question that prompted 'Abdu'l-Bahá's answer as follows: 'Mírzá 'Alí-Akbar [Rafsanjání?] asked ['Abdu'l-Bahá] that in the West it was often stated that in the Bahá'í Cause, work had taken the place of prayer and this had led to the wrong idea that there was no prayer in the Bahá'í Dispensation.'

486 According to Sohrab, this talk also concerned 'the importance of the Covenant', and he writes, 'This was the first time that ['Abdu'l-Bahá] had ever spoken about the Covenant in Paris, because the conditions are different. People do not comprehend the significance and importance of the Covenant. They all love the Master and will do anything he says and obey his commands but the Covenant is a subject that is seldom discussed here.'

487 Sohrab writes that 'Abdu'l-Bahá stayed home and told several stories that evening. His translations of two of these stories appear in the online supplement to this book: https://bahai-library.com/supplement_abdul-baha_europe_1912-1913.

488 According to Sohrab, 'Abdu'l-Bahá addressed these remarks to two ladies who had inquired about His health.

489 Probably a reference to Shu'á'u'lláh Bahá'í (Shua Ullah Behai), son of Mírzá Muḥammad-'Alí, the half-brother of 'Abdu'l-Bahá repeatedly condemned by Shoghi Effendi as 'the arch-breaker of the Covenant of Bahá'u'lláh'. Mírzá Muḥammad-'Alí had sent Shu'á'u'lláh to the United States in 1904 to actively promote schism within the American Bahá'í community, but his efforts proved entirely unsuccessful. The phrase Zarqání has used here, 'benighted Shu'á'', is a play on words, in that Shu'á' means 'ray' (of the sun).

490 Mírzá Badí'u'lláh (1867–1950) was a half-brother of 'Abdu'l-Bahá who sided with his older full brother, Mírzá Muḥammad-'Alí, in opposing 'Abdu'l-Bahá as head of the Bahá'í Faith after the passing of Bahá'u'lláh in 1892. Where 'Abdu'l-Bahá mentions, in the following quote, the 'support' He extended to Mírzá Badí'u'lláh, He may be referring to the money He provided him with in 1903 following a 'reconciliation' between the two – money that Mírzá Badí'u'lláh needed to pay a significant debt he owed to an American missionary. Although Mírzá Badí'u'lláh had ostensibly reconciled with 'Abdu'l-Bahá during this period, supposedly evidenced by a letter of his in which he described the Covenant-breaking activities of Mírzá Muḥammad-'Alí (translated into English by Ameen U. Fareed and published in 1907 as *An Epistle to the Bahá'í World*), in reality he maintained contact with Mírzá

Muḥammad-'Alí the whole time and never truly broke off his loyalty to him. Additional details on the life of Mírzá Badí'u'lláh can be found in Adib Taherzadeh, *The Covenant of Bahá'u'lláh*, passim. In 'Abdu'l-Bahá's *Will and Testament*, he condemned Mírzá Badí'u'lláh in these terms:

Gracious God! After Mírzá Badí'u'lláh had declared in his own handwriting that this man (Muḥammad 'Alí) had broken the Covenant and had proclaimed his falsification of the Holy Text, he realized that to return to the True Faith and pay allegiance to the Covenant and Testament would in no wise promote his selfish desires. He thus repented and regretted the thing he had done and attempted privily to gather in his printed confessions, plotted darkly with the Center of Sedition against me and informed him daily of all the happenings within my household. He has even taken a leading part in the mischievous deeds that have of late been committed. Praise be to God affairs recovered their former stability and the loved ones obtained partial peace. But ever since the day he entered again into our midst, he began afresh to sow the seeds of sore sedition. Some of his machinations and intrigues will be recorded in a separate leaflet. My purpose is, however, to show that it is incumbent upon the friends that are fast and firm in the Covenant and Testament to be ever wakeful lest after this wronged one is gone this alert and active worker of mischief may cause disruption, privily sow the seeds of doubt and sedition and utterly root out the Cause of God. A thousand times shun his company. Take heed and be on your guard. Watch and examine; should anyone, openly or privily, have the least connection with him, cast him out from your midst, for he will surely cause disruption and mischief.

The present translator is unaware of whether or not the leaflet to which 'Abdu'l-Bahá refers, which was intended to describe the 'machinations and intrigues' of Mírzá Badí'u'lláh, has been published.

491 Apparently the residence of Fatḥu'lláh Khán Akbar (d. 1938), an Iranian politician who would go on to serve as Persia's Minister of the Interior (1916) and prime minister (1920–21).

492 A translation of this talk appears in the online supplement to this book: https://bahai-library.com/supplement_abdul-baha_europe_1912-1913.

493 According to Sohrab, Fatḥu'lláh Khán Akbar and 'an unknown Armenian merchant' (Jasion, *'Abdu'l-Bahá in France*, p. 490) were among this group.

494 Zarqání appears to have redacted this person's name. Given the context, it may well be a reference to Fatḥu'lláh Khán Akbar, in which case his name would have been omitted to conceal his identity, probably at 'Abdu'l-Bahá's instruction.

495 'Abdu'l-Bahá is describing the dedication of the Cathedral of the Immaculate Conception in Denver, Colorado, 'which occurred on 27 October 1912' and 'in which 20,000 people participated' (Jasion,

'Abdu'l-Bahá in France, p. 490, n. 1167).

496 Among 'Abdu'l-Bahá's visitors that morning, according to Sohrab, was the Intiẓámu's-Saltanih, for whom He related this story: 'There was a Mírzá Faḍlu'lláh who was looking for a government appointment. He came one day to the Blessed Perfection and begged Him to use His influence before the secretary of one of the departments so that he may become appointed as a clerk. As he was a good and able man this was done and the next day the man took his position as a clerk. Now it so happened that the name of the chief clerk was also Mírzá Faḍlu'lláh and as he was an old man he soon died. By sheer audacity the first man took on his own initiative the place of the chief clerk because of the identity of the names, he signed all the documents and were taken to His Majesty for royal approval. Without noticing the change, the S͟háh approved the papers and after that the man filled this important position for many years and few knew of the change of personality.'

497 According to Sohrab, 'Abdu'l-Bahá actually did this the following day (18 March 1913).

498 At 5:00 a.m., according to Sohrab.

499 Zarqání's account of the following anecdote has 'Abdu'l-Bahá using the word *ruhbán*, or 'monks', while Sohrab's account in English – which is more comprehensive – uses 'nuns' (Jasion, *'Abdu'l-Bahá in France*, pp. 493–5).

500 Siyyid Mihdí Dihají (1836–1920) 'became a Babi in 1268 [AH]/1851 [CE] and lived for a time in Baghdad while Baha'u'llah was there. He visited Baha'u'llah in Edirne in 1867, after which he was directed to live in the house of Baha'u'llah in Baghdad for a while. He fled Baghdad just before the Baha'is there were exiled to Mosul in 1868. Later he established himself in 'Akka and made trips from there to Iran to teach the Baha'i Faith. Baha'u'llah gave him the title Ismu'llah ul-Mahdi (the Name of God the rightly-guided). He arrived in Tehran in 1300 [AH]/1882 [CE] and was among the Baha'is arrested there that year ([cf. Momen, *The Bahá'í Communities of Iran*] 1:35–50). He used to travel under the name of his nephew . . . Siyyid 'Ali Akbar, in order to benefit from British proection. At first, after the passing of Baha'u'llah, he supported 'Abdu'l-Baha and even wrote a treatise against Mirza Muhammad 'Ali. He went to 'Akka, wanting to marry his son to 'Abdu'l-Baha's daughter, and when he failed to achieve this, he went over to the side of Mirza Muhammad 'Ali in mid-1910, writing a treatise attacking 'Abdu'l-Baha. Towards the end of his life, a local man tricked him out of all his money and he was left destitute' (Momen, *The Bahá'í Communities of Iran*, vol. 2, pp. 449–50).

501 Sohrab also has these remarks which 'Abdu'l-Bahá made in praise of Mírzá Abu'l-Faḍl that day: 'He is a most blessed soul. He has sacrificed his life to the Cause of Baha-ollah. He does not think of his own com-

fort, his ease and his life. He is a real monk. He is the embodiment of sincerity' (Jasion, *'Abdu'l-Bahá in France*, p. 495).

502 Sohrab has also attributed these remarks to 'Abdu'l-Bahá, which He apparently made on this same occasion: 'Paris is like a very large, clean stable where many millions of horses are well fed, well-kept and well trained; but you do not expect to find spirituality, the Knowledge of God, the Love of God in a stable. Do you? If you do find [them], then God has worked a miracle.'

503 Sohrab's account seems to suggest that 'Abdu'l-Bahá addressed these remarks, as well as the anecdote that follows, to Claire Bernard on an occasion when she, Alfred Bernard, and Edith Sanderson had visited Him.

504 cf. Bahá'u'lláh, *Gleanings*, CLXII: 'The All-Merciful hath conferred upon man the faculty of vision, and endowed him with the power of hearing. Some have described him as the "lesser world", when, in reality, he should be regarded as the "greater world". The potentialities inherent in the station of man, the full measure of his destiny on earth, the innate excellence of his reality, must all be manifested in this promised Day of God.'

505 According to Sohrab, 'all [their] trunks were transferred to Martha-Pension' at 5:00 p.m. the following day (19 March 1913).

506 This was the Martha-Pension hotel (known today as the Waldorf Trocadéro), which according to Jasion 'was a small hotel, built in 1891 and calling itself a "family hotel"' (*'Abdu'l-Bahá in France*, p. 498). 'Abdu'l-Bahá had moved there the previous afternoon with the help of Hippolyte and Laura Dreyfus-Barney, along with 'several other Persians' (ibid.). Jasion writes that 'Abdu'l-Bahá stayed in room no. 17, Mírzá Maḥmúd Zarqání and Mirza Ahmad Sohrab in no. 18, and Siyyid Asadu'lláh Qumí in no. 20, adding that 'arrangements were made for them to board there, except that 'Abdu'l-Bahá's meal would be cooked at the home of the Dreyfus' and brought to the hotel' (ibid.).

507 According to Sohrab, 'Abdu'l-Bahá left the hotel for Miss Sanderson's home at 9:00 a.m. that day, where He stayed till noon; had His lunch at the Dreyfus residence, where He rested for the afternoon; called on Miss Sanderson again at 4:00 p.m.; and then returned to the hotel at 5:00 p.m. In having been given the title 'Rúḥíyyih Khánum' (which she and her contemporaries would spell 'Roohie'), Miss Sanderson should obviously not be mistaken for Mary Sutherland Maxwell, who would go on to marry Shoghi Effendi and also be known as Rúḥíyyih Khánum, but was only a toddler at this time.

508 The term translated here as 'the five *siyyids*' is *sádát-i-khams*, a title conferred by Bahá'u'lláh on five brothers from the Báqiroff family of Rasht who accepted the Bahá'í Faith and served the Cause with out-

standing devotion. For more information on this family, refer to Handal, *The Khamsis: A Cradle of True Gold.* A biography of the *sádát-i-khams* has also been written in Persian; see Ruhollah Mehrabkhani, *Khándán-i-Sádát-i-Khams.*

509 According to Jasion, these included Tablets to a Mary C. Haybittle in South Africa, Dr Zia Bagdadi in America, Louisa Getsinger in Chicago, and the Báqiroff family in Tehran (*'Abdu'l-Bahá in France*, pp. 499–500).

510 Sohrab writes, 'Siyyid Aḥmad [Báqiroff] and myself went out to buy candies, fruits, nuts and cakes for the Fete. We got two large tables in the salon and decorated them tastily [tastefully] with lilacs, roses and other flowers.'

511 Jasion seems to suggest that these visitors included Ḥájí 'Alí-Qulí Khán, the Sardár-i-As'ad, as well as Ashraf Ashraf, 'Ísá Ṣádiq, and Mírzá Maḥmúd Murshidzádih, all Persians who were studying in Paris at the time (*'Abdu'l-Bahá in France*, p. 500).

512 At Avenue de Malakoff 64.

513 Sohrab writes, 'There were more than [a] hundred young Persians many of them dressed in French army clothes as they are army students. Mírzá Ḥusayn ['Árif] read his poem and toward the end a volume of applause greeted him. The whole embassy was decorated with flags and flowers. Large tables were groaning under the weight of delicacies. It was a lively scene of Persia in the making that one can seldom see anywhere else in Europe. After an hour we said goodbye to the Persian Ambassador.' According to Jasion (*'Abdu'l-Bahá in France*, pp. 503–4), the diplomatic personnel from the Iranian legation and consulate in Paris who attended would probably have included 'Abdu's-Ṣamad Khán (the Mumtázu's-Salṭanih), envoy extraordinary and minister plenipotentiary; Yúsuf Khán Naẓar-Áqá, counsellor; Ardishír Khan Naẓar-Áqá, first secretary; Amír Khán Bahárlú, third secretary; Ḥasan 'Alí Khán, third secretary; Nicolas Sursock, attaché; Prince Fírúz Mírzá Fírúz (the Nuṣratu'd-Dawlih), attaché; and Henri Allard, chancellor. Other likely attendees include these individuals from the Consulate-General, located at ave. Velasquez, 2: Hermann Back de Surany, consul-general; Louis Hohl, chancellor; and Dr. Georges Kendirdjy, secretary.

514 Fortunately, Mírzá Ashraf Ashraf, who was not a member of 'Abdu'l-Bahá's retinue but was present on that occasion, has recorded this summary of His address: ' 'Abdu'l-Bahá extended his solicitude and bounty to all, wished them a Happy New Year and praised their efforts in the pathway of acquiring knowledge and the sciences. He spoke at length about the historical backgrounds of the Arab and European cultures and stated that the latter owed much to the former. He described how knowledge and the sciences of the Arabs had been

passed on to the Europeans through the Spanish. He added, "You must also learn from the Europeans and acquire the qualities and knowledge they have in order to offer them as gifts to Persia. I will pray that you succeed." In complete silence, the audience listened very attentively and with the greatest respect. When 'Abdu'l-Bahá's explanations had come to an end, the Minister invited Him into another room for tea. After a quarter of an hour, the Master came back and we had the honour of seeing Him once again before He left with Mr. Dreyfus' (Jasion, *'Abdu'l-Bahá in France*, p. 502).

515 An English translation of this talk appears in the online supplement to this book:
https://bahai-library.com/supplement_abdul-baha_europe_1912-1913.

516 Sohrab's account suggests that 'Abdu'l-Bahá actually composed this Tablet to Dr Zia Bagdadi the previous morning (of 21 March).

517 A reference to Sargent's Travel School for Boys, a private American school.

518 According to Sohrab, Stanwood Cobb actually called on 'Abdu'l-Bahá the following day (23 March). A partial record of their conversation appears in the online supplement to this book:
https://bahai-library.com/supplement_abdul-baha_europe_1912-1913.

519 Jasion has this somewhat differently: 'Later, ['Abdu'l-Bahá] went by taxi with Ahmad Sohrab and called on Sâlih Münîr Paşa and his wife. Madame Lachenay, several Turks, and a journalist were also present. 'Abdu'l-Bahá gave an exposition on the essential and non-essential parts of religion. He spoke in Turkish and Münîr Paşa translated into French' (*'Abdu'l-Bahá in France*, p. 506).

520 Jasion writes: 'After a short rest, ['Abdu'l-Bahá] received three very prominent Persians. Here we have another case of anonymity, probably at the request of 'Abdu'l-Bahá' (*'Abdu'l-Bahá in France*, p. 506).

521 Bahá'u'lláh, *Summons of the Lord of Hosts*, p. 135.

522 Jasion writes: 'At three o'clock, 'Abdu'l-Bahá went to call on Ahmed Paşa who was not at home. From there, He went to the Bois de Boulogne by taxi and drove around the park, past its meadows, lakes, waterfalls, and throngs of people. A sudden downpour sent the people scattering. When He returned, He found several people waiting' (*'Abdu'l-Bahá in France*, p. 509).

523 The Kitáb-i-Mubín – literally, 'the Lucid Book' – refers to a collection of some two hundred (mostly Arabic) Writings of Bahá'u'lláh prepared by Zaynu'l-Muqarrabín. With the notable exception of the book's first entry, the Súriy-i-Haykal (which includes Bahá'u'lláh's Tablets to Pope Pius IX, Napoleon III, Czar Alexander II, Queen Victoria, and Náṣiri'd-Dín Sháh), the vast majority of its contents have not yet been made available in authorized English translation. Following its initial

publication in Bombay (1890), the book was printed again in Tehran (1964) as the first of seven volumes of Bahá'u'lláh's Writings, compiled by the National Publishing Trust of the Bahá'ís of Iran and composing a series entitled *Á<u>th</u>ár-i-Qalam-i-A'lá* ('Traces of the Supreme Pen'). It was printed a third time in Canada (1996) by the Institute for Bahá'í Studies in Persian (Dundas, Ontario). In their prefatory note to this third printing, the publishers state that Bahá'u'lláh 'almost certainly' (p. 2) reviewed and approved the contents of the initial version of this compilation.

524 Jasion seems to indicate that this actually took place two days later (on 26 March), writing that Hippolyte and Laura Dreyfus-Barney had called at a 'late hour' (*'Abdu'l-Bahá in France*, p. 521) and 'stayed a long time discussing the writings of Mírzá Yaḥyá (Ṣubḥ-i-Azal)' (ibid.).

525 Sohrab's account indicates that Dávúd eventually arrived in Paris on 30 March 1913 and 'had a long interview with the Beloved ['Abdu'l-Bahá]' that day.

526 Henri and Sophie Moser were actually Swiss; see Jasion, *'Abdu'l-Bahá in the West*, p. 304.

527 Sohrab's account suggests that Stanwood Cobb, along with 'Porter Sargent and some of their students' (Jasion, *'Abdu'l-Bahá in France*, p. 519), actually visited 'Abdu'l-Bahá the previous day (25 March) at 5:00 p.m.

528 Sohrab has paraphrased 'Abdu'l-Bahá's remarks to these American students as follows: 'The Beloved welcomed them most cordially. One of them said that they have heard much about the Bahá'í Movement from Mr. Cobb and they think it a great privilege to find themselves in the Presence of 'Abdu'l-Bahá. 'Abdu'l-Bahá said that he was likewise most pleased to meet them, that this Cause has become worldwide. In a short space of time it has permeated throughout all the regions for it has a magnetic power which attracts all the intelligent men and women toward its center. Were a person [to] be informed with the reality of this Cause he would believe in it; for these teachings are the Spirit of this age. The Bahá'í Movement imparts life. It is the Cause of love and amity amongst humankind. It establishes communication between various religions and different nations. It removes all antagonism. Therefore when this Cause is fully spread in Europe, warfare will be a thing of the past, universal Peace will be realized, the oneness of the world of humanity will be practised, religion and science will work hand in hand. Then these various human families will become one family. There will remain no racial distinction such as French, English, American, German, Arab, Turk and Persian. They will become all one. The Bahá'í Movement bestows upon man a new spirit, a new light and a new motion. It enlarges the sphere of thought. It illumines the horizon of the intellect. It expands the arena of comprehension. This

world is like unto an egg. As long as man lives within the shell of the egg he cannot soar heavenward. All the nostrils are afflicted with cold and they cannot inhale the sweet fragrances. All the eyes are blind and they cannot see the rays of the sun of Reality. In brief, the Master talked at length about the intellectual and spiritual powers latent in man and in what manner was man enabled to bring under his contract all the phenomena of nature through this [G]od-given power and how through this heavenly power Divine Civilization will be established. After the meetings they asked questions and received satisfactory answers. Then tea was served and when they left the Master they were all inspired with the noblest ideals of brotherhood. His last words to them were 'I hope each one of you [may] be as luminous as this electric light' and unconsciously they all turned their eyes and looked at the globe of light!'

529 Sohrab has this meeting between 'Abdu'l-Bahá and the Mosers four days later on 31 March at 10:00 a.m.

530 Zarqání is probably referring to Sohrab's daily correspondence with Harriet Magee, a Canadian Bahá'í living in New York at the time, which he kept up until 30 June 1913 when he was in Port Said. This correspondence has yet to be published, but is available upon request from the U.S. Bahá'í National Archives and has been used extensively for these endnotes.

531 In fact, 31 March was the last day of 'Abdu'l-Bahá's sojourn in Paris before departing to Germany.

532 Sohrab's diary indicates that the events in this entry actually took place two days later, on 1 April 1913. Hence, in his reckoning, Zarqání seems to have skipped 30 and 31 March, jumping from 29 March (a Saturday) to 1 April (a Tuesday). Accounts of these missing dates summarized from Sohrab's diary are as follows:

Sunday, 30 March 1913: Mírzá Yuḥanná Dávúd arrived in Paris with a copy of a Tablet of 'Abdu'l-Bahá to Ḥájí Amín in His own handwriting (for which Sohrab includes an English translation) and had a long interview with Him, discussing the spread of the Cause in London, Bahá'u'lláh's prediction about the fall of Edirne, and the nonsensical writings of Mírzá Yaḥyá, from which He read a sample; 'Abdu'l-Bahá also received many other visitors, including an unnamed 'Frenchman of unusual attainment and capacity', followed by two unidentified visitors, and then another unnamed person from London; 'Abdu'l-Bahá had lunch 'with us' (presumably His Persian attendants, with the possible addition of others who were with Him at the time); in the afternoon, Persians, Americans, and Parisians came 'one after another' to hear 'Abdu'l-Bahá speak; at 5:00 p.m., the Sipahdár-i-A'ẓam (Muḥammad-Valí Khán Tunukábuní) called on 'Abdu'l-Bahá, and the two of them had 'a long discussion' on 'the fall of Adrianople and [the]

Persian problem'; 'Abdu'l-Bahá went with Áqá Mírzá Jalál, Dr Muḥammad Khán, and Fu'ád Effendí to visit Rúḥá Khánum at the Maison de Santé, then called on Mr and Mrs Dreyfus-Barney, and returned to the hotel at about 9:30 p.m., taking His dinner in His own room.

Monday, 31 March 1913: An unnamed Englishwoman called on 'Abdu'l-Bahá and told Him that, upon her return to England, she 'desired to have a weekly meeting in her apartment', which elicited 'Abdu'l-Bahá's praise for 'her efforts in the service of the Cause'; 'Abdu'l-Bahá was visited by Beatrice Irwin, who read for Him a poem she had composed called *The Mount* that was 'much admired' by Him, and He then gave her the title Mihrabán ('kind') and 'wrote a very inspiring prayer in her autograph book' (for which Sohrab includes an English translation); at 10:00 a.m., Mr and Mrs Moser called on 'Abdu'l-Bahá, and Zarqání in fact describes that meeting in greater detail than Sohrab (refer back to Zarqání's entry for 27 March 1913, which would have been four days before the visit actually took place); at around 12:00 p.m., 'Abdu'l-Bahá and Sohrab went to Miss Sanderson's residence to say goodbye to her and her mother, and 'Abdu'l-Bahá praised 'the beautiful qualities of Miss Sanderson', with Sohrab writing, 'He declared by Bahá'u'lláh, again He declared by Bahá'u'lláh, that she was His real daughter – that, in His estimation, there was no difference between her and Rúḥá; both were His real daughters'; returning to the hotel, 'Abdu'l-Bahá 'sat at the table with the rest of the friends and ate His lunch most heartily', and then 'after His rest, some letters were read to Him from America and answers were revealed immediately'; at about 3:00 p.m., 'two of the important princes of Persia called on Him and they were most lovingly received in His own room', and He spoke to them about 'America and its natural scenery, especially the mountains of Colorado looking up to the sky', as well as His 'address in the Jewish Synagogue' (presumably His talk at Temple Emanu-El in San Francisco on 12 October 1912); at 5:00 p.m., He instructed His attendants to summon a car, and then went, with Dr Muḥammad Khán and Fu'ád Effendí, to visit Rúḥá Khánum at the Maison de Santé for the last time before He and His retinue left Paris for Stuttgart; returning to the hotel at 7:00 p.m., 'Abdu'l-Bahá met Aḥmad Páshá, who had been waiting for Him, and the two of them spoke for half an hour before 'Abdu'l-Bahá went up to His room; 'Abdu'l-Bahá then called Sohrab and Zarqání to His presence and 'spoke about the wonderful confirmation which will descend upon all those who arise with the deepest sincerity to teach the Cause of God'.

533 Sohrab has this as approximately 8:15 a.m.

534 Sohrab writes, 'The Master went with Mon[sieur] Dreyfus in his auto and we got two taxis for ourselves and other friends.'

535 Sohrab mentions additional details about this train ride: that 'Abdu'l-Bahá and Siyyid Aḥmad Báqiroff rode first class, while the other members of 'Abdu'l-Bahá's retinue were in another part of the train for second-class passengers; that Siyyid Asadu'lláh Qumí prepared 'a fine lunch' consisting of 'rice, chicken, matzoon, etc.'; and that tea was served at about 3 o'clock, shortly after which 'Abdu'l-Bahá wrote Tablets in response to letters from America.

536 'At a time when its people were unaware' is an allusion to Qur'án 28:15. It is worth noting that, according to Alice Schwarz's memoirs (manuscript, p. 2), she had heard from Dr Edwin Fisher on 31 March that 'Abdu'l-Bahá would arrive in Stuttgart the following day and lodge at the Hotel Marquardt.

537 Sohrab notes that 'Abdu'l-Bahá stayed at room no. 150 on the second floor of the Hotel Marquardt.

538 A brief summary of 'Abdu'l-Bahá's first few days in Stuttgart, originally written in German and translated into English, has been published in *Star of the West*, vol. 4, no. 4, pp. 66–69.

539 Sohrab's account differs slightly and mentions additional details: '. . . I telephoned to Mr. Herrigel and Mr. Ekstein [sic] and a letter was despatched by special messenger to Miss Knobloch. When over the phone I told Mrs. Herrigel that 'Abdu'l-Bahá was in Stuttgart[,] I could feel by the vibrations of her voice that she almost jumped up into the air with delight and surprise! "What! What! 'Abdu'l-Bahá here! In Stuttgart! Is this possible!"' On the following day (2 April), 'Abdu'l-Bahá sent the following cablegram: 'With Joy and happiness reached Stuttgart' (*Star of the West*, vol. 4, no. 2, p. 41).

540 More precisely, Sohrab writes that 'Abdu'l-Bahá first received Wilhelm Herrigel and then Adolf Eckstein. Alma Knobloch and Margarethe Döring also came sometime afterwards, but by that point 'Abdu'l-Bahá had already retired for the evening. Jennifer Redson Wiebers has corroborated this, writing that, when Margarethe Döring informed Alma Knobloch that 'Abdu'l-Bahá was staying at the Marquardt in Stuttgart, 'They went directly to the hotel. Sohrab told them that 'Abdu'l-Bahá was resting and asked them to return early the next morning to arrange their meetings, to avoid confusion or conflict' (*Alma Sedonia Knobloch: Maidservant of the Divine Plan*, p. 208).

541 Sohrab's account indicates that he and the other members of 'Abdu'l-Bahá's retinue actually went to a nearby restaurant and then returned to the hotel 45 minutes later.

Germany

542 Both Sohrab's account and German reports suggest that the events in this entry actually took place the following day (2 April).

543 This may have been Alma Knobloch. With regard to 'Abdu'l-Bahá's first morning in Stuttgart, Wiebers writes, 'Alma flew into 'Abdu'l-Bahá's open arms and began to weep. He asked, "Are you happy now? How is everything?" She replied, she had worked so hard her hair had turned grey and He countered, "If your bones had melted it would also be well for such a Cause . . ." 'Abdu'l-Bahá then spoke about the importance of love between believers. Alma recalled that He said:

It is very necessary that love and unity exist between the believers. In New York there were 800 believers at one time and when I arrived there only 80 on account of disunity, petty quarrels. When I left, they were in perfect unity and love, there must be unity amongst Bahá'ís. When the believers are not united the people will say, "If there's no unity among you, how can you teach unity for the whole world?"

In his letters, Ahmad Sohrab recalled Alma's visit to the Master:

Miss Alma Knoblock [sic] came and the Master arose from His seat and greeted her most unusually! Oh, Miss Knoblock [sic]! Oh! Miss Knoblock [sic]! She was very welcome. She loved her very much! His heart was attached to her. In reality, she was the blessed of the Kingdom. Her heart was pure and attracted, otherwise she could not serve the cause so well. Her sincerity confirmed her in the service of the Cause. While in America, He always remembered her, He never forgot her. He was greatly attached to the severed friends who are selfless. Let her thank God that she has attained such a bounty! God willing her heart will become more illumined day unto day. He will ever pray for her and all the German believers so that the confirmations of God may descend upon them. If she taught one soul in a city and he was attracted, after one year he would make ten Bahá'ís. And so on and so on. I can write many more pages but there is no time to write.

Alma remembered what 'Abdu'l-Bahá told her that morning:

I asked if I should return to Leipzig soon & Abdul-Baha said: yes. You must go to many cities & teach. All over Germany, when you have made one good believer in a place, they will then spread the teachings. You must always be the means of keeping the Stuttgart Assembly together, be their support & strengthen the others. When mentioning Leipzig, He said many pure souls will arise who will serve the cause of God in Germany, simply for the love of Bahá'u'lláh. The teachings will be spread all over Germany, the Holy Spirit will illumine this country. The Germans are very susceptible, they are very religious.'

(*Alma Sedonia Knobloch*, pp. 208–09).

544 Sohrab has this as 8:30 a.m. to 1:00 p.m., and writes that 'everyone carried a bouquet of flowers in his or her hand'. He adds that Edwin Fisher, Adolf Eckstein, and Alma Knobloch all translated his English interpretations of 'Abdu'l-Bahá's remarks into German, but also notes that a number of the friends who visited during this time did speak English. Most probably the first to arrive at 8:30 a.m. were Edwin

Fisher and Alice and Albert Schwarz with their daughter, Olly (manuscript A. Schwarz, p. 2). Julie Stäbler notes that she came at 11:15 a.m., carrying a bouquet of lilacs.

545 'During His stay in Stuttgart, 'Abdu'l-Bahá received the friends at the hotel daily from 9 to 11 a.m. His engagements and meetings were planned for the afternoons and evenings. The German believers communicated with 'Abdu'l-Bahá through double translation, Herrigel, Eckstein, Fisher or Alma translating Sohrab's English translation into German' (Wiebers, *Alma Sedonia Knobloch*, p. 208).

546 At 3:00 p.m., according to Sohrab.

547 At about 5:00 p.m., according to Sohrab.

548 Sohrab notes that this group of people also included sculptors, artists, and musicians.

549 'In the car ride back to the hotel, 'Abdu'l-Bahá told Herrigel, "You must thank God that you are sitting in this car with the Centre of the Covenant. The importance of this event cannot be fully appreciated at this time"' (Wiebers, *Alma Sedonia Knobloch*, p. 210).

550 Sohrab's account makes it clear that Consul Schwarz, who had visited 'Abdu'l-Bahá earlier that morning with his wife and daughter, took 'Abdu'l-Bahá to this second gathering in his 'large and magnificent car', which he subsequently offered 'to the Master to use . . . at his discretion'. Sohrab adds that, although it was raining at the time, these friends 'had waited outside for half an hour to be the first ones to greet him'. According to Joseph Hannen, 'Abdu'l-Bahá addressed these remarks to those in attendance on this occasion: 'How attracted and enkindled are the German Bahais! How full of love they are! Love does not need a teacher' ('Abdul-Baha at Stuttgart and Esslingen, Germany'; published in *Star of the West*, vol. 4, no. 9 (20 August 1913), p. 162).

551 Sohrab writes: 'Walking ahead of this large group, I was surprised to see so many people. I am sure there were more than 200, and yet half of the friends are not notified about the Beloved's arrival.' Later on in his notes for this day, Sohrab adds: 'There were so many people that some in the other rooms were standing on their chairs in order to get a glimpse of the Master as he walked to and fro.'

552 'This evening I am united with those souls of God, with people, who have really learned to listen to the call of God, with people, whose faces are enlightened by the rays of the Sun of Truth . . . All nations of this earth have been waiting until this day for the Promised One to appear. The Promised one of the Old Testament was Jesus Christ. The Jews waited anxiously day and night for Him . . . But when His Holiness Jesus Christ appeared, they were deprived of the blessing to understand him. They tormented him with persecution and ill-treatment and at last they crucified him . . . They are still awaiting their Saviour . . . The Saviour

appeared 2000 years ago, but up to the present day, they have not yet recognised him . . . They waited 1500 years for this Saviour and when he came, they denied him . . . We must really thank God that we are to-day aware of the vast importance of the coming of Baha'o'llah. The veil is removed, and you have opened your eyes and sought for truth. Therefore, the light of understanding shines in your hearts . . . You have heard His call. This is the greatest mercy. God hath chosen you for His service. Whilst all others are asleep, you are awakened, the greater number of mankind are blind, but you are seeing . . . If you thank God a thousand times an hour for this mercy, you are nevertheless unable to thank him enough' (quoted in Wiebers, *Alma Sedonia Knobloch*, pp. 211–12).

553 An appellation conferred on 'Abdu'l-Bahá by Bahá'u'lláh in His Lawḥ-i-Arḍ-i-Bá (Tablet of the Land of Bá); see *Tablets of Bahá'u'lláh*, p. 227.

554 Both Sohrab's account and German reports indicate that the events in this entry actually took place the following day (3 April).

555 Sohrab writes, 'Before nine o'clock the friends started to come. I may say there were many "meetings" instead of "interviews" from 9 to 1 o'clock. Every few minutes the room was filled . . .', and notes that Alma Knobloch, Anna Köstlin, and Margarethe Döring were among the first to visit 'Abdu'l-Bahá that morning.

556 With regard to 'Abdu'l-Bahá's remarks that morning, Wiebers writes, 'He talked about the great bounties bestowed upon Stuttgart. He told the friends, "I hope that our happiness will be eternal, I hope we will be together in all the spiritual worlds. We will find refuge and shelter under the protection of the gifts of Bahá'u'lláh. There is a union which has no end, a life which is not followed by death"' (*Alma Sedonia Knobloch*, p. 212).

557 Sohrab's account seems to indicate that the person who made this comment (who actually phrased it as a question: 'What can I say when people ask me: "Whom did you go to see?"') was 'Miss Pollock', a reference to Mrs Susan Pollock, the sister of a Bahá'í living in Washington D.C. by the name of Aseyeh Allen, whom Zarqání has occasion to discuss in his entry for 17 April.

558 At 3:00 p.m., according to Sohrab.

559 To clarify: this is not the royal palace located in the centre of Stuttgart (which can be seen from the Marquardt), but a summer palace situated northwest of the city.

560 Located at Alexanderstraße 3, according to Sohrab.

561 Sohrab states that the original words spoken by 'Abdu'l-Bahá on this occasion 'could not be preserved' as Zarqání was absent, but notes that 'Consul Schwarz had his own special stenographer to take down the address'. Sohrab also writes that 'prominent men and women of Stuttgart were present' at this meeting, which was held in a 'large parlor',

and that one of the attendees was 'the Minister of the Church of the King', who 'spoke English fluently' and 'had a private interview [with 'Abdu'l-Bahá]'. German accounts indicate that Sohrab translated 'Abdu'l-Bahá's talk into English, and that Edwin Fisher provided a German translation (the text of which is published in Gollmer, *Mein Herz ist bei euch: 'Abdu'l-Bahá in Deutschland*, pp. 31–7), but no mention is made of the non-Bahá'í visitors noted by Sohrab. Furthermore, Alice Schwarz has recorded an amusing anecdote from that occasion; she 'knew that in the Orient dogs were not permitted inside the homes, so she locked away the family Dachshund. Despite all her efforts, the dog pushed through a half-opened door and ran into the room where he jumped on her in front of the Master! She begged the Master for forgiveness, to which He replied, "There is no need for apologies, a dog has many attributes. It is loyal, affectionate, watchful, frugal and without wrong"' (Wiebers, *Alma Sedonia Knobloch*, pp. 212–13).

562 At 8:00 p.m., according to Sohrab, who writes that this hall was 'where the first public meeting [in Germany] was to be held'.

563 According to Joseph Hannen, 'more than five hundred persons were present' at the Bürgermuseum ('Abdul-Baha at Stuttgart and Esslingen, Germany' in *Star of the West*, vol. 4, no. 9 (20 August 1913), p. 162). Sohrab writes: 'As we entered the place, there was no room to move. Hundreds, probably five or six hundred Bahais and friends were gathered. With much difficulty a lane was made for the Master to ascend the platform.' Later on in his account for this day, Sohrab notes: 'After the meeting there were so many people who wanted to shake hands with the Master that it was impossible to move around. Everybody rushed forward to kiss his hands, yet in all their movements there was dignity and respect. As the Master came out they filed like a regiment of soldiers and he shook hands with almost every one. Outside around the car they were again gathered together and as he entered it there were hundreds of hands with hats and handkerchiefs waving loving farewell to the Beloved of their hearts!'

564 An English translation of this talk appears in the online supplement to this book:
https://bahai-library.com/supplement_abdul-baha_europe_1912-1913.

Sohrab's paraphrase of 'Abdu'l-Bahá's opening remarks, written in the third person, is as follows: 'He has come to them from a very distant land. He travelled back and forth more than 20,000 miles to reach to Germany. He has been in prison for 40 years. Young he entered the prison, he came out as he stood before them. Notwithstanding the vicissitudes of prison life and the weakness of the body he accepted the hardships and inconveniences of travelling, covering such large distances to come here and behold their illumined faces. His aim was that perchance the world of humanity may be illumined . . . Praise be to

God that the Radiant Century hath come. Praise be God that the spiritual springtime hath pitched its tent. Praise be God this is the age of the discovery of the realities of things. Verily, verily he said unto them[:] This age is the age of lights! This age is the age of sciences! This age is the age of the appearance of truth! This age is the age of the extension of the sphere of thought! This age is the greatest divine age! This age is the age of Everlasting Life! This age is the age of the Breaths of the Holy Spirit! This age is the age of the blossoming forth of all the hidden virtues of the world of humanity!'

565 Sohrab's translation of this prayer is as follows: 'O Thou kind God! This congregation is the sheep of Thy flock and Thou art the real shepherd! These souls are Thy children and Thou art the loving Father! O God! Encircle them with the glances of Thy Mercifulness! Open before their faces the doors of Thy Guidance! O God! descend upon them Thy heavenly Confirmation! Make their eyes seeing and their ears hearing! Quicken their hearts and gladden their spirits: May all of us take a portion and a share from the Sea of Thy Providence! May each one of us be sheltered beneath the Tabernacle of Thy Protection! O God! We are poor, unlock before us the doors of the Treasures of Thy Kingdom! O God! We are humble[,] endear us in Thy Realm! O God! Establish affiliation between the hearts and attract the spirits to each other, so that all humanity may enter beneath the all-inclusive Tent of the oneness of the world of humanity! May wars and rumors of wars be entirely forgotten! May humankind attain to the highest summit of felicity! O God! Answer our prayers! Verily Thou art the Kind! the Giver! the Generous! and the Bounteous!'

566 Sohrab adds an interesting detail on this score: 'When Mr. Ekstein [sic] could not remember the exact word in German, dozens of voices were raised from different corners, giving him the English word, showing that there were quite a considerable number who could understand English.'

567 Sohrab's account indicates that most of the events in this entry actually took place the following day (4 April).

568 Joseph Hannen writes:

April 4th, many groups were seen at the hotel. Among other things Abdul-Baha said that morning, after four hours of consecutive talk: 'I was most happy to see the believers of Germany so holy, so pure and so united. They are the Angels of the Paradise of Abha. You pray that the flame of the Divine Fire may be ignited in all Germany.'

('Abdul-Baha at Stuttgart and Esslingen, Germany', in *Star of the West*, vol. 4, no. 9 (20 August 1913), p. 162).

569 Sohrab's account seems to suggest that this particular visit by Alma Knobloch actually took place the day before (2 April).

570 Alice Schwarz has also recorded these remarks of 'Abdu'l-Bahá from

that morning: 'People thought they could extinguish the Light in Persia but however it begins to shine in every part of the world. This proves that if something is good it can never be extinguished. His Holiness Jesus Christ in His days only attracted 11 followers. At that time the Jews imagined that His light would be extinguished by His Crucification [Crucifixion]' (Wiebers, *Alma Sedonia Knobloch*, p. 213).

571 Sohrab calls this event 'a children's party', and Balyuzi describes it as 'a meeting (which was more like a festival) on behalf of the children whom [Anna Köstlin] taught' (*'Abdu'l-Bahá*, p. 382). Extracts from letters of Alma Knobloch and Mirza Ahmad Sohrab to Pauline Knobloch Hannen, which give firsthand accounts of the children's meeting at Esslingen, have been published in *Star of the West*, vol. 4, no. 9, pp. 155 and 162. Ulrich Gollmer notes that, while Anna Köstlin did indeed hold a regular children's class (or Sunday school) in Esslingen, most of the children who attended this meeting were actually not part of her class, and that the meeting was held at a public building known as the Altes Museum (private correspondence with Ulrich Gollmer dated 15 April 2020).

572 Sohrab writes: '. . . at four o'clock Consul Schwarz with his wife and daughter came with their car to take the Master to Esslingen . . . Another auto was hired for the other Persian friends and after a few minutes we were driving through the most beautiful part of the country . . .'

573 The following account of the children's meeting in Esslingen has been published in *Star of the West*, vol. 4, no. 9 (20 August 1913), pp. 155 and 162:

The most impressive feature of the letters from Stuttgart was the description of the children's meeting, at Esslingen, about which Miss Knobloch wrote as follows:

'We have had some wonderful meetings; the one in Esslingen surpassed them all. It was the children's meeting, last Friday, April 4th, 1913, in the afternoon. They had secured a very pretty hall, which was most beautifully decorated with greens, plants and flowers, with large and small tables near the walls and round tables in the center. About fifty children and eighty adults were present. In a smaller room adjoining the hall the children had been assembled holding flowers in their hands, forming two lines for Abdul-Baha to pass through. It looked most beautiful as Abdul-Baha came upstairs. He passed through a short hall and looked so pleased and delighted to see the dear children.'

Mirza Ahmad Sohrab says of this scene: 'I was overcome with surprise, emotion and joy, and could not contain myself; the tears filled my eyes. It was the most beautiful, the most heavenly, the most artistic picture that I have ever seen in all my life. It was so beautiful! I cannot describe these things; one must feel them, see them. It was a glorious day for these people, in a far-away town in Germany, to see with their own eyes the Beloved of all nations. What love! What attraction! What enkindlement these German believers have!

'The children handed Abdul-Baha their flowers as he came to them and greeted them. When Abdul-Baha's hands were full, he handed the flowers to one of the Persians, and went up one side and down the other. Then he gave them small boxes of chocolates and bon-bons. They were radiantly happy. Then he spoke to them, saying: "These children are of the Kingdom, they are illumined with the Light of God. They have pure hearts, clear as crystal, wherein the rays are reflected. I love them very much. They are mine. I hope they will receive Divine education, that they may receive Heavenly training; become fragrant plants in the Garden of Abha. They are very dear to me. May God guide and protect them, make of them useful men and women for the advancement of the Kingdom on earth."

'Then Abdul-Baha entered the hall. I had to push the people back, for they had come to the door to see what was going on. He seemed greatly pleased, as he entered the hall, to see the decorated tables and the green background. After a little while, he gave an address, which I took down. Tea was then served, and cake and chocolate were on the table. A photograph was then taken of the entire group, a copy of which I am sending you. After this Abdul-Baha got into the automobile, the children crowding around and waving their flowers. Then one after another stepped up and handed their fragrant tokens. O, it looked really beautiful; I cannot describe it, so wonderfully sweet! The children waving their dear little hands, and Abdul-Baha in the auto, covered with flowers, waving his blessed hands to them. Abdul-Baha said that this event would go down in history. The following were his words spoken on the morning of April 5th, at Hotel Marquardt, Stuttgart: "The effect of last night's meeting will be put on record in the world of eternity. The mentioning of it will be throughout centuries and will be recorded in the countries of the Orient. Because these children are tender plants, their hearts are clear and transparent. They have not yet come to the dross of the world; that is why Christ said: 'Blessed are the children, for they are of the Heavenly Kingdom, being pure of heart.' That was a spiritual meeting, a heavenly meeting, the Light of the Kingdom was shining upon it. The Confirmation of the Spirit surrounded that meeting."'

574 Sohrab writes: 'More than one hundred children, boys and girls, most of them dressed in spotless white, each one a bouquet of flowers in his or her hand, waving in the air as a welcome to the King and suddenly the chorus of "Alláh-u-Abhá" was raised from all!'

575 According to Sohrab, these were 'candies in small decorated boxes', which 'Abdu'l-Bahá 'had brought with Him' and which He 'divided amongst [the children]'.

576 Sohrab notes that he translated this talk into English, and Adolf Eckstein translated Sohrab's interpretation into German. Among the remarks 'Abdu'l-Bahá made in His talk were these: 'I recognize my own face on your bright countenances . . . This assembly will be engraven on the book of my memory, it will ever be before me in my thoughts . . .' (Wiebers, *Alma Sedonia Knobloch*, p. 213).

577 According to Sohrab, more than 500 men, women, and children had gathered in front of the hall to take the photograph, and this aroused the curiosity of onlookers, who 'had never experienced such an event in all their lives'. Ulrich Gollmer writes that this figure is 'quite exaggerated', observing that a photograph taken on this occasion shows roughly 150 people in attendance (private correspondence with Ulrich Gollmer dated 15 April 2020).

578 '. . . as ['Abdu'l-Bahá] walked out to the car the children arose to scatter rose petals at His beloved feet. In the end, the children crowded around 'Abdu'l-Bahá's automobile waving flowers' (Wiebers, *Alma Sedonia Knobloch*, pp. 213–14).

579 Sohrab's account suggests that the events in this entry actually took place the following day (5 April).

580 Which 'Abdu'l-Bahá prepared 'with his own hands', according to Sohrab, who goes on to relate this anecdote from that morning: 'A little incident which shows more than anything else ['Abdu'l-Bahá's] extreme courtesy and thoughtfulness was this: He had just given me the cup of tea and I was going to drink it, when he remembered, Sayyid Assadullah had no tea; so he told me, he was going to call him to come in. I put my cup on the table and wanted to go in his place. "No, no" he said, "You drink your tea. It will get cold. I will go and tell him to come." Just think of it! How thoughtful and considerate he is even to his nearest servants – servants who are ready to sacrifice their lives for him.'

581 Sohrab identifies this person only as 'a man' whom 'Abdu'l-Bahá 'picked out from another group'.

582 Meaning 'moon'.

583 Sohrab notes that this boy's name was Hefner, and that he was probably not more than four years old, but that he was nonetheless 'very intelligent and a true Bahai'. Sohrab continues: 'He has been coming every day and receiving much love from the Master. [His parents] told the Master he had already taught all the children of his quarter about the Bahai Cause and was full of love for Abdul Baha."' Ulrich Gollmer has identified the boy as Otto Häfner (1908–1978), who would go on to become the longstanding treasurer of the National Spiritual Assembly of the Bahá'ís of Germany (private correspondence with Ulrich Gollmer dated 15 April 2020). Wiebers writes that Häfner was five years old at the time, and that he 'brought the Master a basket of red

apples decorated with pink carnations' (Wiebers, *Alma Sedonia Knobloch*, p. 214). An obituary for Häfner, which mentions his encounters with 'Abdu'l-Bahá as a child, has been published in *Bahá'í World*, vol. 17, pp. 473–4.

584 An older translation of these words is published in *Star of the West*, vol. 9, no. 18 (7 February 1919), p. 201.

585 According to Sohrab, 'Abdu'l-Bahá's visitors that day included Adolf Eckstein, who came at about noon, and also 'the editor of a monthly German magazine which is published in Switzerland'. Sohrab writes that this editor 'desired to write a monthly article on the Bahai revelation', noting that 'the Master approved of his plan' and that the editor would 'start next month'.

586 Sohrab's account indicates that Edwin Fisher was also present on this occasion.

587 Sohrab notes that 'Abdu'l-Bahá walked through the buildings for two hours, and that at one point He said the following: 'On [the] one hand this wonderful palace shows the high civilization of the Saracens in Spain and on the other hand it makes one sad to contemplate that all these marvellous traces of . . . Arabian civilization are entirely forgotten by the people of the Orient and instead of advancing they have been retrograding.' Sohrab adds that, as they were returning to the hotel, 'Abdu'l-Bahá 'thanked most heartily Frau Consul for giving such a good time in the afternoon', and that He 'evidently enjoyed the outing very much'.

588 Sohrab writes that Consul Schwarz and Wilhelm Herrigel came to 'Abdu'l-Bahá's hotel at 8:00 p.m. to take Him to this gathering.

589 According to Sohrab, Adolf Eckstein's two sons had 'come from another part of Germany to be present' that evening. Also in attendance were Wilhelm and Marie Herrigel, Consul Schwarz, and Susan Pollock.

590 Sohrab writes that, after dinner, 'Abdu'l-Bahá looked at Eckstein, Herrigel, and Schwarz and said, 'You are three fine spiritual champions. I am going to let you wrestle with each other to see which one is the victor.'

591 Sohrab's account indicates that the events in this entry actually took place the following day (6 April).

592 Sohrab writes: 'Being Sunday, before nine o'clock the believers started to come. There were so many that crowds were standing outside ready for the room to be emptied so that they may be able to come in.'

593 Wiebers's account suggests that a cousin of Anna Köstlin's, Bertha Bahnmüller – along with her fiancée, Mr Bopp – may have been among those in this group (Wiebers, *Alma Sedonia Knobloch*, pp. 215–16).

594 Sohrab's account seems to indicate that these words were addressed to 'a girl who desired to enter into the convent as a nun'.

595 The comparison to a lion stemmed from Pfund's physique, which was apparently quite robust, as Zarqání will go on to observe in his entry for 27 April. It is worth noting that Pfund – a Bahá'í from Fellbach, Baden-Württenberg whom Sohrab describes as 'an old man with long flowing beard' – was the father of Marie Herrigel.

596 A lengthier paraphrase of these remarks, recorded by Sohrab, appears in the online supplement to this book: https://bahai-library.com/supplement_abdul-baha_europe_1912-1913.

597 Sohrab writes that the consul came at 3:00 p.m. with his car, and that he took 'Abdu'l-Bahá first to Esslingen, then to 'a portion of the Black Woods', and then through 'the cherry-blossom country'. According to Ulrich Gollmer, however, this is actually a misunderstanding by Sohrab, who probably mistook 'Schwarzwald' (Black Forest) for 'Schurwald'. Gollmer writes: 'In the time available, even a short trip to the Black Forest would not be possible. Even the closest outskirts of the Black Forest lie at a distance of about 50 kilometres from Stuttgart (as the crow flies). The Schurwald lies east of Stuttgart, close to the "Remstal", a fruit-growing area with countless cherry trees' (private correspondence with Ulrich Gollmer dated 16 April 2020).

598 According to Sohrab, this was actually the home of the consul's mother-in-law, where 'all the friends had gathered to take photographs with the Master in the large park of Wangenburgstr 5'. ('Wangenburgstr' is erroneous and should read 'Wagenburg Str.') Since the 1930s, the house and garden are now located at Wagenburg Str 9.

599 Sohrab writes that one of these seven groups consisted exclusively of men.

600 Sohrab notes that Consul Schwarz took these smaller photographs, and that 'Abdu'l-Bahá was standing under a cherry-blossom tree when they were taken.

601 At Karlstraße 25 Zuffenhausen. Zuffenhausen was incorporated into Stuttgart in 1931, and the address is now Friesenstraße 25. Wiebers writes, 'Today the Schweizer house is the home of the Spiritual Assembly of the Bahá'ís of Stuttgart. One room dedicated to 'Abdu'l-Bahá is used for prayer and in it are many of His personal items. National and local teaching projects and events ever continue to be spread from this house' (*Alma Sedonia Knobloch*, p. 216).

602 Sohrab's account indicates that this clergyman actually visited 'Abdu'l-Bahá the following morning (of 7 April).

603 Sohrab writes that 'more than 800 people were present' at this meeting, which he states was 'a public meeting arranged by a committee of Bahai women' and had been held 'in the largest hall of the museum'. Sohrab goes on to say that 'this was the largest meeting ever held in Germany in the Bahai Cause and no doubt its results will be immense in the

future'. German sources note that this meeting began at 8:30 p.m. in the 'Kleiner Saal' (small hall) of the Obere Museum, and that 250 people were in attendance (a number corroborated by Wiebers; see *Alma Sedonia Knobloch*, p. 216), indicating that the estimates given by both Zarqání and Sohrab were quite exaggerated.

604 An English translation of a complete account of this occasion (including Consul Schwarz's opening remarks and 'Abdu'l-Bahá's address), prepared from German stenographic notes, appears in the online supplement to this book: https://bahai-library.com/supplement_abdul-baha_europe_1912-1913.

605 Although Zarqání's entry for this day ends here, Sohrab writes that 'Abdu'l-Bahá and His retinue were then driven to the apartment of Alma Knobloch and Margarethe Döring (at Neue Weinsteige 23) to have dinner. Sohrab goes on to say that, 'The apartment is on the fourth floor and after such a strenuous day it was a little difficult to walk up to the fourth floor but in order to make them happy the Beloved did it with pleasure.' 'Abdu'l-Bahá and His retinue then returned to the hotel when it was 'rather very late', and they all went 'directly to [their] rooms to sleep'. Wiebers offers this account of that evening at the apartment of Alma Knobloch and Margarethe Döring:

'This was the night Alma had been waiting for! Every evening 'Abdu'l-Bahá had spent His time with the other German believers, and she had not been invited, but this evening the Master would come to her home! Alma and Margarethe hired a car to pick up the Master at the Obere Museum and bring Him to their humble home for dinner. Surprisingly, when the car arrived, He preferred to ride in the Schwarzes' car, and upon arrival, He invited the entire Schwarz family to join Him for dinner! Alma and Margarethe had hoped for the chance to serve 'Abdu'l-Bahá privately, and they had not expected so many guests. The small table was set for three, but the Master reorganized the table, sat Consul Schwarz next to Him and organized chairs for the Consul, his wife Alice and daughter Olly. The Master continuously served many helpings to Consul Schwarz, telling him in English, "Eat! Eat!" 'Abdu'l-Bahá filled the room with love and friendship. Alice Schwarz recalled, "It was but a small circle of friends He saw around Him, but He was full of kindest care for all of them and with His blessed hand personally helped those sitting next [to?] Him from the dishes and encouraged them to eat. It seemed to us to have a twofold significance, because He, as our physical father, looked after our bodily welfare, as well as He did after our spiritual welfare, in the capacity of our spiritual shepherd, Who nourished our souls with the water of life and the bread of Divine knowledge."'

(*Alma Sedonia Knobloch*, p. 217)

606 Stark was indeed not a Bahá'í at the time Zarqání was writing this entry, but he did become one later.

607 According to Sohrab, the consul was 'not only the President of the [Bad] Mergentheim baths', but also had 'the controlling share in the company'. For more information, see Guido Ettlich, *Konsul Schwarz: Bankier, Bürger & Bahá'í in Stuttgart und Bad Mergentheim.*

608 Sohrab writes that it was approximately 10:15 a.m.

609 'Two of the finest automobiles of Consul Schwarz', according to Sohrab, who states that he himself, 'Abdu'l-Bahá, the consul, his wife, his daughter, and Edwin Fisher all rode in the first car, while Zarqání, Siyyid Asadu'lláh, and Siyyid Aḥmad Báqiroff rode in the second car.

610 Sohrab notes that it was raining heavily when they left the hotel, but that 'after half an hour driving, the air was cleared'.

611 Sohrab has this as 12:30 p.m.

612 More precisely, Sohrab indicates this was the Hotel Lamm-Post in Hall, known today as Schwäbisch Hall. The hotel burned down in 1945.

613 Sohrab writes that this stop in Schwäbisch Hall lasted for an hour and a half.

614 According to Sohrab, 'Abdu'l-Bahá and His retinue left Schwäbisch Hall at 2:00 p.m. and arrived at 'the most luxurious hotel of [Bad] Mergentheim' at 4:00 p.m. Sohrab writes that the hotel was 'built on the slope of a hill overlooking a vast panorama of other hills and valleys, a most attractive situation.'

615 In fact, this is not entirely correct. Sohrab's account indicates that, before leaving Bad Mergentheim, Consul Schwarz took 'Abdu'l-Bahá and His retinue on a tour of 'his mineral water factory' and introduced Him to 'the physician of the place'. After having breakfast, 'Abdu'l-Bahá inscribed a short prayer in the hotel's guestbook, tipped all the hotel's 'maids and servants', and had His photograph taken in front of the building. It was at that point that 'Abdu'l-Bahá, accompanied by Sohrab (and probably the consul, his wife, his daughter, and Edwin Fisher), departed Bad Mergentheim, but somewhere along the way, it was observed that the other car (probably carrying Zarqání, Siyyid Asadu'lláh Qumí, and Siyyid Aḥmad Báqiroff) was no longer following them. To give them a chance to catch up, 'Abdu'l-Bahá and His companions stopped at Weinsberg, where 'Abdu'l-Bahá rested at the Gasthof zur Traube and briefly visited the Kernerhaus. Eventually, the group telephoned two villages to see whether the other car had gotten into an accident, and after learning that this was not the case, they decided to proceed to Stuttgart. Sohrab goes on to observe that the two groups may have inadvertently parted ways when those in 'Abdu'l-Bahá's car decided to take 'a more picturesque road' to return to Stuttgart, while the other car may simply have taken the same road that they took to get to Bad Mergentheim the day before. The fact that Zarqání was likely to have been travelling in the other car, which went

straight from Bad Mergentheim to Stuttgart, would explain why all these details are missing from his account.

616 At 2:30 p.m., according to Sohrab, who writes that Zarqání, Siyyid Asadu'lláh, and Siyyid Aḥmad Báqiroff had already been there for two and a half hours when he, 'Abdu'l-Bahá, the Schwarzes, and Edwin Fisher arrived.

617 Sohrab's account indicates that 'Abdu'l-Bahá came out of His room at 4:30 p.m. to meet 'several of the friends who had come to see him', including Adolf Eckstein, Anna Köstlin, and Alma Knobloch.

618 Having left the Schwarz residence at 7:00 p.m., according to Sohrab, who writes that it took only 'a few minutes' to reach the railway station.

619 According to Sohrab, 'more than one hundred Bahais were gathered at the station to say godspeed to our Beloved'. Wiebers writes that Alma Knobloch, Anna Köstlin, and Alice Schwarz 'walked 45 minutes on foot to the station' (*Alma Sedonia Knobloch*, p. 219).

620 This included 'the railroad officials and the passengers', according to Sohrab.

621 At 8:00 p.m., according to Sohrab. Ulrich Gollmer writes that the train was scheduled to depart at 7:54 p.m. (private correspondence with Ulrich Gollmer dated 17 April 2020).

622 Alma Knobloch, Anna Köstlin, Annemarie Schweizer, and 'a Bahai young man', according to Sohrab. Ulrich Gollmer writes that the man's surname was Scheuermann, and that the four of them stayed on the train up until the station at Plochingen (private correspondence with Ulrich Gollmer dated 17 April 2020). Wiebers writes, 'They were alone in the first-class wagon; it was joyous, and ['Abdu'l-Bahá] was happy. There was no translator, so they communicated with the few words they shared in common. All the others sat in the second class' (*Alma Sedonia Knobloch*, p. 219).

623 'Anna Köstlin and the Esslingen Bahá'ís had arranged a surprise for ['Abdu'l-Bahá]. Shortly before the train passed through Esslingen, Anna asked 'Abdu'l-Bahá to look out of the window. Just then the Esslingen station platform came into view. It was filled with Bahá'ís waving white handkerchiefs and flowers in the air. Seeing them, His face lit up, "radiant, surprised, happy" as He delightedly waved back. Within seconds, the train had raced through Esslingen, but everyone would remember this moment. 'Abdu'l-Bahá had surprised the German Bahá'ís when He arrived in Germany, but when He left, they surprised Him' (Wiebers, *Alma Sedonia Knobloch*, p. 219).

624 Herrigel accompanied 'Abdu'l-Bahá's retinue on this trip through Hungary and Austria to interpret His talks into German.

625 At 8:10 a.m., according to Sohrab.

626 According to Sohrab, this group consisted of the brother of Siyyid Aḥmad Báqiroff, his wife, and their three children, all of whom 'welcomed the Beloved with happy faces and bouquets of flowers'.

627 Sohrab writes: 'In order to leave for Budapest, we had to go to another station on the other side of the city. We got two taxis and in [a] great hurry speeded along.'

628 At 8:50 a.m., according to Sohrab, who notes that, 'On the way Mr. Herrigel spoke about the Cause with many Hungarians and several were presented to the Master and he spoke to them on the Teachings.'

629 'The train arrived at Keleti [Eastern] station at 1:40 [p.m.], while a delegation was waiting for ['Abdu'l-Bahá] at Nyugati (Western) station. As 'Abdu'l-Bahá was not greeted by the delegation at Keleti station, He and His companions had to go to their hotel alone. From a letter written by Ahmed Sohrab, 'Abdu'l-Bahá's secretary, it became clear that the Master and His companions had to transfer in Vienna from Stuttgart to Budapest. They had very little time for the transfer and there were two trains going to Budapest, arriving at two different stations. They boarded the train bound for the other station, contrary to the itinerary written in the telegram that had been sent to the Hungarian Theosophists' (*In the Footsteps of 'Abdu'l-Bahá in Budapest 1913*, p. 36). Sohrab himself writes: 'It was 8:50 [a.m.] when we pulled out [of the station], but I made a mistake in not taking the train of 9:05 [a.m.], because the latter would have entered the station in which the friends were waiting to greet the Master while the one we took entered another. I did not know Budapest had two stations.'

630 In room no. 47, which according to Sohrab was 'on the second floor overlooking the palace, the noble river, and the country all around'. Remarking further on that room, Sohrab goes on to say: 'I can say that it is one of the most beautiful views we have ever seen. The room was full of light[,] for the sun shone through the windows. The Master pronounced the view as most beautiful and when in the evening the electric lights were lighted, it was sublime!' Sohrab also notes that the hotel itself had only been opened three months before, 'so everything was new and up to date'.

631 At 3:00 p.m., according to the Hungarian Bahá'í community.

632 According to Sohrab, this group consisted of Sardar Umrao Singh, Ignác Kúnos, Edward W. Moore, a certain professor Kovácsné, a journalist by the name of Wilma Balogh, Gyula Germanus, Alexander Simonyi, and 'several other prominent men and women of Budapest'.

633 Sohrab's account seems to suggest this was Lipót Stark.

634 Sohrab notes that he translated the following talk from 'Abdu'l-Bahá into English, and that Lipót Stark translated it from English into Hungarian.

635 György Lederer has referred to this statement as 'not altogether correct', observing that, 'in 1852, the Hungarian papers had covered the assassination attempt made by certain Bábís on the life of the shah of Persia and the subsequent retaliation. Also, at the Theosophical Society in Budapest, Leopold Stark, the society's secretary (an electrical engineer by profession), had given a public lecture on "The Behái Movement" on February 25, 1912, and the text of this lecture had been published in the periodical *Teozófia*' (' 'Abdu'l-Bahá in Budapest', p. 110). To these remarks, Ágnes Ambró adds the caveat that, at least in the case of the former source, the information presented in the papers was cursory and limited strictly to the assassination attempt and the death of the Báb, meaning it 'could not have been a good source of knowledge on the Cause in 1913' (private correspondence with Ágnes Ambró, 1 February 2020).

Hungary

636 Zarqání appears to say that Eigel was employed at an embassy or legation by the name of 'Sar' (*sifárat-k͟háníy-i-sar*). The present translator was unable to determine Zarqání's intended meaning, and opted for a vaguer rendering to err on the side of caution. Sohrab writes that Eigel was 'secretary of the Consul General of Turkey', and phone records from the time (which the present translator is grateful to Ágnes Ambró for locating) confirm that he was serving as secretary to the Ottoman consulate.

637 According to Sohrab, 'Abdu'l-Bahá's visitors during this time also included 'Abdul Latif Effendi, the President of the Islamic Association' and 'the Consul General of Turkey who is at the same time the Persian Consul'. Sohrab adds that all these visitors 'came and payed [sic] their homage and respect to the Beloved and each one stayed a long time with him'.

638 Research by the Hungarian Bahá'í community indicates that these photographs were actually taken the previous day (9 April) at about 4:00 p.m.

639 At approximately 11:00 a.m., according to Sohrab.

640 Sohrab writes that this was a certain 'Mr. O.M.A. Frosell'.

641 For an extensive treatment of Vámbéry's affiliation with the Bahá'í Faith, the reader is advised to consult Miklós Sárközy, 'Arminius Vámbéry and the Baha'i Faith', in *Bahá'í Studies Review*, vol. 18, no. 1 (June 2012), pp. 55–81.

642 At 20 Irányi utca, according to Sohrab. Research by the Hungarian Bahá'í community indicates that this meeting was held at 6:00 p.m. and was attended by about fifty people.

643 According to Sohrab, 'Abdu'l-Bahá said the following in response to Nádler's closing remarks: 'Our hearts like unto pure mirrors receive the

impressions and these spiritual images are reflected from one mirror upon another without the medium of language. As spiritual susceptibilities have encircled us tonight and as the mirrors of the hearts are pure, therefore we can understand each other. No matter how eloquent and oratorical the outward tongue, it cannot adequately express the riches of the spirit. The eloquent tongue is the tongue of consciousness. Praise be to God that that tongue is explaining the real feelings of the hearts and expresses our spiritual susceptibilities. Therefore I too with the tongue of consciousness express my gratitude to you in being so patient and so good to listen to me tonight. I shall never forget this love on your part and I will ever remember you and will beg for all of you divine Confirmations.'

644 Sohrab writes that this was 'a large delegation of the Theosophists belonging to the White Lodge of the Star of the East', who came to see 'Abdu'l-Bahá 'with bouquets of flowers in their hands'. Research by the Hungarian Bahá'í community indicates that the Theosophists came at 9:00 a.m. that morning.

645 Sohrab has translated 'Abdu'l-Bahá's words on this subject as follows: 'Now as to the coming of the great Master. His appearance is dependent upon the realization of certain conditions. Investigate the reality and in whomsoever these conditions are fulfilled, know ye of a certainty that he is the Great Master. Firstly: That great Master will be the Educator of the world of humanity. Secondly: His Teachings must be universal and confer illumination upon humankind. Thirdly: His knowledge must be innate and spontaneous and not acquired. Fourthly: He must answer the questions of all the sages, solve all the difficult problems of humanity and be able to withstand all the persecutions and sufferings heaped upon him. Fifthly: He must be a joy-bringer and the Herald of the Kingdom of Happiness. Sixthly: His knowledge must be infinite and his wisdom all-comprehensive. Seventhly: The penetration of His Word and the potency of influence must be so great as to humble even his worst enemies. Eighthly: Sorrows and tribulations must not vex him. His courage and conviction must be godlike. Day unto day he must become firmer and more zealous. Ninthly: He must be the Establisher of universal civilization, the unifier of religions, the standard-bearer of universal Peace and the embodiment of all the highest and noblest virtues of the world of humanity. Wherever you find these conditions realized in a human temple turn to him for guidance and illumination.' These words were later adapted for publication and printed in *Star of the West*, vol. 6, no. 15 (12 December 1915), p. 117.

646 At 10:00 a.m., according to research by the Hungarian Bahá'í community.

647 This was actually Frosell's brother, according to Sohrab, who describes them both as 'two very excellent young men' who 'are much attracted'.

When on this occasion Frosell asked 'Abdu'l-Bahá whether He had seen any of the sights of Budapest, He replied that He had come 'to see men and not piles of stones and clays'. Sohrab goes on to write the rest of 'Abdu'l-Bahá's response in the third person: 'These buildings you can find everywhere; for his part he was searching for men. Buildings are many, men are few. There are ever so many palaces in this world. There have been great palaces built by the ancient kings and today not a stone has been left to tell the sad story of their decay. The present palaces will go through the same process of destruction. When you lay the foundation of a wonderful palace, at that very moment you must think that a day shall come – it may be a hundred years, one thousand years – ten or 20 thousand years – when not one stone of your palace will be left. But the divine Palace shall never be destroyed, its traces are eternal. He desired them to see that palace. That everlasting palace is the reality of man which reality is indestructible. Therefore he was searching throughout the world to find men and women in whom the divine palace was completed. In the heart of every man and woman the construction of this heavenly palace was going on. Praiseworthy deeds and philanthropic actions were the materials with which the palace was built. Vices and negligence of God's laws were the axes with which the very foundation of this eternal palace laid by the hand of God was uprooted.'

648 Sohrab's record of another conversation that 'Abdu'l-Bahá had that day with this youth, O.M.A. Frosell, appears in the online supplement to this book:
https://bahai-library.com/supplement_abdul-baha_europe_1912-1913.

649 Sohrab calls this 'a delegation of more than 25 young men from the Oriental Commercial University headed by a very excellent orator'.

650 At 11:00 a.m., according to research by the Hungarian Bahá'í community.

651 Among whom, according to Sohrab, were Alajos Paikert along with 'a high military officer and several others'. Paikert asked 'Abdu'l-Bahá on that occasion to 'deliver an address on Monday [14 April 1913] at 6pm before the members of the Touranian Society in the senate chamber of Hungary', which He ultimately did.

652 Following these visits, and before going to the old parliament building that evening, Sohrab notes that, 'long after one o'clock', 'Abdu'l-Bahá went to the studio of Róbert Nádler in 'the natural school of art' (located at Andrássy út 71) to sit for a painting. One hour later, He returned to the hotel to have lunch and rest. At 4:00 p.m., Sardar Umrao Singh accompanied Him to call on Ármin Vámbéry, and then (sometime after 5:00 p.m., according to research by the Hungarian Bahá'í community) visit the home of Ignác Goldziher (at Holló utca 4), where Lipót Stark and Gyula Germanus were also present. All these details are absent from Zarqání's chronicle.

653 This seems to be Zarqání's paraphrase of the following remarks: '. . . Abdul Beha arrived at the Eastern railway station and so the delegation drove to Hotel Ritz. The exotic guest was already there and had booked with his secretary a splendid four-room apartment. He can afford it since he is a multimillionaire' ('A Bábí Próféta' [The Bábí Prophet], in *Pesti Napló* (Budapest), 10 April 1913, p. 10; English translation of this passage published in Egea, *Apostle of Peace*, vol. 2, p. 134). Concerning this particular article, Egea writes: 'While the general tone of the article is sympathetic, the fact that 'Abdu'l-Bahá stayed at the recently inaugurated Ritz and was accompanied by secretaries led this journalist to the wrong conclusion that 'Abdu'l-Bahá was a millionaire' (ibid. p. 133). Sohrab writes that when 'Abdu'l-Bahá learned of this characterization, He joked: 'All right, we have then a good credit? May we borrow a million from the Hungarian national bank?'

654 Zarqání, *Maḥmúd's Diary*, p. 105.

655 At 7:00 p.m., according to Sohrab.

656 Wiebers refers to this as 'a large Esperanto meeting' (*Alma Sedonia Knobloch*, p. 219).

657 Sohrab writes that, when 'Abdu'l-Bahá entered the parliament building, 'there were more than 800 people present and everybody spontaneously arose from his seat'.

658 A report of this address that includes extensive summaries of 'Abdu'l-Bahá's remarks appears in the online supplement to this book: https://bahai-library.com/supplement_abdul-baha_europe_1912-1913.

659 Sohrab's account reinforces this enthusiastic reception and adds this detail: 'It was a remarkable demonstration considering the fact that the words of the Beloved had to be translated by two interpreters and our Hungarian translator was not at all equal to the task. Mr. Stark translated much better the other night.'

660 'In the end, 'Abdu'l-Bahá stood between a Catholic priest and a Jewish Professor holding their hands in His while more than 600 people applauded wildly' (Wiebers, *Alma Sedonia Knobloch*, p. 220).

661 Sohrab writes that those who went to thank 'Abdu'l-Bahá in this separate room included 'many prominent men and women'.

662 At 8:00 a.m., according to research by the Hungarian Bahá'í community.

663 Research by the Hungarian Bahá'í community indicates this visit took place at 10:00 a.m.

664 Sohrab's account of 'Abdu'l-Bahá's remarks to Paikert appears in the online supplement to this book: https://bahai-library.com/supplement_abdul-baha_europe_1912-1913.

665 As mentioned in endnote 652, 'Abdu'l-Bahá actually paid this visit to Ármin Vámbéry the previous afternoon (11 April at 4:00 p.m.).

666 Balyuzi writes that Vámbéry 'had travelled to Bukhárá as Rashíd Effendí, a genuine Osmanli (Ottoman)' (*'Abdu'l-Bahá*, p. 386).

667 According to Sohrab, this meeting was held at 6:00 p.m. by the 'members of the Star of the East in the headquarter[s] of the Theosophical Society'.

668 Sohrab writes that 'Abdu'l-Bahá concluded this address with the following prayer: 'O Thou Compassionate Lord! Illumine these hearts with the light of the Most Great Guidance! Confer life upon these spirits through Thy divine glad-tidings! Enlighten these eyes by beholding the splendours of Thy Sun! Make these ears hearing by hearkening [to] Thy Most Glorious Call! Suffer them to enter in the Kingdom of Thy Holiness! Resuscitate them through the Breaths of Thy Holy Spirit! Grant them eternal life! Bestow upon them heavenly perfections! O God! Sacrifice our lives for Thyself! Give us a new spirit! Clear our vision with Thy spiritual Power! Surround us with Thy eternal joy! Confirm us in the service of the world of humanity! Make us the cause of good fellowship between the hearts! O God! Awaken us from the deep slumber of negligence! Suffer us to become mindful and aware! so that we may become informed with the Mysteries of the Holy Books and comprehend the allegories of the spiritual utterances. Verily Thou art the Powerful, Thou art the Giver! and Thou art the Kind.'

669 While Zarqání's entry for this day ends here, Sohrab goes on to say that 'Abdu'l-Bahá returned to the hotel, where He was visited by Sardar Umrao Singh and his wife, Antónia Gottesmann. They invited 'Abdu'l-Bahá to their apartment the following afternoon, both to have tea and also in hopes that He would bless their baby, Amrita Sher-Gil, who was just two months old. Sohrab writes that Gottesmann said to 'Abdu'l-Bahá: 'I want to bring her up as a Bahai. This is the only religion in the world that I would like her to believe and practice.'

670 Sohrab's account seems to suggest that this group of visitors, who came at 9:00 a.m., also included members of the Esperanto Society and Peace Society.

671 According to Sohrab, 'Abdu'l-Bahá addressed the following words to 'the President of the Star of the East'.

672 It seems 'Abdu'l-Bahá's visitors during this period also included several Ottomans, Arabs, and 'Alí 'Abbás Áqá, a rug merchant who, by Sohrab's account, had been living in Hungary for several years, spoke Hungarian 'quite well', and was the only Iranian residing in Budapest at the time. Research by the Hungarian Bahá'í community indicates that Sándor Giesswein and members of the British-American Literary Society were also present on this occasion.

673 At 2:30 p.m., according to Sohrab, who writes that 'Abdu'l-Bahá was at Nádler's studio for 'more than one hour' that day.

674 Sohrab had accompanied 'Abdu'l-Bahá on this visit to Nádler's studio, and he writes that, on their way back from that place, 'Abdu'l-Bahá spoke to him of His own youth: 'You are young and strong. When I was at your age I never felt the cold. I loved the snow. I was strong enough to wrestle with a bear. Here with my fist I would have liked to go for him!'

675 At Szilágyi Dezső tér 4, according to Sohrab, who writes that 'Abdu'l-Bahá related this anecdote about Bahá'u'lláh on the way: 'For nine years he did not see a green leaf. He loved nature. His sensibilities and powers of observation were marvelous! The tips of his fingers were the most sensitive parts of his holy temple. His sense of smell was most keen. If he walked along this avenue, although his mind was occupied with other thoughts, he would on his arrival home relate most profitably every small detail of the throbbing life. Often he would order us to go and prepare tea five or six miles away from the city, because one could see there a patch of green or a pine tree. He would cut a cucumber into two pieces and smell only its odor and enjoy it as though he had eaten it. While dictating Tablets to his secretary at a rapid rate, he had papers in his hand and writing on some entirely different topic and now and then carried an interesting conversation with those who were present and suddenly he would raise his head and point to us from the window a wonderful, tall, noble tree in a garden far [a] way. One occupation never prevented him from attending to other things.'

676 Sohrab's account of 'Abdu'l-Bahá's visit to the home of Sardar Umrao Singh is as follows: 'Our Indian Sardar had a beautiful apartment, part Oriental and Western. The Master and the rest of the guests were served tea and refreshments. He looked around the large rooms and after blessing the little baby returned to the hotel.'

677 Research by the Hungarian Bahá'í community indicates that this visit lasted from 6:00 to 10:00 p.m.

678 At 9:00 a.m., according to research by the Hungarian Bahá'í community.

679 At 'about noon', according to Sohrab.

680 Sohrab offers this illustration of how 'Abdu'l-Bahá spoke to the consul on that occasion: 'I have seldom heard the Master speaking with such fiery animation; his facial and hand-gestures were the most remarkable. Often when the Master is under the spell of the spirit, every little while, he takes off his turban, arranges his hair and puts it on again. This is done so unconsciously, so gracefully that one is charmed and delighted. He spoke all the time in Turkish, his voice high and sweet, his tone determined and earnest, his face aflame with the light of love and pity, his eyes twinkling like two globes of fire, his countenance now stern, now wreathed with the sun-kissed smiles of the angels, his hands

swiftly moving up and down, now showing the palm, again two or three fingers and at all time[s] portraying most graphically his feelings and emotions!' A fuller account of His remarks, recorded by Sohrab, appears in the online supplement to this book:
https://bahai-library.com/supplement_abdul-baha_europe_1912-1913.

681 At 2:00 p.m., according to research by the Hungarian Bahá'í community.

682 Sohrab's account of this visit by 'Abdu'l-Bahá to the home of Vámbéry is as follows: 'Here again more than two hours they talked together in Persian and Turkish. Prof Vambery telling interesting reminiscences of his journey throughout Oriental countries. He was much interested in the Cause and begged the Master to permit him to write a series of articles in European papers. He is a man that all Europe listens to and his opinion is sought after by the statesmen and diplomats.'

683 'Abdu'l-Bahá wrote Vámbéry this Tablet on 29 June 1913 while in Port Said, according to Sohrab, who has partially translated it in his diary letter of that date as follows:

He is God!

O thou my revered friend, famous throughout the world! From the day of separation up to this time not one moment I have been disengaged from the remembrance of your kindness. Ever your sympathetic face is in my thought and the sweetness of your conversation like unto the delicious honey is in my taste.

During this time I was travelling, therefore correspondence was impossible. Praise be to God that safely and with the enjoyment of good health I have arrived in Port Said. My purpose is to stay and rest for sometimes [some time] in this place – a place isolated and free from the din of occupation; in order that I may get over the hardships and vicissitudes of the journey. Then if it is possible, I shall raise a new melody and sing a new song, vibrant with tumultuous strains and clamorous notes and then probably I shall meet you again. My aim is to render a service to the Reality and make an effort and exertion in the world of humanity.

Praise be to God your intention is humanistic and your object is to serve humankind along the path of prosperity and progress. You have consecrated your life to this glorious object. Consequently I am very pleased with and grateful to you and in order to express this pleasure and happiness I write you this letter and I ever anticipate to receive your good news . . .

(Sig) Abdul Baha Abbas!

The present translator feels fortunate indeed to have stumbled upon this hitherto unpublished Tablet, which the Hungarian Bahá'í community had been attempting to locate for many years.

684 Vámbéry's original letter to 'Abdu'l-Bahá is held at the archives of the

Bahá'í World Centre. A facsimile has been published in *In the Footsteps of 'Abdu'l-Bahá in Budapest 1913*, pp. 32–3.

685 The English translation was produced by Sohrab and appears in his diary entry dated 6 September 1913, where he prefaces his rendering with this note: 'I will translate the letter as a matter of historical interest.' The translation was published shortly thereafter by Jean Stannard in *The Egyptian Gazette* on 24 September 1913, and has since been reprinted in various other publications. This particular version has been taken from *Bahá'í World*, vol. 5, p. 329. A more recent translation is published in Miklós Sárközy, "Arminius Vámbéry and the Baha'i Faith," *Bahá'í Studies Review*, vol. 18, no. 1 (June 2012), pp. 72–73.

686 In his original chronicle, Zarqání reproduces the Arabic translation, but the one quoted here is obviously the English rendering mentioned in the preceding endnote.

687 Intriguingly, the original Persian text of this sentence says precisely the opposite: *man kih jadd-i-válá 'álí-jináb az nazdík dídam*, or 'As for me, who has seen the honourable father of your excellency *up close* . . .' [emphasis added by the present translator]. This discrepancy in the English translation might have originated with the Arabic translation published in *al-Bayán* and quoted in Zarqání's original chronicle, where *az nazdík* (up close) has been rendered as *'an bu'd* (from afar). Hence, it may be that the English translation, produced by Ahmad Sohrab and originally recorded in his diary entry for 6 September 1913 before it was edited and published in multiple places, was actually based on the Arabic translation for some reason, rather than the original Persian text. In any case, Moojan Momen, who has carefully researched the life of Vámbéry, has 'determined that there was no occasion in which he was in the same location as Bahá'u'lláh', and has therefore come to the conclusion that 'what Vámbéry meant in his letter was that, in meeting 'Abdu'l-Bahá, it was as though he had met Bahá'u'lláh' (email from Moojan Momen to the Tarikh listserv dated 21 August 2022).

688 Sohrab's account makes it clear that Alajos Paikert came to the Ritz at 6:00 p.m. to take 'Abdu'l-Bahá to this gathering, which according to research by the Hungarian Bahá'í community began at 7:00 p.m.

689 Sohrab writes: 'Although the weather was inclement yet several hundreds were present.' The Hungarian Bahá'í community has identified Ignác Goldziher, Gyula Pekár, Béla Vikár, Victor Hagara, Károly Rónai, Gyula Mészáros, Rev. Abdul Latif, Sardar Umrao Singh, and Feridun Ömer as attendees on that occasion.

690 A provisional English rendering of the full talk, produced by the present translator, appears in the online supplement to this book: https://bahai-library.com/supplement_abdul-baha_europe_1912-1913.

691 Probably at Váci utca 21, according to research by the Hungarian Bahá'í community.

692 Sohrab names Wilhelm Herrigel and Edward W. Moore as other guests of 'Alí 'Abbás Áqá, and continues: 'There were also several Turks and from 7:30 [p.m.] to eleven thirty the Master spoke to them in Turkish, always illustrating his points with original stories. At 10:30 [p.m.] dinner was served and it consisted of soup, rice, chicken etc. I was glad that even in Budapest there was one Persian who invited the Beloved to his home and spread a very good table for his friends. He ['Alí 'Abbás Áqá] considered this feast as the greatest event of his life. He was a very good young man and the Master was very kind to him.'

693 At 9:00 a.m., according to research by the Hungarian Bahá'í community.

694 Sohrab records several exchanges between 'Abdu'l-Bahá and the Starks that day which are absent from Zarqání's chronicle. Here is one example: 'Mr. Stark asked the Master what books he could translate into Hungarian so that he may publish and circulate [them] amongst the reading public. He said: "Translate the words of Paradise, Tajalliyat, Tarazat, the Bahai Proof [*The Bahá'í Proofs* by Mírzá Abu'l-Faḍl] and other small pamphlets containing short historical accounts. You and your wife have rendered already a great service to the Cause of Bahaullah. I will pray to God that you may always be surrounded with his benedictions. When I leave Budapest you correspond with me and let me hear your news."'

695 Sohrab clarifies that Wilhelm Herrigel asked 'Abdu'l-Bahá how the German Bahá'ís should conduct their meetings in Stuttgart. His response, according to Sohrab, was as follows: 'Gather once a week in a public meeting. Before the meeting begins, one must read a prayer. Afterward they may sing together an anthem or a song. This is optional. They may do it or not according to their tastes. Then one may give an address, on a Bahá'í subject. Then they may read Tablets or extracts from the writings of Bahá'u'lláh such as the Hidden Words, Tarazat, etc. or the news or letters received from other Bahá'í centers. Then with another supplication they may close the gathering. The object is: let the meeting be spiritual and productive of unity and harmony, so that when you leave it you may feel much better than when you entered. Let the meetings be formless as possible. Crystallization of forms will kill the spirit. Let simplicity, progressiveness, naturalness, beauty of ideas, love and fellowship emanate from your meetings. The mother of all the questions is to promote the Cause and spread the Teachings.'

696 Sohrab notes that some Arabs also visited 'Abdu'l-Bahá that day.

697 Among them Alajos Paikert and Ignác Goldziher, according to Sohrab, who writes that the former remarked to 'Abdu'l-Bahá, 'This [Turanian] Society is eternally blessed because it had the favor and distinction of receiving you. Your words of praise and encouragement will inspire all

the future workers of this society,' and also that the latter spoke with 'Abdu'l-Bahá in Arabic on 'the knowledge of divinity, the four criteria of knowledge, [and] the transference of the single atom through all the Kingdoms of life', adding that 'The talk was very long and the professor listened with rapt attention and delight.'

698 At 2:00 p.m., according to research by the Hungarian Bahá'í community.

699 According to Sohrab, this was a reporter from *Az Est*, a Hungarian daily newspaper. Egea notes that he 'has consulted different issues of this periodical and has been unable to find this interview' (*Apostle of Peace*, vol. 2, p. 515, n. 70).

700 At 3:00 p.m., according to research by the Hungarian Bahá'í community.

701 Sohrab writes that Lipót Stark happened to be present during this interview, and that he translated 'Abdu'l-Bahá's words into Hungarian for the journalist.

702 Starting from 4:00 p.m., according to research by the Hungarian Bahá'í community.

703 Sohrab records this detail which took place that day (at 6:00 p.m., according to research by the Hungarian Bahá'í community): 'Mr. Moore brought his gramophone to the hotel and Mirza Mahmoud [Zarqání] chanted through it the beautiful prayer delivered at the Theosophical Society for their future Bahai meetings.' Zarqání may have chosen not to mention this detail in his own chronicle out of humility.

704 According to Sohrab's account, this included 'an old, learned man who was extremely interested in sociology', Alajos Paikert, Sardar Umrao Singh, Edward W. Moore, Lipót and Karolina Stark, and Professor Károly Zipernowsky. Research by the Hungarian Bahá'í community indicates that these visits took place throughout the morning and afternoon.

705 More specifically, Károly Zipernowsky and Ignác Goldziher, according to Sohrab.

706 At Nyúl utca 5, according to Sohrab, who in fact offers a different chronology: A carriage came at 9:00 a.m. to take 'Abdu'l-Bahá to the Stark residence, then Lipót Stark took Him to the home of Károly Zipernowsky (at noon, according to the Hungarian Bahá'í community), then the home of Ignác Goldziher, and then back to the hotel (at 2:00 p.m., according to the Hungarian Bahá'í community), where 'Abdu'l-Bahá invited Stark to have lunch together. Moreover, Sohrab's account indicates that 'Abdu'l-Bahá actually paid all these visits the following day (17 April), insofar as He 'did not go out' on 16 April, owing to the fact that He was 'extremely tired and his voice was a little hoarse'. The remainder of the events recorded in this entry by Zarqání likewise

seem to have actually taken place on 17 April, according to Sohrab, who also writes that 'Abdu'l-Bahá and His retinue had dinner at the home of Edward W. Moore that evening (at 7:00 p.m., according to the Hungarian Bahá'í community, who believe that Moore may have been residing at Belgrade Quay 19 at the time) – a detail which is absent from Zarqání's chronicle. A visit to the Ottoman consul is not mentioned in Sohrab's diary letters of 16 or 17 April.

707 Sohrab writes that 'Abdu'l-Bahá addressed the following words to the Starks at their residence: 'This is a blessed home and will be a very important center in the future. From this home, the lights of guidance have shone forth. From this home, the Call of the Kingdom of Abha has been raised. This is the first home in Hungary in which the name of Bahaullah was mentioned. May it become always a center of guidance! May many Bahai meetings be held here! May the Teachings of the Blessed Perfection be diffused to all parts of Hungary from this home! I have come and sown the seeds. Now you must arise and water them. This is your duty. Be ye confident that Bahaullah shall assist you. He will inspire your hearts. You two are the first man and woman to upraise the banner of [the] Bahai Cause in Hungary. Your station is very great in the Kingdom of Abha! This is not known at present. In the future people will come from all parts to visit this home, because this is the first home from which the glad-tidings of the appearance of the Kingdom of Abha was issued. Years ago when I was travelling toward Tiberias, I saw a large number of people gathered in one place. I asked one why these people have congregated there? He said: It is a matter of tradition that once upon a time, one of the apostles sat on one of these rocks. Now these pilgrims come from all parts of the world and kiss all the rocks, perchance they may kiss the right one[.] Now praise be to God that you are the objects of the Favors of Bahaullah.' For more details on Bahá'í meetings held at the Stark residence, refer to endnote 713.

708 A reference to Wellesca Pollock Dyar, also known as Aseyeh Allen (1871–1940), a trainer of kindergarten teachers who became a Bahá'í in 1900 or 1901 and made a pilgrimage to Haifa in 1907, where she met 'Abdu'l-Bahá for the first time. She then met 'Abdu'l-Bahá again during His visit to Washington, D.C. (20–28 April 1912).

709 Sohrab's account for this day notes that 'Abdu'l-Bahá went to the studio of Róbert Nádler at 8:00 a.m. for His third and final sitting – a detail not mentioned in Zarqání's chronicle.

710 Sohrab writes that this included Sardar Umrao Singh; Dr Victor Hagara, along with his wife and daughter; Edward M. Moore; and Lipót Stark. A key detail which is absent from Zarqání's chronicle is that Moore asked 'Abdu'l-Bahá to intone a prayer into his gramophone, and He consented to this request. An authorized translation of the

Arabic prayer which 'Abdu'l-Bahá chanted on this occasion is as follows:

He is God! O God, my God! I beseech Thee with a heart throbbing with Thy love, and I call upon Thee in the dark of the night, saying: O God! Aid me by Thy grace and mercy, and cause me to utter Thy praise amidst Thy creatures. O God, my God! These are Thy servants who have turned towards the right hand of Thy bounty, who have gathered together and been attracted to Thy call, and who have confessed Thy oneness. O Lord! Cause them to be signs of Thy mercy amongst Thy people and the banners of Thy bounty amidst Thy servants. O Lord! Send down upon them Thy blessings, illumine their hearts with the light of Thy knowledge, gladden their bosoms with the signs of Thy transcendent holiness, and make them as lamps shining with the light of Thy love. Thou, verily, art the Bountiful, the Compassionate. O Lord, my Lord! This is a city wherein have gathered the exalted and prominent ones of the land. Guide them to Thy straight path and solace their eyes with Thy resplendent light. Suffer them to become servants to the cause of the oneness of humanity, standard-bearers of Thy most great bounty betwixt earth and heaven, strivers for peace and amity, and seekers of imperishable glory for all peoples. Verily, Thou art the Bountiful. Verily, Thou art the Compassionate. Verily, Thou art the Almighty.

The present translator was informed by Ágnes Ambró that the Hungarian Bahá'í community has gone to great lengths to locate this recording, but that their efforts have proven unsuccessful thus far.

711 According to Sohrab, 'Abdu'l-Bahá left the Ritz Hotel in Lipót Stark's carriage at 1:00 p.m.

712 Among this group of visitors, Sohrab names Sardar Umrao Singh, Róbert Nádler, Dr Victor Hagara and his wife, the Ottoman consul, and 'more than 20 more friends'.

713 Regarding observations like this one, Lederer writes: 'To the best of my knowledge, this initial optimism about the number of Bahá'ís in Budapest is not supported by any facts' (' 'Abdu'l-Bahá in Budapest', p. 121), and concludes that 'Zarqání must have overestimated the enthusiasm of the Theosophists' (ibid.). Lipót Stark did write a letter to 'Abdu'l-Bahá, dated 29 October 1913 and preserved at the archives of the Bahá'í World Centre, in which he states, 'It is with great pleasure, that I am able to report to Your Holiness, that yesterday, on the 28th of October [1913], the first Budapest Báhai Meeting was held in our home,' and mentions the names of eleven people who attended: 'Abdul Latif, Rev.; E.W. Moore; Prof. Róbert Nádler; Ödön Nérei, K.C.; Iván Sztoits, Minist. Secretary; Umraosing Sher Gil; Dr. Géza Vikár, lawyer; Prof. Charles [Károly] Zipernowsky; Mrs. Anna Zipernowsky [née Kline]; a Lieutenant Colonel and his wife' (of course, Lipót Stark him-

self and his wife, Karolina, were also present). There does not seem to be further documentation of any meetings that followed this one.

714 At 6:30 p.m., according to Sohrab.

715 Sohrab's account indicates that 'Abdu'l-Bahá was driven there by 'a Persian' – probably a member of the Khamsí-Báqiroff family, as the following endnote makes clear.

716 According to Alexander Käfer, this was the Hotel Beatrix, a small hotel in Landstr. Str. 10 in the third district of Vienna, located fifteen minutes from the train station. The Khamsí-Báqiroff family, who lived in a nearby apartment (in the third district of Vienna, Baumannstraße 5, Tur 5), had reserved a number of rooms at this hotel for 'Abdu'l-Bahá (room no. 47) and the members of His retinue (adjoining no. 47). This hotel was destroyed in World War II. See Käfer, *Die Geschichte der Österreichischen Bahá'í-Gemeinde*, p. 27. The present translator is grateful to David Menham for providing him with this information.

717 To clarify: Käfer's account indicates that 'Abdu'l-Bahá felt He would not be able to 'receive visitors in a dignified manner' at the Hotel Beatrix (Käfer, *Die Geschichte*, p. 27; translation of this passage by David Menham). Sohrab reinforces this impression and writes that 'the hotel was neither in a good locality nor what it ought to be', noting that 'Abdu'l-Bahá and His retinue did not actually change hotels until the following morning (of 19 April).

718 According to Sohrab, 'Abdu'l-Bahá initially occupied room no. 221 of the Grand Hotel, but in his diary letter for the following day (19 April), he writes: 'This hotel is so big that our rooms were quite far from the elevator, so we have again moved to another part on the same floor. We have an excellent suite of three connecting rooms nos. 46, 47, 48. The Master is living in front room no. 46 overlooking the broad avenue. We are pleased with our place now and don't think there will be another change.' In this context, a 'front room' is a room situated at the front part of a hotel with a preferred view or location.

Austria

719 Sohrab has recorded this gentleman's surname as 'Cordes', and Jasion states that he was 'Chairman of the Theosophical Society of Austria' (*'Abdu'l-Bahá in the West*, p. 103).

720 In the original chronicle, Zarqání has transliterated this name into the Persian alphabet as 'Tyler'. Sohrab seems to refer to Marie Thaler (without actually naming her) as 'The Secretary of the Theosophical Society', and he notes that 'a few others' also came on this occasion 'to welcome the Master to Vienna'.

721 Sohrab has recorded these remarks of 'Abdu'l-Bahá somewhat differently in his diary: 'The Persians, the Austrians, the Germans, the

French, the Italian, and the English people belong to one common stock of Aryan race. Originally this sturdy race lived along the river of Ganges in India. This people grew rapidly in number and strength. Having become too numerous they migrated to the plateau of Írán – (Persia). From the tableland of Írán, a second migration was set in motion toward [the] Caucasus. After many ages of expansion, the third migration started westward. Then a stream of migration[s] at various periods flowed toward Europe, each one, inhabiting a portion of the land. Lack of intercourse and communication created differences of language and customs. Little by little they were more and more estranged from each other. Now my hope is this: Just as originally these various nations belonged to one family; may they again return to their primal unity. Formerly they were one as regards to their physical life; may they become united in this age as regard to their spiritual life.'

722 Sohrab refers to this as 'Flower Day'.

723 Sohrab's depiction of the event differs only slightly in the details: '. . . all the young girls have little baskets of imitatious [imitation] flowers in their hands with small deposit boxes selling the flowers for charity'.

724 Sohrab writes: 'There were literally thousands of people in the streets and park and everybody stopped to look at the Master, wondering who was this strange man! I have seldom seen anywhere people standing still and looking so intently at him! Thousands of eyes were upon him.'

725 More precisely, Sohrab notes that this was a gathering of Theosophists held at the home of 'Prof. [Lajos, or Louis] Thern' and 'Mrs. [Marguerite] Thern', located at Kastnergasse 11.

726 Sohrab notes that the English interpretation of this talk was translated into German by Johann Kreuz.

727 According to Sohrab, 'there were about one hundred people present' at this gathering.

728 Sohrab's account makes it clear that the details in this paragraph actually pertain to the evening of 21 April: 'Abdu'l-Bahá went to the Thern residence (Kastnergasse 11) on 19 April, and to the lodge of the Theosophical Society at the Lukaneder residence (Johannesgasse 2) on 21 April. In one of His Tablets included in the online supplement to this book (https://bahai-library.com/supplement_abdul-baha_europe_1912-1913), 'Abdu'l-Bahá mentions this exact detail about having to climb a hundred and twenty steps: 'Especially taxing was one night in particular when I went to a place where there were a hundred and twenty stairs made of marble that was cold as ice; I ascended them with exceeding powerlessness and fatigue, and then spoke for two hours without interruption. I promoted the Word of God, and my talk was accompanied by a comprehensive translation' (provisional rendering by the present translator approved by the Research Department at the

Bahá'í World Centre for publication).

729 Sohrab's account indicates that this was the 'Sapahdar Azam' (the Sipahdár-i-A'ẓam), the title of Muḥammad-Valí Khán Tunukábuní, who thrice served as Persia's prime minister and met with 'Abdu'l-Bahá in Paris on several occasions. According to Sohrab, 'Abdu'l-Bahá said the following to Tunukábuní during this particular visit: 'After the ascent [Ascension] of Bahá'u'lláh I was all alone. Enemies within and enemies without had attacked me and a thousand difficulties surrounded me. But my confidence and trust was within, because during the days of His life He explicitly promised me that He will assist me always. I heard this promise from His own lips, therefore I knew that under all circumstances I will be confirmed and all my enemies will be defeated.' Sohrab then adds that, following this, 'Abdu'l-Bahá told Tunukábuní of 'a wonderful dream He had right after the departure [Ascension] of Bahá'u'lláh', but no further details on the dream are given. Sohrab also writes that, at some point that afternoon, 'Abdu'l-Bahá called on Tunukábuní at the Hotel Imperial, but he was not there; his secretary received Him instead, and 'Abdu'l-Bahá asked him to pass on this message: 'Give my greeting to the green mountains and rolling valleys, to the singing nightingales and the cooling springs, to the fragrant rose-gardens and the fresh breeze of Persia. I love them all. Remember me to them.'

730 A lengthier account of these remarks, recorded by Sohrab, appears in the online supplement to this book:
https://bahai-library.com/supplement_abdul-baha_europe_1912-1913.

731 Sohrab's account of 'Abdu'l-Bahá's visit to the Karlskirche is as follows: 'Being a fine day ['Abdu'l-Bahá] called me to have a walk with him. It was Sunday and the people were out going to their churches. He walked toward a church, about three blocks from the hotel. Its outside looked like a palace and its dome rose up to the sky. The Beloved entered the church. All the eyes of the worshippers were upon him. The inside roof contained wonderful paintings, the columns were of marble, the decoration was magnificent and rich. It was a Catholic church, and before the statue of every Saint in the different corners of the Temple candles were lighted and many souls were kneeling. The Master walked around for ten minutes looking intently upon the Statue of the Crucified Christ and the Saints. Coming out he dropped several kronnas [koronas] in the box near the gate. "These people may have thought," he said musingly, "that we are there to ridicule. God forbid! They do not know, how the pictures and statues of Christ affect me. It was better to come out, because I might have prevented them from their worship on account of my strange appearance."'

732 Then located at Prinz Eugenstraße 34, which according to Sohrab was just a five-minute walk from the Grand Hotel.

733 Zarqání appears to have redacted this person's name.

734 Sohrab's account here differs from Zarqání's and sheds more light on 'Abdu'l-Bahá's encounter with this sculptor, a young man by the name of Alexander Engelhardt who made 'statuettes of important personages', including 'King Edward [VII] and other famous men'. He writes that, on the morning of 19 April, Engelhardt had a chance meeting with 'Abdu'l-Bahá in the hotel and 'being attracted by his extraordinary countenance, pleaded [with] him to come and make a model'. 'Abdu'l-Bahá consented to this request; consequently, Engelhardt visited Him at 4:00 p.m. that day and 'for twenty minutes he worked and out of the soft clay he brought out the wonderful face of the Beloved'. Sohrab then notes that Engelhardt was to have a second sitting with 'Abdu'l-Bahá to complete his bust – and he alludes to this again three days later in his diary letter of 22 April, in which he writes that 'the clay model was finished in two sittings, each sitting taking from twenty minutes to half an hour' – but nowhere actually says when the second sitting took place. It may be that the sitting noted here by Zarqání on 21 April refers to that second sitting. In any case, Sohrab goes on to say in his diary letter of 22 April that a few busts based on Engelhardt's clay model would be made in imitation bronze in a week's time, and that he had already ordered two busts: one to be sent to Harriet Magee, the other to Washington, D.C. Writing a few months later on 18 July, Sohrab alludes to the fact that he and Zarqání each had one of these busts, as well, and states that Consul Aḥmad Effendí Yazdí, resident in Port Said, received another one from Wilhelm Herrigel in Stuttgart that day.

735 Sohrab has this as two cars, presumably to accommodate the members of 'Abdu'l-Bahá's retinue.

736 'For more than one hour', according to Sohrab.

737 Sohrab writes: 'One of the most novel sights to be seen was the peculiar arrangement of the trees, so that if one stopped in the beginning of the avenue, one would see a high wall, straight as an arrow, green and verdant!'

738 According to Sohrab, it was 'about 2 o'clock' when 'Abdu'l-Bahá and His retinue returned to the hotel.

739 Sohrab notes that one of 'Abdu'l-Bahá's visitors that afternoon was Marguerite Thern; she brought a book for 'Abdu'l-Bahá, in which He wrote the following inscription: 'O Thou Almighty! Make this Theosophical Society a rose-garden and a meadow through the downpour of the rain of Thy Providence; so that they may become delivered from expectation, behold the rays of the Sun of Reality, become informed with the existence of the invisible world and attain to the Mystery of mysteries. Verily Thou art the Guide! (Sig) Abdul Baha Abbas.'

740 Sohrab writes that, at 7:00 p.m., 'Abdu'l-Bahá was taken to this gathering at the society's lodge (the Lukaneders' apartment at Johannesgasse

2, Wien I) by a certain 'Mr. Eder, the President of [the] Psychological Society and the Vice President of [the] Theosophical Society'. This is probably a reference to David (or M.D.) Eder, a British psychoanalyst and physician.

741 According to Sohrab, 'There were more people present than the other night [presumably 19 April], nearly two hundred all anxious to hear ['Abdu'l-Bahá] speak.'

742 Sohrab describes this talk as 'a wonderful address on the influence of the spirit and the transference of the single indivisible atom throughout all the degrees of the kingdoms' and offers this passage: 'The glory of the world of humanity is not through the body. This is the honour of the animal world; but the glory of man comes through the Spirit. Spirit quickens and regenerates humankind and not the body. Spirit draws man near unto God and not the body. Spirit is the discoverer of the realities of phenomena and not the body. Spirit establishes love and amity amongst the human race and not the body. Spirit will usher in the era of Peace and Salvation and not the body. Spirit attracts the hearts together and not the body. Spirit has drawn me to Vienna so that I may associate with you and not the body. I am Eastern and you are from the West. It is the power of the Spirit that has gathered us together. It is the Spirit that gives wings to man so that he may soar in the immensity of God's Kingdom. Spirit is the Collective Center of all the perfections. Take away the spirit from man and he is an animal!'

743 Sohrab mentions this same detail in his account and adds that, as 'Abdu'l-Bahá was leaving the apartment, He said to Mrs Lukaneder: 'I was most pleased with this meeting because it was a nest for the heavenly birds.'

744 Sohrab writes: 'The audience listened with rapt attention and when ['Abdu'l-Bahá] finished they were so attracted that they clamored for another lecture to be delivered on Wednesday night [23 April]. The Beloved accepted their plea and brought the meeting to a close by delivering a beautiful prayer.' As promised, 'Abdu'l-Bahá did go on to give another talk on the evening of 23 April at the Lukaneder residence. Sohrab's translation of the prayer which 'Abdu'l-Bahá recited to conclude that gathering is as follows: 'O Thou Kind God! The members of this society have turned their faces toward Thee. They are begging to receive the lights from Thy Most Great Guidance. They enjoy spiritual susceptibilities. O God! Quicken the spirits! Extend the horizon of their thoughts. Bestow upon them the Power of the Kingdom! Confer upon them the Confirmations of the Holy-Spirit! O God! Endear these souls and give unto them merciful powers, so that they may illumine this country with Thy Light! May they resuscitate these dead bodies! May they cause the disappearance of the darkness of nature through the rays of Thy Sun! O God! Assist these souls and deliver them from the

darkness of nature. Clothe them with the heavenly body and surround them with spiritual forces. Verily Thou art the Generous! and the Mighty!'

745 Egea writes that, according to Sohrab, this gentleman was 'a representative of *Die Zeit* (Vienna)' (*Apostle of Peace*, vol. 2, p. 149), but adds that he 'has consulted different issues of this periodical and has been unable to find this interview' (ibid. p. 515, n. 72). Sohrab, however, took down his own account of it, mentioned in the following endnote.

746 Sohrab's record of 'Abdu'l-Bahá's conversation with this representative of *Die Zeit* appears in the online supplement to this book: https://bahai-library.com/supplement_abdul-baha_europe_1912-1913.

747 Sohrab's account seems to suggest that 'Abdu'l-Bahá made these remarks in response to this question posed by an unidentified woman: 'How should we gain eternal happiness?' Furthermore, Sohrab's account of 'Abdu'l-Bahá's reply is slightly more extensive than Zarqání's: 'You must enter in[to] the Kingdom of Abhá. In the Kingdom of Abhá, there is light upon light. The darkness of sorrow and pain is banished forever from that region. His Holiness Bahá'u'lláh today has opened the Doors of the Kingdom and people are receiving vision of that far-off palace of happiness. They are made so happy that they sing and dance under the sword. Eternal happiness is all-inclusive. In it is unbraced material happiness. This world is like unto ant-houses. Have you ever observed how the ants are ever busy to gather provisions, sometimes carrying heavier loads than themselves? But once in a while some of these ants grow wings and soar away. I hope you will be like them.'

748 The reader should be advised that, in the 1982 Bahá'í-Verlag reprint of the original text of this volume (currently hosted at http://reference.bahai.org/), the page on which this section begins, page 252, has been switched with page 256; in other words, page 256 appears where page 252 should be (and vice-versa), and the order of these two pages should be reversed. This printing error does not appear in the original 1921 edition of this work.

749 At noon, according to Sohrab. By 'garden' (*bá<u>gh</u>c<u>h</u>ih*), 'Abdu'l-Bahá was apparently referring to the Stadtpark. It may be that, throughout this chronicle, He and Zarqání used this word – along with *bá<u>gh</u>*, a related word – to mean either 'garden' or 'park'.

750 According to Sohrab, this encounter actually took place as 'Abdu'l-Bahá and His retinue were walking back from the Stadtpark to the hotel.

751 Sohrab writes that Áqá 'Alí-Akbar Áqá also went to the Grand Hotel at 5:00 p.m. that day to visit 'Abdu'l-Bahá.

752 According to Sohrab, these were two ladies who each came with a bouquet of flowers in hand.

753 The implication perhaps being that certain technological inventions of the twentieth century, such as automobiles, did not exist a hundred years before.

754 At 5:30 p.m., according to Sohrab.

755 Sohrab's account makes it clear that this was the Persian embassy, and that Siyyid Aḥmad Báqiroff accompanied 'Abdu'l-Bahá on this visit.

756 According to Sohrab, 'Abdu'l-Bahá went to this gathering at approximately 7:30 p.m. directly from the Persian embassy.

757 Sohrab writes that the prayer was not interpreted as 'Abdu'l-Bahá was reciting it because 'the people [preferred] to hear the voice of the Master without interruption', but he does offer his written translation of it: 'O Thou King of Existence! O Thou kind Beloved! The members of this meeting are the lovers of Thy face. They seek after Thee and they long to converse with Thee. They are the investigators of reality and the wooers of Thy countenance! They are thirsty for Thy salubrious stream and have turned their attention toward Thee. O Thou Kind Beloved! Illumine the world of humanity! Enlighten the hearts with the Effulgence of Thy Love! Perfume the nostrils with Thy Sweet Fragrances. Confer upon us a new Bestowal! Give unto us a strong power! Open the eyes! Make the ears hearing! O God! Thirsty are we, Thy grace is the cooling spring! Homeless and shelterless are we, Thy court is the asylum for these poor ones. Indigent are we, give unto us the Treasury of Thy Kingdom. Prisoners are we, free us from aught else save Thee. Nameless and traceless are we, accept us at Thy divine threshold! O God! Do not look upon our desert [i.e., what we deserve]. Have mercy upon us! Be compassionate to us! Grant us Thy favor and guide us to the right path. Verily Thou art the Powerful and the Mighty.'

758 Sohrab's record of the conversation that took place between 'Abdu'l-Bahá and von Suttner appears in the online supplement to this book: https://bahai-library.com/supplement_abdul-baha_europe_1912-1913.

In 1905, von Suttner became the first woman to win the Nobel Peace Prize.

759 To be clear, Karolina Stark came to see 'Abdu'l-Bahá in Vienna the day before (on 23 April). Sohrab's summary of some of her remarks indicates that, by that time, 25 people had expressed their belief in Bahá'u'lláh; that the Hungarian Bahá'ís would have their first meeting upon her return to Budapest (this was eventually held on 28 October 1913, as mentioned in endnote 713); and that they would soon translate the Writings into Hungarian. Sohrab also quotes her as saying: 'Everybody speaks about the Cause with the greatest reverence. They respect us more than ever before because we are Bahais. We will do everything to spread the Cause.'

760 According to Sohrab, 'Abdu'l-Bahá and His retinue left the hotel in two cars at 9:15 a.m., and their train departed Vienna at 10:00 a.m. He notes, moreover, that Siyyid Aḥmad Báqiroff did not accompany them, returning to Persia instead.

761 Sohrab states that 'there were four Bahais waiting to greet the Master' at the station in Esslingen, but does not name any of them. According to German sources, they were Anna Köstlin, the 'Mr Scheuermann' mentioned in endnote 622, Annemarie Schweizer, and Miss Helene Theurer, who boarded the train at Esslingen station.

762 There is a lack of consensus here: While Zarqání has it as 2:00 a.m., Wiebers has 2:15 a.m. (*Alma Sedonia Knobloch*, p. 221), Sohrab has 2:10 a.m., and a German source has 2:05 a.m.

763 Sohrab writes that 'there were more than twelve Bahais' at the station in Stuttgart, among them Consul Schwarz, Mrs Herrigel, Bertha Bahnmüller, Miss Stäbler, Miss Anna Köstlin, Marie Schweizer, Miss Helene Theurer, and a certain 'Mr. Thaunman'. Annemarie Schweizer and Anna Köstlin report that, in addition to the four people who had already entered the train at Esslingen, Consul Schwarz, Elise and Julie Stäbler, Marie Herrigel, and Bertha Bahnmüller were waiting at the station in Stuttgart (private correspondence with Ulrich Gollmer dated 17 April 2020).

764 Regarding the hotel arrangements for this second stay in Stuttgart, Sohrab notes that 'Abdu'l-Bahá occupied room no. 141 on the second floor of the Hotel Marquardt, and that He and His attendants had 'the same number of rooms as before'.

Return to Germany

765 According to Wiebers, these Bahá'ís included Wilhelm and Marie Herrigel; the Schwarz family, who called on 'Abdu'l-Bahá early that morning; and Alma Knobloch, who arrived at 11:00 a.m. (*Alma Sedonia Knobloch*, p. 221). Writing of the Schwarzes, Wiebers states: 'Uncertain whether to bother the Master so early, they finally decided to at least see how he was doing. 'Abdu'l-Bahá Himself answered the door with a big smile and welcomed them' (ibid.). Alma Knobloch has recorded this memorable interaction she had with 'Abdu'l-Bahá on that occasion: 'He took my right hand that he was holding very firmly and placed it into his left hand and held tight shaking hands and did not say goodbye to His guests but remained standing where he stood. Then he opened his arms and held me closely; I snuggling in his arms and he folded me closely to him, after some time it seemed long and heavenly I looked up and the guests were standing at the door spellbound – and others were looking in from the hall – he led me to the door and patted me, 'Blessed, blessed"' (ibid. p. 222). Sohrab has also written down these remarks which the Master made to Alma Knobloch that morning:

'The love of Baha'u'llah is the essence of happiness. Any heart which will become the depository of this love is always happy . . . Therefore you must be very happy because you are living in the Day of the Blessed Perfection. All the prophets longed for this day. They yearned for one moment of this time. Appreciate the value of this age, the more you appreciate these days, the greater will be your blessings.'

766 Sohrab writes that 'Abdu'l-Bahá said the following to those who came to visit Him bearing roses: 'I have come back again to Stuttgart. This shows that Stuttgart has a great deal of capability and the people are worthy of entrance in[to] the Kingdom of Abhá. God willing the Cause of God will advance greatly in Stuttgart and its promotion will be extraordinary, many souls shall accept the revelation and all will be made happy.'

767 The present translator is grateful to Amín Egea for sending him a facsimile of the original article in German, and to Janet Rawling-Keitel for providing him with this direct translation of it into English.

768 According to Sohrab, Wilhelm Herrigel came at 8:00 p.m.; he and the others all walked to the Bürgermuseum, which was nearby.

769 Sohrab writes: 'There were more than 1500 people present and people were coming in, filling the galleries.' Later in this same diary letter from 25 April 1913, Sohrab refers to the audience as 'a waving, moving sea of humanity, all eager to hear the words of the Master', and states that 'many of them had come from the surrounding towns'. German sources indicate that there were actually 600 people present that evening.

770 Namely, Consul Schwarz, Sohrab, and Zarqání himself.

771 Sohrab says this was 'a very good address . . . on the life and ideals of the Master'. In a letter Herrigel wrote to Charles Mason Remey many years later in 1926, he mentions that 'Abdu'l-Bahá had asked him to 'read the translation of the talk He had given at the Temple Emmanuel synagogue in San Francisco' (Wiebers, *Alma Sedonia Knobloch*, p. 223), but that 'Abdu'l-Bahá entered just as he began to read that address (ibid. p. 224). For an English translation of this talk by 'Abdu'l-Bahá, refer to *The Promulgation of Universal Peace*, pp. 361–70.

772 Additional excerpts from this talk appear in the online supplement to this book:
https://bahai-library.com/supplement_abdul-baha_europe_1912-1913.

773 Sohrab writes: 'When we reached the car[,] hundreds of people, those who could not enter the hall[,] had gathered. Hats were raised and the handkerchiefs were waving when they saw the Master coming down from the stairs. The car carried away this King of Kings amidst the rejoicing and happiness of all these devout people!' Sohrab also notes that, while in the car, 'Abdu'l-Bahá said, 'It was a remarkable meeting

and its effect in the Bahai world will be far-reaching.'

774 A fuller account of these remarks, recorded by Sohrab, appears in the online supplement to this book: https://bahai-library.com/supplement_abdul-baha_europe_1912-1913.

775 In his diary letter dated 5 April, Sohrab writes with reference to 'Abdu'l-Bahá's first sojourn in Stuttgart: '. . . before arriving he expected to stay only one day or two, but he found the German believers so warm, so enkindled that he decided otherwise'.

776 Sohrab's account indicates that these visitors were Bahá'ís.

777 Sohrab writes that 'Abdu'l-Bahá gave the following answer in response to a question about whether He was happy.

778 According to Sohrab, this was 'a Bahai farmer who ha[d] come from one of the towns of Switzerland to see the Master'.

779 Sohrab's account indicates that 'Abdu'l-Bahá actually addressed the latter two paragraphs in the following quotation to a group of Bahá'ís who came to visit Him at around noon that day.

780 ' 'Abdu'l-Bahá had stayed in Geneva at the G^{d} [Grand] Hôtel de la Paix on September 2nd–3rd 1911, before proceeding to London' (Balyuzi, *'Abdu'l-Bahá*, p. 390n).

781 A direct English translation of this article from the original German, produced by Rhoda Lane, appears in Egea, *Apostle of Peace*, vol. 2, pp. 151–2.

782 This is a translation of Zarqání's Persian rendering of the excerpt, and the content differs slightly from Rhoda Lane's direct translation of the relevant passage: 'A dignified old man with a long white beard, a high brow and the sharply cut noble eyes of a distinguished aristocratic Oriental, as one might think an Abraham . . .' (Egea, *Apostle of Peace*, vol. 2, p. 151).

783 This is a translation of Zarqání's Persian rendering of the excerpt, and the content differs slightly from Rhoda Lane's direct translation of the relevant passage: '. . . one may welcome the European journey of Abdul Baha, even if in thought one might reject him as a bringer of a higher religion' (Egea, *Apostle of Peace*, vol. 2, p. 152).

784 According to Sohrab, it was Consul Schwarz who 'asked the Master whether he would like to consult a doctor'.

785 Including one of the Bismarck Towers, according to Sohrab. Ulrich Gollmer writes that this was the Bismarckturm, 'a lookout tower with a spectacular view over the whole of Stuttgart valley', named after the German statesman Otto von Bismarck (private correspondence with Ulrich Gollmer dated 21 April 2020). According to Sohrab, 'Abdu'l-Bahá had made these comments on Bismarck earlier that day: 'He was the most wonderful genius in statesmanship. He was a wise, shrewd

and most intelligent diplomat. First he conceived the plan of the confederation of the scattered German principalities into one great empire and then for long many years he worked persistently for its realization till at last his labors were crowned with success. To accomplish such a great task of union was superhuman. Now all this German development and its modern culture owe its origin to the confederation. Notwithstanding all these services, all that is left of him is a name in history and statues erected in his memory here and there. But if he had served one thousandth part the Cause of God, eternally he would have shone forth from the horizon of everlasting glory.'

786 Regarding this excursion, Sohrab writes: 'We had more than one hour drive through the royal park called the "Solitude". There were many old trees, lovely lakes and innumerable deer. On our return the Consul was showing the Master the palace belonging to a Baron. "This is the best private residence in Stuttgart", he said. "No", the Master answered, "the best residence in Stuttgart is yours, because we have been there and have raised the mention of God". Again expatiating on the antiquity of a noble family, the Master answered: "The noble family will be the one which you will found, because you are a believer in Baha-ollah."' According to Ulrich Gollmer, German reports identify "the royal park" as the park that adjoins the Schloss Solitude, and the "lovely lakes" as the lakes around the Bärenschlössle, a royal hunting lodge (private correspondence with Ulrich Gollmer dated 21 April 2020). Sohrab goes on to say that the car made a stop at the office of Edwin Fisher for a few minutes before reaching the home of Consul Schwarz. Gollmer has clarified that this was actually the home of Edwin Fisher, located at Stitzenburgstraße 12 (private correspondence with Ulrich Gollmer dated 21 April 2020).

787 Sohrab writes: 'At four o'clock many prominent men and women of the royal Court of the King of Wurtemberg were invited to meet the Master. Happily [i.e., fortunately] they all understood English and the address of the Master could be made more interesting to them. Many of them were Counts and Countesses, Barons and Baronesses and of the cabinet of the King. It was a very significant meeting and the result of it will be far-reaching for the Cause in Germany. The Consul and his wife were very glad because they were enabled to bring about such a brilliant gathering. They were all most attracted with the Master's address.' Alice Schwarz notes that 'it was a great question whether the beloved Master would be able to address them as He had been requested to be present at a celebration of unity in the Women's Club and had promised to go. 'Abdu'l-Bahá was walking up and down in His room in deep prayer, when He was asked whether He would honour those awaiting Him with a greeting. And how overjoyed they were when the Master entered their midst' (Wiebers, *Alma Sedonia Knobloch*, p. 227).

788 Sohrab notes that Olly Schwarz also brought 'Abdu'l-Bahá a book to sign, and that He inscribed the following prayer: 'O Thou Beauty of Abha! Make Thou this maid-servant of Thy Threshold a radiant lamp so that like unto a star she may shine with the Light of Thy love.'

789 Departing the home of Consul Schwarz at 5:00 p.m., according to Sohrab.

790 According to Sohrab, this was actually a nineteen-day Feast held at the Frauenclub (women's club). Concerning the attendance, Sohrab writes: 'As this [F]east was decided upon only yesterday, therefore all the Bahais did not know about it, notwithstanding there were more than 150 friends . . . Amongst those who were present there were many important men and women in the social life of Stuttgart.' German sources simply have this as 'a meeting with the friends' at the Frauenklub, Kanzleistraße 24, at 5:00 p.m. According to these sources, 'Abdu'l-Bahá began with a prayer; His talk was translated into English by Ahmad Sohrab, then into German by Wilhelm Herrigel, and the German was stenographed by Annemarie Schweizer; the room was decorated with many flowers; and tea and cake were served (private correspondence with Ulrich Gollmer dated 24 April 2020). Wiebers refers to it as a 'Unity Meeting' and adds, 'Although the meeting was planned at very short notice, all four rooms were opened to accommodate the 150 guests' (*Alma Sedonia Knobloch*, p. 227).

791 Additional excerpts from this talk appear in the online supplement to this book:
https://bahai-library.com/supplement_abdul-baha_europe_1912-1913.

792 According to Werner Gollmer, Wieland and Diebold married on 28 April 1913 at 9:00 a.m.; see *Mein Herz ist bei euch*, p. 188. While both Zarqání and Sohrab have recorded Diebold's first name as Eugene in their chronicles, German sources state that it was Jochen.

793 Sohrab writes that 'Abdu'l-Bahá met with this minister on both 28 and 29 April, but that this particular conversation took place on 29 April. Ulrich Gollmer notes that the minister was from Schwäbisch Hall, and that he has been referred to as 'Pfarrer R' in German sources (pfarrer being German for 'pastor'), but that his full name does not seem to have been recorded (private correspondence with Ulrich Gollmer dated 25 April 2020). Wiebers identifies him as 'Pastor Rohleder' (*Alma Sedonia Knobloch*, p. 228).

794 Sohrab writes that this was 'a blind believer' who was 'a man of elderly age', and captures 'Abdu'l-Bahá's remarks to Him as follows: 'Praise be to God that thy insight is open and thou art witnessing the realities with the eyes of perception. Spiritual blindness is worse than material blindness. That is why Christ says: 'These people have eyes but they see not.''

795 According to German sources, there were only a few very brief visits that day.

796 Sohrab writes that 'Abdu'l-Bahá was also visited on that day by Mrs Eckstein, and then Mr and Mrs Schwarz. To Mrs Eckstein He said: 'Your husband . . . is firm and sincere in the Cause and assuredly he shall be confirmed in spreading the glad-tidings of the Kingdom. He is an active Bahá'í. In this Cause there are two kinds of Bahá'ís. The first kind is active and speaking; the second is inactive and silent. These two although Bahá'ís, yet they are wildly different from each other. The former is more beloved than the latter. The body has two hands, one is active, the other paralyzed. Which one do you prefer?' And to Mr and Mrs Schwarz, who had come to inquire after His health, He said: 'Complete physical health is to be enjoyed by the animals. Consider when the animal possesses perfect health, it brays, it rolls on the grass, it grazes in the meadows, it dances and kicks and it does perform all kinds of prank[s]. But man may enjoy the completest physical health, live in the palace and be surrounded with all the luxuries of modern civilization, yet he may not feel happy, mental anxieties attack him, spiritual worries encircle him, he weeps, laments and stalks abroad ghost-like. This in itself shows that man must take greater care of his spiritual health. Again a person may be sick, lying in bed and a piece of good news is brought to him, suddenly he is revived and often he is healed. The happiness of man is through his spiritual health and not bodily health. My spirit is always healthy, therefore I am always happy. You must likewise strive to gain this spiritual health and happiness and thank ye God that ye are living in the age of the Blessed Perfection; ye have heard his resounding call; ye are awakened from the slumber of negligence, ye have attained to the most great bounty and ye have obtained eternal life. If ye had given the treasures of the whole world, ye could not obtain this most great bounty. Consider that Mr. Morgan, the American multi-millionaire died and left behind his wealth but ye shall never die, ye are always living in the Kingdom of Abhá and the traces of your faith and assurance shall ever live.'

797 According to Alice Schwarz, this meeting actually took place the previous day (28 April), beginning at 11:30 a.m. and lasting approximately two hours (private correspondence with Ulrich Gollmer dated 24 April 2020).

798 According to Sohrab, Schweizer was translating *The Brilliant Proof* into German at the time. His account of 'Abdu'l-Bahá's response is largely the same as what Zarqání has recorded in the following quote, with the notable exception of this remark concerning Mírzá Abu'l-Faḍl: 'He is greater even than the apostles [of Christ].' Ulrich Gollmer writes that it is not clear whether Schweizer had already begun to translate *The Brilliant Proof* or simply intended to do so (private correspondence with Ulrich Gollmer dated 25 April 2020). The translation was eventu-

ally published by Zuffenhausen Bahai-Vereinigung under the title *Glänzender Beweis*.

799 Sohrab's account indicates that this visit by the parents and children, as well as the remainder of the events recorded in this entry – with the possible exception of the final detail, concerning the telegram that was sent to Paris – actually took place the previous day (28 April).

800 An older translation of this talk was previously published in *Star of the West*, vol. 7, no. 15 (12 December 1916), p. 142.

801 At noon, according to Sohrab, who has written the physician's name rather illegibly as something like 'Dr. Kahlhas'.

802 According to Sohrab, 'the early callers' who inquired about 'Abdu'l-Bahá's health that morning were Wilhelm Herrigel, Consul Schwarz, Emil Ruoff, and 'several other friends'.

803 Sohrab writes that 'Abdu'l-Bahá addressed the following words to a group of Bahá'ís who had gathered in His presence at about 9:30 a.m.

804 Sohrab writes in his diary letter of 26 April that Faber was 'a celebrated physician of [Bad] Mergentheim who has declared himself publicly to be a Bahai'. His first name does not seem to be known.

805 To clarify: Bebenhausen was formerly a Cistercian monastery, but by the time of 'Abdu'l-Bahá's visit in 1913, it had become a palace for gaming used by King Wilhelm II of Württemberg (not to be confused with Wilhelm II of Prussia, the German Kaiser).

806 'Abdu'l-Bahá wrote the following in the guestbook of Palace Bebenhausen: 'The royal court is empty because I cannot see the face of the king. The green pasture is as if mown down, because it is not adorned with the glorious figure of the Queen. (sig.) Abdul Baha Abbas' (Wiebers, *Alma Sedonia Knobloch*, p. 229).

807 Zarqání's chronology here is phrased confusingly, as it appears to conflate the timing of 'Abdu'l-Bahá's visits to Steinenbronn and Bebenhausen, but Sohrab's account makes it clear that, after departing the Hotel Marquardt, 'Abdu'l-Bahá's car first went to Steinenbronn, then to Bebenhausen, and then returned to the hotel at about 8:00 p.m.

808 Sohrab recounts 'Abdu'l-Bahá's charity while in Steinenbronn through the following anecdote: 'He came down from the car and distributed money and candies amongst a few children and started to walk through the streets. Immediately the rumor was spread that the "King of the East" has come and more than one hundred children were after the Master. He gave me some money and I [ex]changed it in a nearby store and He asked me to distribute it amongst them. I ordered them to form a long line and put a piece of money in the hand of each. When I finished my pleasant "job", the Master told me: "You have now mustered an army and you can fight against any power!"'

809 Both Sohrab's account and German reports make it clear that 'Abdu'l-Bahá addressed the following words to a group of people who actually visited Him the previous day (30 April) at 3:00 p.m.

810 Sohrab identifies this child as Otto Häfner.

811 According to Ulrich Gollmer, 'Abdu'l-Bahá addressed these words to Elise and Julie Stäbler (private correspondence with Ulrich Gollmer dated 9 May 2020).

812 Having left the hotel at 10:30 a.m, according to Sohrab.

813 'Abdu'l-Bahá's entreaties for the confirmation of the German Bahá'ís have been recorded by Alma Knobloch in this account of the moment 'Abdu'l-Bahá left Germany for the last time:

Our beloved left on 1 May at 10:55 AM for Paris. At 10:30 AM our beloved came to the station . . . Oh, such a beautiful sight, our Beloved came out of the center aisle of the depot like – well words fail to express the King of the Universe, majestic and powerful and looking so large and handsome, His oriental robes giving a royal aspect, slowly with a kingly bearing. He advanced several steps behind Him was followed by an immense crowd . . . All of a sudden, He began to speak, and I translated it into German: 'I hope you will become trained in the teachings of Baha'o'llah. I hope the heavenly blessings may descend upon you! That you love each other more, that the Heavenly confirmation may descend upon you! I have sown pure seeds, it depends upon you, what the results will be. It is my hope that they will grow, they will give forth many harvests, I will pray that you may become confirmed in the divine path.' He then asked if the train was ready and a few moments later passengers began to file out and He arose, and the believers formed 2 rows and He passed through. He then got into his car, almost all were crying a sight never to be forgotten. Here we stood for about five minutes. Consul Schwarz, wife and daughter, Dr. Faber and a number of young men from Esslingen and I stood back against the building and all the many believers in front of us and Abdul-Baha at the large window, the Persians in back of him and Mirza Mahmood with an immense bunch of followers [flowers] which He saved. How glorious Abdul-Baha looked so pleased, so happy. And as the train moved out, He turned His blessed face toward the front of the train, for all were crying. (Wiebers, *Alma Sedonia Knobloch*, p. 230)

814 Sohrab has this as 10:53 a.m. German reports indicate that the train was scheduled to depart at 10:52 a.m, but did not actually leave until 11:08 a.m. Alma Knobloch has 10:55 a.m, as mentioned in the preceding endnote.

815 Jasion writes: 'Sohrab estimates about two hundred were at the hotel and later at the station to bid ['Abdu'l-Bahá] farewell' (*'Abdu'l-Bahá in France*, p. 541).

816 An English translation of the remarks 'Abdu'l-Bahá made to this passenger – a 'Mr. H.E. Warneke, of 9 East 37 St., New York City, a merchant of chinaware and bronze statuettes' (Jasion, *'Abdu'l-Bahá in France*, p. 541) – appear in the online supplement to this book: https://bahai-library.com/supplement_abdul-baha_europe_1912-1913.

817 According to Jasion, these were 'Zoroastrians from Bombay . . . two ladies and a young man, on their way to London' (*'Abdu'l-Bahá in France*, p. 542). Sohrab has recorded these remarks which 'Abdu'l-Bahá made to them: 'Persia will advance very rapidly . . . she will be crowned with her former glory and Phoenix-like she will spring up out of the ashes of shame and humiliation. You shall return to your beloved land and you will be respected by all the nations of the world. You will be honoured and loved by everyone. Thirteen hundred years you have wandered over the face of the world. Now it is high time to go back and assist in the reconstruction of your country' (ibid.). He then says that 'Abdu'l-Bahá 'showed them photographs of the Bahá'ís in Stuttgart and explained that all these and even the Bahá'ís in America believe in the divinity of Zoroaster through being Bahá'ís' (ibid.).

818 Sohrab has this as 9:15 p.m.

819 Jasion writes that 'Paul and Mirra Richard, Alice R. Beede, Maud Lillienthal, Edwin and Josephine Scott, Bertha Holley, Edith Sanderson, Mírzá Jalál and others were at the station to greet ['Abdu'l-Bahá]' (*'Abdu'l-Bahá in France*, p. 543).

Return to France

820 Among them Laura and Hippolyte Dreyfus-Barney; Alice Beede, who had recently arrived from New York City and had come with flowers from Maud Lillienthal; and Edwin Scott, according to Sohrab.

821 Jasion writes that, as 'Abdu'l-Bahá was recounting His time in Budapest, He spoke 'in particular about professors Ármin Vámbéry and Ignác Goldziher' (*'Abdu'l-Bahá in France*, p. 544).

822 Sohrab's account makes it clear that 'Abdu'l-Bahá addressed these words to Hippolyte Dreyfus. As part of this conversation, according to Sohrab, 'Abdu'l-Bahá also said, 'The German people are very civilized. They are serious and earnest. They are industrious and energetic.' Later that same morning, in a conversation with Edwin Scott, He remarked, 'The believers of Stuttgart are blessed souls. They shall advance extraordinarily. I was very pleased with them.'

823 According to Jasion, this was 'a copy of the weekly supplement of the newspaper *Le Petit Journal*, dated 4 May' (*'Abdu'l-Bahá in France*, p. 544).

824 The original French caption reads '*Le Nouveau Prophète de l'Islam: Abdul-Baha prêchant l'apaisement et la fraternité dans une mosquée à*

Constantinople,' which more accurately translates to 'The New Prophet of Islam: 'Abdu'l-Bahá preaching calm and brotherhood in a mosque in Constantinople' (ibid.).

825 Sohrab's account makes it clear that 'Abdu'l-Bahá addressed these words to Alice Beede and Maud Lillienthal, who had come to visit Him at 4:00 p.m.

826 Jasion writes: 'Sohrab reports that at the meeting there was a discussion of various forthcoming publications. Horace Holley announced that his book, *Bahaism, the Modern Social Religion*, will soon be published simultaneously in America and Britain, Beatrice Irwin stated that two of her articles had been accepted by London magazines and would be published soon, and the French believer Madame Moro (see endnote 830 for more on her) said that she is "writing a pamphlet on the Cause, especially adapted to the French temperament"' (*'Abdu'l-Bahá in France*, p. 546).

827 'Riḍvániyyih Khánum was a Persian Bahá'í serving in 'Abdu'l-Bahá's household in Acre. She was the daughter of Ḥájí Siyyid Javád and the wife of Mírzá Ḥusayn Ḥájí, the brother of Aḥmad Yazdí' (Jasion, *'Abdu'l-Bahá in France*, p. 498, n. 1181). It seems that she accompanied 'Abdu'l-Bahá and His retinue during their time in France, and Jasion writes that 'she was chosen for this role probably because of her fluency in French' (ibid.).

828 Jasion writes that this was actually the Baltimore Hotel, located on '88bis avenue Kléber at the corner of rue Léo-Delibes' (*'Abdu'l-Bahá in France*, p. 543). He goes on to say: 'For some unknown reason Zarqání states in volume two of his *Kitáb-i badáyi' u'l-áthár* that this was the "Hotel California". Hasan Balyuzi in his very readable biography of 'Abdu'l-Bahá repeats it by stating "Hôtel California in Rue Colbert, near the Bibliothèque Nationale" (p. 391). No listing of any "Hôtel California" in Paris can be found for this period, nor any hotel on rue Colbert' (*'Abdu'l-Bahá in France*, p. 543, n. 1294). Additionally, Sohrab notes that 'Abdu'l-Bahá occupied suites 35–37 of this hotel.

829 Maud Lillienthal and Alice Beede, according to Sohrab, who notes that Dr Muḥammad Khán was also present on this occasion. 'Abdu'l-Bahá had invited the two women to have lunch at 1:00 p.m.

830 Jasion, who spells this woman's surname as 'Moro' (probably based on Sohrab's transcription), writes: 'No information about Madame Moro has surfaced. It is possible that her name was actually spelled Mareau or Moreau' (*'Abdu'l-Bahá in France*, p. 546, n. 1310). Zarqání's transliteration of the name into Persian is ambiguous, such that both of the alternative renderings proposed by Jasion strike the present translator as equally plausible. Thus, the choice of 'Moreau' in this English translation represents a mere guess.

831 5:00 p.m., according to Sohrab.

832 A lengthier account of these remarks appears in the online supplement to this book:
https://bahai-library.com/supplement_abdul-baha_europe_1912-1913.

833 A lengthier account of these remarks appears in the online supplement to this book:
https://bahai-library.com/supplement_abdul-baha_europe_1912-1913.

834 According to Sohrab, 'Abdu'l-Bahá addressed the first few sentences from these remarks to Paul Richard and the remainder to 'a few others'.

835 Jasion has this as 'a French Bahá'í who had been giving lectures at the meetings' (*'Abdu'l-Bahá in France*, p. 553). While Horace Holley, along with his wife and daughter, did visit 'Abdu'l-Bahá that day, Jasion's chronology seems to suggest that these remarks were made to someone else.

836 According to Sohrab, this question was asked by Bertha Holley.

837 An English translation of 'Abdu'l-Bahá's talk appears in the online supplement to this book:
https://bahai-library.com/supplement_abdul-baha_europe_1912-1913.

838 More specifically, Jasion writes that '['Abdu'l-Bahá's] three servants' – presumably, Siyyid Asadu'lláh Qumí, Mírzá Maḥmúd Zarqání, and Mirza Ahmad Sohrab – dined with Him that evening (*'Abdu'l-Bahá in France*, p. 556).

839 This took place in the evening, according to Sohrab.

840 Sohrab's account makes it clear that 'Abdu'l-Bahá actually related these anecdotes the previous morning (of 5 May).

841 This took place at the beginning of the day, according to Sohrab, whose lengthier account of these remarks appears in the online supplement to this book:
https://bahai-library.com/supplement_abdul-baha_europe_1912-1913.

842 Sohrab's account makes it clear that the remainder of the events in this entry actually took place the previous day (5 May).

843 Sohrab attributes these similar remarks to 'Abdu'l-Bahá, apparently spoken at about the same time: 'I do not feel happy in Paris. I do not know whether it is its depressing atmosphere or the effect of the indifference of the people in spiritual things. As I look upon these crowds and these buildings my heart is compressed. I wish to leave this city as soon as possible. I wonder how the people can live in such an atmosphere all their lives and be happy, spending their precious time in hunting, racing, and devising new games and pastimes.'

844 Sohrab's own record makes it clear that he and 'Abdu'l-Bahá actually had this exchange the previous day (6 May).

845 According to Sohrab, 'Abdu'l-Bahá addressed these comments to 'a

Bahá'í who [had] been taught by Mrs. May Maxwell and another by Mr. [Percy] Woodcock' after praising 'both [those] illumined souls'.

846 At around this time, according to Sohrab, 'Abdu'l-Bahá related this anecdote about His skillful marksmanship as a youth: 'When I was young they would light ten candles and at the range of a very long distance I would put out the lights one after another without missing one.'

847 Another version of these remarks, recorded by Sohrab, appears in the online supplement to this book:
https://bahai-library.com/supplement_abdul-baha_europe_1912-1913.

848 Sohrab has this as 'the other day', which is more accurate. The Scotts did pay 'Abdu'l-Bahá this visit on Wednesday, 7 May, and their weekly gathering which 'Abdu'l-Bahá missed that week would have been on the evening of Monday, 5 May.

849 Sohrab states that 'Abdu'l-Bahá recounted this dream the previous afternoon (of 6 May) while on a carriage ride as it was nearing the Seine.

850 Sohrab writes that their train left at 9:00 a.m. that day.

851 According to Jasion, 'It is probable, but not certain, that this was La Maison de Santé du Docteur Blanche at 17, rue Berton' (*'Abdu'l-Bahá in France*, p. 525). In his original chronicle, Zarqání has referred to this hospital with phrases like *dáru'ṣ-ṣiḥḥiḥ* and *baytu'ṣ-ṣiḥḥiḥ*, which both mean 'house of good health,' a literal translation of 'Maison de Santé'.

852 Jasion writes that 'Abdu'l-Bahá addressed this talk to 'some newly arrived Bahá'ís' (*'Abdu'l-Bahá in France*, p. 572).

853 By Sohrab's account, this included Rúḥu'lláh, the son of Varqá. Sohrab attributes these words to 'Abdu'l-Bahá on that occasion: 'When [Rúḥu'lláh] was in 'Akká with his father, I asked him one day, "Tell me, Rúḥu'lláh! What is the greatest desire of thy life?" Immediately he answered, "I long for martyrdom in the path of God." Again I asked him, "Why do you believe in the religion of Bahá'u'lláh?" He answered, "Because I have investigated it for myself. I am not a Bahá'í because my father is one, but because I have thoroughly investigated it!"'

854 Jasion indicates that this was 'Arnold William Rosenthal, the foreign correspondent of the *Pittsburgh Spectator*' (*'Abdu'l-Bahá in France*, p. 570), and that he actually visited 'Abdu'l-Bahá the previous afternoon (of 7 May). Acceding to a request from Rosenthal, 'Abdu'l-Bahá wrote a Tablet for the readers of the *Spectator* on 9 May, which was printed in the paper soon afterward. A rendering of that Tablet into English, produced by the present translator and approved by the Research Department at the Bahá'í World Centre for publication, appears in the online supplement to this book:
https://bahai-library.com/supplement_abdul-baha_europe_1912-1913.

855 According to Jasion, drawing on Sohrab's account, 'Abdu'l-Bahá actually addressed these words to Hippolyte Dreyfus in a separate conversation later in the day.

856 This stroll down the Champs-Élysées actually took place on the previous day (7 May), according to Sohrab, who has recorded this anecdote quite differently from Zarqání: 'The Beloved ['Abdu'l-Bahá] was interested in the artillery and watched it for a long time. Suddenly we observed all the eyes were looking up ward [sic] and as we looked we saw a large balloon floating calmly in the air. It came and stood high up in the middle of the Champs Elysée [sic]. It was a very beautiful sight! Some one [sic] remarked jokingly that it would set at naught all the precautions of the police if just at [the] right time a bomb was thrown from the balloon' (*'Abdu'l-Bahá in France*, p. 567).

857 'A fabulous bird with a perforated bill emitting a musical sound; hence, a symbol of music' (Sulayman Hayyim, *The Larger Persian–English Dictionary*, p. 1023).

858 An English translation of this talk from 'Abdu'l-Bahá appears in the online supplement to this book:
https://bahai-library.com/supplement_abdul-baha_europe_1912-1913.

859 Jasion writes: 'Ahmed Paşa called and talked with 'Abdu'l-Bahá for over an hour. His father had been a great admirer of Bahá'u'lláh when they lived in Edirne. 'Abdu'l-Bahá gave Ahmed Paşa one of His photographs and a copy of the April issue of the *Asiatic Quarterly Review*' (*'Abdu'l-Bahá in France*, p. 575).

860 According to Sohrab, 'Abdu'l-Bahá used this opportunity to take a walk, on which Dr Muḥammad Khán accompanied Him.

861 According to Jasion, this was 'Alice Beede who arrived with a French friend' (*'Abdu'l-Bahá in France*, p. 576).

862 A lengthier account of this reply – which, according to Sohrab, 'Abdu'l-Bahá gave in response to some remarks by Maud Lillienthal, who had told Him about a bird which sang sweetly by her window – appears in the online supplement to this book:
https://bahai-library.com/supplement_abdul-baha_europe_1912-1913.

863 This was 'a walk with Mírzá Ḥusayn 'Árif' that lasted 'for about two hours' (Jasion, *'Abdu'l-Bahá in France*, p. 577).

864 This was a certain 'Mr. Lee', whom Jasion describes as 'most likely an English Bahá'í' (*'Abdu'l-Bahá in France*, p. 577, n. 1386), and Dorothy Hodgson.

865 At that meeting, 'Horace Holley read portions of his book and Hippolyte [Dreyfus-Barney] read a letter from Riḍváníyyih Khánum which she wrote before her departure' (Jasion, *'Abdu'l-Bahá in France*, p. 578).

866 One of these letters was sent from Los Angeles, according to Sohrab,

who only writes, 'The news contained therein about the meetings made the Master very happy.'

867 'A fabulous, monstrous bird, corresponding nearly to the griffin' (Hayyim, *The Larger Persian–English Dictionary*, vol. 2, p. 153).

868 'A fabulous mountain believed to surround the world' (Hayyim, *The Larger Persian–English Dictionary*, vol. 2, p. 511). According to legend, the *símurgh* lives on the summit of Mount Qáf.

869 An English translation of this talk from 'Abdu'l-Bahá appears in the online supplement to this book:
https://bahai-library.com/supplement_abdul-baha_europe_1912-1913.

870 This Tablet was specifically addressed to Mary B. Morrison (1843–c. 1929), a widowed dressmaker living in Denver and an active member of the Bahá'í community there. The following is an early translation of the complete Tablet:

Upon her be Baha'u'llah El Abha!

He is God!

O thou who has[t] turned thy face to the Kingdom of God!

Thy letter was received. Thou has[t] asked regarding the contribution toward the education of the children of the school of Tabriat [Tarbíyát]. Co-operation and mutual assistance are the basis of the religion of God. The East must assist the West and the West must assist the East. Whosoever quotes anything from my tongue, ask [of] him an authority, either with my pen or with my signature. If he has such authority in his hand, all-right; if he has no such authority, do not give any importance to tradition. Keep always this as a criteria [criterion] in view.

Convey the utmost of longing on my behalf to the believers and the maid-servants of the Merciful. I am engaged in their mentioning and beg for them Divine confirmation, so that the power of the spirituality of the Kingdom of Abha may environ the souls, quicken the hearts, deliver them from the hand of self and desire and suffer them to attain to the highest summit of faithfulness.

Then the Sun of the Covenant will shine, flooding the Orient and the Occident with glorious lights. There is no opportunity to write more than this.

Upon thee be Baha'u'llah El Abha!

(Signed) Abdu'l Baha Abbas

Paris, May 10, 1913

('Abdu'l-Bahá to Mary Morrison, 10 May 1913. Typescript. Dwight Barstow Collection, no. 459. The translator may have been Sohrab, as a very similar translation appears in his diary letter to Harriet Magee dated 6 May 1913).

871 Sohrab's own translation of this Tablet appears in his diary entry for 6 May 1913, where he writes that it was composed by 'Abdu'l-Bahá 'just

one day after our departure from New York', which would have been 6 December 1912.

872 The latter was Léa Marie Sophie Inès Cardozo Dreyfus, who 'was very ill' and 'resided at 2, Avenue Hoche, a few blocks away from the Arc de Triomphe' (Jasion, *'Abdu'l-Bahá in France*, pp. 582–3).

873 Sohrab writes, '. . . after talking on the current misfortunes of Turkey, ['Abdu'l-Bahá] told the Pá<u>sh</u>á about His experiences in Calif[ornia], His lectures before various societies, and more interesting than anything else the accumulative incidents which led Him to take the long trip to Calif[ornia] and meet the friends there. The Pá<u>sh</u>á said: "This has been a great service to the world." 'Abdu'l-Bahá replied: "This was through the confirmations of God, otherwise I could not take such a long and arduous journey. I have done my duty. Now may God create the effect."'

874 Sohrab writes, 'We returned home and, as there were present a few of the Persians, the name of Prof. E. G. Browne was mentioned and he became the subject of discussion and his relation to the Bahá'í Cause.'

875 Sohrab has recorded these remarks of 'Abdu'l-Bahá as follows: 'If you have the perception power, as soon as you look in the faces of the people, you can observe what ideals are reigning in their hearts. The other day I walked through the avenues but did not find one face reflecting the spiritual ideals of the heart. In America it was different. Mighty thoughts of philanthropy and illumined ideals of humanitarianism are set in motion and you find their reflections in the faces, because they were lodged in the hearts. One woman told me, she was working day and night to abolish the law of capital punishment; another person told me she desired to have a uniform inter-state divorce law; a third was devoting his time to the betterment of the conditions of criminals in the penitentiaries and the abolishing of capital punishment; another one was trying to introduce a new system of education etc etc. I found these noble ideals have permeated throughout all the classes of America. Civilized and refining influences were at work. Everyone was thinking in terms of progress, and upward march. In the strictest sense of the word, there was no reactionary movement in America. What was called reactionary there will be radical progressiveness in other parts of the world.'

876 According to Sohrab, the first paragraph of these remarks was made in response to an unspecified question that Horace Holley had put to 'Abdu'l-Bahá, while the remainder was addressed to other unnamed inquirers.

877 These were amusing anecdotes, according to Sohrab: 'In the afternoon many Persians came to see Him and He kept them entertained with amusing stories of 'Akká life. I have seldom seen Him enjoying Himself

so much. He spoke uninterrupted for several hours and He laughed and kept others laughing with humorous and funny stories. It was one of the few most enjoyable afternoons that we shall never forget.'

878 This excursion happened at 8:00 p.m., according to Sohrab.

879 Sohrab adds that 'Abdu'l-Bahá showed photographs of the German friends to those who were present and 'said that their faces were illumined, their faith is strong and their future assured'.

880 Sohrab has captured the following remarks made by 'Abdu'l-Bahá on this occasion that were not recorded by Zarqání: 'We have many friends in Scotland, many devoted friends; amongst them is Mrs. Whyte. I was most pleased with my visit to that country. Scotland weather is very invigorating. The city of Edinburgh is beautiful and its inhabitants progressive and deeply religious. Theirs is [a] firm and strong character. They are thirsty for spiritual water. They are not dogmatic but they feel a heartfelt sincerity about their religion. This is good. They have a deep sense for spiritual ideals. While there, they asked me many questions; and several large meetings were organized and we delivered addresses. The people of Edinburgh are intelligent and critical. They investigate. They do not accept anything on blind faith. All their questions were dignified and based upon a desire to learn. A meeting was held in Mrs. Whyte's house for the Oriental students. They were from China, Japan, Persia, India, Turkey, Syria, Arabia, etc. It was a wonderful demonstration of the union of the East and of the West. These were strong, purposeful young men. Another meeting was organized by the Esperantists and one by the Theosophists. Both these meetings were marvelous. Mr. Page, the Secretary of the Esperanto Association and Mr. Graham Pole, the General Secretary of the Theosophical Society were most intelligent and sympathetic. They were very kind and hospitable. In short I met many people in Edinburgh whom I shall never forget.'

881 A reference to the Parable of the Great Banquet, recounted in Matt. 22:1–14 and Luke 14:15–24.

882 A reference to the Parable of the Sower; see Matt. 13:1–30, specifically verses 1–9.

883 An English translation of this story appears in the online supplement to this book:
https://bahai-library.com/supplement_abdul-baha_europe_1912-1913.

884 A reference to the well-known miracle of Jesus recounted in Matt. 14:13–21, Mark 6:31–44, Luke 9:12–17, and John 6:1–14.

885 According to Jasion, 'Abdu'l-Bahá gave 'a lengthy explanation' in response to this question, but it 'was not recorded [by Sohrab]' (*'Abdu'l-Bahá in France*, p. 588). It would seem, therefore, that Zarqání has only quoted a small fraction of 'Abdu'l-Bahá's remarks here.

886 Sohrab's account indicates that 'Abdu'l-Bahá told this story to Hippolyte Dreyfus in particular.

887 'In Shii, Ismaili, and Sufi thought, the Quran is held to contain two aspects: an outer or apparent meaning (zahir) and an inner or secret meaning, often allegorical or symbolic (batin). While the apparent meanings of the Quran are accessed through the traditional discipline of tafsir or exegesis, the batin is made known only through the hermeneutical process known as tawil (interpretation). The notion of secret meanings underlying the Quranic verses is connected to the notion of God as al-Batin, the Hidden One (Quran 57:3), whose absolutely nonmanifest Being underpins the created realm. The Ismailis were also known as the Batinis, presumably on account of their predilection for esoteric interpretations of the divine revelation' ('Batin', in Esposito (ed.), *The Oxford Dictionary of Islam*).

888 Zarqání appears to have redacted this person's name. Sohrab's account suggests it may have been the Iranian envoy, 'Abdu'ṣ-Ṣamad Khán, who 'called and . . . talked with 'Abdu'l-Bahá for about an hour' (Jasion, *'Abdu'l-Bahá in France*, p. 590).

889 Among these friends, according to Jasion, were Edith Sanderson and her mother Margaret, whom 'Abdu'l-Bahá 'thanked . . . again for their hospitality to Rúḥá Khánum and Riḍváníyyih Khánum' (*'Abdu'l-Bahá in France*, p. 590).

890 Among them a woman identified by Sohrab as 'Miss Chevalier', whom Jasion believes to be a very likely reference to Miss Faith Chevallier, 'a Franco-American Bahá'í' who was 'noted for her welfare work among prison inmates in California' (*'Abdu'l-Bahá in France*, p. 591, n. 1418).

891 Jasion's description of the full excursion is as follows: 'The drive was all through the park, past the two lakes with their pleasure boats, through tunnels of luxuriant trees, past green meadows and flower beds decked with an astonishing variety of flowers and colours. Afterwards they went on a walk. Though the names of some of the streets have changed and Sohrab's description is incomplete, it seems that on this day 'Abdu'l-Bahá and His companions went from the hotel down the short street called rue Léo-Delibes to rue Lauriston, turned at Avenue de Malakoff (today Avenue Raymond Poincaré) to the broad Avenue Bois de Boulogne (today Avenue Foch), then along this fashionable street to the Place de Étoile (today Place Charles de Gaulle) and then turned down Avenue Kléber back to the Baltimore Hotel' (*'Abdu'l-Bahá in France*, pp. 592–3).

892 Among them the Intiẓámu's-Salṭanih, according to Sohrab.

893 Sohrab mentions that 'Abdu'l-Bahá told three stories in this vein – one about His early childhood, one about Bahá'u'lláh, and one about 'the charming custom of the lover and loved one in Mazandaran' – but does not go into any further detail.

894 Among them Paul and Mirra Richard, who 'stayed till eleven discussing with 'Abdu'l-Bahá a wide range of topics' (Jasion, *'Abdu'l-Bahá in France*, p. 593).

895 At 1:00 p.m., according to Sohrab.

896 One of these Tablets is as follows:

To the maid servant of God, Miss Edna McKinney, Boston, Mass.

Upon her be Baha'o'llah El Abha!

HE IS GOD!

O thou my beloved daughter!

Thy detailed letter was received. Its contents portrayed the details of the Feast of Nau Roez [Naw-Rúz]. It became the source of infinite joy. Praise be to God that thou art engaged in the service of the Kingdom with an illumined heart, a spirit rejoiced with the Glad Tidings of God and a pure aim. Therefore, rest thou assured that the Breaths of the Holy Spirit shall confirm thee, and day unto day thou shalt become nearer unto the Court of Baha'o'llah and thou shalt obtain [a] greater portion of the Bestowal of Baha'o'llah. I hope that thy tongue may become most eloquent and fluent in teaching the Cause and in the meetings and gatherings thou mayst deliver such addresses as bestow happiness and beatitude upon the audience!

Upon thee be Baha El Abha!

(Signed) Abdul-Baha Abbas!

Translated by M. Ahmad Sohrab,

May 15, 1913,

Paris, France

(Cited in Anise Rideout, 'Early History of the Bahá'í Community in Boston, Massachusetts'.)

897 At about 5:00 p.m., according to Sohrab, who accompanied 'Abdu'l-Bahá on this walk.

898 A reference to Mírzá Fatḥ-'Alí, of whom Balyuzi writes: 'Mírzá Fatḥ-'Alí, surnamed Fatḥ-i-A'ẓam ["the Most Great Victory"] by Bahá'u'lláh, was one of the leading Bahá'ís of Ardistán, near Iṣfahán. He had accepted the Báb, with others in Ardistán, when Mullá 'Alí-Akbar-i-Ardistání and Mullá Ṣádiq-i-Muqaddas passed through the town after their persecution in 1845, with Quddús, in Shíráz. Later, he was one of the Bábís who early recognized the station of Bahá'u'lláh. The horse on which Bahá'u'lláh was mounted as He set off for Constantinople was a gift from Mírzá Fatḥ-'Alí, who was not among those accompanying Him. He returned to Ardistán where he served Bahá'u'lláh as a point of contact for the distribution of Tablets to believers in Írán, often having to use his own judgment as to the intended recipient when no names were given on the Tablets. His son [Áqá Siyyid Shaháb] was married to the daughter of Mullá 'Alí-Akbar. He died shortly before the ascension of Bahá'u'lláh, Who revealed two Tablets of Visitation in his honour'

(*Bahá'u'lláh: The King of Glory*, p. 471). According to Balyuzi, 'Bahá'u'lláh has said of Fatḥ-i-A'ẓam that, all the way from Baghdád to Constantinople, he was with Him in spirit, though not corporeally' (ibid. p. 261). It is worth noting, moreover, that Mírzá Fatḥ-'Alí was the great-grandfather of Hushmand Fatheazam (1924–2013), who served on the Universal House of Justice from 1963 to 2003.

899 A lengthier account of these remarks, recorded by Sohrab, appears in the online supplement to this book: https://bahai-library.com/supplement_abdul-baha_europe_1912-1913.

900 Sohrab's account indicates that the remainder of the events in this entry actually took place the following day (17 May).

901 According to Sohrab, 'Abdu'l-Bahá was speaking here – and later in the quotation, where He says, 'Had that person killed me . . .' – with reference to 'a man who had called himself a Bahá'í, but had embezzled a considerable sum of money' (Jasion, *'Abdu'l-Bahá in France*, p. 598).

902 In Zarqání's original chronicle, this heading reads '7 May', which appears to be a printing error.

903 See Zarqání's entry for 14 August 1912, published in Zarqání, *Maḥmúd's Diary*, pp. 205–08.

904 These remarks, recorded by Sohrab as follows, were apparently prompted by a postcard from Dr Zia Bagdadi, which 'Abdu'l-Bahá had just received: 'Doctor Bagdadi is sincere and faithful in the Cause of God. He is confirmed in the service of the Kingdom. I am well pleased with him. In reality his father was a rare and wonderful soul. Up to the last breath he was faithful in the Covenant of Bahá'u'lláh. Now, praise be to God that he has left behind three sons, each one of whom is a servant of the Cause.'

905 Zarqání's parenthetical remark here seems to suggest that 'Abdu'l-Bahá spoke in a large room (*ṣálun*) at an apartment complex on this occasion, and that He was residing in that complex at the time. In fact, Appendix VI of Jasion, *'Abdu'l-Bahá in France* ('Places Associated with 'Abdu'l-Bahá's Visits to France') makes it clear that 'Abdu'l-Bahá would have still been lodging at the Hotel Baltimore, where He stayed from 1 May to 26 May. He and His retinue did eventually change residence before leaving Paris, when they lodged a second time at the Martha-Pension Family-Hotel (where they had previously stayed from 20 March to 1 April) from 27 May to 13 June, but this had not yet taken place on 18 May. For more information, see Jasion, *'Abdu'l-Bahá in France*, pp. 737–8.

906 Jasion writes that Moore asked 'Abdu'l-Bahá: 'How is it possible to develop the will-power, and, cause it to advance through infinite stages of progress?' (*'Abdu'l-Bahá in France*, p. 604). An English translation of the talk 'Abdu'l-Bahá gave in response appears in the online supplement to this book:

https://bahai-library.com/supplement_abdul-baha_europe_1912-1913.

907 Sohrab's account of this excursion is more descriptive: 'At three o'clock, accompanied by all His Persians, ['Abdu'l-Bahá] drove through [the] Bois de Boulogne. It was a beautiful day of sunshine and warmth and thousands of people were in the park. The Beloved and myself entered the Longchamps where they had the horse race. He watched the race from the grandstand and told the story of a horse race in Persia, a race He had seen when He was 8 years old. He was also interested in a military aeroplane flying over the field. At 5 o'clock the race was over and the people poured out. Such fashion and millinery art seldom one sees anywhere and the Master stood aside and watched the Parade of Manikins [Mannequins].'

908 Sohrab writes that the Richards came to see 'Abdu'l-Bahá at 9:00 p.m. and 'carried along a very brilliant discussion' with Him until nearly 11:00 p.m.

909 This was Siyyid Ja'far Ṣadru'l-'Ulamá, whom Momen describes as 'a covert Azali cleric' who was 'considered as one of the leading reformers in the [Persian] Constitutional Revolution' (*The Bahá'í Communities of Iran*, vol. 1, p. 60).

910 According to Sohrab's account, this was actually an American Bahá'í by the name of Miss Hart, not Lucy Moore. Jasion writes that 'no further information has surfaced about this American Bahá'í' (*'Abdu'l-Bahá in France*, p. 597, n. 1432).

911 Sohrab's account indicates this was an American lady by the name of Mrs Noel, on whom 'no information has come to light' (Jasion, *'Abdu'l-Bahá in France*, p. 609, n. 1464). A record of 'Abdu'l-Bahá's exchanges with this woman, as well as His conversations with other visitors that day, appears in the online supplement to this book:
https://bahai-library.com/supplement_abdul-baha_europe_1912-1913.

912 Sohrab's account suggests that 'Abdu'l-Bahá might have gone out for this stroll and made the following remarks two days before (on 17 May).

913 Sohrab describes these visitors as 'three very important Persians', with whom 'Abdu'l-Bahá discussed 'Persia, Turkey, etc.'

914 At 5:00 p.m., according to Sohrab.

915 Possibly a reference to John 6:38: 'For I came down from heaven, not to do mine own will, but the will of him that sent me.'

916 Additional remarks 'Abdu'l-Bahá made to Fanny Knobloch on this occasion are as follows:

Abdul-Baha listened very attentively to all that was said pertaining to the Sunday School, saying: 'Kheli Khoob! Kheli Khoob! [Very good! Very good!] It is very necessary that the Sunday School be renewed again and be made active.' Then Abdul-Baha asked: 'The Sunday School is very important; then why did the parents become indifferent? It is very essential that the Sunday School be upheld, first, because the children are there taught the Words of Baha'o'llah. Second, because the morality taught there is the true Bahai morality. Third, because the children will there become firmly established in the precepts and truths of the Bahai Cause. Fourth, because the Sunday School is of great value: It is very good and they must attend it with joy and fragrance [radiance] and with enthusiasm.'

(To Miss F. A. K., Paris, 20 May, 1913. Published in *Star of the West*, vol. 9, no. 8 (1 August 1918), pp. 94–5.)

In mentioning the indifference of certain parents, 'Abdu'l-Bahá was alluding to a conversation He had had almost two months earlier with Fanny's sister, Alma Knobloch, in Stuttgart:

Question: 'Is it right that Mrs. H.. . . . has given up the Sunday School work?'

He looked very much surprised and grieved and said: 'Why? No! She must keep it up by all means. Why does she want to give it up?'

I answered that it was too far for most of the children and some were too delicate to walk.

He said: 'If they cannot arrange to go every Sunday, they must go every other Sunday, if not every other Sunday then once a month. But they must come together and must keep up the Sunday School.'

(Words of Abdul-Baha to Miss A. S. K. spoken in Stuttgart, Germany, 2 April 1913. Published in *Star of the West*, vol. 9, no. 8 (1 August 1918), p. 94.)

917 A lengthier account of these remarks from 'Abdu'l-Bahá appears in the online supplement to this book: https://bahai-library.com/supplement_abdul-baha_europe_1912-1913.

918 A partial (but still extensive) English translation of this talk appears in the online supplement to this book: https://bahai-library.com/supplement_abdul-baha_europe_1912-1913.

919 Sohrab's account seems to suggest that one of these respected Persians was the Intiẓámu's-Salṭanih.

920 An early institution of higher education established in the eleventh century by Abú 'Alí Ḥasan ibn 'Alí Ṭúsí, the Niẓámu'l-Mulk, after whom this institution and its counterparts in other cities were named.

921 Sohrab identifies this visitor as a Bahá'í but does not name her.

922 Another record of this exchange, taken down in English, is published in *Star of the West*, vol. 8, no. 11 (27 September 1917), p. 138:

Question: 'How shall I overcome seeing the faults of others – recognizing the wrong in others?'

Answer: 'I will tell you. Whenever you recognize the fault of another, think of yourself: What are my imperfections? – and try to remove them. Do this whenever you are tried through the words or deeds of others. Thus you will grow, become more perfect. You will overcome self, you will not even have time to think of the faults of others. Man is blind, yet he sees far. That is puzzling. We are in Paris and we see the faults of the believers in America and in Stuttgart, but, we are so blind that we cannot see the nose (touching his nose) on our own face. While we are blind we have a far-sighted vision to America, to Germany. You must carry the glad-tidings of the Kingdom wherever you go, and make the people happy, awake them into greater activity – make them active . . .'

(Abdul-Baha: Notes of private interview, Paris, 1913)

923 Sohrab's account suggests that 'Abdu'l-Bahá may have actually made the remarks about Christ the day before (on 20 May).

924 Jasion writes that this was 'the recording studio of Société Pathé Frères at 98, rue de Richelieu' (*'Abdu'l-Bahá in France*, p. 621) where, according to Sohrab, four records of 'Abdu'l-Bahá's voice were produced in all (ibid.). Jasion also notes that 'these records are now in the Bahá'í World Centre Archives, Haifa' (ibid. p. 621, n. 1506).

925 Zarqání appears to have redacted this person's name. Sohrab has identified him only as 'S. ------- S. -------', which Jasion believes to be a reference to Najaf-Qulí Khán, the Ṣamṣámu's-Salṭanih, who served as the prime minister of Persia for two brief periods; see *'Abdu'l-Bahá in France*, pp. 622–3 and 623, n. 1509. His residence in Paris was located at 4, Avenue de Camoëns; Jasion writes that this was 'the exact same flat 'Abdu'l-Bahá occupied during His 1911 visit to Paris', noting that this nobleman 'had such a high regard for 'Abdu'l-Bahá that he rented this very flat for his own use while staying in Paris' (ibid. pp. 622–3).

926 'Abdu'l-Bahá returned to the hotel at 11:00 a.m. and 'found many people waiting to see Him' (Jasion, *'Abdu'l-Bahá in France*, p. 624).

927 Among 'Abdu'l-Bahá's visitors that day, according to Jasion, were Fanny Knobloch and Gottlieb Pfund; see *'Abdu'l-Bahá in France*, p. 624.

928 Jasion writes that, in addition to several Persians who came at 3:00 p.m. and stayed for about an hour, an Iranian prince also visited; he reported on the recent troubles in Persia against the Bahá'ís and 'had a long talk with 'Abdu'l-Bahá' (*'Abdu'l-Bahá in France*, p. 625). Sohrab identifies the prince only by his initials, 'N. S.'

929 Jasion writes: 'In the morning, Gottlieb Pfund, Maude M. Holbach, and Fanny A. Knobloch arrived with flowers for 'Abdu'l-Bahá. Later in the morning, Maud von Lillienthal and Alice R. Beede and many others arrived all bringing roses, pots of flowering carnations, fruit, and candy' (*'Abdu'l-Bahá in France*, p. 625). Sohrab specifies that Holbach and Knobloch arrived at around 7:00 a.m.

930 A translation of 'Abdu'l-Bahá's remarks on this subject appears in the online supplement to this book: https://bahai-library.com/supplement_abdul-baha_europe_1912-1913.

931 A translation of 'Abdu'l-Bahá's remarks on this subject appears in the online supplement to this book: https://bahai-library.com/supplement_abdul-baha_europe_1912-1913.

932 Sohrab writes that 'Abdu'l-Bahá spoke on these subjects at about 11:00 a.m.

933 At 3:00 p.m., according to Sohrab.

934 Sohrab's account suggests that 'Abdu'l-Bahá made these remarks on the education of children in the morning.

935 A reference to the annual Paris Spring Flower Show, or L'Exposition de Printemps de la Société Nationale d'Horticulture de France. That year's show – held in the Cours la Reine, behind the Grand Palais – was covered by *The New York Herald* (Paris); see 'Annual Paris Flower Show held on Cours-la-Reine', 23 May 1913, p. 1. Jasion writes: 'This year's open-air exhibit was dedicated to fruit trees and garden implements. Inside the hothouses were orchids, roses, pinks, pelargoniums (geraniums), etc. How 'Abdu'l-Bahá must have enjoyed walking among the mauve and pink sweet peas, dull-red rhododendrons, and salmon-pink hortensias, which were the highlights of this year's show' (*'Abdu'l-Bahá in France*, p. 630).

936 A lengthier account of this meeting, which includes an English translation of 'Abdu'l-Bahá's talk, appears in the online supplement to this book: https://bahai-library.com/supplement_abdul-baha_europe_1912-1913.

937 Among them 'the report mentioning the activities of Alice Buckton, Isabel Fraser, and Marion Jack in Edinburgh, where they gave many lectures and started a weekly meeting' (Jasion, *'Abdu'l-Bahá in France*, p. 633).

938 According to Jasion, this group of visitors consisted of 'Fanny Knobloch and a number of American Bahá'ís' (*'Abdu'l-Bahá in France*, p. 633), who asked 'Abdu'l-Bahá 'if the activities towards peace by William Jennings Bryan and Woodrow Wilson would bring results' (ibid.). Sohrab's translation of 'Abdu'l-Bahá's response is as follows: 'Of course. These two men are sincere and honest in their aims and purposes and I pray to God that they may become successful. They are the servants of universal peace and the oneness of the world of humanity. America has the capacity of becoming the standard bearer of international peace. Geographically it is a vast continent, far away from the jealous eyes of the envious neighbours; politically democratic and holding aloof from the political complications of Europe. Therefore America is the readiest and freest nation to arise in the service of humanity and initiate new plans of philanthropy and encourage the establishment of

peace throughout all parts of the world. I always pray that the banner of international unity and the solidarity of human race may be hoisted in America . . . I am most pleased with America. I ever supplicate in behalf of America so that the confirmations of His Holiness Baha-ollah may encircle it' (ibid.).

939 Zarqání appears to have redacted this person's name.

940 Sohrab refers to these visitors only as 'three very important Persian gentlemen'.

941 References to the Battle of the Trench and the betrayal of the Banú Qurayẓih, respectively. Refer also to a relevant talk from 'Abdu'l-Bahá recorded by Zarqání in this volume towards the end of his entry for 11 February 1913.

942 Jasion writes that these visitors 'did not leave till almost midnight' (*'Abdu'l-Bahá in France*, p. 634).

943 Among these visitors were Horace and Bertha Holley, with whom 'Abdu'l-Bahá 'spoke about the Bahá'í House of Worship to be built near Chicago' (Jasion, *'Abdu'l-Bahá in France*, p. 634). According to Sohrab, He also made these remarks on singing to another visitor: 'Whenever you sing, be in a state of supplication and prayer. Sing as though you are praying. Let thy song carry with it a spiritual effect, an effect which is lasting and long to be continued' (ibid.). Fanny Knobloch, who was yet another visitor on this occasion, recalls this conversation with 'Abdu'l-Bahá: 'To Miss K. How are you? Are you better? Yes better, very much better. **'Abdu'l-Bahá:** Good! Through the love of Bahá'u'lláh we are always at rest, even though the body is indisposed the soul is strong. While we were in Budapest our body was weak, but our soul rejoiced, could we have remained there for a time many would have been led to God, for the people there are ready to receive. **'Abdu'l-Bahá:** I am very pleased with the Believers in Stuttgart[;] in reality the Believers in Stuttgart are very good. I am very pleased with the Believers in England. I am very pleased with the Believers in America. I will always pray for the Believers in America, in England and in Stuttgart so God will strengthen them ever more' (Fanny Knobloch papers; quoted ibid.).

944 Jasion describes this as 'a short noon-day address to those gathered' (*'Abdu'l-Bahá in France*, p. 635).

945 At approximately 4:00 p.m., according to Sohrab.

946 At 9, rue Val-de-Grace.

947 Jasion seems to suggest that 'Abdu'l-Bahá may have actually paid this visit to Munír Pá<u>sh</u>á the following night (of 26 May), when He 'stayed till eleven pm talking with him, his wife, and a few other invited guests' (*'Abdu'l-Bahá in France*, p. 637).

948 Joseph H. Hannen (1872–1920) was the husband of Pauline Knobloch

Hannen (1874–1939), and thus the brother-in-law of Fanny Knobloch (1859–1949). He was posthumously named a Disciple of 'Abdu'l-Bahá by Shoghi Effendi.

949 According to Jasion, 'Fanny Knobloch called at about seven-thirty in the morning' (*'Abdu'l-Bahá in France*, p. 635); he writes that 'she was on her way to Stuttgart to visit her sister for a few weeks before returning to America' (ibid.). She said to 'Abdu'l-Bahá, 'I am happy, Abdul Baha. I leave your presence with the determination of teaching and spreading more and more the Message of the Kingdom of Abha' (ibid.). As part of His farewell address to her, 'Abdu'l-Bahá said, 'I hope thou wilt leave Paris as a messenger of the divine Joseph. Carry with thyself wherever thou goest the most great glad-tidings. Perfume the nostrils with the Fragrance of the garment of the divine Joseph. Give thou my greetings to all the believers of God. Rejoice their spirits with the heavenly glad News. I always remember them and beg for each one special confirmations. Give my wonderful Abha greetings to each one of the friends, specially thy sisters, Miss A. Knobloch and Mrs Hannen and her two dear sons, I am very happy on account of the services rendered by Mr Hannen. He is my son. I pray to Baha-ollah that the spiritual benedictions and confirmations may encircle him . . . I shall always keep thee in my mind. I hope that thou mayst be always a herald of the cause of God' (ibid. p. 635–6). Fanny Knobloch herself notes that 'Abdu'l-Bahá said, 'Give my greetings to all, especially Miss Alma Knobloch, Pauline, Mrs. Hannen and Mr. Joseph Hannen' (Fanny Knobloch papers; quoted ibid. p. 636).

950 Jasion indicates that there was just one such visitor, 'a lady who was a known singer' (*'Abdu'l-Bahá in France*, p. 636).

951 Sohrab writes that 'Abdu'l-Bahá remarked, 'I spoke much with Ahmad Pasha today. I hope God will create the effect' (Jasion, *'Abdu'l-Bahá in France*, p. 636).

952 Among them Mirra Richard, 'who translated for the French speakers' (Jasion, *'Abdu'l-Bahá in France*, p. 637).

953 According to Jasion, this was 'a reading from *The Seven Valleys*' (*'Abdu'l-Bahá in France*, p. 637).

954 Sohrab writes that, once the meeting had been concluded, 'Abdu'l-Bahá said the following to Edwin Scott: 'Your studio is a radiant place. It is the gathering place of the friends of God. It will have great importance in the future' (Jasion, *'Abdu'l-Bahá in France*, p. 637).

955 A process that lasted from 4:00 to 6:00 p.m., according to Jasion, who notes that '['Abdu'l-Bahá's] room was no. 12 on the first floor' (*'Abdu'l-Bahá in France*, p. 639). According to Sohrab, the Martha-Pension had called the afternoon before (26 May) to inform 'Abdu'l-Bahá, at His request, that three rooms at their hotel were now vacant. Sohrab writes,

'With the Master, we went there to inspect the rooms and He was pleased with them. Arrangement was made to move tomorrow to our former hotel.'

956 According to Jasion, one of these visitors was Dorothy Hodgson, who came 'to say farewell, as she was going to Brittany with her father' (*'Abdu'l-Bahá in France*, p. 638), and to whom 'Abdu'l-Bahá said, 'Thou art my dear daughter. I love thee very much. I have heartfelt attachment for thee. Thou wilt ever be in my memory. Wherever thou goest, teach the Cause. Inform the people about the realities of this Manifestation. The more thou spreads the Glad-tidings, the greater will be thy spirituality. Teaching the Cause of God is like unto the sweet singing of an artist. The Artist enjoys more the song than an indifferent audience, because, she has studied for a long time and knows too well the hardships and the sufferings of the student life' (ibid.). Edith Sanderson and Maud Alice Cruttwell also visited. Cruttwell was 'apparently . . . emotionally overcome with meeting 'Abdu'l-Bahá' (ibid.), Who said to her, 'Praise be to God that the Glances of the Favours of Baha-ollah have encircled thee and thou hast attained to the Knowledge of the Kingdom. The Doors of the Kingdom of God are open before thy face. Happy is thy condition for thou hast entered therein. I hope that thou wilt become one of the elect. Be thou ever firm, ever steadfast. Firmness and steadfastness are the two great attributes of God. Adorn thyself with these spiritual garments. As long as the tree is not well rooted it will not yield luscious fruits. As long as the foundation is not well laid, the building shall not stand forever' (ibid.). Crutwell then knelt before 'Abdu'l-Bahá, Who recited this prayer: 'O Thou Almighty! Direct Thou this traveller toward the Pathway of Thy Guidance. Suffer this thirsty one to reach to the Fountainhead of Thy Bestowal. Confer upon this indigent one an abode in the Neighbourhood of Thy Infinite Mercy. Let this hungry one sit around the Celestial Table of Thy heavenly food. O God! Encircle her with the Glances of Thy Providence! Immerse her in the refulgent sea of Thy glorious lights! Grant her the swift wings of inspiration, so that she may soar toward the real [reality?], of the exalted ideals and universal love! Protect her and guard her from every evil. Verily Thou art the Generous, the Compassionate and the Merciful!' (ibid. p. 639). Jasion notes, moreover, that Maud Lillienthal, Alice Beede, and Laura and Hippolyte Dreyfus-Barney also came to visit.

957 Jasion specifically mentions Aḥmad Pá<u>sh</u>á; he and 'Abdu'l-Bahá 'went to a store next to the hotel where they spoke in length in Turkish' (*'Abdu'l-Bahá in France*, p. 639).

958 At about 8:00 p.m., according to Sohrab.

959 Sohrab writes that these Ottoman visitors included an unidentified 'Turkish gentleman', who spoke with 'Abdu'l-Bahá until noon; a cer-

tain 'Halim Bey', who came at 4:00 p.m., with whom 'Abdu'l-Bahá discussed 'His recent trip' (presumably to Germany, Hungary, and Austria) and to whom He showed 'eight photos of Stuttgart Bahá'ís', and whom Jasion suspects may be a reference to 'the former and future Ottoman minister of justice, Samipaşazade Halim Bey' (*'Abdu'l-Bahá in France*, p. 639); the wife of Munír Páshá; and Samipaşazade Sezaî, 'the Ottoman ambassador in Madrid' (ibid. p. 640). With regard to the last of these visitors, Sohrab writes, 'His father knew the Master. He stayed only a few minutes as he had other engagements.'

960 Sohrab's account seems to specify that 'Abdu'l-Bahá spoke on these subjects with the wife of Munír Páshá and 'several other women'.

961 Jasion writes: 'In the evening, ['Abdu'l-Bahá] went out with Dr. Muḥammad Khán and another newly arrived Iranian and returned about nine o'clock' (*'Abdu'l-Bahá in France*, p. 640).

962 Jasion seems to suggest that one of these visitors was Inayat Khan, who at some point asked a question about nirvana. An English translation of 'Abdu'l-Bahá's response appears in the online supplement to this book:
https://bahai-library.com/supplement_abdul-baha_europe_1912-1913.

963 Zarqání appears to have redacted this person's name. According to Sohrab, this was Fatḥu'lláh Khán Akbar, also known as the Sardár-i-Manṣúr or Sipahdár-i-Rashtí, a wealthy landowner and Iranian statesman who would go on to serve as Persia's Minister of the Interior (1916) and prime minister (1920–21). His residence was located at 42, ave. de La Bourdonnais.

964 A prominent jurist and religious authority of Shí'ih Islam. Concerning him, Bahá'u'lláh has written in His Súriy-i-Haykal: 'Shaykh Murtaḍá – may God exalt his station and cause him to repose beneath the canopy of His grace! – showed forth kindness during Our sojourn in 'Iráq, and never spoke of this Cause otherwise than as God hath given leave' (*Summons of the Lord of Hosts*, p. 119).

965 Jasion writes: 'It was about four o'clock when they departed [the residence of Fatḥu'lláh Khán Akbar]. At five o'clock, ['Abdu'l-Bahá] called on Mrs. Jackson with Dr. Muḥammad Khán and then visited Edith Sanderson. 'Abdu'l-Bahá later visited Rúḥá Khánum at the hospital. He returned to the hotel very fatigued' (*'Abdu'l-Bahá in France*, p. 641).

966 In a similar vein, Sohrab has attributed these remarks to 'Abdu'l-Bahá on this occasion: 'One must eat in moderation. Man is not created for food. He must not indulge in eating too much. Over-eating is the cause of many diseases. Rise from the table always before you are satisfied. One must have been retrograded to the lowest point as to be perfectly satisfied with eating, drinking, and sleeping. The enjoyment of man comes through the unfoldment of his intellect, intelligence, the virtues

of the world of humanity, and the divine characteristics. Man has two aspects; a spiritual and an animal aspect. His animal side is sustained through food and drink like unto other beasts but his spiritual life is fed by the ideal perfections, faith, assurance, the knowledge of God and the love of God. More attention must be given to the latter than the former.'

967 Sohrab's translation of some remarks 'Abdu'l-Bahá made to the Schwarzes on this occasion is as follows: 'I am most pleased to meet you again in Paris. My heart bears testimony to the fact that the Stuttgart Bahais are most sincere. The days of Stuttgart and your hospitality shall never be forgotten. In reality the believers are united and agreed. The Cause shall progress greatly. Your children are always remembered by me. You have an excellent daughter [Olly Schwarz]. She is attracted and enkindled. She will become a great teacher in this Cause. Some souls are withered and they do not become interested and are not set a glow [sic], others receive the fire of the Love of God immediately. During the few days of our stay in Stuttgart you[r] daughter made marvellous spiritual progress' (Jasion, *'Abdu'l-Bahá in France*, p. 642).

968 According to Jasion, 'following 'Abdu'l-Bahá's talk, Consul Schwarz spoke in French about the community in Stuttgart' (*'Abdu'l-Bahá in France*, p. 643).

969 Sohrab's account indicates that this person actually came to 'Abdu'l-Bahá with this request, and that 'Abdu'l-Bahá made the following remarks in response, on the previous morning (of 30 May).

970 Among these German friends were Albert and Alice Schwarz, according to Sohrab, who writes that 'Abdu'l-Bahá called them 'the hundred petalled roses from the garden of Stuttgart'.

971 Sohrab's translation of some remarks 'Abdu'l-Bahá made to Boutaric is as follows: 'When you return, strive in the promotion of the Cause in your midst. Illumine then the souls. Establish in that city the centre of the lights of God. The confirmations of God shall descend upon thee' (Jasion, *'Abdu'l-Bahá in France*, pp. 643–4).

972 Jasion notes that Bey was 'accompanied by two other important Egyptians' (*'Abdu'l-Bahá in France*, p. 643).

973 Jasion writes: 'In the afternoon, ['Abdu'l-Bahá] went to the Baltimore Hotel to call on Consul Schwarz and his wife. He left after half an hour. Later He went out to call on several people, none of whom were home' (*'Abdu'l-Bahá in France*, p. 644).

974 Sohrab adds these details to this excursion: 'Accompanied by myself, the Master drove for nearly two hours calling on different people, and it so strangely happened that no one of them was at home. The last call was on Mrs. Lillienthal and Mrs. Beede in [the] International hotel. He waited for more than half an hour but they did not come, having taken a car ride to Versailles.'

975 According to Jasion, a Bahá'í from Agra, India by the name of Ḥishmatu'lláh Qurayshí was also present on this occasion. Jasion writes that Qurayshí 'became a well-known teacher of the Bahá'í Faith in India and was elected to the National Spiritual Assembly of India 1927–1935. He also worked on the Urdu translation of John Esslemont's *Bahá'u'lláh and the New Era*' (*'Abdu'l-Bahá in France*, p. 644, n. 1565). Additional biographical information on Qurayshí in Persian can be found in Mázandarání, *Táríkh-i-Ẓuhúru'l-Ḥaqq*, vol. 8, part 2, p. 1165.

976 Probably a reference to Munírih Khánum, the wife of 'Abdu'l-Bahá.

977 Sohrab writes that Áqá Mírzá Jalál told 'Abdu'l-Bahá that 'nearly 50 pilgrims from all parts of the Orient [were] anxiously awaiting' His arrival, and that 'some of them [had] been waiting for more than 5 months'.

978 'A believer of wide repute in Shíráz' (Taherzadeh, *The Revelation of Bahá'u'lláh*, vol. 2, p. 115, n. 2), who was given the title Bashír-i-Iláhí ('divine herald') by 'Abdu'l-Bahá. His real name was Mírzá Áqá Khán Bashíru's-Sulṭán (1864–1924), and he was the recipient of several Tablets from Bahá'u'lláh and many more from 'Abdu'l-Bahá. These have been compiled in their original languages by Nasir Bashirelahi in *Alváḥ-i-Názilih bih I'záz-i-Mírzá Áqá Khán Bashíru's-Sulṭán, Mulaqqab bih Bashír-i-Iláhí* (private publication, 2010), appended to which is a short biography of Bashír-i-Iláhí in Persian. Details on his life in English can be found in Momen, *The Bahá'í Communities of Iran*, vol. 2, pp. 272, 283–4, and 372–3.

979 Zarqání appears to have redacted this person's name.

980 Appointed by 'Abdu'l-Bahá Himself as the third trustee of Ḥuqúqu'lláh. Of Ḥájí Ghulám-Riḍá, who would later succeed Ḥájí Amín in this capacity, the Research Department at the Bahá'í World Centre has written: 'The third Trustee of Ḥuqúqu'lláh, Jináb-i-Ghulám Riḍá, was entitled Amín-i-Amín (Trustee of the Trustee). This distinguished soul was born into the wealthy merchant class of Tehran and was brought up to enjoy the comfortable life associated with it. During his youth, the urge to discover spiritual realities led him to the study of comparative religion and, while engaged in his business, he ventured to search out and associate with followers and leaders of religion. Disappointed in what he found, he sought more information about the Bahá'í Faith, which had been introduced to him by his secretary. This enquiry soon developed into a serious study of the sacred Tablets and Writings and his heart was illumined with the light of faith. After embracing the Cause, Jináb-i-Ḥájí Ghulám Riḍá engaged in Bahá'í activities and, at the age of 32, he gave up trade to devote himself fully and freely to the service of the Faith. He developed a special attachment to Jináb-i-Amín and became his constant assistant. In due course he received a Tablet from 'Abdu'l-Bahá urging

him to emulate Jináb-i-Amín and appointing him as Trustee of Ḥuqúqu'lláh. While ever mindful of the responsibilities of his new position, he took the utmost care of Jináb-i-Amín for the remainder of his life. Jináb-i-Ghulám Riḍá held the rank of Trustee of Ḥuqúqu'lláh for eleven years. His home became a centre for the gatherings of the friends and for the administration of the affairs of the Faith. It was during his Trusteeship that initial steps were taken for the registration of Bahá'í properties and endowments in Persia, and he was assiduous in doing his utmost for their protection and preservation. In 1938 he fell ill and passed away' ('The Development of the Institution for the Ḥuqúqu'lláh', March 1987; included in a message addressed by the Department of the Secretariat to all National Spiritual Assemblies, 25 March 1987).

981 Probably a reference to Áqá Siyyid Ismá'íl Sidihí (1848–1917), a celebrated Bahá'í poet from Isfahan more commonly known by his pen name of Síná. A biography of him and his older brother, Áqá Siyyid Maḥmúd Sidihí (1846–1909), known to most Bahá'ís as Nayyir, has been published in Sulaymání, *Maṣábíḥ-i-Hidáyat*, vol. 1, pp. 93–172. Details on the lives of both brothers in English can be found in Momen, *The Bahá'í Communities of Iran*, vol. 2, pp. 50–53, 55, 56n, 97, 154, 162, 222–3, 236, 318, 353n, and 439.

982 A reference to Muḥammad Káẓim Qazvíní (1844–1918), more commonly known to Bahá'ís as Shaykh Káẓim Samandar, an early Bábí and later a prominent Bahá'í. A biographical account of Samandar has been published in Balyuzi, *Eminent Bahá'ís*, pp. 191–215.

983 'Believers living in Tbilisi, Georgia, whose father Ḥájí Aḥmad met the Báb in Tabríz and hid the remains of the Báb after His martyrdom' (Afroukhteh, *Memories of Nine Years in 'Akká*, p. 428). Details on the lives of the Aḥmadov family can be found in Momen, *The Bahá'í Communities of Iran*, vol. 1, pp. 377, 390, and 398.

984 A reference to Mullá Bahrám Akhtar-Khávarí (1859–1930), a prominent early Zoroastrian convert to the Bahá'í Faith. A biographical account of Mullá Bahrám, written in Persian, has been published in Sulaymání, *Maṣábíḥ-i-Hidáyat*, vol. 4, pp. 376–446. Details on his life in English can be found in Momen, *The Bahá'í Communities of Iran*, vol. 2, pp. 101, 195, 371, and 378.

985 A reference to Ḥájí Mihdí Arjumand (1861–1941), also known as Áqá Rifú'á, an early Jewish convert to the Bahá'í Faith. A very brief account of his life has been published in Arsalan Geula, *Iranian Bahá'ís from Jewish Background: A Portrait of an Emerging Bahá'í Community*, pp. 126–9. Additional details can be found in Momen, *The Bahá'í Communities of Iran*, vol. 2, pp. 186, 190, 191–2, 193, 195, 209, 214, and 215. A more extensive biographical account of Arjumand's life, written in Persian, has been published in Sulaymání, *Maṣábíḥ-i-Hidáyat*, vol. 4, pp. 447–67.

986 A reference to Muḥammad Muṣṭafá Baghdádí (1837/8–1910), an early Bahá'í of Iraq and Apostle of Bahá'u'lláh who has been eulogized in 'Abdu'l-Bahá, *Memorials of the Faithful*, pp. 131–4. His sons were Dr Zia Bagdadi, Ḥusayn Iqbál, and 'Alí Iḥsán.

987 A reference to Ḥájí Siyyid Mihdí Shírází, an Iranian immigrant to Burma and one of the first members of its Bahá'í community. Several anecdotes about Shírází are published in the memoirs of Siyyid Muṣṭafá Rúmí, prepared by Iran Furútan Muhájir under the title of *Siyyid Muṣṭafá Rúmí: Hand of the Cause of God, Apostle to Bahá'u'lláh*.

988 A reference to Áqá Siyyid Muṣṭafá Rúmí (1846–1945), the early Bahá'í and builder of the Burmese Bahá'í community who was eventually martyred for his faith and posthumously appointed a Hand of the Cause by Shoghi Effendi. As mentioned in the preceding endnote, his memoirs have been published.

989 Áqá Mírzá Riḍá Manẓar (d. 1914), known as Mírzá Maḥram, was an Iranian Bahá'í who travelled throughout Persia, and eventually to India and Burma, to teach the Faith. Details on his life can be found in Momen, *The Bahá'í Communities of Iran*, vol. 2, pp. 51–4, 56n, 323, and 399. An account of his time in South Asia, written by Siyyid Muṣṭafá Rúmí, has been published in Furútan Muhájir, *Siyyid Muṣṭafá Rúmí*, pp. 71–84.

990 Concerning the Bahá'ís of India, Sohrab writes, 'The name of Mírzá Muḥammad-Riḍá Shírází was mentioned, who recently has made an extensive trip throughout India, spreading the message and preparing the way for the coming of 'Abdu'l-Bahá. "Yes," the Beloved said, "I read about it in an English newspaper when I was in London. Consider what a glorious effect has the power of teaching the Cause! I intend to make a voyage to India. I [would] like very much to do so if divine destiny agrees with my plan."'

991 This is probably a reference to Mírzá Ismá'íl Kitábfurúsh, who wrote poetry under the pen name 'Mishkát'. At the instruction of 'Abdu'l-Bahá, he lived in Izmir for a time to teach the Faith, until the Iranian population there rose up in opposition against him, at which time he was dispatched to the Caucasus to resume his teaching efforts. He continued to reside in that region and teach the Cause there, primarily in Baku and Tbilisi, until he eventually passed away in Tbilisi in 1336 AH (1917–18). For more biographical information on Mírzá Ismá'íl and a sample of his poetry (both in Persian), see Mázandarání, *Táríkh-i-Ẓuhúru'l-Ḥaqq*, vol. 8, pp. 62ff. Other possible candidates include Ismail Asadulaogli, mentioned in Soli Shahvar et al., *The Bahá'ís of Persia, Transcaspia, and the Caucasus*, vol. 2, p. 104, or Áqá Ismá'íl, the son of Ustád 'Alí-Ashraf Karímov, mentioned in Ali Nakhjavani, *Mírzá 'Alí-Akbar Nakhjavání*, p. 116; both were very early members of the Bahá'í community in Baku.

992 Given the context, this is likely a specific reference to the 1903 upheaval of Yazd, one of the bloodiest to occur in the ministry of 'Abdu'l-Bahá. A few of the incidents from that upheaval are listed in *Bahá'í World*, vol. 18, pp. 385–6. Additional details can be found in Momen, *The Bahá'í Communities of Iran*, vol. 2, pp. 380–91. Perhaps the most comprehensive account of this period, written in Persian, is published in Ḥájí Muḥammad Ṭáhir Málmírí, *Táríkh-i-Shuhadáy-i-Yazd* (1923).

993 Sohrab offers more details on this particular topic: 'A French woman was present and asked questions about the return of Christ and the expectation of the Theosophists. The Master gave her comprehensive answers and she was made most happy.'

994 A reference to 'Abbás 'Alí Khán (1867–1940), who wrote poetry under the pen name Bínish ('insight'). Details on his life can be found in Momen, *The Bahá'í Communities of Iran*, vol. 2, pp. 240, 245, and 316. A short biography of Bínish and a sample of his poetry (all in Persian) have been published in Ni'matu'lláh Dhuká'í Bayḍá'í, *Tadhkariy-i-Shu'aráy-i-Qarn-i-Avval-i-Bahá'í*, vol. 1, pp. 228–35.

995 This was Mírzá Hádí Shírází, the father of Shoghi Effendi. He married the eldest daughter of 'Abdu'l-Bahá, Ḍíyá'íyyih Khánum, in 1895.

996 A short biography of Mas'úd Qazvíní (c. 1859–1919) and a sample of his poetry (all in Persian) have been published in Bayḍá'í, *Tadhkariy-i-Shu'aráy-i-Qarn-i-Avval-i-Bahá'í*, vol. 3, pp. 370–83.

997 Sohrab's account does not include any of the foregoing discussion about poetry, but he does mention several details following 'Abdu'l-Bahá's talk at the public gathering that day which are absent from Zarqání's chronicle. At 3:00 p.m., 'Abdu'l-Bahá and Sohrab took a car to see Prince Muḥammad-'Alí Bey (the brother of the Khedive) at the Hotel Imperial on Rue Christopher Colombe, where 'Abdu'l-Bahá read for Him 'the Arabic text of His address in Oxford and spoke upon other interesting subjects' (this Arabic text was printed in *The Christian Commonwealth* and a facsimile of it has been published in Brendan McNamara, *The Reception of 'Abdu'l-Bahá in Britain: East Comes West*, Leiden: Brill, 2021). Afterwards, He visited the Ottoman Minister to Spain, who was sojourning in Paris at the time, and with whose father 'Abdu'l-Bahá was acquainted from the days when Bahá'u'lláh was conducted to Istanbul. Tea was then served at 15 Rue de la Nople, and 'Abdu'l-Bahá spoke on Ottoman political parties and current events. From there, 'Abdu'l-Bahá and Sohrab drove to the Dreyfus-Barney residence; since they were away, 'Abdu'l-Bahá rested for a few minutes and then returned to the hotel, where 'one of the celebrated Persian editors was waiting, and the Master received him with due courtesy and took him to His room to speak with Him'. Following this, Albert and Alice Schwarz came in; they 'asked many questions about the

meetings and how they should be conducted', to which 'Abdu'l-Bahá gave 'satisfying answers', and they left His presence with conspicuous joy. 'Abdu'l-Bahá then sent Sohrab to call on 'S.M.' (presumably the Sardár-i-Manṣúr) and he returned late, at which time he 'had the privilege of eating with Him' as Áqá Mírzá Jalál and Mírzá 'Alí-Akbar Nakhjavání were giving Him 'further news about their trips'.

998 A reference to Áqá (Muḥammad) Riḍá Shírází (d. 1912), also known as Áqá Riḍá Qannád ('confectioner'), discussed in endnote 14.

999 A reference to Mírzá Maḥmúd Káshání (d. 1912), 'a selfless and trusted companion of Bahá'u'lláh throughout His exile from Baghdád to 'Akká' (Taherzadeh, *The Revelation of Bahá'u'lláh*, vol. 2, p. 400). Brief episodes from the life of Mírzá Maḥmúd have been published in Taherzadeh, *The Revelation of Bahá'u'lláh*, vol. 1, pp. 288–9. A eulogy for him by 'Abdu'l-Bahá is also published in *Memorials of the Faithful*, pp. 39–41.

1000 A reference to Mírzá Ja'far Yazdí (d. 1891), 'a learned divine' who 'attained the presence of Bahá'u'lláh and became filled with a new spirit' (Taherzadeh, *The Revelation of Bahá'u'lláh*, vol. 1, p. 289). Taherzadeh further writes: 'On the way to Constantinople he served the friends in every possible manner' (ibid. pp. 289–90). Brief episodes from the life of Mírzá Ja'far have been published ibid. pp. 289–91. Additional details on his life can be found in Momen, *The Bahá'í Communities of Iran*, vol. 2, pp. 350–1.

1001 Among them Sulṭán-Mas'úd Mírzá, the Ẓillu's-Sulṭán, who governed the province of Isfahan for several decades. Sohrab writes that he came to see 'Abdu'l-Bahá at 3:00 p.m. and was taken to His room, where 'they were together for about an hour'. Sohrab then adds that 'Abdu'l-Bahá 'told [him] some of the things they talked about', but does not recount any of those details in his diary.

1002 Jasion believes this to be Ḥájí Khusraw Khán, the Sardár-i-Ẓafar, an Iranian politician and brother of Najaf-Qulí Khán, the Ṣamṣámu's-Salṭanih (*'Abdu'l-Bahá in France*, p. 646). Sohrab refers to him as 'S.Z.' and notes that he called on 'Abdu'l-Bahá sometime in the morning accompanied by 'three other Persians'.

1003 Sohrab writes, 'For two hours ['Abdu'l-Bahá] spoke on the Cause, on His historical address in [the] San Francisco Synagogue, and on the life and teachings of Bahá'u'lláh. Toward the end, He told them the story of an assassin who had killed 75 Bahá'ís and while the Blessed Perfection was in Baghdád He came there and took refuge at the holy Threshold because he was haunted by his enemies. Bahá'u'lláh protected him and he would go everywhere with perfect security, declaring that he was the freedman of Bahá'u'lláh.'

1004 Sohrab notes that one of these people who gave an 'interesting talk' was Mirra Richard.

1005 A lengthier account of the words 'Abdu'l-Bahá spoke on this occasion appears in the online supplement to this book: https://bahai-library.com/supplement_abdul-baha_europe_1912-1913.

1006 Sohrab's account includes several details following the gathering at the Scott residence which are absent from Zarqání's chronicle. First, 'Abdu'l-Bahá took a car to see the mother of Hippolyte Dreyfus, Léa Marie Sophie Inès Cardozo Dreyfus, who was 'in bed and very weak physically', and Sohrab writes that He 'read over her a short, beautiful prayer and most touchingly kissed her forehead'. From there, He went to the home of Hippolyte Dreyfus himself to rest for a few minutes and have a cup of coffee. Following this, He went to see Mary 'Edith' Jackson, with whom He spoke 'very beautifully about the glories of the other life and how He hoped that they will meet each other there; in that world of light wherein there will be no separation', eventually parting with the words 'I will always remember you and will pray for you'. Following this, 'Abdu'l-Bahá went to the Hotel International, where He, Albert Schwarz, Alice Schwarz, Hippolyte Dreyfus, Laura Dreyfus-Barney, Áqá Mírzá Jalál, Mírzá 'Alí-Akbar Nakhjavání, Zarqání, Sohrab, and others were the dinner guests of Maud Lillienthal. By Sohrab's account, they were all seated at the table by 8:45 p.m. with 'Abdu'l-Bahá sitting at the head. After dinner, everyone went into the reception room, 'where coffee was served and for nearly an hour reincarnation was the topic of discussion'. 'Abdu'l-Bahá then 'thanked most beautifully Mrs. Lillienthal for her reception' and walked back to the hotel with His attendants.

1007 This may be the 'member of the theosophical society, The Order of the Star in the East' who visited 'Abdu'l-Bahá that morning, according to Jasion (*'Abdu'l-Bahá in France*, p. 648).

1008 Jasion states that the Schwarzes 'were on their way to the train station to catch the nine o'clock train to Stuttgart' (*'Abdu'l-Bahá in France*, p. 649). Sohrab writes that the Schwarzes 'had brought a box of chocolate for the Beloved and He accepted it, blessed it, and gave it back to them to carry with them and, on His behalf, give one to each of the Bahá'ís and two to each one of their children. He showered upon them His wonderful blessing and, on their departure, He embraced Consul Schwarz and kissed Him many times.'

1009 A lengthier account of the words 'Abdu'l-Bahá spoke on this occasion appears in the online supplement to this book: https://bahai-library.com/supplement_abdul-baha_europe_1912-1913.

1010 Sohrab's account suggests that 'Abdu'l-Bahá actually spoke these words to the Schwarzes as part of His farewell address to them. Furthermore, regarding Mary Magdalene, Jasion mentions a detail that is notably absent from Zarqání's chronicle: 'The Dreyfuses, who were present, told ['Abdu'l-Bahá] about a play about Mary Magdalene then playing in Paris and invited Him to go with them to see it. He immediately accepted, and at a quarter to nine they arrived in their automobile and went to see the play. *Marie-Magdeleine* was performed at the prestigious Théâtre du Châtelet, located at 2, rue Edward Colonne, where it had premiered on 28 May' (*'Abdu'l-Bahá in France*, p. 650).

1011 At approximately 2:00 p.m., according to Sohrab, who writes that 'Abdu'l-Bahá was accompanied by Áqá Mírzá Jalál on this visit, and that He returned at about 4:00 p.m.

1012 Jasion writes: 'At five o'clock Sardár-i-Mansur with his brother, Mubassiru'l-Mulk Asaduláh Khán, called. With them, He drove to the Hôtel Imperial, 4, rue Christophe Colomb, to call on Prince Ali Muhammad Bey. 'Abdu'l-Bahá introduced the Persian politicians to the Egyptian prince. After staying a short time, 'Abdu'l-Bahá returned to His hotel' (*'Abdu'l-Bahá in France*, p. 649). Sohrab adds these details to that meeting: 'They started to talk on the closer union of the East and of the West, the better relations between the various nations and religions of the Orient, and the removal of misunderstanding from amongst them. The Beloved spoke at this important meeting in very eloquent Turkish, reciting stories of ancient times illustrating the valor, the civilization, and the courage of those old nations under all emergencies.'

1013 The present translator has not been able to definitively identify the person Zarqání is referring to here. Sohrab's diary letters make no mention of anyone by the name of 'Abdu'l-Karím around this time, nor does Jasion's extensive research on 'Abdu'l-Bahá's stay in France make any allusions to such a person. It could be a reference to Ustád 'Abdu'l-Karím Báqiroff, a member of the Báqiroff family, which had connections to 'Abdu'l-Bahá's travels throughout Europe, or possibly a certain Ḥáj 'Abdu'l-Karím Qazvíní, who is known to have met 'Abdu'l-Bahá in Egypt (Mázandarání, *Ẓuhúru'l-Ḥaqq*, vol. 8, p. 614). It could not refer to Mírzá 'Abdu'l-Karím Ardabílí (Asadov), who played a significant role in acquainting the Russian orientalist Alexander Tumanski with the teachings of the Bahá'í Faith, since he passed away in 1897 (Momen, *The Bahá'í Communities of Iran*, vol. 1, p. 434). Similarly, it could not refer to Ḥájí 'Abdu'l-Karím Ṭihrání – a Bahá'í merchant who was sent by 'Abdu'l-Bahá to America in 1900 to try and neutralize the seditious activities of Ibrahim Kheiralla, to whom Ṭihrání had taught the Faith – as he died in 1906 (Vahid Rafati, *Ma'ákhidh-i-Ash'ár dar Áthár-i-Bahá'í*, vol. 3, p. 100).

1014 At about 11:00 a.m., according to Sohrab.

1015 Sohrab writes, 'With Mírzá Jalál[,] ['Abdu'l-Bahá] went out and paid a long call on Rashíd Páshá who has moved from his old apartment to a new quarter. On His return He took His simple lunch in His own room, and at 3 o'clock I found myself sitting beside Him in automobile driving toward the Imperial Hotel to call again on the brother of Khedive. Here the Master met a Syrian naturalist and had a lively discussion with him on divine and natural philosophy. The naturalist become very much interested but after half an hour in company with the brother of Khedive, the Master called on Sardar Mansur by appointment. Tea was served and for two hours happy and intimate conversation continued. The apartment of Sardar Mansur is beautifully furnished with Oriental draperies and Persian rugs and these interesting objects were shown to the brother of Khedive before we left. Sardar Mansur's personal automobile was waiting for us downstairs and after the exchange of true Oriental courtesies we were again driven to our hotel. He rested for half an hour and then he went out followed by me to call on Mon. [Monsieur] and Madame Dreyfus. They were not in and we returned.'

1016 Sohrab has this as cherries, rather than money; he writes: 'On our way [back to the hotel], ['Abdu'l-Bahá] bought some cherries, but before reaching the hotel He had distributed them amongst the children in the street. The children know Him by this time and every time they see Him they gather around him. He said: "These are my friends. Their parents may not understand the love that I entertain for them. They may ask of themselves, why this Eastern man loves so much our children, while in reality there exists between us no racial or family relations!" And He gave the last handful of cherries to a little girl and kissed her on both cheeks.'

1017 More specifically, Jasion writes that the report was typewritten, in twelve pages, by Joseph Hannen, and that 'Abdu'l-Bahá requested it 'be translated into Persian and several copies be made of it for Sardár-i-Mansur, Sardár-i-Zafar, and for the Bahá'í assemblies in the East' (*'Abdu'l-Bahá in France*, p. 651). Sohrab adds that he himself was the one who translated the report into Persian, and that Zarqání transcribed copies of this Persian translation for Sardár-i-Manṣúr and Sardár-i-Ẓafar.

1018 This sentence appears to be 'Abdu'l-Bahá's Persian paraphrase of a passage from an untranslated Arabic Tablet of Bahá'u'lláh that has been published in *La'áli'u'l-Ḥikmat*, vol. 2, pp. 44–7 (see p. 45 for the original text of this specific passage).

1019 In addition to the members of 'Abdu'l-Bahá's retinue, Jasion writes that this group also included Mírzá 'Alí-Akbar Nakhjavání, Dr Muḥammad Khán, Áqá Mírzá Jalál, and Ḥishmatu'lláh Qurayshí (*'Abdu'l-Bahá in France*, p. 652).

1020 Sohrab writes, 'The Beloved enjoyed the supper very much and it was about half past ten when we walked back to the hotel behind [Him].'

1021 The story 'Abdu'l-Bahá proceeds to tell can also be found in Nabíl Zarandí, *The Dawn-Breakers*, pp. 137–38. It should be noted, however, that the roles are reversed in Nabíl's portrayal: it is Mírzá Muḥíṭ who seeks to have a secret audience with Bahá'u'lláh, and Kayván Mírzá – 'one of the Persian princes who dwelt in Ba<u>gh</u>dád' (ibid. p. 137) – who serves as his intermediary. This version of events is supported by Mázandarání in *Ẓuhúru'l-Ḥaqq*, vol. 4, p. 192, n. 1, where he states that Mírzá Muḥíṭ died of meningitis (*sarsám*), rather than typhus (*muḥriqih*). In fact, 'Abdu'l-Bahá Himself relates that same portrayal elsewhere: a pilgrim's note recorded in Persian by Mírzá Badí' Bu<u>sh</u>rú'í and dated 17 June 1915 (Badí' Bu<u>sh</u>rú'í, *Dar Ẓill-i-<u>Sh</u>ajariy-i-Mí<u>th</u>áq*, pp. 98–9), in which He attributes the death of Mírzá Muḥíṭ to 'a fever' (*tab*).

1022 Mullá Muḥammad-Ja'far Naráqí, whose name is sometimes shortened to Mullá Ja'far Naráqí (as 'Abdu'l-Bahá has done here), was a *mujtahid* who became a <u>Sh</u>ay<u>kh</u>í and student of Siyyid Káẓim Ra<u>sh</u>tí, and then a Bábí after meeting with Mullá Ḥusayn in Ká<u>sh</u>án in 1844. He introduced the religion to his native village of Naráq and converted many people there. Following the execution of the Báb in 1850, Naráqí became a staunch supporter of Mírzá Yaḥyá and a promoter of reprehensible behavior who more than once denied his allegiance to the Bábí religion in order to protect himself. At one point, he advanced a claim to be 'Him Whom God shall make manifest' and ordered that every Bábí pay him *<u>kh</u>ums* (a 20% tax on annual surplus income and certain items), a command that some Bábís obeyed. When this matter was brought to Bahá'u'lláh's attention, He revealed the following in one of His Tablets: 'Mullá Ja'far was not permitted by anyone to do this; he spoke and gave orders out of selfish desire . . . From that very order Mullá Ja'far gave, it is clear that he hath not inhaled a single fragrance wafting from the gardens of detachment. He is even as one who washeth the dead and is yet focused, at that moment, on stealing their clothing . . .' (www.bahai.org/r/255697647; provisional rendering by the present translator). According to one source, Naráqí once took all the possessions of two young children from their uncle, ostensibly for safekeeping, but he ran off to Baghdad and the family fell on hard times as a result. After being exiled twice to Iraq and returning to Iran both times, Naráqí fell ill and eventually died, apparently by poisoning or strangulation, on 18 July 1869. In a prayer 'Abdu'l-Bahá composed several decades later for a Bahá'í who had recently passed away, He writes that the deceased 'avoided the root of sedition, the idol of Naráq', an allusion to Naráqí (Fáḍil Mázandarání, *Tárí<u>kh</u>-i-Ẓuhúru'l-Ḥaqq*, vol. 8, part 1, pp. 383–84; provisional rendering by the present translator). For a more detailed account of Naráqí's life in English, see Momen, *The Bahá'í Communities of Iran*, vol. 2, pp. 120–24; and for a shorter account in Persian, refer to Músá Amánat, *Bahá'íyán-i-Ká<u>sh</u>án* (Fundación Nehal, 2012), pp. 55–56.

1023 Jasion writes: 'In the evening ['Abdu'l-Bahá] went to a meeting organized by Ahmed Paşa with leading Ottoman politicians. No doubt this was in preparation for the forthcoming Arab-Syrian Congress, which was to be held in Paris 18 – 23 June' (*'Abdu'l-Bahá in France*, p. 652).

1024 This included 'Abdu'l-Bahá's Burmese servant Áqá Khusraw, according to Sohrab, who has captured 'Abdu'l-Bahá's remarks as follows: 'Khosrow is in reality very sincere. On our first trip he served most willingly all the Persian friends. He washed and mended their clothes and shined their shoes. He would laughingly say, when I return to Palestine, people will come and ask me "you have been in Paris, what did you see? How is Paris like?" I would say, "Paris is like a kitchen, a small narrow kitchen." This because he was most of the time in the kitchen and did not have an opportunity to go out sightseeing. However, he was loved by everyone. I was sorry to lose him in Naples' (Jasion, *'Abdu'l-Bahá in France*, p. 653).

1025 Refer to 'Abdu'l-Bahá's eulogy for Shaykh Salmán in *Memorials of the Faithful*, ch. 4.

1026 'Alavíyyih Khánum (born Ḥamídih) and Mullá 'Alí Ján were a Bahá'í couple who opened Bahá'í schools in the early 1880s in the northern Iranian village of Máhfurúzak. Drawing on multiple Bahá'í histories, Momen writes that the latter 'was responsible for the conversion of some 1,500 in the area' (*The Bahá'í Communities of Iran*, vol. 1, p. 292), and that 'he and his wife instituted major reforms in the life of Mahfuruzak' (ibid.). As a result of malicious misrepresentations of their activities by Muslim clerics and other enemies of the Bahá'ís, Mullá 'Alí Ján was publicly executed on 28 June 1883 (ibid. p. 295). Following his death, 'Alavíyyih Khánum rose up to take her husband's leading place in the local Bahá'í community, continuing the educational reforms they had started, undertaking numerous teaching trips, and eventually dying in 1921 (ibid. p. 296). A brief account of the lives of 'Alavíyyih Khánum and Mullá 'Alí Ján has been published ibid. pp. 292–97. A more extensive biography of the latter in Persian, which concludes with two Tablets of visitation by Bahá'u'lláh revealed in his honor and one prayer by 'Abdu'l-Bahá written in praise of him, has been published in Sulaymání, *Maṣábíḥ-i-Hidáyat*, vol. 4, pp. 499–537.

1027 Born Fáṭimih Bagum, later surnamed Rawḥání ('spiritual') by Bahá'u'lláh, and more commonly known as Bíbí Rawḥání (or Rawḥáníyyih), Rawḥání Bushrúyi'í was born to Bábí parents and went on to become an active promoter of the Bahá'í Faith. A brief account of her life has been published in Momen, *The Bahá'í Communities of Iran*, vol. 1, pp. 220–21.

1028 In the vein of great women, Sohrab notes that 'Abdu'l-Bahá made these comments on Joan of Arc to an unidentified Bahá'í that day: 'The voices that she did hear from childhood were not outward, physical voices. They were spiritual revelations in her heart. It is very strange that the Popes in the beginning anathematized and excommunicated her from the church, but now they have canonized and made her a saint. At first, they said that she was deprived from the favors of God and the denial lived in the center of her; now they say she intercedes before the Throne of the Almighty for their sins! Under any circumstance, the Popes change if opinion shows conclusively the fallibility of their judgment.'

1029 At 3:00 p.m., according to Sohrab.

1030 Sohrab's account suggests that 'Abdu'l-Bahá received all these visitors in His room, rather than the reception room of the hotel.

1031 According to Sohrab, this was Sulṭán-Ḥusayn Mírzá, the Jalálu'd-Dawlih and brother of Sulṭán-Mas'úd Mírzá, the Ẓillu's-Sulṭán.

1032 Sohrab notes that Aḥmad 'Izzat Pá<u>sh</u>á was accompanied by his son. Furthermore, Jasion writes: 'A few minutes later and Sâlih Münîr Paşa's wife and brother were shown in. Madame Sâlih Münîr Paşa brought a bundle of copies of the issue of the journal *La Vie* that contained articles about the Faith. Sohrab reports that 'Abdu'l-Bahá praised her exceedingly and that she will be a great force for good' (*'Abdu'l-Bahá in France*, p. 656).

1033 Sohrab writes that Áqá Mírzá Jalál, Mírzá 'Alí-Akbar Na<u>kh</u>javání, and Siyyid Asadu'lláh Qumí accompanied 'Abdu'l-Bahá to dinner that night.

1034 Zarqání appears to have redacted this person's name. Sohrab's account indicates that it was Fatḥu'lláh <u>Kh</u>án Akbar, the Sardár-i-Manṣúr (or Sipahdár-i-Ra<u>sh</u>tí).

1035 According to Sohrab, 'Abdu'l-Bahá addressed these words to Ida A.M. Benjamin and a certain Mrs Heriot, both from London.

1036 This was the theme of His noonday talk, according to Sohrab.

1037 This would have included Ida A.M. Benjamin and Mrs Heriot, both mentioned in endnote 1035. Jasion also writes: 'In the morning four believers arrived from England to meet 'Abdu'l-Bahá. Mírzá 'Alí-Akbar-i-Rafsanjáni arrived from London with Lutfu'lláh Hakím' (*'Abdu'l-Bahá in France*, p. 656).

1038 Sohrab states that 'Abdu'l-Bahá told Ida A.M. Benjamin and Mrs Heriot to 'to carry His greeting and love for the London Bahá'ís' and give them the following message: 'Praise be to God that the lights of Bahá'u'lláh have environed you. I am most pleased with you, because you have arisen faithfully to diffuse the Glad tidings of the Kingdom of God. You will become greatly assisted and you shall, with the aid of Bahá'u'lláh, hoist the banner of goodwill amongst all the nations of the world. You are very beloved to me. I always remember you. I hear testimony that you are sincere and that your faces are turned toward the Kingdom of Abhá. Arise with ye with the greatest effort to serve the Cause, to create love in the hearts and to promulgate the word of God.

Praise be to God that ye are the active members of the Cause. Increase your activity in the path of God. Through great joy, you must soar toward the heaven of reality. All the prophets and sanctified souls have yearned for this day and you have attained to it without any labor on your part. Therefore appreciate it.'

1039 Sohrab writes, 'This morning the Beloved sent me to call on three important Persians to deliver His messages of love and to show them the translation of the report of the Mashriqu'l-Adhkár Convention in New York as written by Mr. [Joseph] H. Hannen. They were all very interested and thought the feasts must have been very wonderful and the Bahá'í Cause taking greater hold of the people.'

1040 According to Sohrab, 'Abdu'l-Bahá first went to the home of Aḥmad 'Izzat Páshá before paying this visit to Munír Páshá at 4:00 p.m., and then called on Edith Sanderson and her mother afterwards.

1041 The Richards came by the hotel at 10:00 p.m., according to Sohrab.

1042 Following a visit to Rúḥá Khánum at 4:00 p.m., according to Sohrab.

1043 Sohrab writes that 'Abdu'l-Bahá spoke with these Jews about 'the coming of the Lord of Lords in this latter day'.

1044 A reference to the road built by the Báqiroff family that connected Tehran to Rasht by way of Qazvin. According to Mehrdad Amanat, since the Báqiroffs owned the rights for collecting tariffs on merchandise and travellers on that road, and also controlled all road services such as lodging, this group of Jews – which may well have been acting as a delegation – might have been requesting 'Abdu'l-Bahá to ask the Báqiroffs to show more favourable treatment to the Jewish merchants who were active in the northern trading route with Russia (private correspondence with Mehrdad Amanat dated 1 June 2020).

1045 Most likely a reference to Qazvin, which according to Mehrdad Amanat had a declining Jewish community at the time (private correspondence with Mehrdad Amanat dated 1 June 2020).

1046 Further to the preceding endnote: Given that the Bahá'ís of Jewish background were involved in trade with Tehran via Hamadan and Basra, this Jewish delegation may have been asking 'Abdu'l-Bahá whether the Jews of Qazvin could also participate as agents in this trade (private correspondence with Mehrdad Amanat dated 1 June 2020).

1047 These visitors included Alfred and Claire Bernard, according to Jasion (*'Abdu'l-Bahá in France*, p. 662).

1048 These were probably the same Jews who called on 'Abdu'l-Bahá the day before.

1049 Zarqání appears to have redacted this person's name.

1050 Sohrab has this as 7:30 a.m., and writes that they were taken to the train station via omnibus.

1051 Jasion writes that more than fifty people had come to see 'Abdu'l-Bahá off (*'Abdu'l-Bahá in France*, p. 665).

1052 Sohrab has this as 9:15 a.m.

1053 Sohrab writes, '['Abdu'l-Bahá] got acquainted with a young Frenchman and, in my absence, He carried along with him an interesting conversation, inviting him to come to Haifa.'

1054 Sohrab has this as 10:45 p.m.

1055 According to Jasion, this was the Hotel Terminus at Gare de Marseille Saint-Charles, where 'Abdu'l-Bahá stayed in room no. 26 (*'Abdu'l-Bahá in France*, p. 665).

1056 Sohrab has this as 10:00 a.m.

1057 The abbreviation for the Peninsular & Orient Steam Navigation Company.

1058 Jasion writes that 'Abdu'l-Bahá's room was on the starboard (right-hand) side of the ship (*'Abdu'l-Bahá in France*, p. 668).

1059 Jasion writes: 'The other four members of ['Abdu'l-Bahá's] entourage shared one cabin' (*'Abdu'l-Bahá in France*, p. 668).

1060 According to Jasion, these were two young French Bahá'ís: a young lady by the name of Marguerite Chazalviel and a young man whom Sohrab identifies only as 'Albert' (*'Abdu'l-Bahá in France*, p. 668). Sohrab notes that 'Abdu'l-Bahá wrote them a Tablet on 16 August 1913 while in Egypt that included these words: 'Praise be to God that you have not forgotten the time of our meeting and that your hearts and souls are attracted to Baha-Ullah. I hope that you will obtain complete concentration of thought; so that you may have no idea and conception save Baha-Ullah. Then you shall make extraordinary progress and the Confirmation of the Kingdom of God shall descend upon you. You shall develop a seeing eye and a heart overflowing with the Love of God. Your breaths shall have influence upon others and your tongues will become the interpreters of the holy Books. Therefore, strive as much as you can to attain to this station' (*Abdul Baha in Egypt*, p. 200).

1061 Sohrab's record of the words which the Richards asked these two young Bahá'ís to convey is as follows: '. . . the last loving thought sent to you from France is ours and these two small French Bahais are bringing to you the loving greeting of all the people of France. This is a good sign' (Jasion, *'Abdu'l-Bahá in France*, p. 668).

1062 Jasion refers to this as a 'radiogram', a telegram sent by radio (*'Abdu'l-Bahá in France*, p. 668).

1063 Sohrab's transcription of their message is as follows: 'A thousand regrets to see you parting and not being able to accompany you. We hope that your voyage will be agreeable and we trust to find you again soon. Rooha [Rúḥá <u>Kh</u>ánum] is well. In thought she joins with us to send you affectionate greeting' (*'Abdu'l-Bahá in France*, p. 668).

1064 Sohrab has recorded the following words, which 'Abdu'l-Bahá addressed to the members of His entourage on that occasion: 'You must not remain idle here. You must teach the Cause. There are many young Indian students on the ship with whom Mirza Mahmoud [Zarqání] is quite at home, because he speaks their language. The laborers on the ship are likewise Mohamadan Indians, because this is an English Company' (*'Abdu'l-Bahá in France*, p. 668).

1065 According to Jasion, this was 'a young Indian lawyer returning to India to start his practice' (*'Abdu'l-Bahá in France*, p. 668), whom Sohrab identifies as 'Nawabzada Mohammad Yousaf' (ibid. n. 1616). A record of a conversation 'Abdu'l-Bahá had with Yousaf that day appears in the online supplement to this book:
https://bahai-library.com/supplement_abdul-baha_europe_1912-1913.

Voyage to Egypt

1066 According to Sohrab, this Indian was Nawabzada Mohammad Yousaf, mentioned in the preceding endnote. Sohrab's lengthier account of 'Abdu'l-Bahá's remarks to him on this occasion appears in the online supplement to this book:
https://bahai-library.com/supplement_abdul-baha_europe_1912-1913.

1067 Jasion writes that 'Abdu'l-Bahá 'went to the second class section of the ship and spoke about the teachings of Bahá'u'lláh with the many Indians, and there was one Arab from Aden' (*'Abdu'l-Bahá in France*, p. 671).

1068 'The phrase is derived from the custom of the ancients of keeping genealogical records (Nehemiah 7:5, 64; 12:22, 23) and of enrolling citizens for various purposes (Jeremiah 22:30; Ezekiel 13:9). So, God is represented as having a record of all who are under His special care and guardianship. To be blotted out of the Book of Life is to be cut off from God's favor, to suffer an untimely death, as when Moses pleads that he be blotted out of God's book – that he might die, rather than that Israel should be destroyed (Exodus 32:32; Psalms 69:28). In the New Testament it is the record of the righteous who are to inherit eternal life (Philippians 4:3; Revelation 3:5; 13:8; 17:8; 21:27). In the apocalyptic writings there is the conception of a book or of books, that are in God's keeping, and upon which the final judgment is to be based (Daniel 7:10; 12:1; Revelation 20:12, 15; compare Book Jubilees 39:6; 19:9) (Orr, 'Book of Life', in *International Standard Bible Encyclopedia*, 1915).

1069 Jasion writes that Meyer 'asked many questions about the Báb, the history of Bahá'u'lláh, the relation of Islam to Bahá'í, polygamy, divorce, obedience to government, etc.' and that ' 'Abdu'l-Bahá answered all his questions satisfactorily' (*'Abdu'l-Bahá in France*, p. 672).

1070 Sohrab writes that this was a copy of *The Asiatic Quarterly Review*, and according to Jasion (*'Abdu'l-Bahá in France*, p. 672 and ibid. n. 1621), it was probably the issue featuring a transcript of the following talk by 'Abdu'l-Bahá: 'On the Importance of Divine Civilization', translated by Ahmad Sohrab, *The Asiatic Quarterly Review* (London) n.s., vol. 1, no. 2 (April 1913), pp. 224–37. This article has been reproduced in the online supplement to this book: https://bahai-library.com/supplement_abdul-baha_europe_1912-1913.

1071 Sohrab writes that Meyer asked 'Abdu'l-Bahá to pray for him and his daughter, and that 'Abdu'l-Bahá replied: 'You are my true son and your daughter is my own daughter. There is no difference. I will pray for both of you and from the Threshold of God will beg for each divine confirmation and assistance. May His benediction ever encircle you! May you ever be the means of the happiness and comfort of the people! May you render a mighty service to the world of humanity' (Jasion, *'Abdu'l-Bahá in France*, p. 672).

1072 According to Jasion, the first of these Indians to call on 'Abdu'l-Bahá was Nawabzada Mohammad Yousaf (mentioned in endnotes 1065 and 1066), who was followed by 'another young man from India, Moganbhai C. Patel' (*'Abdu'l-Bahá in France*, p. 672).

1073 A lengthier account of these words from 'Abdu'l-Bahá – which according to Sohrab were spoken not in the morning, but 'in the evening as He was sitting on the deck' (Jasion, *'Abdu'l-Bahá in France*, pp. 673–4) – appears in the online supplement to this book: https://bahai-library.com/supplement_abdul-baha_europe_1912-1913.

1074 Jasion identifies this visitor only as 'an Indian student' (*'Abdu'l-Bahá in France*, p. 673).

1075 As this wording suggests a prior acquaintance, this may have been the same unnamed Jew who called on 'Abdu'l-Bahá two days before (on 14 June).

1076 In the original Persian, the following words read more like poetic prose than actual poetry. The present translator, however, felt that strict fidelity to that form would read awkwardly in English, and thus opted to recast the words into a poem instead.

1077 At approximately 12:30 p.m., according to Sohrab.

1078 Sohrab has this as 'bread, cheese, and salad'.

1079 Jasion writes: 'The *Himalaya* arrived in Port Said in the late morning. At one thirty the ship anchored in the harbour and shortly afterwards 'Abdu'l-Bahá was taken by a motor launch to shore' (*'Abdu'l-Bahá in France*, p. 674).

1080 A reference to Ḥájí Muḥammad Yazdí, an Iranian Bahá'í who took up residence in Egypt during the lifetime of 'Abdu'l-Bahá and worked as a merchant in Alexandria (Ḥájí Muḥammad Ṭáhir Málmírí, *Kh͟áṭirát-i-Málmírí*, p. 47).

1081 A reference to Mírzá Munír Zayn, son of Mullá Zaynu'l-'Ábidín, also known as Zaynu'l-Muqarrabín, who was an Apostle of Bahá'u'lláh. A Persian-language biography of Zaynu'l-Muqarrabín has been published in Sulaymání, *Maṣábíḥ-i-Hidáyat*, vol. 5, pp. 416–472; additional details in English can be found in Momen, *The Bahá'í Communities of Iran*, vol. 2, pp. 59–61 and passim. In Habib Taherzadeh's obituary for Yúnis K͟hán Afrúk͟htih (*The Bahá'í World*, vol. 12, p. 680), he mentions that Mírzá Munír Zayn was the person who took down the original words 'Abdu'l-Bahá spoke in response to the questions of Laura Barney – responses that were eventually compiled and published under the title *Mufávaḍát* and then translated into English as *Some Answered Questions.*

1082 A Burmese Bahá'í who served as one of 'Abdu'l-Bahá's attendants, discussed in endnote 1024.

1083 Sohrab has 'Mirza Mohsen – son-in-law of Abdul Baha – Ahmad Yazdi, Haji Mohamad Yazdi, Mohamad Taki Esphahani and about 12 other Persian Bahais'.

1084 According to Sohrab, 'Abdu'l-Bahá dictated a cablegram that evening to be sent to New York, Washington, Chicago, San Francisco, and Montreal, which read: 'With joy and fragrance [radiance] safely arrived in Port Said.' A date of 19 June 1913 was later appended to this cablegram and published in *Star of the West*, vol. 4, no. 6 (24 June 1913), p. 104. The following brief report by Sohrab was also published in the subsequent issue of *Star of the West*: 'PORT SAID, EGYPT – Abdul-Baha and suite arrived June 17 on board the steamship *Himalaya.* He sent a telegram to Haifa, instructing the many pilgrims awaiting his return to come to Port Said. On account of the great numbers who came and there being no room in the hotel large enough to hold them, a large tent was erected on the roof in which to hold meetings' (vol. 4, no. 7, p. 121).

1085 Sohrab notes that this hotel was 'not far away' from the home of Consul Aḥmad Effendí Yazdí, and that 'it belongs to a Persian whose picturesque name is El Haj Ali Hossein Esphahani'.

Egypt

1086 In his diary letter of 18 June, Sohrab writes that 'Abdu'l-Bahá 'has rented a house for one month; so we know that we will be here as much and probably longer'. On 24 June, he writes that this house was still 'being slowly furnished', and that the eventual plan was for Mírzá Munír Zayn, Mírzá Maḥmúd Zarqání, and Sohrab himself to occupy the first floor, while 'Abdu'l-Bahá and the members of His family would take the second floor. That plan appears to have changed by 1 July, when Sohrab writes: 'As the "Greatest Holy Leaf" . . . will arrive from Haifa to be with the Master, and as the present house is small and rather unfurnished, another apartment consisting of four rooms and a kitchen is rented for us. "Us" means Mirza Mahmoud [Zarqání], Sayad Assad-Ullah [Qumí], Mirza Moneer [Zayn] and Ahmad Sohrab' (*Abdul Baha in Egypt*, p. 7). He then writes that he and the others mentioned in the preceding quotation moved into that separate apartment two days later on 3 July (ibid. p. 13). In his unpublished diary entry for 22 October 1913, Sohrab writes that 'Abdu'l-Bahá 'gave up His house in which He and His family have been living since His arrival in Ramleh' that day and moved into a hotel, which he later identifies in his entry for 27 October as the New Victoria Hotel (probably synonymous with the 'Hotel Victoria'), where 'Abdu'l-Bahá occupied room no. 26.

1087 Held on the afternoon of 18 June, according to Sohrab.

1088 Naturally, these pilgrims expected that 'Abdu'l-Bahá would return to the Holy Land at once, but when His plans changed and He decided to remain in Egypt for an extended period, He summoned them to His presence there instead.

1089 The flag of Persia featured the emblem of the lion and the sun at this time, and also well before it.

1090 A provisional English rendering of the full talk, produced by the present translator, appears in the online supplement to this book: https://bahai-library.com/supplement_abdul-baha_europe_1912-1913.

1091 Áqá Mírzá 'Ináyatu'lláh was one of the six Aḥmadov brothers, mentioned in endnote 983, who 'controlled an important commercial empire trading with the Caucasus and beyond until the time of the Bolshevik revolution, which ruined them' (Momen, *The Bahá'í Communities of Iran*, vol. 1, p. 398). He also served as 'a member of the Tabriz local assembly and the Baha'i National Assembly of Persia' (ibid.). His father, Ḥájí Aḥmad Mílání, along with his uncle, Ḥájí Muḥammad Taqí, were both early Bábís and 'prominent and wealthy merchants in the town [of Mílán], owning a silk-weaving factory' (ibid. p. 396). For an account of the state-sponsored persecution of the Bábís of Mílán, which took place in August 1852 as a consequence of the ill-conceived Bábí plot to assassinate Náṣiri'd-Dín Sháh and affected both Ḥájí Aḥmad and Ḥájí Muḥammad Taqí, see ibid. p. 396–7.

1092 Sohrab's account seems to suggest that 'Abdu'l-Bahá actually delivered the following address two days before (on 19 June).

1093 A very similar (but somewhat different) Persian transcript of this same talk has been published in *Majmú'iy-i-Khiṭábát*, pp. 779–80. The present translator's provisional English rendering of that transcript appears in the online supplement to this book: https://bahai-library.com/supplement_abdul-baha_europe_1912-1913.

1094 Sohrab describes Darvísh Karam-'Alí as an old man and states that he had come to Egypt from the environs of Luristan, a province of Iran. He goes on to mention this anecdote from that morning: 'With the dramatic simplicity and the naturalness of an epic story-teller, he told me of the tyranny of the chiefs, the rapacity of the enemies, and the lack of education in those parts.' Sohrab then writes that, sometime before noon that day, 'Abdu'l-Bahá summoned Darvísh Karam-'Alí and wrote the following Tablet for his two sons at his request:

To Nasser and Mansour the two honourable sons of Darveesh Karamali upon them be Baha-ollah El Abha

He is God!

O ye godlike Nasser and Mansour! His honour, your father, has traversed through the desert and crossed the ocean until he reached the Holy Land and attained to the visit of the Radiant Tomb. At this time on the shore of Egypt, in the city which is built between the two oceans, he is the companion and associate of Abdul Baha. He showed me the letters of those two young plants of the garden of his hope. The perusal of those two letters gave me such happiness that immediately I occupied myself with the writing of this Epistle. Thank ye God that ye are trained and educated in the arms of such a father who hath guided you to the Kingdom of Holiness and who illumined your hearts like unto the lamps with the light of the Most Great Bestowal. Appreciate the value of this father and convey to all the friends the utmost longing of Abdul Baha! (Signed) Abdul Baha Abbas!

Following this, Sohrab writes that 'Abdu'l-Bahá summoned him at 5:00 p.m., and that he found Darvísh Khandán in 'Abdu'l-Bahá's presence when he arrived. It was to Darvísh Khandán specifically, according to Sohrab, that 'Abdu'l-Bahá made the remarks about Shaykh Salmán, since he had travelled to Egypt from Hindiján. Sohrab writes that Darvísh Khandán told 'Abdu'l-Bahá about a certain Mírzá Yaḥyá (not to be confused with the half-brother of Bahá'u'lláh), 'a good Bahai teacher who for the last 18 years has lived in those parts [near Hindiján] and has taught the Cause to more than 400 families, but he deplored the lack of school for the children and begged the Master to write a Tablet about this matter'. In response, 'Abdu'l-Bahá said, 'The matter of education is most important. The Bahai children must be given the best and the most complete education and the friends of God all over Persia must exert themselves to open schools for both boys and girls.' Sohrab states that 'Abdu'l-Bahá proceeded to write the following Tablet 'with his own hand':

Through Aga Mirza Yahya. Hendeyan [Hindiján].

To the friends of God. Upon them be Bahaollah El Abha.

He is God!

O ye believers of God!

In the commencement of the dawn of the Morn of Reality, Hendeyan caught the splendour of light. The names of the believers of Hendeyan often were mentioned in the most holy Court of the Blessed Perfection. Consequently, they are dear and near; beloved and related to his holiness Salman. They are accepted and favored. At this time we have returned from the journey to America and Europe and have met his honour Darveesh [Khandán]. Therefore I sent you this message and I beg of God that infinite Bestowals may surround the believers of Hendeyan. May they become confirmed to spread the Fragrances, to promote the manifest signs and to organize a school for the children. This is the irrefutable, the irrefragable command of the religion of God and must be put in practice without delay. In this Divine Dispensation this is incumbent upon all . . . (Signed) Abdul Baha Abbas!

According to Sohrab, 'Abdu'l-Bahá then handed the above Tablet to Darvísh Khandán and told him, 'Now you must show an effort, go there and create enthusiasm and exhilaration amongst the Bahais. Return from this place with attraction, enkindlement, praiseworthy morality, and noble characteristics.' He also writes that Darvísh Karam-'Alí and Darvísh Khandán left Egypt for Bombay on the afternoon of 26 June.

1095 By 'the principal seat of the Christian priests', 'Abdu'l-Bahá meant Vatican City. What has been quoted from Him here is, in fact, an excerpt from a longer talk, the full text of which has been provisionally rendered into English by the present translator in the online supplement to this book:
https://bahai-library.com/supplement_abdul-baha_europe_1912-1913.

1096 Sohrab's account indicates that these Christians actually called on 'Abdu'l-Bahá three days later (on 27 June). He writes: 'There were three Baptist American missionaries . . . two women and one man. They are living in Port Said and have a missionary school . . . They were exceedingly dogmatic and narrow and they rather liked to argue than to be informed.'

1097 Sohrab describes their departure rather differently: 'They left ['Abdu'l-Bahá's] presence quite confused and displeased because they did not expect such an overwhelming power, knowledge, love, and radiant influence.'

1098 Sohrab's account indicates that this banquet was held the night before (26 June).

1099 Surnamed 'Raḥmání' (roughly meaning 'divine' or 'heavenly') by 'Abdu'l-Bahá, Mírzá Ja'far Shírází was a Bahá'í businessman who was originally from Shiraz and later moved to 'Ishqábád, eventually settling in Kokand in today's Uzbekistan. A biography of Mírzá Ja'far Shírází in Persian has been published in Hádí Raḥmání Shírází, 'Sharḥ-i-Aḥvál-i-Mutaṣá'id ila'lláh Jináb-i-Áqá Mírzá Ja'far-i-Hádíoff Raḥmáníy-i-Shírází', *Áhang-i-Badí'*, year 28, nos. 11 and 12 (Bahman–Isfand 1352, corresponding to February–March 1974), pp. 6–21; available online here: https://bahai-library.com/bahailib/1166.pdf.

1100 A provisional English rendering of the full talk, produced by the present translator, appears in the online supplement to this book: https://bahai-library.com/supplement_abdul-baha_europe_1912-1913.

1101 Sohrab writes: 'In the center of the Tent, on the roof, the largest table was prepared around which more than 75 guests sat.'

1102 This was rock candy, according to Sohrab.

1103 In his diary letter of 28 June 1913, Sohrab writes that, on that morning, 'Abdu'l-Bahá 'gave a farewell talk to 22 of the pilgrims who left an hour later for Alexandria, there to meet our revered teacher Mirza Abul Fazl and then take the steamer direct for Constantinople'. Sohrab's English translation of 'Abdu'l-Bahá's address appears in the online supplement to this book: https://bahai-library.com/supplement_abdul-baha_europe_1912-1913.

1104 Sohrab's account suggests that 'Abdu'l-Bahá did this the following day (30 June). In his diary letter for that date, we read: 'The Master has also moved into the new house and everybody was invited both in the morning and afternoon to take tea and listen to his divine Words.'

1105 According to Sohrab, 'Abdu'l-Bahá actually went for this stroll the day before (30 June). Ferdinand de Lesseps (1805–1894) was a French diplomat famous for building the Suez Canal.

1106 This was the Casino Palace Hotel, according to Sohrab, who writes: 'We returned toward the Casino Palace Hotel. ['Abdu'l-Bahá] ascended the stairs and we followed him. He sat on a chair and bade us also to seat [sit]. The casino faces the sea and has a most beautiful outlook. He ordered Turkish coffee to be brought for each, after which he dictated several wonderful Tablets, then he spoke about the former glory of Islam and its present decadence illustrating it by a striking story of the time of Byzantine Emperors in Constantinople.'

1107 Sohrab's partial translation of this talk into English appears in the online supplement to this book: https://bahai-library.com/supplement_abdul-baha_europe_1912-1913.

1108 This was Mawlví Maḥbúb 'Álam, who according to Sohrab met with 'Abdu'l-Bahá on 5 and 6 July (*Abdul Baha in Egypt*, p. 28), and is discussed further in the biography of Zarqání included in the online supplement to this book: https://bahai-library.com/supplement_abdul-baha_europe_1912-1913.

1109 At 8:00 a.m. by train, according to Sohrab (*Abdul Baha in Egypt*, p. 52). As to the members of 'Abdu'l-Bahá's retinue: neither Zarqání nor Sohrab accompanied Him on His move to Ismailia, and Siyyid Asadu'lláh Qumí, after gaining His explicit permission, left Egypt the day before on 10 July to teach the Cause in the Caucasus (ibid. pp. 48–50).

1110 'Abdu'l-Bahá may have been contemplating this move as early as 4 July, according to Sohrab, who writes on that date: 'For the last few days ['Abdu'l-Bahá] has been complaining about the weather and he may shortly leave for Ismailia, which is the summer resort of Egypt. The Port Said weather at this season is most humid' (*Abdul Baha in Egypt*, p. 23). The plan had become definite by 10 July, when Sohrab writes: '['Abdu'l-Bahá] said that the weather in Port Said had not agreed with him, and that he expected to leave tomorrow for Ismailia, a town about one hour and fifteen minutes from this city. He is going there for two or three days and if all goes well, he will send for us. Ahmad Yazdi and Khosro will accompany him' (ibid. p. 50). Elaborating on this plan the following day, Sohrab writes: '['Abdu'l-Bahá] will stay there [in Ismailia] two or three days. If the weather agrees with him, he will rent a house and send for us. If not, he will return, and go either to Alexandria or Ramleh' (ibid. p. 52). 'Abdu'l-Bahá had reconsidered this plan by 14 July, according to Sohrab, who writes on that date: 'The first two days ['Abdu'l-Bahá] had not felt well, but now he is resting better. While there he had met an old friend of his, a famous doctor who had prescribed a regime of rest and diet to be followed strictly. The Master has decided to remain a week; if the weather agrees with him he will send for all of us, if not, he will return and then may go to Ramleh' (ibid. p. 64). By the next day, 'Abdu'l-Bahá seemed resolved to stay in Ismailia: 'To-day a letter was received from Mirza Moneer who is in Ismailia, giving the news of the well-being of the Master, and saying that he will soon send for us; he is looking for a house large enough to accommodate all' (ibid. p. 70). Sohrab then writes on 16 July that he and the other attendants received permission to visit 'Abdu'l-Bahá in Ismailia the following day (ibid. p. 72), which they did, departing Port Said by train on 17 July at 8:00 a.m. and arriving in Ismailia at 10:00 a.m. (ibid. p. 76). They visited 'Abdu'l-Bahá at the hotel of a certain J. Bosta, where He was staying in room no. 13, and found Him 'in bed in a weakened condition' (ibid. p. 77). It took everyone by surprise when 'Abdu'l-Bahá then informed them that He would be leaving for Ramleh, where He planned to stay for one week (ibid. p. 79). Similar to how He had initially conceived His plan for Ismailia, His idea for this move, according to Sohrab, was as follows: 'If the weather agreed with him, he would send for us; if not, he would return to Port Said and together we would all go to Haifa' (ibid. p. 80). 'Abdu'l-Bahá, Mírzá Munír Zayn, and Áqá Khusraw left Ismailia for Ramleh at 2:30 p.m. that day, and the attendants who had travelled to Ismailia to visit 'Abdu'l-Bahá returned to Port Said by train at 9:30 p.m. (ibid.).

1111 Unlike the other date headings used in the chronicle, this one is absent from the original Persian; it has been added by the present translator to more clearly distinguish 'Abdu'l-Bahá's brief stay in Ismailia from His time in Ramleh.

1112 Sohrab seems to indicate that 'Abdu'l-Bahá arrived in Ramleh on 19 July (*Abdul Baha in Egypt*, p. 84). On 24 July, he and the other attendants received permission from 'Abdu'l-Bahá (via telegram) to leave Port Said and relocate to Ramleh; they took the 1:00 p.m. train that day, changing trains in Benha at 4:30 p.m. and finally arriving at the Sidi Gaber station at 7:30 p.m. (ibid, pp. 105–06). By 26 July, Sohrab writes that 'Abdu'l-Bahá was resolved to stay in Ramleh in spite of some persistent ailments: '['Abdu'l-Bahá] spoke of the weather and of the state of his health saying that he had not been feeling well, in Ramleh, but that for the present he would not move to any other place, no matter what might happen' (ibid. p. 115). This held true up until His eventual departure to Haifa on 2 December, though Sohrab does write on 8 November 1913 that, shortly after 7:00 p.m. that day, he and 'Abdu'l-Bahá set sail from Ramleh on the *Jerusalem*, a Russian steamer, for a brief sojourn in Port Said, where they arrived the following morning (of 9 November). While there, 'Abdu'l-Bahá stayed at the home of Consul Aḥmad Effendí Yazdí once again, and Sohrab lodged at the same room of the Hotel Sulṭání that he had occupied earlier that year. 'Abdu'l-Bahá had initially planned to be away from Ramleh 'for three to five days', and eventually returned more than a week later on 17 November.

1113 See Balyuzi, *'Abdu'l-Bahá*, p. 401, where it is notably mentioned that Shoghi Effendi accompanied his mother (Ḍíyá Khánum) and the Greatest Holy Leaf on this visit to Egypt. Shoghi Effendi and his mother left for Haifa on 3 October 1913, according to Sohrab's unpublished diary entry for that date. The Greatest Holy Leaf, along with Áqá Mírzá Jalál, left for Cairo one week later on the evening of 10 October, according to Sohrab, who writes that they returned to Ramleh on 18 October.

1114 Sohrab writes that, when he and the other attendants first arrived in Ramleh, the residence of Mírzá Abu'l-Faḍl in Alexandria was an hour's drive away from where 'Abdu'l-Bahá was living in Ramleh (*Abdul Baha in Egypt*, p. 108). An 'almost adjacent' house was found on 25 July, which Abu'l-Faḍl personally inspected that day and was evidently pleased with (ibid. p. 110). The ensuing pages of Sohrab's account suggest that Abu'l-Faḍl moved into that residence a few days later. According to Isabel Fraser, who met with Abu'l-Faḍl in Ramleh, 'Abdu'l-Bahá rented for him 'the upper part of a two-story house set in a garden of date palms' (*Star of the West*, vol. 4, no. 19 (2 March 1914), p. 316).

1115 Isabel Fraser's account of Mírzá Abu'l-Faḍl's time in Ramleh, 'A

Glimpse of Mirza Abul-Fazl at Ramleh', is published in *Star of the West*, vol. 4, no. 19 (2 March 1914), pp. 316–17.

1116 Zarqání uses the word *miṣr* here, which in this context refers not to the country of Egypt (since Abu'l-Faḍl was already in that country, and could thus not 'return' there), but to its alternative meaning of Cairo. This is corroborated in a report on his passing by Hussein A. Afnan dated 2 February 1914, which states: 'A few days before Abdul-Baha's departure from Egypt to the Holy Land, Mirza Abul-Fazl went to Cairo' (*Star of the West*, vol. 4, no. 19 (2 March 1914), p. 315).

1117 The following is one brief account of a memorial service for Mírzá Abu'l-Faḍl: 'On Sunday night, February 1, the spacious parlors of Mme. de Lagnel's apartment were quite filled with the Bahais of Washington, D.C., who assembled in a meeting of Memorial for Mirza Abul-Fazl. Many present had been taught by this great soul. Ish'te'a'l Ebn-Kalanter [Ali Kuli Khan] and Mme. [Madame] [Laura] Dreyfus-Barney were the speakers of the evening. Brief addresses were also made by others who had known Mirza Abul-Fazl, including Mrs. F. J. Woodward [presumably the wife of Frederick J. Woodward, named here only by association to her husband]. Prayers were chanted by Ghodsea [Qudsíyyih] Ashraf and by Ish'te'a'l Ebn-Kalanter. The utmost spirituality and unity prevailed, and an undercurrent of deep reverence pervaded the meeting' (*Star of the West*, vol. 4, no. 19 (2 March 1914), p. 319).

1118 According to the aforementioned report by Hussein A. Afnan, when 'Abdu'l-Bahá first learned of the passing of Mírzá Abu'l-Faḍl, He sent this telegram immediately: 'VERILY THE EYES HAVE SHED TEARS AND THE HEARTS HAVE BURNED BECAUSE OF THIS GREAT AFFLICTION. BE YE POSSESSED WITH THE BEAUTY OF PATIENCE IN THIS MIGHTY CALAMITY' (*Star of the West*, vol. 4, no. 19 (2 March 1914), p. 315). The Persian transcripts of four eulogies for Abu'l-Faḍl given by 'Abdu'l-Bahá are published in Mehrabkhani, *Zindigániy-i-Mírzá Abu'l-Faḍl-i-Gulpáygání* (3rd ed.), pp. 300–05. Three of these have been translated into English by Sohrab and published in different issues of *Star of the West*: the first in vol. 9, no. 3, p. 25; the second in ibid. p. 26; and the third in vol. 8, no. 6, p. 66. The fourth eulogy was also translated by Sohrab and appears in his diary entry dated 13 February 1914 but seems not to have been published anywhere.

1119 In his unpublished diary entry for 3 October 1913, Sohrab offers this detailed account of daily life in Ramleh:

. . . the Master's family – in a Bahai sense – is very large, very large indeed. He and His own family live in one house; the Secretaries, with as many pilgrims as they can accommodate, live in another house; and there is besides these two houses a third which is rented only for the pilgrims. The American and European Pilgrims live in the New Victoria Hotel, as well as prominent Persian nobilities. There is another hotel at Bacos station, which is brought into service when there is an overflow of pilgrims. All these houses and hotels are used at this time for the accommodation of the friends who are constantly coming from the four corners of the earth to welcome the King of Kings and Lord of Lords. The secretariat house is like a club house, and a common ground for all the pilgrims. Except during the sleeping hours, they spend all their time here. Here in the East everybody arises very early, so that between 5 and 6 o'clock we are out of our beds, with the word 'Allah-o-Abha!' on our lips, greeting each other.

There are four morning customs that have impressed me deeply, and are the significant signs of the religious nature of these people.

First: Their uniform early rising. Although in the West it is taught, 'early to bed and early to rise,' it is seldom practiced.

Second: No sooner do they open their eyes than the Holy Name of God is on their lips, thanking Him for all His past graces and future Bestowals.

Third: Their quiet, solitary prayer and concentration from ten to thirty minutes, according to the religious spirit of the individual.

Fourth: As soon as they have finished their individual prayer, and before taking their breakfast, they assemble in the reception room and pray to God, read Communes or sing anthems. They will then gather round the table to partake of the material food.

After the performance of the above rites, it is about 6 or 6:30 [a.m.], and then the friends start to arrive from the other house and hotels to take their breakfast with us. When everybody is present, we all go to the reception room and have a ten to fifteen minutes [sic] prayer meeting, and then thus refreshed with our spiritual food, we go to the dining room. We sit around a very large table, over which the samovar is brewing, and Aga Jamal, our faithful cook, is ready to dispense tea. Our breakfast consists of native bread and cheese, and tea, nothing else; easterners as a rule do not give much attention to the morning repast. Everyone drinks from one to three cups of tea, helps himself to a piece of bread and cheese, and in a few minutes we are all through. Then the pilgrims go to the veranda and sit around; often Mirza Abul Fazl comes and talks with them. Within half an hour someone from the Master's house comes, giving the news that the pilgrims are summoned. They go and return laden with the Jewels of the Kingdom. Some mornings the Beloved pays us a visit. On their return, the pilgrims are then free; some go to the city, a few sit down and write letters home or copy Tablets and the Master's Western addresses, while another group is engaged in conversation, imparting and in turn receiving the news of the progress of the Cause in their respective countries . . . Our lunch is simplicity itself, only one kind, either Persian soup called 'Ab-Gousht', or fried egg-plants, etc., with large, round, native bread. When there are many friends, they are divided into two parties. The first party sit down and eat(?), and when they have finished the rest partake of the food. The Secretaries are always included in the second party, and the guests and pilgrims in the first. Often we have fruits, such as grapes, pomegranates, figs, cantaloupes, watermelons, etc. . . . After lunch, they are all again scattered, most of them taking their usual naps . . . Between 3 and 4 [p.m.] tea is served, and then the friends come. We read Tablets and talk about the Cause. Then, forming different groups, they saunter out, but always near and around the house, in the hope that the Master may come. Meanwhile, He may be either dictating Tablets in the adjoining rose garden, or calling on Mirza Abul Fazl, or entertaining some Pashas in His home, or calling on some learned or simple person. At eight o'clock we are again gathered in the dining room, and eat the one course dinner, the articles changing now and then, but always one course. After dinner, we are generally free, and may make our own choice, either going out to take a walk, or sitting in the house to read or converse with others. Before midnight everyone is in bed. Our house is the rendezvous for all the beggars. Every day several of them call with petitions for Abbas Effendi. None of them goes away empty handed.

1120 According to Sohrab's unpublished diary, this included Isabel Fraser, Alice Beede, Maud Lillienthal, Emogene Hoagg, a certain 'Mrs. Wise' (possibly Harriet Wise), Ibn-i-Aṣdaq, and Mírzá Maḥmúd Furú<u>gh</u>í.

1121 The same institution where Shoghi Effendi studied, known today as the American University of Beirut.

1122 According to Sohrab's unpublished diary entry for 2 November 1913, these were 'Sheikh Asad and another Pasha, two members of the Turkish Parliament from Syria' who had just arrived from Istanbul. Sohrab describes them as the Master's 'old friends', and notes that He went to Alexandria to receive them and bring them to Ramleh that day. With reference to them, Sohrab writes: 'Although not Bahais, they love the Master very sincerely and will do anything for him. From him they receive light and guidance and they are deeply grateful. His praise is on their lips, his love in the depths of their hearts.'

1123 'Abdu'l-Bahá met with the Khedive on 17 August, according to Sohrab, who writes on that date: 'This was an important date in the Bahai calendar because Abdul Baha and the ruler of Egypt met each other for the second or third time. Beyond this bare announcement I have no other information. The Master may give us, later, an account of the meeting, and thus in our imagination we may construct a picture or he may not divulge any of the details. None of the believers were with him. For the present it is enough to know that on this day, between three and six p.m., the sovereign of Egypt had the honour and privilege of talking with Abdul Baha' (*Abdul Baha in Egypt*, p. 201).

1124 'During the last days of our stay in Egypt, we went to Tanta for the repair of the tomb of Ḥájí Abu'l Qásim and from there went to Mansurih. In Tanta one of the English officials was our friend, who held us in great honour and showed us great respect everywhere. Observing this, the natives were more respectful and polite to us than even to the said officer, and throughout the town, everyone, young and old, even the policemen in the street, saluted us. But, at another time when we went alone to Mansurih, because the people did not observe outward riches, they did not pay any attention to us. This is the condition of hypocritical people who only look to outward appearances' (Zarqání, *Maḥmúd's Diary*, p. 14).

1125 Certain passages from this excerpt had been previously translated into English by Balyuzi (*'Abdu'l-Bahá*, p. 136), and those renderings have been incorporated into this fuller translation. The present translator is grateful to Ruwa Pokorny for her assistance with translating the remaining passages. An alternative translation of the article into English has been published in Egea, *Apostle of Peace*, vol. 1, p. 60. A typescript of this article in the original Arabic has been published in Suheil Bushrui, *'Abbás Afandí fí al-dhikrá al-mi'awíyah li-ziyáratihi ilá Misr (1910–1913)*, p. 118. A translation of this article from Arabic into Persian, by Nahid Rouhani, has also been published in Suheil Bushrui, *'Abdu'l-Bahá 'Abbás: bih Yádbúd-i-Ṣadumín Sálgard-i-Dídár-i-Ḥaḍratash az Miṣr: 1910–1913*, p. 122.

1126 'al-Bahá'íyyah' in the original Arabic.

1127 Another suburb of Alexandria close to Ramleh.

1128 Also known as Mírzá Muḥammad Mahdí Khán, the Za'ímu'd-Dawlih.

1129 A reference to *Miftáḥ-i-Bábu'l-Abváb* (Cairo: Maṭba'at Majallat al-Manár, 1903). This polemical work was later translated into Persian by Ḥasan Faríd Gulpáygání under the title *Miftáḥ-i-Bábu'l-Abváb, Yá, Táríkh-i-Báb va Bahá* (Tehran: Kitábkhániy-i-Shams, 1961).

1130 Allusions to the Persian Constitutional Revolution (1905–11) and the Young Turk Revolution (1908), respectively.

1131 Refer to the Lawḥ-i-Ra'ís (Bahá'u'lláh, *Summons*, pp. 159–73), especially the opening paragraphs.

1132 From the Súriy-i-Ra'ís: 'The day is approaching when the Land of Mystery [Edirne, formerly known as Adrianople] and what is beside it shall be changed, and shall pass out of the hands of the King, and commotions shall appear, and the voice of lamentation shall be raised, and the evidences of mischief shall be revealed on all sides, and confusion shall spread by reason of that which hath befallen these captives at the hands of the hosts of oppression. The course of things shall be altered, and conditions shall wax so grievous, that the very sands on the desolate hills will moan, and the trees on the mountain will weep, and blood will flow out of all things. Then wilt thou behold the people in sore distress' (Bahá'u'lláh, *Summons*, p. 143). Though similarly named, the Súriy-i-Ra'ís and Lawḥ-i-Ra'ís are two different Tablets of Bahá'u'lláh.

1133 Refer to the preceding endnote.

1134 'And We hear the lamentations of Berlin, though she be today in conspicuous glory' (Bahá'u'lláh, *Kitáb-i-Aqdas*, para. 93).

1135 'O banks of the Rhine! We have seen you covered with gore, inasmuch as the swords of retribution were drawn against you; and you shall have another turn' (Bahá'u'lláh, *Kitáb-i-Aqdas*, para. 93).

1136 The reader should bear in mind that World War I had not yet broken out at the time of this writing.

1137 'Mirza 'Abdu'l-Husayn Khan Qallati Shirazi Tamaddun ul-Mulk was a prominent Baha'i who had been educated in Europe and knew English well. He represented 'Abdu'l-Baha at the Universal Races Congress in London in 1911 and accompanied 'Abdu'l-Baha on his first trip to Europe as a translator. 'Abdu'l-Baha was not happy with his translations, however. Upon the return of the party to Haifa, Tamaddun ul-Mulk felt slighted when he was offered the same accommodation as other Baha'is and went off aggrieved. Upon his return to Tehran he set up an Assembly of Unity (*maḥfil-i-ittiḥād*) and started to give instructions, which he said came from 'Abdu'l-Baha, that for the time being all propagation activities should cease. His actions caused disruption of the community. Eventually 'Abdu'l-Baha was forced to telegram to Tehran expelling Tamaddun ul-Mulk from the community' (Momen, *The Bahá'í Communities of Iran*, vol. 1, pp. 103–04).

1138 According to one source, Tamaddunu'l-Mulk was 'about four feet high' (Juliet Thompson, *The Diary of Juliet Thompson*, p. 156).

1139 The details of this move are given by Sohrab in his unpublished diary entry for 13 October 1913. According to Sohrab, Aboukir was 'a little town half an hour away from Ramleh' at the time, and he writes that Mírzá Munír Zayn and Áqá Khusraw accompanied 'Abdu'l-Bahá there. Sometime after 'Abdu'l-Bahá's departure, His attendants in Ramleh received a letter in Persian from Mírzá Munír Zayn, which Sohrab translates as follows: 'Praise be to God! The Divine Temple ['Abdu'l-Bahá] arrived safely in the small town of Aboukir, and this locality became adorned with the Blessed Feet of the Beloved. There are hardly any signs of busy city or the progressive thrift of even a small town. It looks like a country without fertility. The only scene that strikes upon the retina of the eye is the ever shifting Sahara of sand and the groves of palms, the dates of which are beginning to ripen. The weather is, however, clear and fine. About fifteen minutes to eleven [in the morning] the Master left Ramleh for Aboukir. From the windows of the train the Beloved Temple looked at the natural scenes, gardens, orchards and palm groves, and the very slight change of air reacted upon His tender constitution, and He felt much better. I hope the weather will agree with Him. The manager of the hotel has seen the Master in Ramleh, and is very considerate and kind. The patrons have already left, and everything is very quiet . . . I do not know when the blessed Temple shall return to Ramleh. He may stay for a week.' Sohrab goes on to say that Mírzá Munír Zayn briefly returned to Ramleh on 14 October to convey 'the good news of the health of the Beloved', and then left for Aboukir again a few hours later. Much to everyone's surprise, 'Abdu'l-Bahá returned to Ramleh on the morning of 15 October after having stayed in Aboukir for just two days, and gave these reasons later that day: 'I did not find any difference between the weather of Aboukir and here, therefore, I preferred to return. Beside this, there was nobody there, and the manager was anxious to close the doors of the hotel and go away, for this was at the very end of the season.'

1140 The maternal relatives and descendants of the Báb.

1141 In his unpublished diary entry for 4 December, Sohrab writes that 'Abdu'l-Bahá travelled first class on the *Baron Call* and stayed in cabin no. 9.

1142 Sohrab writes that Port Said had come into view from a distance by 7:00 a.m.

1143 According to Sohrab's unpublished diary entry for 4 November 1913, Ḥájí Siyyid Javád was a man of very advanced age who had previously come from Cairo to Ramleh on 3 November to visit 'Abdu'l-Bahá.

1144 Though Zarqání uses the word *iskilih* (pier) here, Sohrab, writing on 4 December, indicates that Jaffa did not actually have a harbour of any kind: 'Our steamer anchored off the shore of Jaffa at 8:30 a.m. in the midst of a rough sea. Having no harbour, all the ships drop anchor in deep sea, or as near Jaffa as they dare to go, which is often quite far.'

1145 In his unpublished diary entry for 4 December, Sohrab refers to the first of these three men as 'a good Baha'i in Jaffa by the name of Abdassamad Nohass' and then vaguely alludes to 'two others', whom Zarqání seems to have identified here. Sohrab then goes on to say: 'They were notified by Mirza Jalal in a letter that the Master is on the steamer, and so they came in that awful weather, bringing with them two baskets full of oranges. We were delighted to see them, but they stayed only for half an hour.'

1146 At 9:00 a.m, according to Sohrab.

1147 Sohrab writes: 'By eleven o'clock the Monastery of the Monks could be seen on the summit of Mt. Carmel.'

1148 In his unpublished diary entry for 5 December, Sohrab writes: 'Thanks to the knowledge and familiarity of Mirza Jalal, we were landed quickly, but the Master stayed on board to land at 5 o'clock . . .' He does not say when exactly the attendants disembarked, but given that he mentions earlier in that same entry that it was a five-hour voyage from Jaffa to Haifa, that they set sail from the former city at 9:00 a.m., and that they were walking through the rose-garden by the house of 'Abdu'l-Bahá at approximately 2:30 p.m., it can be reasonably inferred that it was probably at around 2:00 p.m.

1149 At 7:00 p.m., according to Sohrab.

1150 Probably a reference to Munírih Khánum.

1151 Probably at 7:00 p.m., according to the original plan mentioned by Sohrab, who writes that news was first given at around 6:30 p.m. that 'Abdu'l-Bahá had just arrived at His house and was ready to receive His guests in the main hall, but when everyone rushed there to meet Him, they found that 'it seemed it was a false alarm'.

1152 In the 'large, spacious hall' of His house, according to Sohrab.

1153 Sohrab writes that 'more than one hundred men' were 'prostrating to the ground, their foreheads touching the floor'.

1154 Sohrab writes: 'A chair was arranged for the Master, but he sat like the others on the floor and began to speak in his clear, resonant voice.'

1155 Sohrab writes that 'Abdu'l-Bahá 'asked Mirza Mahmoud Foroughi to chant a supplication, which he did in his great big voice, with wonderful color and rich diapason'. For a short biography of Mírzá Maḥmúd Furúghí (d. c. 1927), the only Iranian Bahá'í known to have met face-to-face with a Qájár Shah (Muẓaffari'd-Dín Sháh), refer to Balyuzi, *Eminent Bahá'ís*, pp. 156–170. Additional details can be found in Momen, *The Bahá'í Communities of Iran*, vol. 1, pp. 184–7 and passim. A more comprehensive account of Furúghí's life, written in Persian, has been published in Sulaymání, *Maṣábíḥ-i-Hidáyat*, vol. 3, pp. 417–83.

1156 Sohrab writes: 'After the meeting, fruit and candies were given around, and we retired with thanksgiving to the Pilgrims' Home near the top of Mount Carmel.'

The Holy Land

1157 Corroborating this detail, Sohrab writes in his diary entry dated 6 December 1913: 'In the front toward the side of the building [the Shrine of the Báb], facing the sea, there is a large reception room, the floor of which is carpeted with one single, large, multi-colored rug, and here the Master received the pilgrims. They wanted to throw themselves at his feet, but he forbade them emphatically.'

1158 According to Sohrab, these were 'three members of Haifa's Civil authorities'.

1159 Sohrab indicates that 'Abdu'l-Bahá had also given this same order the day before while He and various pilgrims were at the reception room of the Shrine of the Báb. Writing on 6 December, he states: '. . . ['Abdu'l-Bahá] spoke a few other words, and commanded all the believers to go to Acca to-morrow, to the Holy Tomb of Baha'u'llah'.

1160 By this, Zarqání means to say that 'Abdu'l-Bahá took a later train to 'Akká and did not travel with the large group of Bahá'ís. This is made clear by Sohrab's unpublished diary entry from 7 December 1913, in which he writes the following after having made pilgrimage to the Shrine of Bahá'u'lláh: 'When we reached the Station [in 'Akká], we heard that the Master was coming on the next train to visit the Holy Tomb and stay in Acca for one or two nights.'

1161 Sohrab writes: 'One of the believers who knows how to pull the inside strings goes [went] to the Inspector and asks [asked] him to give us two [train] cars to ourselves – each car holding fifty persons. He is [was] kind enough to give us this accommodation, and at 8 o'clock [in the morning] the whistle blew and the train started Acca-ward.'

1162 An anniversary which had taken place about a week before.

1163 'Andalíb, which means 'nightingale', was the sobriquet of Mírzá 'Alí-As͟hraf of Láhíján (1853–1919), a well-known Bahá'í poet. A biography of 'Andalíb has been published in Balyuzi, *Eminent Bahá'ís*, pp. 60–74. Additional details on his life can be found in Momen, *The Bahá'í Communities of Iran*, vol. 1, pp. 351–3 and passim. A more comprehensive account of his life in Persian has been published in Sulaymání, *Maṣábíḥ-i-Hidáyat*, vol. 7, pp. 142–225. An extensive selection of his poetry in Persian has been published in Bayḍá'í, *Tad͟hkariy-i-S͟hu'aráy-i-Qarn-i-Avval-i-Bahá'í*, vol. 2, pp. 356–94.

1164 Baṣṣár, meaning 'perceptive' and implying sightedness, was the sobriquet of Mírzá (Muḥammad) Báqir Bihis͟htí (c. 1852–1915); it was given to him by Bahá'u'lláh and he adopted it as his pen name for writing poetry. Sohrab refers to Baṣṣár as 'a blind poet of Rasht' (blinded as a result of his imprisonment in 1883 for being a Bahá'í), writing that one poem of his in particular – whose refrain was 'the Center of the Covenant has returned!' – 'was chanted with vim and spirit . . . by young and old', and that 'its echoes reverberated through the mountain on one side and the sea on the other'. A biography of Baṣṣár in Persian has been published in Sulaymání, *Maṣábíḥ-i-Hidáyat*, vol. 5, pp. 473–507. Additional details on his life in English can be found in Momen, *The Bahá'í Communities of Iran*, vol. 1, pp. 334–6 and passim. An extensive selection of his poetry in Persian has been published in Bayḍá'í, *Tad͟hkarih*, vol. 1, pp. 163–94.

1165 Sohrab writes that the train left Haifa at 8:00 a.m. and stopped near the gate of 'Akká one hour later.

1166 Bahá'u'lláh, *Summons of the Lord of Hosts*, pp. 133–5.

1167 In his own diary, Sohrab corroborates the fact 'Abdu'l-Bahá reviewed the second volume of Zarqání's chronicle. In his entry for 18 June 1914, he writes: 'Mírzá Maḥmúd brought for ['Abdu'l-Bahá's] perusal the second volume – in manuscript – of accounts of the Beloved's journeys through Europe after His departure from America. It consists of about 500 pages in His excellent, artistic handwriting, and a fine contribution to the Bahá'í literature for all the ages to come. "You have worked very diligently," He told him, "over the compilation of these two volumes. During the first journey to Europe no one was thinking to do this work. Now and then Mírzá Báqir Khán, who was a member of our party, wrote down a few addresses and dates, but no systematic attempt was made in this direction. Hence many addresses were delivered which were not at all reported. The aim was to proclaim the Appearance of the Kingdom of Abhá which, praise be to God, was accomplished. We have scattered the seeds. Now God will cause its growth. It is assured that they will grow and reach the stage of fruition. As the Movement is endowed with hidden, creative energy, it will suffer these seeds to germinate in the earth and push up their heads in the shortest possible length of time. The seeds which were sown by the Apostles of Christ yielded their fruits after 300 years, but the results of the activities of the believers of God have become evident in these very days. This is because the power and protection of the Blessed Perfection are with us under all circumstances."'

1168 From a *g͟hazal* by Ḥáfiẓ; translation by Joshua D.T. Hall.

1169 The wording of this sentence, written in Arabic, is almost identical to, and is clearly a paraphrase of, the following passage from a Tablet of Bahá'u'lláh: 'Every good thing is of God, and every evil thing is from yourselves' (*Gleanings*, LXXVII).

INDEX

'Abbás Ḥilmí Pá<u>sh</u>á, Khedive of Egypt 488, 749
'Abdu'l-Bahá (the Master)
  in 'Akká 55-6, 61, 85, 94, 101, 112-13, 138, 159, 175, 188, 194, 253, 319, 391, 427, 476, 489, 491, 501-3, 528, 561, 584, 634, 708, 711, 754
  and Bahá'u'lláh, relationship with 64, 272, 275, 308, 339, 384, 471, 638
    dream of 382
  Centre of the Covenant viii, 6, 36, 39, 40, 61, 68, 83, 87, 117, 273, 290, 474, 496, 665, 754
  childhood and youth 218, 238, 263-4, 281, 306, 396, 427, 446, 708, 718
  clothing of, remarks on 327, 442-3
  Disciples of 527, 535, 571, 721
  happiness of 14, 62, 100, 101, 108, 147, 165, 193, 198, 215, 225, 238, 270, 274, 277, 289, 464, 467, 471, 477, 487, 488, 611, 630, 632, 642, 649, 663, 668, 676, 684, 702, 704, 710, 721, 728, 732, 742
  unhappiness, heavy-heartedness of 129, 136, 193, 207, 379, 396, 707, 751
  health, ill-health of 17, 73, 124, 135, 201, 202, 204, 206, 207, 216, 218, 224, 226, 227, 235, 236, 247, 267, 311, 312, 335, 338, 340, 341, 342, 343, 345, 356, 361, 369, 396, 462, 471, 473, 480, 485-6, 496, 648, 653, 684, 745, 746, 752 *see also* physicians
  humour of 16, 18-20, 47, 131, 151, 152, 182, 212, 284-5, 346, 401, 403, 427, 615, 651, 681, 711-12
  imprisonment 6-7, 21, 28, 61, 62, 80, 94-5, 101, 112-13, 139, 194, 195, 227, 264, 306, 337, 362, 427, 491, 502, 645, 667
  inscriptions in books 89, 90, 675, 693, 694, 701, 703
  joy of 10, 16, 17, 67, 91, 104, 112-13, 140, 164, 165, 188, 205, 215, 237, 270, 272, 320, 382, 386, 398, 400, 427, 429, 432, 435, 471, 484, 498, 602, 611, 663, 714, 740
  love for
    Mírzá Abu'l-Faḍl 17, 131, 237-8, 354, 487, 631, 656-7, 702, 746-7
    Bahá'ís in Europe 101, 213, 216, 273, 268, 269, 298, 344, 361-2, 365, 373, 453, 455, 460, 42, 463, 649, 665, 670, 679, 722
    children 146, 187, 278, 346, 442, 669-70, 701, 732 *see also* children
    nature 662, 692
    see also love
  meals 10, 13-14, 16, 17, 20, 71, 182, 186, 204, 335, 375, 381, 405, 426, 427, 440, 662
    áb-gú<u>sh</u>t 71, 202, 617, 748
    bread 71, 395
    cheese 471
    chicken (and rice) 17, 408, 625, 663, 686
    coffee 381, 730
    fruit 471
    ice cream 93
    khoresh 27, 121, 483, 600
    milk 395
    rice 15, 20, 27, 121
    sharbat 31 and n, 93, 118, 181, 278, 418

sweets 18, 52, 181, 244, 278, 285, 306, 483
tea 134, 294, 385, 398, 403, 671 *(and many other entries)*
yogurt 15
paintings of 305, 617, 680
and palmist 521, 616
prayers of *see* prayer
recordings of His voice 192-3, 644, 645, 688-9, 718
self-sacrifice of 309, 342, 612
Servant of Bahá, of God 23, 64, 102, 209, 624, 638
service by *see* service
sleep, lack of 17, 71, 135, 160, 186, 206, 215, 235, 318, 319, 335, 496, 497, 612
Tablets revealed by 15, 17, 49n, 119, 139, 157, 189, 194, 208, 230, 232, 242, 247, 326, 376, 388, 395, 398, 479, 574n, 633, 663, 691, 725, 744, 748, 749
to Mírzá Abu'l-Faḍl 131
to Ḥájí Amín 601, 661
to Ḥájí Ghulám-Riḍá 725-6
to Zia Bagdadi 248, 658
to Bahá'ís of Denver, Colorado 388, 710
to Bahá'ís of Fars 478
to Bahá'ís of Fruitport, Michigan 388, 710-11
to Lua Getsinger 658
to Mary C. Haybittle (South Africa) 658
to Bahá'ís of Hindiján 742-3
to Bahá'ís of Honolulu 236
to Bahá'ís of Qum 647
to Bahá'ís of the West 232
to Báqiroff family 247, 658
to Edward Granville Browne 652
to Marguerite Chazalviel and 'Albert' 737
to Faraju'lláh Káshání 650
for Manúchihr Khán 647
on Thomas Kelly Cheyne 208-9
to Thomas Kelly Cheyne 211
to sons of Darvish Karám-'Alí 742
to Khusraw Bimán 645
to Edna McKinney 714
to Mary Morrison (and Bahá'ís of Denver, Colorado) 388, 710
to readers of *The Christian Commonwealth* 119
to readers of the *Pittsburgh Spectator* 708
to Sakínih Sulṭán 648
to Ármin Vámbéry 308, 684
of Visitation 645
to Jane Whyte 214
talks vii-viii, ix
published
Paris Talks 563
Some Answered Questions 286, 528, 634, 708
for subjects of His talks in Europe see individual entries
travels in the West vii-viii, ix, 2, 9, 38, 60, 65, 110, 135, 145, 165, 198, 301, 311, 373, 389, 391, 393, 432, 470, 473, 489, 502, 504, 667, 694, 731
anecdotes recounted by 133, 137, 179, 194, 393
significance ix, 2, 9, 65
walks, strolls taken by 3, 15, 18, 25, 32, 36, 50, 54-5, 59, 100, 104, 124, 135, 137, 142, 151, 169, 189, 217, 219, 228, 233, 271, 289, 296, 294, 321, 322, 325, 327, 375, 379, 381, 384, 386, 395, 398, 403, 405, 406, 432, 463, 465, 471, 484, 613, 672, 674, 683, 692, 703, 709, 713, 714, 719, 730, 732
'Abdu'l-Ghaffár Khán 544-5, 624
'Abdu'l-Ḥamid II, Sultan 140 and n, 194, 207, 337, 377, 427, 451, 491
'Abdu'l-Karím, Mírzá 440, 731
Abdul Latif Effendi 294, 308, 310, (317), 678, 683-4, 685, 689
'Abdu'ṣ-Ṣamad, Áqá 497, 752
'Abdu'ṣ-Ṣamad Khán (Mumtázu's-Salṭanih) 131, (213, 226, 395), 557, 636, 648, 652, 655, 658, 713
áb-gúsht 71, 202, 617, 748
Aboukir, Egypt 496, 751-2
Abraham 1, 262, 344, 355n, 439n, 699
Abú 'Alí Ḥasan ibn 'Alí Ṭúsí (Niẓámu'l-Mulk) 717

Abú Ayyúb Anṣarí 203
Abú Dhar Ghaffárí 203
Abú Ḥamid al-Ghazálí 126n
Abú Sufyán 331, 420
Abu'l-Faḍl *see* Gulpáygání
Abu'l-Ḥasan Amín *see* Ardakání
Abu'l-Qásim, Ḥájí, tomb of 750
Abu'l-Qásim Faráhání *see* Qá'im-Maqám
Adíb, Áqá 'Alí Khán ('Alí ibn Adíb) 122, 136, 236, 440, 507
Adam 48, 119, 449
Adana massacre 630
Adrianople (Edirne) 251, 337, 377, 427, 430, 436, 503, 661, 750
advancement(s)
- of the Cause 373, 387, 698
- of civilization 47, 93, 99, 643
- and divine confirmations, necessity of 195
- of Easterners 241, 299
  - of Eastern women 382
- through faith 390
- of Germany 165, 373, 698, 705
- of humankind 50, 82, 190, 261, 301, 328, 414, 611
- of Kingdom on earth 670
- of the masses 18
- of minds 50, 457, 646
- of nations 205, 358-60
- of peoples 360, 485
- in Persia 82, 129, 142, 184, 643, 705
- of personal interests 24, 128, 234, 251, 496
- of souls 50, 330, 389, 651
- spiritual 47, 389
- of this age 456
- of universal peace 10
- in the West 47, 241, 297
- of the world of being 469
- *see also* progress

aeroplane 357, 384, 716
al-Afghání, Siyyid Jamál al-Dín 490
Afnán family 496, 498
Afnán, Hádí Shírází 434, 728
Afnán, Hussein A. 747
Afnán, Muḥsin 471, 472, 483, 740
Afnán, Nayyir 507
Africa 49 and n, 50, 158, 550 *see also* South Africa
Afrúkhtih (Afroukhteh), Yúnis Khán 145, 633, 740
agriculture 129, 142, 184, 351, 359, 693
Aguilar, Alejo 507, 555, 645
Aḥmad 'Izzat Páshá (Furgaç) 448, 449, 451, 562, 735, 736
Aḥmad Khán, Áqá 545
Aḥmad Khán, Dr 545, 626
Aḥmad Páshá and family 135, 248, 382, 394-5, 424, 426, 561, 662, 721, 722, 733
Aḥmadov brothers 433, 726
Aḥmadov, 'Ináyatu'lláh 477, 741
Akbar, Fatḥu'lláh Khán (Sardár-i-Manṣúr or Sipahdár-i-Rashtí) (427, 452), 507, 655, 723, 729, 731, 732, 735
Akhtar-Khávarí, Mullá Bahrám 433, 726
'Akká 15, 137, 200, 224, 476, 493, 496, 498, 502, 603, 633-4, 656, 754
- 'Abdu'l-Bahá in *see* 'Abdu'l-Bahá
- Bahá'u'lláh in *see* Bahá'u'lláh
- Mufti of 253
- Mutaṣarrif of 253
- railway station 754

'Alavíyyih Khánum 449, 734
al-Bayán magazine 308, 685
alcohol 148, 214, 376
Alexandria, Egypt 155, 308, 474, 483, 485, 486-9, 497, 515, 530, 565, 740, 744, 745, 746, 749, 750
Alfassa, Mirra ('The Mother') *see* Richard, Mirra
Alfonso XIII, King of Spain 381 and n
Alhambra 281
'Alí 'Abbás Áqá (Budapest) 310, 682, 686
'Alí-Akbar Áqá (Vienna) 327, 695
'Alí-Akbar Rawḥání Mílání (Muḥibbu's-Sulṭán) 173, 225-6, 638
'Alí-Aṣghár Khán (Amínu's-Sulṭán) 199
'Alí Effendi 497
'Alí ibn Adíb 122, 236, 507
'Alí Ján, Mullá 449, 734
'Alí-Qulí Khán (Sardár-i-As'ad) 545, 658
'Alí Yúsuf, Shaykh 489
Alláh-u-Abhá 271, 272, 273, 277, 291, 363, 366, 670, 748

Allard, Henri 509, 658
Allen, Mary Sophia 509
Allen, Aseyeh 666, 688 *see also* Dyar, Wellesca
Alliance Spiritualiste, Paris 190, 514, 643, 648
Amanat, Mehrdad 736
Ambró, Ágnes 678, 689
America, Americans 2, 3, 4, 9, 21, 25, 55, 60, 87, 138, 152, 179, 193, 195, 202, 216, 243, 244, 254, 271-2, 300, 305, 310, 312, 331, 366, 376, 383, 394, 429, 451, 493, 503, 512, 513, 602, 654, 659, 660, 661, 731
  and 'Abdu'l-Bahá, mentioned by 13, 18, 22, 23, 24, 27, 31, 45-7, 49n, 65, 100, 123, 133, 137, 147, 160, 193, 171, 181, 193, 233, 242, 249, 251, 259, 266, 276, 319, 352, 355, 357, 389, 393, 406, 413, 415, 418, 423, 425, 453, 456, 501, 601, 603-4, 609-10, 630, 651, 653, 662, 705, 711, 718, 719-20
  Bahá'ís 7, 14, 129, 158, 159, 172-3, 180, 194, 195, 212, 218, 235-6, 238, 248, 259, 263, 271, 276, 314, 317, 326, 355, 368, 371, 384, 385, 388, 394, 395, 398, 406, 408, 410, 413, 418, 423, 430, 444, 456, 487, 489, 641, 653, 658, 662, 663, 664, 666, 705, 713, 716, 721, 747
  freedom in 47, 603, 610, 719
  newspapers, magazines 165, 370-71, 383, 526,
American University (Syrian Protestant College), Beirut 138, 487, 532, 581, 648, 749
Amín, Ḥájí *see* Ardakání
Amír-'Alí, Ṣáḥib (Sir Syed Ameer Ali) 107, 508, 626
'Andalíb ('Alí-Ashraf of Láhíján) 501, 754
Andalusia 182, 281
animal(s) 12, 96, 110, 114, 125-6, 158, 185, 212, 307, 321, 325, 350, 400-01, 635, 702
  aspects in man 158, 160, 401, 635, 724
  kingdom 32, 130, 205, 316, 385, 453, 694
  see also bird(s), camel, cow(s), dog, lion(s), sheep, wolf
Anṣárí, Shaykh Murtaḍá 427, 723
Apostle(s)
  of Bahá'u'lláh 510, 598, 602, 628, 727
  of Christ 12, 161, 197-8, 203, 329, 383, 392, 393-4, 457 and n, 688, 702, 755
Arabia, Arabs 2, 96, 182, 246, 255, 281, 294, 308, 393, 408, 419, 421, 433, 474, 497, 640, 658, 660, 672, 682, 686, 712, 734, 738
Arabic language 56, 66, 67, 126n, 129, 189, 303, 407-8, 429, 437, 476n, 518, 522, 586, 598, 609, 633, 639, 647, 659, 685, 687, 689, 728, 732, 750, 755
Arab-Syrian Congress 734
archbishop 90, *see also* cardinals, clergy, ministers, priests
Ardabíli, 'Abdu'l-Karím (Asadov) 731
Ardakání, Ḥájí Abu'l-Ḥasan (Ḥájí Amín or 'Amín-i-Iláhí') 36, 122, 131, 140, 144, 199, 433, 509, 602-3, 604, 609-10, 631, 633, 661, 725-6
Ardaláni, 'Alí Khán 624
'Árif, Ḥusayn 154-5, 244, 246, 510, 658, 709
Aristotle 323
Arjumand, Ḥájí Mihdí Rifú'á 433, 726
Ark
  of the Covenant 18
  of the Kingdom 11
Armenians 128, 569, 624, 630, 655
Armour, Mrs 25, 599
art, arts 139, 182, 188, 241, 293, 359, 409, 508, 523, 524, 525, 526, 539, 540, 541, 556, 572, 610, 642, 643
Arundel, Sir Arundel Tagg 510
Arundel (née Sim), Dame Catherine Helen 510
Arundel, Mr 616
Asad, Sheikh (487-8), 749
Asadulaogli, Ismail 727
Asadu'lláh, Siyyid *see* Qumí
asceticism 175, 189, 293

Ashkabad ('Ishqábád) 433, 550, 556
Ashraf, Ashraf 511, 642, 658
Ashraf, Ghodsieh 511
Áshtíyání, Siyyid 'Alí-Akbar 19
Asia, Asians 155, 202, 421, 556, 580, 619, 727
Asiatic Quarterly Review, The 106, 552, 626, 709, 739
Asquith, Lady, Cynthia 610
Assyria 2
Astarábádí, Ja'far 264
Atta Ullah, Sheik 511
Aurelian, Emperor 398
Austria, Austrian Empire, Austrians 298, 319-35, 368, 373, 396, 511, 534, 549, 571, 572, 580, 582, 608, 676, 690-97, 723
Avicenna 323
Aws (Arab tribe) 203
Azalis 4, 16, 26, 164, 168, 206, 405, 447, 495, 598, 599, 600, 640, 716
Azerbaijan 433, 477, 512, 558, 646

Báb, the 69, 101, 170, 199, 337, 407, 418, 501, 623, 647, 649, 678, 714, 726, 733, 738, 752
  Covenant of 598
  Declaration of 416-17
  Shrine of ix, 477, 484, 493, 500, 505, 533, 753, 754
Bábís ix, 168, 264, 337, 446, 509, 568, 599-600, 640, 641, 656, 678, 714, 726, 733, 734, 741
Bábu'l-Abváb 490-91, 750
Back de Surany, Hermann 511, 658
Bacon, Francis Herbert 511, 624
Badasht, Conference of 208
Baden-Baden, Germany 290
Badiei, Amir vii
Badí'u'lláh 232, 634-5
Bad Mergentheim, Germany 288-90, 571, 675-6, 703
Bagdadi, Dr Zia 248, 658, 659, 715, 727
  Tablets from 'Abdu'l-Bahá (244), 248, 657, 659
Baghdad 74, 85, 114, 168, 193, 206, 248, 257, 338, 381, 409, 416, 427, 429n, 430, 436, 445, 493, 598, 656, 715, 729, 733
Baghdádí, Muḥammad Muṣṭafá 248, 404, 433, 727
Bahá'ís
  'Abdu'l-Bahá's love for *see* 'Abdu'l-Bahá
  becoming 136-7, 348, 371, 708, 725
  duties of 142, 688
  of the East *see* East
  persecution of 79, 80, 109, 112, 197, 376-7, 415, 455, 714, 741 *see also* calamities
  qualities of 116, 231, 336, 344, 364-6, 386, 454-5, 478, 600, 601, 613, 631, 638, 662, 664, 698, 704, 722, 724, 735-6, 743
  sorrow of, at 'Abdu'l-Bahá's departure 118, 121, 291, 317, 332, 366, 452, 461, 704
  station of 203, 220, 227, 330, 343, 631
  steadfastness of *see* steadfastness
  two devoted believers in every city 399
  unity among 87, 188, 365, 434, 437, 664, 686
  see also individual place entries
Bahá'í Committee, London 525
Bahá'í Faith, Cause ix, 27, 48, 79, 85, 94, 159n, 166, 236, 258, 329, 330, 334, 337, 352, 453, 633, 641, 660, 725, 736 *see also* Cause of God
  teaching the *see* teaching
  teachings of the 48, 107, 312, 331, 336, 348, 375, 620, 652, 654, 660 *see also* Bahá'u'lláh,
Baha'í Society
  Budapest 334
  London 568
Bahai Temple Unity 514, 523, 535, 537, 541, 583
Bahárlú, Amír Khán (Emir Khan de Beharlou) 512, 658
Bahíyyih Khánum *see* Greatest Holy Leaf
Bahnmüller, Berta *see* Bopp
Bahá'u'lláh (Blessed Beauty, Abhá Beauty, Ancient Beauty)
  'Abdu'l-Bahá's relationship with 64, 272, 275, 308, 339, 384, 471, 638, 666
    in dream 382

in Adrianople (Edirne) 656
advent of 39
adversities, afflictions, persecution, tribulations suffered by 216-17, 260-61, 337, 413, 438, 455, 647 *see also* calamities, *and below*, imprisonment and exile
in 'Akká 112-13, 248, 253, 257, 337, 476, 492-3, 502, 503, 509, 599, 729
Apostle(s) of 510, 598, 602, 628, 727
ascension, passing of 476, 640, 641, 654, 692
assistance and protection of 9, 137, 226, 301, 377, 446, 471, 647, 692, 729
  under shade of 113, 203, 369, 477
in Baghdad 168, 656, 714-15
bounties of 20, 25, 173, 207, 269, 286, 377, 385, 411
Cause of 6, 273, 305, 329, 330, 355, 364
  established foundations of divine civilization, universal peace 53, 162
commandments, laws, ordinances of 37, 77, 282
companions of 598, 729
confirmations of 27, 301, 339, 377
Covenant of 63, 94, 121, 203, 236, 310, 365, 387, 715
dispensation, greatness of 62, 117, 118, 123, 143, 150, 157, 181, 183, 211, 239-40, 253, 275, 449
family of (Holy Family) 432, 496, 498
greatness of 171, 173
handwriting of 407
imprisonment and exile of 70, 168, 217, 218, 248-9, 254, 257-8, 264-5, 337, 455, 492-4
independence of 445
Kingdom of 365, 695
love for 147, 363, 698, 720
love of nature 683
loved ones of 7, 15, 198, 222, 362, 402, 438, 447
in Mazandaran 173-4
perfect Man 413
on Persia, Persians 183, 251, 258, 332, 439, 460, 478
as physician for world 630
power of 47, 94, 123, 214, 254, 269-70, 355, 445, 446
prophecies by 123, 175, 250-52, 490-91, 503
Promised One ix, 493-4
Revelation of 370
  for action 354
Shrine of 15, 16, 314, 477, 501, 502, 525, 754
in Sulaymáníyyih, Kurdistan 168, 228, 395, 445
teachings of 7, 9, 39, 65, 68, 86, 95, 175, 178, 221-2, 257, 258, 286, 292, 373, 390, 400, 444, 447-8, 449-50, 605, 758 *for subjects see individual entries*
Writings 206, 221-2, 254, 258, 445, 458, 483n, 500n, 629, 633, 642, 659-60, 666, 683, 686, 714, 725, 734
  Hidden Words 354, 390, 423, 575, 605, 620, 686
  Kalimát-i-Firdawsíyyih 629
  Kitáb-i-Aqdas 37, 251, 491, 524, 565
  Kitáb-i-Mubín 251, 659
  Lawḥ-i-Arḍ-i-Bá 666
  Lawḥ-i-Dunyá (Tablet of the World) 183, 441
  Lawḥ-i-Ra'ís 123, 750, 751
  poems 407
  prayers 144, 148, 165, 229, 408
  Seven Valleys (424), 721
  Súriy-i-Haykal 659, 723
  Súriy-i-Ra'ís 258n, 750, 751
  Tablets 143, 145, 191, 214, 221-2, 315 and n, 382, 409, 447, 450, 458n, 460, 500n, 633, 638, 642, 683, 686, 714, 725, 732, 733, 755
    to kings and rulers 123, 174-5, 250, 251, 258, 491, 659
    to Náṣiri'd-Dín Sháh 413, 492-3, 503-4
    to Ottoman rulers 130, 250-51, 258, 490

of Visitation for individual Bahá'ís 714, 725, 735
Bahjí, Mansion of 476, 502
Baku (Bádkúbih) 433, 512, 558, 727
Balkan League 47n, 561-2
Balkan states 25, 120
Balkan War 22 and n, 25, 32, 47, 120, 342, 561-2
balloon 709
Balogh, Vilma (Wilma) (Bánoczi Lászlóné) 292, 512, 677
Balyuzi, H.M. vii, 611, 648, 652, 669, 682, 706, 714, 715, 746, 750
baptism 51, 274, 280, 609
Báqiroff family 247, 657-8, 677, 690, 731, 736
Tablet from 'Abdu'l-Bahá 247
Báqiroff, 'Abdu'l-Karím 231, 731
Báqiroff, 'Abdu'lláh 122
Báqiroff, Siyyid Aḥmad 122, 213, 243, 244, 251, 266, 319, 512, 544, 658, 663, 675, 676, 677, 696, 697
Báqiroff, Siyyid Naṣru'lláh 122, 188, 434 and n, 435, 512
Barbour, Dr Alexander 621
Barclay, Sir Thomas 39, 512, 604-5
Barnes, Rev. Isaac Edmestone 513
Barney, Alice Pike 513
Barney, Laura Clifford *see* Dreyfus-Barney
Barney, Natalie Clifford 513, 550, 560
Baron Call, ship 497-8, 752
Bashir Uddin, Shah 514
Ba<u>sh</u>íru's-Sulṭán, Áqá <u>Kh</u>án (Ba<u>sh</u>ír-i-Ilahí) 433, 725
Basil Hall, Mary (née Blomfield) 30, 586, 627
baths 13, 136, 289-90, 328, 675
Battersea Park, London 54-5, 59, 613
Bayán, the 221
Baudry (née Sacy), Mercedes 159, 194, 514, 646
Beauchamp, Jeanne 190, 514, 643
Bebenhausen, Palace of 361, 703
Bedouins 188
Beede, Alice R. 370, (425), 514, 582, 705, 706, 709, 718, 722, 724, 749
Beirut 137, 195, 530, 531, 561, 633
Beloved of Martyrs *see* Muḥammad-Ḥusayn
Benjamin, Ida A. M. 514, 735
Berlin, Germany 491, 751
Bernard, Alfred 147, (457), 515, 657, 736
Bernard, Claire 147, 148, 418, (457), 515, 647, 657, 735, 736
Bhawani Singh Bahadur, Maharaja of Jhalawar 57, 113, 115, 516, 611, 624, 627, 628
bigotry 292, 421, 465, 493 *see also* prejudice
Bihi<u>sh</u>tí, Muḥammad Báqir (Baṣṣár) 501, 754
Bimán, Mihtar <u>Kh</u>usraw 192, 644-5
Tablet from 'Abdu'l-Bahá 645
Bíni<u>sh</u>-i-<u>Sh</u>írází, 'Abbás 'Alí <u>Kh</u>án ('Imád-Ábádí) 434, 728
bird(s) 12, 80, 158, 316, 325, 372, 384, 386, 607, 613, 635, 650, 694, 709, 710
of the Kingdom 364-5
Bismarck, Otto von 699-700
blacks 49n, 352-3, 513
Blavatsky, Helena 553
Blech, Charles 170
Blomfield, Lady, Sara Louisa Ryan ('Sitárih <u>Kh</u>ánum') 30-31, 47, 56, 66, 69, 91, 105, 117, 507, 509, 513, 516-17, 518, 519, 522, 525, 531, 533, 536, 537, 545, 548, 552, 556, 560, 563, 564, 566, 570, 574, 576, 578, 582, 584, 604, 610, 611, 612, 617, 623, 624, 626, 627
Blumenthal, Vera de (142) 632
body, physical, human 58, 159, 168, 186, 205, 255, 334, 374, 378, 390, 424, 428, 694
of 'Abdu'l-Bahá 227, 322, 653, 667, 720
relationship with spirit and soul 147, 162, 167, 358, 452, 453, 694
boats 396, 713 *see also* ships
Bolshevik Revolution 741
Bombay, India 115, 251, 523, 533, 644, 660, 705, 743
Bopp (née Bahnmüller), Berta (283), 517, 672, 697
Bopp, Mr (283), 672
Bristol, England 102-5, 518, 564, 617

Clifton Guest House, 17 Royal York Crescent 102-5, 564, 625
Bourlet, Carlo 166, 517
Boutaric, Henri 431, 517, 724
Britain, British 26, 81, 104, 105, 136, 267, 441, 508-9, 604, 608, 610, 656 *see also* 'Selected Biographical Notes'; England; Scotland; Wales
British-American Society, Hungary 637
British Empire 6, 627
British Museum, London 169, 252, 637
brotherhood 32, 40-42, 83, 101, 125, 170, 258, 267, 301, 302, 454-5, 619, 620, 661, 706
Brotherhood Church, N.J. 300
Browne, Edward Granville 24, 26, 31, 33-4, 35, 221-4, 232, 508, 517-18, 546, 568, 599, 601, 620, 652, 711
Bryan, William Jennings 331 and n, 719
Buckton, Alice Mary 38, 518, 571, 605, 607, 624, 719
Budapest, Hungary 165, 287-9, 290-92, 294-317, 319, 322, 334, 335, 338, 368, 512, 530, 531, 534, 535, 538, 549, 553, 555, 558, 560, 562, 573, 576-7, 578, 580, 581, 587, 637, 677, 678-90 passim, 705, 720
Places visited by 'Abdu'l-Bahá:
Andrassy út 71 (Nádler studio) (299, 305, 317), 680, 682
Belgrade Quay 19 (Moore home?) 688
Buda Castle 294
Danube River 294, 312
Holló utca 4 (Goldziher residence) (299), 680
National Museum 310
Nyúl utca 5 (Stark home) (313) 687
railway stations 291, 317, 677, 681
Ritz Hotel 291-2, 294, 531, 576, 587, 677, 681
Esperanto Society 637 *see also* Esperanto
Old Parliament 300-01, 681
Szilágyí Dezső tér 4 (Umrao Singh home) 306, 683
Váci utca 21 (home of Áqá 'Alí-Abbás) (310), 685
see also Esperanto, Ottoman Society, Peace Society, Theosophical Society, Turanian Society
buildings 76, 124, 150, 261, 271, 372, 399, 488, 672, 680, 707
Bulgaria, Bulgarian 541-2, 622
Burújirdí, Jamálu'd-Dín 175-6, 199 and n, 200 and n, 640
Byfleet, Surrey 518, 571

cablegrams 495, 653, 663, 740 *see also* telegrams
cab 160
Caesar 196, 255
Cairo, Egypt 487, 511, 514, 515, 516, 527, 530, 540, 746, 747, 752
calamities 12, 33, 38, 111, 258, 359, 378, 414, 460
endured by
'Abdu'l-Bahá 61, 164, 206, 263
Bahá'ís 7, 99, 112, 179
Bahá'u'lláh 45, 157, 168, 193, 248, 265, 438, 492, 502
Manifestations of God 288, 444, 448, 452
Muhammad, Prophet 195
suffered for Cause of God 79, 206, 263, 415
California 47, 219, 234, 383, 388, 515, 520, 521, 523-4, 532, 533, 535, 537, 541, 555, 570, 578, 626, 706, 713
see also San Francisco, Los Angeles
camel 172, 188, 444
camera obscura 76, 619
Campbell, Hilda May 518
Campbell, Mary Elizabeth Slack 518
Campbell, Rev. Reginald John 107, 518, 519, 616, 626
Canada, Canadian 234 511, 540, 541, 542, 551, 583, 660, 661
capacity 11, 147, 260, 272, 326, 338-9, 340, 386, 504, 661, 719
cardinals 234, 646 *see also* archbishop, clergy, ministers, priests
Carnegie, Andrew 24 and n
Carpenter, Dr Joseph Estlin 61, 519
carpet *see* rugs
carriages 76, 138, 396, 410, 472, 636, 687, 689, 708 *see also* trains

Cart, Théophile 176, 519-20, 640
Cathedral of the Immaculate Conception, Denver, Colorado (234) 655
Caucasia, Caucasus, 140, 259, 320, 432, 562, 691, 727, 741, 745
Cause of God 40, 57, 77, 92, 100, 149, 151, 157, 159, 161, 165, 189, 200, 257, 279, 289, 327, 340, 376, 430, 465, 473, 492
allegiance to 333
banner of 377, 445
calamities that befell the 79
centre of 491
devotion to 276, 399
dissension in 236, 302, 394, 446
embodiment of every divine principle 313
exaltation, fame, glory, renown of 31, 54, 63, 81, 109, 112, 118, 123, 168, 206, 242, 305, 438
faithfulness to 715
firmness, steadfastness in 270, 364, 456, 462, 487
foundation of 413, 438, 454, 492
greatness of 26, 67, 81, 171, 177, 188, 207, 331, 344, 477
history and teachings of 92, 393
and Holy Land 435
influence of 5, 93, 118, 121, 122, 146, 157, 415, 429, 434, 502
nature of 436
opposition to 405
physician for 'Abdu'l-Bahá 345
power, might of 22, 134, 137, 302, 312, 387, 438
progress, advancement of 165, 272-3, 336, 236, 302, 394, 446, 698
promulgation, promotion, proclamation, spread of 7, 28, 29, 112, 131, 145, 175, 184, 252, 306, 311, 336, 387, 412-13, 438, 473, 643, 698
protection of 437, 446
rejection of 206
sacrifice of 'Abdu'l-Bahá for 342
shoreless sea 485
teaching the *see* teaching
triumph of 502
uprooting, destruction of 249, 400, 655
vitality of 468
Caxton Hall, Westminster 31, 92, 98, 511, 523, 545, 552, 624
Cedric, RMS 565, 583
Celtic, RMS 9-22
Central Africa, inhabitants of 49 and n, 50, 158
century, the momentousness of this 78, 153, 183, 219, 225, 293, 295, 503
Chaldea 2
Chamberlain, Isabel Fraser 29, 520, 600, 601, 604, 605-6, 609, 622, 625, 626, 634, 641, 719, 746-7, 749
Chamberlain, Samuel Selwyn 520
charity, acts of 175, 245, 691, 703
Charteris, Mary (Lady Elcho, Countess of Wemyss) 578, 601, 610
chastity 350
Chevallier, Faith 520, 713
Cheyne, Elizabeth Gibson 61, 521, 614
Cheyne, Thomas Kelly 60-65, 208-11, 521, 614
Tablet from 'Abdu'l-Bahá 211
Chicago 155, 581, 582, 604, 658, 720, 740
Child, C. W. 521, 616
children
'Abdu'l-Bahá's meetings with 51, 54, 55, 78, 146, 149, 187, 272, 276, 277-9, 231, 288, 290, 331, 336, 345, 346, 348, 354, 361, 366, 398, 404, 416, 442, 609, 610, 618, 651, 669-71, 677, 703, 724, 730, 732
attack on 'Abdu'l-Bahá (in childhood) by 264
comparisons to 162, 357, 390, 409
desire to have 314-15
education and training of 53, 55, 78, 187-8, 346, 354, 375, 398, 404, 416-17, 610, 710, 717, 719, 742-3
of humanity 356, 441
of Israel 44, 61
of the Kingdom 355 and n, 439 and n, 670
orphans 454
prayer for 620-21
prohibition on striking of 96

raising others' 417
spiritual 213, 650
in times of war 261, 359
China, Chinese 473, 550, 604, 623, 712
cholera 255n, 476
Christ *see* Jesus Christ
Christianity, Christians, Christendom 5, 6, 9, 37, 43, 44, 50, 64, 77-8, 79, 81, 85, 106, 138, 177, 182, 194, 209-10, 234, 250, 258, 260, 262, 283, 309, 330, 337, 347, 480-81, 534, 559, 567, 568, 603, 605, 612, 641, 743
Christian Commonwealth 48, 63-4, 119, 209-11, 416, 520, 526, 542, 544, 551, 608, 609, 624, 628, 728
Christmas 48, 50, 55, 119, 611
churches 65, 147, 210, 234, 243, 261, 371, 383, 692, 735
Anglican (Church of England) 511, 519
Catholic 65, 210, 226, 510, 511, 569, 646, 681, 692
Lutheran 640
New Congregational, Woolwich, London 101, 565
Protestant 555
United Free Church of Scotland 544, 548, 577, 584
Unitarian 519, 529, 542
see also individual entries
Church House Westminster 43, 518
civilization
age, century of 79, 420
ancient 731
Arabian 672
divine 2, 6, 47, 53, 99, 181-2, 186, 297, 312, 326, 363, 368, 372, 661, 739
Eastern 93, 296, 297, 306, 421, 642, 653
European 182, 368, 421, 438
foundation of 642
heavenly 275
history of 127
material 6, 34, 47, 52, 80, 93, 99-100, 181-2, 297, 368, 372, 643
modern 702
spiritual 52, 80, 93, 95, 99-100, 297, 312
universal 679
Western 77, 87, 93, 363, 450, 603, 653
see also 614
Clark, Sir John Maurice 522, 620
Clayton, Margaret Honor Blomfield 522
clergy, clergymen 66, 79, 87, 109, 145, 192, 201, 226-7, 511, 513, 519, 529, 542, 543, 551, 567, 575, 583, 618, 648, 658 *see also* archbishop, cardinals, ministers (religious), priests
clerics (Muslim) 446, 716, 734
Clifton *see* Bristol
climate 121, 135, 290, 320, 476, 485, 496, 503, 617, 653
clothes, clothing 234, 245, 266-7, 321, 327, 442-3, 444, 658, 733, 734
Cobb, Stanwood 248, 254, 522, 570, 659, 660
Cobden-Sanderson, Anne (Annie) 523, 624
Cochrane-Baillie, Charles Wallace Alexander Napier (Lord Lamington) 50, 107, 523, 546, 608, 626
cognizance 180, 485
Colby Ives, Howard 300
colours 21, 52, 58, 130, 278, 320, 384, 460, 713
comfort 11, 12, 14, 85, 104, 113, 124, 131, 160, 214, 234, 241, 264, 289, 359, 376, 394, 413, 428, 442, 464, 468, 484, 503, 725, 739
commerce 142, 184, 240, 351, 359, 373, 375, 381, 643
communists 10, 18, 526, 561
concord 46, 132, 266, 302, 358, 485
universal 58, 166, 170
constancy 51, 66, 336, 503
conscience 316, 637, 638
freedom of 389
Constantinople (Istanbul) 106, 168, 178, 257, 369, 484, 488, 522, 525, 561, 562, 576, 651, 706, 714, 715, 728, 729, 744, 749
Constitutional Revolution (Iran) 140, 182, 252, 459, 495 and n, 547, 579, 599, 648, 716, 750

Cooper, Eleanor (Ella) Frances Goodall 219, 387, 523-4, 535
Coppin, Marie Elénore (194), 524, 569, 646
Copts 488
Costa Rica 507, 555, 645
courage 12, 175, 237, 283, 309, 329, 348, 358-9, 679, 731
Covenant 236, 287, 387, 434, 437, 654, 710
  Ark of the 18
  of the Báb 598
  of Bahá'u'lláh (Abhá Beauty) 63, 94, 121, 203, 236, 310, 365, 387, 715
  Centre of the viii, 6, 36, 39, 40, 61, 68, 83, 87, 117, 273, 290, 474, 496, 665, 754
  firmness in the 36, 116, 173, 203, 236, 285, 437, 487, 504-5, 638, 649, 655, 715
  of God 22, 87, 116, 127, 152, 224, 377, 437, 451, 482, 498, 649
  influence of the 152, 224
  Kingdom of the 455
  power of the 3, 22, 63, 77-8, 81, 94, 121, 122, 127, 177, 293, 387, 451
  servants, signs of 227, 601
Covenant-breakers 16, 138, 163, 164, 206, 377, 495-6, 585, 597-8, 641, 654-5
cows 27, 114, 601, 631
creation
  becoming a new 153, 205, 329, 346, 402, 451, 602
  elements of 20, 85-6
  eye of 90
  and God 20, 82, 85-6, 156, 219, 429
  Intermediary between God and His 157, 323
  Lord of 492
  and man 257, 293, 350, 395, 401, 428, 607, 723
  mysteries of 46, 378
  purpose of 73, 135, 396
  world of 19, 111, 219, 233, 358, 394
Crete 130
Crookes, Sir William 524, 626
Cruttwell, Maud Alice Wilson (425) 524, 722
customs and practices 227, 261, 419, 476, 615, 653, 691, 748
customs office 23, 131
Cuthbert, Arthur 525
Cyprus 168, 607

dancing 32, 68, 348, 376, 501, 695, 702
D'Astre, Georgine d'Ange 525, 648
Daváfurúsh, Ghulám-'Alí 494
Dawlatábádí, Yaḥyá 26, 599-600, 640
Dawson, Albert 525
Dáwúd (Dávúd), Yuḥanná 254, 256, 526, 660, 661
Day of Revelation 43, 44
dead, the 113, 733
  as metaphor 32, 279, 390, 396, 404, 429, 453, 460, 469, 473, 483, 694
death 39, 145, 172, 186, 279-80, 342, 414, 449, 450, 606, 702
  angel of 235
  of a child 467
  fear of 11-12
  life after 277, 652, 666, 730
Denver, Colorado (234), 388, 556, 655, 662, 710
Despard, Charlotte 39-40, 69, 526, 616
detachment 13, 68, 72, 162, 168, 230, 238-9, 242, 364, 386, 427, 445, 456, 468, 469, 479, 487, 733
  meaning of 175, 238-9, 329
Devil, the 49, 112, 119 *see also* Satan
Dickinson, Giselle (née Sacy) 159, 527
Diebold, Jochen (Eugene) 350, 701
Dihají, Siyyid Mihdí 237, 656
diseases 115, 374, 476, 723
  spiritual 304, 374
disorder 4, 77, 421, 490, 49 *see also* order
disunity 222, 230, 664
diversity 57-8, 303, 320, 368, 390
divine power 87-8, 95, 128, 129, 190, 195, 214, 491, 613
divines 444
  Christian 9, 75, 81, 350
  Muslim 74, 112, 141, 174, 250, 304, 460

divorce 37, 603, 711, 738
Ḍíyá'íyyih Khánum 486, 728, 746
doctors 218, 338, 340, 619, 699, 745
see also Muḥammad Khán (Dr); physicians
dog (in Schwarz family) 667
Doré Art Gallery, London 118, 628
Döring, Margarethe 527, 540, 663, 666, 674
dreams 279, 382, 441, 458, 692, 703
Dreyfus, Léa Cardozo 288, 527, 711, 730
Dreyfus-Barney family 121, 122, 193, 206, 215, 228, 408, (425), 426, 463, 550, 648, 657, 660, 705, 722, 730
Hippolyte, 23-6, 27, 29, 40, 121, 143, 154, 157, 161, 63, 171, 174, 222, 228, 246, 263, 372, 386, 418, 429, 527-8, 567, 599, 600, 631, 637, 639, 649, 654, 659, 662, 705, 709, 713
Laura Clifford 193, 222, 227, 513, 528-9, 602, 747
residence 126, 143, 144, 150, 161, 174, 193, 205, 217, 230, 246-7, 369, 385, 386, 398, 410, 411, 418, 429, 444, 633, 636, 657, 662, 728, 730, 732
Drower, Ethel Stefana (née Stevens) 529, 603
Drummond, Rev. Robert B. 80, 529
Dublin, Ireland 516, 526, 529, 564
Dublin, New Hampshire 403, 518, 549, 571, 574
Dundee Courier, The 620
Dunlop, Daniel 70-71, 529, 616-17
Dúst Muḥammad Khán (Mu'ayyiru'l-Mamálik) 103-4, 106, 123, 545, 625
duty 96, 142, 162, 176, 204, 255, 394, 417, 421, 429, 711
Dyar, Harrison Gray 314 and n
Dyar, Rawshan and Gulshan 314-15
Dyar, Wellesca Pollock (Aseyeh (Ásíyih) Allen) 314-15, 666, 688

Eager Heart, play 43, 518, 607
ease *see* comfort
East, the 3, 5, 14, 35, 38, 47, 53, 67, 69, 83, 85, 106, 110, 138, 166, 186, 189, 194, 197, 200, 214, 225, 229, 232, 241, 256-7, 260, 270, 279, 292, 297, 303, 306, 308, 331, 332, 365, 370, 379, 382, 422, 428, 431, 434, 436, 440, 443, 448, 452, 456, 463, 465, 651, 748
Bahá'ís of 94, 95, 98, 131, 140, 143, 145, 157, 173, 179, 242, 388, 401, 432, 479, 480, 602, 732
Sun of Truth rises in 143, 198, 257, 463, 464, 478
and West ix, 1, 2, 7, 9, 23, 25, 26, 28, 31-2, 36, 48, 56, 65, 66, 73, 80, 82, 91, 92, 93, 95, 103, 108, 112, 113, 129, 131, 143, 206, 211, 214, 216, 224, 226, 233, 245, 256, 269, 297, 299, 300, 301, 305, 308, 310, 320, 332, 355n, 356, 362, 368, 378, 387, 388, 390, 429-30, 432, 439 and n, 452, 463, 479, 487, 498, 503, 614, 621, 710, 712, 791
Easterners 67, 140-42, 151, 152, 171, 180, 207, 208, 229, 241, 249, 251, 327, 331, 370, 412, 420, 748
unity with Westerners 95, 301, 388, 614
Eckstein, Adolf 275, 282, 530, 663, 664, 665, 671, 672, 676
Eckstein, Agatha 530, 702
economics 36, 63, 88, 312, 403, 416, 531, 543, 612, 646
Eder, David (325), 693-4
Edinburgh, Scotland 71, 74-5, 76-90, 100, 166, 296, 392, 522, 529, 533, 536, 543-4, 560, 563, 567, 583-4, 615, 619, 620, 712, 719
Places visited by 'Abdu'l-Bahá:
Charlotte Square (No. 7, Whyte residence) 75-90 passim, 584
College of Art 620
Freemason's Hall, 96 George St 77, 620
Great King St (No. 28, Theosophical Society) 87-8, 621
Holyrood (Queen's Park, King's Drive) 76-7, 619
North Canongate School, 5 New St 620

Outlook Tower 76, 79, 533, 618, 619
Princes Street station 75, 90, 622
Rainy Hall, New College 79, 621
Roxburghe Hotel, 38 Charlotte Square 79, 89-90, 618
St Giles Cathedral 84, 621
Edinburgh Evening Dispatch 81, 620
Edirne *see* Adrianople
education 22, 45, 46, 49-50 and n, 52, 58, 86, 114, 126, 172, 176, 180, 241, 248, 295, 300, 358, 372, 409, 450, 711, 742
of children 53, 55, 78, 187-8, 346, 354, 375, 398, 404, 416-17, 610, 710, 717, 719, 742-3
divine 22, 126, 451, 670
of humanity 49, 57, 59, 184, 414, 642, 679
material 126, 181, 226, 443
moral 543
secular 53
spiritual 47, 181, 226, 346, 354, 398, 404, 443
of women 35, 40, 42, 86, 214, 559, 601
Edward VII of Great Britain 693
Edward VIII of Great Britain 267
Eger, Gustav 531, 636
Egypt, Egyptians vii, ix, 2, 27, 61, 82-3, 104, 106, 140, 142, 155, 159, 189, 431, 432, 433, 465, 473-99, 508, 514, 515, 516, 520, 530, 534, 564, 569, 575, 581, 582, 585, 600, 619, 630, 640, 724, 731, 737, 739, 741, 742-3, 744, 745, 746, 747, 749, 750
Egyptian Gazette, The 685
Eigel, Ferdinand (Nándor) 294, 531, 678
elements 20, 39, 86, 358, 397
enemies 36, 32, 49, 142
of the Bahá'í Cause 4, 19, 36, 79, 157, 164, 236, 249, 251, 263, 377, 391, 435, 437, 446, 490, 492, 495, 573, 679, 692, 734, 742
of Christ 234
of Islam 163, 241
of human development 605
of the prophets 234
of the state 142
Engelhardt, Alexander (324-5), 693
England, English 18, 21, 25-73, 92-121, 244, 302, 303, 412, 466, 599-618, 623-8, 660, 662, 738
Christians 64, 209
government and officials 168, 750
love of 'Abdu'l-Bahá for believers in 101, 455, 720
people from 61, 94, 103, 106, 152, 305, 429, 430, 451, 453, 455, 691, 701 *see also individual entries*
rule in Cyprus 607
see also Britain, Bristol, London, Oxford
English language 267, 275, 286, 308, 564, 586, 598, 628, 633, 644, 655, 667, 668, 674, 677, 691, 700, 701, 751
Enthoven, Garielle 108, 531, 626
equality 69, 293
of men and women 35, 40, 52, 69, 86, 181, 357, 431
of the rights of men and women 35, 69, 86, 181, 357
Esperanto, Esperantists, 640
Hungary 305, 534, 637, 682
London 34, 556, 564, 601, 618, 620, 622
Paris 165-7, 517, 519-20, 640
Scotland 77-8, 90, 165-6, 618, 620, 622, 712
Stuttgart 276-7, 282, 681
Esphahani, Ali Hossein 740
Esslingen, Germany 277, 280-81, 284, 291, 335, 429, 531, 548, 549, 572, 669-71, 673, 696, 697, 704
Altes Museum 669-71
railway station 291, 335, 676, 697
Ethiopia 561
Europe, Europeans 87, 133, 165, 211, 388, 391, 684
and 'Abdu'l-Bahá, mentioned in talks by ii, 14, 27, 46-7, 65, 130, 140, 148, 156, 180, 182, 183, 211, 231, 241, 249, 284, 295-6, 305, 315, 316, 320, 322, 330, 360, 362, 368, 393, 409, 415, 420-21, 425, 601, 603, 604, 643, 649, 658-9, 660, 691, 719
calendars 416

children 55
dress 266-7
languages 320, 633
material civilization of 47, 182, 241, 368
materialism 27, 322, 601, 603
rejection of religion by 34, 204
European languages 320, 633
evil 126, 221, 309, 450, 505, 600, 650, 722, 755
evildoer 406
Exodus, Book of 481-2, 738

Faber, Dr 357, 703, 704
Faḍlu'lláh, Mírzá (story of) 656
fairness and fair-mindedness 2, 87, 100, 120, 177, 199, 211, 223, 240, 293, 315, 341, 385, 503 *see also* justice
faith 116, 143, 191, 196, 236, 280, 364, 390, 411, 439, 441, 445, 448, 454, 615, 702, 712, 724, 725
faithfulness 66, 109, 110, 115, 119, 163, 263n, 276, 401, 402, 423, 450, 600, 602, 651, 710, 715, 735
fame 24, 74, 148, 211, 359, 439, 440, 451, 469, 495
of 'Abdu'l-Bahá 368-9, 490
of Cause, Word of God 81, 109, 293, 305
fancies, idle 5, 44, 115, 241, 261, 339 *see also* imaginings, vain; superstitions
Faráhání *see* Qá'im-Maqám
Farley, John Murphy 234n
Farmánfarmá'íyán, Muḥammad-'Álí Mírzá 194, 531, 646
farmers 71n, 373, 580, 699
Fars, Iran 433, 478, 532, 554
Fatḥ-'Alí (Fatḥ-i-A'ẓam) 399, 714-15
Fatḥ-'Alí Sháh 132, 555, 557
Father Christmas 611
Fáṭimih 173-4
Fírúz, Fírúz Mírzá (Núṣratu'd-Dawlih) 194, 532, 646
Fisher, Edwin 158, 212, 276, 532, 663, 664-5, 667, 672, 675, 676, 700
flock(s) 45, 257, 280, 292, 293, 356, 372, 668 *see also* sheep
flowers 21, 52, 58, 108, 116, 184, 235, 244, 255, 267, 277, 278, 279, 287, 288, 321, 325, 336, 346, 351, 358, 365-6, 370, 380, 381, 384, 416, 417, 422, 430-31, 461, 467, 615, 667, 669, 678, 679, 719
Paris Flower Show 417, 719
'Flower Day', Vienna (321), 691
food 55, 67, 114, 188, 191, 428, 430, 635, 723-4, 748
at gatherings 67, 349, 614, 730, 749
healthful 114, 400-01, 228, 395
as metaphor 191, 622, 722, 748
moderation in 723-4
see also 'Abdu'l-Bahá, meals of; vegetarianism
forgiveness 14, 33, 96, 364
four criteria of comprehension 133, 324, 687
four kinds of love 617 *see also* love, degrees of
Fraser, Rev. Donald B. 25
Fraser, Ethel Patterson 377, 533
Fraser, Isabel *see* Chamberlain
freedom 315-16, 390
of 'Abdu'l-Bahá from prison 7, 94-5, 139, 194, 337, 491, 502
of action 316
in America 47, 603, 610, 719
of children from guile and deceit 345
of conscience 389
divine 315
and divine confirmations, necessity of 195
from dogma and superstition 611
of the heart from attachments 238-9
of humanity 316, 403
of individual 38, 283, 450
of inquiry 65, 210
of Manifestations of God 415
political 128, 315
from selfish defilements 422
from sorrow 38, 277, 316, 442
of thought 316
of Universal Reality 397
of women 47, 69, 86, 523, 526
of the world of nature 315-16
from the world 347, 351
free will 450
Frosell, O. M. A. (294), 296, 678, 679-80

Fruitport, Michigan 388, 710-11
Fu'ád Effendi 662
Furúghí, Maḥmúd 749, 753

Gabriel, angel 114 and n
Gail, Marzieh vii
Gamble, Annie Eliza 58, 533, 611
Ganges river, India 320, 691
Garden of Eden 119, 449
Geddes, Sir Patrick 76, 78-80, 533, 619, 621
Geneva, Switzerland 344, 368, 511, 515, 575, 699
George V, King 105
Germanus, Gyula (Julius) 294, 534, 677, 680
Germany, Germans 157-8, 165, 205, 212, 213, 225, 229, 254, 267-8, 269-91, 302, 303, 305, 335, 336-67, 368, 378, 396, 408, 429, 430, 439, 491, 608, 650, 652, 663-78, 697-705, 718, 723
  Bahá'ís, believers in 269, 271, 273, 276, 278-80, 284-5, 288, 290-91, 336-8, 342, 344, 345, 346-9, 350-51, 353-6, 361, 366 *see also individual entries;*
  love of 'Abdu'l-Bahá for 213, 268, 298, 341, 343, 365, 391, 649, 668, 670 *see also individual entries*
Getsinger, Lua (244), 657
Ghaffárí, Abú Dhar 203
Ghaffárí, Mihdí Khán 534, 632
al-Ghazálí, Abú Ḥamid 126n
Ghálí 237 and n
Ghani, Abdul 534
Ghulám-'Alí 433
Ghulám-Riḍá, Ḥájí (Amín-i-Amín) 433, 725-6
Giesswein, Alexander (Sándor) 294, 300-01, 534, 682
gifts, offered to 'Abdu'l-Bahá 5, 7, 89-90, 138, 243, 300, 308, 349
God
  advent of 492
  and adversity 492, 611
  aid and assistance of 73, 89, 156, 247, 342, 377, 454, 502, 694
  Ancient Being 397
  attachment to 639
  attributes, perfections of 33, 86, 323, 426, 722
  belief in 262, 481
  bestowals, blessings, bounties, favours, gifts of 1, 33, 42, 104, 120, 149, 175, 216, 332, 369, 382, 406, 429, 502, 610, 735
  Book(s) of 52, 230, 314, 492, 738
  call of 154, 438, 473, 484, 501, 665
  City of 416, 493, 719
  capacity, capability given by 11, 147, 293, 383
  Cause of *see* Cause of God
  closeness, nearness to 346, 347, 611, 694
  command of 500n
  confirmations of 6, 44, 68, 156, 181, 200, 216, 245, 256, 313, 377, 408, 447, 457, 469, 613, 649, 664, 711, 724, 737
  Covenant of *see* Covenant
  and creation 82, 156, 157, 219, 323, 401
  Day of 657
  decree of 447
  enemies of, thwarted 178
  Essence of 51, 53, 57, 315, 397, 426
  eternal dominion of 616
  Faith of 222
  fear of 32, 316, 441
  fragrances, effulgences of 59, 73, 136, 137, 147, 149, 151, 227, 334
  glad-tidings of 269, 274, 284, 351, 385, 714, 735
  good-pleasure of 101, 444, 494
  grace of 171, 217, 328
  guidance of 44, 492, 670
  healing by 374
  Hidden One 169, 713
  human race as handiwork of 293, 401
  image of 22
  inattention to 601
  kindness of 292, 668, 694
  Kingdom of 9, 11, 48, 82, 110-11, 139, 161, 275, 276, 283, 298, 327, 330, 346, 347, 351, 355 and n,

375, 393, 394, 431, 439 and n, 442, 469, 603, 608, 621, 627, 631, 639, 710, 722, 735, 737
knowledge of 72, 110-11, 162, 186, 313, 375, 380, 384, 430, 441, 483, 604, 606-7, 613, 622, 626, 638, 657, 674, 687, 689, 721, 724
law(s) of 246, 315-16, 350, 390, 680
light of 12, 280, 286, 460, 670, 724
lion of 348
love of *see* love
loved ones, of, friends, favoured ones of 54, 94, 188, 231, 252, 272, 345, 380, 381, 386, 399, 435, 459, 498, 721, 742
Manifestations of *see* Manifestations of God
method of 1
mysteries of, revealed to 'Abdu'l-Bahá 80
oneness of 83, 262, 292, 458, 606, 639, 689
One True 437
path of 7, 112, 122, 164, 179, 247, 348, 383, 414, 492, 708, 736
plan of 493
poverty beloved by 50
power of 7, 97, 128, 160, 171, 241, 254-5, 259, 269, 308, 313, 316, 447, 463, 479, 503, 682
praise of 148, 410, 453, 464, 667-8
prayers to *see* prayer
prerogative to contravene human rules 476
promises of 196
proofs of existence of 158, 312
protection of 650, 670
protector of orphans 454
purpose of 476
refuge in 363
rejection of 141, 204
reliance on 230
religion of 31, 72, 227, 257, 262, 309, 313, 316, 341, 388, 456, 710, 743
remembrance, mention, mindful of 203, 231, 261, 326, 352, 381, 454, 461, 632, 700
sanctified from incarnation 387
Servant of *see* 'Abdu'l-Bahá
service to *see* service
signs of 360, 423, 456
snow-white hand of 504
sovereignty, reign of 27, 196, 224
Spirit of 77, 78, 351, 609 *see also* Holy Spirit
splendours of 363, 378
sweet savours of 10, 13, 101, 279, 311, 317, 339, 347, 431, 440, 467
teachings of 119-20
thanks to 20, 346, 410, 411, 453, 464, 466, 478, 504, 664, 665, 666, 702, 742, 748
and thoughts, cast into human minds 479
threshold of 108, 152, 199, 289, 376, 433, 454, 739
True Shepherd, Father 257, 292, 357
trust in 72
trustees of 447
universality is of 28, 167
Voice of 168, 339
Will of 26, 44, 210, 218, 219, 239, 310, 441
Word of *see* Word of God
worlds, realms of 213, 277, 313, 441, 442, 453, 646
worship of 261, 262
Goldziher, Ignác 301, (310), 534, 535, 680, 685, 686, 687, 705
Gollmer, Ulrich 669, 671, 673, 676, 699, 700, 701, 702, 704
Goodall, Helen 219, 377-8, 387, 523, 535
Gospel(s) 149, 194, 283, 392, 408, 416, 434, 481 *see also* New Testament
Gottesmann-Baktay, Antónia 306, 535, 573, 682
governance 96, 180
gratitude 3, 63, 90, 203, 293, 343, 347, 417, 499
to 'Abdu'l-Bahá, *throughout*
Great Britain 267, 585, 604, 608 *see also* Britain, England, Scotland
Greatest Holy Leaf (Bahíyyih Khánum) 263, 283, 432, 486, 498, 586, 740-41, 746
Greatest Name 9, 51, 272, 287, 455

Greco-Turkish War 130 and n
Greece, Greek(s) 50, 130, 147, 525, 562, 571
Gregory, Louis 352 and n.
Gulpáygání, Abu'l-Faḍl 17, 131, 140, 237-8, 354, 433, 483, 487, 598, 631, 632, 633, 648, 656-7, 686, 702, 744, 746-7, 748-9
  Brilliant Proof, The 354, 702
  Tablet from 'Abdu'l-Bahá 131

Haack, Vana K. (142), 632
Hagara, Viktor (310, 317), 535, 685, 688, 689
Hague, The 201, 512, 534, 543, 557, 571
Haifa 26, 27, 138, 224, 435, 482, 493, 496, 497, 498-9, 500, 507, 533, 535, 536, 540, 541, 542, 603, 633, 688, 713, 737, 740-41, 745, 746, 751, 753, 754
  Pilgrim House 482, 753
Häfner, Otto 281, 362, 671-2, 704
Ḥajjáj (al Ḥajjáj ibn Yúsuf?) 132, 631
Ḥakím-Báshí, Músá Khán (Ḥakím-i-Iláhí) 140, 433, 536, 602
Ḥakím, Luṭfu'lláh 73, 536, 617, 622, 625, 735
Hall, Mary Basil (née Blomfield) 30, 536, 627
Hall, Joshua D.T. x, 134n, 148n, 600, 617, 755
Halpérine-Kaminsky, Nina (142), 632
Hamadan, Iran 377, 427, 433, 457, 532, 652, 736
Hammond, Eric 537, 616, 624
Hanbury-Tracy, Charles 609
Hands of the Cause 433, 507, 510, 540, 557, 581, 602, 628, 630, 727
Hannen, Joseph 423, 537, 665, 667, 668, 720-21, 732, 736
Hannen, Pauline (née Knobloch) 423, 537, 548, 549, 669, 720-21
Haybittle, Mary (244), 657
happiness 37-8, 45, 46, 65, 216, 220, 241, 287, 316, 328, 365, 376, 383, 409, 441-2, 664, 674, 698, 707, 714, 721, 739
  of 'Abdu'l-Bahá *see* 'Abdu'l-Bahá, happiness of
  of humanity 86, 215, 329
  lack of 37, 639, 702, 707, 751
  divine 154, 375, 441
  of people in presence of 'Abdu'l-Bahá 29, 75, 79, 84, 187, 297, 458, 467, 670, 677, 698
  spiritual 38, 73, 280, 702
  see also joy
harmony 119, 151, 190, 244-5, 252, 320, 325, 459, 485, 613, 686
Ḥasan-i-Adíb, Hand of the Cause 433, 507
Haṣan Kaj-Damágh 264
Ḥaydar-'Alí, Ḥájí Mírzá, Iṣfahání, 131, 140, 176, 225, 433, 585, 630-31
healing 3, 308, 330, 352, 374-5, 480, 619, 630, 702
  through prayer 374
health 131, 186, 187, 189, 229, 237, 375, 378, 382, 429, 442, 483, 487, 702
  poor 60, 112, 115, 131, 267, 296, 303, 416, 428, 711
  of 'Abdu'l-Bahá *see* 'Abdu'l-Bahá, health of
  and food 228, 395
Hearst, Phoebe 523
heat 47-8, 115, 188, 476, 484, 492, 601, 644
  of fever 486
  of the sun 346, 351, 473
hedonism 228, 232, 236, 379
Heine, Heinrich 65, 210
Heriot, Mrs 735
Herod Antipas 43
Heron, Louise 537, 610-11
Herrick, Elizabeth 29, 537-8, 541, 601
Herrigel, Marie 205, 273, (335, 336), 538, 562, 650, 663, 672, 673, 697
Herrigel, Wilhelm 158, 205, 267, 271, 273, 275, 278, 291, 324, 327, (336), 338-40, 538, 650, 652, 663, 665, 672, 676, 677, 686, 693, 697, 698, 701, 703
Hieston, Lilian Haydon 180, 538, 641
Higher Thought Society, London 118
Himalaya (P&O ship) 462-72, 515, 553, 739, 740
Hindiján (Hendeyan) 478, 479n, 742-3

Hindus 508, 515, 538, 567
Hoagg, Emogene 749
Hodgson, Dorothy (425), 538-9, 649-50, 709, 722
Hohl, Louis 539, 658
Holland (Netherlands) 542, 571, 627, 636
Holley, Bertha (422), 539, 705, 707, 720
Holley, Hertha 187, 398, 539
Holley, Horace 187, 374, (422), 540, 706, 707, 709, 711, 720
Holy Family 432, 496, 498
Holy Land ix, 314-15, 473-4, 497, 498, 500-05, 523, 586, 645, 652, 741, 753-5
  Bahá'ís of 140, 225, 382, 432, 433, 472, 486, 496
  banishment of Bahá'u'lláh to 249, 493-4
  mentioned by 'Abdu'l-Bahá 15, 110, 177, 225, 237, 432, 435, 465, 484, 499, 742
Holy Spirit 41, 116, 158, 192, 274, 280, 286, 322, 351, 352, 355, 369, 393, 453, 612, 613, 622, 642, 643, 664, 668, 670, 682, 683, 694, 714
honesty 17, 49, 90, 237, 240, 344, 398, 719 *see also* truthfulness
Honolulu 116, 235
  Bahá'ís of 116, 627
  Tablet to Bahá'ís of 236
honour 38, 141, 213, 304, 308, 358-9, 412, 417, 419, 446, 448, 451, 452, 455, 489, 694
hotels
  Astoria, Paris 653
  Bad Mergentheim 675
  Baltimore, Paris (370), 533, 556, 706, 713, 715, 724
  Beatrix, Vienna (317), 690
  California (*see* Baltimore), Paris
  Casino Palace, Port Said (484), 744
  Grand, Vienna 317, 690, 692, 695
  Grand, de la Paix, Geneva (344), 699
  Grand, du Parc, Thonon-les-Bains 540, 554
  Imperial, Paris 728, 731
  Imperial, Vienna (324), 692
  International, Paris 730
  Lamm-Post, Hall, Germany 675
  Marquardt, Stuttgart 267, 285, 335, 663, 666, 668-70, 697, 703
  Martha-Pension Family Hotel, Paris 242, 265, 425, 510, 524, 536, 545, 546, 547, 552, 554, 556, 557, 561, 562, 570, 571, 657, 715, 721-2, 728
  Midland Adelphi, Liverpool (now Britannia Adelphi) 24, 25, 29, 599
  Moderne, Paris 165-6, 517, 519
  Ritz, Budapest 291-2, 294, 531, 576, 587, 677, 681, 685, 689
  Roxburghe, Edinburgh 79, 89-90, 618
  Sulṭání, Port Said 472, 484, 740, 746
  Terminus, Marseille 462, 737
  Victoria (New), Ramleh 486, 489, 741, 748
  Westminster Palace, London 39, 512, 518, 526, 604
Huguenin, Edmée (née Sacy) 159, 540
humanity, humankind
  advancement, progress of 50, 82-3, 110, 130, 184, 190, 261, 301, 328, 414, 485, 495, 611, 684
  asleep 346
  bounties, kindness of God to 5, 42, 292-3, 406, 429
  brotherhood of 32, 42, 125, 170, 301, 302
  character, improvement of 45, 49, 180-81, 184, 190, 234, 261, 313, 316, 350, 358, 420, 441, 642
  and civilization 53, 80, 99, 326, 635
  conflict, dissension, enmity in 120, 257, 286, 309, 455
  customs and practices of, befits purpose of God to violate 476
  destiny of 181
  differences in 86
  distinction of 326
  disunity of 230
  and divine teachings 3, 25, 36, 39, 59, 82-3, 109, 117, 189, 223, 306, 357, 450, 476, 630, 660, 679

duty to 162, 417, 431
education of 49, 57, 59, 184, 414, 642, 679
eternal life of 457
first duty of 394
glory of, born of love for God 110, 694
happiness, felicity of 86, 215, 329
love for *see* love
mirror of 389
needs of 341, 436
nobility, excellence of 14, 119, 280, 359
oneness of 14, 40, 42, 70, 72, 99, 101, 103, 107, 117, 125, 151, 216-17, 257, 262, 275, 278, 282, 288, 292, 298, 300, 317, 320, 330, 349, 356, 358, 369, 383, 402, 438, 453, 454, 462, 467, 471, 476, 489, 660, 668, 689, 719
particular matters of 28, 167, 615
peace, security, tranquillity of 23, 46-7, 86, 99, 117, 205, 259, 292, 301, 302, 320, 340, 358, 446, 630
powers of 205, 322, 325
prosperity of 99, 100, 127, 205, 261, 262, 267, 309, 313, 320, 328, 406, 440, 684
protection of 454
realities of 5, 6, 88
salvation of 48, 49
scattered sheep 356-7
second reality of 66, 88, 125, 621-2
service to *see* service
sickness of 630
single family 97, 299
spiritualization of 22, 47, 73, 226, 230, 270, 326-7, 328, 330, 392, 424, 694, 724
unity of *see* unity
and veils 144
virtues and perfections of 357, 415, 417, 436, 454, 470, 668, 679, 723-5
well-being, welfare of 73, 86, 100, 358, 385, 446
world of 130, 389-90, 424, 440
see also service to, unity of
human nature 49
human realm 119
human rights 359
Humáyún, 'Alí Khán Iḥtishám 540, 624
humidity 113, 480, 484, 485, 745
of ignorance 180
humility 159, 237, 399, 451, 639, 687
toward Bahá'í Cause 94, 103, 146, 206
toward 'Abdu'l-Bahá, *throughout*
humour *see* 'Abdu'l-Bahá, humour of
Hungary, Hungarians 291, 294-317, 334, 368, 373, 396, 511, 512, 531, 534, 535, 549, 553, 558, 560, 562, 576, 578, 580, 581, 582, 587, 608, 676, 678-90, 713
Bahá'í community
following 'Abdu'l-Bahá's visit 317, 696
love of 'Abdu'l-Bahá for 298, 679
present-day 677-89 passim
Andrassy út 71 (Nádler studio) (299, 305, 317), 680
British-American Society 637
Esperanto Society 637 *see also* Esperanto
Holló utca 4 (Goldziher residence) (299), 680
Old Parliament 300-01, 681
Oriental Commercial University 680
Orientalist School 637
National Museum 310
Peace Society 637, 682
Hungarian language 293, 299, 677, 681, 682, 686, 687, 696
Ḥuqúqu'lláh 509, 581
Ḥusayn, son of 'Abdu'l-Bahá 187
Ḥusayn 'Árif 154-5, 244, 246, 510, 658, 709
Ḥusayn, Ḥájí 239, 547, 706
Ḥusayn Iqbal 727
Huvaydá, Ḥabíbu'lláh ('Aynu'l-Mulk) 16, 598

Ibn-i-Abhar, Hand of the Cause 433
Ibn-i-Aṣdaq, Hand of the Cause (487), 557, 749
ibn-i-Adíb *see* Adíb, Áqá 'Alí Khán

Ibráhím Gúrkání (Ibráhím Khán, Ibtiháju'l-Mulk) 213, 433, 650
Ismá'íl, Ḥájí 327
Ismailia, Egypt 485-6, 744, 745, 746
imagination, power of 603, 749
imaginings 30, 241, 255, 413, 496
vain 5, 44, 52, 58, 72-3, 82, 98, 103, 109, 114-15, 127, 144, 145, 178, 204-5, 216, 227, 426
see also fancies, idle; imitation; superstitions
Imám(s) 234, 543, 618
'Alí 139, 399
Hidden 382n
Ḥusayn 264n
imitation
blind 3, 23, 29, 30, 44, 81, 82, 84, 88, 98, 103, 109, 127, 144, 178, 204, 205, 227, 228, 257, 275, 286, 322, 444, 452, 455, 465, 466, 481
harmful 292
idle 443
illusory 261
outworn 72
immorality 164, 259, 401
immortality, of the soul 142 *see also* life, eternal
Inayat ('Ináyatu'lláh) Khán 139, 154, (426), 546, 634-5, 723
India, Indians 5-6, 115, 192, 200, 489, 533, 534, 553-4, 585-6, 601, 613, 727
meetings with 'Abdu'l-Bahá 82, 106, 107, 113, 139, 154, 159, 216, 295, 305, 312, 317, 463-4, 465-6, 469, 471, 474, 508, 516, 534, 543, 546, 558, 566, 573, 585, 619, 644, 651, 683, 712, 725, 738, 739
mentioned by 'Abdu'l-Bahá 114, 115, 258, 320, 473, 611, 691, 727
industry 79, 129, 142, 153, 156, 184, 351, 359, 373, 375, 381, 456, 606
insistent self 49
intelligence, intelligent 100, 149, 191, 281, 282, 331n, 600, 601, 602, 603, 613, 660, 671, 700, 712
intellect 30, 46, 49n, 87, 307, 354, 378, 403, 622, 646, 660, 661, 723
International Bahá'í Council 526
interpreters 21, 75, 143, 153, 226, 602, 634, 681, 732 *see also* translators
Intiẓámu's-Salṭanih (Mír Siyyid Muḥammad) 123, 145, (179-80, 409), 557, 641, 656, 717
inventions 397, 601, 696
Iram of the Pillars 235
Iran *see* Persia
Iraq 218, 581, 617-18, 723, 727, 733
Íráni, Mihdí (Muḥammad Mahdi Khán, Za'ímu'd-Dawlih) 490-91, 750
irreligion 204, 222, 226-7, 257, 451 *see also* religion
Irwin, Beatrice 424, 431, 451, 662, 706
Isaiah, prophet 61, 92, 352, 623
Isfahan, Iran 159, 198, 199n, 546, 547, 554, 574, 633, 647, 714, 726, 729
Iṣfahání, Muḥammad-Taqí 131, 471
Isfandíyár, Kay-Khusraw 115 and n.
'Ishqábád (Ashkabad) 433, 550, 556
Islam 9, 29, 79, 84, 90, 138, 142, 245, 309, 319, 369, 394, 413, 480-81, 488, 723, 738, 744
divines of 74, 112, 141, 174, 250, 304, 460
history and traditions of 132, 163-4, 173-4, 195-6, 235, 246, 250, 255, 260-61, 331-2, 419-20, 279, 489, 720, 744
jurisprudence and doctrine 427
pilgrimage in 313-14
Ismailia, Egypt 485-6, 744, 745-6
Israel, Israelites 1, 9, 44, 61, 163, 182, 235, 262, 392, 393, 409, 481-2, 548, 748
Istanbul *see* Constantinople

Jábulqá and Jábulṣá 382 and n
Jack, Marion 52, 537, 541-2, 609, 623, 719
Jackson, Edith 415-16, 426, 542, 723, 730
Jaffa 497-8, 752-3
Jalál, Áqá Mírzá *see* Shahíd
Jalál, Siyyid (son of Síná) 483
Jamaica 513
Japan, Japanese 82, 383, 473, 508, 539, 550, 559, 712

Jasion, Jan x, 507, *multiple references in Notes* 597-755
Javád, Ḥájí Siyyid 497, 547, 706, 752
Jenkyn, Daniel 542, 611
Jerusalem 9, 250, 465, 485, 526, 533, 603
Jerusalem (Russian steamer) 746
Jesus Christ
discussed in talks given by 'Abdu'l-Bahá 9, 11-12, 13, 43, 44, 50, 51, 71, 77, 97, 99, 112, 147, 149, 161, 177, 197-8, 233-4, 250, 260, 262, 273, 283, 305, 323, 329, 342, 343, 347, 350-02, 355, 360, 369, 370, 371, 373, 383, 386, 390, 392-4, 408-9, 411, 414, 416, 434, 439, 442-3, 477, 481-2, 610, 641, 646, 665, 669, 670, 692, 701, 702, 712
other mentions 1-2, 64, 78, 82, 99, 194, 209, 457n, 712
return of, second coming of 273, 434, 439, 603, 728
Jews, Judaism 9, 43-4, 64, 65, 79, 112, 149, 163, 209, 210, 221, 235, 254, 303, 309, 337, 433, 457, 458, 465, 469, 487, 493, 511, 526, 581, 616, 662, 681, 726
discussed in talks given by 'Abdu'l-Bahá 9, 43-4, 79, 112, 149, 163, 190, 256, 258, 260, 262, 386, 465, 481, 662, 665, 669
see also synagogues
Joan of Arc 734-5
John the Baptist 48
Johnson, Rev. Henry Harold 542
Jones, Sir Tracey French Gavin 543
Jones, Captain 624
Joshua 483
Jounet, Albert (190), 201, 643, 648
journalists 104, 512, 520, 524, 526, 538, 551, 552, 562, 567, 585, 636, 659, 677, 681, 687 *see also* reporters
joy 11, 32, 38, 52, 277, 320, 328, 351, 354, 359, 360, 376, 400, 401, 679, 682, 736
of 'Abdu'l-Bahá *see* 'Abdu'l-Bahá
see also happiness
justice 46, 120, 198, 199, 240, 293, 316, 359, 385, 421, 496 *see also* fairness, fair-mindedness

Ka'bu'l-Aḥbár 234-5
Kamal-ud-Din Khwaja 543
Kanno, Takeshi 383
Karam-'Alí, Darvís<u>h</u> 478, 742
Tablet from 'Abdu'l-Bahá to his sons Nasser and Mansour 742
Karbala, Iraq 264n, 617
Karímov, Ustád 'Alí-A<u>sh</u>raf 727
Ká<u>sh</u>ání, Faraju'lláh <u>Kh</u>abbáz 122, 142, 160, 215, 225, 543, 546, 547, 632, 636
Tablet from 'Abdu'l-Bahá 650
Ká<u>sh</u>ání, Maḥmúd 436, 729
Kayván Mírzá 445, 733
Kazimayn, Iraq 617-18
Kelman, Rev. John 77, 80, 543-4
Kendirdjy Georges 544, 658
Kerman, Iran 433, 532
Kermanshah, Iran 427, 526, 532, 554
<u>Kh</u>aḍraj (Arab tribe) 203
<u>Kh</u>alílu'lláh <u>Kh</u>án Ra<u>sh</u>tí (Ḥájí Áqá <u>Kh</u>alíl) 221, 566
<u>Kh</u>amsí-Báqiroff, Siyyid Mihdí Riḍá and family 544, 690
Khan, Ali Kuli 747
<u>Kh</u>andán, Darvís<u>h</u> 478, 742-3
Khedives of Egypt 488, 515, 728, 732, 749
Kheiralla, Ibrahim George (<u>Kh</u>ayru'lláh) 159 and n, 242, 568, 731
<u>Kh</u>iḍr 55, 399n, 483n
Khurasan (Khorasan), Iran 252, 406
<u>Kh</u>usraw (Persian king) 196, 255
<u>Kh</u>usraw, Áqá, Burmese servant of 'Abdu'l-Bahá 471-2, 497, 734, 740, 745, 751
<u>Kh</u>usraw <u>Kh</u>án (Sardár-i-Ẓafar) (436), 546, 729, 732
Kingdom of God 9, 11, 48, 82, 110-11, 139, 161, 275, 276, 283, 298, 327, 330, 346, 347, 351, 355 and n, 375, 393, 394, 431, 439 and n, 442, 469, 603, 608, 621, 627, 632, 639, 710, 722, 735, 737
King of Martyrs *see* Muḥammad-Ḥasan
kings (and rulers) 11-12, 47, 76, 105,

109, 147, 161, 174, 244, 278, 362, 447, 457, 475, 502, 629, 680
Bahá'u'lláh's Tablets to 123, 174-5, 250, 491
see also Persia: Shahs
Kinnaird, Arthur Fitzgerald 543
Kirmání, Mírzá Muḥíṭ 445, 732-3
Kitáb-i-Aqdas 37, 524, 565
Kitábfurúsh, Ismá'íl (Mishkát) 433, 727
Knobloch, Alma 158, 212-3, 267, 276, (336), 408, 423, 537, 548, 549, 636, 650, 663, 664, 665, 666, 668, 669, 674, 676, 697, 704, 717, 721
Knobloch, Fanny 408, (418, 422), 423, 537, 548-9, 716-17, 718, 719, 720, 721
Tablet from 'Abdu'l-Bahá 716-17
knowledge 62, 68, 80, 127, 180, 201, 282, 329, 354, 359, 378, 386, 388, 392, 399, 425, 435, 443-4, 448, 450, 467, 485, 487, 490, 603, 610, 646, 658, 679
of 'Abdu'l-Bahá 170-71, 176, 308, 342, 425, 489, 743
about the Bahá'í Faith 491
of Bahá'u'lláh 491
acquired 1, 34, 49, 394, 443, 642, 658-9, 679
four criteria of 687
of God 72, 110-11, 162, 186, 313, 375, 380, 384, 430, 441, 483, 604, 606-7, 613, 622, 626, 638, 657, 674, 687, 689, 721, 724
innate 180, 679
spiritual 454
Köstlin, Anna 205, 277, (335), 549, 6636, 666, 669, 672, 676, 697
Kovácsné, Professor 292, 677
Kreuz (Cordes), Johann 319-21, 334, 549, 690, 691
Krishnamurti, Jiddu 295 and n
Krupp guns 100
Kúnos, Ignác 294, 534, 549, 677
Kurdistan 445, 554

Lacheny (Lachenay), Emmanuelle 550, 659
Lagente, Gabrielle (née Sacy) 159, 550
Lagnel, Mrs de 747
Lake Mohonk Conference 46, 551
Lamington, Lord *see* Cochrane-Baillie
Landor, Arnold Henry Savage 550
Lane, Rhoda 699
Lausanne, Switzerland 26, 515, 530, 639-40
language
of the spirit 479, 604, 679
universal 78-9, 166, 282, 300, 382
La Vie, journal 735
law(s)
of the Bahá'í Faith 77, 181, 282
of capital punishment 711
concept of 156
conducing to peace and order 10
divine 316, 450
of divorce 37, 711
of Europe 128, 316
of God 131, 315, 316, 350, 390, 680
international 512
of love 191
in/for Persia 128, 183, 460
of nature 62, 95, 191, 218, 358, 622
and order 128
of religion 62, 153, 275, 304, 444
renewal of 315, 393, 456
spiritual 152, 389
Lebanon 507
Lederer, György 678, 689
Lee, Mr (386), 709
Légion d'Honneur 511, 516, 528, 573
Leipzig, Germany 548, 652, 664
Leitner, Henry 550-51, 626
Le Leu, Louis (190), 643
Lesseps, Ferdinand de 484, 744
Lesser Peace 103, 223
Lewis, Alice 551
Lewis, Rev. Edward William 59, 551, 608, 611, 612
Lewis, John 551, 616
life 11-12, 171, 342, 348, 375-6, 390, 445, 660
Book of 465, 738
after death 652, 730
eternal, everlasting 1, 11, 41, 45, 129, 135, 158, 161, 175, 181, 220, 250, 266, 275, 277, 280, 329, 351, 356, 390, 424, 442, 457, 469, 668, 682, 702, 730,

738 *see also* soul, immortality of
goal, purpose of 110, 154, 162, 200, 283, 375-6, 381, 399, 428, 445, 708
longevity of 280
new 1, 153, 327, 393, 424, 646
physical 37, 39, 110, 126, 128, 148, 186, 264, 372, 390, 428, 449, 635, 691
spiritual 3, 11, 108, 110-11, 157, 208, 361, 370, 390, 392, 396, 439, 443, 483, 601, 613, 639, 666, 724
useful 229
water of 609, 674
way of 189, 404
Lillienthal, Maud (von Behr) 370, 388, (425), 582, 705, 706, 709, 718, 722, 724, 730, 749
lion(s) 126, 283, 348, 475, 673, 781
Liverpool, England 9, 21, 22, 24, 25-9, 520, 537, 538, 567, 584, 599, 600
Midland Adelphi Hotel 24, 599
London, England 4, 21, 22, 25, 29-73, 75, 80-102, 104-121, 122, 123, 135, 136, 159, 165, 169, 207, 223, 254, 412, 441, 466, 606, 608, 615, 624, 628, 644, 649, 652, 661, 706, 727, 751 *see also* 'Selected Biographical Notes'
Bahá'ís, believers in 22, 24, 28, 30-31, 33, 52, 65-6, 67, 70, 90, 91, 92, 101, 102, 105, 106, 107, 111, 116, 118-19, 455, 735
love of 'Abdu'l-Bahá for 101, 455, 735
places associated with 'Abdu'l-Bahá:
Battersea Park 54, 59, 613
Bloomsbury Square (No. 33) 94-8, 578, 624
British Museum and Library 169, 252, 637
Cadogan Gardens (No. 97) 30, 91, 509, 516, 517, 529, 545, 554, 570, 615 *see also* Blomfield, Lady
Caxton Hall, Westminster 31, 92, 98, 511, 523, 545, 552, 623
Cedar Club House, 106A High St, Battersea 55, 610
City Temple 519
Church House Westminster 43, 518
Cosmos Club 66, 615
Cromwell Road (No. 59) 113, 627
Elm Park Road (No. 80), Chelsea (Moscheles home) 117, 556, 628
Essex Hall 69
Great Peter Street (Salvation Army Centre) 50-51, 575, 609, 615
Hyde Park 603
King's Weigh House, London 58-9, 551, 611-12
London Library 169, 637
New Congregational Church, Parson's Hill, Woolwich 101, 565, 624
Passmore Edward's Settlement, Tavistock Place (in 1911) 568, 575, 576, 578
Sinclair Road (No. 74), Kensington 568
Warrington Crescent (No. 16), Maida Vale 613
Westminster Palace Hotel, London 39, 512, 518, 526, 604
White Lodge, 8 Sunnyside, Wimbledon 70, 616, 620
William IV Street (Chandos St) 615
see also railway stations
London Peace Conference 46, 120, 608, 628
Lorge, Mr 603
Los Angeles, California 231, 473, 520, 521, 532, 535, 574, 616, 707
Louis, Kings of France 398
love 32, 41-2, 60, 147, 221
for 'Abdu'l-Bahá 64, 147, 161, 185, 214, 247, 272, 276, 290, 320, 434, 460, 482, 602, 654
by children 146, 272, 345, 671
of 'Abdu'l-Bahá 45, 210, 216, 232, 317, 332, 344, 365, 400, 460, 480, 722
for Mírzá Abu'l-Faḍl 17, 131, 237-8, 354, 487, 632, 632, 656-7, 702, 746-7
for Bahá'ís in Europe 101, 213, 216, 273, 268, 269, 298, 344, 361-2, 365, 373, 453, 455,

460, 42, 463, 649, 665, 670, 679, 722
for children 146, 187, 278, 346, 442, 669-70, 671, 701, 732
for German Bahá'ís 213, 268, 298, 649, 665, 670
for Hungarian Bahá'ís 298, 679
for nature 662, 692
among Bahá'ís 129, 143, 220, 272, 279, 343, 361-2, 365, 664, 774
for Bahá'u'lláh 147, 363, 664, 698, 720
and brotherhood 41-2, 101
and capacity 147
Cause of God founded on 454
for Christ 147, 646
and Covenant 638, 654
degrees, kinds of 68, 412, 435, 617
divine 41, 147, 230, 280
eternal, perpetual 298, 365
familial 41, 33
and fellowship 23, 32, 35, 40, 56, 174, 222, 247, 257, 269, 352, 362, 364, 383, 431, 453, 454, 457, 686
for followers of all religions 142
for God 1, 32, 47, 64, 72, 73, 110, 133, 151, 161, 162, 180, 210, 222, 257, 262, 276-8, 326, 339, 345-6, 348, 366, 382, 441, 453, 458, 613, 622, 626, 631, 657, 689, 737, 743, 749
fire of 1, 144, 181, 239, 274, 276, 280, 285, 317, 330, 344, 346, 355, 387, 460, 604, 609, 639, 643, 647, 653, 724
for humanity 32, 41-2, 46, 56, 73, 79, 142, 166, 214, 226, 257, 267, 288, 337, 398, 403, 450-51, 660
law of 191
light of 73, 110, 159, 683
nationalistic 41, 259, 303, 488
among nations 40
among one's own kind 41, 259
power of 96, 115, 269
pretensions to 402
racial 41, 259
spiritual 143, 170, 298, 431, 694
and unity 23, 59, 144, 457, 654
universal
Lukaneder, Mrs, and Paul Lukaneder 332, 333, 551, 691, 694
Lycurgus 187

Macdonald, Ramsay 552, 616
Madrid, Spain 723
Magee, Harriet 620, 650, 661, 693, 710
Maḥbúb 'Álam, Mawlvi 744
Máhfurúzak, Iran 734
Mamaqan, Iran 474
Manchester, England 28, 543, 560, 561
Mandeans 529
Manifestations, Prophets of God 1, 483n, 491, 492, 607
in talks by 'Abdu'l-Bahá 27, 45, 46, 47, 48n, 49, 50, 57, 59-60, 72, 75, 83, 97, 98, 99, 103, 108-10, 129-30, 133, 144, 161, 170, 171, 182, 184, 194, 198, 207, 208, 219, 222, 231, 241, 253-4, 262, 273, 282, 288, 315, 323, 340, 360, 362, 402-3, 413, 415, 444, 448, 452, 455, 458, 483, 492, 616, 642, 722
calamities endured by 288, 444, 448, 452
Mann, William MacCarthy 552, 626
Mansurih, Egypt 488, 750
Manú<u>ch</u>ihr <u>Kh</u>án Gurjí (Mu'tamidu'd-Dawlih, 198-9, 647
Manẓar, Riḍá (Áqá Mírzá Maḥram) 433, 727
Margoliouth, David Samuel 552, 624
Markovitch, Marylie (Amélie de Néry) 552
marriage 350
interracial 352
Marseille, France 236, 461-2, 515, 527, 528, 574, 654, 737
Gare Saint-Charles 462, 737
Hotel Terminus 462, 737
martyrs 79, 122, 163, 181, 197, 337, 379, 383, 399, 433, 449, 497, 554, 573, 580, 581, 623, 628, 641-2, 647, 648, 708, 727
martyrdom 337, 383, 415, 707
of the Báb 69, 649, 726
of Imám Ḥusayn 263-4n

of Jesus Christ 43, 393
of Manifestations of God 414
Mary, mother of Jesus 173-4, 283, 408, 607
Mary Magdalene 43, 147, 383, 439, 730
Mas͟hriqu'l-Ad͟hkár (Bahá'í House of Worship), Wilmette 368, 388, 406, 720
Mashhad 406, 554
materialism 27, 164, 228, 322, 327, 347, 601, 603, 629, 631
materialists 6, 10, 20, 44, 227, 322, 631
Mathew, Louise 352 and n.
Maxwell, Mary (Rúḥíyyih K͟hánum) 547-8, 567, 570, 657
Maxwell, May 231, 551, 708
Mazandaran, Iran 163, 173, 218, 396, 399, 474, 478, 554, 713
Mazra'ih 253
McKinney, Edna
Tablet from 'Abdu'l-Bahá 714
McNamara, Brendan 625-6, 728
Mead, George, R. S. 553
meat 67, 114, 400, 600
Mecca 203, 255, 261, 313 and n
medicine 113, 228, 353, 374, 619, 633-4
spiritual 343, 374, 619, 630
Medina 203, 255, 420
Mendelssohn, Felix 556
Merrick, David 623
Messiah 23, 604
Messiah (oratorio by Handel) 84
Mészáros, Gyula (310), 553, 685
Meyer, Cicely (Cicelia) 466, 553, 739
Meyer, William Stevenson 466, 553, 738, 739
Mihdí K͟hán (baker) 140, 546, 632
Mihdí K͟hán (Mus͟híru'l-Mulk) 546-7, 604, 624, 633, 647, 650, 653
Mílání, Aḥmad Áqá 477
Mílání, Ḥájí Aḥmad 741
mind, the 10, 48, 191, 214, 224, 230, 241, 293, 314, 329, 352, 393, 404, 420, 435, 438, 442, 445, 457, 479, 605, 637
discourse on mind, soul and spirit 139
mindfulness 406
mineral
hot springs 288-90, 675
kingdom 130, 453
ministers (political) 25, 74, 77, 131, 132-3, 244, 286-7, 532, 545, 546, 557, 561-2, 580, 583-4, 604, 607, 623, 658, 659, 723, 728
prime 141, 180, 199 and n, 507, 547, 551, 552, 565, 579, 610, 629, 648, 650, 655, 692, 718, 723
ministers (religious) 4, 25, 28-9, 80-81, 107-8, 176-7, 286, 300, 350, 519, 542-3, 543-4, 564-5, 662, 667, 701
see also archbishop, cardinals, clergy, priests
moderation 37, 42, 175, 227, 242, 316, 359, 390, 398, 419, 449-50, 723
Mohammedans 64, 310 *see also* Muslims
Momen, Moojan 600, 609, 613, 615, 640, 656, 685, 716, 741, 751
monasticism, monks, nuns 236-7, 283, 656, 657, 672, 752
Monnier, Henri, Pasteur 176, 555, 640, 641
monogamy 246
Montealegre, Ricardo 507, 555, 645
Monte Carlo 634
Moody, Dr Susan 388, 536, 555
Moore, Edward W. 292, (312, 317), 555, 677, 686, 687, 688, 689
Moore, Lucy A. 404, 406, 556, 715, 716
morality 99-100, 166, 642, 717, 753
moral(s) 64, 210, 229, 259, 269, 485, 604, 635, 643
education 543
Moreau, Mrs 372, 404, 556, 706
Morgan, John Pierpont 266 and n, 376 and n, 378, 702
Morrison, Mary B. 556
Tablet from 'Abdu'l-Bahá 710
Moscheles, Felix 67-8, 97-8, 117, 556, 615, 617
Moser, Henri and Sophie 254, 256, 258, 556, 557, 660, 661, 662
Moses 1, 64, 155, 209, 262, 339, 481, 483 and n, 627, 738
mosques 19, 261, 262, 706
S͟háh (Masjid S͟háh), Tehran 19 and n

Shah Jahan, Woking 106, 466, 508, 510, 511, 514, 516, 518, 523, 524, 543, 550, 552, 553, 558, 564, 576, 579, 580, 585, 626
Most Great Prison 7, 28, 306, 492, 502, 503 *see also* 'Akká
motion 233, 360, 484, 660, 711
Mount Carmel ix, 237, 254, 493, 498, 499, 500, 505, 533, 752, 753
  Monastery of the Monks 752
Mount Lebanon 476
Mount Qáf 387, 710
Al-Mu'ayyad newspaper 489
Mu'ávíyyih 235
Mu'ayyiru'l-Mamálik *see* Khán, Dúst Muḥammad
Mudie, Harold 34, 601
Muhammad (Prophet) 2, 9, 44n, 48n, 90, 97, 115n, 163, 172, 195-6, 203, 208n, 246, 261, 309, 331, 337, 419-21, 446n, 478n
Muḥammad-'Alí (half-brother of 'Abdu'l-Bahá) 177-8, 640, 641
Muḥammad-'Alí Bey, Prince 431, 515, 724, 728, 731
Muḥammad-Ḥasan, King of Martyrs 181, 379, 399, 497, 641-2
Muḥammad-Ḥusayn, Beloved of Martyrs 399, 641-2
Muḥammad-Ibráhím Kalbású 199
Muḥammad Iṣfahání, Siyyid 446
Muḥammad Karím Khán, Ḥájí 112
Muḥammad Khán, Dr 152, 226, 228, 405, 425, (444), 547, 630, 644, 645, 648, 662, 706, 709, 723, 732
Muḥammad, Mír Siyyid (Intiẓámu's-Salṭanih) 123, 145, 557 (+79-80), 641, 656
Muḥammad-Qulí (faithful half-brother of Bahá'u'lláh) 263
Muḥammad Ṣáliḥ Effendi 151, 530
Muḥammad Ṣandúq-Dár 264
Muḥammad Sháh Qájár 124, 555, 629
Muḥammad-Taqí (*mujtahid*) 173-4
Mu'ín, Jináb-i- 421
Mullá Ḥusayn 399, 733
Munír Páshá, Ṣáliḥ and family 135, 219, 423, (426) 427-8, 456, 550, 561-2, 646, 651, 659, 720, 723, 735, 736
Munírih Khánum (wife of 'Abdu'l-Bahá) 239, 432, 498, 547, 548, 725, 753
murder 49, 80, 96, 114, 128, 260, 261, 348, 415
Murshidzádih, Maḥmúd 558, 658
music 13, 19, 84, 139, 154, 323, 360, 384, 423-4, 546, 599, 635, 709
  effect of 19, 108
  spiritual 360, 627
Muslim(s) 106, 107, 114, 123, 138, 141, 143, 164, 170, 178, 196n, 207, 234-5, 237n, 250, 258, 260, 262 and n, 294, 303, 304, 306, 331, 369, 409, 420, 422, 478n, 480-81 and n, 488, 491, 508, 734 *see also* Islam; Mohammedans
Muẓaffari'd-Dín Sháh 646

Nádler, Róbert A. (294), 296, 305, 306, (317), 558, 678, 680, 682, 688, 689
Na'ím *see* Sidihí, Muḥammad
Naimutullah, Shah Mohammad 558
Najaf, Iraq 617
Najaf-Qulí Khán (Ṣamṣámu's-Salṭanih) 411-12, 545, 546, 547, 718, 729
Nakhjavání, 'Alí-Akbar 122, 432, (444), 462, 558-9, 729, 730, 732, 735
Napoleon Bonaparte 160, 398
Napoleon III 659
Naráqí, Muḥammad-Ja'far 446, 733
Naruse, Jinzō 559, 613
Náṣiri'd-Dín Sháh 19, 123, 199, 413, 446, 492, 503, 545, 554, 555, 659, 741
National Bahá'í Convention
  America 368, 443, 514, 524, 535, 537, 541, 736
  India 533
National Spiritual Assembly (Assemblies) 598, 726
  British Isles 536
  Egypt 530
  Germany 671
  Germany and Austria 549, 571, 572
  India 566, 725
  Persia 581, 634
  United States vii
  United States and Canada 540, 613
nations 1-2, 5, 23, 40, 46, 50, 96, 103,

120, 127, 153, 191, 194, 216, 260, 261, 293, 295, 302-3, 358-60, 380, 421, 440, 496, 503-4, 621, 660, 665, 670, 691, 705, 719, 731, 735
advancement of 205, 358-60
nationalism 41, 259, 303, 488
nature
characteristics of 358
darkness of 110, 286, 322-3, 342, 363, 373, 694-5
defects of 628
dictates of 125-6
divine in 607
human 49
laws of 62, 95, 191, 218, 358, 622
phenomena of 661
second 404
world of 110-11, 127, 148, 316, 322, 325, 342, 347, 358, 373, 385, 389, 397, 454, 456, 466
see also Bahá'u'lláh, love of nature; scenery
Naw-Rúz 244-7, 512, 558, 714
Naẓar-Áqá, Ardi<u>sh</u>ír <u>Kh</u>án 559, 629, 658
Naẓar-Áqá, Yúsuf <u>Kh</u>án 559, 632, 658
Nazareth 347
Nérei, Őd ̄on (317), 689
Netherlands *see* Holland
Newhaven (port) 628
New Jersey 300, 514
New Testament 53-4, 108, 481, 738 *see also* Gospel(s)
newspapers
featuring 'Abdu'l-Bahá's visit 48, 60, 64, 77-8, 81, 87, 100, 103, 106, 119, 142, 165, 189, 190, 210, 293, 294-5, 299, 307, 308, 326, 336-7, 338, 344, 369, 485, 489, 512, 600, 626, 705, 727
current affairs in, commented on by 'Abdu'l-Bahá 25, 136, 140, 172, 232, 267, 342, 379, 641
New York 9-10, 11, 24, 243, 368, 406, 423, 443, 513, 514, 515, 518, 520, 527, 532, 539, 540, 542, 553, 558-9, 567, 569, 570, 572, 574, 581, 582, 583, 604, 645, 651, 661, 664, 705, 711, 736, 740
Nice, France 146, 511, 542, 580, 634, 653
Nicolas, A.L.M. 648
Nineteen Day Feast 59, 613, 701
Nineveh 156
Nirvana 723
Niẓámíyyih 409, 717
Niẓámu'd-Dawlih 145
Nobel Peace Prize 512, 556, 557, 582, 696
Núr-'Alí <u>Sh</u>áh (Muḥammad-'Alí Ṭabasí) 74, 617
Núrí, Mírzá 'Abbás (Mírzá Buzurg) 557, 629
Núrí, Áqá <u>Kh</u>án 199 and n

obedience 87, 93, 166, 173, 177, 185, 241, 272, 313, 339, 448, 459, 638, 640, 654, 733, 738
Omër, Feridun (310), 685
oneness 3, 180, 190, 259, 269, 302
of the divine religions 48, 83-4, 85, 117, 412
of existence 489
of God 83, 262, 292, 458, 606, 639, 689
of humanity *see* humanity, humankind
of the Manifestations of God 48n
of races and nations 440, 496
spirit of 159, 258, 269
see also unity
opposition 42, 86, 190, 204, 227, 241, 269, 295-6, 331, 415, 490, 617
to Bahá'ís, Bahá'í Cause 26, 31, 109, 112, 168, 189, 330, 405, 446, 489, 640, 641, 727
to Christ 112
to Islam 77, 196 and n, 303
to religion(s) 227, 256-7
orchestra 13, 19, 423-4
order 10, 49, 128, 132, 254, 316, 330, 359, 360
of the world 72, 156, 441, 451
see also disorder
Oriental Commercial University, Budapest 680
Orientalist School, Budapest 637
orphans 78, 454, 621

Ottomans 19, 25-6, 33, 47n, 120, 123, 130, 136, 168, 195, 207, 233, 251, 255 and n, 258, 294, 295, 319, 337, 490-92, 494, 630, 682
visitors to and visited by 'Abdu'l-Bahá 100, 189, 135, 194, 196, 215, 294, 298-9, 308, 310, 311, 313, 319, 324, 326, 425, 426, 429, 465, 678, 682, 688, 689, 722-3, 728, 733 *see also individual entries*
see also Turkey, Turks
Ottoman-Persian War (1821-23) 255 and n
Ottoman Society, Budapest 299
Outlook Tower Society, Edinburgh 76, 79, 533, 618, 619
Oxford, England 60-63, 519, 521, 614, 728
Manchester College (Harris Manchester) 519, 614
Parks Road (No. 17) 60, 614

Pagan, Jessie Osborne 560, 770
Page, Mr (Esperantist) 622, 712
Paikert, Alajos 302, 307, (312), 560, 680, 681, 685, 686, 687
Paisa Akhbár newspaper 485
Pankhurst, Christabel 560
Pankhurst, Emmeline 560
Pankhurst, Sylvia 561
painters, painting 78, 305, 508, 528, 541, 550, 556, 558, 568, 572-3, 583, 617, 623, 680, 692
Pakistan 534, 543, 550, 585, 586
palmistry 521, 616
Paris 4, 22, 24, 110, 118, 121, 122-266, 267, 299, 356, 357, 368-461, 462, 463, 468, 476, 599, 602, 628-63, 705-38
'Abdu'l-Bahá's ill-health in, reason for 218
'Abdu'l-Bahá's statements on 160, 245, 255, 396, 422, 456, 461, 476, 630, 631-2, 643, 653, 657, 707
'Abdu'l-Bahá's statements on Parisians 124, 134, 135, 137, 147-8, 164, 165, 171, 181, 186, 197, 198, 203, 207, 220, 221, 226-7, 232, 379, 381, 393, 396, 401, 425, 428, 453, 631-2, 707
'Abdu'l-Bahá's unhappiness in 129, 136, 193, 207, 379, 396, 707
Bahá'ís, believers in 121, 123, 126, 127, 129, 143, 146, 153, 155-6, 181, 191-2, 193, 202, 217, 220, 227, 247, 252, 261, 263, 266, 368-70, 372, 373-5, 379, 300-81, 383, 384, 386, 389, 391, 393, 407, 416, 418, 422, 424, 425, 426, 428, 431, 433, 437, 441, 449, 452-4, 455, 456, 457, 458, 460, 461, 462, 632 460, 462, 463, 632 *see also individual entries*
'Abdu'l-Bahá's love for 216, 220, 273, 373, 453, 460, 462, 463, 722
Easterners in, visiting and visited by 'Abdu'l-Bahá 124, 125-6, 127, 131-4, 135, 137, 139, 140, 142-3, 145, 150, 151, 154-5, 158, 159, 163, 167, 171, 176, 179, 182-5, 188, 189, 193, 194-5, 196-7, 200, 207, 208, 213, 215, 216, 219, 221, 229, 232, 233, 240, 244, 245-6, 248, 251, 254, 263, 265, 370, 384-5, 388, 393, 395, 407, 409, 411-12, 419, 422, 423, 424, 425, 426, 427-8, 429, 431, 436-7, 440, 442, 448-9, 451, 452, 456, 459-60, 692, 728
newspapers in 369, 379
prayer for 220
visits of German Bahá'ís to 205, 212-13, 429, 439, 724
places associated with 'Abdu'l-Bahá:
avenue de la Bourdonnais (No. 59) 507, 637, 723
avenue de Camoëns (no. 4) 511, 514, 527, 530, 532, 536, 540, 547, 549, 550, 554, 565, 569, 572, 573, 575, 718
avenue des Champs-Élysées (228), 384, 653, 709
avenue Greuze (No. 15) *see* Dreyfus-Barney
avenue Hoche (No. 2), 388, 711, 730

avenue Kléber 370, 379, 389, 706, 713
avenue de Malakoff (No. 46) (now Raymond Poincaré) 569, 634, 658, 713
avenue Victor Hugo (228), 653
Bois de Boulogne 151, 229, 251, 391, 396, 410, 659, 713, 716
Bld. Arago (No. 83) (176), 640
Bld. Montparnasse 180, 538, 641
Carnival 148, 634
Cours-la-Reine, Grand Palais (Paris Flower Show) (417), 719
Eiffel Tower 158, 228, 325, 637, 651
Hôtel Astoria 653
Hôtel Baltimore, Paris (370), 533, 556, 706, 713, 715, 724
Hôtel Imperial, Paris 728, 731
Hotel International 724, 730
Hôtel Moderne, 10 place de la République 165-7, 517, 519, 637
Library 169
Longchamps racecourse (405), 716
Lumina Studio, 12 ave. de la Grande Armée (179), 641
Maison de Santé, rue Berton (No. 17) 382, 411, 425, 548, 662, 708
Martha-Pension Family Hotel *see* hotels
Montmartre, Cimitière 527, 528
Pathé Frères, 98 rue de Richelieu (192), 645
Pont d'Iéna 651
rue Boissonade (No. 17, Scott residence) 133, 150, 181, 191, 197, 212, 379, 407, 424, 437, 456, 573, 634, 636, 631, 634, 636
rue Lauriston 239, 265, 425, 713
rue de Nople 728
rue Saint-Didier (No. 30) 121, 510, 515, 524, 531, 532, 534, 546, 547, 557, 561, 565, 566, 628, 635
rue de Sontay (16ème) 134, 631
rue de La Trémoille (No. 26) (Ṣáliḥ Munír Pá<u>sh</u>á residence) (219), 550, 561, 562, 651
rue de Trévise 190, 643
rue Val-de-Grace (No. 9) (Richard residence) 423, 700
Salle de Troyes 514
Seine river 651, 708
Théâtre du Châtelet, 2 rue Edward Colonne 731
see also railway stations
parks, visits of 'Abdu'l-Bahá to 54, 59, 321, 327, 603, 613, 619, 659, 691, 695, 700, 713, 716 *see also individual entries*
parliament, parliamentarians
America 604
Britain 75, 512, 533, 552, 563, 577, 583, 616
Hungary 535, 294, 300, 301, 680, 681
Persia 494, 531-2
Turkey 749
Pársís *see* Zoroastrians
Parsons, Agnes 173 and n, 571, 653
Patel, Moganbhai C. (466), 739
Paul (Apostle) 350-51, 621
peace
of humankind *see* humanity, humankind
Lesser 103, 223
of mind 132, 290, 389
universal 10, 21, 23, 26, 46-7, 51, 53, 65, 72, 83, 95, 101, 103, 107, 151, 170, 201, 241, 258, 259-60, 267, 278, 292, 300, 302, 317, 334, 340-41, 349, 358, 380, 440, 462, 467, 471, 616, 660, 679, 719
world 40, 613
Peace Society,
London 117, 624
Hungarian 637, 682
Pekár, Gyula (310), 562, 685
Pembroke Chapel, Liverpool 25, 28
perception, power of 194, 212, 306, 307, 701, 711
Peter, apostle 82, 197-8, 392, 457, 621

Persia, Persians 24, 33-4, 37-8, 54, 73, 79, 82-3, 92, 122, 125, 127-9, 133, 136, 140, 142, 154, 156, 180, 182-3, 184, 186, 240, 252, 254-6, 257-8, 267, 330-32, 355, 363, 395, 412, 415, 418-19, 429, 451-2, 455, 459-60, 478, 491, 494-5, 601, 604-5, 635, 642-3, 658-9, 669, 692, 705, 716, 718, 741
  'Abdu'l-Bahá's retinue *see individual entries*
  Bahá'ís in 16, 17, 69, 112, 145, 195, 201, 225, 259, 348, 362, 381, 389, 432, 4, 435, 444, 456, 468, 489, 495, 602, 726, 742
    women 35, 329, 444, 456
  divines of 112, 141, 460
  enemies of Cause in 4, 112, 330, 415, 447
  government 19, 184, 240, 246, 415, 492
    officials 24, 38, 124, 131, 132-4, 140, 141, 145, 160, 179-80, 199 and n, 213, 233, 237, 246, 252, 255, 324, 393, 436, 459, 599, 604, 629, 648, 650, 678, 718, 731 *see also individual entries and* 'Selected Biographical Notes'
  history of 124-5, 244, 320, 691 progress of 129, 136, 240-41, 643
  princes of 237, 267, 337, 436, 451-2, 554, 646, 658, 662, 718, 733
  prosperity of 104, 140, 180, 182, 184, 252, 256, 330, 459
  Shah(s) of 124, 258, 296 and n, 361-2, 555, 678 *see also* Fatḥ-'Alí Sháh, Khusraw, Muḥammad Sháh Qájár, Muẓaffari'd-Dín Sháh, Náṣiri'd-Dín Sháh, Tahmasp I
  students in Europe 142, 176, 183-4, 221, 240, 409, 604, 619, 622, 640, 642, 653, 658
  visitors to 'Abdu'l-Bahá *see individual entries*
  see also Constitutional Revolution
Persia Society, London 508, 512, 518, 523, 545, 547
Persian-American Educational Society 522, 535, 537, 542, 566, 574
Persian language 14, 40, 100, 141, 148, 171, 172, 192, 218, 275, 303, 308, 407-8, 426, 443, 586, 598, 601, 609, 614, 617, 644, 684, 685, 732
Pfund, Gottlieb 283, 348, 538, 562, 673, 718
Pharaoh 482, 488
philosophers 2, 4, 20, 60, 99, 182, 184, 206, 211-12, 296, 303, 308, 322-3, 397, 426, 732
philosophy 312, 324, 642
  divine 72, 193, 436, 469, 732
  of the Greeks 50
  natural 193, 435, 732
photographs 179, 192, 625, 641, 645
physicians 242, 487, 630, 633-4, 675, 694, 703
  treating 'Abdu'l-Bahá 202, 215, 227-8, 338, 340, 353, 355-6, 361, 653, 745
  see also doctors
pilgrimage, pilgrims
  of 'Abdu'l-Bahá 15, 146, 500, 754
  Bahá'í 15, 477, 500, 501, 502, 523, 528, 535, 579, 688, 725, 747-9, 753-4, 740, 741, 744
  Christian 645, 688
  Islamic 263n, 313-14, 618
Pilgrim House
  Bahji 502
  Haifa 482, 493, 753
Pittsburgh Spectator (383), 708
  Tablet from 'Abdu'l-Bahá 708
Platt, Beatrice 562-3, 623
plays *see* theatrical performances
poems, poetry ix, x, 55, 148, (151), 154-5, 172, 215, 434-5, 470, 488, 501, 564, 628, 629, 633, 634, 635, 658, 662, 727, 728, 739, 754
  of Bahá'u'lláh 407
poets 145, 154-5, 215, 244, 246, 383, 434, 501, 510, 513, 521, 541, 528, 560, 585, 617, 626, 628-9, 633, 658, 662, 726, 727, 728, 754
Pokorny, Ruwa 750
Pole, David Graham 87, 392, 563, 621, 622, 712
Pole, Jessie Hair Pagan 563, 770

politics 180, 195, 216, 292, 303, 351, 373, 443, 459, 599, 605
Pollen, Dr John 107, 564, 626
Pollock, Susan 666, 672
polygamy 26, 168, 245-6, 315, 554, 738
Ponsonaille, Victor and Fanny (146), 634
Pontius Pilate 4
Pool, Rev. John James 101, 564, 624-5
poor, the 5, 24, 50-51, 55, 78, 84-5, 94, 105, 131, 146, 149-50, 175, 239, 243, 255, 300, 321, 369, 371, 417, 454, 464, 602, 610, 611, 615, 621, 625 *see also* poverty
Popes 65, 210, 603, 659, 646, 734-5
Port Said, Egypt 225, 229, 444, 462, 471-2, 474-85, 497, 585, 599, 652, 661, 684, 693, 739, 740, 743, 745, 746, 752
Portugal 520, 527
Pound, Ezra 513, 528
poverty 6, 50, 74, 141, 316, 388, 611, 639 *see also* poor
prayer(s) 108, 173, 220, 374, 408, 433, 654, 673, 686, 720, 748
 of 'Abdu'l-Bahá 89, 90, 171, 175, 275, 332, 620-21, 637-8, 639, 644, 662, 668, 675, 682, 687, 688-9, 694, 696, 700, 722, 733, 734
 of the Báb 407
 of Bahá'u'lláh 66, 144, 148, 165, 229, 408
 chanted, recited by
  'Abdu'l-Bahá 29, 40, 62, 66, 70, 142, 171, 175, 275, 326, 332, 410, 637, 688-9, 694, 696, 701, 722, 730, 747, 748
  Maḥmúd Zarqání 129, 687
  others 56, 60, 66-7, 71, 76, 101, 129, 131, 134, 144, 145, 149, 150, 153, 160, 161, 164, 171, 174, 177, 192, 193, 206, 217, 226, 228, 244, 250, 338, 370, 395, 424, 429, 437, 461, 499, 747, 753
 Christian 612, 618
 to God 40, 47, 62, 89, 98, 101, 108, 116, 120, 134, 148, 247, 248, 280, 326, 344, 618, 620-21, 637, 639, 651, 668, 682, 686, 689, 694, 696, 719, 722, 748
 inscribed by 'Abdu'l-Bahá 89, 662, 675, 700
 of Khiḍr 399 and n
prejudice 3, 6, 115, 164, 185, 292, 319, 322, 333, 352, 360, 371, 386, 421, 480, 482, 484, 488
 detrimental effects of 72, 113, 189-90, 256, 258, 292, 302, 452, 465, 485, 605
 elimination of 51, 56, 72, 83, 86, 103, 113, 143-4, 151, 216, 261-2, 490
 see also bigotry
priests 59, 61, 79, 101-2, 164, 194, 204, 480, 511, 641, 646, 681, 743
 see also archbishop, cardinals, clergy, ministers (religious)
professions, engagement in 80, 376
progress 130, 328
 age of 293
 in America 271-2, 711
 of the Cause 165, 200, 743
 in Germany 271-2, 724
 century of 114, 260
 of the construction of the Mashriqu'l-Adhkár in Wilmette 37
 in the development of human perfections 376, 389, 454
 in East and West 241
 in France 128
 of God's chosen ones 343
 Holy Spirit, religion, role of in 182, 205, 262, 642
 of humankind *see* humanity, humankind
 of India 611
 of industry 79, 153
 in learning Persian 407-8
 in the love of God 344
 material 34, 47, 93, 182, 187
 of minds 46, 293
 of peoples of the world 39, 205, 611
 of Persia 129, 136, 240-41, 643
 physical 42, 255, 328
 of science 153
 of souls 293, 321, 424

spirit of 79
spiritual 42, 66, 182, 328, 724
of will-power 715
of women 42
see also advancements
Promised One ix, 109, 249, 298, 382n, 458, 492, 493, 665
prophecies ix, 143, 159, 192, 219, 249, 250, 252, 273, 458, 465, 466, 469, 482, 492, 493, 494, 568
by Bahá'u'lláh 123, 175, 250-52, 490-91, 503, 661
prosperity 1, 6, 7, 30, 32, 34, 104, 122, 135, 180, 195, 241, 258, 292, 296, 327, 331, 356, 359, 368, 414, 438, 442, 480
of Persia 104, 140, 180, 182, 184, 252, 256, 330, 459
of humankind 99, 100, 127, 205, 261, 262, 267, 309, 313, 320, 328, 406, 440, 684
prostration 500-01 and 500n
psychic phenomena, research 524, 571, 609, 616
Ptolemy 165
Pune, India 192, 644
punishment 32, 43, 49, 156, 403, 451
capital 711
Punjab, India 115, 295, 485, 534, 573, 585
purity 38, 71-2, 159, 237, 240, 270, 276, 350, 365, 374, 393-4, 399, 408, 413, 446, 447, 449, 450, 460, 478, 610, 642, 668, 704
of heart 52, 58, 72, 82, 105, 205, 215, 276, 278, 284, 345, 349, 352, 382, 452-3, 623, 664, 670, 678-9
of motive, intention 156, 198, 245, 441, 714
of spirit 336
of soul 358, 487, 664

Qá'im-Maqám, Abu'l-Qásim Faráhání 124-5, 198, 395, 530, 565, 629
Qá'im-Maqámí, Mírzá Áqá Khán 122, 225, 396, 565, 624, 630
Qaráquzlú, Abu'l-Qásim (Náṣiru'l-Mulk) (213), 650
Qazvin 16, 140, 163, 433, 457, 536, 602, 736
Qazvíní, Ḥáj 'Abdu'l-Karím 731
Qazvíní, Mas'úd (Áqá Mírzá Báqir Qazvíní) 434, 728
Qazvíní, Muḥammad Khán 66, 122, 565
Quddús 399, 714
Queenstown, NY 20
Qum, Iran 141, 200, 565, 647
Qumí, Áqá Siyyid Asadu'lláh 10, 15, 23, 244, 266, 381, 462, 565, 611, 625, 641, 657, 663, 675, 702, 707, 735, 741, 744
Qur'án 44, 115, 123, 128, 141, 164, 196, 199, 208, 235, 246, 250, 253, 262, 313, 339, 392, 398, 481, 483, 611, 663, 713
Quraysh, tribes of 163
Qurayshí, Ḥishmatu'lláh (432, 444), 566, 725, 732

racetrack (Longchamps) 405, 716
Ra'fat Páshá, Mrs (142), 632
Rafsanjání, 'Alí-Akbar 122, 142, 143, 144, 145, 150, 164, 169, 174, 175, 566, 639, 656, 735
Raḥmání, Ja'far Shírází (Hádíoff) 482, 743-4
Raḥmatu'lláh, Áqá 497, 752
railroad man, addressed by 'Abdu'l-Bahá 608
railway carriages 90, 335, 501 *see also* trains
railway (train) stations
'Akká 502-3
Bacos, Ramleh 748
Bristol, England 105
Budapest 291, 317, 677, 681
Esslingen, Germany 291, 335, 676, 697
Euston, London 73, (91)
Gare de l'Est, Paris (266), 367
Gare de Lyon, Paris 461
Gare de Marseille Saint-Charles, Marseille 462, 737
Gare Saint-Lazare, Paris 121, 628
Lime Street, Liverpool 29, 599
Maẓlúm Páshá, Ramleh 486

Oxford 60
Paddington, London (60), 102, (105), 625
Plochingen, Germany 676
Princes Street, Edinburgh 75, 90, 622
Sidi Gaber, Ramleh 746
Stuttgart 267, 290, 335, 366, 676, 697, 704
Vienna 291, 319, (335), 677
Victoria, London (120-21), 628
Rajab-'Alí, Ḥájí 263
Ramleh, Egypt 308, 485-97, 582, 741, 745-52
Ras͟híd Mumtáz Pás͟há 137-9, 176, 195, 248, 388, 393, 419, 561, 646, 731
Rasht, Iran 140, 150, 213, 433, 566, 579, 585-6, 632, 634, 650, 657, 736, 754
rationality 39, 149, 178, 204, 385, 633
see also reason
Rawḥání Bus͟hrúyi'í (Bíbí Rawḥání, Fáṭimih Bagum) 449, 734
reality
of animals 321
of the Cause 660, 722
divine 118
essential, inner, of things 5, 6, 57, 111, 184, 293, 380, 381, 385, 394, 397, 668, 694
heaven of 736
holy, sanctified 216, 358, 390
investigation of 394, 679, 696
light, relationship to 33, 120, 742
of man 5, 6, 95, 321, 615, 657, 680
of the Manifestations of God 129-30, 483n, 722
natural 125
second 66, 88, 125, 621-2
spiritual 125, 701, 725
Sun of 72, 627, 638, 639, 643, 661, 693
Universal 397
reason 190, 358, 434, 435, 606-7
science and 30, 178, 204, 227, 257
see also rationality, understanding
Red Cross 525, 528, 531
reincarnation 51-2, 312, 313, 609, 616, 730
religion
aversion to, disinterest in 127, 204, 223, 226-7, 260, 303, 330, 333, 345
divine 6, 63, 205, 209, 228, 403, 436, 446, 450, 463
Founders of 448, 455 *see also individual entries*
of God 31, 72, 205, 227, 262, 309, 313, 316, 341, 388, 441, 710, 743
influence of 642
leaders of 176, 178, 204-5, 226-7, 314, 350, 360, 444, 452, 456, 458, 725
laws of 62, 153, 275, 304, 444
people, followers of 23, 227, 257, 322, 329, 409, 712
prejudices of 216, 261, 292, 605
purpose of 22, 222, 257
and science 178, 204, 257, 605, 660
true 448, 605
unity of 286, 299
universal 166, 309
see also 47, 63, 88, 257, 659; *and* irreligion
Remey, Charles Mason 173 and n, 525, 698
repentance 500n, 655
reporters 23, 30, 36, 45, 58, 85, 293, 299, 312, 383, 416, 483, 687 *see also* journalists
revenge 96 *see also* vengeance
Rhine river 491, 751
Rice, Alice 566
Rice, Nellie 566
Richard, Mirra (Mirra Alfassa, 'the Mother') 149, 161, 174, 393, 405, 416, 423, (424), 432, 456, 462, 508, 539, 634, 639, 647, 705, 714, 721, 729, 736, 737
Richard, Paul Antoine 416, 423, 432, 456, 462, 567, 705, 707, 714, 736, 737
riches
earthly, worldly 6, 7, 145, 316, 329, 442, 479, 611, 750
of God 447
of the spirit 679

see also wealth
Riḍá Khán 163 and n, 343
Riḍá Qannád (Muḥammad-Riḍá Shírází) 16, 113, 146, 436, 598, 729
Ridgway, Sarah Ann 28, 567
Riḍván-'Alí 169
Riḍváníyyih Khánum 239, 370, 382-3, 547, 706, 709, 713
ringstone 412
Ríyáḍ Salím Effendi 151, 530
Robb, Rev. Alexander B. 80, 567
Robinson, Mary Letitia 59, 613
Rohleder, Pastor, 350, 701
Rome, Romans 43, 123, 195, 234, 250, 623, 625
Rónai, Károly (310), 685
Rosenberg, Ethel 30, 101, 568, 615, 627
Rosenthal, Arnold William (383), 708
roses, rosegarden 1, 74, 85, 615, 658, 671, 692, 698, 718, 719
  as metaphor 96, 113, 116, 184, 255, 256, 404, 422, 615, 693, 724, 743, 749
Rúdakí (poet) 154, 384
rugs 85, 100, 287, 308-9, 310, 577, 624, 682, 753
Rúḥá Khánum (daughter of 'Abdu'l-Bahá) 202, 229, 236, 239, 242, 244, 251, 265, 379, 382, 383, 386, 411, 425, 440, 444, 547, 548, 569, 648, 652, 654, 662, 713, 723, 736, 737-8
Rumelia 257, 493
Rúmí, Jalál al-Dín 48n, 429n, 438n
Rúmí, Siyyid Muṣṭafá 433, 586, 727
Ruoff, Emil 703
Russia, Russians 142, 432, 556, 558, 579, 580, 581, 632, 668, 731, 736, 746
  Bolshevik Revolution 741

Sabeans 262, 481
Sacy, Gabriel 159-60, 194, 524, 568, 569, 636
Sacy, Madeleine and daughters 159-60, 194, 524, 527, 540, 550, 568-9, 580, 636 *see also* Baudry, Dickinson, Huguenin, Lagente
sacrifice 179, 197, 198, 292, 348, 383-4, 386, 414, 438, 445
  of self 19, 95, 108, 115, 309, 342, 390, 487, 646, 656, 671, 682
safety 45, 53, 222, 263, 359, 364, 413, 435, 476
see also security
Ṣádiq, 'Ísá (244), 569, 658
Ṣádiq-i-Muqaddas, Mullá 714
Ṣadru'l-'Ulamá, Siyyid Ja'far 405-6, 716
Sakínih (Sikkínih) Sulṭán 202, 648
Salman (the Persian) 478
Salmán, Shaykh 449, 478-9, 734, 742-3
Salt Lake City 610
Salvation Army 50-51, 575, 609, 615, 624
Samandar, Shaykh Káẓim (Muḥammad Káẓim Qazvíní) 179, 433, 726
Samarra, Iraq 617
Samipaşazade Halim Bey (426, 431), 723, 724
Samipaşazade Sezaï (426), 723
Sanderson, Edith 146, 151, 200, 220, 239, 242, 244, 372, 382, 385, 407, 409, (425), 569, 570, 632, 648, 657, 662, 705, 713, 722, 723, 736
Sanderson, Margaret 569, 570, 713, 736
San Francisco, California 520, 523, 535, 566, 569, 617, 651, 662, 698, 729, 740
Santa Claus 611
Sargent, Porter Edward 570, 660
Sargent's Travel School for Boys 254, 522, 570, 659
Sarkar 'Azíz Aḥmad 294
Satan 48-9, 119-20, 236, 261, 280-81, 402 *see also* Devil
Save the Children Fund 517, 583
Saysan, Iran 474
Scatcherd, Felicia 570
scenery 12, 105, 157, 158, 285, 662
  Schepel, Annette 571
Scheuermann, Mr (335), 697
scholars 211, 409-10, 444, 451, 489, 598
Schwäbisch Hall 675, 701
Schwarz, Albert, Consul 275, 281, 285, 288, 289, 290, 335, (336, 340, 345), 348-9, 429, (430), 439, 571, 572, 665, 666, 669, 672, 673, 674, 675, 697, 698, 699, 700, 701, 702, 703, 704, 724, 728, 730

Schwarz (Solivo), Alice 275, 285, 288, 289, (336), 348-9, 429, (430), 439, 571, 572, 665, 667, 668-9, 674, 675, 676, 697, 700, 702, 704, 724, 728, 730
Schwarz, Olly 349, 665, 669, 674, 675, 697, 701, 704, 724
Schwarz residence 275, 285, 290, 348-9, 666-7, 676, 700, 701
Schweizer, Annemarie 205, 285, (335), 572, 636, 673, 676, 697, 701
Schweizer, Friedrich 335, 353-4, 572, 702
Schweizer house 285-6, 673
science(s) 30, 35, 53, 153, 178, 182, 188, 191, 204, 227, 241, 257, 293, 297, 351, 359, 409, 427, 443, 456, 602, 605, 610, 642, 660, 658, 668
Scotland 71, 73, 76-91, 100, 214, 392, 512, 520, 523, 525, 529, 533, 543, 548, 552, 560, 563, 567, 577, 583, 584, 618-23, 712
Scotsman newspaper 620, 621
Scott, Edwin and Josephine 133, 150, 181, 191, 197, 205, 212, 379, 381, 407, 424, 437, 456, 572-3, 634, 705, 721, 730
sculpting, sculptors 78, 324-5, 528, 693
security 205, 233, 251, 306, 359, 364, 446, 729, *see also* safety
self 45, 53, 126, 201, 242, 280, 339, 350, 351, 386, 400, 413, 425, 428-9, 446, 453, 456, 469, 710, 718
  -effacement, selflessness 175-6, 399, 664, 729
  insistent 49
  -sacrifice 19, 95, 108, 115, 309, 342, 390, 487, 646, 656, 671, 682
  -mortification 428
selfish desires, interests, motives 5, 44, 54, 97, 143, 255, 295, 422, 440, 496, 629, 655, 733
Selim II, Sultan 296 and n
senses, the 20, 130, 683
Serbia 525
service 27, 90, 121, 159, 173, 188, 192, 237, 276, 441, 438, 610
  by 'Abdu'l-Bahá 27, 90, 155, 289, 290, 340, 311, 391, 428, 468, 684, 711
    of tea, etc., to others 348, 294, 465, 483, 674
  of Americans 651, 719-20
  to Bahá'ís 207, 237, 368, 436, 491, 612, 729, 734
  to (Cause of, Kingdom of) God 2, 14, 23, 90, 93, 102, 152, 199, 226, 283, 289, 292, 304, 313, 314, 320, 340, 352, 376, 383, 399, 423, 428, 432-3, 455, 460, 477, 495, 610, 662, 664, 666, 700, 715
  to Christ 439
  to humanity, humankind 162, 189, 292-3, 299, 310, 376, 391, 396, 398, 423, 441, 456, 495, 600, 621, 682, 684, 689, 719, 739
  to the Orient–Occident Unity 388
  of the material world 396
  to Persia 184
  to the poor 51, 612
  public 494, 647, 699-700
  in raising children of others 417
  spirit of 159
  at the (divine) threshold of Bahá'u'lláh, of God 31, 155, 199, 289, 440
Shaddád bin 'Ád 235 and n
Shahíd, Áqá Mírzá Jalál 202, 239, 265, 367, 379, 382-3, 432, (444), 497, 498, 548, 573, 654, 662, 705, 725, 729, 730, 731, 732, 735, 746, 752
Shah Jahan Mosque, Woking 106, 466, 508, 510, 511, 514, 516, 518, 523, 524, 543, 550, 552, 553, 558, 564, 576, 579, 580, 585, 626
Shahmírzádí, Ḥájí Mullá 'Alí-Akbar (Ḥájí Ákhund) 36, 141 and n, 199, 602
Sháh Mosque (Masjid Sháh), Tehran 19 and n
sheep 45, 114, 125, 126, 257, 292, 293, 356, 384, 631, 668 *see also* flock(s)
Sher-Gil, Amrita 573, 682
Sher-Gil, Sardar Umrao Singh 295-6, 306, (310), 312, (317), 535, 573, 677, 680, 682, 683, 685, 687, 688, 689
ships 9-23, 423, 462, 464-72, 497, 498, 737-8, 739 *see also* boats

Shiraz, Iran 16, 159, 251, 493, 714, 725, 743
Shírází, Mírzá Hádí Afnán 434, 728
Shírází, Ja'far (Hádíoff) 482, 743
Shírází, Siyyid Mihdí 433, 727
Shírází, Muḥammad-Riḍá (Riḍá Qannád) 16, 113, 146, 436, 598, 729
Shoghi Effendi viii, 510, 540, 541, 543, 548, 567, 570, 573, 581, 585, 598, 602, 628, 630, 641, 648, 654, 657, 721, 727, 728, 746, 749
Shu'á'u'lláh Bahá'í 231, 654
Sidihí, Muḥammad (Na'ím) 145, 633
Sidihí, Siyyid Ismá'íl (Síná) 433, 483, 585, 726
Sidihí, Siyyid Maḥmúd (Nayyir) 585, 726
Sidley, J. W. 67, 70, 576, 615, 617
Sidley, Mrs 624
Simon, apostle 457 and n
Simonyi, 292, 677
símurgh 387, 710
Sinai 43, 247, 492
Síná *see* Sidihí
Síyáh-Chál, Tehran 264-5
Skrine, Francis 574, 627
Skrine, Helen 627
sleep 11, 52, 85, 115, 148, 186, 232, 347, 376, 389-90, 723
  'Abdu'l-Bahá's lack of *see* 'Abdu'l-Bahá
societies
  secret 394
Sohrab, Ahmad 10, 21, 22, 23, 29, 73, 144, 146, 199n, 232, 244, 263, 266, 275, 333n, (340), 379, 462, 497, 545, 552, 574 and n; *multiple references in Notes* 597-755
Solomon 255, 363
song(s), singing 13, 84, 278, 282, 289, 401, 501, 618, 686, 692, 720, 722
  as metaphor 2, 386, 418, 467, 684
soul(s), human 378
  advancement, progress of 50, 293, 321, 330, 389, 424, 651
  ascension of the 51
  edification of the 41
  exclusive individuality of the 52
  if not athirst 356
  immateriality of the 142
  immortality of the 142 *see also* life, eternal
  influence, powers of in this world 167, 378, 414
  of Paris 238
  wicked 236
  see also spirit
South Africa 378, 513, 533, 541, 549, 658
Spain 381, 672, 728
Spencer, Col. John 575, 609
spirit
  of 'Abdu'l-Bahá 702
  of (contingent) world 162, 186
  divine 147, 220, 274
  of devotion, humility, supplication 126, 159, 164, 237, 312
  Faithful, the 114
  of God 77-8, 351, 609
  influence of the 152, 694
  of joy, gladness 41, 100, 102, 132, 146, 159, 257, 332, 714
  of knowledge and assurance 425
  of living things 152, 325-6
  love and fellowship, brotherhood, unity 23, 32, 174, 180, 222, 352, 457, 458
  and man 12, 19, 162, 186, 327, 336, 358, 390, 429, 442, 452, 460, 643, 660, 694, 748
  second reality of 66, 88, 125, 621-2
  power of the 72, 390, 429
  of progress 79
  of prophethood 393
  of service 158 *see also* service
  world of the 385, 389, 443
  see also Holy Spirit; soul; spirituality
spiritualists 191, 191, 514, 524, 581, 643, 648
spirituality 6, 56, 73, 74, 101, 102, 133, 160, 171, 204, 231, 298, 322, 349, 422, 642, 710, 722, 747
  contempt for, rejection of 34, 204, 226
  countries in need of 312, 635
  distinction of humanity 326-7, 441
  lack of 134, 207, 324, 327, 657
  and prayer 408
Sprague, Sydney 115

Sri Aurobindo 508, 567
Stäbler, Elise (Lisa) (335), 575, 697, 704
Stäbler, Julie (335), 575, 665, 697, 704
Stanford University 47
Stannard, Jean 391, 575, 685
Stapley, Annie Jenner 94, 106, 575-6
Stapley, Sir Richard 67, 94-5, 97-8, 106, 576
Stark, Karolina 165, 291, 306, 311, (312), 313, (317), 334, 576, 581, 687, 688, 696
Stark, Lipót (Leopold) 165, 288, 291, 306, 311, (312), 313, (317), 334, 576, 581, 674, 677, 678, 680, 681, 686, 687, 688, 689
Starkoff, Véra (142), 632
steadfastness 17, 36, 101, 116, 179, 197-8, 225, 230, 238, 268, 270, 364, 383, 404, 449, 456, 462, 478, 487, 649, 722
Steinenbronn, village 361, 703
Stuttgart, Germany 157-8, 205, 212, 219, 225, 262, 266-90, 298, 324, 335-66, 368, 391, 408, 429, 439, 516, 517, 527, 530, 531, 532, 536, 538, 548, 549, 562, 571, 572, 575, 581, 582, 649, 652, 653, 654, 662, 663-77 passim, 686, 693, 697-705 passim, 717, 718, 720, 721, 723, 724, 730
  Bahá'ís, believers in *see* Germany; *see also individual entries*
    love of 'Abdu'l-Bahá for 213, 268, 269, 298, 344, 361-2, 365, 649, 665, 670
  places visited by 'Abdu'l-Bahá (see also illustration):
  Alexanderstr. (No. 3) (Schwarz residence) 275, 285, 290, 348-9, 666-7, 676, 700, 701
  Bärenschlosse 700
  Bismarckturm (Bismarck Tower) (349), 699
  Bürgermuseum 275, 337, 339, 667, 698
  Hotel Marquardt 267, 285, 335, 663, 666, 668-70, 697, 703
  Kanzleistr. (No. 24), Frauenclub (Women's Club) (349), 700, 701
  Neue Weinsteige (No. 23) 674 (Knobloch and Döring residence)
  Obere Museum 287, 674
  Oberer Schlossgarten 271
  railway station 267, 290, 335, 366, 676, 697, 704
  Schloss Solitude 275, 666 (n559), 700
  Schurwald (Stuttgart region) 673
  Stitzenburgstr. (no. 12) (349), 700 (Fisher residence)
  Wagenburgstr. (283), 673
Stuttgarter Neues Tagblatt 336-7, 344
Suez Canal 744
Sufism, Sufis 52, 178, 219, 237, 313, 387, 397, 405, 432, 456, 546, 617, 713
suffragists 509, 521, 523, 526, 537-8, 560, 561, 602, 617, 624
Sulaymáníyyih 168, 193, 228, 395
Sulaymán Khán (martyr) 197
Sulṭán-Ḥusayn Mírzá (Jalálu'd-Dawlih) 554, 735
Sulṭán-Mas'úd Mírzá (Ẓillu's-Sulṭán) (436), 554, 641, 729, 735
supernatural, the 10, 34, 62, 70, 121, 250, 307
superstitions 30, 50, 257, 603, 605, 611
  see also fancies, idle; imaginings, vain
Sursock, Nicolas 577, 658
Suttner, Bertha von *see* von Suttner
Swabia, Germany 289 *see* Schwäbisch Hall
Switzerland, Swiss 26, 175, 343-4, 511, 515, 520, 530, 556, 557, 566, 569, 570, 639, 660, 672, 699
Symonds, Annie 613
synagogues 9, 23, 31, 45, 65, 142, 179, 210, 233, 262, 304, 501
  Temple Emmanuel, San Francisco 617, 662, 698, 729
Syria, Syrians 2, 159, 195, 432, 521, 548, 562, 568, 712, 732, 734, 749
Syrian Protestant College (American University), Beirut 138, 487, 532, 581, 648, 749
Sztoits, Iván (317), 689

Tabriz, Iran 150, 159, 310, 327, 474,

531, 557, 577, 579, 580, 634, 726, 741
Tabrízí, 'Alí 'Abbás Áqá 587
Ṭáhirih (Qurratu'l-'Ayn) 69, 181, 552, 623
Tahmasp I, Shah 296 and n
Tamaddunu'l-Mulk ('Abdu'l-Ḥusayn Qalátí) 495-6, 751
Tanta, Egypt 488, 750
Taqí Khán (Amír Kabír) 180, 199 and n
Tarbíyát schools, Tehran 388, 440, 555, 710
Tbilisi, Georgia 726, 727
teaching
the Bahá'í Cause, Cause of God 9, 112, 175-6, 200, 212, 227, 242, 276, 281, 283, 300, 336, 353, 369, 383, 385, 386, 408-9, 431, 433, 440, 457, 463, 468, 469, 566, 598, 622, 639, 651, 656, 662, 664, 714, 722, 724, 727, 735, 738, 745
children *see* children
spiritual principles 468
unity 664
teachings
of Bahá'u'lláh *see* Bahá'u'lláh
of Christ 11, 77, 85, 250, 260, 392
secondary, of religion 62-3, 84, 85, 153, 164, 205, 315, 455
telegrams 25, 131, 173, 202, 226, 266, 291, 356, 418, 444, 465, 473, 479, 487, 494-5, 529, 638, 677, 737, 740, 746, 747, 751 *see also* cablegrams
telegraph 136, 140, 232, 357, 479
telephone 31, 265, 267, 319, 357, 419, 663, 675
Tehran 188, 251, 368, 388, 405-6, 443, 457, 474, 493, 494, 495, 510, 579, 580, 581, 653-4, 640, 656, 658, 660, 725, 736, 751
mentioned by 'Abdu'l-Bahá 4, 17, 19, 141, 175, 180, 200, 218, 237, 238, 251, 493
in connection with His childhood 218, 238, 263-4, 306, 396, 427, 446
Sangilaj 263
Shimírán 263
Síyáh-Chál 264-5
Spiritual Assembly of 634, 638
Temple Emmanuel, San Francisco 617, 662, 698, 729
Tennant, Edward 577-8
Tennant, Pamela 577-8
tests, trials, and tribulations 38, 79, 94, 99, 113, 117, 168, 206, 378, 394, 411, 450, 647, 679
of Bahá'u'lláh 216-17, 413, 438, 455, 647
Thaler, Marie 319-21, 333, 578, 579, 690
theatres, theatrical performances 43, 44, 148, 150, 518, 531, 607, 731
Thaunman, Mr (335), 697
theology, theologians 9, 489, 519, 551, 555, 614, 649
Theosophy, Theosophists 28, 295, 298, 304, 232, 319, 322, 324, 328, 529, 551, 558, 563, 566, 576, 578, 581, 600, 608, 616, 712, 728, 730
Theosophical Society
Austria 321-2, 325, 326, 334, 549, 551, 578, 690, 691, 693, 694
Prayer of 'Abdu'l-Bahá for 693
France 170-71, 325-6, 439, 458, 637
Hungary 296-7, 304, 305, 311, 334, 558, 576-7, 582, 677, 678, 682, 687, 689
Altruism branch 582
Apollo 558
White Lodge of the Star of the East 679, 682, 730
Liverpool, England 25-7
London, England 70-71, 526, 529, 553, 617
Scotland 87-9, 90, 296, 392, 560, 563, 618, 622, 712
Stuttgart, Germany 276-7, 296-7
United States 617
Thern, Lajos (Louis) (321), 578, 691
Thern, Marguerite (321, 325), 578, 691, 693
Theurer, Helene (335), 397
Thornburgh, Harriet 578
Thornburgh-Cropper, Mary (Minnie) 31, 54, 65, 93, 537, 578-9, 607, 608, 609, 611, 615, 616, 617, 624
Tiberius, Emperor 43 and n, 44

Ṭihrání, ʻAbdu'l-Karím 731
Titus, Emperor 250
Topakyan, H. H. 24 and n
Torah 149, 481-2
Toulouse, France 431, 517
train journeys 21, 60, 73-4, 90-91, 105, 121, 266-7, 290-91, 317, 335, 366-7, 461-2, 501-2, 600-01, 622, 625, 628, 663, 676, 677, 697, 704, 730, 745, 746, 751-2, 754
train stations *see* railway stations
tranquillity 3, 18, 32, 37, 46-7, 54, 71, 83, 100, 130, 163, 186, 217, 234, 236, 238, 241, 251, 292, 320, 357, 359, 384, 413, 442, 451, 455
translators 175, 527, 530, 538, 552, 553, 574, 580, 581, 623, 676, 681, 710, 751 *see also* interpreters
travelling to other planets 183
True Shepherd 45, 257, 292, 357
trustworthiness 17, 90, 240, 398, 400, 401, 599
truth
  Beauty of 627
  bereft of, distant from 324, 381
  century of 260
  discernment, recognition of 88, 261, 411
  ensigns of 475
  independent investigation of 27, 169, 228, 257, 298, 394
  of ʻAbdu'l-Bahá's words 86-7, 144, 368
  of Bahá'u'lláh's words 3, 36, 315, 447
  of the Cause of God 68, 81, 159, 329, 494
  of divine religion 107, 205
  Horizon of 171, 411
  of Islam 9, 884, 90, 138, 142, 413, 419, 481
  of the Manifestations of God 198, 414
  oneness of 228, 257, 323, 455
  secrets, mysteries of 280, 286, 606
  seekers of 177, 394
  Sun of 3, 7, 46, 57, 75, 88, 89, 98, 108, 116, 119, 127, 143, 180, 198, 247, 274, 286, 323, 363, 366, 385, 393, 445, 452, 464, 478, 615, 665
  vindication of 437, 494
truthfulness 237, 401, 455, 459 *see also* honesty
Ṭúbá Khánum, daughter of ʻAbdu'l-Bahá 472
Tudor Pole, Alexander 563, 617
Tudor Pole, Wellesley 102-5, 518, 564, 617, 625
Tumanski, Alexander 731
Tunukábuní, Muḥammad-Valí Khán (324), 579, 648-9, 650, 661, 692
Tunukábuní, Sulaymán Khán (Jamál Effendi) 199-200n
Turanian Society, Turanians, Budapest 302, 305, 307, 310, 560, 680, 686-7
Turkey, Turks 128, 130 and n, 317, 508, 534, 581, 604, 607, 640, 651, 678, 711, 712, 716, 722 *see also* Ottoman
Turkish language 189, 192, 303, 484, 624, 644, 659, 683, 684, 686, 722, 731

Umayyads 631
understanding 1, 12, 68, 109, 127, 152-3, 192, 280, 300, 373, 448, 449, 666 *see also* reason, rationality
unification 1, 247, 358, 370, 382, 384, 414, 465
unifying agencies 302-3
unity 1, 3, 39, 46, 51, 57, 59, 67, 68, 83, 95, 117, 144, 180, 190, 201, 249, 259, 282, 317, 369, 418, 430, 606, 638, 720
  among Bahá'ís 87, 188, 365, 434, 437, 664, 686
  of the Bahá'í Faith 236
  of God, Manifestations of God 357, 383, 483, 606 *see also* oneness of
  of humanity, humankind 10, 21, 23, 26, 51, 53, 65, 83, 86, 117, 119, 201, 214, 216-17, 247, 259, 320, 340, 438, 471, 660
  among peoples of the world 1, 21, 27, 40, 70, 71, 85, 86, 106, 117, 151, 302, 337, 358, 402, 454-5, 457
  and politics 691
  primal 691
  of religion 29, 48n, 62, 70, 86, 164, 286, 299, 337, 369, 605

tabernacle of 1, 217
of Westerners with Easterners 95, 301, 388, 614
see also oneness
Universal House of Justice vii, viii, 223, 536, 559, 598, 715
Urdu language 566, 585-6, 725
Urosov, Prince Lev Pavlovic 579, 580
Urusova Paraskov'ia Aleksandrovna (142), 579, 580, 632
Uzbekistan 743

valour 163, 175, 358-9
Vámbéry, Ármin 296, 303, 305-6, 308-9, 534, 549, 580, 678, 680, 681, 682, 684, 685, 705
Tablet from 'Abdu'l-Bahá 308, 684
Varqá, 'Alí-Muḥammad 122, 628
Varqá, 'Azízu'lláh Khán 122, 136, 140, 580, 581
Varqá, Rúḥu'lláh 708
Varqá, Valíyu'lláh Khán 122, 501, 580-81
Vatican City (480), 743
Vaucamps, Valentin (179), 641
Vesel, C. Jessie 581
vegetable kingdom, vegetables 130, 453
vegetarianism 114, 400-01
vengeance 43, 156, 176 *see also* revenge
Versailles 512, 513, 558, 569, 573, 724
Palace of 154
Victoria, Queen 605
Vienna, Austria 291, 317-35, 368, 511, 538, 544, 549, 551, 576, 578, 579, 582, 587, 677, 690-97 passim
Bahá'ís in 332 *see also individual entries*
places visited by 'Abdu'l-Bahá:
Hotel Beatrix (317), 690
Grand Hotel 317, 690, 692, 695
Hotel Imperial (324), 692
Johannesgasse (No. 2) (322, 325), 691, 693-4 (Theosophical Society and Lukaneder residence)
Karlskirche (St Charles Church) 324-5, 692
Kastnergasse (no. 11), (321), 691 (Thern residence)
railway stations 291, 319, (335), 677
Prinz Eugenstr. (No. 34) (324), 692
Schönbrunn 325
Stadtpark 321, (327), 691, 695
Vikár, Bela (310), 581, 685
Vikár, Dr Géza (317), 581-2, 689
von Behr, Maud *see* Lillienthal
von Suttner, Bertha, Baroness 334, 582, 696

Wales 625
war 2, 23, 25, 58, 94, 120, 130, 223, 224-5, 258, 357-60, 443, 463
Balkan 22 and n, 25, 32, 47, 120, 342, 561-2
elimination of 23, 25, 58, 224-5, 359, 605
Franco-Prussian 491, 751
Greco-Turkish (1897) 130
'holy' 260
instruments of 341
in Islam 261, 420
Ottoman-Persian (1821-23) 255 and n
as a spiritual metaphor 342
world 22
First 438, 509, 515, 528, 531, 560-62, 564, 579, 751
Second 544, 572, 690
Warneke, H. E. 366, 582, 705
Washington, D.C. 525, 528, 548, 574, 604, 688, 734, 740
Bahá'ís of 172-3, 314, 522, 537, 549, 653, 666, 747
wealth 5, 6, 7, 12, 106, 189, 239, 266, 329, 359, 371-2, 398, 454, 479, 503, 702, 725, 741 *see also* riches
weapons 100, 361, 450
Weardale, Philip 582
Weinsberg, Germany 675
West, the 4-5, 6, 38, 77, 80, 82, 87, 93, 99, 117, 125, 146, 182, 198, 229, 233, 241, 297, 300, 308, 363, 377, 450, 452, 653, 654, 748
'Abdu'l-Bahá's travels in *see* 'Abdu'l-Bahá
significance of ix, 2, 9
Bahá'ís in 7, 48, 66, 73, 91, 92, 129, 143, 144, 232, 337, 388, 479, 597, 615 *see also entries for individual cities and countries*

and East *see* East and West
Westerners 67, 300, 452, 523
unity with Easterners 95, 301, 388, 614
Whyte, Dr Alexander 75, 82, 84, 90, 544, 583-4, 618, 619, 622
Whyte, Sir Frederick 75
Whyte, Jane Elizabeth 74-5, 78, 84, 89-90, 584, 618, 622, 712
Tablet from 'Abdu'l-Bahá 214
Whyte, Lancelot 584
Wieland, Helen 350, 701
Wilhelm II of Prussia, Emperor of Germany 287, 703
Wilhelm II of Württemberg 703
Wilhelma palace, Germany 281, 672
Wilkins, Mr and Mrs 652-3
Wilmette, Illinois 37, 524, 565
willpower 404
Wilson, Woodrow 719
wine 201, 305 and n, 393
as spiritual metaphor 68, 91, 108, 281, 315, 339, 393, 467, 492, 629
Wise, Mrs 749
wives 26, 168, 246, 314-15, 554
Woking, England 106-7, 625-6
Oriental Institute 626 *see also* Shah Jahan Mosque
wolf, wolves 45, 125, 126, 293, 384
women
activists 42, 602
of America and Europe 47, 357
Eastern 35, 329, 382
education of 35, 40, 42, 86, 214, 559, 601
equality with men 35, 40, 52, 69, 86, 181, 357, 431
rights of 35, 37, 39-40, 42, 69, 86, 181, 214, 300, 357, 602
see also suffragists
Women's Freedom League 69, 523, 526
women's movement 528, 606
Woodcock, Percy 583, 708
Woodcock, Aloysia 583
Woodward, Mrs 747
Word of God 63, 67-8, 92, 128, 135, 380, 414, 473
all-compelling 403
effects of 434
exaltation of 147, 227, 238, 311, 317, 445, 451, 455, 492
influence of 127, 151, 343, 451, 491
meaning of 52, 108, 192
power, might of 5, 57, 250, 269, 302, 313, 314, 352, 362, 429, 441, 503, 619
promotion, promulgation of 7, 206, 283, 293, 334, 354, 374, 387, 423, 691, 735
raised up 195
sacrifice to 487
shade of 70, 224, 316, 384
sustaining 249
triumph over opponents 172, 492
work 12, 18, 148, 172, 187, 189, 190, 191, 201, 385, 468, 488, 611, 612, 614, 654
workers' rights 18, 464
world, contingent (or contingent realm) 86, 110-11, 186, 295, 315, 358, 397, 449
Wyndham, Pamela (Lady Glenconner) 577-8, 624

Yaḥyá, Mírzá (Ṣubḥ-i-Azal) 16, 26, 167-8, 169-70, 206, 252, 446, 597-8, 599, 640, 660, 661, 733
Yaḥyá, Áqá Mírzá (of Hindiján) 742-3
Tablet from 'Abdu'l-Bahá 743
Yálrúd, Iran 173
Yandell, Maud 584
Yazd, Iran 433, 550, 554, 648, 728
Yazdí, Aḥmad Effendi (Mírzá Aḥmad Yazdí, Consul) 25, 29, 471, 472, 475, 484, 497, 547, 584-5, 601, 603, 693, 706, 740, 745, 746
Yazdí, Ḥájí Muḥammad 471, 472, 739, 740
Yazdí, Ḥájí Mullá Mihdí 629
Yazdí, Ja'far 436, 729
Yazdí, Muḥammad Riḍáy-i-Muḥámmad-Ábádí 17, 237-8, 598-9
Yehya, Shah Mahomed 585
Young Men's Christian Association, Paris (190), 643
Young Turk Revolution 7, 137, 750
Yousaf, Nawabzada Mohammed (463, 465, 466), 738, 739

Zafar Ali Khan, Maulana 585
Zarqání, Maḥmúd ibn-i-Ismá'íl vii-x, 10, (312, 340), 505, 625, 662, 666, 675, 676, 687, 693, 698, 704, 707, 730, 738, 740-41, 744
  chants prayer 687
  diary, 'Abdu'l-Bahá's comments on 755
  poetry ix
Zayn, Munír 471, 740, 741, 745, 751, 752
Zaynu'l-'Ábidín (Zaynu'l-Muqarrabín) 659, 740
Zaytun, Egypt 490
Zeit, Die newspaper (326), 695
Zipernowsky, Anna (Kline) (317), 689
Zipernowsky, Prof. Károly (312, 317) 687, 689
Zoroaster, Zoroastrians (Pársís) 64, 65, 97, 115, 192, 209, 210, 258, 309, 366, 433, 644, 705, 726
Zuffenhausen (Stuttgart) (285) 572, 673
  Friesenstr. (No. 25) 285, 673